THE SINGAPORE MIRACLE, MYTH AND REALITY

SECOND EDITION

RODNEY KING

Dedication

This book is dedicated to Singapore's Samsui women. They came from China and laboured long and hard for low pay in miserable conditions to build modern Singapore. When they were too old to work their adopted country let them live their final years in poverty and deprivation. The Singapore Miracle did little for them.

The cover shows the Singapore skyline at night with the Esplanade Bridge in the foreground: Photograph by Michael Haxholdt.

About the author

Rodney King lived and worked in Singapore for most of 15 years and currently resides in Perth, Western Australia. This is his third book. The others were 'Armed Revolution' and 'Your Guide to Investment Trading – with Special Reference to Singapore and Malaysia'.

ACKNOWLEDGMENTS

The assistance of the following in the preparation of this book is gratefully acknowledged. Ian Kerr, Michael Thorpe, Garry Rodan, Jim Minchin, Andre Malan and Peter Mack for the many useful and corrective comments they made on reading various drafts of the manuscript; Ray King for patiently filing mounds of newspaper clippings into over 90 large scrapbooks; "Kevin" for his insightful comments on Singaporean construction practices and Chris Beyrer for his help with the AIDS section; Jon Ostenfeld for assiduously removing shoals of typos and other errors from the entire manuscript and also Olga de Moeller and Richard Brouwer for editorial help with various sections; Simon Wheeler and again Richard for useful inputs on the cover design; Simon again for IT help; Lesley Tunnecliffe for guidance on publication and distribution, and finally "Jane" the typesetter for patiently wading through endless changes and corrections and for providing useful IT advice on indexing the book.

CURRENCY EXCHANGE RATES

The Singapore dollar exchange rate fluctuated widely during the years covered by this book. The exchange rates in US, Australian and Hong Kong dollars, British Pounds and Malaysian ringgits for the 1995 – 2006 period are listed below.

	1995	2000	2004	2006
US dollar	1.41	1.72	1.69	1.59
Malaysian ringgit	0.56	0.45	0.44	0.43
Australian dollar	1.05	1.00	1.24	1.20
British Pound	2.18	2.58	3.09	2.93
Hong Kong dollar	0.18	0.22	0.22	0.20

CONTENTS

PREFACE

The idea for this book was conceived in the mid-1990s. By then I had lived and worked in Singapore for nearly a decade. During this time I was constantly exposed to endless claims about the success of the Singaporean model. Singapore was depicted as an affluent, cutting-edge city-state of superlative efficiency, excellence and competitiveness which had delivered the good life to its citizens.

Official propaganda regularly proclaimed the Republic's successes to the world and suggested that it was an example of successful development. Almost weekly, the local media would obediently herald the findings of yet another survey from some ratings agency or Western think-tank showing this. Singapore was again tops in yet another attribute, whether it was international competitiveness, economic freedom, being a good place to do business, transparency, lack of corruption, good governance or having the best workforce in the world. Foreign journalists and visiting experts would also praise Singapore's housing, pension and health schemes as world-class, if not the best.

I eventually came to believe that Singapore's exulted international reputation and much-praised economic miracle deserved critical scrutiny. Although much has been written about Singapore, this has not really been done.

Most books about modern Singapore focus on its nation-building successes, the policies and personality of its formidable founder-leader Lee Kuan Yew, or the often repressive, authoritarian nature of its political system and lack of press freedom. Other works have covered the island's rich and varied history from the time it was established as a major trading centre in 1819 by British colonist Stamford Raffles. But to me, the full story of the legendary Singapore Miracle had not been told. Had Singapore really been transformed from an underdeveloped island-port into a world-class metropolis of cutting-edge excellence and efficiency? Clearly, such flattering claims required rigorous analysis, especially when my experience and that of other expatriates in Singapore so often seemed to contradict them.

My determination to embark on such an enterprise was enhanced by the hubris that so much praise had generated in Singaporeans. The country's leaders, especially Lee Kuan Yew, felt free to patronise their lesser-developed neighbours and sneer at the West's failings. Often Singaporeans would mirror this arrogance, which has generated widespread resentment towards Singapore in South East Asia. They and their miracle were definitely ripe for some vigorous scrutiny. How much of their miracle was myth and hype, and how much reality?

So I set to work and began amassing massive amounts of material about Singapore. The task proved far greater than I had imagined. There was so much to be said; so many untested claims had been made about Singapore and its miracle. The book eventually grew to 33 chapters.

Another problem was the constant need to integrate a continuous stream of new data into the existing manuscript. There was not only so much to say about the Singapore Miracle, but endless amounts of additional information to do this with. New information that would strengthen the book's arguments demanded inclusion. But the book's length also required a time period to be imposed. I decided the book would cover Singapore's development from the early 1960s to early 2005.

Inevitably, the book will date in this fast-changing world, but its main observations about the Singapore Miracle should remain valid for some time. After all, they are not only based on extensive research about modern Singapore, but the result of my having lived and worked in Singapore for most of the 15 years from 1986 to 2004. Residing in the country for so long in a variety of circumstances, both employed and self-employed, and mixing with a wide range of the locals, gives one special insights into its values and lifestyles, strengths and weaknesses, myths and realities.

Rodney King
Perth, Western Australia,
November 2006

PREFACE TO THE SECOND EDITION

The first edition of my book examined the Singapore Miracle till the end of 2004. This second edition, which extends the analysis till early 2008, has been extensively revised and updated. The changes include a far more detailed account of Temasek Holdings and the Government of Singapore Investment Corporation. There are also updates on Singapore's R&D and entrepreneurial capacities, Biopolis and the Shorvon-National Neuroscience Institute controversy.

In addition, the newest data on Singapore's growing income gap, rising poverty levels and worsening AIDS problem are included, along with the city state's most recent rankings for competitiveness, economic freedom, transparency and attractiveness to foreign capital. Among other changes are updates on Japan's halting recovery and revised scenarios about Singapore's future.

Rodney King
August 2008

GENERAL INTRODUCTION

Foreign political leaders regularly visit the Republic of Singapore and hail its remarkable achievements. Dazzled by the city-state's success, they readily agree that it has much to teach the world.

Occasionally, unfriendly reports of political repression, a compliant judiciary, denial of civil liberties and ceaseless hounding of opposition politicians leak out. Singapore responds by defending its Asian-style authoritarian democracy. Its most vocal defender is Singapore's ex-prime minister, Lee Kuan Yew, who suggests that other developing countries should follow Singapore's example. Lee usually expresses an almost petulant impatience with Western notions of liberty, democracy, and civil rights. They are "inappropriate" for countries still seeking to drag themselves out of poverty and political chaos, he contends.

Lee is always carefully listened to, and rather too politely, by countries such as Australia, which have often been the target of his criticisms. Lee's seemingly brilliant 31-year reign over Singapore (1959-90) and his often wise and penetrating comments about world affairs ensure he gets a more-than-fair hearing from many. His views and lectures often receive reverential attention from opinion leaders, American think-tank experts and others who often have little direct first-hand knowledge of Singapore.

Lee himself is accorded special status by many sympathetic Western journalists and editors. They often bestow such terms as Asia's "senior", "elder" or even "great statesman" on him.[1] Such deferential treatment emboldens Lee to offer gratuitous and sometimes insulting advice to other countries. He once told Australians they would become "the white trash of Asia" unless they bucked up.

Lee has also been a major player in the Asian values debate since its emergence in the 1970s. Prominent US commentator Samuel Huntington, author of *The Clash of Civilisations*, depicted Lee as a prophet of rising Sinic and Asian civilisations. Lee is extensively mentioned in Huntington's book, whose index lists Lee ten times – more than any other individual mentioned. Lee's main message is that Asian societies should emulate Singapore's authoritarian rule rather than Western liberal democratic models. Certainly, attention must be paid to Singapore and Lee. Despite its 3.2 million population and tiny size, Singapore really does "punch above its weight" internationally.

Under Lee's People's Action Party (PAP) Government, Singapore has been reputedly transformed from a "mosquito infested swamp" to a modern industrial economy of apparent First World status. This achievement is often deemed an economic miracle. Singapore's economic strategies have been widely studied. Many believe they should be copied by underdeveloped countries. Even developed countries could learn from Singapore, claim its Western neo-con fans. Singaporean economist Linda Low notes that Singapore's

> *partnership with MNCs [multinational corporations] and direct foreign investment in industrial restructuring, infrastructural support in education and public housing, which doubles as a social function and a provision of social security, are sufficiently universal for others to emulate.*[2]

A wide array of international ratings agencies and think-tanks has been selling Singapore's miracle to the world for many years. They constantly rank Singapore top or near-top for efficiency, competitiveness, transparency and freedom from corruption. The best-known ratings bodies are the World Economic Forum (WEF), Institute for Management Development (IMD), Business Environment Risk Intelligence (BERI), Political and Economic Risk Consultancy (PERC), Transparency International (TI) and Heritage Foundation (HF). IMD and WEF measure nations' international competitiveness while BERI gauges government proficiency; PERC, business risk; TI, the degree of corruption and transparency; and HF, economic freedom.[3]

IMD and WEF rankings are the most cited. They usually rate Singapore in the world's best two or three for competitiveness. Singapore also gets top rankings for economic freedom by HF and equally flattering scores for transparency and lack of corruption by TI. Meanwhile, PERC ranks Singapore the best place in Asia to do business. Such ratings bodies also give Singapore top marks for:

- Being the world's most globalised economy
- Providing one of the world's the most profitable investment venues
- Having the world's best workers
- Practising good governance and economic management, and possessing bureaucratic efficiency and leadership quality.

Singapore's high growth rates since the 1960s have enhanced its glowing global reputation. From 1964-84, annual GDP growth was in double-digit figures and it has averaged eight per cent since then. Even the island's Tiger beer has won top awards.[4] As Singapore's reputation thrived, increasing numbers of foreign political and business leaders visited the city-state from the 1980s to learn the secrets of its success. So keen was the world's interest in Singapore that by 1994 its Foreign Ministry had created 80 positions to deal with inquiries and tours. In 1990, 48 foreign dignitaries came to study the Singapore model; by 1993 the figure was 231.[5] One such visitor in 1996 was Tony Blair, then Britain's opposition Labour Party leader. He praised the Republic's "stake-holder economy" where economic growth accompanied a strong commitment to social cohesion and full employment. He hoped to introduce this idea into Britain.[6] Following Blair's visit, effusive articles about Singapore appeared in the British press. Typical was one by the London *Daily Mail*, which gushingly described the island's Changi airport as having "a permanent traffic jam of Western politicians, whey-faced with awe (and not a little fear) at the astonishing growth" which the former colony of "coolies" had achieved. The Republic was the place to find "the Big Idea" which would "save exhausted Western political and social systems from drowning in the choppy seas of the global economy". [7]

Such sentiments have encouraged Singapore's rulers to think their island state is an example for everyone to follow. Surviving the 1997/8 Asian financial and SARS crises better than the other Asian Tigers proved the superiority of the Singapore model, they contend. This view is readily endorsed by Singapore's many foreign supporters.

Developing countries could duplicate the Singapore Miracle's "good governance and a people-centred economic strategy of growth with equity," claimed Professor Tommy Koh, the Republic's ambassador-at-large. [8] "Thirty years ago, Singapore was a backward developing country, with high unemployment, slums, poor public health, corrupt officials and industrial unrest," he asserted. Yet since then "we have caught up with many of the OECD countries". [9] In 2001, Singapore was labelled a "brand state" in a *Foreign Affairs* article by European scholar Peter Van Ham, who warned that unbranded states would find it difficult to attract economic and political attention. Proudly citing this, Singapore's Prime Minister Goh Chok Tong said the Singapore brand was an excellent one and must be kept that way. [10]

China is one state that Singapore has beguiled. China's love affair with the city-state first became apparent in 1992, when Deng Xiaoping, China's then paramount leader, called for Chinese officials to learn from Singapore. In March 1996, Singapore was being hailed as a model for "constructing spiritual civilisation" by China's leadership. [11] Communist leaders had directed cadres to study party publications on Singapore's success. The party admired how Singapore's leadership had apparently attained both economic progress and moral rectitude.

Singapore remains a model for China, especially as the Chinese economy continues to expand and becomes more globalised. In 2001, a 1996 program for training senior Chinese officials in public administration, urban planning, and financial management was extended to 2005. [12] Joint Singapore-China projects such as industrial parks at Suzhou and elsewhere in China seek to implement Singaporean managerial, financial and town-planning expertise. Lee and other PAP leaders like to see this as exporting Singapore's nation-building "software".

Many other developing countries have also looked to Singapore for inspiration. During a 1997 visit to Singapore, Hungary's Prime Minister Gyala Horn, praised Singapore's apparent success in blending ancient cultural traditions with 20th century technology, adding that "we see with sincere admiration that you have already succeeded in entering the 21st century ahead of others". [13] He hoped Hungary would emulate the Republic's success and also become an economic hub.

In March 1999, Ramos Horta, then foreign minister for East Timor's independence movement, also believed his people could learn from Singapore:

> *We want to learn from a country like Singapore. Look at how Singapore started off. It was in a very similar situation to what Timor faces today. It was poverty stricken, kicked out of Malaysia, had no resources and faced hostile enemies.*

It had only one thing – a resilient and creative leadership. ...When we get our independence, we will ask Singapore to help us develop and manage our airport and harbours.[14]

In 2003, the prime minister of the tiny African country of Sao Tome visited Singapore to learn from its experience in tourism and human resource development.[15] Singapore attracts representatives from countries, large and small, well-known and obscure, to impart the secrets of its seeming success.

Singapore has even organised conferences to teach developing countries how it succeeded. In November 1993, 25 African leaders attended a three-day conference in the Republic to discuss how Africa could learn from Singapore.[16] Singapore has also come to see itself as an expert on world affairs, especially in Asia. As Singapore's Ambassador to the USA in 2001, Professor Chan Heng Chee, explained:

Singapore is often seen as a brains trust by other countries. We have ideas, we see things with clarity. We are able to analyse what is happening in Asia.[17]

Prominent foreign academics and development experts have echoed similar sentiments about Singapore, including Massachusetts Institute of Technology professor Jagdish Bhagwati, a noted authority on globalisation. He saw Singapore as "providing an exemplary role model on the economic dimension" and described it as "an empire by example".[18] In similar vein, were the comments of the CEO of the London-based Securities and Investment Institute (SII) Simon Culhane.[19] "All I saw convinced me that everything works excellently in Singapore," he concluded, after a visit to the city-state in 2006.

It is not surprising that such praise encourages Lee Kuan Yew to dispense advice, often unsolicited, to other countries. An impressive mythology, both historical and economic, has arisen to extol the "Singapore model" and explain its achievements. Tales of spectacular economic success and survival against great odds are regularly told.

The myth-making process was well-established by the early 1970s when Buchanan's book, *Singapore in Southeast Asia*, appeared in 1972.[20] Buchanan showed that Singapore's achievements had already assumed a mythic quality during its first 13 years of PAP rule. Since then, the city-state's achievements have mutated into a widely promoted nation-building doctrine.

The Singapore Government's well-oiled public relations machine works constantly to sell the Singapore Miracle to the locals as well as to MNCs and the globalisation lobby. Endless statistics are churned out to illustrate tales of wondrous success, of a cutting-edge economy ceaselessly reinventing itself. But perhaps Singapore's greatest success has been to sell itself so well to the world as a nation-building example to follow. Copy Singapore's formula and achieve your own miracle is the message. How justified are such claims? This book aims to assess them. It examines how much substance there is to the Singapore Miracle, how much is reality or myth, and to what extent Singaporeans have benefited from it.

References

1. Rodan, Garry: *Transparency and Authoritarian Rule in Southeast Asia* (London, RoutledgeCurzon, 2004), p. 92.
2. Low, Linda: *The Political Economy of a City State* (Singapore, Oxford University Press, 1998), p. 5.
3. The rankings of these and other ratings bodies are systematically examined throughout this book.
4. *The Sunday Times* (Perth, Western Australia), May 2, 1999. In 1998 it was voted the best lager in the world at the biennial brewing awards in London.
5. Naisbitt, John: *Megatrends Asia* (London, Nicholas Brealey Publishing Ltd, 1995), p. 148.
6. *The Straits Times* (ST), January 7, 1996.
7. As quoted in *The Straits Times*, January 14, 1996.
8. ST, July 20, 1998.
9. Ibid.
10. ST, September 2, 2001.
11. ST, March 7, 1996.
12. ST, April 3, 2001.
13. ST, April 18, 1997.
14. ST, March 14, 1999.
15. ST, March 16, 2003.
16. ST, March 3, 1999.
17. ST, June 11 2001.
18. *The Sunday Times* (Singapore), September 26, 2004.
19. Business Times, June 24, 2006.
20. Buchanan, Ian: *Singapore in Southeast Asia* (London, Bell and Sons, 1972).

....

Myths Historical and Developmental

S urviving against great odds, then achieving stunning economic success: these are the two fundamental claims of the Singapore Miracle. Alone and vulnerable after being ejected from the Malaysian Federation in 1965, Singapore hung on during the early and supposedly perilous years to forge ahead under Lee Kuan Yew and the PAP's determined rule to achieve decades of sustained double-digit growth. By 1995 Singapore was being seen as a developed country as well as a model for developing countries. This section begins by examining Singapore's true situation in 1965 after being ejected from the Federation; then Singapore's nation-building strategies are examined, along with widespread perception that Singapore is a developed "First World" country.

Note:
The Malaysian Federation ("Malaysia") grew out of the Malayan Federation, which achieved independence from Britain in August 1957 and consisted of Peninsula Malaya. In subsequent years a campaign was waged by Singapore and Malaya for the Malayan Federation to be expanded to include Singapore and the British Borneo territories of Sarawak and Sabah. It was this enlarged entity that became the independent state of Malaysia on September 16, 1963. Previously Singapore had been a British self-governing colony which from May 1959 had been ruled by the PAP Government headed by Lee Kuan Yew.

CHAPTER 1

....

THE MYTH OF '65

One of Singapore's most enduring myths is that when ejected from Malaysia in 1965 it was little more than a poverty-stricken swamp, alone and defenceless against large and hostile neighbours. This myth, perpetuated by the PAP Government and its many foreign sympathisers, is often swallowed by Western journalists. Even Stan Sessor, one of Singapore's more perceptive observers, echoed this view when he wrote:

When Lee Kuan Yew took power, he found himself governing a mosquito-infested swamp dotted with pig and chicken farms, fishing villages and squatter colonies of tin-roofed shacks. [1]

According to Singapore's mythology, it was only the heroic efforts of Singapore's leader Lee Kuan Yew and his PAP comrades that pulled this 25km by 40km island out of the "swamp" and transformed it into a gleaming metropolis. Lee was "an authoritarian Asian leader who transformed a fishing village into an economic powerhouse," claimed *Far Eastern Economic Review* correspondent Faith Keenan.[2] Not surprisingly, Singapore has acquired the "political image of a country without resources struggling against hunger, privation, and internal and external threats," notes Singapore sociologist Chua Beng Huat.[3]

1. Up from the Swamp?

While Singapore's progress has been impressive since 1965, it was already one of Asia's most developed centres at the time, along with Japan and Hong Kong – a fact usually ignored by the Republic's propagandists. In 1963, a Singapore Government publication painted this rosy picture of the island:

Singapore is one of the few cities in South East Asia where everything keeps ticking – and on time.

The roads and streets are broad, clean and filled with orderly traffic. They are well lit at night – in fact better than most major cities of the East.

The city is packed with well-laid out modern public buildings and office blocks. And the telephones, the water taps, the electric and gas fittings and modern sanitation work as they should – without any nasty surprises.

The city works efficiently as a centre of world communications and
trade. Its port facilities, its international airport, its banking insurance and
commercial facilities are the first in South East Asia.

The standard of living – one of the highest in Asia – is visible in the people
on the streets, the shopping centres, the satellite towns and in the villages.

These panoramic views of typical sectors of Singapore present a fair idea of
a city which has earned the name of the New York of Malaysia. [4]

Malaysian prime minister Tunku Abdul Rahman echoed these sentiments in a
December 1964 speech when he described the island as the "New York of Malaysia
... Singapore is a great city. It is the pride of Malaysia. Here trade, commerce and
business flourish".[5] Lee Kuan Yew also underlined Singapore's pre-eminence when
he stated in July 1963 that while only one-fourteenth the size of Malaysia, the island
accounted for 40 percent of the Federation's purchasing power.[6] And in September
1965, a month after Singapore had separated from Malaysia, Lee said, "One hundred
years ago, this was a mudflat, swamp. Today, this is a modern city. Ten years from
now, this will be a metropolis. Never fear!".[7] Singapore in 1965 was hardly a swamp
where most people were living in poverty. Moreover, as Singaporean academics Tan
and Lam note:

Besides strong PAP leadership there were many factors that have contributed to
Singapore's remarkable economic growth. They include: the strategic location
of Singapore as an international port, access to relatively open global markets
and thus the ability to adopt an export-led growth, a regional balance of
power maintained by the US, the deterrence offered by the Five Power Defence
Pact (Singapore, Malaysia, Britain, Australia and New Zealand), peaceful
relations with its neighbours, a reliable state bureaucracy inherited from the
British colonial masters, and a hardworking population. [8]

The PAP state rarely acknowledges such facts, which tend to diminish its
achievements since independence. But what was Singapore's real situation in the late
1940s to 1965 when it was severed from Malaysia? To answer this question, Singapore's
level of natural resources and economic development, its living standards, its political
and strategic situation and the lucky breaks it has enjoyed will be considered.

2. Resources, Natural and Otherwise

Singapore's magnificent position at the bottom of the Malay Peninsula has always
been the country's greatest natural resource and has underwritten its prosperity and
development.

Soon after Singapore's founding in 1819 by Stamford Raffles, it became – and
still is – a major Asian port. The island's strategic position on the main Europe-Far East
shipping route prompted Raffles to establish it as a port. By the mid-60s Singapore
was the natural convergence point for about 50 maritime nations and more than 200
shipping lines: [9]

Singapore's geographic location gave it a natural base to build sea and air transport facilities that served to establish its competitive position as a regional hub for physical production and transport (manufacturing, entrepot trades and distribution).[10]

Geographic position, a magnificent harbour and extensive British-built shipyard repair facilities made Singapore the pre-eminent anchorage for South East Asia. As Lee himself recalled, Singapore had "a natural world-class harbour sited in a strategic location astride one of the busiest sealanes of the world".[11] For these reasons – and because of its extensive docking and ship-repair facilities – Singapore's capture by the Japanese in 1942 was a disaster for the Allies.

When the British withdrew militarily in 1971 they gave all these facilities to Singapore gratis, as well as their private title real estate and all fixed assets.[12] As George recorded, "When Britain decided to close its enormous naval base in Singapore, the [PAP] Government ... began converting the dockyard into a veritable commercial bonanza. Enlisting the active involvement of British and Japanese companies, Singapore became the best ship-repair centre between Japan and Europe".[13]

Besides its geographic position, Singapore had other natural assets in 1965. Despite its limited land area (639 sq km) inhabited by two million people, Singapore had a sizable agricultural sector, which made it largely self-sufficient in food production. Many Singaporeans grew their own food in small backyard plots, and even by 1969 Singapore still produced enough to meet all of its pork, poultry, egg and fish needs, and 40 per cent of its vegetable requirements. About 20,000 farms covering 138 square kilometres generated this produce.[14] In 1969, there were 54,000 active farmers, 4000 fishermen and 60,000 part-time primary producers.[15] Singapore was also a significant primary products exporter in the early 1960s. "The farming communities of Singapore have ... become major exporters of poultry, eggs and pigs," reported a government publication.[16]

Finally, there is Singapore's greatest asset to consider: its people. Even in 1965, Singapore had one of Asia's most educated and literate populations, capable and hardworking. Dr Albert Winsemius, an industrial economist sent to Singapore by the UN, was one of the first to recognise the capacities of Singapore's work-force. Heading a UN survey team that came to Singapore in October 1960, Winsemius witnessed Singaporeans' resourcefulness. During a stroll down Beach Road, he found all sorts of metal workers operating from little shop-houses repairing many types of machinery with very simple tools. Although without spare parts, they got the machines working again. He studied how family-based work-teams near Kallang could service and repaint ships at sea when striking dock workers would not. The way the teams did this was "a beautiful piece of organisation", he said. In his 1961 report to the Singapore Government, Winsemius praised the island's workforce. Singaporean workers were industrious, quick learners and a great asset for industrialisation.[17] Joseph Tamney, too, observed that Singaporeans had traditional values that aided modernisation:

"They valued education and hard work, gave high status to state bureaucrats, and believed the state is responsible for perfecting society".[18]

These observations described Singapore's workforce as it was in the early 1960s. This book will be considering how valid they still are.

3. Economic Development to 1965

Singapore's entrepot trade grew rapidly in the 19th and 20th centuries, especially in relation to the Malay Peninsula. By 1949, Singapore handled 71 per cent of Malaya's imports and 63 per cent of its exports.[19] As the Peninsula's chief port and trading centre, Singapore became the headquarters for numerous commercial enterprises from import-export firms to agency houses, banks, shipping and insurance companies. They branched out from Singapore to all parts of the Malayan peninsula and the Borneo territories.

Even before World War Two Singapore had a significant industrial capacity. In 1926, Ford set up a car assembly plant on the island (it was in this factory that British and Allied forces surrendered to the Japanese on February 15, 1942). Even so, industrial development was initially tied to Singapore's entrepot role. A 1947 census of the labour force showed that 72.4 per cent were in tertiary industry. Manufacturing and construction accounted for only 19.1 per cent and primary production for 8.4 per cent.[20]

However, by the late 1950s the island had developed a sizable manufacturing sector. In 1959, Singapore had 530 factories employing 10 workers or more and this had risen to 750 by 1963.[21] Among these factories were modern shipyards and a steel mill with a 20-ton blast furnace (the largest in South East Asia), two cement plants, three oil refineries, several textile mills, a basic chemical complex, a sugar refinery, an integrated fertiliser plant, plywood factories and a tyre plant. In addition, there were factories producing refrigerators, air-conditioners and cookers, condensed milk, metal louvres, wheat flour, chocolate products, chewing gum, wire nails, television aerials, animal feed, steel pipes and tubes, plastic products, office furniture, cables, calcium carbide, vegetable products and matches. By the mid-50s, secondary and tertiary industry was more important to Singapore than to other Asian economies.[22] By 1960, commerce, manufacturing and transport accounted for 60 per cent of the total Gross Domestic Product (GDP).[23]

A further measure of Singapore's economic strength was shown in May 1959, when the PAP's Finance Minister designate, Goh Keng Swee, revealed that the island had S$300 million invested abroad.[24] Moreover, a decade earlier, Singapore had been providing grants and loans to the Federation of Malaya. In 1949, a S$4.3 million grant was given to the Federation and in 1953 the Federation received, from Singapore, a S$30 million, 25-year loan with the first 10 years interest free. [25]

Singapore was also the region's main film-making centre. In 1965, the island had four cinematic companies that produced films for Singapore and Malaysia. From

1955-65, the Cathay-Keris Film Organisation and Shaw Brothers made an average of 19 films a year and also 20 feature films in Malay, Mandarin and Hokkien.[26] About 120 films were produced by Cathay-Keris before it closed in 1968.[27]

When separation from Malaysia came in August 1965, Singapore was a significant economy in its own right, not merely in the Federation but throughout South-east Asia. But Lee Kuan Yew and the PAP leadership were unconvinced of this. One who sought to vigorously remind them of Singapore's advantages, now it was independent, was Winsemius. When he arrived in August 1965 he found "to my amazement" that "a discussion had started: can Singapore survive?. Almost the whole of Singapore was behaving like a beaten dog, as if they had no future". He admitted that this was the only time he got really angry in Singapore, and told them, "Now you have your hands free – use them!" He said it was "the best thing that had happened during the whole period from 1960 until today [1981]".[28]

Winsemius clearly saw Singapore's potential as a foreign investment locale from the beginning. In time, Lee and the PAP did too and began ably, sometimes brilliantly, often with Winsemius' guidance, as the next chapter will show, to exploit its substantial resources. But they had a firm economic foundation to build on, not a mosquito-ridden swamp. Moreover, their economic success was no greater than that achieved by Hong Kong, Taiwan and South Korea, not to mention Puerto Rico. A member of Winsemius's 1960 team to Singapore was Juan Gaztambide, from Puerto Rico, which by then had had almost had two decades of industrial growth (the Caribbean country had in 1942 also started from scratch with supposedly few natural resources; but by 1960 it had 2500 factories, of which 600 were major concerns).[29]

4. Living Standards

Singapore had one of the highest living standards in South East Asia, boasted the PAP Government in 1963. Living in one of Asia's most developed centres, Singaporeans were more affluent than most other Asians, as per capita income and other statistics reveal. In 1968, Singapore's per capita income was US$751, second only to Japan's, which was US$1405.[30] Indonesia's per capita income for 1969 was US$80, Thailand's $165, South Korea's $191, Taiwan's $304, Malaysia's $326 and Hong Kong's $680. In 1959, Singapore's per capita income was US$411, and in 1965 it was US$534. Moreover, while some of these countries' 1960-67 growth rates exceeded that of Singapore's, in 1968 its per capita GDP was still second to Japan's.[31]

The preceding shows that Singapore's living standards were among the highest in Asia in 1959 when the PAP assumed power and after Separation in 1965. Even so, significant poverty still existed in Singapore in 1965 and was widespread there in the late 1950s. Chapter 25 cites a major survey showing that between 22 and 25 per cent of households in Singapore were below the poverty line, defined as having sufficient income to pay for minimum housing, utilities, food, clothing, transportation and education. Also, in 1960 unemployment was 13.2 per cent and in 1965 more than half the population lived in slums.[32] Other poverty indices showed that in 1960 there was one doctor for every 2573 people[33] while the infant mortality rate (IMR) was 43.7 per 1000 births in 1958.[34] By 1963 the IMR had fallen to 28,[35] which by 1960's standards was quite low.

5. Political and Strategic Situation

A vulnerable little Singapore, standing all alone in a big and threatening world, is another heroic PAP image for 1965. The fledgling republic was facing a large and hostile Indonesia, which would continue to wage its Confrontation campaign against Malaysia and Singapore until 1966. Confrontation was a campaign of armed opposition launched against the formation of Malaysia in 1963 by Indonesian president Sukarno. He saw the creation of the Federation as a neo-colonialist plot by Britain to divide Asia and thwart the rise of Asian nationalism, of which Sukarno believed he was the leading figure. During Confrontation, armed clashes occurred in Borneo between Indonesian military forces and those from Malaysia and Commonwealth countries.

Again, an embittered Malaysia lay just across the Johor causeway while further away was an aggressive China engulfed in the Cultural Revolution. How serious were such threats to Singapore, and was it really alone in facing them?

At Separation in August 1965, Singapore's most immediate threat was Indonesia and its Confrontation campaign. But this menace soon diminished when Singapore left Malaysia. Indonesian President Sukarno hailed Singapore's departure as vindication of his Confrontation policy and immediately recognised Singapore. Britain also quickly recognised Singapore and set about building up Lee "as a leader of world stature, even to the extent of making" Malaysia's ruling Alliance leaders complain that Britain was more sympathetic to Singapore than to Malaysia.[36] What remained of the Confrontation threat had ceased by 1967, when Suharto forced Sukarno from power and became Indonesia's new leader.

The other threat to Singapore was from the Malaysian military forces still in Singapore. The Malaysians believed they had a right to stay there because they were obliged to defend the island. The Malaysian Government did not want a Cuba at their feet if the Communists ever took power in Singapore. On one occasion, Malaysian forces refused to vacate barracks to accommodate Singaporean troops returning from Sabah in Borneo. Such disputes were unsettling, considering Malaysia's post-Separation resentment towards Singapore and the presence of Malaysian troops on the island.[37]

Overall though, Singapore's security was underwritten by Britain, Australia and New Zealand, who returned to Singapore after the Japanese surrender in 1945 and from 1948-60 fought the Communists during the Malay Emergency. Afterwards, forces from all three countries remained on the island ready to defend it against future threats. Any attack on Singapore would have been met by Allied as well as Malaysian forces. Also, all four countries still had troops in Borneo fighting Indonesian infiltrators.

Lee revealed that during confrontation, there were 63,000 British servicemen, two aircraft carriers, 80 warships and 20 squadrons of aircraft in South East Asia to defend the Federation, including Singapore.[38] Even after Britain withdrew East of Suez in 1971, the Royal Australian Airforce (RAF) retained a base on the island which had a British battalion with a squadron of helicopters, together with Australian and New Zealand battalions. The last British troops left in late 1975.

Singapore's security was further underpinned by the Anglo-Malayan Defence Agreement (AMDA), "which did help to buy time for the development of an external defence as well as deterrent capability".[39] Separation did not affect the treaty's defence provisions, which were stretched to cover Singapore. With the British withdrawal in 1971, Singapore became part of a five-power alliance comprising Australia, New Zealand, Britain, Malaysia and Singapore. The Five Power Defence Arrangement was inaugurated in April 1971, bringing Singapore under the protective shield of Australian, New Zealand and British forces.[40]

British support for and protection of Singapore and Lee Kuan Yew was demonstrated in other important ways. First, Lee was clearly the golden-haired boy for several British foreign ministers and governors of Singapore. "He was so much head and shoulders above the others," proclaimed one governor, Sir Robert Black. "Outstandingly the ablest chap on the local political scene," enthused British Colonial Office official Sir Angus MacKintosh.[41] Britain's political and bureaucratic establishment believed Lee was the man to lead Singapore.

Whitehall also ensured Lee's personal security. By May 1965, Lee had managed to arouse deep and almost murderous hatred against himself by prominent Malaysian political leaders. Some were talking about imprisoning him. The Tunku said that his cabinet "wanted me to arrest Kuan Yew".[42] Lee's intelligence network (which included British MI5 operatives) also reported plans by some Malaysian Alliance leaders to arrest him.[43] Lee suspected that an "accident" would be arranged to remove him. Britain's prime minister at the time, Harold Wilson, told Drysdale in 1980 that Lee's "liberty was in jeopardy and his life too". There was a fear that if Lee was imprisoned "there would be an accident one morning and it would be written off as suicide...Easiest thing in the world to organise". To head off any threats to Lee, Wilson privately told the Tunku that if his government ordered the arrest and detention of Lee, the Tunku would not be welcome at the forthcoming Commonwealth Prime Ministers' Conference in London. "British defence had acted as a constraint," Wilson stressed.[44]

Lee was also protected by British-trained Gurkhas who acted as his personal bodyguards. They were "a godsend for Lee when he felt threatened from the Chinese extreme Left, the [Malaysian-Chinese Association] 'hit men' and the Malay 'ultras'," noted Minchin.[45] Malaysian-Chinese Association leaders and the Ultras (extreme Malay nationalists) were among Lee's deadliest enemies. Lee had come to power in 1959 under the 140-year-old British umbrella, which continued to nurture and protect him and his regime for over a decade.

In any case, Singapore had always been well placed to fight insurgencies. Being a small, crowded island with little jungle, Singapore provided an adverse environment for insurgency. Malaysia, by comparison, had extensive jungles and highlands that could provide shelter and bases for protracted guerrilla warfare. Besides its size, Singapore's urbanised environment greatly enhanced anti-insurgent measures.

6. Lucky Breaks

Luck also did much to ensure Singapore's success.

America's involvement in the Vietnam War until 1975 created big export markets for Singapore. This was especially so after the US war effort accelerated in 1965. From then on, Singapore had an increasingly lucrative trading relationship with South Vietnam. By 1967 Singapore's exports to South Vietnam were US$100 million, and indirect exports were estimated to be US$33 million. In the 1960s this represented a sizeable market for a small country of two million people. Weapons produced in Singapore accounted for much of the exports trade with Vietnam.[46]

In addition, US involvement in Indo-china restored confidence in Asia's future stability, attracting more foreign investors to Singapore and neighbouring countries.[47] Fortune again smiled in the late 1960s when some MNCs chose Singapore over Hong Kong and Taiwan because of the chaos of the Cultural Revolution then engulfing China.

The acquisition of British military bases from 1968 further boosted Singapore's development. The departing British left behind military and other facilities "ranging from fully equipped and staffed ship-repairing capabilities to the largest offshore British military hospital".[48] While the bases' closure made many Singaporeans jobless, substantial economic benefits were conferred on Singapore. In 1968, the Sembawang Shipyard took over from the Royal Naval Dockyard, while the Singapore Electronic and Engineering Private Ltd replaced the dockyard's Weapons and Radio Organisation. Moreover, British air force operations in Singapore were taken over and expanded by the Singapore Aerospace Manufacturing and Engineering Company, Air Charter Enterprises, Saber Air, Helicopter Services and Singapore General Aviation Services.[49] Singapore also caught the right time in the 1960s' product cycle when it launched its MNC-run electronics industries.

* * * * * * * * *

In 1965, and well before, Singapore was one of Asia's most developed countries. Its economic development, literacy levels and living standards were well ahead of its neighbours'. Lee and his PAP Government were protected and nurtured by the British and Allied military presence. Britain's donation of extensive docking further helped Singapore's development. Singapore clearly was no underdeveloped, mosquito-ridden swamp in 1965. "Post-war Singapore was never a backward fishing village waiting to be transformed by Lee Kuan Yew into a modern economy," note Peebles and Wilson.[50] This refutes claims to the contrary by the PAP and numerous foreign journalists and commentators.

But while Singapore was not the backwater many claim, its economic viability had been reduced following separation from Malaysia. To deal with this problem the PAP Government launched a range of economic and developmental strategies to ensure Singapore's long-term survival. What they were, and how they made Singapore what it is today, is the focus of the next two chapters.

References

1. Sessor, Stan: *Lands of Charm and Cruelty* (New York, Vintage Books, 1994), p. 11.
2. *Far Eastern Economic Review*, December 18, 1997.
3. Chua, Beng Huat: *Communitarian Ideology and Democracy in Singapore* (London, Routledge, 1995), p. 74.
4. *Social Transformation in Singapore* (Singapore, Ministry of Culture, 1964), p. 105.
5. Drysdale, John: *Singapore: Struggle for Success* (Singapore, Times Books International, 1984, 1996 reprint), p. 372.
6. Ibid, p. 342.
7. Han, Fook Kwang; Warren Fernandez, and Sumiko Tan: *Lee Kuan Yew, The Man and His Ideas* (Singapore, Times Editions, 1998), p. 82.
8. Tan, Kevin Y. L. and Lam Peng Er, editors: *Managing Political Change in Singapore* (London, Routledge, 1997), pp. 7-8.
9. George, T.J.S.: *Lee Kuan Yew's Singapore* (London, Andre Deutsch, 1973), p. 95.
10. Toh, Mun Heng and Tan Kong Yam: "Macroeconomic Perspectives of Competitiveness", p. 30 in *Competitiveness of the Singapore Economy*, edited by Toh and Tan (Singapore, Singapore University Press, 1998).
11. Lee, Kuan Yew: *From Third World to First* (Singapore, Times Media, 2000), p. 24.
12. Drysdale, p. 402.
13. a) George (1973), p. 5;
   (b) quoted by Cheng Siok Hwa in "Economic Change and Industrialization", p. 196 in *A History of Singapore* edited by Ernest C.T. Chew and Edwin Lee (Singapore, Oxford University Press, 1991).
14. Buchanan, Ian: *Singapore in Southeast Asia* (London, Bell and Sons, 1972), p. 82.
15. Ibid.
16. *Social Transformation in Singapore*, p. 99.
17. Drysdale, pp. 250-1.
18. Tamney, Joseph B.: *The Struggle for Singapore's Soul* (Berlin, Walter de Gruyter, 1995), p. 8.
19. Cheng, Siok Hwa, in Chew and Lee, p. 183.
20. Ibid, p. 185.
21. *Social Transformation in Singapore*, p. 26.
22. Cheng in Chew and Lee, p. 187.
23. Ibid, p. 199.
24. Drysdale, p. 215.
25. ST, December 4, 1998.
26. Chen, Ai Yen: "The Mass Media 1819-1980", p. 305 in Chew and Lee.
27. Brazil, David: *Insider's Singapore* (Singapore, Times Books International, 1999), p. 124.
28. Drysdale, p. 404.
29. Ibid, p. 250.
30. Buchanan, p. 56.

31. While Singapore's growth rate was 11 per cent from 1960-7, South Korea's was 20.4 per cent, Taiwan's 18.6 per cent and Hong Kong's 16.3 per cent. (Buchanan, pp. 65-6).

32. Tamney, p. 59.

33. Ibid.

34. Tan, Nalla: "Health and Welfare", p. 347 in Chew and Lee.

35. Buchanan, p. 224.

36. George, p. 91.

37. Drysdale, 395-6.

38. Lee, Kuan Yew: *The Singapore Story* (Singapore, Times Editions, 1998), p. 20.

39. Chin Kin Wah: "Singapore: Towards Developed Country Status – The Security Dimension", p. 292 in *Singapore, Towards A Developed Status*, edited by Linda Low (Singapore, Oxford University Press, 1999).

40. Chan, Heng Chee: "Political Developments, 1965-1979", p. 163 in Chew and Lee.

41. Drysdale, pp. 148-9

42. Ibid, p. 387.

43. Minchin, James: *No Man Is an Island* (Sydney, Allen and Unwin, second edition, 1990), p. 147 and p. 157.

44. Drysdale, pp. 386-7.

45. Minchin, pp. 227-8.

46. George, 165.

47. Peebles, Gavin and Wilson, Peter: *Economic Growth and Development in Singapore* (Cheltenham, UK; Edward Elgar Publishing, 2002), p. 49.

48. Low Linda: *The Political Economy of a City State* (Singapore, Oxford University Press, 1998), p. 44.

49. Cheng, Siok Wah, pp. 213-4 in Chew and Lee.

50. Peebles and Wilson, p. 26.

Chapter 2

Strategies for Survival

Suddenly on August 8, 1965, Singapore was independent. No longer part of Malaysia, it would have to fend for itself. Although protected by Commonwealth forces, having substantial port and ship repair facilities and being the most developed economy in South East Asia, Separation was still a traumatic moment for Lee Kuan Yew and his government. So devastated was Lee by this event that he had "a minor breakdown" and spent six weeks recuperating.[1] During this time he was unable to perform his normal duties, though he still attended regular cabinet meetings. [2]

After Singapore's ejection from Malaysia, gloom enveloped the island. This prompted Dutch economist Winsemius's angry remonstrations with the PAP leadership, and his call for them to exploit their freedom now they were free from Malaysia. His insistence that Separation was the best thing that could have happened to them was based on his belief that Singapore had great potential as a profitable venue for Western capital.

As the previous chapter shows, the island's substantial resources and the protective defence umbrella provided by Britain and her allies made it far more viable than Lee and his team apparently first realised. Eventually they adopted Winsemius' view. His optimistic assessment of Singapore's situation certainly lifted their spirits. It gave them confidence to chart a constructive course for Singapore instead of impotently fuming at the Malaysians. Even so, according to Minchin, "Only well into 1966 could Lee...begin to talk calmly of the future".[3]

When Lee recovered his composure, he and his ministers devised a blueprint for developing Singapore, opting for four basic strategies to assure its survival:

- Rapid industrialisation
- Export-based development
- The state to operate strategic industries and establish enterprises that foreign capital or the private sector could or would not start
- The development of financial reserves and assets to weather adverse times.

These strategies often reflected Winsemius's proposals. They not only led to open-door policies for foreign capital but to the establishment of a network of state enterprises (SEs) and a forced savings program through the Central Provident Fund (CPF).

1. Luring the MNCs

The MNCs were to be the key to achieving an export-oriented industrialisation strategy (EOI). An open-door policy was launched to lure them to Singapore. Before Separation, Singapore's PAP rulers had envisioned the Malaysian Federation as a protected market for the island's industrial goods. But following Separation they decided to make the world a substitute for Malaysia. Moreover, the MNCs, not local entrepreneurs, were seen as best for driving this strategy because of MNC access to world markets. As Doshi and Coclanis remarked.

> The government's hospitable policy towards foreign investment has been accompanied by the recognition that, given the absence of a nascent class of domestic industrialists, only large multinational firms possessed the requisite technological and marketing capabilities to successfully penetrate competitive world markets.[4]

– a view echoed by Murray and Perera:

> The official perception in the early 1960s was that it would be a long and tedious process to transform small domestic commercial traders into export-oriented industrial entrepreneurs. Export manufacturing could be more readily achieved by relying on direct foreign investment, particularly on MNCs with their in-situ global networks.[5]

Lee Kuan Yew insists that the open-door policy to the MNCs was Singapore's only realistic option in the 1960s:

> Had we waited for our traders to learn to be industrialists we would have starved. It is absurd for critics to suggest in the 1990s that had we grown our own entrepreneurs we would have been less at the mercy of rootless MNCs.[6]

Singapore's leaders believed foreign capital would enable Singapore "to leapfrog over the difficulties of acquiring technology and markets in the competitive international environment," observed Lee and Low.[7] The PAP Government did not share the antipathy of other Third World states to foreign capital and its neo-colonialist connotations. The city-state's rulers readily accepted Winsemius's pro-foreign capital views. Now they were out of Malaysia, they could easily open their doors to foreign capital, he told them. In recalling Winsemius's role, Lee said, "He recommended, yes, proceed. Dr Goh discussed it with him and I discussed it with Dr Goh and met him". Lee had also suggested forming the Economic Development Board (EDB) to sell Singapore to America, Europe and the world.[8]

Singapore's decision to become a financial centre was prompted by advice from Winsemius's banking associates and Singapore began trading in Asian Currency Units in 1968. PAP minister Hon Sui Sen got the idea from one of Winsemius's banker friends, recounted Lee: "True it wasn't all his [Hon Sui Sen's] idea. But he had the good sense to listen to people with ideas. So a Dutch banker called Van Oenen, who had worked for Bank of America, who was a friend of Winsemius, said, 'Try'. But we made it work".[9]

Winsemius also apparently gave the PAP Government the idea to build a big international airport and an equally sizeable container port. On the airport, he said:

My advice was to build an airport where the largest planes can land and let everyone know they are welcome to land here. In other words, do not use landing rights to protect your own Singapore Airlines. [10]

The airport was built and became one of Singapore's biggest successes. "And thanks to this initiative, Singapore has become a tourist centre too, especially for short visits," Winsemius recalled.

Winsemius had also had much experience advising the Dutch Government on shipbuilding. He had seen the enormous growth of container transport between the US and Europe, initially concentrated at Rotterdam. "So I advised that a big container terminal in the harbour of Singapore be constructed ...The advantage was evident: Singapore would be the only harbour in the region with container facilities." Today Singapore has the world's second-busiest container harbour.

In addition, Winsemius provided Singapore with a blueprint for industrial development. He identified industries to develop and recommended a single coordinating agency be set up to attract foreign investors. So in August 1961 the EDB was established for this purpose, and it has since played a central role in Singapore's development.[11] Singapore's largely Winsemius-inspired decision to opt for MNC-led development was vigorously implemented. "Export markets, foreign capital, and cheap labor were the essential ingredients of the new approach, and the PAP Government pioneered among Third World governments in devising packages of incentives that would attract the multi-nationals," said Bello.[12]

Initially Singapore's main attraction was cheap labour. First the Government ensured this by destroying the independent trade union movement and bringing the unions under state control. Second, the Government instituted a free trade with minimal import and export tariffs and permitted unrestricted repatriation of profits and investments and 100 per cent foreign ownership of firms. Third, the Government provided industrial estate sites with efficient infrastructure. Finally, foreign firms were offered many tax incentives. By 1988, foreign investors were receiving 18 separate tax incentives.

The Government's pro-MNC policies produced double-digit growth from the 1960s to the '80s. Manufacturing output soared from S$455 million in 1965 to S$2.2 billion in 1977 (at constant 1968 prices).[13] Trade leapt from S$3.29 billion a year during 1960-4 to S$16.37 billion annually for the 1975-7 period.[14] GDP growth was also spectacular from 1966. Real GDP grew between 10.6 and 14.3 per cent from 1966 to 1973 and from 6 to 9 per cent to the mid-1990s.[15] But this rapid, largely MNC-driven growth also led to heavy dependence on foreign capital, as coming chapters will show.

2. Statist Policies

While the MNCs' role was to industrialise Singapore through export-led manufacturing, much else also had to be done to transform Singapore into a viable economy. As growth accelerated so did the economy's transport, communication and other infrastructure requirements. Moving the people out of kampongs and into high-rise flats became another major priority. Building infrastructure, housing the people and other nation-building imperatives, required heavy state involvement in the economy. A network of SEs comprising statutory boards and Government Linked Companies (GLCs) were developed to do this.

Statutory boards were wholly-owned government bodies created to produce the community goods and provide the economic and social infrastructure that the private sector could not supply. By the end of the 1960s Singapore had statutory boards for industrialisation, telecommunications, utilities, port development, public housing and industrial training. In the 1970s and the '80s they moved into monetary and financial activities, productivity, research and development (R&D), tourism, urban renewal, broadcasting, trade, construction, mass rapid transit and civil aviation. By 1998 there were over 80 statutory boards.[16] These included the CPF, the Housing Development Board (HDB), the EDB, the Public Utilities Board (PUB) and the Monetary Authority of Singapore (MAS).

The boards also began to spawn GLCs to fulfil specific functions. The GLCs themselves are companies in which the boards had a controlling interest, usually one quarter or more equity. Often the GLCs would become sizeable entities in themselves and breed their own groups of GLCs. The Ministry of Finance (MOF) oversees them through holding companies.

Over the years four holding companies have been identified in the labyrinthine SE system that dominates Singapore's domestic sector. They are: Temasek Holdings Pte Ltd, Singapore Technologies (Private) Limited (which has since been absorbed by Temasek), Ministry of National Development (MND) Holdings Pte Ltd and Health Corporation of Singapore Pte Ltd.[17] In addition to these is the Government Investment Corporation (GIC), a large and autonomous entity that is responsible for investing Singapore's huge national reserves. The GIC also operates under MOF auspices.

GLCs first appeared in the manufacturing sector. They started with food, textiles, and garments and progressed to petrochemicals, biotechnology and aerospace. In the service sector, GLCs began with trading activities and later entered the financial, property and development, transportation and warehousing fields.

Over the decades GLCs have rapidly proliferated along with their holding companies. With about two dozen statutory boards, the GLCs form a complex web of enterprises and organisations that pose a challenge for researchers to quantify. Varying estimates exist on how many SEs, especially GLCs, Singapore has. According to Linda Low, GLC figures hit 720 by 1994 but declined to 592 by 1996.[18] Worthington identified more than 800 GLCs, of which he deemed 657 to be significant enterprises. But he estimated that there were about 2000 GLCs with a lot registered outside Singapore. Many were incorporated in Hong Kong, Cayman Islands, Panama, Ireland, Luxembourg and other countries, making it too costly in time and money to identify them.[19] The task of researching Singapore's SEs is made difficult because of government reluctance to release information about them. As this book will repeatedly show, Singapore's governmental secrecy is a constant problem for researchers.

Initially, the Government's open-door policies to MNCs and the proliferation of SEs may have been driven by nation-building concerns. The local private sector may have lacked the capacity to meet such challenges. But political reasons are likely also to have prompted the Government to rely on MNCs and SEs to develop Singapore. MNCs must depend on government approval to operate in the country. They, along with SEs, including GLCs, are much easier to control than independent local enterprises. Better to have the economy run by compliant MNCs and SEs than by private indigenous concerns that could provide strong backing for anti-government parties.

Lee and his team have never forgotten the support that the Singaporean magnate Tan Lark Sye and the Chinese business community gave to the PAP's left-wing opponents, the Barisan Sosialis, in the early 1960s. The business community "virtually wrote its obituary" when it did this, said Chee. "Since then, the PAP has understood that to control the economy, especially in a city-state like Singapore, is to ensure long-term political hegemony."[20]

3. Forced Savings

Generating large amounts of development capital for the fledgling state was another government priority. Forced-saving policies were instituted to do this, initially through the CPF scheme. The scheme's ostensible aim was to provide retirement security for all employees. The scheme required both employers and employees to contribute monthly amounts to the fund. The accumulated contributions would then be paid out to employees on reaching the age of 55.

When first introduced under British colonial rule in 1955, the CPF required total monthly contributions of 10 per cent of an employee's wages from both employer and employee, with each paying 5 per cent. By 1971 the contribution rate had risen to 20 per cent, then 30 per cent in 1974; it finally hit 50 per cent in 1985.[21] But with the 1985/6 recession, the employers' contribution was cut to 10 per cent to help business recover. Since then employer/employee contributions have fluctuated. By July 2007, the total contribution was 34.5 per cent, with employers contributing 14.5 per cent and employees 20 per cent.

Being a compulsory scheme, the CPF has been a form of state-imposed forced savings. CPF contributions have been a major source of national development capital and have also done much to increase national savings dramatically. Singapore's savings soared from negative 2.4 per cent of GDP in 1960, to 15.7 per cent of GDP in 1966, to 41.6 per cent by 1985, to 51.5 per cent by 2000.[22] Such stupendous savings rates had given Singapore savings of US$25,614 a head by 2000, the highest per capita savings by far in the world. This was almost double its nearest rival, Hong Kong, whose per-capita savings were US$13,748.[23] By comparison, Switzerland's were US$5189, Norway's US$5100 and Taiwan's US$4827.[24]

The preceding measures, especially the open-door policy towards foreign capital and the expansion of the CPF scheme, did much to generate high growth rates.[25] Because of such rapid growth Singapore came to be perceived as a developed country by the 1990s. By 1995 its GNP per capita income was US$26,730. This was the world's eighth highest out of 133 countries covered by the World Bank's World Development Report for 1997.[26] Singapore's high GNP prompted the OECD (Organisation for Economic Cooperation and Development) to consider classifying Singapore as a developed country at times. Besides

Singapore's high GNP, its industrialised and urbanised economy and apparent affluence would have made such a promotion seem reasonable. But it may be premature to see Singapore as developed, as the next chapter shows.

References

1. Barr, Michael: "Lee Kuan Yew: *The Beliefs Behind the Man* (Surrey, UK; Curzon, 2000), p. 75.
2. Ibid, p. 93.
3. Minchin, James: *No Man Is an Island: A Portrait of Singapore's Lee Kuan Yew* (Sydney, Allen and Unwin, second edition, 1990), p. 163.
4. Doshi, Tilak and Peter Coclanis: "The Economic Architect: Goh Keng Swee", p. 33, in *Lee's Lieutenants, Singapore's Old Guard,* edited by Lam Peng Er and Kevin Y.L. Tan (Sydney, Allen and Unwin, 1999).
5. Murray, Geoffrey and Audrey Perera: *Singapore: the Global City State* (Surrey, China Library/Curzon Press Ltd, 1996), p. 97.
6. Lee, Kuan Yew: *From Third World to First* (Singapore, Times Media, 2000), p. 86.
7. Lee, Tsao Yuan and Linda Low: "Entrepreneurship Policy", p. 176 in *Local Entrepreneurship in Singapore: Private and State* edited by Lee Tsao Yuan and Linda Low (Singapore, Times Academic Press, 1990).
8. Han, Fook Kwang, Warren Fernandez and Sumiko Tan: *Lee Kuan Yew, The Man and His Ideas* (Singapore, Times Editions, 1998), p. 340.
9. Ibid.
10. *The Straits Times,* September 21, 1997.
11. Peebles, Gavin and Peter Wilson: *Economic Growth and Development in Singapore* (Cheltenham, UK; Edward Elgar Publishing, 2002), p. 35.
12. Bello, Walden and Stephanie Rosenfeld: *Dragons in Distress: Asian Miracle Economies in Crisis* (London, Penguin, 1990), p. 291.
13. Cheng, Siok Wah: "Economic Change and Industrialization", p. 203, in *A History of Singapore,* edited by Ernest (C.T.) Chew and Edwin Lee (Singapore, Oxford University Press, 1991).
14. Ibid, p. 202.
15. Peebles and Wilson, p. 273.
16. Worthington, Ross: *Governance in Singapore* (London, RoutledgeCurzon, 2003), p. 172.
17. Ibid, p. 203.
18. Low, Linda: *The Political Economy of a City State* (Singapore, Oxford University Press, 1998), p. 161.
19. Worthington, p. 202 and pp. 321-2.
20. Chee, Soon Juan: *Your Future, My Faith, Our Freedom* (Singapore, Open Singapore Centre, 2001), p. 56.
21. Ibid, p. 141.
22. Peebles and Wilson, pp. 273-4.
23. Ibid, p. 226.
24. Ibid.
25. Peebles and Wilson, p. 273.
26. *World Development Report 1997* (New York, Oxford University Press).

CHAPTER **3**

....

A DEVELOPED COUNTRY?

From Third World to First was the title of Volume Two of Lee Kuan Yew's autobiography published in 2000. Such a title implied that Singapore had reached the status of "First World" or developed country. In February 2007, Lee Kuan Yew asserted that Singapore was already in the "lower half" of the First World and in the next 10-20 years would move into the upper half. [1] As a heavily industrialised, urbanised, and seemingly affluent society, Singapore could reasonably be regarded in that light. Certainly the PAP Government did then and still does everything possible to promote Singapore as a modern cutting-edge IT-smart country of superlative efficiency.

But in 1995 PAP leaders were curiously reluctant to endorse media reports that the OECD was about to confer developed country status on Singapore. This was an odd response from rulers ever ready to trumpet Singapore's achievements to the world: Singapore lacked several features of a developed country, they admitted.

According to Prime Minister Goh Chok Tong, Singapore's relative weakness in technology was one reason why it "was not throwing a party" after foreign and local media reports of its having reached developed status. [1a] Any developed country status for Singapore would relate to per capita GNP only, he said. Singapore had yet to develop an economic structure resembling that of a developed country. "We also lag in terms of educational levels, skills, and the capability of generating ideas and technology." [2] Goh's doubts about Singapore's true level of development were justified, as this chapter will show. But there may have been other reasons for Goh's tepid response to reports of Singapore's imminent developed country status. Singapore has always wanted to enjoy the kudos, but not the obligations of a developed country. As Norbert Wagner noted:

Surprisingly, given the otherwise omniscient striving for excellence and being No 1 in every endeavour, Singaporean officials have been cautious or even reluctant to acknowledge that Singapore has already attained the status of a developed country.

Is it because being a developed country brings with it not only prestige but also burdens and responsibilities? Is it because developed countries don't receive aid from other countries, but, on the contrary, are expected to grant aid to poorer ones? Is it because developed countries don't receive trade preferences but instead have to compete with other developed countries on an equal footing?[3]

Lee Kuan Yew had adroitly sought to avoid this fate during visits to the UN and Commonwealth meetings. Unlike other Third World leaders he was canny enough to not travel on special aircraft and be driven in luxury cars on arrival.

Those African presidents whose countries who were then better off, like Kenya and Nigeria, also had special aircraft. I wondered why they did not set out to impress the world they were poor and in dire need of assistance. Our permanent representative at the UN in New York explained that the poorer the country the bigger the Cadillacs they hired for their leaders. So I made a virtue of arriving by ordinary commercial aircraft, and thus helped preserve Singapore's Third World status for many years. However, by the mid-1990s the World Bank refused to heed our pleas not to reclassify us as a "High Income Developing Country", giving no Brownie points for more frugal travel habits. We lost all the concessions that were given to developing countries.[4]

Lee had faced similar problems with the Japanese in the 1970s. He had protested to Japan's Prime Minister Fukuda that Japanese officials were talking of Singapore as an industrialised, not a developing country and thus no longer entitled to soft loans from Japan. If Japan treated Singapore as already industrialised when it was not, then the European Economic Community (EEC) and the US would do the same. Singapore would lose its General Scheme of Preferences (GSP) and other advantages. Fukuda took note of Lee's objections and Japanese officials ceased to do this, Lee said.[5]

By the mid-1990s Singapore's "developing country" pose was no longer of use in receiving preferential treatment in trade and other areas. No pleas from Lee and his government, no denials that Singapore was a developed country, had any effect.

But while Singapore had lost the trade and loan benefits it previously enjoyed, it continued to minimise its foreign aid expenditure, an obligation expected of developed countries. Despite having the world's eighth-highest GNI in 1999, Singapore contributed only 0.07 per cent to international aid. Other developed countries, including Australia, were giving 0.2-0.3 per cent of GNI to international aid.[6] Singapore's mean-minded mentality was also reflected in regulations limiting the percentage of charity money raised in Singapore that could be used abroad. In January 1995, the Government passed the Charities Act 1994 which rules that only 20 per cent of money raised for foreign charities in Singapore can be sent to such charities. The remaining 80 per cent must be spent on charities in Singapore.[7] Such regulations would not be countenanced in a truly developed country. Rich Western countries often feel they have humanitarian obligations to help poor countries. Singapore's rulers have yet to experience similar stirrings of conscience, despite their country's affluence – disaster relief for natural catastrophes in the region notwithstanding. Singapore's humanitarian deficiencies reveal that culturally it lacks developed country values.

But usually a country's development levels are measured by economic and other more mundane benchmarks. When assessed by such criteria, perceptions that Singapore is a developed country are found to be misconceived.

1. Assessing Singapore's Development

As Prime Minister Goh noted, development involves more than GDP levels. It includes adequate levels of research and development, literacy and skills, and capacities for innovation, he said. Another basic measure of development is a country's degree of economic independence.

In countries like Singapore, development can be more apparent than real. High per capita GNP (or GNI as it has been termed since the 1990s), extensive manufacturing and service sectors, and sophisticated transport, shipping and communications infrastructures can disguise significant underdevelopment. While Singapore's strengths are readily apparent, its heavy dependence on foreign capital, technology and expertise and world export markets is not so obvious.

Singaporean economist Linda Low summed up the contradictory nature of Singapore's development:

> The general consensus is that by conventional standards set by Western industrialized developed countries, Singapore has yet to become developed. [But its] economic indicators as traditionally measured may reflect or even do better than those in developed countries.[8]

Moreover, "its capability and technology to sustain the industrial structure and dynamism of a developed nation are more in doubt as it is extremely dependent on the global economy".

Singapore's economic dependence can be measured by examining such factors as:

- The degree of MNC involvement in the economy
- Dependence on exports produced by MNCs
- Entrepreneurial capacities, especially of the SME sector
- Extent of indigenous R&D
- The workforce's educational and skill levels.

MNC-Dominated Manufacturing

Singapore depends heavily on foreign capital and world markets for economic survival.

By the mid-1980s foreign companies in Singapore were accounting for 70 per cent of gross manufacturing output, over 50 per cent of manufacturing employment and 82 per cent of direct exports.[9] By 1998, foreign firms produced 77.3 per cent of Singapore's manufacturing output, and were responsible for 50.5 per cent of manufacturing employment and 88.32 per cent of direct exports.[10] Moreover, by 2000 foreign companies held 71 per cent of total assets in the manufacturing sector.[11] Overall, by 2000 more than 7000 firms had set up business in Singapore.

By 2005, foreign direct investment (FDI) in Singapore had hit US$186.9 billion.[12] The biggest investor was the UK with US$30.2 billion while the US was second with US$25.7 billion, Japan third with $24.7 billion and the Netherlands fourth with $19 billion.[13] Collectively the European Union's total FDI in Singapore was $62.7 billion while Australia's was $11.9 billion.[14]

In terms of assets and output, most of Singapore's manufacturing sector is foreign-owned. Few countries have such a high degree of foreign ownership, as Oxford economist Sanjaya Lall revealed in 2002 when he measured the foreign direct investment as a percentage of gross domestic investment for Singapore and 13 other Third World countries. [15] Singapore's score was 24.5 per cent, while those for the other countries were: Malaysia (18%), Mexico (17%), Argentina (12%), Chile (10.5%), Philippines (9%), Hong Kong (8.5%), China (8%), Indonesia (6.5%), Brazil (5%), India (4.5%), Thailand (3%), Taiwan (2.5%) and South Korea (1.5%). (Also, in Singapore's case, 41.5 per cent of its GDP was produced by foreign enterprises in 1998, as Chapter 14 shows.) Low remarks:

> One not often realized fact is that the concentration of MNCs in Singapore must be among the highest, if not the highest in the world. As much as this is the formula that it has chosen to industrialize and gain technology and markets quickly and effectively, it has put itself in a permanent bind with the MNCs.[16]

For years the PAP Government hoped that this dependence on foreign capital would be reduced by the spinoffs the MNC would give local firms. But as Bello and Rosenfeld note:

> When it opted for a strategy of making multinationals the engine of growth, the PAP technocratic elite envisioned a situation in which the foreign corporations would stimulate the growth of the local industries that would service them. This has clearly not happened.[17]

By the mid-80s, foreign firms were sourcing only 25 per cent of their input from local companies. The MNCs have also failed to develop Singapore's technological capacities, as is shown below.

MNC-Dependent Trade

Exports have done much to drive Singapore's rapid expansion since Separation. Double-digit export growth occurred from the mid-1960s to the mid-1990s. The MNC-dominated electronics sector was the major contributor to export growth, being responsible for 55 per cent of Singapore's total domestic exports.[18] Moreover, the electronics sector still accounts for more than half the island's total manufacturing output and a third of its total employment.

Not only are Singapore's exports, electronic and otherwise, produced by MNCs: the electronic export sector is heavily dependent on disk drive manufacture. Singapore is the world's biggest exporter of disk drives. Murray and Perera note that, "There is no exaggeration in saying that this sector is seen as Singapore's lifeline to continued prosperity",[19] adding that some "worry that the heavy dependence on such a narrow band of products, especially in a sector known to be highly volatile, and sensitive to exchange-rate pressures, is not good for long-term economic health".[20]

Singapore's export vulnerability is accentuated by its heavy dependence on the US market and economy. Singapore's trade with the US totalled S$27 billion in 1995; US investment in Singapore was S$30 billion, and American companies employed 91,000 Singaporeans and paid $1.3 billion a year in wages. "Thus, Singapore is clearly still very dependent on the financial health of the US, as it was in 1985," wrote Murray and Perera in 1996.[21]

However, the Singapore economy, especially its manufacturing sector, has diversified over the last decade.

While electronics made up 51.4 per cent of Singapore's manufacturing output in 1995,[22] they only accounted for 32 per cent in 2006.[23] Again, pharmaceuticals, chemicals, gases and paints generated 6.1 per cent of manufacturing output in 1995,[24] But by 2005 pharmaceuticals alone contributed 7.7 per cent to output and various chemical products (excluding petroleum) 12.3 per cent.[25]

Despite such diversification Singapore remains very dependent on foreign capital and its exports to the US. Singapore's electronics, pharmaceutical and chemical industries remain overwhelmingly in MNC hands and the export markets they service. And while the US only took 9.9 per cent of Singapore's exports in 2006,[26] compared to 18.2 per cent in 1995,[27] Singapore is still vulnerable to US downturns. This is because Singapore's other major trading partners such as China (9.7 per cent of Singapore's exports) and Hong Kong (10 per cent) also heavily depend on their US export markets.[28] In the fourth quarter of 2007, Singapore's economy contracted 3 per cent, when US demand for its exports was slack. The US's dot.com crash in 2001 also adversely affected Singapore and its electronics exports. Whenever the US economy sags, so does Singapore's.

Limited Innovative Capacities

Substantial indigenous R&D capacity, which yields significant technological innovations, is another key feature of developed economies. Here too Singapore's PAP leadership has been busy image-making. According to one Sintercom columnist "Acidflask":[29]

> *The Singapore government has been lauding Singapore as a technologically advanced nation and world-class leader in research and development...*

Singapore's rulers have striven mightily to transform it into such a nation through the pursuit of various strategies. Until the 1980s, they saw the MNCs as the means for providing new technologies as well as business prospects for the economy. Singapore R&D expert and NUS academic, Wong Poh Kam, described Singapore's industrial development as one,

> ... *emphasising government facilitation of MNC-induced technological learning. Through the Economic Development Board ... the Singapore Government has encouraged MNCs to bring in successive waves of new technologies to their subsidiary operations in Singapore.*[30]

The Government hoped MNCs would share their technologies with local firms, especially following the launching of Singapore's Second Industrial Revolution for 1980-85 whose aim was to upgrade the economy from labour-intensive to high-tech manufacturing. But little technological transfer or increased R&D materialised, especially from the Japanese. As Lee Kuan Yew sourly noted, "the Japanese are miserly in passing on their technology".[31]

The new industrial revolution failed to significantly upgrade production processes, boost R&D investment or elicit more R&D operations from MNCs. Only 59 out of 4300 wholly or majority-owned foreign firms were conducting R&D in Singapore in 1981-2, rising to 60 firms in 1984-5.[32] The "Mark II" revolution also did little to boost indigenous technological innovation. In 1990, foreign inventors were awarded 99 per cent of all patents issued for Singapore.[33] Singapore remained almost devoid of indigenous R&D capacity, a strange outcome for a country that even then epitomised supposedly successful national development.

Even so, while the Government had been banking on technological transfer from the MNCs, it had also been taking steps to develop an indigenous technological capacity. Government R&D spending rose from S$36.1 million in 1981 to S$262.2 million in 1990.[34] Then from 1991-6 the first National Science and Technology Plan (NSTP) was implemented.[35] The plan aimed to develop technology infrastructure, encourage private sector R&D and the training of RSEs (research scientists and engineers). The National Science and Technology Board (NSTB) was also set up to develop and fund 13 research institutes and centres in industry-specific areas. By 1996, nine of these had been launched.

A S$2 billion R&D fund was established to finance the NSTP and by 1994, government R&D spending had hit S$438.8 million. Also by 1994, 148 patents had been approved since 1990, of which 51 were in 1994.[36] The Government launched a second NSTP for 1996-2000 to further boost RSE numbers and overall R&D spending.

Total R&D expenditure rose to 1.65 per cent of GDP in 1998 (it had only been 0.26 per cent of GDP in 1981).[37] RSEs rose to 65 per 10,000 employees in 2000, from 47.5 in 1995.[38] By 2001, Singapore had matched the developed world in the allocation of R&D resources. In 2001, R&D spending had reached 2.1 per cent of GDP, passing the R&D world benchmark figure of 2 per cent of GDP.[39] Also, its 1998 RSE figure of 65 per 10,000 workers was almost equal to the 70 RSEs/10,000 workers deemed necessary for a technology-intensive industrial society. By 2006, Singapore's total R&D expenditure was S$5 billion and represented 2.39 per cent of GDP [40] while RSE numbers had reached 87.4 per 10,000 workers. [41] Of this, private sector expenditure accounted for 66 per cent (S$3.293 billion).

Surging R&D spending and RSE numbers saw patent activity leap in Singapore. Between 1993 and 1999 patent numbers increased four-fold to 673. [42] By 2003, they had reached 3027 and 5436 by 2006. [43] While this may look impressive, soaring patent numbers are only one sign of increased R&D capacity. Their true worth can only be assessed by first ascertaining what percentage were produced by Singaporean, rather than foreign, enterprises.

Till the mid-1990s, the bulk of Singapore's patents were produced by (and assigned to) foreign firms in Singapore. But by 2000, more patents were being assigned to Singapore inventors than to foreign enterprises. [44] Out of 299 patents, 179 were assigned to Singaporeans and 120 to foreigners in Singapore. There was also a further 20 Singapore patents by foreign inventors that were assigned to Singaporean organisations. In 2003, there were 291 Singapore assignee patents and 273 foreign.[45]

Table 3.1 – Singapore patent numbers

	1995	2000	2003	1976-2006
Patents by Singapore inventors				
Singapore assignee	30	179	291	1478
Foreign assignee	51	120	273	1376
Patents by foreign inventors assigned to Singapore organisations	3	20	24	173
TOTALS	84	319	588	3027

Singapore's patent numbers were not only soaring but by 2003 over half had been produced by Singaporeans and/or Singapore organisations. Though impressive, the explosive growth in Singapore's patent numbers, both foreign and local, raises the question of whether this was anything more than a quantitative phenomenon. Did the quality of Singapore's patents increase where significant innovations and breakthroughs were achieved?

Most of Singapore's MNC-produced patents continue to be trivial adaptions of existing products to suit local conditions, rather than cutting-edge innovations. The emphasis was still on applied R&D for the incremental meeting of current industry needs, noted Wong. [46] MNCs "tend to retain their fundamental research and design activities at home, using their Singapore R&D centres mainly for adapting products for local needs," observed Professor Andy Green, a UK competitiveness expert from the University of London. [47] MNCs keep their main R&D effort for their home countries, he said. Elsewhere, including Singapore, they modify their products for local markets. MNCs are reluctant to share their technologies with their host country. Few MNCs will transfer R&D facilities to local subsidiaries. As Singaporean economists Hu and Shin noted in 2002, "There is no complementary asset that local governments can provide to attract core R&D capability, however hard and earnestly they try". [48]

The MNC sector has always dominated Singapore's R&D agenda, where product modification, rather than major innovations, is the focus. As Wong noted, "An institutional culture that is used to responding to the needs of large MNCs and promoting technology deployment [as opposed to technological innovation] cannot be transformed into one that stresses technopreneurial start-ups and basic research overnight". [49]

Such a situation has probably done much to stunt the development of Singapore's indigenous R&D capacities which billions of dollars have yet to correct. While Singapore's patent numbers, both local as well foreign, continue to soar the quality of the patents remains questionable. One measure of a patent's quality is the number of times it is cited in other patents. Cited patents are the "shoulders" upon which subsequent patents in the same field will stand. A patent that represents a major breakthrough will attract the most citations. However, few Singaporean patents have so far reached this quality, noted Acidflask. [50]

> *Conventional wisdom claims a strong correlation between the number of citations and the relative importance of a paper in that field, particularly when compared with that field's average....citations are one of the most powerful forms of evaluation in terms of what peers think of one's work.*

However, Singapore's patenting achievements are still mediocre by developed-world standards, according to Thomson Scientific's Essential Science Indicators. Thomson Scientific publishes the Web of Knowledge, one of the world's most important citation databases for patents – and the scientific papers they contain. For the years 1999-2003, Singapore scored below average in terms of impact factors in 19 out of 21 fields tracked by Thomson Scientific. [51] The only above-average disciplines were mathematics (10 per cent above the global average) and agricultural science (48 per cent above). By contrast, engineering and the physical sciences, which Singapore boasts as its strengths, performed poorly. Materials science was 5 per cent below average, chemistry (−11%), computer science (−18%), engineering (−18%), physics (−38%) and geosciences (−52%). "This contrasts with statistics suggesting prolific scientific output in computer science, engineering, materials science, physics and mathematics in particular, in sheer numbers of papers published," said Acidflask. [52]

Singapore was ranked 36th in numbers of papers published in all disciplines out of 145 countries, but only 92nd in terms of relative impact (citations per paper). "We are very good at producing unstimulating scientific research [and] wasting trees." [53]

Apologists for Singapore claim that its undistinguished R&D performance is due to limited human and natural resources and a late start in developing R&D capacities. However, comparing Singapore "with other countries quickly debunks such entrenched self-pitying beliefs". [54] Israel has a population of about six million, the fewest natural resources of any Middle-Eastern country, has constantly been embroiled in wars since 1948 and must spend huge sums on defence just to survive. Yet citation statistics rank Israel 16th for patent productiveness and 24th for relative impact. Belgium, another small country, had 9.43 citations per paper and was ranked 19th for their impact. By comparison Singapore's ranking was not only 92nd but had only 4.58 citations per paper. Even Lebanon, wracked by civil war for 16 years till 1991, beat Singapore in computer science (supposedly one of Singapore's greatest strengths) with 1.12 citations versus Singapore's 1.03 per paper. [55]

Despite huge increases in R&D spending and RSE numbers and in patent numbers, both indigenous as well as foreign, Singapore's capacities for technological innovation remain modest by developed economies' standards. Even so, Singapore's rulers realise that the development of a significant innovation capacity remains central to Singapore's long-term survival and prosperity. The Biopolis project, described in Chapter 13, represents the latest PAP Government strategy to achieve this end by trying to transform Singapore into a world-class biomedical research centre.

Below-average Entrepreneurial Capacities

Besides innovative capacities, economic independence depends very much on entrepreneurial ability. The extent to which an economy can develop and market new products and services significantly determines its potential for indigenous economic development and independence. Singapore scores poorly on such criteria.

Singapore's entrepreneurial deficiencies have been regularly revealed in the annual Global Entrepreneurship Monitor (GEM) reports. The reports have been published by Babson College in the US and the London School of Economics since 1999 and rank countries according to their levels of entrepreneurial activity. The GEM criteria for measuring entrepreneurial activity in its 2006 report were: levels of nascent and early-stage entrepreneurial activity, and numbers of new and established business owners. [56] In the 2000 report, 21 countries were surveyed for entrepreneurial activity and Singapore was ranked third from the bottom. "Despite higher-than-average GDP growth," the report noted that Singapore "showed the lowest rates of entrepreneurial activity". [57] In the 2003-2006 GEM reports, Singapore's average ranking was 36th for entrepreneurial activity out of 55 countries surveyed. [58] The reports showed that during these years an average of 5.9 per cent of people surveyed in Singapore were involved in some form of entrepreneurial activity. The world average was 9.5 per cent for 2003-6, the reports noted. Singapore's below-average levels of entrepreneurial activity have limited its ability to develop new products and services for both domestic and export markets. Harvard economist and Singapore Government advisor, Professor Michael Porter, noted that despite Singapore's rapid growth since the 1960s, its own companies have hardly made a dent in the global market place, the only exceptions being Singapore Airlines (SIA) and the Singapore software company, Creative Technology.[59]

A key component of a developed economy is a vibrant SME sector. In most modern market economies the SME sector is seen as the major source of innovation and entrepreneurial endeavour. From the SMEs spring many great companies, famous brand names and future tycoons. But as will be shown Singapore's private and SME sector remains stunted, lacking the small firms that usually play key pioneering roles in developing new products and services in most developed market economies. When successful, SMEs produce the well-known consumer products of the future and make their countries world-class economies. Singapore's underdeveloped SME sector mainly explains why the country has failed to achieve this.

The Government likes to blame Singapore's low entrepreneurial capacities on the risk-averse mentality of local firms, but other factors have greatly contributed to their stunted growth since the 1960s. These are ones the Government would rather not acknowledge, and include crippling SE and to some extent MNC competition, which coming chapters examine.

Deficient Skill and Education Levels

For a country which had the world's eighth-highest per capita GNI in 2001,[60] Singapore's literacy and education levels have been surprisingly low. In 1998, Singapore was 37th out of 49 countries for literacy.[61] In 1995, when its GNI was the world's seventh highest,[62] 26 per cent of Singapore's 1.7 million workforce only had Primary 6 (six years of schooling) or less education.[63] Moreover, 43 per cent of its workforce had less than secondary education, compared to 30 per cent in Britain and 12 per cent in the US.[64] Singapore's workforce is also deficient at the tertiary level. In 1999, only 14 per cent of Singaporeans had university degrees or higher qualifications, compared to 35 per cent of the German workforce [65] and – in the 1990s – 17 per cent of the Japanese and 25 per cent of the US workforce.[66] Singapore also lags in skills upgrading. In 1995, only 10 per cent of workers aged between 20 and 49 were undergoing education and training that would lead to formal qualifications, admitted Singapore's National Productivity Board's chief, Mr Lee Suan Hiang. By contrast, up to 40 per cent of the adult population in the US and Europe took part-time courses, he said.[67] Reasons for the workforce skill deficits in Singapore are explored in Chapters 10 and 11.

Over the last decade Singapore has made sustained efforts to improve the education and skill levels of its workforce. But by 2002 only 35 per cent of Singapore's workforce still had post-secondary education and above compared to 75 per cent of the workforce in developed countries, according to Spring Singapore (formerly the Productivity and Standards Board). [68]

Singapore has been handicapped by its relatively unskilled workforce, observes Dr Hermann Franz, retired chairman of global engineering giant Siemens and advisor to the Singapore Government. Singapore must create a core of research and technological strength which is the key to a KB economy, he said. [69] But Singapore is still far from this stage.

The preceding discussion has shown that Singapore falls short of being a developed country in several important ways, despite appearances to the contrary. A highly industrialised country is not "developed" when MNCs account for over 70 per cent of the output of its key manufacturing sector, most of its total exports and the bulk of its patents. Limited indigenous entrepreneurial and innovative capacities (EICs) and the deficient skill and education levels of its workforce further demonstrate that Singapore is far from developed country status. Clearly, in many important ways Singapore is neither a developed nor an economically independent economy; but there are different types and degrees of development and dependence, as Singapore also shows.

2. Dependent and Underdeveloped

Economies normally described as dependent rely heavily on foreign capital and technology and have limited EICs; they also display widespread poverty and have weak states easily dominated by MNCs and major capitalist economies. These views, propounded in the 1960s and '70s by such dependency theorists as Gunder Frank, dismiss Third World states as the servants of foreign political and economic forces. They are "dependent financially, technologically, institutionally, ideologically, militarily, in a word politically, on the international bourgeoisie(s) and their metropolitan states," argued Frank.[70] He contended that the world's advanced capitalist economies progress by "underdeveloping" the Third World, especially Latin America. Their growth and prosperity depended on enfeebling and impoverishing the Third World and relied on pliant comprador elites to facilitate this process.

However, emergence of many newly industrialising countries (NICs) in the Third World prompted a revision of Gunder Frank's dependency theories by such writers as Cardoso. Cardoso modified dependency theory by contending that NICs exhibit a dependent or "associated" development that served the developmental interests of international capital.[71] He cited the case of Brazil, noting that despite the growth of its manufacturing sector it still depended on the technology of advanced countries.

A major criticism of dependency theories, including Cardoso's revised version, is that they deny the capacity of Third World states to influence industrialisation and economic development, even on occasion to successfully bargain with international capital. Since the 1980s such theorists as Deyo and Rodan have extended the critique of dependency theory in recognition of how such countries as Singapore have maximised the benefits from foreign capital. Both describe how Singapore successfully exploited the new industrial division of labour (NIDL) that emerged in the 1960s as major corporations of the developed countries began out-sourcing their manufacturing to cheap-labour economies in the Third World. The pro-foreign investment policies of Singapore's leaders enabled them to take advantage of expanding NIDL opportunities in ways that produced rapid growth and prosperity for Singapore. A proactive PAP state also pursued national development strategies that created the infrastructure for a modern industrial economy.

Superficially, Singapore has little in common with Gunder Frank's classic dependent state. Through well-targeted foreign investment and export oriented industrialisation (EOI) policies, the PAP state has adroitly exploited the NIDL and maximised the benefits of foreign investment. Moreover, Singapore has managed to protect its banking sectors from foreign competition for many years. Only with the signing of free trade agreements in the late 1990s has Singapore been compelled to open up its banking sector to foreign competition.

Singapore's development programs have established the infrastructure for an industrial state while its statist policies have spawned a formidable network of state enterprises that dominate the local economy. In addition, Singapore's per capita income equals that of most developed countries. Despite all this, Singapore remains an underdeveloped and dependent state. Over 40 per cent of its GDP is produced by foreign concerns and it remains heavily reliant on foreign technology and expertise. Singapore's limited EICs further restrict its economic independence. Singapore's large SE sector has yet to generate the EIC levels of a developed economy. Moreover, Singapore still depends strongly on foreign markets. Its EOI has produced rapid growth, but the cost has been a heavy dependence on world export markets, especially for the electronic products manufactured by Singapore's MNCs. When world, especially US, demand for these products plunges, so does Singapore's economy.

By the early 2000s, MNCs, despite the economic downturn, were still the locomotive driving the Singapore economy. Singapore had yet to build a dynamic capitalism on its own, one that had a solid locally-owned manufacturing base driven by home-grown entrepreneurs. Singapore remains very reliant on the calculations and whims of MNCs. It lives in fear of MNCs moving to better investment venues elsewhere in the region. Should sufficient MNCs do this, the Singapore economy would be as devastated as it would be by a plunge in world demand for its MNC-produced electronic and other goods.

Singapore is neither developed nor economically independent by developed country standards. Coming chapters examine the reasons for this, along with the many other claims made about the Singapore Miracle. The next section assesses Singapore's much-touted reputation for efficiency.

References

1. *The Bangkok Post* (AFP), February 26, 2007.

1a. *The Straits Times* (ST), December 8, 1995. In fact, the OECD was not about to upgrade Singapore to being a developed country but had decided to remove it from a list of countries receiving "official development assistance" from OECD members. From January 1, 1996, Singapore was to be moved to the "more advanced developing country" list, so that any OECD countries who gave aid to Singapore would no longer be able to call it official development assistance. (ST, January 17, 1996)

2. ST, December 8, 1995.

3. Wagner, Norbert: "When Will Singapore Become A Developed Country?" p. 169 in *Debating Singapore*, edited by Derek da Cunha (Singapore, Institute of Southeast Asian Studies, 1994).

4. Lee, Kuan Yew: *From Third World to First* (Singapore, Times Media, 2000), p. 407.

5. Ibid, p. 568.

6. ST, September 2, 2001.

7. ST, May 23, 1995.

8. Low, Linda: "The Elusive Developed Country Status", p. 376 in *Singapore: Towards a Developed Status*, edited by Linda Low (Singapore, Oxford University Press, 1999).

9. Bello, Walden and Stephanie Rosenfeld: *Dragons in Distress: Asian Miracle Economies in Crisis* (London, Penguin, 1990), p. 293.

10. Ho Kong Weng, Koh Ai Tee and Shandre M. Thangavelu: "Enhancing Technopreurship: Issues and Challenges", p. 331 in *Singapore Economy in the 21st Century*, edited by Koh Ai Tee et al (Singapore, McGraw Hill Education, 2002).

11. *Singapore's Corporate Sector 1999-2000* (Singapore Department of Statistics, December 2002), p. 6.

12. *2008 Investment Climate Statement – Singapore* (US Department of State – www.state.gov) p. 5.

13. Ibid.

14. *Singapore Country Brief* (Department of Foreign Affairs and Trade, Australian Government, April 2006), p. 8.

15. Lall, Sanjaya: "Globalization and development, perspectives for emerging nations", BNDES 50th Anniversary Seminar, Rio de Janeiro, Brazil, September 12, 2002), p. 13.

15a. Peebles, Gavin and Peter Wilson: *Economic Growth and Development in Singapore* (Cheltenham, UK: Edward Elgar Publishing, 2002), p. 14.

16. Low, Linda: *The Political Economy of a City State* (Singapore, Oxford University Press, 1998), pp. 176-7.

17. Bello and Rosenfeld, p. 295.

18. Murray, Geoffrey and Audrey Perera: *Singapore the Global City* (England; China Library/Curzon, 1996), p. 129.

19. Ibid.

20. Ibid, p. 130.

21. Ibid, p. 257.

22. *Economic Survey of Singapore 1995*, (Singapore, Ministry of Trade and Industry), 1996, p. 132.

23. Au, Alex: "Singapore joins banking top table", *AsiaTimes Online*. Jan 12, 2008 www.atimes.com, p. 2.

24. *Economic Survey of Singapore 1995*, p. 132.

25. *Economic Survey of Singapore 2005*, (Singapore, Ministry of Trade and Industry), 2006, p. 178-9.

26. Au, p. 2.

27. *Economic Survey of Singapore 1995*, p. 150.

28. Au, p. 2.

29. "How is Singapore Science Really Doing?", by "AcidFlask", March 28, 2005; p. 1. www.newsintercom.org.

30. Wong, Poh Kam: "Upgrading Singapore's Manufacturing Industry" p. 131 in *Competitiveness of the Singapore Economy*, edited by Toh Mun Heng and Tan Kong Yam (Singapore, Singapore University Press, 1998).

31. Lee Kuan Yew (2000), p. 585.

32. Bello and Rosenfeld, p. 298.
33. Lingle, Christopher: *The Rise and Decline of the Asian Century* (Hongkong, Asia 2000 Ltd, second edition, 1997), p. 73.
34. Wong, Poh Kam: "From Leveraging Multinational Corporations to Fostering Technopreneurship: The Changing Role of S&T Policy in Singapore", p. 78 in *Singapore Inc, Public Policy Options in the Third Millenium*, edited by Linda Low and Douglas M. Johnston (Singapore, Asia Pacific Press/Times Media Private Limited, 2001).
35. Hu, Abert G. and Shin Jang-sup: "Climbing the technology ladder: Challenges facing Singapore in a globalised world", p. 312 in *Singapore Economy in the 21st Century* (2002) edited by Koh Ai Tee et al.
36. Wong in Toh and Tan, p. 65-6.
37. Wong in Low and Johnston, p. 76.
38. Hang Chang Chieh: "What It Takes to Sustain Research and Development in a Small, Developed Nation in the 21st Century", p. 26 in *Singapore: Towards a Developed Status* edited by Linda Low (Singapore, Oxford University Press, 1999).
39. ST, October 26, 2002.
40. *National Survey of R&D in Singapore 2006*, (Agency for Science, Technology and Research, Singapore, November 2007), p. 1.
41. Ibid, p. 4.
42. ST, August 26, 2000.
43. Wong Poh Kam and Annette Singh: "From Technology Adaptor to Innovator: The Dynamics of Change in Singapore's National Innovation System" (Entrepreneurship Centre, National University of Singapore, August 2005), p. 14. **and** *National Survey of R&D in Singapore 2006*, p. 6.
44. Wong, and Singh, p. 14.
45. Ibid.
46. Wong in Low and Johnston, p. 64.
47. ST, April 19, 2001.
48. Hu and Shin in Koh et al, p. 303.
49. Wong in Loh and Johnston, p. 64.
50. "How is Singapore Science Really Doing?", p. 1.
51. Ibid.
52. Ibid.
53. Ibid, p. 3.
54. Ibid.
55. Ibid.
56. *Global Entrepreneurship Monitor 2006, Summary Results* (Babson College, USA; London Business School, UK; 2007) p. 6.
57. ST, January 17, 2001.
58. *Total Entrepreneurial Activity (TEA) Ranked by Country*, Internationalentrepreneurship.com.
59. ST, August 11, 2001.
60. *World Development Report 2003* (New York, Oxford University Press).
61. *The World Competitiveness Yearbook 2001* (Lausanne, Switzerland, Institute of Management and Development).
62. *World Development Report 1997* (New York, Oxford University Press).
63. ST, April 19, 1995.
64. ST, November 16, 1995. In Singapore, primary-level education does not end at primary six for many of the slowest students but may extend to primary seven and eight. Hence there will be larger numbers of students with primary education who have not proceeded to secondary school.
65. ST, November 14, 1999.
66. PSB Corporation press release, October 31, 2002, www.tuv-sud-psb.sg/news_release
67. Chee, Soon Juan, p. 48.
68. ST, November 5, 1995.
69. ST, November 14, 1999.
70. As quoted in Martin Carnoy, *The State and Political Theory* (Princeton University Press, 1984), p. 189.
71. Rodan, Garry: *The Political Economy of Singapore's Industrialization: National State and International Capital* (London, Macmillan, 1989), p. 10.

Section Two

The Efficiency Myth

One day in the mid-1960s Lee Kuan Yew found a button in a government building that wouldn't work. He didn't know what the button was supposed to do, but "when you have a button, there must be a purpose," he insisted, fuming that he would not tolerate such sloppiness:

> I want to make sure that every button works. And even if you are using it only once in a while, please make sure every morning that it works. And if it doesn't when I happen to be around, then somebody is going to be in for a rough time because I do not tolerate sloppiness.

"More than three decades later, it is rare to find a button in Singapore that does not work," Barr remarks.[1] Lee has always displayed a ruthless intolerance for inefficiency and incompetence, and has stamped this attitude on the Singaporean consciousness. Efficiency has obsessed Lee since he first became Prime Minister in 1959; and "Striving for Excellence" is one of the more abiding slogans of Singapore Inc.

Singapore displays many stunning examples of efficiency. The island's Changi Airport keeps winning awards for the world's best airport year after year. Changi is modern, spotlessly clean, spacious and state-of-the-art. Arrivals and departures from the airport are pleasurable and trouble free. Banking and financial transactions are completed with the same ease and promptness as in any Western country. Telecommunications are the latest and best; public transport, especially the Metropolitan Rail Transit (MRT), is quick and efficient.

Newly-arrived foreign journalists are often smitten with Singapore's seeming efficiency and ask why. Two US journalists posed this question to Brigadier General Lee Hsien Loong (BG), Lee's eldest son, when he was deputy prime minister. "What makes it special?" asked the Brigadier rhetorically. "The only thing that makes it special is that the place is revved to 99 per cent of what it is capable of."[2] BG's smug musings aside, efficiency and Singapore seem synonymous to many, and the country's image-makers constantly push this line. As Low notes:

> Singapore is marketed as a product signifying efficiency and sterling performance in the regionalization drive.[3]

The IMD and WEF have frequently rated Singapore first or second for international competitiveness. Such rankings are often taken as proof of Singapore's efficiency in social and political as well as in economic areas. By 2000, BERI had been ranking Singaporean workers as the world's best for 20 years.[4] The following chapters will analyse Singapore's claims to efficiency, beginning with an assessment of its overall productivity levels.

References

1. Barr, Michael: *Lee Kuan Yew: The Beliefs Behind the Man* (Surrey, UK, Curzon, 2000), p. 111.
2. Kelly, Brian and Mark London: *The Four Little Dragons* (New York, Simon and Schuster, 1985), p. 387.
3. Low, Linda: *The Political Economy of a City State* (Singapore, Oxford University Press, 1998), p. 218.
4. *The Straits Times*, May 2, 2000.

CHAPTER **4**

··

ASSESSING SINGAPORE'S PRODUCTIVITY

I f the various ratings agencies are to be believed, Singapore is efficiency personified, at both general and workforce levels. The Singapore Miracle is supposedly the result of a single-minded pursuit of efficiency. But in the mid-1990s several economists began questioning the rapid growth that Singapore and the other Asian Tigers had achieved. All was not as it seemed, they claimed.

1. The Krugman View

Stanford academic Paul Krugman was one of the most prominent economists to query the Singapore Miracle. His 1994 essay in the prestigious US journal *Foreign Affairs* sparked debate about productivity in Singapore.[1] Krugman's views were based on work by another Stanford economist, Lawrence Lau, and MIT economist Alwyn Young.

Lau's study of the Soviet economy found that its rapid growth was input-driven. Huge amounts of capital had been invested and a vast population mobilised to raise production, making rapid growth, initially at least, inevitable. However, there were declining increases in output. The law of diminishing returns took hold; the Soviet Union could not sustain its high economic output and eventually stagnated. "Mere increases in inputs, without an increase in the efficiency with which those inputs are used – investing in more machinery and infrastructure – must run into diminishing returns; input-driven growth is inevitably limited," argued Krugman.[2] Lau applied his findings to Asian economies and found a similar pattern. Some, including Singapore, had high growth but little increase in productivity.

A 1993 paper by Young comparing the economic development of Singapore and Hong Kong added fuel to the Asian productivity debate.[3] Young's paper examined Singapore's and Hong Kong's growth from the 1960s to 1990. He found that increased capital and labour, not productivity, could explain most of Singapore's growth. In comparing each country's growth for 1970-90, Young argued that the growth of Singapore's manufacturing was primarily due to increased capital and labour. The total factor productivity (TFP)[4] had actually dropped by 6 per cent for this sector, while Hong Kong's TFP increases accounted for 56 per cent of manufacturing growth from 1970-90. Moreover, MIT Professor Robert Solow concluded that in the US, technological progress explained 80 per cent of the rise in per capita income. Increased capital investment was responsible for only the remaining 20 per cent.[5]

Thus, according to the "Krugman School", Singapore's growth was initially fuelled by a huge increase in inputs, primarily labour and capital. High unemployment in the 1960s meant a large labour surplus was available to increase the labour input. Meanwhile, the capital input was being dramatically boosted by vast amounts of capital generated by the Government's forced savings strategy, spearheaded by the CPF program; but as Singapore reached full employment, capital was the only input that could continue to increase under the CPF scheme.

Via the CPF (and rising government charges), Singapore's total savings rocketed from a negative 2.4 per cent of GDP in 1960 to over 50 per cent by 1996.[6] In the three years from 1997-99 Gross National Savings (GNS) averaged as much as 54 per cent of GNP, the highest ratio in the world.[7] But while Singapore's savings rate soared, its efficient use of capital plummeted. Return on capital fell from 40 per cent in the 1960s to 11 to 12 per cent by the late '80s. This was "one of the lowest rates in the world," notes Low.[8]

The performance of the corporate sector demonstrates that Singapore's use of capital is mediocre at best. In 2000, the return of capital employed (less weighted average cost of capital) was only 3.38 per cent – well behind that of comparable countries.[9] Returns on capital by Hong Kong's corporate sector was 11.59 per cent, South Korea 12.2 per cent, Taiwan 11.28 per cent and the US 15.95 per cent. However, an IMF study of 42 countries found that in 2002 the return on assets by Singapore's non-financial corporate sector was 3.96 which was just above the global median of 3.75 per cent. [9a] Even so, Singapore's lagged behind its Asian competitors (India, Thailand, Malaysia, Hong Kong, South Korea, Taiwan and the Philippines) in terms of profitability. Their median return on assets was 5.29 per cent, well above Singapore's. If Singapore's local corporate sector had been considered separately from foreign companies, its returns on capital would have been even lower. Singapore's foreign firms have always had a higher return on equity (ROE) than local concerns. In 1991, the ROE of foreign firms was about 27 per cent while that of the locals was about 9 per cent.[10] In 1999, the respective ROEs were 17 per cent and 11 per cent. While the gap between local and foreign enterprises has significantly narrowed, it was still sizeable in 1999.

2. Comparisons with Hong Kong

Other comparisons have been drawn with Hong Kong to further illustrate Singapore's inefficient use of capital. Between 1960 and 1985, Hong Kong saved and invested 20 per cent of its GDP[11] but by 1972, Singapore had surpassed this rate and was saving 24.5 per cent of its GDP. By 1985, Singapore's savings were 41.6 per cent of GDP and by 2000 were 51.5 per cent.[12]

While Hong Kong, like Singapore, has achieved rapid growth since the 1960s, its capital investment has remained a constant percentage of GDP. Moreover, Hong Kong has been using its capital more efficiently than Singapore. In September 2004, a Standard & Poor report found that Singapore's investment strategy had netted a simple annual return of 1.7 to 4 per cent from 1999 to 2003. By comparison, Hong Kong efforts had yielded a 6.1 per cent return during the same period.[13] If Singapore had performed as well as Hong Kong it would have been S$17 billion richer during this period. In addition, Hong Kong's investment returns in **real** terms were even more impressive: 9.1 per cent, versus Singapore's 1.0 to 3.5 per cent.

While Singapore's savings have been higher, it has been using them less efficiently than Hong Kong. Unlike Singapore, Hong Kong had achieved GDP growth by increased TFP, not by ever-greater capital inputs – especially after its excess labour surplus had been soaked up. From 1970 until the late 1980s, Hong Kong's increase in output per worker came from a rise in its TFP. Singapore's TFP fell by 6 per cent over the same period. According to Low:

> *Hong Kong appeared to have grown by being more efficient in the way it used people, capital and technology. Singapore prospered through higher taxes, forced savings and dependence on favoured MNCs...[14]*

She adds that the, "Singapore worker is not psychologically geared to be independent minded and resilient as the Hong Kong worker". Increased productivity is very dependent on worker attitudes and initiative. A workforce lacking these attributes has little capacity to improve its productivity.

The differences between Singapore and Hong Kong are duplicated on the managerial and entrepreneurial levels. Singapore's economic development has been overwhelmingly state-directed and has largely crippled the SME sector. But Hong Kong has pursued a laissez-faire approach, providing a climate conducive to risk-taking and innovation. Jones has noted that "it was risk-taking, Chinese merchant entrepreneurs in SMEs, that largely accounted for the double-digit growth that Hong Kong achieved between 1960 and 1980".[15] This factor, plus a more innovative labour force, explains Hong Kong's much higher productivity than Singapore's.

3. The Productivity Debate

Given the standing of Young and Krugman, their views were taken seriously by Singapore's policy-makers, especially when Krugman compared Singapore's growth experience to that of the defunct Soviet Union:

> *Singapore's growth can be explained by increases in measured inputs. There is no sign of increased efficiency. In this sense, the growth of Lee Kuan Yew's Singapore is an economic twin of the growth of Stalin's Soviet Union – growth achieved purely through mobilization of resources.[16]*

Krugman's comments miffed Lee and the PAP leadership. Singapore's carefully cultivated reputation for efficiency was being questioned. Spurred by Krugman's comments, Singaporean economists began scrutinising their country's productivity. Several groups of local economists became involved, some supporting the Krugman/Young view, others the government position that Singapore had indeed experienced increased growth through productivity.

A 1995 study by two Singaporean economists, Rao and Lee, supported the PAP Government view.[17] They found that while the country's TFP had fluctuated significantly in the 1960s and 70s, it had taken off during the 1987-94 period. While TFP had only reached 1.3 per cent from 1966 to 1973, and dipped to 0.6 per cent during 1976-84, it had soared to 2.6 per cent in 1987-94, they contended. Productivity had accounted for 30 per cent of GDP growth in the last eight years, compared to only 7 per cent in 1976-84 and 10 per cent in 1966-73, they claimed.

Other studies of Singapore's manufacturing sector came to opposite conclusions, including a 2000 study of 28 manufacturing industries by Mahadevan and Kalijiran. Using different methods from Rao and Lee they found that TFP's contribution declined in the late 1980s and became negative in the 1990s.[18] A 2000 study by Bloch and Tang of the manufacturing sector from 1975-94 found that this sector had displayed low efficiency. Increased capital input "accounts for almost all the rapid output growth in Singapore manufacturing," they said.[19] The contribution of technical progress was "either very low or negative".

Singapore's bureaucrats' own calculations confirmed the low productivity findings. The MAS's 1994 annual report revealed that the TFP contribution to Singapore's growth was modest. Between 1991-3, increased productivity accounted for only 2 per cent of the 7.5 per cent growth that the economy had experienced.[20] The rest was due to a higher employment rate (3.8 per cent), greater capital intensity (1.2 per cent) and cyclical factors (0.5 per cent). The report showed that despite significant increases in productivity, Singapore's economic growth was still mostly being driven by labour and capital inputs.

A study of the 1960-86 period done by the MAS in 2000 again put the TFP contribution to GDP growth at a low 0.9 per cent.[21] A similar TFP figure of 1.0 per cent was calculated for the 1973-96 period by the Department of Statistics (DOS) in 2000.[22] For the 1985-90 period the TFP contribution was a high 3.8 per cent, but during 1990-96 it dropped back to 1.8 per cent.

These studies, made by Singapore's technocrats to disprove Young and Krugman's claims that Singapore was inefficient, more or less confirmed them. As Peebles and Wilson note, the technocrats "did their own calculations trying to show that things were not as bad as the earlier studies had shown...All quite civilised and progressive".[23]

While the MAS technocrats accepted the findings with good grace, the Government's reaction was not so gentlemanly, especially when reports about Singapore's low productivity began to appear in the local press. One PAP cabinet minister professed to be "saddened" that *The Hammer*, the journal of the local opposition Workers' Party, had reproduced articles on Young's study from an August 1992 edition of *The Economist*.[24] *The Hammer* was reproducing articles "written by foreigners against Singapore," he complained. BG Lee also attacked Young's article.

The Economist may have suffered for publishing such material. In August 1993, *The Economist*'s circulation was restricted in Singapore by the Government, following another dispute with the magazine.[25] But Francis Seow contends that the magazine's 1992 publication of Young's findings influenced the Government's decision.

Despite their public opposition to the Young/Krugman findings, PAP leaders such as Lee Kuan Yew reportedly came to accept them by 1995. Lee reportedly told Krugman, "you're right so far, but our total factor productivity growth will be much higher in the future because of the investments we're making in education".[26] But future chapters will consider whether Lee's confident predictions about Singapore's productivity – and education policies that aim to raise it – are justified.

4. Singaporean Productivity, Real and Imaginary

BG Lee's boastful 1986 claim that Singaporeans work at 99 per cent efficiency was an example of Singapore spin. It most often involves making exaggerated claims about the superiority of the Singapore model – usually to receptive and unquestioning Western journalists and neo-cons. Selling Singapore to the world is the prime aim, particularly the city-state's claims of efficiency. Yet most studies of Singaporean productivity, including those of its government economists, show that Singapore's TFP was only about one per cent from 1960-96. They clearly reveal that Singapore is not operating at 99 per cent efficiency, nor at anything remotely like that.

Flattering ratings from such compliant ratings agencies as BERI greatly facilitate Singapore's constant image-making. Singapore's overall productivity, including that of its workforce, is very average compared to that of other countries'. In 2000, Singapore was ranked 26 out of 49 countries for overall labour productivity by the IMD.[27] In the industrial and service sectors, the IMD ranked labour productivity at 22 and 18 respectively – about average by world standards.[28] How BERI has managed to rank Singapore's workers as the world's best in 2000 is deeply mysterious. By comparison, the IMD ranked the US fifth for general labour productivity, third for industrial labour productivity; and fourth for service productivity while Australia's rankings were 12, 14, and 11. Singapore's unimpressive labour productivity levels are matched by its inefficient use of capital. But these are only overall productivity figures for Singapore. To get a fuller picture of Singaporean efficiency, a survey of how various sectors of its economy perform is required, beginning with the public sector.

References

1. Krugman, Paul: "The myth of Asia's miracle", *Foreign Affairs*, Vol 73, No. 6, November/December 1994.

2. Ibid, p. 67.

3. Young, Alwyn: "A Tale of Two Cities: factor accumulation and technical change in Hong Kong and Singapore", in *NBER Macroeconomics Annual* (Cambridge, Massachusetts; MIT Press, 1992), pp. 13-54.

4. TFP is the total combined productivity of labour and capital. Productivity itself measures how much production (i.e. GDP) is growing independently of any quantitative increase in labour or capital (or land).

5. Krugman, p. 68.

6. Tan Khee Giap and Lee Wee Keong: "Beyond Regionalization, Basis for Sustainable Growth and Potential

Sources of Expansion", p. 98 in *Singapore: Towards A Developed Status*, edited by Linda Low (Singapore, Oxford University Press, 1999).

7. Peebles, Gavin: "Saving and investment in Singapore", p. 375 in *Singapore Economy in the 21st Century*, edited by Koh Ai Tee, et al (Singapore, McGraw Hill, 2002).

8. Low, Linda: *The Political Economy of a City State* (Singapore, Oxford University Press, 1998), p. 34.

9. Bhaskaran, Manu: *Re-inventing the Asian Model: The Case of Singapore* (Singapore, Times Media, 2003), p. 22.

9a. Singapore: Selected Issues: IMF Country Report No. 04/103, April 2004, (Asia-Pacific Department, International Monetary Fund, Washington D.C.), pages 17 and 22.

10. Ibid, p. 23.

11. Low, p. 34.

12. Peebles, Gavin and Peter Wilson: *Economic Growth and Development in Singapore* (Cheltenham, UK; Edward Elgar Publishing, 2002), p. 275.

13. *Business Times*, October 1, 2004.

14. Low, p. 35.

15. Jones, David Martin: *Political Development in Pacific Asia* (Cambridge, UK; Polity Press, 1997), p. 89.

16. Krugman, p. 71.

17. Rao, V. V. Bhanoji and Christopher Lee, "Sources of growth in the Singapore economy and its manufacturing and service sectors", *The Singapore Economic Review*, 40 (1), April 1995 (cited in Peebles and Wilson).

18. Mahadevan, Renuka and Kali Kalirajn; "Singapore's manufacturing sector's TFP growth: A decomposition analysis", *Journal of Comparative Economics*, 28 (4), December 2000 (cited in Peebles and Wilson).

19. Bloch, Harry and Sam Tang, "Estimating technical change, economies of scale and degree of competition for manufacturing industries in Singapore", *The Singapore Economic Review*, 45 (1) April 2000 (cited in Peebles and Wilson).

20. *The Straits Times*, August 7, 1995.

21. Peebles and Wilson, p. 64.

22. Ibid.

23. Ibid.

24. Seow, Francis: *The Media Enthralled: Singapore Revisited* (Boulder, Colorado: Lynne Rienner, 1998), pp. 132-3.

25. Ibid, p. 172.

26. Peebles and Wilson, p. 61.

27. *The World Competitiveness Yearbook 2001* (Laussanne, Switzerland; Institute for Management Development).

28. Ibid.

CHAPTER 5

PUBLIC SECTOR PRODUCTIVITY

An expectation of efficiency in all areas, including high capital productivity, would seem reasonable in such a modern and seemingly cutting-edge economy as Singapore. But as already shown, its corporate sector returns lag behind those of such industrialised economies as Hong Kong, Taiwan, Korea and the US, as does its overall yield on capital. Singapore's use of capital was also found to be very inefficient, especially compared with most other industrialised countries.

Moreover, the yields that Singapore has been getting from its publicly-controlled capital resources in the form of national financial reserves and state-run pension funds have been unimpressive. The Economist estimated that the real return on pension funds in Singapore between 1983 and 1993 was 2.3 per cent per annum, the lowest of 18 countries surveyed. [1]

To understand the reasons for Singapore's inefficient use of capital – and to see to what extent this is still the case – first requires an examination of Singapore's state enterprises (SEs). Collectively they are the domestic economy's biggest players, and as Chapter 14 shows, account for most of the 30 per cent or more of GDP generated by the economy's public sector. Also, SEs (in the form of GLCs) made up 40 per cent of the market capitalisation of the Singapore Stock Exchange (SSE) by October 2004, according to US Government estimates. [2]

The SE sector controls most of Singapore's financial and other capital reserves through its two biggest SEs, Temasek Holdings and the Government of Singapore Investment Corporation (GIC). The term sovereign wealth fund (SWF) has also been applied to them. SWFs are investment arms some states have used to invest their financial reserves and earnings. Over 20 nations have sovereign funds. In Asia these include China, Brunei, South Korea and Malaysia, as well as Singapore. SWFs were estimated to control anywhere from US$1.9 trillion to US$2.9 trillion in assets worldwide. [3]

In Singapore's case Temasek controlled US$108 billion (S$164 billion) in assets by mid-2007. [4] But with the far more secretive GIC estimates vary on its total funds. The GIC will only say that they are "over US$100 billion" but the *Financial Times* reports them at US$140 billion (S$212 billion) [5] while in February 2008, Morgan Stanley calculated them at about US$330 billion. [6]

1. Temasek

Temasek Holdings was set up in 1974 as a holding company by the Ministry of Finance to hold and manage government investments in GLCs. At that time 36 GLCs were transferred to Temasek's control.[7] Since then Temasek, and the number of GLCs it controls, has expanded enormously. Temasek's structure has become vast and complex. It directly controls 22 first-tier GLCs, all of which have subsidiaries and associate companies. These in turn often have third-tier subsidiaries and so on.

Most of Singapore's 600 or more GLCs would fall under Temasek's auspices, one way or another. Other holding companies have included MND Holdings (owned by the Ministry of National Development). But MND was taken over by the Ministry of Finance and the bulk of its GLCs were transferred to Temasek.[8] In addition to these Temasek-listed companies (TLCs) there are also a number of GLCs fully or majority-owned by statutory boards.

Many TLCs are listed on Singapore's stock exchange and, by October 2007, the top six accounted for nearly 22 per cent of the SSE's total market capitalisation.[9] Six of the biggest TLCs (and the degree of Temasek's ownership in them by March 2006) were: Singapore Power (100%), Singapore Telecommunications (Singtel) (56%), Capitaland (42%), Neptune Orient Lines (67%), Singapore Airlines (57%), Keppel Corporation (31%) and Sembcorp (50%).[10] GLCs are, on average, almost ten times bigger than non-GLCs in terms of capital stock (fixed assets).[11]

Investment Locations and Strategies

Temasek companies are involved in a wide range of activities. But "Traditionally, Temasek likes to downplay the extent to which its companies dominate Singapore's economy," noted the *Far Eastern Economic Review* (FEER).[12] Since Temasek's formation its companies have "penetrated every key segment of the [Singapore] economy from ports, telecoms, stockbroking and shipping to power, food, the media, logistics, airlines, engineering, property, healthcare, education and even zoos and aviaries".[13]

Till the 1990s, most of Temasek's investments had been in Singapore. Even in 2004, 52 per cent of Temasek's investments were still in Singapore, though by then 32 per cent were also in OECD countries – with a strong Australian bias – and 16 per cent in Asia, excluding Japan.[14] But over the last decade, Temasek has been aiming to reduce its Singapore assets to one third of its total portfolio. By March 2006, its Singapore assets had fallen to 49 per cent and to 44 per cent in 2007.[15] Overall, 80 per cent of Temasek's assets are in Asia, including Singapore.[16] Australia has become a prime venue for Temasek investments. By 2007, Singapore's total state-controlled assets in Australia (including those of Temasek's) were almost Aus$30 billion.[17] TLCs' Australian investments, include Optus (bought by Singtel in 2001); Australand (by Capitaland, 1995); the Victorian electricity transmission business, Powernet (Singapore Power, in 2000); TXU's Australian energy portfolio (Singapore Power, 2004); Alinta gas distributor (Singapore Power, 2007), and a stake in ABC Learning (2007).[18] GIC investments in Australia include a 50 per cent stake in Westfield Parramatta (2007) and another in the Melbourne Myer complex (2007).

Temasek adopts a long-term approach to investments with a focus on both listed and private companies and real estate investments. About 60 per cent of its investments are in the financial and communication sectors, reflecting the Singapore Government's aim to enhance Singapore's role as a regional communication's centre. Often Temasek takes large stakes in enterprises it invests in. About half of Temasek's portfolio consists of holdings in companies in which it has more than 50 per cent. [19]

Disappointing Deals

Temasek's performance, as reflected by the returns of its major GLCs, has often been disappointing. "Returns by GLCs have been poor in the past decade despite impressive economic growth and a substantial improvement in corporate governance," noted Daniel Lian a Singaporean economist with Morgan Stanley Dean Witter in December 2001. [20] Lian's comments about Singapore's GLCs would seem justified when considering their performance from 1992 to 2002. The lacklustre performance of the mostly Temasek GLCs was revealed in a *Business Times* survey of 17 of them which had been listed on Singapore's stock exchange.[21] The survey found that from 1992-2002 their total shareholder returns were 4.4 per cent per annum – less than half the Singapore share market's 9.2 per cent average for the period. A 2004 survey by UK consulting firm LEK found that Temasek's 22 listed companies had made an average return of only 1.7 per cent a year since their respective listings.[22]

The losses of major Temasek GLCs have also been widely publicised. Much attention has been focused on the disastrous performance of Singtel, one of Singapore's largest and most prestigious companies. In 2001, Singtel was ranked as one of the world's biggest value destroyers by consulting firm Stern Stewart. Singtel had wiped out nearly US$30 billion of wealth to June 30, 2001. [23]

Singtel, in which Temasek had a 65 per cent stake in 2001, had been engaged in a number of loss-making off-shore deals. There have been abortive acquisitions with Cable & Wireless, Hong Kong Telecommunications and later with Malaysia's Time Engineering. Both deals fell through: the first when Singtel was outmaneouvred by Richard Li, son of Hongkong billionaire Li Ka-shing; the second when the Malaysian government got cold feet about its flagship telecommunications company partnering with Singtel because it was a Singapore government-controlled corporation. [24]

From the mid-1990s Singtel had been lurching from one bad deal to another and this had hit its share price hard. After debuting at S$3.60 in 1993, Singtel's share price fell from a high of about S$4 in 1996 to S$1.20 by the end of 2002. [25]

Bad investment decisions explained much of the price drop. Initially Singtel's purchase of Optus in September 2001 was Singtel's worst acquisition. Singtel paid S$12.9 billion for Optus when its book value was only S$3.2 billion. [26] A telecommunications analyst for Kim Eng Ong Asia said: "Optus was bought at the peak of the technology bubble, and that was why there was such a huge amount of goodwill paid for it ... [Singtel] got carried away and overpaid for the company". [27]

By February 2002, it was clear that Singtel had paid 50 per cent (about S$5 billion) too much for Optus, concluded market analysts. By February 2003, Singtel was still carrying S$9.56 billion in debt, largely because of the Optus acquisition. [28] The telco had to sell stakes in two subsidiaries – Singapore Post and Yellow Pages – to reduce the debt. Singtel's cash hoard which had once been more than S$7 billion was severely depleted. [29] Only several years later did the Optus deal eventually came right for Singtel, though in late 2005 Optus was losing market share to aggressive smaller players Vodafone and Hutchison in Australia. Singtel has finally made substantial gains from Optus, which has become its crown jewel. But Singtel still paid several billion too much for Optus despite high profits from 2004.

Moreover, by early 2006, Optus was being handicapped by "the penny-pinching bureaucracy and glacial decision-making of its owner, Singapore Telecommunications," noted Michael Sainsbury, a financial correspondent for *The Australian*. [30] "Optus is being strangled by mama at a time when its bigger rival, Telstra, is making a much bigger fist at getting its broadband plot together," he said.

Other Singtel investments have also taken a long time to come good. It was five years before Philippines Globe Singtel turned a profit after Singtel acquired it. Also, it took Singtel over three years to reap a profit from its stake in Bharti, an Indian telco.[31] Again, in March 2004, Singtel sold Lycos Asia, a US$50 million joint venture for US$1. In recent years other foreign ventures by Temasek companies have often lost hundreds of millions of dollars.

- In January 1998, it was revealed that Micropolis, a US disk-drive manufacturing company, taken over by one of Singapore's biggest GLCs, Singapore Technologies, sank with losses of S$575 million. [32]
- The Development Bank of Singapore (DBS) then 37 per cent government-owned through Temasek, admitted in March 2000 that it had lost heavily in acquiring the Thai Danu Bank in 1998. The CEO of DBS acknowledged that the acquisition was an "expensive mistake". [33] The size of this mistake was revealed when the bank said that it was raising provisions for its stake in the Thai bank from S$241 million to S$763.4 million.
- SIA, one of Temasek's and Singapore's biggest GLCs, made an abortive take-over for Air New Zealand in April 2001, during which SIA acquired 25 per cent of a troubled airline. The New Zealand carrier was suffering financial and operational troubles. This caused its share price to nose-dive, forcing the New Zealand government to bail out the airline, diluting SIA's share to 5 per cent. By October 2004, SIA was estimated to have lost NZ$500 in this ill-fated foray, according to the investment director for Macquarie Equities NZ. [34]
- Further SIA ineptness was revealed in its acquisition of 49 per cent of Virgin Atlantic which was bought at the height of the tech boom in 2001 for Aus$1.6 billion. Virgin boss Sir Richard Branson must have been laughing all the way to

the bank, because he got top dollar and retained control of the airline.[35] Paying top price for 49 per cent of Virgin while leaving Branson in charge was seen by many business analysts as showing poor business acumen.

- Chartered Semiconductor Manufacturing, a hi-tech company which Temasek has a 60 per cent share in, bled money from 2001-4.[36] Having inferior technology to Taiwanese rivals, the company has not made a profit since 2000.[37]

These loss-making ventures by Temasek GLCs would account for much of Temasek's unimpressive performance – and Singapore's mediocre capital yields generally – to the early 2000s.

Madam Ho to the Rescue

Temasek's debacles to 2002 demonstrated that it and its companies needed better leadership. In May 2002, Ho Ching, the wife of Deputy Prime Minister Lee Hsien Loong, was appointed to head Temasek. Her brief was to perk up its performance. Madam Ho's appointment was seen as nepotistic by some, but others thought it was a smart move. Having married into the Lee family she was seen as having the political clout to make the sometimes painful decisions required to transform Temasek into a more profitable operation. After two years at the helm Ho was being praised by Singapore financial analysts for having galvanised Temcsak. "Temasek-linked companies are much better investment propositions than ever before," said one Singapore-based CLSA research head.[38]

The results of Ho's leadership were contained in the first annual report that Temasek had ever released in its 30-year history. In 2004, Temasek wished to sell bonds and to do this needed an international credit rating from Standard and Poor and Moody's Investors Services. To get a good credit rating required far greater transparency than Temasek had previously practised. After the report appeared in October 2004, both S&P and Moodys obliged and gave Temasek a triple-A debt rating.[39] The report showed that over 30 years Temasek's total shareholders' return (TSR) had been 18 per cent, but in the past 10 years had only been 3 per cent.[40] The low returns to 2004 had been due to such factors as the 1997/8 Asian financial crisis, the September 11, 2001, terrorist attacks, and the 2003 outbreak of severe respiratory syndrome (SARS) in Asia, claimed Temasek. Also, during the year ended March 31, 2004, Temasek's TSR had leapt to 46 per cent.

However, the Temasek report got a sceptical response from financial commentators, both foreign and local. The London-based *Financial Times* noted that the 3 per cent return was well below both the Singapore stock market average and that of the top 50 Asian companies as measured by CLSA brokerage.[41] Even the 46 per cent shareholder return chalked up by Temasek for the year to March 2004 was not as impressive as it seemed, noted foreign business media. *Bloomberg News* reported that for the same period, the Morgan Stanley Capital International Asia-Pacific Index gained 59 per cent in Singapore dollars.[42]

Some local analysts were also lukewarm about Temasek's results. A CSLA analyst in Singapore remarked, "Temasek's performance in the past decade has been pretty mediocre, very unimpressive ... In spite of its reputation for having well-managed companies, the figures do not support that". [43] Temasek had underperformed, not only against listed non-state private companies in Singapore, but also against the top 50 Asian companies outside Japan, and state-owned companies in India and Malaysia.

Again, a later Temasek report showed that its total shareholder return from March 2000 to March 2005 was a mere 1 per cent a year, compared with 2.7 per cent for the *Straits Times Index* (STI). [44] However, the share market was high in March 2000 because of the dot.com boom and was then followed by market lows in 2001 and 2003, due to terrorism threats and the 2003 SARS crisis. Only by 2005 was the Singapore stock market at 2000 levels again, including the prices of listed Temasek companies. Many would have only returned to their 2000 price levels by 2005. Even so, Temasek had still only scored 1 per cent to the STI's 2.7 per cent.

However, Temasek's reports show its performance was improving and continued to do so through to 2007. In 2006, TSR was 24 per cent, the same as for the STI, [45] and in 2007, Temasek's TSR was 27 per cent. [46] In 2007, Temasek was claiming a compounded return of 18 per cent since its inception.

Ho's energetic management has been cited as the main reason for Temasek's improved performance. In June 2002, *Business Week* reported that "Many analysts insist that only an outsider can break up the cozy corporate culture of patronage widely blamed for the lethargy of the ... GLCs". [47] Previously Temasek had been generally content to supervise its GLCs at arm's length. But with Ho, Temasek has adopted a more interventionist approach with its companies and taken greater risks with overseas investments. Temasek chairman, S. Dhanabalan said that Ho was not chosen to head Temasek because she was Lee's wife, but for "a willingness on her part to take calculated risks". [48] However, some analysts in Singapore's financial community "warn that Temasek's strategy of buying big chunks of companies exposes it to potentially deep loses if markets turn," noted *Reuters*. [49] One former Temasek advisor said: "Temasek's strategy is similar to that of a big private equity investor and could well end up producing lower returns than the big index-tracking funds", adding "You can't just become George Soros or Warren Buffett overnight." [50]

On-going Debacles

Temasek has already come a cropper several times since 2006 with its more risk-taking strategies. The first was its purchase of the Thai telco, Shin Corp, in March 2006. Temasek paid US$2 billion for a controlling interest in Shin Corp which was owned by the family of Thai Prime Minister Thaksin Shinawatra. Temasek then quickly snapped up most of the rest of Shin Corp on the stock market through Thai nominee companies, giving it 96 per cent control of the conglomerate. While Temasek claimed it had done everything by the book, the Thai authorities saw the deal as having violated their country's 49 per cent foreign investment laws.

Questions also arose as to where Temasek had paid Thaksin his US$2 billion, considering that Thailand's central bank limits personal cash transfers to US$1 million a year. Was it a foreign tax haven, avoiding Thai regulations altogether? Far from being the great buy Temasek claimed, the deal ignited six months of political turmoil. This culminated in the September 2006 coup which ousted Thaksin from power. The deal also enraged the Thais who boycotted Shin Corp's television, airline, finance and technology businesses. The Thais were angry that a foreign state-controlled company had acquired control of their leading telco by methods they deemed questionable. The country's military were particularly aggrieved that a foreign power would control the telco they used for military communications.

An effigy of Ho Ching was even burnt during the anti-Thaksin demonstrations. By October 2006, Temasek was facing a US$2 billion paper loss on the Shin Corp purchase, along with fines of up to US$2 billion if it was proved that Thai licensing laws had been breached. [51] In its 2007 report, Temasek did not specify its losses from Shin Corp but recorded a loss of S$830 million from associated companies which included Shin. [52] Temasek also said that its net profit had fallen by 29 per cent compared to the previous year, from S$12.8 billion to S$9.1 billion.

After the Shin Corp fiasco, another one erupted for Temasek in Indonesia in 2007 regarding its stakes in two telcos there – Indosat and Telkomsel. Because the pair controlled 80 per cent of the country's mobile-phone market, Temasek was found guilty of violating Indonesia's anti-monopoly laws by a Jakarta business court and was fined US$3 million. This was despite the fact that Temasek had only had indirect minority holdings in both companies, which had been acquired in 2001 and 2002. However, the belated court-action could have been because the share values of both companies had increased five times, making them far more valuable to Indonesian business interests. As Temasek had also discovered in Thailand, foreign-ownership of a country's telcos can arouse strong nationalist sentiments. Indonesia too believed Singapore could tap into its military communications through Temasek. Temasek has appealed against the court's ruling. [53]

Again, by April 2008, Temasek was also sitting on paper losses of US$1.3 billion from its investments in Barclays and Merrill Lynch. [54] Temasek invested US$1.9 billion in Barclays in July 2007, whose share price had then fallen 38 per cent within nine months, and US$5 billion in Merrill Lynch in 2007, whose price was down 11 per cent. Financial analysts have criticised Temasek for making premature investments in Western financial institutions at the height of the global credit crunch. [55]

Accounting Issues

Despite some setbacks, Temasek's performance may have improved in recent years. But Temasek's only partial transparency still generates questions about its returns. Under the Singapore Companies Act, Temasek is an "exempt private company" and is not required to publish audited financial statements. [56] But under Ho, Temasek started doing it anyway because of the need to gain a S&P and Moody's credit rating. Even so, the statements are limited. As the *Wall Street Journal* noted:

> *Temasek releases only consolidated accounts, so cash flows between its subsidiary investments and the holding company aren't detailed. Historical financials are provided only back to 2001, which means some claims such as the 18 per cent compounded shareholder return – can't be independently verified.* [57]

Singapore correspondent for the *Financial Times* John Burton reported that: "There have been some complaints by people in the finance sector that ... it makes it difficult to independently verify claims about investment yields that Temasek has been able to return for [its] investments." [58] Moreover, the media have been repeatedly denied access to Ho Ching and senior managers at Temasek. FEER sought interviews with Ho in November 2002, but its request was denied. [59] Also, Temasek promised to schedule interviews with other executives, but failed to deliver. FEER submitted a list of detailed questions, but a spokeswoman said Temasek didn't feel "quite comfortable with the angle of [the] story" and declined to respond. "The questions largely pertained to Temasek's business strategy, the performance of its companies and the benchmarks it uses to measure their performance." [60] These were the types of questions that securities analysts would want to know of companies they cover and which any board chairman or CEO would need to answer from his shareholders. But such questions require Temasek to divulge more information than it would wish to about its activities.

What Temasek publishes "are figures drawn from summaries of audited accounts of its constituent companies, some of which are listed," noted Philip Bowring of the *Asia Sentinel.* [61] "Thus the published figures could be considered the truth but perhaps not the whole truth." [62] Nonetheless, *Asia Times Online* cites independent financial analysts who mention the use of "accounting gimmicks that diverge from internationally accepted norms" by Singapore SEs "who buy and sell among themselves at undisclosed transfer prices, obscuring their profit and loss profiles". [63]

Transactions of assets between GLCs at below market prices could also inflate their profits, including those of Temasek's. For example, in November 2004 Temasek acquired HDB Corp (a wholly-owned HDB subsidiary) for S$117 million, whose normal market value would have been about S$200 million, based on local housing industry estimates. Also, no tenders were called for the HDB Corp transaction. (Details of this transaction are described in Chapter 15). Such cosy deals provide easy ways for Temasek – and other SEs – to boost their profits.

Hand-outs by the PAP Government to selected GLCs have also greatly increased their profitability. After liberalising the telecommunications industry in 2000 the Government paid Singapore's existing telcos (both GLCs) S$2 billion as compensation for the introduction of competition to their local market. Singtel was paid S$859 million despite having S$6.3 billion in net cash. [64] Singtel announced it would redistribute the payout to shareholders as a special dividend. The other company Starhub, then run by Ho Ching, was given S$1.08 billion. Starhub had just started operations and had yet to draw any revenue. The billion-dollar payout was to allow it to cover losses in the first years of operation.

An Uncertain Future

Even so, while inhouse deals may have lifted Temasek's profits and TSR, its performance in the last few years seems to have improved. Some may attribute this to Ho and Temasek's new risk-taking strategies. But, as already noted, Ho has yet to prove she is Warren Buffett. She "has become increasingly adventurous perhaps, some suggest, to the point of being carried away by the bullish attitudes of the investment bankers who flock to give advice or sell participation in some private equity fund". [65] Till the credit crunch hit world financial markets in late 2007, Temasek was investing far and wide in the midst of global financial liquidity. Besides its Barclays and Merrill Lynch purchases, Temasek has been buying into Chinese state banks and ventures in Vietnam and Russia, etc.

However, such adventurous forays were being executed during world bear markets by early 2008. They could become loss-making prospects as Temasek's Barclays and Merrill Lynch investments have already done. Temasek has been a relative newcomer to Asian and world financial markets with,

> *...its big investments beginning in 2003 rather than in the immediate aftermath of the Asian financial crisis when asset prices were at their nadir. Since then almost all Asian markets have been on a sharp uptrend. [The] quality of investment decisions has yet to be tested.* [66]

Global bear markets could significantly reduce Temasek returns to the mediocre levels – or even worse – that prevailed pre-2003/4.

2. The GIC

The GIC, which invests Singapore's financial reserves, is a far more opaque entity than Temasek. Only in 2006 did the GIC reveal its investment returns for the first time since its foundation in 1981. Over 25 years till March 2006 the GIC said it had achieved an average return of 9.5 per cent in US dollar terms, or 5.3 per cent over global inflation. [67] In 1981, the GIC was set up to invest Singapore's financial reserves, about which various estimates have been made. The International Monetary Fund (IMF) calculated that Singapore's "gross official reserves" were US$136.3 billion in 2006.[68] Meanwhile, the *CIA World Factbook* estimated that the Republic's "reserves of foreign exchange and gold" were US$157 billion by December 2007. [69]

The GIC was Lee Kuan Yew's idea. He decided to set up the fund in 1981 because he thought the government was not investing the country's reserves for the best long-term returns. Lee was the GIC's founding chairman and still is. His son, and current prime minister of Singapore, Lee Hsien Loong, is the GIC's deputy chairman. All but one of its 13 board members are current or former government officials. The GIC has about 900 staff working for it in its offices around the world and invests in more than 40 countries.

About half of GIC investments have been in equities, 30 per cent in bonds and the rest in property, private equity, hedge funds and commodities. About 80 per cent of the portfolio has been invested in the US, Europe and Japan.[70] The GIC is barred from investing in Singapore because of fears that its huge size would distort local financial markets.

Previously, the GIC had adopted a cautious investment policy, going for low though safe returns. But while the GIC says its 9.5 per cent returns are beating world inflation by 5.3 per cent, this may be harder to do in future. GIC annual returns would likely range from 6 to 8 per cent in coming decades, with a return above inflation of 3 to 4 per cent, said the fund's public markets director.[71]

To boost future yields, the GIC seems to have followed Temasek's lead and begun taking more risks. Like Temasek, the GIC has started buying equity in large but troubled banks who have been embroiled in the US sub-prime financial crisis. In December 2007, the GIC invested US$9.75 billion for a 9 per cent stake in the giant Swiss bank USB. In September 2007, USB posted a loss of US$712 million, its first ever annual loss.[72] GIC invested the money as the major part of a rescue package for the ailing bank, whose losses had reached US$37.4 billion by April 2008. This loss was the highest of the 14 banks that had been hit by the sub-prime mortgage crisis.[73] Again, in January 2008, the GIC invested US$6.88 billion in Citigroup – the bank which by April 2008 had the third highest losses of US$21.1 billion.[74] And in April, just a few months after its massive capital raising exercise that involved the GIC, UBS was seeking more emergency capital from shareholders.

Both the GIC and Temasek's investments in ailing banks have alarmed some financial analysts in Singapore, including US investment guru Jim Rogers, who co-founded the famous Quantum Fund with George Soros in the 1970s. Rogers, who now lives in Singapore, said: "It grieves me to see what Singapore is doing. They are going to lose money."[75] Rogers, the long-time commodities bull, was shorting investing banks on Wall Street in early 2008. He said Wall Street had to work off ten years of excesses and predicted that the losses linked to risky mortgages would eventually spread to credit card bills, student loans and other debt.

In April 2008, the GIC's deputy chairman, Tony Tan, sought to allay Singaporeans' fears about the GIC's parlous bank investments. "We regard our investments in UBS and Citigroup as long term investments which will give us good returns when markets stabilise and economic conditions return to more normal levels," he said.[76] But as always, only time will tell whether the GIC and Temasek bank purchases were good long-term investments. And it could be a very long time before these investments turn a profit, if Rogers' forecasts are accurate. Till then the GIC and Temasek will be saddled with heavy paper losses.

Moreover, the GIC, like Temasek, has made some past bad investments, but its opacity has ensured that publicity about them was minimised. Pereira reports that,

> There were few reports in the press or even in parliament about the activities of the GIC. As far as the GIC was concerned, no news was good news.[77]

But despite the GIC's opacity, during the 1997-7 Asian financial crisis, reports began leaking out that,

...the GIC was financially 'struggling'. With most private investment houses openly declaring they were hurting as a result of the Crisis, there were rumours that the GIC was also in trouble. Furthermore, the GIC was named as creditor of many investment houses, industrial enterprises and real estate projects in the region when these were declared bankrupt as a result of the Crisis.[78]

For example, the GIC was named as a major investor in Guangdong International Trust and Investment Corporation (CITIC) which collapsed in 1999. The GIC was reportedly owed S$390 million.

In another bad deal the GIC purchased 15 million shares in Australia's Macquarie Corporate Telecom in 2000 at about three dollars a share, making it the biggest shareholder in a company which was on a downward slide. A year after the GIC purchase, the telco announced it was losing money and its share prices tumbled sharply. The GIC was left with depreciated shares and had to sell 14 million of them at 18 cents a share.[79]

If it's true that the GIC was struggling with losing investments during the 1997/8 Asian crisis, the same could have been occurring again during the sub-prime crisis in early 2008. The GIC's higher-risk strategies have taken it into stormy waters where big losses may be as likely as big profits. The question is whether the GIC and its staff have the risk-taking astuteness to come out on top in turbulent markets. By early 2008, the GIC had already taken heavy paper losses on its USB and Citigroup investments that may take some time to come right.

3. The Transparency Problem

Assessing the true profitability of Temasek is still difficult, despite its greater transparency since 2004. But doing the same for the much less transparent GIC is even harder.

The studies cited earlier showed that returns on Singapore's capital assets up to the early 2000s were modest. Singapore lagged behind developed countries in both corporate and pension fund returns. Also, GLCs had lower total shareholder returns than those of non-government concerns for the decade to 2002. But the question is how efficiently has Singapore's state sector used capital in recent years through its TLCs and other SEs and the GIC.

Temasek's returns indicate that its TSR has been rising since around 2004, but the big losses it was facing in early 2008 could significantly cut this. And Temasek's only partial transparency would make it difficult to definitely confirm by how much. This could only be done if Temasek provided the same degree of disclosure as normal public-listed companies. And only then could it be ascertained whether its returns matched those of private-sector enterprises and the corporate sectors of developed economies.

The same could be said about the GIC. It too was facing large paper losses by early 2008, with its more high-risk investment strategies. But how far this will effect the GIC's long-term profitability would be almost impossible to say for as long as it continues to display much greater opacity than even Temasek. While one can get some general idea of Temasek's real returns, the same can not be said for the GIC. Prime Minister Lee Hsien Loong has previously rejected calls to publish details on GIC investments on the grounds that it would reveal information useful to currency speculators. His father, GIC Chairman Lee Kuan Yew, declared: "It is not in the people's interests, in the nation's interests, to detail our assets and their yearly returns".[80]

However, this continued opacity feeds Singaporean suspicions that Temasek and the GIC especially have lost heaps of the country's national reserves in bad deals. Singaporeans bloggers regularly make such claims. One blogger said the "government has lost too much monies on foreign investments and poor management in GLCs".[81] Only much greater transparency by the GIC especially could disprove such allegations.

Assessing Temasek and the GIC's performance in recent years ranges from difficult to impossible because of their lack of transparency. But Temasek's past lacklustre returns – perhaps matched by some equally modest ones from the GIC – have significantly depressed Singapore's capital yields. And both SEs' more high-risk strategies could result in an even more inefficient and wasteful use of the country's capital resources. Their managements have yet to demonstrate they have the investment savvy and adroitness required to achieve good TSRs in the more volatile world markets they have now entered.

References

1. Peebles, Gavin and Peter Wilson: *Economic Growth and Development in Singapore* (Cheltenham, UK: Edward Elgar Publishing, 2002), p. 228.
2. *Doing Business in Singapore: A Country Commercial Guide for U.S. Companies* (US and Foreign Commercial Service and Department of State, 2005), p. 2.
3. Devlin, Will and Bill Brummitt: "A few sovereigns more: the rise of sovereign wealth funds" (the Macroeconomic Group, the Australian Treasury, Canberra, 2007), p. 119.
4. *Bloomburg*, August 2, 2007.
5. *The Financial Times* (FT), September 4, 2007.
6. *Reuters* (Factbox), April 21, 2008.
7. Ramirez, Carlos D. and Ling Hui Tan: "Singapore Inc. Versus the Private Sector: Are Government-Linked Companies Different?" (IMF Working Paper, IMF Institute, July 2003), p. 4.
8. Ibid.
9. *2008 Investment Climate Statement – Singapore* (US Department of State – www.state.gov) p. 1.
10. Goldstein, Andrea and Pavida Pananond: "Singapore and Thailand" (A contribution to the ICRIER Intra-Asian FDI Flows project; the OECD Development Centre and Thammasat University, Thailand, 2007), p. 10.
11. Ramirez and Tan, p. 7.
12. *Far Eastern Economic Review* (FEER), November 7, 2002.
13. Ibid.
14. Wood, Justin: "Translucent Temasek", November 2004, (CFO Asia.com).
15. *Bloomburg*, March 2, 2007.
16. Devlin and Brummitt, p. 124.
17. Mayne, Stephen: "Eaten by Singapore", July 22, 2007, www.theage.com.au
18. Ibid.
19. Devlin and Brummitt, p. 124.

20. *Asian Wall Street Journal* (AWSJ), December 26, 2001.
21. *Weekend Business Times* (Singapore), November 9-10, 2002.
22. *The Economist*, August 14, 2004.
23. AWSJ, December 26, 2001.
24. Chee, Soon Juan: Your Future, My Faith, Our Freedom (Singapore, Open Singapore Centre, 2001), p. 58.
25. *Business Times* (BT), March 26, 2004.
26. *The Straits Times* (ST) July 27, 2003.
27. Ibid.
28. ST, July 22, 2003.
29. ST, March 3, 2003.
30. *The Australian*, February 23, 2006.
31. BT, March 26, 2004.
32. ST, January 16, 1998.
33. ST, March 7, 2000.
34. ST, October 6, 2004.
35. *The Australian*, February 16-17, 2002.
36. *The Economist*, August 14, 2004.
37. *The Australian*, October 28, 2004.
38. *International Herald Tribune* (IHT), January 27, 2005.
39. Ibid, January 27, 2005.
40. ST, October 15, 2004.
41. Ibid.
42. Ibid.
43. *The Australian*, October 14, 2004.
44. *Reuters* (Singapore), January 24, 2006.
45. IHT, July 27, 2007.
46. *Temasek 2007 Report*, www.temasekholdings.com.
47. Shari, Michael: "Can Ho Ching Fix Singapore Inc"?, *Business Week*, June 24, 2002.
48. *Reuters*, July 27, 2007.
49. Ibid.
50. Ibid.
51. Ellis, Eric: "Mdm Ho's Temasek in firing line after Thai coup", *Fortune*, September 25, 2006.
52. Forbes.com, August 2, 2007.
53. *The Economist*, November 29, 2007 and Tempo, November 26-December 3, 2007.
54. IHT, April 15, 2008.
55. FT, April 15, 2008.
56. *Temasek Review 2007* "Creating Value", p. 24.
57. "The Temasek Model" *The Wall Street Journal On-line*, March 21, 2007.
58. FT, May 18, 2007.
59. FEER, November 2, 2002.
60. Ibid.
61. Bowring, Philip: "Singapore's Temasek hits hard going", *Asia Sentinel*, August 4, 2007.
62. Ibid.
63. Crispin, Shawn W.: "Fiscal finangling in Singapore", *Asia Times On-Line*, April 13, 2007.
64. *South China Morning Post*, September 12, 2000.
65. Bowring, August 4, 2007, *Asia Sentinel*.
66. Ibid.
67. *The Government of Singapore Investment Corporation 2007*, (www.gic.com.sg/).
68. IMF Public Information Notice (08/34), Article IV Consultation with Singapore, March 17, 2008 (IMF External Relations Department).
69. CIA World Factbook, Singapore, www.cia.gov/library.
70. FT, September 4, 2007.
71. *Bloomburg*, September 6, 2007.
72. *Business Day*, April 21, 2008, SMH.com.au.
73. *BBC News Channel*, April 1, 2008, news.bbc.co.uk.
74. Ibid.
75. *Reuters*, March 5, 2008.
76. *Reuters*, April 21, 2008.
77. Pereira, Alexius: "Revitalizing National Competitiveness: The Transnational Aspects of Singapore's Regionalization Strategy (1990-2000)": (Faculty of Arts & Social Sciences, Department of Sociology, National University of Singapore, Working papers), No. 161, 2001, p. 16.
78. Ibid.
79. *The Age* (Melbourne), April 11, 2001.
80. FEER, December 2004.
81. www.newsintercom.org: Blogger comments on "Open your books, Temasek Holdings".

CHAPTER 6

. . . .

SOME KEY INDUSTRIES SURVEYED

S ingapore's state enterprises clearly perform below par. Can the same be said for other major sectors of the economy such as the construction, banking, investment and service industries?

1. Construction

The construction sector's low productivity is well known in Singapore. A 1995-9 study showed that the productivity of this sector was much less than that of such countries as Japan, Australia and Hong Kong. Productivity was calculated by using construction volume and total employment to arrive at volume per worker.[1] The study also found that the productivity of Singapore's construction industry from 1995-9 had declined by 13 per cent.

A 1989 study by the country's Construction Industry Development Board (CIDB) compared construction cost efficiencies between Singapore and Perth. The study revealed that while basic building materials cost 60 per cent more in Perth and wages were four to five times higher, luxury apartment, office and hotel construction costs ranged from as little as 5 to 11 per cent more to build than in Singapore.[2] Again, in Dallas, Texas, it was found that while materials cost 80 per cent more and wages were nearly six times higher, unit construction costs were only 2 to 15 per cent greater.

In Singapore, construction projects take two to three times longer to complete than in Australia and other developed countries. This became apparent to me while watching the progress of two apartment buildings being built near where I lived in Singapore. One small three-storey block (comprising six units and a parking basement) took a year to build while a five-storey apartment block nearby, with a parking basement, took 21 months. Australian builders who saw these blocks said that in Australia the first would take three to four months to build and the second six to eight months. I also noted that it took over a year for three hundred metres of sewerage pipe (in a three-metre wide trench) to be laid in my street.

Public works projects in Singapore never seem to end. This was evident during upgrading projects in Orchard Road and New Bridge Road in Chinatown. The Orchard Road project, which involved the building of footpaths and two new pedestrian tunnels, dragged on for 18 months. The Chinatown project, which included construction of an MRT station in the middle of New Bridge Road, took four years. While this project required road-widening and diversion of a canal, the delays and endless inconveniences to pedestrians and businesses in the areas affected would not be tolerated in most Western countries. In both projects pedestrians had to dodge hoardings and other obstacles, and walk on planks, for years. Chinatown retailers were hit hard. Some said their trade had been halved during the construction.[3]

In commenting on the 1989 CIDB study, the Minister for Manpower blamed low-skilled foreign workers for the construction sector's low productivity. Despite getting low pay in Singapore, their use had not reduced construction costs, he said. Only 7 per cent of foreign workers in Singapore were skilled, compared to 30 to 40 per cent of Australian and Japanese workers.[4] In 2003, Singapore's construction productivity was still "low relative to developed countries," admitted the Ministry of Manpower (MOM).[5] This despite efforts to upgrade foreign workers' skills since 1998.

Singapore's foreign workers are unfairly blamed for low building industry productivity. Most of the onus lies with deficient construction practices and poor management of foreign labour by Singaporean supervisors, who themselves often lack proper construction skills. While this is not something the Minister for Manpower would like to admit, it is a view readily endorsed by an Australian construction supervisor who has worked frequently in Singapore.[6] He said the poor treatment of foreign workers, plus the lack of planning, organisation and construction skills, largely explained Singapore's inefficient building industry.

In commenting on the way Chinese Singaporean supervisors treated the foreign workers greatly reduced productivity (few Singaporean Malays or Indians worked as supervisors), Kevin recalled:

> All the Chinese builders would shit on their workers. You can't get the best from people if you treat them like that. They could not see that you get more work from them if you treat them with respect.

Kevin did what he could to help his foreign workers. Many lacked proper tools to do their jobs. He spent S$800 of his money to buy tools for them. He also trained the most promising workers and even managed to get higher pay for a couple of the best. Normally, foreign workers were paid S$16 a day when Kevin was working in Singapore, but he was able to get his best Thai worker's daily rate increased to S$30, and an Indian worker's to S$18. Within a month of Kevin's departure the pay rates of these promising workers had dropped back to S$16 a day. "All I could do with the Indian worker before I left was to give him my work boots," he sighed.

Wasteful construction methods on Singaporean building sites also irked Kevin, who felt that they went a long way to explaining why Singapore's building costs were often much higher than those in Australia. On one site wastage cost was about S$20,000 a week. About 25 per cent of form work (scaffolding etc) that had been hired would not be returned because it had been lost, buried or covered in concrete. Other wastage was due to on-site incompetence. Work had to be constantly re-done, along with patching up cracks and other building flaws. "There were screw-ups every day," Kevin said. A recurring problem was wrongly-sized concrete columns. They were always about 30mm too tall. Jack-hammers would have to be used to chip them down to the required size. "I suggested that if they poured them to the right size to begin with they wouldn't have to do that." Kevin's boss exclaimed, "Oh that's a good idea – I hadn't thought of that."

Singaporean engineers and supervisors lacked not only initiative and common sense but basic building skills. Kevin said construction supervisors in Singapore were poorly trained. They did a six-month course, but it was mostly theoretical, with little practical training. By comparison, supervisors in Australia have to do a four-year apprenticeship, including a two-year course, with emphasis on practical training. When Kevin mentioned this to his Singaporean construction colleagues he was sneeringly told that Australians were "slow learners". But he found that Singaporean supervisors often "just didn't know what to do".

Kevin found that many Singaporean supervisors were not only poorly trained and incompetent but lazy. They would spend much of their time in nearby coffee shops or the worksite canteen. Part of the problem was that there were too many Singaporean supervisors. Government regulations stipulate that there must be one Singaporean hired for every five foreign workers. Kevin considered that many of these Singaporean supervisors were surplus to requirements on construction projects.

Since leaving Singapore, Kevin has not returned, despite being well paid and being asked to come back. "It was the most frustrating time in my life," he said. "I just hated the whole deal."

Kevin's comments reveal that the low productivity of Singapore's construction industry is primarily due to poor quality supervisors. Although the mostly foreign workforce they oversee is often under-skilled, their own shortcomings greatly reduce its productivity. Not only is their training inadequate, but their hierarchical attitudes to foreign workers greatly reduce workforce morale. Even apart from a callous disregard, even contempt, for subordinates, especially lowly foreign workers, workforce morale on Singaporean worksites is reduced by the fear Singaporean managers have of getting their hands dirty. Building supervisors must often get down with their workers to help with jobs, but Singaporean foremen and supervisors find this demeaning.

The comments of a foreign worker from China are also instructive. He said he made up to S$3000 a month doing jobs which Singaporeans wouldn't touch with a ten-foot pole. These included plastering cement on brick walls, laying bricks and building partitions under a hot sun at construction sites.[7] Sometimes foremen and supervisors must "plug gaps" at building sites and help when workers are short. Managerial reluctance to do this delays work and reduces productivity. As Lee Kuan Yew himself noted:

Our graduates don't like to go to the factory floor and soil their hands. They don't know what happens on the factory floor. So how can they order more efficient work?[8]

NTUC head, Lim Sway See, notes that Singaporeans do not display "enough pride" in their jobs:

This seems to be so in technical jobs as compared with managerial positions. Many in the technical area are anxious to move into management because it is seen as more prestigious. However, a premature switch from technical positions to the managerial track will deprive us of the deepening of expertise and experience in key technological fields.[9]

The lack of hands-on experience of Singaporean managers and supervisors is the result of hierarchical attitudes as well as exploitative treatment of foreign workers, especially non-Chinese Asians such as the Thai, Indian, Filipino, Bangladeshi or Burmese. Such managerial behaviour adversely affects worker morale and productivity. Workers work better for bosses who respect and consider them than for those who don't. Only when Singapore's construction industry realises this is its productivity likely to increase appreciably.

2. Banks

Singapore's banks and other financial institutions have frequently won international recognition for the high quality of their supervision, probity and the discharge of their banking obligations. An ING Barings Securities banking study found that Singapore had the best banking supervision policies of eight major Asian banking markets surveyed.[10] Singapore beat Malaysia which was ranked second while Hong Kong was ranked 3, Taiwan 4, Indonesia 5, Korea 6, Philippines 7 and Thailand 8. Singaporean banks have a reputation for being financially very sound and low-risk compared to other Asia-Pacific banks. They have a strong capacity to meet deposit and other financial obligations on a timely basis.

In 2001, the IMD ranked the policies of Singapore's central bank (the MAS) as first among the central banks of 49 countries for having "a positive impact on the economic development" of the country.[11] Singapore was ranked 9 on the adequacy of the "legal regulation of financial institutions" to ensure "financial stability".[12] But Singapore's locally owned banks have earned few accolades for efficiency. Doubts about this were expressed by Lee Kuan Yew as early as 1997, when he realised how unprepared they were to face competition from the foreign banks that were coming to Singapore. In 1994, during brainstorming sessions with managers of foreign banks in Singapore, Lee was told that the Republic's banking policies were over-cautious. They were preventing its financial centre from growing and catching up with more developed centres.[13]

Lee gained further insights into how far Singapore lagged behind big Western banks after joining the advisory board of J.P. Morgan, a blue-ribbon US bank. He saw how they were preparing for globalisation by upgrading their operations, especially in the field of information technology. "I concluded that Singapore was light years behind them," he said. After discussions with local bankers, Lee felt,

> *they were not awake to the dangers of being in-bred and of failing to be outward and forward looking in an age of rapid globalisation. They were doing well, protected from competition. They wanted the government to continue to restrict foreign banks from opening more branches or even ATMs...*[14]

Lee told them that under trade agreements with the US and possibly the World Trade Organisation (WTO), Singapore would have to open up its banking industry and stop shielding local banks from foreign competition. They had been protected since 1965 when the Government prevented foreign banks from coming into Singapore. For "30 years, I protected these family-owned banks," Lee admitted in a May 1999 speech.[15] He said the local banks were not "thriving because they are wonderful bankers. It's because I protected them along with Koh Beng Sen [Deputy managing director of the MAS]," and added that he had prevented the foreign banks from opening branches and having ATMs and had allowed local banks to spread their ATMs and their branches throughout the HDB estates.[16] But this benign situation could not continue, Lee warned. Singapore banks were "headed down the hill". They risked being "wiped out" on their home ground, through technological challenges and the foreign competition that liberalisation would bring.

Lee's comments came two years after he had initiated measures intended to improve the performance of local banks in anticipation of the liberalisation of Singapore's banking sector in fulfilment of trade agreements with the US and other countries. Foreign banks would have freer access to the local banking sector, and qualifying foreign full banks could open more branches and ATMs. Limits were also lifted on foreign ownership of local bank shares.[17]

Singapore's banks were slow to adapt themselves to foreign competition, as Lee noted in May 1999 when he castigated their tardy progress. He blamed this on their family management: "each one has got a son in waiting".[18] Again, in August 1999, Lee expressed his exasperation at local banks' slow response to liberalisation. In noting how Americans did their banking at supermarket kiosks, he asked:

> *Why haven't we done that? Because we are protected from competition and lack that cutting edge. Within three to five years, the local banks [had] better shape up or else we are in trouble.*

The banks responded by lobbying to prevent further liberalisation, protesting that Singapore was already open enough to foreign banks. Local bankers' fears were justified. By 2003, it was apparent that foreign banks were beating them. A *Straits Times* columnist noted that local banks' "defence of the market they have traditionally dominated has looked pretty weak".[19] The foreigners had "raced ahead by introducing innovative products" whereas the locals "had not been innovative". Singapore's banks were clearly not world class in terms of efficiency. Until recently, the same could be said about their low levels of transparency, which lagged behind those of Western banks and of many in Asia. But US Free Trade Agreements (FTAs) from 2000 have forced Singaporean banks to be less opaque, as Chapter 15 explains.

3. The Investment Industry

By April 2004, Singapore was the world's fourth-largest derivatives trading centre, having a turnover of US$125 billion per day. Singapore was also the second-biggest forex centre outside Japan in Asia.[20] The Singapore International Monetary Exchange (SIMEX) is reported to be one of the world's best-run and most successful futures and options exchanges. The Singapore Stock Exchange (SSE) has won similar accolades.

Singapore hosts one of the world's largest offshore financial markets, the Asian Dollar Market (ADM). "This is the equivalent of the Eurodollar market except that it is located in Asia and plays a key role in channelling capital to corporations and government agencies for development in the Asian region," note Peebles and Wilson.[21]

Singapore also aspires to be a major centre for venture capital management. In 2004, the MAS reported that funds in Singapore managed S$462 billion in assets, about half that of Hong Kong's.[22] Besides having a sizeable fund management industry, Singapore has impressive legal, technical and investment-market infrastructure; yet despite all this the returns of Singapore's fund management sector have, for many years, been less than those achieved in Western countries, according to National University of Singapore (NUS) economist Mohammad Ariff.

From 1979-95, a Singapore unit trust investment grew by 7 per cent a year after deducting fees and charges. In the same time period, a direct investment in the portfolio of shares which make up *The Straits Times Industrials Index* (STII) would have grown by 17 per cent, assuming reinvestment of dividends: Singapore's fund managers achieved only 41 per cent of the STII's rate of return from 1979-95. By comparison, Australian fund managers achieved a net return of 10 per cent a year against the share market's 13 per cent – 77 per cent of the market's return during the same period. Meanwhile, US fund managers averaged 9 per cent a year against the total market's 12.5 per cent – 72 per cent of the market's return.[23]

Higher funds costs was one reason for the lower return of Singapore funds, Dr Ariff said. But while front-end fees charged by some Singapore funds were 4-5 per cent in 1988, they had dropped to 3 per cent in 1992 and 2.2 per cent in 1996. This improved the performance of Singapore's unit trust industry. For the 1988-95 period, 12 CPF-approved funds achieved a return of 64 per cent of STII. But "this remains below the comparative short-term performance of US and UK fund managers," Dr Ariff notes. "When the impact of short-term cycles is washed out of the results, the Singapore fund management industry appears to fall further short of this benchmark than its counterparts elsewhere in the world."[24]

Singapore funds' mediocre results are in part the result of the relative lack of solid investment information in Singapore compared with what is available in more mature Western investment markets. Dr Ariff points out that "in a small and volatile share market like Singapore's, stock picking is less of a science than it is in large and mature markets". In addition, the secretive nature of GLC and government business operations greatly hampers the free flow of business information in Singapore required for making informed investment decisions.

A strong risk-averse mentality among Singapore's unit trust managers further explains the poor performance of its unit trusts. Risk-averseness generally accounts for the lower returns of funds in the US, Australia and elsewhere compared to the market average, or share market index, which records the fluctuations in the collective value of a stock market's counters.

Numerous studies have shown that investors who randomly chose shares by throwing the proverbial dart at a daily newspaper's stock market pages got better returns than highly-trained unit trust experts. Only a quarter of US funds manage to beat the Wall Street stock market indexes. The same applies in Australia and the UK, and even more so in Singapore.

Share market commentators believe excessive caution largely explains the dismal performance of unit trusts. Fund managers fear losing investors' money. Failure means career setbacks. High staff turnovers and frequent sackings occur when funds do poorly in the markets; bad decisions usually mean the sack. Not surprisingly, most fund managers play it safe and follow the consensus view. Blame is shared when fund managers fail conventionally. While such thinking afflicts fund managers everywhere, it is particularly obvious in Singapore where risk-averse behaviour is far more prevalent than in Australia and the US, as this book will repeatedly show. The greater caution of Singaporean unit trusts combined with less market information than is available to a mature securities market, does much to explain their poorer results compared to those in the West.

4. The Service Sector

Availability and performance are the key criteria for assessing service quality. Availability is measured by the range of services offered, while performance is gauged by how well they are delivered. By the early 2000s, Singapore was lagging behind most developed countries on both counts.

Singapore has lacked many personalised and innovative services. Even by 2001, Singapore did not have facilities for cinema ticket booking by phone complete with home print-out. It lacked mobile laundry services and websites common in developed countries for locating play tickets or booking flights.

Manpower costs and lackadaisical attitudes explain such deficiencies, observe local service industry experts. "Some companies see it as an investment but most think that going the extra mile for their customers means extra costs," commented the director of a Singapore institute for improving service standards.[25] "It is not in the culture of many companies here to give value-added services," she said. Besides deficiencies in availability, the delivery of customer service has been poor in Singapore.

Indifferent Service

In 2000, Prime Minister Goh condemned Singapore's "indifferent service", adding:

> I have been to many countries. I can say that generally, the quality of service in Singapore does not match that in many places I have visited.[26]

He recalled coach drivers in Australia who doubled as tour guides, and public-relations officers in France who received VIPs at airports, handled customs and immigration procedures, drove guests to the lounge and even made them coffee. Goh said the service sector needed to buck up and become more efficient and offer quality customer service. He recalled that while in Paris a woman taxi driver went out of her way to carry his heavy luggage out of the boot.

Such a scenario would be "light years" away in Singapore, complained a local dress-shop manager. She had had to fire two salesgirls in the previous three months when they refused to deliver clothes to customers. One told her that it was not in her contract to be a delivery girl; the other just said no.[27]

Many Singaporeans would claim that local taxi drivers are also light years behind their Parisian counterparts in service quality. One Singapore taxi driver unabashedly told *The Straits Times* that he never helped passengers carry their bags:

> I don't see why I should help carry the passengers' luggage or shopping bags. I am just a taxi driver. I am not getting any extra money, so why should I do it?[28]

The Straits Times spent two days observing cabbies at work at four shopping centres in town and noted that many did not come out of their vehicles to assist passengers with heavy luggage.[29] Service was much better at the airport, with nine in ten cabbies helping with passengers' bags. Singapore's cab companies have felt compelled to severely discipline cabbies who fail to help airport passengers.

Besides helpfulness, another measure of customer service is product knowledge. Here too Singaporean sales staff score poorly. A US university study of workers' sales motivation in nine countries found that Singaporeans place product knowledge low on their list of priorities.[30] Only six per cent of Singaporean staff cited product knowledge as the most important ingredient for sales success, compared to 25.5 per cent of Chilean staff, 25 per cent of New Zealand and 23.3 per cent of Australian staff.

Singaporeans regularly complain about service quality in Singapore. After *The Straits Times* published an article about deficient service, the paper was deluged with 120 letters endorsing the article's views. The rudeness of retailers was a recurring theme. "That some retailers here are so bold with their customers is shocking, but what may be worse is that there seems to be so little redress from them," the article noted. [31]

One reader recalled seeing a computer shop in Sim Lim Square with a notice which said: "$1 for each question about my stuff if you're not buying". Another vexed reader suggested, "Grab the thing you want, go to the counter and pay for it. No talk, no questions, no problems".

Favoured Foreigners

Foreigners, especially Westerners, tend to get better service than locals in Singapore's shops and restaurants. Singaporeans in the service industries say this is because Westerners appreciate good service much more than the locals. As one contributor to a local newspaper forum on customer service said, "I think our problem is that our culture is not appreciative of good service.... Why waste your time when customers just give you a blank stare in return, and occasionally, a really lousy thank you?"[32] Another Singaporean noted that "quality service is a mutual thing", adding that:

> Singaporean consumers should learn to respect others in order to get respect and quality service in return. People want others to smile and greet them, but they don't smile or return a greeting. It's like serving wine. If I know you can't appreciate good wine, I'll just serve you plonk.[33]

Lack of appreciation kills good service, noted a Singaporean back from Australia. He believed it was a cultural problem:

> I suspect part of the problem is that, unlike the Japanese, Thais and Australians, we lack a culture to bind us together within circle of social graciousness. After my years of study in Australia, I thought I might be able to bring some of the politeness back here. After a while I gave up ...No, I gave in – I surrendered.[34]

A Singaporean *Streats* columnist noted:

> Perhaps service staff in Singapore are not always to blame for bad service. The cold and less-than-friendly customer has to take the rap. [35]

He himself admitted to being cold and unappreciative of service staff. "I'm one of those people who are oblivious to the existence of service staff, but yet are fond of criticising them for their bad service." A *Today* columnist expressed similar sentiments:

> I think we Singaporeans get the customer service we deserve. We complain about the sales girl who did not smile at us and pulled a long face when we entered the store. We mess up the display bin and then complain when everything is so hard to find....you get what you give. I have seen Westerners chat and laugh with salespeople and get good treatment in return.

Of course when that happens, we locals immediately say: "You see, you see? The salesgirl discriminates between locals and foreigners. I want to see the manager right now! [36]

A saving grace of Singaporeans is they sometimes have few illusions about themselves.

Low Incentives = Poor Service

Besides poor customer appreciation, low pay and status discourage courteous service. A Singaporean service institute director said, "Many see it as an unglamorous job. It's hard work, the hours are long and the pay is not that attractive. That's why it is difficult to keep good staff in the industry." *Straits Times* columnist Warren Fernandez remarked:

Ask service workers and many will say that paltry pay, lack of job prospects and low social status all result in service jobs being far down on the list of choice careers. Underlying all this is the question of "face". Put simply, in our social context, it is better to be served than to serve, which some attribute to Singapore's Asian cultural values. [37]

In September 2001, service-sector employers were "baffled" to find it so difficult to hire workers, even when unemployment was rising. [38] In August 2001, only 120 jobs out of 1000 that were offered at a government-organised job fair were taken. One retail chain went to the fair looking for 10 to 20 trainee supervisors and sales assistants. Of the 30 shortlisted, only 10 came for interviews. Eight were offered jobs but four rejected them; of the four who started work, one quit within a week. A chain spokesman complained that applicants were being too choosy. They were asking "unrealistic salaries" of over S$1000. But S$1000 a month for shop assistants in countries such as Australia would be unacceptable. There, new sales staff earn the equivalent of S$2000 to S$2500 a month. This is despite the fact that Australia has a similar per capita income to Singapore's.

Singaporeans who have held retail jobs in Australia notice how this salary gap affects customer service. One Singaporean working in Australia said that his friend earned S$15 an hour working in MacDonalds in Melbourne, while he got S$12.50 an hour in a buffet restaurant. [39] Previously he had been "really happy" with S$5.50 an hour in Singapore. If he worked in a Singapore restaurant again he would probably bring back some of his "good service" habits. But after a while he would probably cease practising them. "You pay peanuts you get monkey service," he said.

After being in countries like Australia, many Singaporeans realise how bad service is in Singapore. After returning to Singapore, one Singaporean "felt a bit offended by the poor service offered by sales people here". [40] In Singapore if you ask sales people for something they will tell you: "it's all there on the shelf. If not there, means we don't have". But in Australia "they'll take the trouble to help you find it," he said.

Low Skill Levels

In Singapore low skill levels, including poor English, also explain deficient service. Westerners find this a particular problem in Singapore:

- Singaporean shop assistants, despite being taught English at school from Year One, do not understand what you want, despite your repeated explanations in simple clear English. A few days before writing this, a young female shop assistant in a kitchenware shop could not understand me when I asked for a kettle, carefully repeating the word three times. Eventually she got the supervisor who immediately directed me to where many kettles were displayed in the shop.

- A waitress asks if you want chillie sauce or tomato sauce. You say "tomato sauce". She repeats "chillie or tomato sauce" again. You say "tomato sauce" again – as clearly as possible. And she still brings you chillie sauce.

Such experiences make Westerners think they have a speech impediment.

Poor stock-taking is another problem in Singapore shops. Lines that are in demand run out quickly and it may be months before they are replenished. One UK woman who worked in Singapore's retail sector said she found this was a constant problem. "If I see something I want that's advertised I rush down to buy it straight away, before it runs out," she said.

Singapore bookshops have peculiar stocking practices. Local book distributors have told me how some bookshops refuse to re-stock steadily selling titles which have sold out. This was certainly the experience of one Singaporean writer. His book had sold out, and when he suggested the bookshop manager order more he was told, "Oh, but we've already sold that book". Re-ordering sold-out titles was apparently an alien concept.

Service sector efficiency is becoming increasingly important in modern economies, especially highly urbanised ones like Singapore's with its large retail, hospitality and tourist industries. Poor customer service in these areas can be very damaging economically. For example, in the retail sector Singaporeans are shunning local stores and shopping abroad, spending at least S$7 billion overseas. A Singapore retail expert, Dr Lynda Wee, says that "Singapore retailers must begin to acknowledge that they are not trading in Singapore – they are trading in South-east Asia".[41] Regional competitors like Thailand have a service edge: "Salesgirls in Thailand may not speak English well, but their warm smiles and pleasant service more than make up for it".[42] One Singaporean executive said, "I go to Australia and Thailand to do all my shopping. Sure, I spend a little more but I get treated like a queen and feel good about it". Another Singaporean noted Singapore lacked the "dynamic spirit in the provision of service" which she found in Hong Kong. "From bazaar stalls and small eateries to hotels and expensive shops, no effort was spared to ensure customers received top service, even if they did not make a purchase," she said. But after "days of being pampered, it is hard to adjust to the robotic faces of people running my neighbourhood supermarket".[43]

Singaporean polytechnic students made similar discoveries when they studied service quality in Japan and Australia.[44] In face-to-face interviews and visits to retail outlets they found that Singaporean staff lacked courtesy and product knowledge, passion and spontaneity, compared to those in Australia and Japan.

"Indifferent service" cuts sales and reduces profitability. Surly, unhelpful staff discourage people from buying and erode profit margins. In Singapore, this largely explains the service sector's mediocre performance.

The preceding survey of several major sectors of Singapore's economy has revealed that low productivity is not confined to the SE sector but prevails in other major sectors of the economy. Even Singaporean icons such as SIA display severe shortcomings, as the next chapter shows.

References

1. *The Straits Times* (ST), October 21, 1999.
2. ST, November 6, 1996.
3. ST, April 20, 2002.
4. ST, November 6, 1996.
5. *Streats* (Singapore), February 25, 2003.
6. Private interview by the author.
7. ST, October 21, 1999.
8. Han, Fook Kwang; Warren Fernandez, and Sumiko Tan: *Lee Kuan Yew, The Man and His Ideas* (Singapore, Times Editions, 1998), p. 355.
9. Mahizhnan, Arun and Lee Tsao Yuan: *Singapore: Re-engineering Success* (Singapore, Oxford University Press, 1998), p. 46.
10. ST, February 16, 1997.
11. *The World Competitiveness Yearbook 2001* (Laussanne, Switzerland; Institute for Management Development), p. 414.
12. Ibid, p. 430.
13. Lee, Kuan Yew: *From Third World to First* (Singapore, Times Media, 2000), p. 98.
14. Ibid, p. 99.
15. ST, May 22, 1999.
16. *Business Times* (BT), May 7, 1999.
17. Lee, p. 101.
18. BT, May 7, 1999.
19. ST, December 24, 2003.
20. ST, September 29, 2004.
21. Peebles, Gavin and Peter Wilson: *Economic Growth and Development in Singapore* (Cheltenham, UK; Edward Elgar Publishing, 2002), p. 230.
22. *Today*, September 24, 2004.
23. "Laggards" by Louis Beckerling. *Singapore Business*, October 1996, pp. 42-44.
24. Ibid.
25. ST, August 21, 2001.
26. ST, October 29, 2000.
27. ST, August 21, 2001.
28. Ibid.
29. ST, March 16, 2001.
30. *Streats*, January 7, 2004.
31. ST, March 3, 2001.
32. *Project Eyeball*, November 1, 2000.
33. Ibid.
34. *Streats*, June 9, 2003.
35. *Streats*, August 1, 2003.
36. *Today*, September 24, 2004.
37. ST, September 8, 2001.
38. ST, September 20, 2001.
39. *Project Eyeball*, November 1, 2000.
40. Ibid.
41. ST, November 28, 2002.
42. Ibid.
43. ST, July 27, 2002.
44. ST (*City Weekly*), September 8, 1995.

CHAPTER 7

TARNISHED ICONS

If indifferent productivity plagues Singapore's state and major industrial sectors, are such Singaporean icons as Singapore Airlines (SIA) similarly afflicted? This chapter examines the performance of SIA and another major well-known GLC, *The Straits Times*. SIA is a Temasek GLC, while both Temasek and MND Holdings together hold controlling shares in *The Straits Times*, a Singapore Press Holdings (SPH) company.

1. SIA – The Greatest Way to Fly?

SIA is one of Singapore's proudest achievements. Well known for being "A great way to fly" with its pretty kebaya-clad "Singapore girls", SIA basks in business travellers' acclaim. As Singapore's flag-carrier, the airline has won many international awards for excellence. In October 2000 readers of two London newspapers voted SIA as the world's Best Scheduled Airline.[1] SIA also won the *Business Traveller* magazine's Best Long Haul Airline award in October 2000, and in 2003, the Airline of the Year award sponsored by travel information provider OAG, Best Leisure Airline by the UK newspapers *The Guardian* and *The Observer*, and Best Airline by *Global Finance* magazine.[2] In April 2004, SIA won the Skytrax Airline of the Year award, beating more than 130 airlines.[3]

In addition, SIA was voted the top Singapore company for the 11th consecutive year in an annual poll conducted by the *Far Eastern Economic Review* (FEER) in 2003.[4] The runner-up was Singtel! FEER readers ranked the companies of 12 Asian countries on five criteria: quality of services and products, managerial vision, responsiveness to customer needs, financial soundness and capacity to inspire emulation by other companies. SIA was voted tops for service quality, long-term vision and emulative potential.

How deserved are these accolades?

Fatal Flaws

SIA has won numerous awards for the reputed quality of its in-flight service and punctuality. But an airlines's safety record is surely the most fundamental criterion by which to rank it. Flying passengers from A to B without killing or maiming them is an airline's primary responsibility. Here SIA, and its subsidiary airline Silkair, have less than spotless records. Each has had recent crashes resulting in the deaths of 187 people. A Silkair plane crashed in Sumatra in December 1997, claiming 104 lives. At Taipei Airport in October 2000 an SIA plane crashed into some construction equipment on the runway, killing 83 people.

In the Silkair crash, the plane suddenly dived into the Musi River, near Palembang. An Indonesian inquiry into the tragedy ruled in December 2000 that there was insufficient evidence to ascertain what caused the crash, whether pilot error or mechanical failure. A Singaporean court came to a similar conclusion in October 2001, when families of the victims sued the airline for compensation. However, US and Australian aviation experts concluded that the crash was due to suicide by its pilot, Captain Tsu Way Ming. He had deliberately put the plane into a steep dive and crashed it, they said. A report by the US National Transportation Safety Board rejected the Indonesian findings. Critical facts about the crash and events leading up to it had been ignored or explained with disingenuous logic in the Indonesian report, the board noted. It contended that circumstantial evidence showed the pilot had deliberately crashed the plane. The board's conclusions were based on evidence of Tsu's chequered flying record and financial problems.

The Indonesian hearings revealed that Captain Tsu Way Ming had made three mistakes as a pilot in the nine months before the December 1997 crash. The third one had occurred on November 20 – only 29 days before the December 19 crash. After the second mistake in June 1997, he was demoted from Line Instructor Pilot to Captain.[5] One former Silkair captain told the inquiry that he had complained to the airline's management about Tsu's unsafe behaviour. He had asked for a meeting to discuss the matter, which had been scheduled for December 23, 1997 – four days after the crash.[6]

Tsu had taken out a S$1 million mortgage-reduction insurance policy several days before the crash.[7] The policy was attached to the loan for a new house that he and his family had moved into in June 1997. Normally such policies cover mortgage payments if home-owners fail to make payments. Tsu posted the cheque for the insurance premium on December 16, three days before the crash. The policy took effect on December 19, the day of the crash. Despite this evidence, the Singapore police probe concluded, "There is no indication that he had committed suicide in order that his family might gain from the policy".[8] The insurance policy would have taken effect on the day of the crash and indicated a suicide motive to many.

US and Australian investigators claimed there was a cover-up regarding Tsu's financial problems. They said that the Indonesian investigators had refused several requests by US and Australian investigators to see a confidential report about Tsu's financial affairs. "This is a major cover-up," a former Australian investigator said. "If Tsu Way Ming's financial problems were not grave and a motive, they would have made the report public or at least shown it to the US investigators."[9] But the head of the Indonesian inquiry reportedly said he did not want to upset authorities or governments. This cast doubt on the inquiry's objectivity and suggested it was trying to protect Tsu.

Whether or not Tsu deliberately crashed the plane, the whole episode reflected badly on Silkair. Despite having reprimanded him three times and demoting him, Silkair continued to let him fly its planes. After the reprimand on November 20 for the third offence, it would have been appropriate to ground him. Silkair's failure to do this was a glaring oversight.

Interestingly, while Singaporean pilots supported their colleagues accused of negligence in the Taiwan crash, they would not back Tsu. At an Internet forum on the crash some pilots expressed concern at the Indonesian findings. One pilot said the inquiry "was denying what we all know: that serious worries and stresses in a pilot can and do affect actions and performances".[10] Whether because of suicide or mere incompetence, the consensus was that pilot error could well have played a key role in the crash.

The Taipei tragedy exposed SIA's deficiencies and inefficiencies. The disaster occurred when SIA flight SQ006 was using the wrong runway. The plane hit construction equipment as it taxied down the runway for take-off, and 83 passengers died when it was engulfed in flames.

Investigations revealed that pilot error was the cause, compounded by the pilot's decision to take off in driving rain and winds of 50kpm. Other planes had decided not to take off from Chiang Kai-shek Airport that night. SIA's CEO, Cheong Choong Kong, said the airline took full responsibility. "They were our pilots. It was our aircraft, the aircraft should not have been on the runway and we accept full responsibility," he said.[11] However, pilot error was not solely to blame. Singapore's Ministry of Transport (MOT) pointed out flaws in the airport's design, layout, and facilities and also criticised the actions of the airport controllers.[12] "It was an accident waiting to happen," said a MOT spokesman. Had runway-closure markers and barriers been in place, in accordance with international standards, the accident would not have occurred, contended the MOT. This view was supported by the International Federation of Air Pilots' Associations (IFALPA), which emphasised how difficult Chiang Kai-shek airport was for pilots.

Despite this, after an 18-month study, Taiwan's Aviation Safety Council (ASC) claimed that of the eight probable causes of the tragedy, seven were due to pilot error. Only one – the bad weather that night – was not. In July 2002, SIA sacked two of the three pilots of the plane, confirming that pilot error had contributed to the tragedy. "The two investigation reports did not exonerate the two pilots concerned completely, notwithstanding the fact that there were serious deficiencies at Chiang Kai-shek Airport that fateful day," announced SIA.[13]

While the Sumatran crash revealed severe managerial flaws in Silkair, an SIA subsidiary, the Taiwan tragedy revealed not only pilot error but cabin crew deficiencies, especially when flames from the petrol tanks began to engulf the stricken plane. Several passengers described how fear immobilised some staff as fireballs exploded inside the aircraft. One passenger remembered watching business class hostesses sitting stunned.[14] When smoke entered the top-deck section, one of the hostesses, urged on by 28 passengers, tried to open the escape hatch but lacked the strength to do so. A passenger immediately stepped forward and yanked it open. Similar problems occurred opening the exit hatch at the plane's tail. A British passenger said, "There were two passengers trying to wrestle it open and the stewardess is next to them and doesn't know what to do. We asked her how to open the door and she was just standing there looking at us. She was in shock. She's like 18."[15] Eventually, directing a stewardess in front of him, he and the other passengers escaped through a hole in the fuselage.

Besides this major disaster SIA has also had minor accidents, including one in March 2003. *The Straits Times* reported:

The pilots of a Singapore Airlines plane made basic errors during a take-off at a New Zealand airport in March, causing the tail of the 747 to drag almost 500m along the runway, a damning safety investigation has found.

The mishap was blamed on pilot error. "That error caused the pilots to calculate a take-off speed that was too slow, hence the aircraft's tail struck the runway before the aircraft became airborne," reported SIA.[16]

PR Failures

The airline's flaws are not confined to pilot and cabin staff inadequacies.

SIA's PR handling of the Taiwan tragedy was also defective. Families of the dead passengers first heard the news through the media, instead of from SIA. While CNN was breaking the news that SIA Flight 006 had crashed, SIA was still issuing statements that there were no known casualties.[17] This massive oversight was dramatically highlighted during SIA news conferences in Taiwan and Singapore two days after the crash. During the Taiwan conference, a Singapore woman whose relative was on the flight burst in and angrily confronted the airline's officials for not keeping her informed about the fate of her relative. Soon after, a distraught man broke in on the SIA news conference in Singapore, screaming that he wanted to know the truth about his brother who had died in the crash. "You are the ones who tell me that you all can give us first-hand news. Well, we end up getting news from all the newspaper reporters," he sobbed.[18]

What these incidents demonstrate is that while SIA may be one of the world's better airlines, it is not the best, especially in terms of passenger safety. Only airlines such as Qantas with accident-free records deserve that accolade, certainly not SIA with error-prone pilots, ineffectual in-flight staff and inadequate management.

The youth of SIA stewardesses is also a concern, with many no older than 18. The minimum age for hostesses on other airlines, such as British Airways, is 21. During the Taipei crash some SIA hostesses had neither the maturity to guide panicky passengers to safety, nor the physical strength to perform such critical safety procedures as opening exit hatches. On other airlines, such as Qantas, cabin crew are usually older and have more male staff. This provides not only a more mature flight staff, but one more likely to have the brute strength necessary to open escape hatches during emergencies.

A S$35m Fraud

Besides in-flight and managerial deficiencies, SIA has displayed weak financial controls. In July 2000, a SIA employee received a 24-year jail sentence for embezzling S$35 million from the airline. An administration supervisor moved this huge sum from an SIA account into personal bank accounts over a 13-year period before being caught.[19] He spent about S$21 million on properties and cars and S$8 million on a Malaysian mistress.

Some Singaporeans were irate that SIA had failed to detect the fraud for so long, especially by an employee on a salary of S$2994 a month. One Singaporean said SIA "has some explaining to do because this case implies that it is not able to detect huge discrepancies". It was amazing that "SIA appeared to be unaware and had to be alerted by another company". While insignificant sums might escape detection, those involving big amounts should have been detected. "Were the superiors of the accused sleeping on the job?" he asked.[20] This is a reasonable question considering the magnitude of the fraud.

Indifferent In-flight Service

SIA's in-flight service may be ranked the best by travel bodies, but many Singaporeans think otherwise. In 2000, there was a flurry of complaints on how passengers were treated on SIA flights. "On Singapore Airlines it is so blatantly obvious that the stewardesses treat *ang mohs* [Westerners] better," one Singaporean angrily wrote to *The Straits Times*. He said he was only offered coke or orange juice while Westerners were automatically given wine. He noticed he was not discriminated against when flying on any European carrier. "On carriers like British Airways and Virgin, wine is liberally distributed regardless of race."[21] One Singaporean who contributed to a *Project Eyeball* forum on good service wrote that while Singapore was "renowned for our first-class airport terminals", SIA's onboard service was not really up to standard. "The air stewardesses can be quite rude and it takes ages for them to get something to you. And when they do they're not polite," she said.[22]

Three years later the same complaints were still being made about SIA's service. In June 2003, Singaporean columnist Conrad Raj noted that on a Bangkok-Manila flight "the food was lousy and the service so-so despite the plane being less than two-thirds full".[23] Complaints about Westerners being favoured over Singaporeans also persisted. As one Singaporean woman noted, "I think most Singaporeans would agree that the best service is sadly reserved for the fairer-skinned foreigners".[24]

By 2003, international ratings for SIA's cabin service began to reflect more accurately the airline's service quality. In the annual Skytrax's Cabin Staff of the Year survey for 2003, SIA slipped from third to ninth place for its cabin service.[25] The survey polled 1,822,503 passengers worldwide. Criteria included cabin crew efficiency, attentiveness, friendliness and consistency.

SIA's high air fares have also attracted strident complaints. Conrad Raj wrote, "Many people ... prefer to fly SIA despite its higher fares because of its service and reputation".[26] But some believe they have not been getting value for money, including an irate business traveller who said he had flown 600,000 miles on SIA. "I am often astonished by the airline's belief that it can charge almost farcically high prices. On almost all sectors that I fly SIA is not just marginally more expensive it is many times more so." Although wanting to support SIA and Singapore, he added, "I am not willing to pay a premium for what have become average products, or put up with arrogant customer service in the process," adding that the new business class seats were "simply terrible". "Whoever designed them obviously doesn't fly much as they are uncomfortable, almost always broken, have tray tables designed for primates and are very good at depositing your drink on your lap."[27] By comparison, British Airways, which had the best business class seats, charged only half of SIA's price for the Sydney-Singapore run, he said.

Despite such complaints SIA somehow keeps winning awards for being one of the world's best airlines.[28] The mystery is why this is so, considering the criticisms of SIA's in-flight service by Singaporeans, its less-than-perfect safety record and occasional managerial failings. Staff morale problems could significantly explain such shortcomings.

Low Staff Morale

Low staff morale has been a perennial SIA problem. The airline has been dogged by high staff turnover and constant industrial unrest for decades. One of the first to publicise these problems was Lee Kuan Yew. In a 1981 speech he recalled how he had sent Devan Nair (then a PAP MP and later President of Singapore) to sort out SIA's management problems. It was "human relations gone wrong", Lee stated. "Even a successful company can begin to go sour when human relations go wrong, and they can improve in spite of their good performance if they get the human relations right." [29] Nair found that SIA employees felt little bond with the company. As Lee recounted in the following garbled passage:

There is no identification with the company because the management do not identify themselves with the workers, and human relations are poor. Pilots: "This is a second-class hotel; since I am flying a 747, equal to Pan Am, BA, Qantas, I want first-class, five-star hotel," and so they got it. So the cabin crew, you know the girl that appears in the advertisements – millions of dollars – [Lee was disjointedly referring to SIA's Singapore Girl advertisements] *she goes into a three-star hotel, the captain and pilots – cockpit crew – go into a five-star hotel. That has been put right. Captain is the captain, he is in charge, including cabin crew. And Devan discovered that when the executives meet with the unions, everybody on the executive side wears a necktie, to the lowest clerk, to show they are executives, you see. Everybody on the union side, open-neck shirt. There is something wrong with their psychology.* [30]

While disjointedly lambasting SIA, Lee took a stroll down memory lane, fondly recalling the PAP's egalitarian past:

The first thing we did in 1955 was to campaign with open neck shirts to make it possible for the worker to identify himself with me [sic]. *If I am with a necktie and a coat and he doesn't own one, it's difficult isn't it? If you cast your mind back to 1959, we changed the rules of Parliament to allow members to go without neckties.* [31]

Lee related Nair's experiences in Japan, a nation which has always impressed Lee. When visiting a Japanese shipyard, Nair,

saw a man in overalls with a helmet talking to him [sic], *and he said, "Who are you?"* [as you do] *and he said "I am the personnel manager". And he looked just like the other workers. And so did six other divisional directors. And one of the rules of the Japanese management system is, everybody wears the same.* [32]

Lee then praised Korea and Taiwan, eagerly noting that Japan had ruled them for 40 and 50 years respectively. When "you go into their enterprises, they have learnt. They all wear the same. They all eat in the same canteen. But not in SIA; executives eat in a different canteen. All this makes for trouble, isn't it [sic]?" [33]

Lee expressed these sentiments in the early 1980s, yet SIA remained afflicted by industrial problems and low morale. In July 1997, industrial relations between airline management and its five unions, representing 15,000 members, were still poor. To solve the problem, the Government had a minister, Mr Lim Boon Heng, secretary-general of the government-controlled National Trade Union Congress (NTUC), appointed to the SIA board.[34] Lim said the Prime Minister had authorised his appointment "in the national interest". Because SIA was a national symbol, known world-wide, its success must be maintained. "In a sense, it reflects Singapore, it is Singapore. We are entering a more competitive environment. If SIA succeeds, it gives us all that much more confidence that we can succeed against global competition," he declared.[35]

His role was to improve SIA's industrial relations when the airline needed to cut costs, improve service, and raise productivity to meet stiffer competition. But the essential problem was the airline's management culture, which had to change if it were to rally every SIA employee to meet global competition. The current SIA culture was "very much bottom-line oriented and at least as far as its employees are concerned, there is insufficient attention given to human aspects of work," Lim said.[36] Workers had to feel that their ideas were useful to management if they were to contribute. He would facilitate union-management communications by getting unions to see the big picture and understand management aims while listening to staff complaints and feeding them back to the management. At least that was what Lim claimed.

However, within weeks it became clear that Lim's appointment to the SIA board was meant to ensure that the airline implemented cost-cutting measures to make it more competitive and to crush any union opposition that might arise.[37] Lee himself had stressed the need to cut costs as Air France and BA had done. But he noted that both airlines had experienced strikes as a result. "Singapore Airlines simply cannot afford this," he warned. To ensure union compliance, the government had installed its NTUC chief on to the board. Reducing costs and short-circuiting union opposition at SIA was the real agenda, and little thought was given to the negative effect this would have on employee morale – as would soon be apparent.

By December 1999, staff resignations had soared by nearly 50 per cent in the second half of the year compared with the second half of 1998.[38] Resignations rose after management decisions to cut recruitment, presumably to reduce costs. This left many flights short of crew, and increased pressure on existing in-flight staff. In November 1999, more than 25 per cent of SIA flights from Changi Airport were down by one or two staff. Cabin crew said that a shortage of even one or two crew members could be hard on those working. "We've to cover for one missing crew member and it can be an ordeal. In some cases we are not able to provide prompt service," said one flight attendant, who "spoke on condition she was not named," *The Straits Times* reported.[39] Clearly, the increased pressure on flight crews was a major factor in staff resignations. SIA belatedly began recruiting more staff again in late 1999, to plug the gap: so much for reducing cabin-crew staff to cut costs. Such staff shortages may explain why cabin service had worsened, not improved, by mid-2003.[40]

Other management-employee problems surfaced in February 2001 when SIA and the Airline Pilots' Association of Singapore (Alpa-S), representing 1500 pilots, appeared before the Industrial Arbitration Court to resolve their differences.[41] The management-union agreement that was hammered out during 65 meetings over 26 weeks had been rejected by 90 per cent of the pilots in January. The pilots claimed that other airlines paid their pilots much more. Another pilot-management dispute dragged on until August 2002 over six rounds of talks. [42] This time the dispute was over whether pilots could take in-flight breaks in economy instead of business-class seats. For 13 years pilots had used business-class seats; but now management wanted them to use economy seats because the introduction of Space-beds meant fewer business seats were available. The pilots objected, and the squabble dragged on until it was resolved with Ministry of Labour mediation. Both sides then resolved to strive for a better working relationship.

But hopes of a better union-management relationship at SIA were dashed by the Iraq war and the February-May 2003 SARS crisis. SARS hit the Asian tourist industry and airlines especially hard. By June 30, 2003, SIA had lost S$312 million for the year – its first-ever net loss. [43] SIA's response was to start sacking staff. Some 414 staff were laid off and a further 145 made to retire early from SIA subsidiaries. Of those sacked, 156 were SIA cabin crew and 26 were pilots. The cabin crew had averaged seven to eight years' service. [44] While SIA had planned to cut S$200 million from wage costs, [45] its retrenching of 414 staff only saved S$14.5 million. [46] This was a small fraction of the S$176 million which had been saved by wage-cuts and no-pay leave. [47] Despite staff readiness to accept less pay and unpaid leave, over 400 were still retrenched.

The retrenchments began to provoke outrage when the SIA subsidiary, Singapore Airlines Terminal Services (SATS), began hiring 400 security workers just a month after it had axed 196 jobs during the retrenchments. Although some of the 196 sacked staff had held security positions, none was offered a new position. They did not meet the "job profile" and were unsuitable, was the glib response from a SATS spokesman. [48] The retrenchments aroused even more anger when SIA's fortunes quickly recovered. The June 2003 passenger traffic rose by nearly 50 per cent on the previous month. The lay-offs could easily have been avoided because passenger loads were picking up, said one Singaporean corporate analyst. [49]

Siasu, the union representing SIA's rank and file staff, was irate at how the retrenchment exercise was conducted. Although told by SIA the previous week that there would be lay-offs, the union was only given details of the lay-offs a few hours before the retrenchment letters were handed out. Siasu president Eddie Chew said, "We are very unhappy at the way it was done. We had no chance to prepare. There must be some trust in one another." [50] Siasu officers had to "scramble" to SIA offices to counsel and help those laid off to get new jobs.

The union was also disappointed that SIA had "forgotten the sacrifices" of cabin crew. They had been the first group to agree to unpaid leave. Pilots' union Alpa-S echoed these sentiments, saying pilots had recently agreed to the wage cuts and no-pay leave arrangements. Like Siasu, Alpa-S believed that the management had been "too hasty" in implementing retrenchments.

Pilot and staff discontent intensified as SIA's fortunes kept improving and new staff were hired. SIA's turnaround was confirmed when it made a S$306 million profit for the July-September quarter. But the airline refused to give preference to the 26 pilots and 156 cabin crew who had been axed in July. [51] This angered the airline's unions. Two weeks later the pilots ditched their union leaders for giving in too easily to management on wage cuts and retrenchments.[52] Their resentment was deepened by SIA's third-quarter profits. The pilots expected the new leaders to be tougher with management.

The ousting of the Alpa-S leadership alarmed the government, who saw it as "confrontational". The government feared that this militancy would spread to other unions, jeopardising its control over them. Government ministers began condemning Alpa-S leaders.

In early December, the Government removed the rights of Alpa-S members to have the final say in any negotiations with SIA management. Previously the union's leaders had had to get the approval of members before they could conclude any agreement or settle a dispute with SIA management. Leaders of other Singapore unions can make deals with managements that bind members. The Government changed the Trade Union Act to impose the same rule on Alpa-S.[53] The Government also had a Malaysian pilot – an Alpa-S member – expelled from Singapore because he had supposedly been a "prime mover" in getting the pilots to sack their union leaders.[54] SIA pilot Ryan Goh, a Singapore permanent resident [PR] for 23 years, lost his PR status in March 2004 because the Government deemed him an "undesirable migrant".

In November 2003, Lee Kuan Yew warned of "broken heads" if escalating management-pilot tensions were not resolved. This undermined SIA's competitiveness when it was facing greater competition from budget carriers, but Lee's real target was the pilots. He repeated his 1980 warning to them that he "won't let anyone do Singapore in". He attacked the pilots, accusing them of having "big egos" because of their greater bargaining power due to high training costs. It cost S$500,000 to S$700,000 to train a pilot who was then contracted to serve for six to seven years before he could quit to work for another airline.[55] It was easier and cheaper for airlines to poach pilots from rival airlines when their contracts finished, rather than to train them from scratch. It also made pilots more mobile and gave them greater bargaining power, Lee said, and it explained the greater conflict between management and the pilots' union than occurred between management and other SIA unions.

Since 1980 there have been 20 pilot-management disputes,[56] but superior bargaining power only partly explains the pilots' militancy. SIA management is also largely to blame for its insensitivity to employee demands, made worse by a government headed by such anti-union leaders as Lee, who sees SIA as his personal fiefdom: "Nobody knows the history of SIA like I do. I nurtured this company, and without my personal intervention there would be no SIA." [57] Lee clearly thinks SIA cannot survive without him.

Lee has also been behind SIA's readiness to sack employees during temporary downturns and has done much to exacerbate its inept and thoughtless managerial style. Retrenchments undermine morale in organisations, especially when badly handled. Singapore management consultant Patrick Lambe said the way SIA dealt with its employees "will be the critical trust factor for the future, not necessarily the retrenchments themselves".[58] Retrenchments can easily breed a sense of betrayal in an organisation. This occurred with the big US companies IBM and General Electric. "Both organisations undertook very painful cuts in the 1980s and 1990s. The cuts were handled very badly and there was a deep sense of betrayal. They took years to recover their credibility as employers," Lambe points out. SIA might face the same reaction with its handling of retrenchments.

Few acts reduce employee morale more than managerial betrayal, a feeling that was widespread among SIA staff by July 2003. After the retrenchments SIA pilots who still had jobs with the airline left to work for other carriers. By November more than 20 pilots had resigned.[59] Unhappiness over wage cuts and job losses were the common reasons given. Between November 2003 and November 2004, 100 pilots and engineers resigned to join the likes of Malaysian Airlines, China Airlines, Emirates, and Dragon Air, according to SIA union leaders.[60]

During 2004, an NTUC survey of non-pilot SIA staff found that employee morale had continued to sink. Unions representing non-pilot staff complained of low morale. A "culture of fear" had spread because of increased "accountability". Workers feared making mistakes and were often threatened with the sack.

The SIA union leaders accused the SIA management of bullying unions, using "divide and rule" tactics in negotiations and paying union leaders scant respect. "Their gestures and tone are humiliating," unionists said. They also complained of managerial factions, lack of information-sharing and little appreciation for staff sacrifices. They attacked management's self-serving behaviour, such as when profit-sharing bonuses were given to newly-employed management officers but not to SIA workers.[61] Such high-handed elitism is typical of Singaporean managements, but a better managerial style could be expected from Singapore's most prestigious local enterprise. SIA's managerial failings largely explain SIA's chronically low staff morale, which had been falling for many years even before 2004. Certainly Lim's 1997 appointment to the SIA board achieved nothing in this regard. His promises to develop a more open management style and greater management-staff trust failed, as constant industrial disputes since 1997 have shown. This is not surprising: Lim and the SIA board embody an elitist and arrogant managerial culture that afflicts not only SIA but most Singaporean organisations, demoralising employees and undermining efficiency. *The Straits Times* also displays these problems.

2. The Straits Times

While not having the same iconic status as SIA, *The Straits Times*, founded in 1845, is one of Singapore's oldest and best-known companies. Although regularly derided as a PAP government propaganda sheet, the paper's production values make it one of Asia's best. Its extensive coverage of international, and especially Asian, news is well-known and often better than most Australian newspapers. In August 2002, *The Straits Times* was named the Pacific region's best newspaper by the Pacific Area Newspaper Publishers' Association (PANPA).[62] The citation for the award commended the paper for its ability to connect with its local community and its extensive foreign overage and analysis. The paper's layout, graphics and design are world-class. In 2003 and 2004 the paper won top awards for printing, infographics and design at Ifra's Publish Media Awards for Asian newspapers.[63] Moreover, the paper and the SPH group generally is highly profitable. Enjoying a monopoly position as Singapore's only morning newspaper has meant *The Straits Times* has always been a lucrative cash cow for SPH. Yet despite all this, the paper has had severe productivity problems.

In November 1991, SPH chairman Lim Kim San belittled SPH's journalistic staff for low productivity.[64] Lim said he was concerned about rising staff costs, which were not matched by corresponding productivity increases.

Low Productivity

The Straits Times' low productivity has always been apparent to the paper's expatriate journalists. During my time in Singapore the paper would struggle to get one edition out by 12.30am. By contrast, *The West Australian,* where I had previously worked could get out a first edition by 8.30pm, a second out by 11pm and a revised second edition out by 12.30pm. Despite being obsessed with efficiency, *The Straits Times* was often very inefficient.

Periodic (and very expensive) efficiency surveys which resulted in the reorganisation and re-arrangement of tasks did little to improve productivity. Once, the paper's editor gathered us all together to give us the results of one of these surveys. The survey showed that the average *Straits Times* journalist wrote one story a day and 0.3 of a feature per week. In Australia, journalists on a major morning newspaper could expect to write several stories a day while features writers would produce a couple of features a week. Besides low productivity, *The Straits Times* and its affiliated publications display other shortcomings.

Being Scooped

To be scooped is the ultimate humiliation for any self-respecting newspaper. The foreign media regularly do this to *The Straits Times.* Often stories about Singapore will appear in foreign publications first, before being lamely followed up by the paper. To be fair to the paper, Lee Kuan Yew and Prime Minister Goh regularly give interviews on Singapore political and business matters first to such foreign publications as the *Asian Wall Street Journal* (AWSJ), *Business Week, The Economist,* the BBC and Reuters TV. For example, Goh initially talked to the AWSJ about his retirement plans and the appointment of Lee family members to head Temasek. Lee Kuan Yew also spoke first to foreign media on plans for greater transparency for the GIC. A *Today* columnist in Singapore noted:

> *It's hard to avoid the impression that the local media keeps being "scooped" by their foreign counterparts. More so, because each time such interviews are done, they break new ground.* [65]

Unlike foreign journalists, locals fear asking Singapore's leaders about democracy and human rights issues, the treatment of opposition politicians, or the use of the judiciary for political purposes. Sometimes there is too much deference towards leaders by local journalists, notes Dr Ooi Giok Ling, senior research fellow at Singapore's Institute of Policy Studies.[66] Dr Ooi's comments suggest that local journalists are afraid to ask tough questions for fear of offending the Government and being seen as anti-PAP. As long as *Straits Times* journalists have such attitudes – and as long as PAP leaders occasionally give preference to foreign publications – foreign rivals will continue to scoop the paper and other SPH newspapers.

A Misguided Chairman

Chairman Lim made the interesting suggestion that productivity could be increased by training reporters to work with minimum supervision, but this would undermine one of the paper's most fundamental editorial principles: reporters must be closely supervised to ensure that they write only what the paper and the Government want. To this end, layer after layer of copy checkers, sub-editors, check subs and finally senior editorial staff are constantly supervising, overseeing, chastising, checking and re-checking everything that the paper's reporters do and write. Moreover, sensitive issues must first be cleared with government ministries. Former *Straits Times* executive Lyndley Holloway describes the procedure:

> *When sensitive issues are involved, journalists must check with the relevant ministry press officers first to seek confirmation or further confirmation. If the officer says that the story cannot be run and the editors accept the reasons given for not printing it, the newspaper will abide by the decision. If the editors disagree – which is quite rare – they take it to higher levels and if the minister vetoes the report, the newspaper must weigh up the risks of ignoring him.* [67]

To cease exercising such close editorial supervision would be unacceptable to the paper's editors and to the Government. Chairman Lim clearly didn't know what he was talking about when he suggested that reporters be subject to less supervision. Nor did he consider that reporters used to close supervision would find it difficult to practice initiative, especially after being educated and raised in a society that discourages this.

The fear of publishing anything that could upset the Government (and the Chairman) constantly worries senior editorial levels and delays decision-making. A page can be held back for hours until senior editors think it's safe to let it go. Such consensus decision-making spreads the blame if anything goes wrong.

The same principle applies to processing *Straits Times* editorials. As Seow explains:

> *Writers put up drafts of leaders, etc., and circulate them among a committee of three or five persons for discussions and approval at the editorial conference...if an editorial or a leading article sometimes appears to the reader rather vapid, uninspiring or lacking in spontaneity or conviction, the plus side is that any political fallout is shared equally amongst the members of the editorial staff. "Two heads are better than one", and "safety in numbers" are not idle proverbs in Singapore's risky media circles.* [68]

Constant checking of editorial content undermines efficiency and seriously delays publication. A couple of ex-*Straits Times* sub-editors now working on Australian publications say how much freer they are to work without constant supervision and checking from numerous superiors. "You can just get on with the job here," said one. But *Straits Times'* editors feel they can't do that with their reporters and sub-editors. Its many editors live in dread of offending the Government.

An experience I had when I worked on the paper illustrates this. One day I was subbing a story and came across the insipid phrase that some PAP MPs had "gently ticked off" the Government on some issue or other. Believing that one word is better than three, I changed this phrase to "chided", which means to mildly criticise. Next day all hell broke loose. The MPs who made this mild comment contacted the paper and insisted that they hadn't meant to attack the Government in such strong terms. They wanted a retraction – and got it. Bewildered *moi* was taken aside by a senior editor who apologetically explained to me the reason for the paper's action.

Crippling supervision is accompanied by punitive and sometimes callous treatment of staff by management and also does much to reduce productivity.

In late 1998, an intimidating memo was issued to the paper's editorial staff. It described what would happen to reporters who made mistakes in their stories. Under the heading "Publicising the Seriousness of Errors", the memo threatened:

> *Management has agreed that from this year the number of people who did badly in performance appraisal banding because of errors will be made public. The number of people who suffered bonus cuts will also be made public.* [Bonus cuts at the ST were usually inflicted on those whose performance had been deemed below par.]

Journalists to get this treatment were those whose "published errors" had required "either file [pre-publication] or published corrections". Under another heading, "Taking Personal Responsibility for Errors", the memo described what erring journalists could expect.

> *The person responsible for the error will have to write directly to the newsmaker concerned, owning up and apologising for the error, in addition to writing the correction for the error. He could also be required to experience the inconvenience caused to the newsmaker, for instance being present to apologise to a newsmakers' clients or customers who have been inconvenienced by the erroneous report. He will also be asked to go to the [editor's] office to apologise personally for having added to the error count.*[69]

Perhaps six-of-the-best should have been thrown in for good measure.

The memo outlined further humiliating procedures the error-prone could expect, revealing a punitive mentality more likely to undermine than enhance efficiency. Fear of making mistakes can induce risk-averse behaviour that cuts productivity. Stories become fewer, shorter and written more slowly to avoid mistakes. An obsession with factual accuracy means duller, less well-written stories. Obviously factual accuracy is critical for newspapers, but if pursued obsessively journalistic paralysis, rather than greater efficiency, will result. Often, managerial attitudes are merely callous and uncaring rather than punitive, to editorial staff who get little consideration from their superiors. Reporters are often kept hanging around for hours after their knock-off time, waiting for some editor to return at his/her leisure to check their stories. Overtime is rarely paid, and staff who dare put in for it are regarded as lacking *esprit de corp.*

Journalists are often summarily demoted, even sacked, for quite small offences. A middle-aged sub-editor was sacked by his section chief for not keeping his shorthand up to speed. As a copy taster on the foreign desk, knowledge of shorthand was as useful to him as Latin; but that was the ostensible reason for sacking him. A middle-aged sub-editor was also sacked because his subbing was deemed inadequate. The fact that he had never been a sub before, and had defective eyesight which made it difficult for him to see what he was editing on a computer screen, was apparently not considered an excuse. He had once been a good police roundsman in Singapore, but no effort was made to find him a more suitable position at the paper.

These examples illustrate the indifference that management and upper editorial levels showed to staff. While similar abuses are increasingly common on Australian and British newspapers, their journalists can seek redress through effective unions and industrial tribunals. The victimised in Singapore have no such recourse, for few such mechanisms exist. Most employees have few rights in Singapore, unless they have highly sought-after skills. Mistreated employees often have minimal redress either through unions or courts, and are rarely in as strong a position such as SIA pilots – and only then if they act as a group – and the efficacy of that has already been seen! The Singapore Journalists' Association is regarded as a joke by local journalists.

The Straits Times' low productivity has been mainly caused by too much time-wasting supervision and a punitive atmosphere that has bred risk-averse attitudes that inhibit innovative reporting. Both factors, combined with managerial indifference to employees' needs, have also reduced morale. This has prompted high staff turnover and further reduced productivity. Happy employees stay put. Staff morale was so low one year that no one wanted to organise an annual staff party, one of the paper's expatriate journalists told me.

Despite *The Straits Times'* low productivity and journalistic shortcomings, it remains one of Asia's best newspapers. Although not unreasonably seen as a government mouthpiece, the paper is still a mine of information about PAP Singapore. Much of the material for this book comes from this paper and others produced by SPH. Buried in the paper's detailed and factual articles is much information that raises serious questions about the Singapore Miracle and PAP policies.

While productivity may be low, the paper is a major information resource on Singapore and Asia and the quality of its printing, lay-out and design remains high. But greater efficiency and better staff management could yield the same results with fewer staff and resources. As early as 1991 Chairman Lim correctly noted that the paper suffered from low productivity, and it is a problem that continues to afflict the paper. Constant efforts to improve productivity have had limited success.

Like SIA, *The Straits Times* has an organisational culture that sabotages efficiency. While both generally produce a quality product, such a culture prevents them from doing better with less and, in SIA's case, undermines its inflated reputation as a Singaporean icon.

On more mundane levels too, Singapore's claims to cutting-edge efficiency can be challenged, as the next chapter shows.

References
1. *The Straits Times* (ST), October 21, 2000.
2. *Streats*, July 31, 2003.
3. ST, April 25, 2004.
4. ST, December 19, 2003.
5. ST, December 15, 2000.
6. ST, July 18, 2001.
7. Ibid.
8. Ibid.
9. *The West Australian*, January 23, 2001.
10. ST, December 16, 2000.
11. *The Australian*, December 16-17, 2000.

12. ST, April 27, 2002.
13. ST, August 16, 2002.
14. *The Australian*, December 16-17, 2002.
15. Ibid.
16. ST, December 16, 2003.
17. Chee, Soon Juan: *Your Future, My Faith, Our Freedom* (Singapore, Open Singapore Centre, 2001), p. 183.
18. ST, November 3, 2000.
19. ST, July 9, 2000.
20. ST, July 4, 2000.
21. ST, January 14, 2000.
22. *Project Eyeball*, November 1, 2000.
23. *Streats*, June 23, 2003.
24. ST, July 26, 2003.
25. *Streats*, July 31, 2003.
26. Ibid, June 23, 2003.
27. ST, July 26, 2003.
28. For what it's worth I have found SIA in-flight service quite good. But then I'm easy to please. I even like airline food! Unfortunately for most airlines, many of their passengers are not so easy-going.
29. Han, Fook Kwang, Warren Fernandez, and Sumiko Tan: *Lee Kuan Yew, The Man and His Ideas* (Singapore, Times Editions, 1998), p. 360.
30. Ibid.
31. Ibid.
32. Ibid, p. 361.
33. Despite his disapproval of Singlish (Singaporean English), Lee sometimes lapses into it. In Singlish "Isn't it" is often used in place of "Doesn't it".
34. ST, July 20, 1997.
35. Ibid.
36. Ibid.
37. ST, August 8, 1997.
38. ST, December 25, 1999.
39. Ibid.
40. Low cabin staff morale could also be explained by SIA's authoritarian staff culture. Former SIA hostess Margaret Tan, now a Singapore university lecturer, said that behind "the beautiful images of the Singapore Girl was a very disciplined, very manufactured system of reward and punishment," where "You were under constant checks – there were only certain shades of red lipsticks you could use; your hair, nail polish and weight...were all under scrutiny. You had to conform to a certain image and role." Such regimented and authoritarian workplaces breed unhappy, stressed-out employees. (ST, June 6, 2003)
41. ST, February 23, 2001.
42. ST, August 24 and 27, 2002.
43. ST, July 31, 2003.
44. ST, July 22, 2003 and *Streats*, June, 20, 2003.
45. ST, July 22, 2003.
46. *Today*, June 26, 2003.
47. ST, July 31, 2003.
48. *Streats*, July 22, 2003.
49. ST, July 22, 2003.
50. ST, July 22, 2003.
51. ST, November 6, 2003.
52. ST, November 20, 2003.
53. ST, December 1, 2003.
54. ST, March 19, 2004.
55. ST, December 2, 2003 and January 6, 2004.
56. ST, December 1, 2003.
57. *Business Times* (BT), November 9, 2004.
58. *Today*, June 26, 2003.
59. ST, November 20, 2003.
60. BT, November 9, 2004.
61. ST, February 25, 2004.
62. BT, August 15, 2002.
63. ST, July 2, 2004.
64. ST, November 9, 1991.
65. *Today*, June 29-30, 2002.
66. Ibid.
67. Seow, Francis T.: *The Media Enthralled: Singapore Revisited* (Boulder, Colorado; Lynne Rienner, 1998), pp. 212-13.
68. Ibid.
69. *Straits Times* internal staff memo issued in about October 1998. It was given to me by a former *Straits Times* staff member.

CHAPTER **8**

....

ENDEMIC INEFFICIENCIES

Inefficiency not only prevails at the state enterprise and macro-corporate levels in Singapore but also at more mundane levels. Persistent inefficiencies have been noted by both Singaporeans and expatriates in many diverse services and businesses. This chapter examines the complaints that have been made about taxi and public bus services, book publishing, swimming pool management, cinema projection, government accounting, locally produced goods and local tradesmen. Deficient laboratory procedures and inadequate tuberculosis control are also scrutinised.

1. Taxis

In a commendable fit of candour, *Straits Times* columnist Monica Gwee admitted that she had "been bragging about the Republic's 'world class' virtues with services to match to would-be visitors for so long, it never occurred to me to check my claims". But an American visitor had told her that the island's taxis "never seemed to know how to get where we wanted to go" and "didn't even know how to get to our hotel". He suggested she take taxis for a week to confirm his experience. Ms Gwee did, and found that it was,

> *increasingly clear that there are far too many cabbies on Singapore roads who really shouldn't be taxi drivers because they have no clue where some of the city's most well-known landmarks and public buildings are. And it's not because the buildings are new, it's because the drivers obviously haven't been given a thorough enough orientation.*[1]

She discovered that four out of seven taxi drivers did not know where to find the Phoenix Hotel, a well-known three-star hotel in the central Orchard Road shopping and leisure belt. They also lacked knowledge of other well-known destinations, including those in Chinatown. When asked why they don't know, their "constant refrain is: 'I'm new'." But "New to what?" she indignantly asked. "Your own country? Hey friend, a tourist is even newer than you, you know? How many 'new' cabbies are there cruising the streets and what sort of training do they get?" While New York cabbies often got lost because they were foreigners in a city of eight million, there was no excuse for native-born Singaporean cabbies to do so in a city of only four million, she said.

During my years in Singapore I found that ten to 15 per cent of taxi drivers don't know destinations, even though you speak slowly and carefully to them, patiently repeating directions two or three times. Many don't even have road maps in the taxi to guide them. One taxi driver who spoke reasonable English told me that he was attending a taxi board evening course in improving customer service – and then took me to the wrong hotel despite my having repeated its name three times to him!

Expats often stridently criticise Singapore taxis. "Why is it so difficult for taxi companies to provide an acceptable level of service in this country?" one Western expat exasperatedly asked.[2] He had travelled all over the world but found "the standard of taxi service in Singapore is way behind many third-world countries". He was particularly upset at the "changing shift" practice of Singapore taxis between 5pm and 6pm, where unoccupied taxis refuse to pick up passengers because the driver is going home:

> *I find it quite unbelievable that a forward-looking country such as Singapore is prepared to put up with such an appalling lack of judgement on behalf of the taxi companies which allows all their drivers to go home at exactly the same time. Surely it does not take a great deal of thought to improve the service by preventing taxi drivers from changing shift at such peak times.*

Often he had to wait 45 minutes or more for a taxi to take him home after work at 5pm. "If it is raining, it is impossible to get through to any taxi switchboard and very nearly impossible at this time, even if the sun is shining." Many other expatriates would agree.

Paradoxically, there are swarms of empty and desperate-for-business taxis everywhere after midnight. They may blithely ignore customers during the day, but at night they have an almost supernatural ability to see you from 100 metres away and often pester you. You can be standing beside a road waiting to cross, and a taxi will suddenly swerve to a halt in front of you waiting for you to get in even though you have not hailed it. You should stand stock-still at such times. One twitch and they will pull up next to you.

It must be admitted that while Singapore's taxis are inefficient, they are much more numerous than in countries such as Australia. Even in remote parts of Singapore, day or night, you can usually get a taxi quickly (outside rush hours in the CBDs), usually driven by friendly if not always capable drivers. Try finding an unoccupied taxi in an average Australian suburb. In Singapore there are 4.6 taxis per 1000 people, compared to 1.5 in Paris, 2.7 in London and 1.0 in Sydney.[3]

The onerous shifts imposed on Singapore's taxi drivers should also be recognised. They usually work seven days a week, 10 to 12 hours a day, for a take-home pay of S$1500-S$1700 a month. This discourages competent people from being taxi drivers, often only leaving the less able for the job, notwithstanding the fact that there are some taxi drivers in Singapore who can often give shrewd insights into PAP Singapore and how it functions.

Many of the shortcomings of Singapore's taxi drivers may be blamed on deficient taxi company management. Failure to ensure reasonable wages and working conditions and proper rostering of cabs largely explains the mediocre quality of Singapore's taxi services. Similar observations can be made about its bus services.

2. Bus Companies

Frequent complaints about Singapore's bus services suggest they too are far from world-class. One Singaporean, after living in Switzerland for five years, bought a car on returning to Singapore to avoid having to use local buses. This was a very expensive decision, because cars cost several times more in Singapore than in most Western countries. "We felt that the level of bus service in Singapore was unacceptable after what we experienced in Switzerland [where we] never once experienced the heavy and sudden braking, lack of anticipation and excessive acceleration and cornering so common in Singapore public buses."[4] Singapore's bus companies should visit Switzerland to learn how to run a world-class bus company, she said.

Singapore's bus drivers certainly have a lurching stop-go mode of driving and can be impolite and unhelpful, but much of the problem is again probably managerial. One bus driver described the enormous pressures that unreasonable managements impose on drivers. Very tight schedules left no room for road contingencies, and breaks between runs were also very short:

> *This means that if we are late, we either have to sacrifice our rest time or delay the start of the next run. We may also face disciplinary action if we deviate from our timetables by more than three minutes. In this kind of scenario we literally have to "run". We are in a hurry to close the doors and speed off. We apply our brakes hard when approaching bus stops so as to minimise the time spent at each stop. We drive as if possessed.*[5]

Drivers were subjected to unrealistic directives by managers who had no first-hand experience of the conditions drivers faced on the roads. Management knew about drivers' problems but did nothing about them, he said. Once again, an uncaring Singaporean management seemed to be the source of much stress, low morale and the reduced efficiency this causes.

Even so, like its taxis, Singapore's bus services make up in quantity what they lack in quality. In central areas, buses to most destinations arrive every few minutes. There are also TVs on buses for those who can't bear the boredom of staring out the window and day-dreaming. But for those who do, the TVs are an irritating intrusion.

3. Swimming Pools

A deficient swimming pool safety culture has attracted complaints in Singapore. A Western expat, commenting on a recent swimming pool fatality, described how he and another swimmer had rescued a weak swimmer who had been swept under by some passing swimmers in a university pool. He had told the pool staff but they claimed to have seen nothing.

> *This incident simply underlines the fact that there is no "culture of safety" in Singapore pools. The guards at a local community pool where I swim regularly can usually be found sitting and chatting at the base of a tall chair, on which another one is slumped, occasionally casting a lazy glance towards the pool. I don't recall ever seeing any one of them walking around the pool.*[6]

One Singaporean who supported the expat's comments said they were "spot on". He asked, "How often do you see lifeguards remaining perched on their lookout chairs around public pools?"[7] He did not think some guards were competent swimmers. Authorities should examine "the professionalism which lifeguards bring to the job," he said.

4. Cinema Projection

Substandard cinema projection has also aroused expat ire. A Western expat owner of a film company in Singapore said that while the city-state had one of the world's highest per capita numbers of cinema patrons, its cinema projection often lacked professionalism.8 Three times in 12 months he and Singaporean friends had walked out of films because of projection faults. Films running out of sync for 20 minutes, defective projector lenses, and part of the film missing the screen, were problems that had remained uncorrected by cinema management. "Human mistakes occur in any industry, but only in Singapore cinema do they go unnoticed by the staff and management for so long," he lamented.

5. Publishing

Often books and magazines published in Singapore have typos and grammatical errors that would not be accepted in developed countries. Even government publications and books containing Lee Kuan Yew's numerous speeches contain such errors. In the Singapore-published English translation of *Crows*, a novel by Chinese woman writer Jiu Dan, a quick reading of the book reveals about 80 grammatical and spelling errors in its 290 pages. Such sloppiness is common among Singapore-published books.

A *Straits Times* survey found that 16 primary school assessment books being sold by major book stores were littered with blatant grammatical and factual errors.[9] The survey also discovered mistakes in test papers. The newspaper listed 50 mistakes from assessment books and test papers.

6. Government Accounting

Many Singaporeans were stunned to learn that the Auditor-General's 1999/2000 report found that S$1.1 billion of payments by the Defence Ministry had not been properly reported.[10] Overpayments to suppliers featured strongly. The Auditor-General noted that "To cover up mistakes or omissions raised by Audit, alterations and insertions were made". As one irate Singaporean complained:

> I wonder what has happened to the internal controls of the Government authorities. Such irregularities should not be happening in Singapore at all, especially in Government departments.[11]

Singaporeans deserved a full explanation on how this occurred and the officers responsible should be punished, he said. But his appeal evoked little response from officialdom. As with SIA's S$35 million fraud, it seemed no action, at least publicly, was taken against those responsible.

7. Local Manufactured Goods

Both Singaporeans and MNCs in Singapore have reservations about locally manufactured goods. Singaporeans are reluctant to buy domestically-made electronic products, such as TVs and washing machines. Several Singaporeans have told me that they prefer foreign products because they last longer than local ones. One Singaporean in the products development field sadly noted, "the local civil servants and engineers do not always put their faith in products designed and manufactured locally".[12]   An NUS study, which included surveys of 32 MNCs and 70 SMEs in Singapore, found that 91 per cent nominated "quality deficiency" as a problem with Singapore-based suppliers.[12a] A problem for a further 83 per cent was "failure to deliver goods on time". While these problems were not exclusive to local SMEs, 39 per cent of the study's respondents claimed that "the incidence of such difficulties was higher among Singapore-owned companies than foreign-owned companies".

8. Local Tradesmen

An Australian bar owner in Singapore once told me that he got Australian tradesmen to renovate his bar, having little faith in the locals. Indifferent workmanship is widespread in Singapore. The problem was even raised in Parliament by PAP MP, Dr Tan Cheng Bock:

> *When I was renovating my house, it took the local contractor four times to get my wash basin right. I thought his workers were all foreign workers but when I heard that they were all Singaporeans, I was very, very disappointed. I asked them whether they were proud of the job. The contractor's reply was: "Everyone also do like that".[13]*

Windows crashing to the ground from high-rise flats, especially HDB units, are common. Casement windows – windows which open outwards – accounted for more than 200 cases of falling HDB windows from 2000 to December 2004.[14] In 2003, alone a total of 106 windows had fallen. HDB owners have complained about poor workmanship, one saying:

> *Recent incidents involving loose windows in Housing Board flats have generated concern over a seeming decline in the quality of HDB workmanship. Friends and colleagues I have spoken to agree there is a vast improvement needed in the design of HDB flats, but other aspects such as quality of workmanship and materials used have taken a plunge.[15]*

Apart from loose windows, complaints have been made about cracked walls, peeling paint and poor tiling in HDB units. Such defects were often discovered when owners moved into their flats. Of the 44 flat-owners in one HDB block, 40 asked for chipped tiles, hairline cracks and stained door handles to be rectified.[16]

9. Laboratories

An international team of investigators found serious shortcomings in several Singapore government laboratories in September 2003.[17] The team's visit was prompted when a researcher who was infected with SARs several months after the main SARS outbreak had been eliminated in Singapore. The researcher contracted the SARS virus at an Environmental Health Institute laboratory. Initially laboratory officials strenuously denied that he could have got the virus there, but the investigating team declared that he had; and that unclean equipment was a possible cause.

The team also found three other government laboratories had deficient procedures. The laboratories were at Singapore General Hospital, the Defence Science Organisation, and the National University of Singapore. All three had inadequate safety standards. The team believed Singapore needed to develop a "safety culture" in research work and also uniform standards for all its laboratories. Although Singapore won world accolades for its handling of the SARS epidemic, it would get few for laboratory safety.

10. Tuberculosis Control

In Western countries tuberculosis is seen as a disease of the past that afflicted the poor who lived in crowded slums. In Singapore and other affluent Asian countries, TB is still a significant health problem. In March 1999, there were 58 TB cases for every 100,000 people reported in Singapore, compared to six per 100,000 in Australia and eight in all of the US.[18]

Singapore is not alone in its unimpressive record on TB control. In 2000, Japan had 33 cases per 100,000 people, while Hong Kong had 75, Malaysia 68 and South Korea 47; though Singapore's cases had fallen to 43 by then.[19] WHO said that such TB rates were very high for an affluent country and much worse than in developed countries. Clearly, anti-TB efforts by Singapore and other wealthy Asian states lag well behind those in the West.

* * * * * * * * *

A society's efficiency is reflected in capital and labour productivity figures and also at the micro level, right down to whether or not lift buttons work for Lee Kuan Yew. This section has shown that Singapore's efficiency is questionable at both macro and micro levels. Singapore is much less efficient than popularly believed. Mediocrity so often prevails, whether considering the low yields on its capital reserves or faulty HDB windows, defective laboratories or school books littered with mistakes.

The next section considers the political, economic and sociological reasons for this.

References

1. *The Straits Times* (ST), April 29, 1999.
2. ST, March 31, 2000.
3. ST, September 16, 2000.
4. ST, December 4, 1999.
5. ST, July 31, 2000.
6. ST, September 29, 2001.
7. ST, October 1, 2001.
8. ST, March 31, 1999.
9. ST, August 1, 1999.
10. ST, September 20, 2000.
11. ST, September 21, 2000.
12. ST, November 14, 1998.
12a. Perry, M. and Tan Boon Hui: "Global manufacturing and local linkage in Singapore" (Economic and Planning A 1998, Vol 30) p. 1612.
13. ST, September 2, 2003.
14. ST, December 7, 2004.
15. ST, December 30, 2003.
16. ST, April 9, 2004.
17. ST, September 24, 2003.
18. ST, March 24, 1999.
19. ST, February 18, 2002.

Section THREE

Probing the Efficiency Myth

Productivity is essentially determined by how well the basic factors of production (traditionally regarded as land, labour and capital) are allocated, organised and used to produce the goods and services that society needs.

Entrepreneurs, managers and workers are the three main economic agents who perform these operations. Entrepreneurs mobilise and allocate the factors of production, while managers supervise their operation and workers use them to produce the goods and services required by society. Economic efficiency is determined by how well these economic agents perform their respective roles. In Singapore, neither entrepreneurs, managers, or workers perform them particularly well.

Lee Kuan Yew voiced his concerns about Singapore's indifferent efficiency as early as 1981. He had been disturbed by criticism from foreign and local corporate executives about the Republic's entrepreneurs, managers and workers. The most worrying point of their submissions to the Singapore National Productivity Board (SNPB) "was that if we had to depend on Singapore entrepreneurs we would not have today's Singapore. It's a damning admission for me as prime minister to tell you this".[1]

The submissions to the SNPB compelled Lee to make damning admissions about the quality of Singapore's managers and workers. Of its managers, he said, "We have been traders, but we do not understand management," adding that "Our managers do not understand productivity".[2] Lee made similar humbling confessions about Singaporean workers. He agreed with the MNC submissions that they lacked dedication and company loyalty.

The submissions made to the SNPB will be examined in this section, along with the failings of Singapore's entrepreneurs, managers and workers and the political, economic and sociological reasons for their shortcomings. The section concludes with an account of government efforts to raise productivity.

References

[1] Han, Fook Kwang, Warren Fernandez and Sumiko Tan: *Lee Kuan Yew, The Man and His Ideas* (Singapore, Times Editions, 1998), p. 356.

[2] Ibid, p. 357.

91

CHAPTER 9

ENTREPRENEURIAL DEFICIENCIES

Singapore has been getting low marks for its entrepreneurial capacity in recent years. It was not only ranked 18th out of 21 countries for entrepreneurship by GEM in 2000, but was ranked 28th out of 49 countries for entrepreneurship by the IMD in 2001.[1] Such mediocre rankings reflect the substandard performance of Singapore's entrepreneurs, bureaucratic and otherwise. It partly explains Singapore's low yields on capital and why, for example, its GLCs produced returns of only 4.4 per cent per annum from 1992 to 2002. Such returns reflect limited entrepreneurial capacities, as do the many failed deals of Singapore's SEs during the 1990s.

1. Defining Entrepreneurial Capacity

An economy's ability to efficiently mobilise and allocate capital is a prime measure of its entrepreneurial capacity. This applies to both the organising (or mobilising) of resources to launch new ventures and the allocation of resources to sustain existing enterprises.

For the launching of new enterprises especially, risk-taking is seen as a key attribute. The readiness and ability to take risks are critical requirements for entrepreneurs. They must have the business acumen to spot new market demands and a readiness to risk the capital and other resources necessary to exploit them.

Entrepreneurship can be of the "venture" or "administrative" variety. Venture entrepreneurs mobilise and allocate resources to launch new businesses and projects. This is the popular image of the entrepreneur. But there is also the administrative entrepreneur. He works within an organisation, allocating resources to maintain or improve current operations rather than to start new ones. His entrepreneurial ability depends on how efficiently he allocates resources, rather than on the readiness to take risks. His entrepreneurial role is an allocative one, done within an existing organisation to maximise its productivity. (In reality however, the role of administrative entrepreneur is just one of several that senior managers must perform in organisations).

The more an economy has people who have entrepreneurial ability – and the freedom to exercise it – the greater its entrepreneurial capacity. Various factors determine how many entrepreneurs an economy has. The first of these is the degree of state control of the economy. Free-market economies breed more entrepreneurs than those where state control predominates. Entrepreneurs cannot easily develop in countries where risk-averse attitudes, limited business acumen and heavy controls discourage entrepreneurial activity. In state-run societies bureaucrats operate most of the economy, often in response to political policies rather than to market demand. They mainly decide how an economy's resources will be mobilised and allocated to meet society's demands. Political, organisational, even ideological considerations often prevail over the need for economic efficiency, the demands of consumers and market realities: the demands that dictate the decisions of private-sector entrepreneurs.

In communist states especially, resource mobilization and allocation have been shown to be less efficient than in free market economies. Private sector enterprises usually perform these entrepreneurial functions more efficiently than state concerns, as the low yields of Singapore's SEs show. Moreover, within the state sector, especially government bureaucracies, mis-allocation and wasteful use of resources is common. As Loh noted when writing about the Singapore economy:

> Productivity is found to lag in the public sector. Bureaucrats take leisure on the job and produce less than is possible with given inputs. There is little incentive to keep costs down since there is no personal benefit from any savings and it is better to maintain or increase budgets in following years to allude to same or more work done...[2]

Similar sentiments are expressed by senior Singaporean public servant Lim Siong Guan in describing the comfortable and potentially fatal situation that bureaucrats, Singaporean and otherwise, find themselves in:

> There is no profit bottom line in much of public service work to give warning of impending trouble, and to communicate to workers that their livelihoods are at stake if they do not keep up with productivity improvements. It is difficult to motivate people to deliver the best service possible when there is no competitor offering the same service, when the service provided is something the public cannot go elsewhere to get, and when no one else knows how much can be improved because the public does not know the processes and policies to be able to say how much better the service can be. Not having a bottom line means one instrument less to encourage improvement and induce change...[3]

Civil servants lack the incentive to maximise productive use of resources. This, combined with their minimal free-market experience, limits their entrepreneurial capacity to efficiently allocate and manage resources. An economy which has a large public sector with civil servants performing such functions has a greatly reduced entrepreneurial capacity.

Nonetheless, key sections of an economy need to be state run. Privatisation has not always been the answer to increasing productivity, as many Western economies have found since the 1980s. State concerns, especially in utilities and other basic sectors, have often been more efficient and reliable than private companies that have replaced them.

Besides the size of the state-controlled sector, other major factors that dictate an economy's entrepreneurial capacities include an entrepreneurially and culturally supportive environment that must:

- Provide a level playing field to ensure fair competition, especially for SMEs, from state concerns and MNCs
- Ensure adequate venture capital for all viable entrepreneurial prospects
- Minimise unnecessary red tape

- Have values that promote risk-taking, especially in the economic sphere.

A level playing field which includes equal access to new business prospects is critical for SMEs. As seedbeds of innovation, SMEs often pioneer new products and services that become future brand names. But while SMEs play a vital entrepreneurial role in a market economy, big enterprises, including SEs and MNCs, can easily poach promising prospects from them. SMEs need opportunities to grow and develop. A level playing field prevents "the big boys" using their superior power to monopolise new prospects at the expense of smaller businesses.

Ready access to venture capital is also critical to entrepreneurial development. Promising ventures cannot be exploited without adequate finance. In the US, venture capital is relatively easy to raise; but in countries such as Singapore it requires substantial security. Again, the regulatory environment imposed on businesses also determines how easily new ventures can be launched and run. Too much red tape impedes this.

Finally, cultural factors can also do much to determine how entrepreneurially supportive an economic environment is. Societies vary greatly in how far their values foster risk-taking and other entrepreneurial activities. Some societies discourage risk-taking; others encourage it. Some cultures place higher priority on making money, others on fulfilling religious and kin obligations and maintaining community harmony. Thus a country's entrepreneurial capacity overall depends on the size of its public sector and the cultural and economic environment in which business must function. Singapore's entrepreneurial deficiencies will be assessed in the light of these two basic factors.

2. Singapore's Entrepreneurial Deficiencies

The PAP Government likes to blame local private companies for Singapore's entrepreneurial deficiencies, claiming they are risk-averse and lack entrepreneurial zeal. But a large state sector and an adverse business environment for SMEs, as well as cultural values that discourage risk-taking, largely explain Singapore's limited entrepreneurial capacities.

A Bureaucratised Economy

After the separation from Malaysia, Singapore's SEs multiplied and progressively assumed a leading role in the local economy. They took on entrepreneurial and investment functions normally left to the private sector. As a result, Singapore's SEs and therefore much of its local economy became largely run by civil servants and government appointees.

Civil Service Entrepreneurs

Public servants not only run statutory boards but dominate Singapore's GLCs. A detailed study by Ross Worthington revealed that, in 1991, 70.7 per cent of GLC directorships were public sector appointees who were public servants, PAP ministers and MPs, and retired military personnel.[4] By 1998 this figure had risen to 74 per cent.[5]

In Singapore, the holding companies and statutory boards controlling the GLCs are run by senior public servants and in several cases by Lee family members. In 1998, the Government's four holding companies (Temasek Holdings, MND Holdings, the Hospital

Corporation of Singapore and Singapore Technologies) were chaired by permanent secretaries and staffed mainly by civil servants.[6]

The CEO for one of Singapore's biggest GLCs was Lee Hsien Yang, Lee Kuan Yew's second son. Like his elder brother, Lee Hsien Loong, he is a former brigadier general. Hsien Yang was one of Singapore's high-flying technocrats "parachuted" into a top GLC position. Another Lee family member to enjoy rapid promotion was Ho Ching, Hsien Loong's wife. After leaving the army as a major she joined Singapore Technologies in 1976 and rose to became its chief executive in 2001. In May 2002, she was appointed executive director of Temasek Holdings. Finally, Lee Kuan Yew himself heads the GIC, Singapore's biggest SE.

The bulk of Singapore's GLCs are run by CEOs and directors who have been appointed by the Government in the Japanese *amakudari* style. *Amakudari*, which means "descend from heaven", describes how Japan's senior public servants are given high-level corporate positions in the private corporate sector. This has produced a civil service-business complex which plugs into the ruling Liberal Democratic Party (LDP). According to Low:

> *"Amakudari" is also perceived in Singapore as more and more retired civil servants are despatched to statutory boards and GLCs. Because of younger aspirants and the need for faster promotion to invigorate the bureaucracy, more senior bureaucrats are opting for early retirement and to be put under GLCs instead.[7]*

But Low added that "this growing network should not be under scored as a web of semi-government influence." Others may disagree with her, especially considering that the Government decides who will sit on GLC boards. Directors are appointed and their activities monitored under the Government's Directorship and Consultancy Appointments Council (DCAC). Besides ex-civil servants, numerous retired politicians and military officers sit on GLC boards. As such, much of the local economy and most of Singapore's biggest domestic enterprises are run by government-approved appointees, usually ex-civil servants and politicians. Many of the civil servants appointed to Singapore's SEs are from the Administrative Service (AS), the Republic's civil service elite.

The Best and Brightest?

Singapore's rulers pride themselves on recruiting the country's best and brightest for the civil service, especially the AS elite. The AS's job is to help the political leadership spot trends, meet needs, maintain standards and formulate and implement policies for Singapore's security and success. Sometimes termed the "mandarinate", the AS's "heaven-born" appointees, rarely number more than 300 officers.[8] In 1997, there were 247 AS officers in GLCs, of whom 24 were permanent secretaries and the remainder deputy secretaries.[9]

Singapore's civil servants enjoy a high international reputation. Even commentators from Hong Kong, one of Singapore's biggest rivals in Asia, have paid homage to its bureaucrats. Singapore's practice of grooming a first-rate civil service under Lee Kuan Yew should be copied by Hong Kong, claimed a prominent *Hong Kong Economic Times* journalist, Mr Yau Shing Mu.[10] The quality of Singapore's civil servants was part of its recipe for success, he said. They had abilities summarised by the acronym "Hair", a favourite term of Lee Kuan Yew's. Lee bestows this term on those having a Helicopter view, Analytical power, Imagination and a sense of Reality.

Through extensive control of the economy, including most of its biggest local enterprises, Singapore's civil servants have had ample opportunity to demonstrate their abilities, Hair or otherwise, especially in entrepreneurial areas. But the mediocre yields from the state sector and a string of ill-judged foreign deals have revealed how failure-prone Singapore's entrepreneurial bureaucrats are. Their ignorance and lack of street smarts are largely to blame.

Singapore has naive bureaucrats running or regulating too many of its enterprises, according to US academic Philip Anderson, entrepreneurship professor at Insead's Asian campus in Singapore:

> Many of the people who regulate entrepreneurship here have absolutely no experience in the private sector. They are honest, smart and efficient, but they're naive. It's simple naivity. They have no idea how to run private enterprise.[11]

Professor Anderson says that only practical experience in the private sector could banish such naivety. But the average bureaucrat, Singaporean or otherwise, usually lacks such experience. Few have the street smarts that are best developed in the rough and tumble of the open market. Running privileged and protected statutory boards in Singapore ill prepares its senior bureaucrats or SE chiefs for foreign ventures. As PAP MP Inderjit Singh caustically remarked:

> Our GLCs are late in going global and the consequences can be seen in their failure to compete successfully and being "taken for a ride" in certain high-profile acquisition transactions. If the Government fails to realise this negative impact on our GLCs from staying in their old roles, we will see many more sad stories...[12]

Others to question the capacity of Singapore's SEs to compete and innovate in the real world include Harvard Business School Professor Michael Porter. His sentiments on business matters were approvingly quoted by Prime Minister Goh Chok Tong during his 2001 National Day speech. Porter said it was the same story everywhere: companies not fully subjected to market discipline were less able to compete when the crunch came.[13] Singapore's GLCs had been useful for increasing economic efficiency but not for fostering innovation, he said. Companies structured like GLCs "will not support" the promotion of highly advanced, knowledge-based activities.

Singapore's local economy is dominated by GLCs and other SEs, which constitute a large state sector though estimates on its size vary. The local private sector produces only about one third of GDP, the state sector supposedly a quarter and MNCs over 40 per cent, according to Singapore government figures. But the state share could be higher, as Chapter 14 shows. Even so, civil servants and public sector appointees operate the biggest and most important enterprises in the local economy. Like most bureaucrats, they are cautious and risk-averse. Such attitudes worry Singapore's leaders.

Over the years Prime Minister Goh railed against the attitudes of Singapore's bureaucrats while Deputy Prime Minister Lee Hsien Loong said the civil service had to dispense with its over-cautious conservative attitudes. Lee Hsien Loong acknowledged that the Government was often seen as being "too cautious and risk-averse" and civil servants appeared "conservative and resistant to new ideas".[14] The Singapore civil service's elitist system was the core of the problem and required review, said one ex-civil servant:

> *It is a fact that scholars and administrative-service officers are on a fast-track career. This system tends to breed precisely the incumbent attitude that PM Goh was talking about.*[15]

He found that such officers focused on avoiding mistakes that would jeopardise their fast-track status. Moreover, the short stints they served in different positions did not give them sufficient experience to make risky judgements. He was not impressed by civil servants he worked with, noting that "for some of them...their sense of self-preservation was so strong that it often clouded their decision-making".

Risk-averse bureaucrats continue to exercise widespread control of Singapore's economy through an extensive system of SE bureaucrats, past and present, and other government appointees, including retired PAP ministers. The term "mandarin bureaucrats" or "scholar mandarins" has been used to describe many such functionaries, reflecting the government belief that they are Singapore's best and brightest. They are paid high salaries and enjoy lavish perks, especially at more senior levels, to encourage them into the SEs.

Getting the latest data on what Singapore's senior civil servants are paid is not easy, but Worthington found that in 1995 the base rate (excluding bonuses and CPF contributions) ranged from S$7600 to S$25,000 a month for the eight Superscale divisions.[16] CPF and performance bonuses boosted these rates by about 30 per cent. Moreover, these salaries were not confined to senior officers: an overwhelming majority of Division 1 officers (about 28 per cent of the civil service) and some Division 2 officers (about 30 per cent of the civil service) got them. Public servants also received subsidised rental of holiday homes, low-interest loans for housing, cars and other purchases, low membership fees for the Civil Service Club which has lavish sport and recreation facilities, generous subsidised health benefits, group insurance cover, interest-free study loans and generous leave entitlements.[17]

Such highly-paid public servants tend to develop feelings of entitlement and elitist arrogance. As Singaporean commentator Cherian George noted:

> *The scholar mandarins....function in an increasingly rarified environment from their late teens. There is a danger that by the time these individuals reach highly influential positions, some will imagine themselves to be god's gift to Singapore.*[18]

Despite their lack of real world experience and limited chances to develop entrepreneurial skills, the Government has great confidence in them. "Never having been tested in the private sector, [one] can only take the government's word that they would excel in practically any field and therefore deserve top dollar," George said.[19] They are frequently isolated from the demands of the real world and the performance tests imposed on private sector recruits. Even Singapore's PAP MPs face elections or have grass-root responsibilities which make them answerable to ordinary citizens.

Given this, it is debatable whether the Government is hiring or retaining the best available talent to run its civil service and SEs, even from among those in the elite AS. Moreover, despite high remuneration, growing numbers of AS officers have been leaving for the private sector since the late 1980s. The main reason given is that "officers were disenchanted with the political system and the nature of their work with ministers," notes Worthington,[20] who interviewed past and present AS officers. The AS has had increasingly to rely on recruits from the Singapore Armed Forces (SAF) to maintain its numbers.[21]

By mid-2000 the exodus of talent from the public service was increasing. Some 267 officers from the Senior Officer Service resigned in 1999, and a further 284 officers (12 per cent of its staff) left the service within the first five months of 2000.[22] Imminent major pay rises failed to stem the departures. In 2000, all civil servants got a 13 per cent pay rise while mid-level AS officers got hikes of up to 50 per cent, yet the AS continued to suffer resignations. Eight AS officers left in the first half of 2000 amid a growing exodus from the civil service. Their ages ranged from 26 to 38.[23] Three of them said they knew of the pay rise but had not even waited to learn of its size before they quit. More pay would not induce them to stay. They had left for the private sector for new experiences, not more money, they said.[24]

One said he would have left no matter how large the pay increases were. He preferred being a private-sector player to operating "behind the scenes" in the civil service. The AS officer was "the oil inside the engine that keeps the country going," he said. "I would prefer to work on the outside, as one of the gears." [25] He started a company that helped SMEs build websites and sell products online. Being his own boss meant that he could no longer depend on supervisors for guidance and he was aware that his mistakes would affect both him and his employees. Although uncertainty was much greater, he enjoyed the increased sense of personal control. Two other ex-AS officers also started a company where they were earning much less: they too wanted to break out of the "comfort zones" and be in the new economy.

These sentiments are those of budding entrepreneurs – the sort of people the Government supposedly wants for Singapore. But they have found that working for the civil service is too limiting, as most real entrepreneurs would. High pay, scholarships, and other benefits are what budding bureaucrats, not embryonic entrepreneurs, yearn for. Such inducements have little appeal to red-blooded entrepreneurs. As Low aptly remarks:

> One may even argue...that true entrepreneurs cannot be nurtured through formal education. Risk-taking requires more gut feelings and animal instincts. Business opportunities must be seized quickly and entrepreneurs can ill afford the deliberations and careful weighing of opportunity costs, towards which educated scholars are perhaps more inclined.[26]

Such "educated scholars" would remain in the public service. The typical bureaucrat lacks the hungry restless mindset that drives the typical entrepreneur. Being good at passing exams, playing office politics and conforming to public service-corporate stereotypes do not top entrepreneurs make.

The Singaporean "scholar-technocratic hybrid of entrepreneurship is probably most desirable" for running state monopolies such as statutory boards, notes Low,[27] but they are not entrepreneurial abilities. Her scepticism about the capacities of Singapore's bureaucratic entrepreneurs is shared by US academics Philip Anderson and Michael Porter.

The Government keeps recruiting top graduates for the civil service with ever more extravagant pay rises, but the mandarin mentality they acquire in the public service is not conducive to developing entrepreneurial skills, which include humility when dealing with others. Singapore's state entrepreneurs apparently lacked this in the industrial park project in Suzhou. Their arrogance towards the Chinese did much to undermine the project, as explained in Chapter 13.

Poor people skills as well as other deficiencies of Singapore's state entrepreneurs do much to explain the corporate debacles of its SEs – and the resulting low returns on national reserves.

An Uneven Playing Field

Singapore's SMEs have faced crippling SE/MNC competition over the years. This has stunted not only their growth but also the development of indigenous entrepreneurial capacity. Both SEs and MNCs regularly poach business prospects from SMEs. Complaints about the predatory behaviour of SEs, particularly the GLCs, have grown louder since the 1980s. SEs have had few scruples about encroaching on private sector prospects and their greater resources have enabled them to muscle out SMEs. Many SMEs are afraid of partnering a GLC for fear it will steal their ideas. As Chapter 16 will show, their concerns are justified.

MNCs have posed similar problems for Singapore's SMEs. Since the 1960s, MNC competition has squeezed out many local firms because of superior financial, marketing and other resources, especially in the construction industry, as Chapter 16 will also show. While MNCs may establish new businesses, these have often been poached from local private firms – although they have provided out-sourcing business opportunities for local firms on occasion. But much of what MNCs have given Singapore has been at the expense of local entrepreneurial ventures. Most MNC profits go abroad and, as shown earlier, the MNCs have conferred few technological benefits or innovations on Singapore that would make it more economically independent.

Barriers to Private Enterprise

Adequate venture capital and freedom from unnecessary regulations are requirements for entrepreneurial development. Singapore's SMEs are often denied both.

Venture Capital Shortages

While Singapore's SEs have ready access to substantial government capital, its SMEs often struggle to finance new ventures. The conservative lending policies of Singapore's banks are largely to blame.

SMEs regularly criticise the banks' unsympathetic attitudes to them. One SME spokesman to voice such complaints is Mr Ong Joon Koon, president of the Rotary Club of Singapore. The club has about 1000 members, many heading listed and unlisted companies. Mr Ong said that "nine out of 10 times" a bank would turn down a loan application or demand to see better financial figures before approving it. "But under the current circumstances who can improve the business?" he asks. "Most of the banks maybe do not go to the market...and understand the real needs of businessmen." [28]

The lack of support from banks was revealed in a 2004 survey of SMEs by the former Productivity and Standards Board (now renamed Spring Singapore).[29] The survey found that banks rejected 56 per cent of SME bank loan applications during the first six months of 2004. It confirmed the widespread SME belief that Singapore's banks refuse to lend without collateral, sometimes even for amounts as small as S$50,000.

Unhelpful banks have forced Singapore's SMEs to resort to unorthodox means to raise capital. One survey found that SMEs usually finance new ventures with seed money from family savings or loans from "business angels".[30] Although the Government has launched programs to help SMEs with loans, the results so far seem modest, as Chapter 16 will also show.

Strangled by Red Tape

The acronym "Nuts" was used by a PAP MP to describe an over-governed and regulated Singapore. "Nuts" means "No-U-turn-syndrome". It describes a traffic situation where no reversal in direction is permitted unless there is a sign specifically saying you may, explained the MP, Leong Horn Kee.[31] In many countries, motorists are allowed to make U-turns unless expressly forbidden. For Leong, "Nuts" demonstrated the need for Singaporeans who are used to "being led, guided and spoon-fed by the Government" to break out of the old mould. He was attacking the PAP mentality that forbids Singaporeans from doing what the Government has *not* said they can do.

The PAP's obsessive desire to control all aspects of the Singaporean economic and social life has bred a plethora of rules and regulations which strangle entrepreneurial activity. Business has "to navigate through myriad regulations in many things they do" wrote *Straits Times* columnist Tan Tarn How.[32] The proliferation of statutory boards accounts for much of the red tape engulfing Singapore. As *Today* columnist Lee Han Shih exclaimed:

> Since Singapore entered the 21st century, the Civil Service has acted as if it is on Viagra: It is spawning new stat boards at an average of one every three to four months. Today there are close to 70 stat boards in this small country of less than four million people.[33]

To justify their existence, statutory boards keep devising new rules and regulations. "Very often this simply means more running around for people or businesses to get things done in Singapore," Lee said.

MNCs have expressed concern at the problems of starting a business in Singapore. One MNC complained that it needed licences and/or permission from 15 different departments to set up a factory. Red tape hits small and micro businesses hard.[34] They "have to spend valuable resources to get all the stamping done before they can start to make a living". For example, food vans need at least three licences to operate in car parks and the licences' conditions are so restrictive as to make the food vans uneconomic. Once when 33 people were given food-van licences, they found they could only operate between 7am and 10.30am although they needed to trade for at least 12 hours to cover costs and make money.[35]

With so many approvals required it can take up to a year to start a business, even the smallest one. It took more than a year to set up a 13-square-metre snackbar at a Singapore MRT station, according to PAP MP Mrs Yu-Foo Yee Shoon,[36] one of several MPs to condemn the red tape strangling business activity in Singapore.

Another Singaporean MP related the problems she faced in launching a business to train health-care workers. Dr Gan See Khem said, "We need the Nursing Board's approval before we can get the NTUC and the Skills Development Fund to approve the courses for training and subsidy....So all these approval processes took six months, nine months and, you know, we are still working on it today."[37] Official approval times were too long and costly for SMEs, she argued, urging the Government to speed up the streamlining of approval processes. "If the Civil Service...does not implement these measures fast enough, we shall see many, many more SMEs failing."[38]

Singapore business people complain bitterly about excessive red tape. Singaporean journalist Conrad Raj has devoted several columns to red tape problems, including those faced by restaurateurs. One Indian restaurateur was so fed up with bureaucratic obstacles to hiring staff that he was thinking of returning to India. "The Government tells us to be entrepreneurs, but then you have its various departments putting all sorts of obstacles in your way," he said.[39]

In response to this tide of criticism the Government has been trying to reduce red tape for years. In 2000, it established the Pro-Enterprise Panel (PEP) to promote a more pro-business environment. By March 2003, the red-tape busting agency had received 500 complaints, half of which have resulted in rule changes.[40] A panel of permanent secretaries was also overseeing efforts by ministries to revise their rules by the end of 2004. But there still seems a long way to go, according to some Singaporeans. As one told *Streats*, "We hear rhetoric about how Singapore is going all out to cut costs of doing business here and getting more efficient and better organised than our competitors."[41] Not only did land costs, rents, utilities and licensing fees, levies and carpark charges not seem to be falling, but red tape remained a problem. Each "statutory board staunchly defends its turf and fees," he said. Despite government claims to being pro-business and lowering costs, Singapore was still more expensive and less competitive than its neighbours.

Starting businesses in Malaysia is much quicker, as Singaporean IT firm Creative Technology found. CT's Malaysian subsidiary Cubic Electronics set up and helped staff a special IT-training campus for a Malaysian university in two months. CT founder Mr Sim Wong Hoo, one of Singapore's most admired entrepreneurs, was amazed at the speed with which the campus was approved and launched. "It would never have happened so fast in Singapore," he said.[42] Red tape seems to restrict entrepreneurial activity less in Malaysia than in Singapore.

As a modern industrialised society, Singapore has all the physical, financial and legal structures required for entrepreneurial activities. But these must be balanced against excessive red tape, the often crippling SE/MNC competition SMEs face and the lack of venture capital.

Risk-averse Values

Till the mid-1960s Singapore probably had as much entrepreneurial talent as other Asian economies, as Winsemius's descriptions of Singaporeans' resourcefulness suggest. But the risk-averse mentality fostered under authoritarian PAP rule has since discouraged many Singaporeans from entrepreneurial careers. The PAP state has conditioned Singaporeans to conform, not ask questions, and accept top-down decision-making. Such thinking cripples the development of the free-wheeling creative mindsets required by successful entrepreneurs.

Singapore has often been called the "one mistake society": one slip and you're finished. The Government often portrays Singapore as being on a tightrope or knife-edge. No margin for error, is the message. As Low observes:

> It is a common perception that the old political leadership was intolerant of mediocrity and had no time for fools. Considering how small the country is, and how young its culture, it is hardly surprising that the intolerance of failure had filtered down to every fibre of local society.
>
> There is little or no room to be exceptionally daring or non-conformist in terms of education and job prospects. The culture breeds risk-aversity and cautiousness right from the very start.[43]

Such attitudes discourage risk-taking, the first key requirement for entrepreneurial activity. NUS sociologist Bjorn Bjerke observes, "Singaporeans attach tremendous stigma to failure; the idea of learning from mistakes is practically unknown".[44] Failure is seen as more shameful in Singapore than in more forgiving societies. As Dr James Lee, a director of a digital lab company in Singapore, noted:

> If you run a company in Taiwan or the United States and if you fail, that failure is like a medal – an asset which represents battle experience, and people will actually want to work with you. But in Singapore, if you fail, that's it, people won't talk to you anymore.[45]

Bankrupts quickly discover this in Singapore. They face not only the trauma of being in deep financial trouble, "but the bleak prospect of going back to normal life even after they have discharged their debts," wrote one Singaporean columnist.[46] Not only do they find it hard to borrow money or get credit cards, but employers are reluctant to offer them jobs.

The case of a 25-year-old Singaporean systems engineer is typical. Three years after being declared bankrupt he found no employer would hire him.[47] He felt so ashamed he never told his girlfriend, even when she became his fiancée. The engineer survived by doing freelance work for over two years before landing a job as an IT executive earning S$37,800 a year. He worked his way out of bankruptcy, but two months after he was discharged, four banks rejected his applications for credit cards. "Once a bankrupt, always a bankrupt – that is the way I was made to feel," he said. He appealed, but the banks still rejected him and he believed he had little chance of getting a bank loan. "I am thinking of migrating to Australia," he said.

Fear of failing and risk-aversion are mindsets the PAP Government has been fighting since the 1980s, recognising how they undermine innovation and productivity. Such mindsets have deep cultural roots in Singapore and are further perpetuated by a range of government policies and practices, as this book will continue to show.

The strength of the stigma attached to failure was demonstrated by the NSTB when it launched the Phoenix Award in 2000.[48] The award was to be given to comeback technopreneurs who, like the mythical bird, had risen from the ashes of their failure. The award was created to fight the fear of failure generated by risk-averse values and to encourage entrepreneurs to keep going despite failure. Removing the shame from business failures would, it was hoped, encourage more risk-taking entrepreneurs. But the NSTB found the award had few contenders. "It has been difficult to get people to go for the award," sighed the NSTB director. "We approached technopreneurs whom we felt were suitable for the award, but many hesitated. Some don't see any benefit to sharing their failure stories; others just don't feel like talking about it."[49] The award was part of the Government's efforts to change this mind-set and encourage greater risk-taking. In 2001, the EDB took over the award's operation.[50] That year the message was, "it's OK to fail".

If Singapore's private sector business people, like their civil service counterparts, are somewhat risk-averse, they cannot be accused of an inefficient use of capital. Life is tough for Singapore's private firms in an MNC/SE-dominated business environment. Only those with considerable acumen survive and prosper. Anyone who has business with Singaporeans in the private sector knows that they are shrewd operators who astutely exploit opportunities and make efficient use of their own (or someone else's) capital resources. When it comes to buying and selling, bargaining and negotiating, minimising risk and maximising gain, they have few equals. They manage money well and use capital efficiently. Singapore's capital productivity would likely be higher were they to allocate and manage the bulk of its capital resources, despite Lee Kuan Yew's disparaging comments about them in the early 1980s.

Even so, a risk-averse mentality continues to dominate Singaporean thinking. Cultural values change slowly, especially when they continue to be buttressed by authoritarian PAP attitudes. Despite claiming to be more liberal, the PAP state keeps intimidating Singaporeans and encourages their already strong risk-averse attitudes.

Singaporeans' play-it-safe thinking is strengthened by lucrative positions (for graduates) in the MNC and state sectors. Attractive prospects in these sectors further encourage low-risk career paths. For many Singaporeans, the latter are more preferable to starting one's own business with its many drawbacks, five of which Bjerke lists: [51]

- Uncertainty of income
- Risk of losing one's savings or capital
- Long hours and hard work
- Lower quality of life until the business gets started
- Complete responsibility.

Those who don't relish risk for its own sake must be adequately compensated for such drawbacks. The benefits of entrepreneurship compared to those of employment must at least be sufficient to counter the risk of starting a business. High rewards for state employment greatly lower this differential. In Singapore, good salaries, attractive conditions and career opportunities in the Government and MNC sectors tilt the risk-reward trade-off away from entrepreneurship and so discourage it. This keeps down the numbers of entrepreneurs in Singapore.

Risk-averse attitudes have encouraged many Singaporean companies to stick to traditional businesses and the property sectors, deterring them from devising and manufacturing new products and services or venturing aboard. In 1993, a Singapore government committee noted that many thought Singaporean companies were not sufficiently developed to compete abroad compared to Western companies or those in Hong Kong and Taiwan.

> The largest local companies tend to be concentrated in traditional sectors such as banking, property development and food and beverages....Most local companies are small and have concentrated on serving the local market...[52]

In 1996, Prime Minister Goh spoke admiringly of Scandinavian countries and how a long-standing emphasis on R&D had enabled them to produce technologically high-quality goods that had achieved global success. A sense of adventure had led them to venture abroad and seek out business opportunities. He said these were qualities that Singapore should emulate. "The lesson for Singapore is that we can't depend on property development for the future. We can't just be a nation of property agents."[53] Goh also did not want Singapore to merely be a launching pad for foreign firms to establish markets in Asia, with Singapore acting as a broker and collecting commissions. "Again, there's no depth, you are merely trading." A large amount of local business activity involves property speculation and trading. Developing new products and marketing them overseas has been beyond the entrepreneurial and technological capacity of most Singaporean firms, and their risk-averse nature has been blamed for this. In 1996, Murray and Perera remarked:

> Despite all the financial incentives to Singaporean companies to move overseas, there is still evidence of some reluctance to do so. One key aspect, identified by government officials, is that life has become so comfortable – 'cushy' – at home, that Singaporeans are loath to move abroad to take risks or live in a less comfortable environment. One could argue that this is inevitable, particularly for a generation that has been raised on total government paternalism, with everything laid on the plate for the man or woman willing to conform. Being a pioneer in these circumstances requires a difficult psychological transition.[54]

Recently Singapore's private sector, including the SMEs, has been increasingly venturing abroad. Adverse economic conditions for private firms in Singapore have compelled them to seek foreign markets. Necessity has countered their risk-averseness, forcing them to be more entrepreneurial. Even so, ongoing competition from the state and MNC sectors, venture capital shortage and restrictive red tape continue to stunt the growth of the private sector's entrepreneurial and innovative capacities. Moreover, most of Singapore's domestic capital resources remain under SE control. Bureaucrats and state appointees with limited entrepreneurial capacities still dominate the allocation and use of capital in Singapore.

Singapore's entrepreneurial deficiencies are damaging enough, but they only partly explain its mediocre productivity. The lacklustre quality of its managers and workers is also to blame, as the next chapter shows.

References

1. *The World Competitiveness Yearbook 2001* (Laussanne, Switzerland; Institute for Management Development).
2. Low, Linda: *The Political Economy of a City State* (Singapore, Oxford University Press, 1998), p. 283.
3. Lim Siong Guan: "PS21: Gearing up to the Public Service for the 21st Century", p. 130 in *Singapore: Re-engineering Success*, edited by Arun Mahizhnan, and Lee Tsao Yuan (Singapore, Oxford University Press, 1998).
4. Worthington, Ross: *Governance in Singapore* (London, RoutledgeCurzon, 2003), p. 190.
5. Ibid, p. 204.
6. Ibid, p. 194.
7. Low, p. 210.
8. Worthington, p. 46.
9. Ibid, p. 171.
10. *The Straits Times* (ST), November 10, 1998.
11. ST, November 8, 2003.
12. ST, August 28, 2002.
13. *The New Paper*, August 28, 2002.
14. ST, July 12, 2000.
15. ST, August 28, 2000.
16. Worthington, pp. 142-3.
17. Ibid.
18. George, Cherian: *Singapore: the Airconditioned Nation* (Singapore, Landmark Books, 2000), p. 77.
19. Ibid.
20. Worthington, p. 47.
21. Ibid, p. 239.
22. ST, June 30, 2000.
23. ST, July 6, 2000.
24. Ibid.
25. Ibid.
26. Low, Linda: "State Entrepreneurship", p. 160 in *State Entrepreneurship in Singapore, Private and State*, edited by Lee Tsao Yuan and Linda Low (Singapore, Times Academic Press, 1990).
27. Ibid. p. 161.
28. ST, June 23, 2003.
29. ST, September 3, 2004.
30. Tan Khee Giap and Lee Wee Keong: "Beyond Regionalization, Basis for Sustainable Growth and Potential Sources of Expansion", p. 115 in *Singapore: Towards A Developed Status*, edited by Linda Low (Singapore, Oxford University Press, 1999).
31. ST, March 11, 2003.
32. ST, March 11, 2003
33. Today, August 8, 2003.
34. Ibid.
35. Ibid.
36. ST, March 12, 2003.
37. ST, March 11, 2003.
38. Ibid.
39. *Streats*, February 24, 2003.
40. ST, March 11, 2003.
41. *Streats*, July 24, 2003.
42. ST, August 10, 2003.
43. Lee, Tsao Yuan and Linda Low: "Entrepreneurship Policy", p. 192 in Lee and Low (1990).
44. Bjerke, Bjorn: "Entrepreneurs and SMEs in the Singaporean Context", p. 276 in *Competitiveness of the Singapore Economy*, edited by Toh Mun Heng and Tan Kong Yam (Singapore, Singapore University Press, 1998).
45. ST, September 23, 1998.
46. *Streats*, December 12, 2002.
47. Ibid.
48. ST, June 30, 2000.
49. Ibid.
50. ST, July 12, 2001.
51. Bjerke in Toh and Tan, pp. 258-9.
52. Murray, Geoffrey and Audrey Perera: *Singapore: the Global City State* (Surrey, China Library/Curzon, 1998), p. 79.
53. ST, June 10, 1996.
54. Murray and Perera, p. 258.

CHAPTER 10

....

MEDIOCRE MANAGERS, DEMORALISED WORKERS

Besides entrepreneurs, managers and workers are the two other economic agents involved in the productive process. Their performance is as central to productivity as that of entrepreneurs. In Singapore, managerial and workforce deficiencies have added to entrepreneurial shortcomings to undermine productivity.

The failings of Singapore's managers and workers have worried Lee Kuan Yew as much as its limited entrepreneurial capacities. Once again the 1981 MNC submissions to the SNPB sparked his concern. The MNC submissions criticised both Singapore's managers and workers. Two decades later the performance of each has improved little despite repeated exhortations from PAP leaders.

1. Managers

Since the early 1980s, Singaporean managers have not scored well in international surveys. The IMD ranked Singaporean managers 21st for managerial competence out of 47 countries surveyed in its 2000 report.[1] Various studies provide reasons for Singapore's second-rate managers and confirm Lee's 1981 admission that Singapore's managers don't understand management.

Uncommunicative, Unappreciative and Bureaucratic

Singaporean bosses were deemed "uncommunicative, unappreciative and bureaucratic" by Singaporean workers, according to a September 2002 *Straits Times* poll. The paper interviewed 30 workers and found that "most feel employers have, in the pursuit of the bottom line, neglected the personal touch, like forming bonds with their staff". They also "lacked the charisma to motivate their employees and fail to provide for their career development". Most of the bosses "were considered bad" by the workers interviewed.[2]

A world-wide two-year survey of employee opinion of bosses conducted by International Survey Research (ISR) reached similar conclusions about Singaporean managers. In Singapore, the ISR interviewed 60,000 Singaporeans from despatch riders to managing directors. ISR senior consultant Peter Record said that "Singaporean employees are telling us they are not well led," noting that "Employees see their leaders as lacking the intellectual capital to craft aspirational goals and the emotional intelligence necessary to achieve them". They are also unhappy with the lack of development opportunities in their companies, not being given enough authority to do their jobs and the poor management skills of their supervisors.[3]

Another weakness of Singaporean managers is an inability to listen to staff when talking with them. A survey of Singapore managers by a US human resource consultant found that they scored lower on listening skills than managers in Thailand, the Philippines, Indonesia, Malaysia and Brunei. The consultant based this conclusion on 200 managers he had tested in Singapore over three years.[4]

Unready for the KB Economy

Singaporean managers' unreadiness for dealing with knowledge-based economy personnel, especially in the IT sector where highly trained innovative people are required, was also noted by a 1999 ISR survey, which interviewed 20,000 workers in Singapore. Managers failed to properly communicate with employees and share information or explain the reasons for decisions to them.[5] Such managerial flaws especially affect knowledge workers' performance.

IRS president John Stanek said that typical knowledge workers needed a clear view of company roles and freer access to information, but many Singaporean employers were unwilling to provide this and often avoided explaining the reasons for corporate decisions. A survey of Silicon Valley workers showed that they were motivated by bosses who gave them clear goals and freedom to choose how they wanted to do their jobs. They also tended to resent structured authority and interference by bosses who they felt were not as familiar with their jobs as they were. "There's a lot of people [in Singapore] who may not know how to handle such workers," noted Stanek. "If you don't know what they need, they'll just leave and go next door." [6] People skills are important and Singaporean managers often lack them.

Traditional Managerial Methods

The traditional managerial methods of many Singaporean businesses hinder skill development, especially in the local sector. Bjerke caustically notes:

> Chinese enterprises may often appear impressive in terms of market capitalisation and growth. But looking under the hood, management may look like a mess in Western eyes...There is no formalised personnel management to speak of...and constant supervision of staff is common.
> And the employees expect it.[7]

Koh made similar observations:

> It would seem that while firms in the advanced economies have changed, management style in Singapore remains particularly archaic. Not many employers have redesigned jobs to fit people to work part-time. Neither have they redesigned jobs to fit older people who have retired from the full-time workforce.[8]

A survey by the Singapore National Employers Federation (SNEF) showed that only 31 (8.8%) of 350 Singaporean companies offered flexible working arrangements. More than half (58.3%) had a five-day work week, while only five allowed job-sharing and one offered alternative workplace arrangements.[9]

Lack of flexible hours for workers reduces productivity. A US study revealed that companies who practised flexi-time showed a 10 to 40 per cent increase in productivity, according to Singapore's Manpower Minister Lee Boon Yang. A UK study found that 77 per cent of firms had more efficient employees after introducing such flexi-time measures as telecommuting or working from home.[11] "Compared to the developed countries, our employers have been slow to adopt alternative work arrangements and employee benefits," the minister said.[10]

Singaporean managers are generally indifferent to employees' requests and lack pro-family policies. A *Straits Times* survey of 20 working couples said their bosses often rejected requests for time off to deal with family emergencies.[12] Only five couples were happy with their employer's stance on this issue. The rest said their bosses treated requests for time off with suspicion and hostility.

Lack of flexible work arrangements, the archaic and authoritarian attitudes of Singapore management, poor communication with workers, and managers' reluctance to share information with or show respect to workers undermine staff morale and create disloyal, lazy and job-hopping employees, which all combine to reduce productivity. Much of the job-hopping at SIA and *The Straits Times* was due to low morale caused by poor management.

More PAP Lectures

PAP leaders other than Lee Kuan Yew have recognized the shortcomings of Singaporean managers. Lee's despairing 1981 remark that Singapore's managers didn't understand management and productivity was endorsed by NTUC chief and PAP Labour Minister Lim Boon Heng. When commenting on the low IMD ranking in 2000 for Singapore's managers, he proclaimed, "The current state of affairs is unhealthy".[13] Singapore managers needed new tools to supervise people in the emerging knowledge-based economy. Warming to his theme, Lim exclaimed:

> *Forget about the well-pressed suit and the passion for issuing orders. Today's manager needs the flexibility of a gymnast, the quickness of a panther and the mastery of a few foreign languages.*[14]

Managers also needed to be more entrepreneurial and less authoritarian. "Anyone inclined to wait for orders or follow established procedures will be left behind," declared Lim. No one can lecture like PAP ministers. He described the skills that managers need for the new economy. Managers have to spark innovations, motivate staff, tap into their strengths, provide continuous learning for them and bring out their best by being flexible in such areas as working hours. In other words, managers have to motivate workers to work hard and innovate. Managers also have to exploit their strengths by giving them tasks they are best at, ensure they are adequately trained and maintain their morale by showing consideration for their needs through such means as flexible working hours. But Singaporean managers usually lack the people skills to treat staff in these ways, especially in local companies.

Many of the organisational defects of Singaporean firms stem from managerial people-skill deficiencies. However, Singaporean managers seem to improve their people skills when working for MNCs in Singapore, which usually practice much better management-staff relationships than local firms. Annual surveys of the best firms to work for in Singapore confirm this.

Two such surveys have been conducted by the consulting firm Hewitt Associates and *The Straits Times Recruit* since 2001. In the 2003 survey, 30 organisations took part, comprising 16 MNCs, four government agencies and 10 GLCs and private companies. Of the ten companies voted the best employers by their employees, nine were MNCs. In 2003, the first Singaporean organisation made it into the top ten – ranked tenth on the survey's list of the best employers.

A Hewitt Associates spokesman said that Singapore's top employers invested in people, even during the tough times. "They continued to relentlessly develop the best talent, communicate their long-term focus, provide clarity as to the current business situation and pay attention to employees' views," he said.[15] As a result the best employers had more engaged employees, greater profitability and higher share prices, even in lean periods. But SIA clearly failed to follow such an approach in 2003, ruthlessly laying off employees and significantly demoralising many who remained. The fact that only one Singaporean firm scraped into the top ten demonstrates the extent to which Singaporean-managed organisations lag behind world standards in their treatment of employees. Singaporean organisational culture largely explains the poor showing of local concerns in these surveys. When working for MNCs, Singaporean managers are weaned off this culture and their managerial abilities seem to improve: for while it is clear that most MNCs beat the local companies for being best employers, it should be noted that Singaporeans often are the senior managers in these MNCs. When exposed to MNC managerial philosophies and practices they become much better managers.

Overall, however, the Hewitt/*Straits Times* surveys confirm that Singaporean organisations and their managers are clearly defective in their treatment of employees. Their surveys also show that Lee's forlorn observations about Singaporean managers remain as valid today as they were in the early 1980s. More than 20 years of PAP Government exhortations have apparently had a limited effect on their performance. This is not surprising: many Singaporean managers may well think that some PAP ministers have little right to lecture them on how to be good managers, considering the high-handed, threatening way that Lee Kuan Yew – supported by NTUC chief Lim Boon Heng – has repeatedly intervened in SIA staff-management disputes in recent years. Lee's intervention aggravated these disputes and worsened SIA staff morale. In exhibiting all the authoritarian attitudes of traditional Singaporean managers, Lee is hardly a role model for good management.

2. Workers

The deficiencies of Singapore's workers are often obscured by the high scores they receive by such ratings agencies as BERI. From 1980 to 2006 BERI ranked Singapore workers as the world's best in its workforce rankings, against up to 50 other countries it usually measures.[16] Yet while BERI has been giving Singapore's workers No. 1 rankings since 1980, other ratings agencies have not been so flattering, as the IMD's 2001 rankings for the productivity of Singaporean workers showed in Chapter 4.[17]

Decades of Complaints

For decades both Lee Kuan Yew and the MNCs in Singapore have been complaining about the mediocre quality of its workforce. Lee cited a 1981 German submission to the SNPB which said:

> The Singapore paradox...it is well known throughout the world that the workers of Singapore are busy and industrious. One can easily see this when looking around the Kallang area – small maritime wharves build ships with the highest skill. One finds this in any area where demand for performance matches the ability to perform and the worker concerned can identify with the fate of the enterprise involved.

However,

> Touring the shopping centres, factories, office buildings, one often observes that operators or clerks are not in the least interested in the fate of the enterprise; just chatting and being non-productive...To be successful you must instil a sense of loyalty, a sense of trustworthiness...[18]

Lee then reported what the Japanese said about Singaporean workers. One Japanese company had invited its 3500 Singaporean employees to a gathering to celebrate the company's anniversary. "Nobody came!" Lee exclaimed. They were not interested in the company's future. This shocked the Japanese company. They came from a society where employees showed strong company loyalty and where their bosses took a significant personal interest in them, even attending their weddings.[19]

Well before the 1981 submissions Lee had been dazzled by Japanese organisational methods. During a visit to Japan in 1967 he quizzed Japanese managers about their worker-management relations. One Japanese shipping company vice-president told Lee that "Japanese executives and engineers start work on the factory floor. They had to understand the top-level workers to lead them effectively before they can rise from the ranks."[20]

In 1987, Lee asked a Japanese CEO in Singapore to compare the workers of both countries:

> He assessed the Singaporean's productivity at 70 per cent. The reasons: Japanese workers were more skilled and were multi-skilled, more flexible and adaptable, had less job-hopping and absenteeism. They accepted the need for life-long learning and training. All workers considered themselves grey-collar workers, not white or blue-collar. Technicians, group leaders and supervisors were willing to soil their hands.

The CEO also told Lee that,

> the Japanese worker would cover for his work-mate who had to attend to other urgent business; the Singapore worker looked only after his own job.[21]

Singaporean workers have changed little over the years. Lee's 1981 disenchantment about Singapore's workers was recalled in 1999 when he again complained about their poor work attitudes and lack of teamwork:

> Foreign investors complained to the EDB that our workers shunned shift work, did not think it part of their job to prevent defects and took little or no interest in things

beyond their job function. None took any initiative to safeguard the company's interests. Job-hopping was rampant. [22]

Lee also noted that Singaporean workers were not well educated. He said that only 40 per cent of workers had secondary education or more and only 30 per cent had completed primary education, while the rest had no qualifications, he said.

Lee's criticisms of Singapore's workers are justified, as the following examination of their low job commitment, job-hopping propensities and lack of initiative and skill, as well as educational deficiencies, illustrate.

Minimal Job Commitment

In the early 1980s Lee correctly described the malaise gripping worker-management relations in Singapore. The snobbish hierarchical attitudes of management were matched by the lack of company loyalty and job-dedication in the workers. Little has changed since then. Not only are Singaporean managements still hierarchical, but workers (and often managers) display little loyalty to their companies.

Managerial attitudes are a prime cause of the low job commitment of Singapore's workers, according to the ISR's 1999-2001 survey of employee opinions. The survey found that Singaporean workers were among the world's least committed and they blamed this on alienating and distant top bosses.[23] Most workers had little faith in their employers, whom they felt lacked the brains and heart to inspire them. Of the 12 countries surveyed, Singapore was ranked 11. Other countries were Brazil (1), Spain (2), Germany (3), Canada (4), Italy (5), US (6), France (7), Hong Kong (8), Britain (9) and China (10).

A September 2003 Gallup survey produced similar negative findings about Singaporean workers.[24] The 11-country survey found that only six per cent of Singaporean workers could be classified as "engaged" – i.e. loyal, productive and satisfied with their work. Singapore ranked equal bottom with France on this factor. The US got the top score with 30 per cent of its workforce being rated as engaged.

The Gallup survey found that 17 per cent of Singaporean workers were "actively disengaged employees". Such workers were "disenchanted and disaffected" and "often vocal and/or militant in showing their negative attitudes to their work and employer". Moreover, employment disenchantment was getting worse. Singapore's 17 per cent figure was 5 per cent higher than in the previous year.

The survey also revealed that unhappy workers were costing Singapore's economy S$4.9 billion a year, based on such factors as reduced productivity and days employees took off. Gallup's regional coordinator said this figure was conservative for Singapore: "In company after company, we have found the cost of disengagement is really high and it has very serious financial implications for business." [25]

A year later a Gallup survey found the percentage of disengaged workers in Singapore had fallen to 9 per cent of the workers polled.[26] This mysterious turn-around was mainly ascribed to the economic upturn. Employees had been rather negative in the previous three years because of economic downturns. Lower wages and the fear of losing their jobs had been dominant, remarked one Singaporean union official.[27]

A spokesman for a local human resource institute said that workers' mentality had changed, noting "they tend to treasure what they have in job security". Fear of losing one's job can quickly transform a disengaged worker into an engaged one, but job commitment based on fear is a poor substitute for dedication and loyalty to one's employer – which good managements are best at cultivating. The 2004 Gallup survey found employee disaffection due to managerial shortcomings was still strong. Disengaged workers were still costing Singapore S$4 billion a year, Gallup calculated. Singapore's deficient managerial culture and its Government's low-wage policies are likely to perpetuate this situation for some time.

Singapore's unhappy workers are therefore likely to continue to express their dissatisfaction by constant job-hopping, which could be viewed as a substitute for union militant action. In Western democracies workers can often get redress for grievances through their unions. But the PAP's repressive union policies restrict Singaporean employees from doing that, as the SIA union-management sagas showed.

Job-Hopping and Fussy

Low worker commitment often leads to job-hopping. Singaporean employers constantly complain about it. Ratings agencies such as PERC have noted that it is a serious problem for Singapore.[28] In 1997, Ministry of Labour figures showed that the monthly resignation rate for the first quarter was 3.2 per cent, making this an average turnover of 38.4 per cent a year, according to the calculations of Toh and Tan.[29] By comparison, a nationwide study of the Australian workforce in 2002 by Aon Consulting, called Australia Work, found that 12.3 per cent of the nation's workers had changed employment at least once in the previous year.[30] The greater the staff turnover, the more managers have to hire the inadequately qualified. Singaporean workers are prone to job-hopping but are demanding and fussy about working conditions, especially shift work. PAP MP Inderjit Singh has experienced both problems. He complained that more than 20 per cent of workers employed by his semiconductor factory quit within three months. They left because they did not want to work in a clean room, disliked the job or were unwilling to work shifts.[31] This was despite gloomy employment prospects at the time. Mr Singh said he had designed the workers' compensation package to be as attractive as, if not better than, those of such MNCs in Singapore as Seagate and Motorola, yet could not retain workers. Other employers had told him that some of their workers had left on the first day.

A constant turnover of workers cuts productivity when new inexperienced workers replace experienced workers. Not only must they learn the job but extra resources have to be expended to train them, as the managing director of Aon, which did the Australia Work survey, noted: "When you consider the costs associated with recruitment, training and loss of production, the estimated cost of staff turnover is around 1½ times average salary costs. . . . That makes losing staff a very expensive exercise."[32]

Singapore's leaders are concerned at the negative impression that job-hopping gives to MNCs. A workforce that job-hops will drag Singapore down with MNCs, warned Mr Lim Swee Say, managing director of the Economic Development Board.[33] With their big investment in Singapore MNCs sought workers who would stay longer than two or three years or would lose faith in the workforce. High staff turnover meant higher retraining costs and stopped companies building up expertise and experience.

Foreign companies in Singapore regularly have the discouraging experience of training local staff only to see them leave soon after. Singaporeans call it the TBQ syndrome: they undergo Training, collect their Bonus and Quit. One story told to me well illustrates this syndrome: a British computer engineer with many years' experience applied for one of two positions with a big German company in Singapore. The German personnel manager was keen to employ him because of his obvious competence and background but was told by his superiors that Singaporeans had to be hired; so they were. The jobs required the new recruits to attend a six-week training course in Germany. The two Singaporeans did the course and then returned to Singapore, only to resign a month or two later, saying that the job was "too hard". The personnel manager suspected that they had simply used the company to get a free trip to Germany and some useful training before looking for brighter prospects elsewhere.

Of particular concern in recent years has been the bond-breaking phenomenon of young Singaporeans joining the civil service. In return for a Public Service Scholarship (PSC) they agree to work for the Government for six years. But many break their bonds or plan to do so. Out of 30 scholarship holders interviewed by *The Straits Times*, 25 did not see a problem in doing this and 11 said they would not serve out their six years. One said the scholarship was a trophy. It looked good on your resume.[34] The scholarships cost about S$350,000 each and are awarded to straight-A students to finance their studies at top US and British universities. The students want to break their bonds because they believe they must move around to advance their careers. As one ambitious 21-year-old due to study economics at a top US Ivy-league university arrogantly stated:

How can they expect us to commit our "prime" years to them? As they say, it's the new economy. We need to move around by our second year of working life, to broaden our job scope in order to rise faster. [35]

The naked opportunism of Singapore's brightest young people is partly matched by that of the average Singaporean worker. The almost full-employment situation that the country has enjoyed for many years has enabled Singaporeans to pick and choose their jobs, as Singaporean employers constantly complain. Koh notes:

The tight labour market encouraged employees to be choosy, hence bringing about high job turnover, which in turn worsens labour shortage at the firm level. [36]

Low wages also explain Singaporeans' chronic job-hopping, especially in the manufacturing and service industries. Singaporeans constantly switch jobs to get themselves better-paid positions. The low pay many Singaporeans receive in the lesser-skilled jobs, as Chapter 23 will show, significantly explains their job-hopping propensities.

Besides endemic job-hopping, Singaporeans are notoriously choosy about what jobs and working conditions they will accept. For example, few Singaporeans will work graveyard shifts in factories. Only foreigners do the 10pm to 6am shifts.[37] Not even the high jobless levels during the 2002/3 recession changed Singaporeans' fussy job-seeking habits. Although unemployment levels were 4.5 per cent by mid-2003, the highest since the 1985 recession, Singaporeans were still far too picky about jobs, fumed Lee Kuan Yew.

While there were 89,000 unemployed Singaporeans in March 2003, 200,000 foreigners were working in the manufacturing and services sector, he said. [38]

Singapore's managers display similar choosy job-seeking attitudes. A 1999 survey of 160 Singapore university graduates, mostly married and aged between 31 and 40, revealed that 30 per cent were unwilling to leave Singapore.[39] Only 39 per cent of those prepared to work abroad would do so for more than one year, and preferred developed countries such as the US, Australia or Japan, and/or culturally similar ones like China, Taiwan or Korea. Only a minority chose other ASEAN or Third World countries. Four years later Singaporean managers' reluctance to work abroad had changed little, despite a 4.5 per cent jobless rate. "We've seen an increase in the number of executives willing to go overseas but it's a very small number," said a manager from a Singapore job executive search firm.[40] Indian, Taiwanese and Malaysian Chinese managers in their countries were far more willing to take overseas positions.

Singaporean aversion to overseas postings could be affecting Singapore's competitiveness. Both Singaporean and foreign companies need local staff prepared to work abroad. Singaporean companies going global require locals to effectively represent them offshore, and MNCs must have locals in the host country also prepared to work abroad. But Singaporeans' reluctance to do this has worried MNCs.

Ever sensitive to MNC needs, Singapore's EDB commissioned Insead to study the problem. The study canvassed the Singaporean subsidiaries of more than 300 MNCs and found there was a shortage of locals willing to accept foreign postings. Some MNCs said getting Singaporeans to take such postings was a struggle. These were not even hardship postings they were being asked to accept, the MNCs said. A Siemans CEO in Singapore remarked, "For us, it's a fact that it's difficult to make employees go on long-term assignments."[41] MNCs still rate Singaporean workers higher than those of lesser-developed countries because of their technical competence and higher education levels, but a picky and job-hopping workforce undermines efficiency and negatively affects Singapore's productivity. While high employment levels may partly explain this, low pay and poor management are also to blame.

Low Initiative

Besides commitment (and loyalty), another major factor that determines workforce productivity is employee initiative. Poor initiative is a common complaint made of Singapore workers. This partly stems from the punitive risk-averse atmosphere of so many Singaporean workplaces, but it is also a result of the compartmentalised thinking that prevails in Singaporean organisations.

Doing your own assigned job and nothing more is the essence of compartmentalised thinking, the "It's not my job" refrain. In most organisations employees may sometimes have to accept tasks they don't normally do, or perform existing tasks in new ways. Flexible, innovative and loyal employees are most likely to do this. They are also quick to notify superiors of potential problems and propose ways of improving productivity. Despite being deluged with Quality Circles in their workplaces, few Singaporean workers are like this. Lee's early 1980s complaints about them still apply – not thinking it was their job to correct defects and showing no interest beyond their immediate job. Such lack of initiative is typical of uncommitted workers who have little attachment to their jobs or their employers.

Compartmentalised thinking restricts both the freedom as well as the desire to display initiative. Professor Neo Boon Siong, dean of Singapore's Nanyang Business School, uses the football term "striker" to describe people who make decisions, take action and make a difference. "A common organisational culture problem here is: Are potential strikers allowed to strike out?" he asks. Many employees aspire to make a difference but are not allowed to because of organisational rules and boundaries. They are told, "This is not your job", or "You're too junior, wait until you accumulate some years and grey hairs".[42] Such attitudes chip away at employee motivation.

Poorly Educated, Under-skilled

Lee's complaints in 1981 about the literacy levels of Singaporean workers have remained valid for many years. As Chapter Three shows, 26 per cent of Singapore's workers had only Primary Six or less education in 1995, while 43 per cent had less than secondary education. The Singapore workforce was also deficient in tertiary education compared to such developed countries as Germany, Japan and the US.

A trained workforce is central to productivity, a US study has shown. A Federal Department of Education survey of managers and owners of about 3000 businesses employing 20 workers or more found that improving the educational levels of a company's workforce by 10 per cent boosted productivity by 8.6 per cent. Increasing the value of tools and machinery or capital stock by 10 per cent only improved productivity by 3.4 per cent.[43] The educational deficiencies of Singapore's workforce do much to undermine its productivity.

The experiences of Australian builder Kevin on Singapore's construction sites demonstrate the direct relationship between training and productivity. Poorly trained Singaporean building supervisors lacked the skills to perform basic tasks, resulting in much wastage. Moreover, the failure to train foreign workers further reduced efficiency.

Singapore's leaders constantly stress the need to upgrade workers' skills to raise productivity. NTUC deputy head Lim Boon Heng said that Singapore's lower skill levels compared to Western countries' explained its lower productivity. "Workers in the West are better trained and even multi-skilled," he said, adding that for every three Singaporean workers needed to repair oil refining equipment, firms in the West only needed one or two.[44]

Significant barriers to training and retraining the workforce still exist in Singapore. The SMEs especially, who employ about half of the country's workforce, are very reluctant to train employees. SNEF vice-president Bob Tan said it was a "hard slog" to get SMEs to commit to staff training. The "lack of management support" was the No. 1 problem as SME CEOs were simply "too busy" to organise workers' training. The CEOs were their SMEs' human resource department but were not HR-savvy. They did not even know how to identify training programs. In 2003, only one in ten SME workers received training, compared to the national average of one in four.[45] The Government's Workforce

Development Agency (WDA) has roped in two business organisations to pressure the SMEs to train more workers. In December 2004, the WDA appointed SNEF and the Singapore Business Federation (SBF) – which have 2400 SME members between them – to be joint "Training Champions" for SMEs. Their task was to have 15,000 SME employees trained over the next two years.

Low SME commitment to workforce training is one of the barriers the Government must overcome to boost workforce productivity and prepare workers for the knowledge-based economy.

Analysing the BERI Rankings

Despite the obvious inadequacies of Singapore's workforce, BERI has continued to give its workers top rankings year after year. Not even Lee Kuan Yew has done this.

The four criteria that BERI uses to construct its rankings are relative productivity, legal framework, workers' attitudes and technical skills. [46] The rankings are compiled from surveys of 43 countries. In 2000, BERI scored Singapore:

- First for workers' relative productivity (because of wage cuts which boosted Singapore's cost competitiveness, explained BERI)

- First for its legal framework whose rating depends on fair and transparent laws giving employers the flexibility to hire and fire and workers the right to influence management decision-making.

- Third, behind Japan and Switzerland, for worker attitude, which BERI calculates based on work lost through labour disputes and absenteeism.

- Seventh in technical skills, for which Singapore scored 98 out of a perfect score of 100. Six countries which got the perfect 100 were Japan, Switzerland, the US, Holland, Germany and Sweden. Singapore tied with Denmark.

Overall, Singapore scored 85 out of 100, 10 points ahead of the next country, Switzerland. BERI deemed Singapore's workers to be better than Switzerland's.

Since 2000, BERI has continued to give Singapore's workforce top rankings. In 2005, Singapore was ranked (1), the US (2) and Ireland (3), with Switzerland slipping to (4).[47] In 2006, the rankings were Singapore (1), Hong Kong (2), New Zealand (3) and Australia (4)[48] and in 2007 they were Singapore (1), US (2), Taiwan (3) and Belgium (4).[49]

The strong evidence of Singaporean workforce inadequacies soundly refutes the high rankings BERI gives its Singapore's workforce. Why the difference? Analysis indicates that the BERI criteria significantly reflect corporate concerns such as keeping wages down, freedom to hire and fire workers and the advantages of a docile workforce. While these considerations may be of corporate importance, they have little bearing on a workforce's efficiency in terms of its degree of engagement, capacity for initiative, and company loyalty.

The BERI criteria that do relate to workforce efficiency seem to have been assessed inaccurately for Singapore. First, the hierarchical nature of Singaporean organisations severely limits the right of employees to influence management decision-making. Yet BERI ranks Singapore first for this, along with employers' right to hire and fire. Next, Singapore's ranking of seventh for technical skills seems questionable, considering the low educational levels of its workforce compared to those of other industrialised societies. While many Singaporean workers may have technical qualifications that is no guarantee of their skill levels, as Singaporean construction supervisors show.

The BERI criteria are poor measures of workforce quality. They either reflect corporate/MNC concerns about having a passive, easily controllable workforce, or they wrongly measure technical skills and other factors that determine workforce efficiency. Either way, little credence can be given to BERI's habit of constantly ranking Singapore's workforce as the world's best. Singapore's workforce is far from this.

* * * * * * * * *

Managerial shortcomings significantly account for the failings of Singapore's workforce. Uncaring, uncommunicative and uninspiring managers do much to undermine worker morale, loyalty, and so productivity. But managers cannot fully be blamed for the deficiencies of Singaporean workers, including those resulting from educational shortcomings. There is a stratum of underlying cultural and political/structural factors that adversely affect managerial and workforce performance in Singapore, as the next chapter shows.

References

1. *The World Competitiveness Yearbook 2001* (Laussanne, Switzerland; Institute for Management Development), p. 471.
2. *The Straits Times* (ST), September 11, 2002.
3. ST, September 7, 2002.
4. ST, April 3, 1995. Inability to listen seems widespread in Singapore. "In one ear and out the other" is how they seem to treat the comments of others. I once mentioned this to a Canadian acquaintance. Was it just me, I asked him. He assured me it wasn't. "They don't hear you because they are thinking about what they want to say most of the time."
5. ST, November 9, 1999.
6. Ibid.
7. Bjerke, Bjorn: "Entrepreneurship and SMEs in the Singaporean Context", p. 276 in *Competitiveness of the Singapore Economy*, edited by Toh Mun Heng and Tan Kong Yam (Singapore, Singapore University Press, 1998).
8. Koh, William: "Human Resource Management for the New Competitive Environment", p. 349 in *Competitiveness of the Singapore Economy* (Singapore, Singapore University Press, 1998), edited by Toh Mun Heng and Tan Kong Yam.
9. Ibid.
10. ST, May 2, 2000.
11. Ibid.
12. ST, October 25, 2000.
13. ST, August 31, 2000.
14. Ibid.
15. ST, April 17, 2003.
16. Lim Yoon Foo, "Singapore Workforce Tops BERI Rankings Yet Again" Productivity Digest June 2002, *and* BERI Labour Force Evaluation Measure (LFEM) rankings for 2003-7.
17. *World Competitiveness Report 2001*, pp. 462-3.
18. Han, Fook Kwang, Warren Fernandez, and Sumiko Tan: *Lee Kuan Yew, The Man and His Ideas* (Singapore, Times Editions, 1998), p. 357.

19. Ibid.
20. Lee Kuan Yew: *From Third World To First* (Singapore, Times Media, 2000), p. 581.
21. Ibid, p. 580.
22. ST, April 10, 1999.
23. ST, September 7, 2002.
24. *Today*, September 19, 2003.
25. *Streats*, September 18, 2003.
26. *Business Times*, December 3, 2004.
27. *Today* (Weekend Edition), December 4-5, 2004.
28. ST, March 16, 1999.
29. Koh in Toh and Tan, pp. 321-2.
30. *The West Australian*, October 22, 2002.
31. ST, March 16, 1999.
32. *The West Australian*, October 22, 2002.
33. ST, August 9, 1996.
34. ST, July 9, 2000.
35. Ibid.
36. Koh in Toh and Tan, pp. 321-2.
37. ST, February 7, 2003.
38. *Streats*, July 24, 2003.
39. Campbell, Kathleen H., Donald J. Campbell, and Audrey Chua: "Regionalisation: Policy Issues for Singapore", p. 118 in *Singapore Inc: Public Policy Options in the Third Millenium,* edited by Linda Low and Douglas M. Johnston (Singapore, TimesMedia, 2001).
40. *Streats*, March 26, 2003.
41. ST, October 27, 2003.
42. ST, August 30, 2000.
43. ST, May 15, 1995.
44. ST, October 28, 1998.
45. *Today*, December 2, 2004.
46. ST, May 2, 2000.
47. Lim Yoon Foo and BERI LFEM rankings 2003-7.
48. Ibid, 2006.
49. Ibid, 2007.

CHAPTER 11

LOOKING FOR CAUSES

The previous chapter identified how managerial and workforce inadequacies have adversely affected Singapore's productivity. These inadequacies are, in their turn, adversely affected by fundamental cultural values and from structural factors resulting from the Government's educational and union policies.

1. Cultural Factors

Hierarchical values, low-trust attitudes and risk-averse mentalities have already been identified as reducing productivity. How they do this in relation to Singapore's managers and workers will now be examined.

Hierarchical Values

Hierarchical thinking is ingrained in Asian societies. Egalitarianism is an alien concept, "regarded as a time-wasting, inefficient, directionless affair," according to Byrnes. Such thinking is displayed even by liberal pro-democracy elements in Asia. A notable feature of the 1989 Tiananmen Square events in Beijing "was students who lectured, with pointed fingers, groups of ordinary citizens around the streets of the city".[1]

> The students, through their demonstrations, were acting out their hierarchical roles as leaders of society. On the square itself, the students formed barriers to entry against ordinary people...There was more hierarchy than democracy on Tiananmen Square. [2]

The pervasive hierarchical attitudes in Asia, including Singapore, do much to crush innovation and initiative, both critical ingredients for improving efficiency. As Bjerke notes, in Singaporean firms staff are constantly supervised:

> Chinese management is even in modern times a top run, one-man show by an autocratic boss assuming authority for all management functions...The Chinese manager is very "boss-centred"...but also self-reliant.[3]

Chinese culture is very hierarchical and power-centred, notes Hofstede.[4] The belief in an unequal order prevails: everyone has a place, high or low. A few may be independent but most must be dependent. Other people are a potential threat to one's power and can rarely be trusted. These class-based, hierarchical and low-trust values are ingrained in Chinese life and workplaces. Bjerke summarises the observations of several theorists on Chinese values:

Dependence on 'class' and importance of power is shown in many different ways among Chinese. One is a general lack of communication across positions, particularly in a vertical downward direction....Withholding information to gain or maintain power is acceptable among Chinese... Openness is, in fact, often considered to be a sign of weakness in the Chinese culture.[5]

Hierarchical attitudes are also prevalent in Singapore's Indian and Malay communities. The rigid caste-and class-based Indian cultures and the hierarchical feudalistic values of Malays, still strongly affect these peoples.

Pearson and Chatterjee report that managerial studies of Indian managers show that they place great importance not only on job satisfaction but also on "dignity, prestige, security and power".[6] These findings reflect those of Hofstede who finds that Indian managers are mainly concerned with rules, power distance and masculinity. They are also risk-averse and rate family and status highly. The emphasis on such values as prestige, status and "power distance" reflects hierarchical attitudes.

Many Malay values resemble the conservative and hierarchical ones of Indian managers. The Malay kampong was formed in the image of the family, where the headman was a father-figure respected and obeyed by his "children", remarks Tamney:

Rebellion against authority figures was forbidden. Each person must act in accordance with his station. Hormat *is a Malay term expressing the respect due to a social position and thus the person holding that position. It is unthinkable that one would be free, unbound by ties of dependence, and standing outside the hierarchical order of social positions.*[7]

Tamney adds that "the Malays in Singapore live out a modernized version of their culture".[8] In so doing they exhibit similar hierarchical and risk-averse attitudes as the Chinese and Indians.

Hierarchical values clearly dictate Singaporean behaviour, especially where traditional values are strongest, such as in the SME sector. Many SMEs are family-run companies where patriarchal top-down practices and centralised decision-making prevail, according to a Singapore Institute of Management study of 177 SMEs. "SMEs are very autocratic and paternalistic. They follow the chain of command closely, following a comprehensive set of written rules and standard procedures," said the study's compiler.[9] They have military-type structures in which top managers decide everything and junior employees "simply carry out directives", lowering worker morale and stifling creativity.

A more egalitarian corporate culture prevails in large Singaporean companies, but hierarchical values still adversely affect management-labour interactions and impede efficiency in most Singapore companies and organisations. Strong organisational stratification reduces interactions between superiors and subordinates. This slows down communication, hinders mobilisation of skills and abilities and impedes efficiency.

In more egalitarian organisations, a much narrower management-staff gap facilitates communication between both levels. Management is readier to listen to and even accept criticism from staff who in turn feel freer to suggest ways of improving efficiency. In hierarchic organisations, staff must constantly defer to superiors and are made to feel that it is "not their place" to make proposals, let alone to criticise the organisation. Bosses who rarely receive honest and sometimes critical feedback from subordinates continue to perpetuate inefficient practices and policies.

In hierarchical organisations, employees' initiative is stifled because they constantly wait for orders from above instead of acting on their own initiative when necessary. Staff develop an "it's-not-my-job" mentality. Such compartmentalised thinking stultifies their capacity to act independently, causing organisational inflexibility and inefficiency.

Hierarchical organisations also reduce efficiency and staff morale in more insidious ways. Hierarchical managers see subordinates as inferiors, deserving little respect and not worth listening to; mere "cogs" or "digits" to be used as managers see fit. This breeds demoralised and disloyal workers who do as little work as possible, "screw the company" when they can, and job-hop whenever better prospects appear. Their often poor pay, especially in such areas as the service industry, coupled with inconsiderate treatment from their bosses, goes far to explaining Singaporeans' job-hopping. Such behaviour indicates low staff morale and dissatisfaction. It also explains the poor showing of Singaporean firms in the Best Employers survey mentioned earlier.

Hierarchical managers demoralise workers, discourage their job commitment and initiative and increase their propensity to job-hop. Being made to feel like under-valued cogs in an uncaring organisation undermines employee motivation. Low management/labour trust levels have similar effects.

Low Trust Levels

Trust is the lubricant of economic and social relations. Based on the concept of reciprocity, it assumes that each party in a relationship, business or otherwise, will fulfil their obligations and promises to the other, whether they be such matters as gaining business credit and loans or employer-worker agreements.

Trust can significantly affect efficiency levels, especially between labour and management. As Fukuyama argues in his book *Trust*:

> *If people who have to work together in an enterprise trust one another because they are all operating according to a common set of ethical norms, doing business costs less. Such a society will be better able to innovate organizationally, since the high degree of trust will permit a wide variety of social relationships to emerge....*[10]
>
> *By contrast, people who do not trust each other will end up cooperating only under a system of formal rules and regulations, which have to be negotiated, agreed to, litigated, and enforced, sometimes by coercive means. This legal apparatus, serving as a substitute for trust, entails what economists call "transaction costs".*
>
> *A high trust society can organize its workplace on a more flexible and group-oriented basis, with more responsibility delegated to lower levels of the organization. Low-trust societies, by contrast, must fence in and isolate their workers with a series of bureaucratic rules. Workers find their workplaces more satisfying if they are treated like adults who can be trusted to contribute to their community rather than small cogs in a large industrial machine designed by someone else.*[11]

Specifically, workforce productivity is significantly influenced by the degree of labour-management trust that exists. How far workers trust management can greatly determine their company loyalty and productivity. Managers can build trust in several ways, according to Anna Murphy, editor for *Worklife Asia*. These include reducing red tape of a controlling nature, giving employees more freedom to make decisions, standing by employees and supporting rather than censuring them when a plan fails and implementing such innovations as flexi-time and job-sharing.[12] Singaporean managers score poorly in these areas and their reluctance to give staff time off to handle family crises has already been noted. This not only reveals employer distrust of their workers, but also undermines workers' trust in their bosses. As Murphy observes:

> *Employees seldom see formal, rigid bosses as being trustworthy. They usually beget people who are unhappy working with them. When workers feel that their needs and emotions are being marginalised in favour of rules and regulations, they become disillusioned. And you can bet they'll be leaving right after they pick up their bonuses.*[13]

Singaporean managers easily fit this description with their hierarchical rule-based attitudes and readiness to punish rather than back employees when something goes wrong. But other factors besides hierarchical managers account for low trust levels in Singaporean organisations.

Fukuyama talks of high and low trust societies. He sees Japanese and North American and most West European societies as high-trust, while non-Japanese Asian societies, especially Chinese societies, are low-trust. In Asia lack of trust is endemic not only to Chinese, but to virtually all societies, whether Thai, Malay, Indonesian, Filipino, Korean, Indian, Sri-Lankan, Pakistani – or, in Singapore, whether Chinese, Indian or Malay. Those who have done business in Asia for a few years understand this. Distrust is widespread while trust is hard won and quickly lost. Singapore is no exception with its low-trust Chinese, Malay and Indian "familiaristic" societies which Fukuyama describes as frequently having,

> *weak voluntary associations because unrelated people have no basis for trusting one another. Chinese societies like Taiwan, Hong Kong and the People's Republic of China itself are examples; the essence of Chinese Confucianism is the elevation of family bonds above all other social loyalties.*[14]

Fukuyama's comments apply equally to Indian and Malay societies – especially in business matters. In all three cultural traditions, family and kin remain paramount, even in modern industrial Singapore. As such, as in other low-trust societies, Singaporeans have little trust in (or often respect for) people outside their own immediate group of kin, clan or race.

Before assessing the economic effects of such attitudes, the operation of familiaristic values requires further examination. In Chinese and most other Asian businesses, management keeps employees at a distance, especially non-family ones. Traditionally, Chinese enterprises favour the proprietor's family. "There is a very strong inclination on the part of the Chinese to trust only people related to them, and conversely to distrust people outside their family and kinship group."[15] This includes non-kin employees. As Taiwan-Chinese writer Bo Yang recalls:

Many Chinese people in the [US] have told me that if their boss is Chinese, they constantly have to be on their toes. Chinese bosses never promote their Chinese employees, and when people are being laid off, they are always the first to go.[16]

This breeds disloyal employees and discourages them from staying with the company. As Fukuyama notes:

They know that they will probably not be accepted into top management as fully trusted and equal partners, nor do they feel comfortable in a relationship of day-to-day dependence with their employers. Employees in Chinese firms therefore tend to switch employers readily and ultimately hope to accumulate the capital to start their own businesses.[17]

But nepotistic managements are only one problem in family-oriented societies. Another is that non-kin often get little consideration. This is not only from bosses to non-kin subordinates, but from non-kin to each other. Frequently Singaporeans operate on the premise that anyone outside one's family is "fair game", whether they be colleagues, superiors or subordinates. Much opportunistic and ungracious behaviour in Singapore stems from such thinking. Singaporeans' opportunism is more than making the most of one's opportunities; it also involves cynically using non-kin people or groups for one's own ends and then discarding them when they are no longer of use. Graciousness, which is essentially gratitude shown for favours rendered or for loyalty and support given, is often withheld from non-kin in familiaristic societies such as Singapore's.

Opportunism is endemic in Singaporean "use or be used" society though is now becoming more so in Western societies. The TBQ experience of the German company hiring and training two Singaporeans who then left illustrates this sort of behaviour, as does bond-breaking by Singaporean graduates.

Opportunism compounded by ungraciousness destroys trust between people. While such behaviour is increasingly common in all modern societies, in Singapore it is particularly noticeable.

Singaporeans' lack of courtesy and graciousness has concerned their PAP rulers since the 1970s. In 1979, Prime Minister Lee Kuan Yew launched Singapore's annual courtesy campaigns. The aim was to transform Singapore into a "gracious society". The courtesy campaigns have become an annual event in Singapore, each with a different theme. The 1987 campaign was particularly noteworthy because its target was ingratitude. Singaporeans were urged "to make the first move at courtesy rather than just be passive recipients of other people's thoughtfulness".[18] So far the courtesy campaigns have had little effect on Singaporeans' manners, as they and their leaders gloomily note. But Singaporeans seem less likely to spit in the street than they were in the 1970s, according to local commentators. The need to hold annual courtesy campaigns demonstrates how discourteous Singaporeans still are.

Opportunistic and ungracious behaviour not only undermines trust but destroys relationships and ends friendships. In the workplace it reduces trust between workers and management, cutting productivity and efficiency. In low-trust organisations, suspicion and paranoia prevail. This cripples cooperation and communication, the sharing of ideas, employee initiative and creativity. In low-trust organisations, defensive risk-averse and compartmentalised thinking flourishes, as does job-hopping. Together they all undermine productivity. The job-hopping that afflicts low-trust organisations run by uncaring managements also indirectly inhibits workforce training. Worker readiness to job-hop generates even more managerial distrust and discourages businesses from training their workers. Who wants to train workers likely to leave once trained?

A negative spiral of distrust develops where distrust breeds further distrust. This situation significantly explains the skill deficits of Singaporean workers, especially in the SME sector. As explained earlier, the low training levels of workers in SMEs is supposedly because their CEOs lack the time to train workers. But not having time is a standard excuse for inaction. The job-hopping tendencies and TBQ syndromes of workers are a more likely and real reason for the reluctance of the CEOs of Singapore's SMEs to train workers.

By comparison, in Japanese companies where management-worker trust is higher, a much better retraining environment exists. Because workers are loyal and unlikely to job-hop, companies are far more ready to train them. This partly explains why Japanese workers are more productive than Singaporean workers.

To summarise, low worker-management trust levels, like hierarchical attitudes, reduce worker commitment and increase job-hopping. While low trust is partly the result of hierarchicalism, other factors independently reduce trust levels in Singapore. These include familial values, which encourage nepotism and opportunism by both workers and management. Managers and workers act in thoughtless and opportunistic ways toward each other. The effect of non-kin values gives rise to a use-or-be-used, low-trust society that ultimately undermines efficiency.

Risk-averseness

Risk-averse attitudes reduce the performance not only of Singapore's entrepreneurs but also of its managers and workforce. To some extent, such attitudes are due to hierarchical and low-trust values which discourage initiative, innovation and risk-taking by both groups. But punitive organisational and cultural values are also to blame in Singapore, especially the one-mistake mentality that authoritarian PAP rulers have traditionally displayed, especially under Lee Kuan Yew.

Demands that something must be got right every time, and an intolerance of mistakes, produces careful risk-averse behaviour, especially at middle-management and employee level. The punitive organisational culture of SIA and *The Straits Times* demonstrates this. Memos that threaten humiliating punishments for errors committed only encourage risk-avoiding behaviour to minimise the chances of making a mistake. As little work as possible is done to reduce the potential for mistakes and rules are strictly followed to avoid being blamed if anything goes wrong. Such behaviour undermines both management and staff initiative, reducing productivity. The irony of the one-mistake mentality is that it reduces efficiency and probably breeds more mistakes in the long run.

2. Structural Factors

Besides cultural values, structural factors resulting from the PAP Government's educational and union policies have also reduced productivity.

A Defective Education System

For a highly industrialised country, the educational and literacy levels of Singapore's workforce are surprisingly low. As Chapter Three shows, 26 per cent of Singapore's workers had only Primary Six or less education in 1995 while 43 per cent had less than secondary education. Singapore's illiteracy levels were still almost Third-World in the 1990s. IMD figures for 1998 show Singapore was ranked 37th for illiteracy, with 6.9 per cent of the population over 15 being illiterate. The Philippines, ranked 36th, beat Singapore with an illiteracy rate of 5.4 per cent.[19] The teacher-pupil ratio for government schools in Singapore was 1:40, reported Rahim in 1998,[20] while in March 2003 Primary 1 and 2 class ratios were still 1:40.[21] In Australia, primary school class ratios are between about 1:20 and 1:26 in such states as South Australia, New South Wales and Victoria.[22] Most Scandinavian and West European countries also have low class numbers.

The literacy deficiencies of Singapore's workforce may be partly due to inadequate resources for subnormal students. These are the physically handicapped, the autistic and the academic "failures", notes Rahim. Such students are mainly catered for by privately-run special education schools that "tend to be poorly funded, overcrowded, and offer poor educational facilities," she says. The demand for them far outpaces supply. Although the state pays half the education costs of handicapped pupils, their school fees are three times those of mainstream schools. "The government's parsimonious funding of special education schools stands in stark contrast to its generous funding of programmes for 'gifted' children." [23] Classes are much smaller and resources more lavish compared to government schools, which are under-resourced and overcrowded.

The top schools are funded at the expense of state schools. This reflects the PAP's elitist education policies, which favour the most talented students. Inevitably, heavy spending on the brightest students is at the expense of average and subnormal students, many of whom enter the workforce functionally illiterate. While Singapore's elitist education methods favour the academically gifted, they impede the development of an educated workforce. They have produced a generation of under-educated workers who will keep down labour productivity for some time.

Weak Trade Unions and Low Pay

Reports of Singapore's "disciplined labour force" with its modest pay demands are sure to please MNCs and local enterprises and earn high BERI rankings. Business likes nothing better than compliant workers who meekly accept below-average wages.

The PAP Government proudly informs foreign capital that Singapore's unions are kept under a tight leash. No companies, foreign or local, need fear strikes or other labour unrest. Unions are controlled by the NTUC, which is run by government-appointed ministers and bureaucrats. The NTUC, which prevents workers from controlling union policy, is concerned with holding down wages and stops collective action and other measures to please the MNCs.

While the business sector may benefit from the Government's anti-union measures in the short term, such policies undermine workforce productivity over time. Poorly paid, maltreated and unappreciated workers soon become demoralised and unproductive.

Disgruntled employees are bad for productivity, because they lack commitment, don't perform to capacity and are prone to job-hopping. Were they able to press their demands more effectively, the company might be compelled to meet their requests. Although this might produce a larger wages bill, it would also result in a more content and productive workforce.[24] Had the SIA unions been stronger, for instance, the airline could not have retrenched the staff it did because of a short-term profit plunge. A tougher union would have stopped the retrenchment and forced SIA to adopt fairer measures to deal with the crisis. As it was, the SIA unions could not save the jobs of over 400 of their members, who bitterly complained of union inability to protect them.

Had SIA been prevented from retrenching the sacked workers its wages bill would have been higher but staff morale would have been better, their trust in management stronger and readiness to do their best for the airline greater. (Their in-flight service might also have improved, especially for fussy Singaporeans.) Moreover, SIA would not have had to hire and train new staff, as it had to do when business recovered and job-hopping would have been reduced.

The same applies to many other organisations in Singapore where weak unions have let managements ride rough-shod over staff with resultant falls in employee morale and productivity. The Government boasts that Singapore's unions and management cooperate to boost productivity, but the mediocre productivity of Singapore's workforce suggests otherwise.

A restructuring of Singapore's trade union movement in which government control was cut back would indirectly boost workforce productivity. By being much freer to fight for their members' interests, unions would likely improve workers' pay and conditions. This would boost workers' morale and increase their job commitment and reduce job-hopping in ways that would improve their productivity.

The factors that undermine managerial and workforce efficiency in Singapore are many and complex. Such cultural factors as hierarchical company structures, low-trust levels and risk-averse attitudes are largely to blame, along with a range of counterproductive behaviours they breed in organisations. These include compartmentalised thinking, a lack of initiative, a refusal to take responsibility for correcting defects and narrow self-seeking behaviour. It is a challenge to identify them and describe how they interact with each other. The picture is further complicated by such structural factors as a substandard education system and a weak union movement that cannot properly fight for employees.

Such factors would also account for many of Singapore's endemic inefficiencies in such areas as taxi and bus services, the operation of laboratories and swimming pools, TB control, local manufacturing, publishing, cinema projection, and government accounting. So many of these deficiencies are due to uncaring hierarchical managements that encourage obedience and passivity and foster "it's not my job" compartmentalised thinking. Such thinking saps managerial and employee initiative. It also discourages tradesmen and factory workers from practising quality control and removing production-line defects. Moreover, all these failings are exacerbated by inadequate education, which discourages initiative and ill-prepares many Singaporeans to be literate and competent employees.

A complex web of factors, then, depresses Singapore's efficiency at both macro and micro levels. On the political-economic level are PAP government policies, including those which have permitted a large and inefficient state sector to develop at the expense of an innovative and vibrant SME sector. But various cultural, organisational, educational and other factors have significantly contributed to Singapore's inefficiencies and indifferent productivity.

* * * * * * * * * *

While low productivity, along with risk-averse entrepreneurs and a demoralised and job-hopping workforce, are regularly agonised over in Singapore, this soul-searching seems to have largely escaped international attention. The world financial and business community appears oblivious to Singapore's chronic shortcomings, preferring to see it as the most successful and durable of the Asian tigers. How Singapore has disguised such unflattering realities about itself is considered in the next two chapters.

References

1. Byrnes, Michael: *Australia and the Asia Game* (Sydney, Allen and Unwin, 1994), p. 33.
2. Ibid.
3. Bjerke, Bjorn: "Entrepreneurs and SMEs in the Singaporean Context", p. 269, in *Competitiveness of the Singapore Economy* (Singapore, Singapore University Press, 1998), edited by Toh Mun Heng and Tan Kong Yam
4. Geert, Hofstede: *Culture's Consequences* (California, Sage Publications, second edition, 1984), pp. 97 and 104.
5. Bjerke in Toh and Tan, p. 270.
6. Pearson, Cecil, and Chatterjee, Samir: "Managerial goals and organizational reform in India" in *Asia Pacific Journal*, Vol 3, No 1, June 1999, p. 80.
7. Tamney, Joseph B.: *The Struggle for Singapore's Soul* (Berlin, De Gruyter, 1996), p. 114.
8. Ibid.
9. *The Straits Times* (ST), December 9, 2003.
10. Fukuyama, Francis: *Trust: The Social Virtues and the Creation of Prosperity* (London, Penguin, 1995), p. 27.
11. Ibid, p. 31.
12. ST, April 28, 2000.
13. Ibid.
14. Fukuyama, p. 29.
15. Ibid, p. 75.
16. Yang, Bo: *The Ugly Chinaman and the Crisis of Chinese Culture* (Sydney, Allen and Unwin, second edition, 1992), p. 13.
17. Fukuyama, p. 187.
18. "Courtesy: More than a smile" (Singapore, Ministry of Information and the Arts, June 1999), p. 14.
19. *The World Competitiveness Yearbook 2001* (Laussanne, Switzerland; Institute for Management Development), p. 437.
20. Rahim, Lily Zubaidah: *The Singapore Dilemma: The Political and Educational Marginality of the Malay Community* (Kuala Lumpur, Oxford University Press, 1998), p. 135.
21. ST, March 21, 2003 and March 30, 2003.
22. *The Australian*, May 12, 2003.
23. Rahim, p. 148.
24. Foreign banks in Singapore have demonstrated the positive correlation

between higher wages and greater productivity. Consultants KPMG compared the performance of six of Singapore's foreign banks with those of three of the biggest local banks (*Business Times*, April 26, 2004). The survey found that in 2002 the top foreign bank (Citibank) had an operating profit per employee of US$285,000, which was 30 per cent higher than that of United Overseas Bank, the most profitable local bank. Three of the six foreign banks surveyed (Citibank, HSBC and Stanchart) all had higher profits per employee than the three leading local banks (UOB, Development Bank

of Singapore and Overseas Chinese Banking Corporation).

The irony was that local banks were seeking to recruit staff from foreign banks even though the latter were drawing higher salaries. "Local banks hope that they will continue to work their higher productivity magic after switching over," commented *Business Times*. But it could be a forlorn hope. The organisational culture of Singaporean banks would probably sabotage whatever benefits ex-foreign bank staff would bring with them.

CHAPTER 12

EFFICIENCY REAL AND APPARENT

While many foreign commentators may criticise Singapore's authoritarian regime and lack of democratic freedoms, they still pay homage to its efficiency. The only foreigners to realise the often mythical nature of Singapore's efficiency are those who have lived and worked there. As an Australian expatriate once told me, Singapore was "the best-managed stage show on earth", cleverly disguising its often lacklustre reality. A British expatriate who had lived in Singapore since the early 1960s once used the term "unrelieved mediocrity" when describing the place to me. But several years' living in Singapore is usually required to achieve such insights. Singapore has some conspicuous strengths that delay such realisations and disguise its economic and other weaknesses.

1. Real Strengths

While Singapore may be a dependent, underdeveloped and a not-so-efficient economy, its very visible efficiencies seem to contradict such realities.

The Changi Arrival

Singapore displays some stunning examples of cutting-edge excellence. Visitors first encounter it on landing at Changi airport, which constantly wins awards for the world's best airport. Changi is modern, spotlessly clean, spacious and state-of-the-art in every respect. Arrivals and departures from the airport are pleasurable and trouble-free. Passing immigration and customs is smooth and hassle-free, especially for Westerners. Even the taxi drivers there are more helpful and efficient than elsewhere in Singapore. Newcomers landing at Changi from Asia's lesser-developed countries think they have encountered an oasis of brisk efficiency and cleanliness in a region often lacking both.

Other Visible Efficiencies

On leaving Changi a clean green island greets visitors. Numerous parks, tree-lined roads and gleaming modern high-rises meet one on the smooth, comfortable ride to the city. Further positive experiences usually await visitors whenever they deal with officialdom in Singapore. Overall, Singapore's civil service is as efficient as those of most Western countries, and probably better than some. Moreover, banking and financial transactions are completed with the same ease and promptness as in any Western country. Singapore is also the world's fourth-largest forex trading centre and one of Asia's main financial centres.

Telecommunications are the latest and best. Public transport, especially the Metropolitan Rail Transit (MRT), is quick and efficient. The MRT usually amazes visitors to Singapore. It provides a first-rate rail service to over 50 stations throughout the island, moving millions of people daily.

Singapore's port is also impressive. In tonnage and efficiency it rivals Rotterdam as the world's top port.

Singapore's health care is regarded as Asia's best. About 200,000 people a year come to Singapore for medical treatment, mostly from surrounding countries. Some even travel from Europe and North America to be treated.[1]

Adroit Crisis Management

Singapore's reputation usually soars when dealing with crises because of the apparently quick and efficient way it responds to them. As a small, densely populated and easily controllable island ruled by often astute rulers with wide-ranging authoritarian powers, Singapore is well placed to react rapidly to crises.

Singapore's reputation for crisis management was enhanced by its handling of the Asian 1997/8 financial downturn. The Government's adroit response was seen as a key reason for Singapore surviving the crisis better than its Asian neighbours. Singapore also got kudos for practising policies which had made its economy financially sound. These included the accumulation of huge cash reserves, a healthy balance of payments, an absence of foreign debt, lack of large liabilities in foreign currency among its banks and limits on the amount of Singapore dollars that local banks could lend to foreigners. Together these measures greatly protected the country's currency from the speculative attacks that had undermined the currencies of other Asian countries. Moreover, Singapore's capital inflows were dominated by foreign direct investment, which is far more productive than speculative "hot money". The success of Singapore's fiscally conservative measures during the crisis confirmed its global reputation for fiscal rectitude and prudent management.

More recently the world was impressed by Singapore's seemingly rapid response to the SARS (Severe Acute Respiratory Syndrome) emergency from March to June 2003. While SARS badly hit the tourist industry and economy, Singapore's handling of the crisis earned international acclaim. Although Singapore's SARs death toll was nearly 40, the outbreak was contained by early June.

However, Singapore deserves no more than qualified praise for its handling of the SARS outbreak. After a slow start, Australian political scientist Michael Barr reported:

The Singapore government eventually responded to this epidemic with exemplary vigour, throwing the resources of not just the Ministry of Health, but also that of the Army, police and the networks of government-linked "grassroots organizations", into the task of tracking down suspected carriers, enforcing rigid quarantines, and maintaining supplies of food to unfortunates who were quarantined in their homes.[2]

Nonetheless, Barr, who was in Singapore during the whole of the SARS crisis, also noted that,

the government's response was painfully slow in coming. In the first five weeks of the SARS outbreak (13 March to 20 April 2003), it was clear that there were no protocols or contingency plans to deal with the epidemic, and the responses were ad hoc and reactive.[3]

This "rudderless period" only ended when responsibility for handling the crisis was taken from the Minister for Health and given to two ministerial committees ("combat teams"). "It even took 5 weeks before the government began supplying free ambulances to take suspected SARS cases to hospital. Until then, SARS suspects generally made their way to hospital by taxi or public transport." [4]

After a slow start, effective anti-SARS measures were quickly implemented. Airline passengers were checked for signs of the virus when arriving and leaving Singapore. Schools were closed, and anyone known to have been in contact with SARS cases was isolated. They were put under "home quarantine" and told not to return to work or school until daily health checks found them free of the virus. Those disregarding quarantine orders were fined S$5000.[5] When, by early April, 12 people were found to have broken quarantine orders, the health authorities installed surveillance cameras in the homes of 490 people under quarantine.[6] They had to report in front of the camera several times a day. If they were out when health workers called, an electronic tag was put on their wrist to keep track of them. Later, more draconian measures were introduced to punish quarantine-breakers, such as arrest without a warrant, a S$10,000 fine and six months jail.[7]

Singapore's tough measures won it world-wide praise. The BBC lauded Singapore for having "the toughest measures in the world" to halt SARS.[8] On a prime-time news program, millions of Britons saw what the Republic was doing to combat the virus.[9] The program gave a detailed account of the steps Singapore had taken, commenting, "Authoritarian, maybe, but it might just beat this alarming virus".[10] The program also quoted a WHO official praising Singapore's anti-SARS efforts: "I think the Singapore Government has done an excellent job and I really would not characterise it as draconian," he said. A Massachusetts public health director who had visited Singapore during the outbreak stated:

Singapore's citizens should be proud. They beat this disease. And Singapore can be used as a real-life showcase on how to handle such contagious threats to public health. I know I will be citing Singapore as a model for disease-control in my conversations with peers.[11]

A PERC survey found that Singapore was the best prepared country to handle a SARS-type medical crisis. PERC surveyed 1072 expatriate business executives working in 12 Asian countries. "In all the Asian countries, expatriates in Singapore expressed the greatest degree of confidence in the medical system's ability to treat major illnesses," reported PERC. [12] The PERC findings were published in *The Straits Times* on April 12, 2003 – over a week *before* the Government had implemented any plans to deal with the epidemic, Barr noted. So much for the accuracy of PERC's latest accolade. Perhaps Singapore's hype about how well it was handling the SARS crisis influenced the responses of the PERC respondents. Certainly, as the "government ramped up its handling of the SARS crisis, the response contained many stage-managed displays designed purely for international and domestic audiences rather than to combat SARS". [13]

Predictably, Lee Kuan Yew took every opportunity to promote Singapore and justify PAP policies during the SARS crisis. He proudly cited a Taiwanese e-mail supporting Singapore's tough anti-SARs measures. The e-mail, widely circulated in Taiwan, was written by a Taiwanese who had lived in Singapore. He said that in Singapore there was "no finger-pointing among government officials – only full cooperation". Calls to respect human rights when fighting SARs in Taiwan had only hindered anti-SARS efforts. The tough Singapore approach was much better, he claimed.[14]

While "the government was singularly unprepared to deal with an epidemic and had to learn on the run," observed Barr, "it did learn quickly and is likely to handle the next threatened epidemic much better".[15] Singapore now has stringent quarantine laws and procedures for handling any future epidemics. It has transformed its Communicable Diseases Centre into a large state-of-the-art facility to contain such epidemics. One may confidently expect Singapore to handle any such threats with the same adroitness as those of a financial nature.

Technical Competence

Singaporeans' abilities are strongest at the technical level, where they often display impressive competence. Performing complex technical operations seems to best suit their mindset where the close following of rules and established procedures is required. Using computers and other equipment is Singaporeans' forte. They also make every effort to keep up with the newest developments and advances in these areas and quickly acquire the latest IT skills. An April 2002 survey revealed that 950,000 Singaporeans access broadband from homes, offices and community organisations.[16] By late 2002, the National IT Literacy program launched in June 2001 had trained over 100,000 people.

Though the skill and educational levels of Singapore's workforce are below those in most Western countries, Singaporeans' IT expertise is considerable. When combined with regular exposure to the country's conspicuous strengths the impression of an efficient cutting-edge society becomes overwhelming. Several apparent rather than real Singaporean strengths fortify this image.

2. Apparent Strengths

Singaporeans' readiness to work long hours, mouth the latest human resource development (HRD) buzzwords and gain qualifications does much to accentuate Singapore's image as a progressive 21st century society.

12-hour Days

Singaporeans at managerial and professional levels have a reputation for hard work and putting in 12-hour days. Their almost masochistic pride in working such long hours helps sustain their reputation as a diligent and dedicated people. But working hard is one thing, working smart another – as Singapore's mediocre levels of workforce productivity show. Often professional and executive-level Singaporeans hang around at work to avoid being seen as slackers if they leave on time. But long hours mean little if not much is done.

Buzz Word Experts

Throngs of Singaporeans attend workshops and seminars where they readily swallow the glib theories of management gurus, mainly from the US. Soon such Singaporeans are mouthing the latest managerial and HRD terms – "creativity", "synergy", "lateral thinking", "Emotional Intelligence". Their understanding of such concepts is often superficial. As one Japanese industrialist in Singapore said:

> *Singaporeans are clever, but the bad thing is that they don't have much patience. They learn things a little bit, and already they think they are experts. Very shallow thinking.* [17]

While good at gaining cursory knowledge of the latest HRD and managerial ideas, Singaporeans usually have little success implementing them. This is partly because of their limited understanding but also because of the Singaporean cultural and organisational factors already described. *The Straits Times* was a hothouse for HRD strategies, but higher productivity rarely materialised. Its organisational culture saw to that.

PAP leaders are often the first to espouse the newest imported HRD ideas, as this book repeatedly shows. Until the mid-1990s many such ideas came from Japan. As Lee Kuan Yew recalls:

> *I learnt from the Japanese the importance of increasing productivity through worker-management cooperation, the real meaning of human resource development. We formed the National Productivity Board in 1972. ...we built up an effective productivity organisation that gradually got the unions and management working together on improving productivity.* [18]

Lee was particularly captivated by Japan's extensive use of Quality Control Circles (QCCs) as a means of raising productivity in manufacturing enterprises. The QCC consists of groups of workers and management working together to improve productivity and achieve zero defects. QCCs were rapidly introduced into Singapore at Lee's behest. Quantitatively, the QCC push has been a big success. In April 1999, Lee delightedly reported that Singapore had 20,000 QCCs involving 170,000 workers. One in ten workers belonged to QCCs, the highest participation rate in the world, he crowed.[19] From 1988-98, QCCs had saved their organisations S$380 million and helped cut industrial disputes referred to the Industrial Arbitration Court from 122 in 1980 to 10 by 1993.

Lee also asserted that productivity had doubled in the 18 years to 1999 and implied that QCCs had significantly contributed to this; but productivity studies suggest otherwise, as this book has already shown. Either Singapore's productivity was abysmal in the early 1980s, or the QCCs had far less effect than Lee liked to think. Considering the powerful managerial and workforce failings that undermine Singapore's productivity, the latter is more likely.

Despite being inundated with QCCs, Singapore's productivity lags behind most developed countries', including Japan's. Nevertheless, claims of 20,000 QCCs can impress foreign HRD experts.

Qualified But Not Educated

Getting prestigious well-paid jobs is an abiding obsession of Singaporeans. Academic qualifications, the more exalted the better, are seen as the means to this end. Passing exams and getting some initials after their names is what's important. Understanding their subjects and developing skills for further education doesn't mean much to them. Their qualifications may appear initially impressive until one realises how little they understand.[20] As Lee Kuan Yew once lamented:

We are turning out students, graduates...polytechnic students, who think that their moment of achievement has arrived when they get a diploma or their degree. And they all take pictures with their caps and gowns, and that's the summit of their career. But any American will tell you that's the foothill and you then begin the climb up the mountain.[21]

In commenting on the Singaporean Chinese, Bjerke noted that for them knowledge is useless if it does not help you make money, get a better job or "gain face", the acquisition of which "leads to strong feelings of satisfaction, pride and confidence".[22] Apart from gaining face, knowledge, for Singaporeans, "is narrowly seen as 'talent' or 'expertise' for wealth creation in a 'knowledge-based economy'," note Singaporean sociologists Kwok and Ali.[23] Pragmatism dominates Singaporean students' mindsets, contends Singaporean educationalist Arlene Bastion:

Forget about learning for knowledge's sake, or the quest and thirst for knowledge. The only quest and thirst is for good grades in the right subjects.

Students are only being pragmatic. These are the scores and subjects that will get them ahead in the job market and society.[24]

Lifelong learning and the passion to understand are concepts "too bizarre" for pragmatic Singaporean students to comprehend, Bastion says.

A seemingly hard-working population desperately trying to acquire educational qualifications looks good to outsiders. But closer examination reveals the hollowness of these efforts, as does Singaporeans' propensity to work long hours and their familiarity with the latest HRD/managerial jargon. Singapore's strengths, real, apparent and imaginary, do much to obscure its deep-rooted inefficiencies, as does its well-oiled PR machine.

However dubious Singapore's claims to efficiency may be, it is brilliantly efficient at promoting itself. Few other countries work on their image so assiduously. Since the 1960s, Singapore has constantly sold itself as a safe stable haven for foreign capital where superlative efficiency prevails. The PAP state has always believed that being seen as Number One was critical to Singapore's survival and independence. Its reputation is its greatest asset, and must be nurtured and advertised. Singapore lives on its image. By such means Singapore has successfully attracted – and usually kept – the foreign capital and expertise so central to its survival. As a dependent economy it has few other options. Singapore's strengths are therefore vigorously promoted and its weaknesses hidden, especially from international eyes.

Since the 1960s Lee Kuan Yew has been central to the very slick PR operation that Singapore has developed to sell itself to the world. His "statesmanlike" standing, especially in Western neo-con political circles, has made him one of Singapore's best advertisements as he travels the world dispensing nation-building advice and selling the Singapore Miracle to anyone who will listen.

Also central to Singapore's ongoing PR offensive is the vast amount of statistics churned out to publicise its success and hide its deficiencies. Since coming to power in 1959, the PAP Government has systematically used statistics to boost Singapore's reputation. International ratings agencies have accepted Singapore's official data uncritically, lacking the capacity or inclination to scrutinise and analyse them, as future chapters will show.

Should anyone, foreign or domestic, question Singapore Government statistics, draconian defamation laws and other threats usually silence them. For many years the PAP Government has muzzled not only political opposition but any domestic and foreign media outlets who dare criticise official data and policies. This does much to ensure widespread acceptance of PAP statistics that disguise the country's economic deficiencies.

Singapore has been less successful in disguising the illiberal, quasi-authoritarian nature of the PAP state to many in the West. Reports have been regularly published in the Western media about the Government using its politically compliant judiciary to persecute, bankrupt and silence its critics and political opponents. Accounts of dissidents being interrogated while kept standing under air-conditioners for 12 hours or more to force bogus confessions have received wide coverage.[25]

However, such revelations are usually of little concern to MNCs unless they have activist shareholders back in their home countries who raise such matters at company AGMs. A politically stable and profitable economic climate is the MNCs' prime concern. But do they worry about Singapore's efficiency levels? While they may do so, Singapore is still so profitable for them that its second-rate managers and mediocre workforce can be lived with. This is not so for Singapore's rulers, who have been concerned about its inefficiencies for decades. They have striven mightily to overcome them, as the next chapter shows.

References

1. *The Straits Times* (ST), November 26, 2003.
2. Barr, Michael: "Singapore", p. 168 in *Comparative Health Policy in the Asia-Pacific,* edited by Robin Gauld (England, Open University Press, 2005).
3. Ibid.
4. Barr, p. 169.
5. ST, March 25, 2003.
6. ST, April 11, 2003.
7. ST, April 25, 2003.
8. ST, April 27, 2003.
9. ST, April 27, 2003.
10. Ibid.
11. *Streats,* June 4, 2003.
12. ST, April 14, 2003.
13. Barr, p. 168.
14. ST, May 12, 2003.
15. Barr, p. 169.
16. *2002 Economic Survey of Singapore* (Singapore, Ministry of Trade and Industry, 2003), p. 90.
17. Da Cunha, Derek: "Self-congratulation: hallmark of the Singapore arts scene", p. 117 in *Debating Singapore,* edited by Derek Da Cunha (Singapore, Institute of Southeast Asian Studies, 1994).
18. Lee, Kuan Yew: *From Third World to First* (Singapore, Times Media, 2000), p. 583.
19. ST, April 10, 1999.
20. Dissertations Singaporeans write for degrees and PhDs often reveal shallow thinking, poor conceptualisation and limited writing skills. Minimal ability to compile and use data to develop an argument is also evident, as I and other expatriate Westerners have discovered, having edited and even re-written dissertations compiled by Singaporeans. The country's rote-learning education system has failed to teach Singaporeans how to think, analyse and critically examine ideas.
21. Han, Fook Kwang, Warren Fernandez, and Sumiko Tan: *Lee Kuan Yew: The Man and His Ideas* (Singapore, Times Editions, 1998), p. 357.
22. Bjerke, Bjorn: "Entrepreneurship and SMEs in the Singaporean Context", p. 276 in *Competitiveness of the Singapore Economy,* edited by Toh Mun Heng and Tan Kong Yam (Singapore, Singapore University Press, 1998).
23. Kwok, Kian Woon and Mariam Ali: "Cultivating Citizenship and National Identity", p. 116 in *Singapore: Re-engineering Success,* edited by Arun Mahizhnan and Lee Tsao Yuan (Singapore, Oxford University Press, 1990).
24. Bastion, Arlene: *Singapore in a Nutshell* (Singapore, Prentice Hall, 2003), p. 105.
25. Seow, Francis: *To Catch a Tartar: A Dissident in Lee Kwan Yew's Prison* (New Haven, Connecticut, Yale Center for International and Areas Studies, 1994).

CHAPTER 13

DELUSIONS, DIVERSIONS AND RE-ENGINEERING WITHOUT REFORM

Despite some highly visible efficiencies, Singapore's rulers know its overall efficiency levels are mediocre. Various government programs have been trying to boost the country's productivity for years. Raising productivity has become a national obsession – hence the calls for Singaporeans to be more entrepreneurial, creative and innovative; for managers to perform better; for workers to cooperate with management and do their best, and for all Singaporeans to strive for excellence. But as can be seen, a range of powerful factors, economic, political and cultural, sap Singapore's entrepreneurial capacities and managerial and workforce efficiency.

Many of these are the result of government policies that have stunted the development of SMEs, preventing them from being the seedbeds of innovation they are in most other market economies. The strength of the SME sector significantly determines an economy's entrepreneurial and innovative capacities (EICs). In Singapore, government policies have permitted crippling SE/MNC competition and excessive red tape to stunt SME expansion. Their plight has been made worse by venture capital shortages. A weak SME sector and risk-averse values have combined to greatly limit the growth of Singapore's EICs.

EICs, however, only relate to the efficient mobilisation and allocation of capital. Efficiency is also determined by managerial and workforce performance. In Singapore the performance of both is second-rate, and this has reduced efficiency. Once again, deeply rooted cultural factors are operating. Singapore's risk-averse values have stunted the development of EICs while its hierarchical and low-trust behaviours undermine managerial and workforce efficiency.

Boosting both EIC levels and management-workforce efficiency would require major governmental and cultural changes. To increase EICs significantly the Government would first have to create a much better environment for SMEs. This would require the reversal of pro-SE and MNC policies and a major restructuring of the economy; such a task would be beyond the current PAP state. The MNCs drive the economy and the large SE sector gives the Government enormous economic and political control. To relinquish such control would jeopardise its hegemonic style of rule, which depends upon a monopoly on power.

Almost as difficult would be the changing of long-held values that undermine EIC and organisational efficiency.

First, there would need to be a genuine political and economic liberalisation and a ditching of authoritarian policies which discourage risk-taking. This would be more than Singapore's present PAP rulers could countenance, for political reasons. Were the Government to genuinely restructure and liberalise the economy, Singaporeans' hierarchical, low-trust and risk-averse values bred by ingrained cultural attitudes, plus PAP authoritarian policies, would also have to be changed. Such values and policies do much to independently discourage entrepreneurial endeavours and undermine organisational initiative and efficiency and blunt government reform measures. It will take time for Singaporean organisations to evolve into more egalitarian concerns where higher trust levels and greater readiness to share information prevail. Deeply rooted cultural attitudes change slowly.

Thus, cultural factors as well as political and economic ones pose major barriers to the type of structural change that Singapore needs in order to become innovative, entrepreneurial and competitive. Singapore's leaders desperately want the country to develop these attributes, knowing that failure to do so will leave Singapore uncompetitive. But because they also want to retain hegemonic control of the economy and society, they face a great dilemma. Attempts to resolve this dilemma have produced three types of response from the Government, ranging from delusory utterances to cynical diversions to sustained efforts to re-engineer Singapore without major reform.

1. Schizoid Behaviour

PAP leaders regularly urge Singaporeans to think outside squares and push envelopes etc. Such appeals for Singaporeans to be more creative, innovative and risk-averse often have a surreal, almost schizophrenic quality. If acted upon, such appeals would undermine the PAP regime. Prime Minister Goh told Singaporeans in 2000 that they must be "insurgents and not incumbents",[1] and behave like "revolutionaries" in the next decade.[2] The term "insurgent" was repeated in 2004 by Defence minister Teo Chee Hean while extolling the virtues of risk-taking: "We should be prepared to think like 'insurgents'," he proclaimed. "Taking too little risk is the greatest risk of all."[3] Lee Kuan Yew himself has called for "a mental revolution", arguing that old ways of thinking and working must be changed.[4] Lee has also spoken of the need to build the new economy through the "creative destruction" of the old.[5]

Over time Lee's exhortations in the name of productivity, creativity and innovation have become even more peculiar. In February 2002 he said that Singapore must have "little Bohemias ... where you can do you own thing". He cited Holland Village (an upmarket expatriate hang-out) as a place where the academic and professional community gather for the ambiance and to "do odd things".

> If you are that way inclined, you want to be an artist, you want to do odd things, provided you don't go and offend the more conservative people in the HDB heartlands, just carry on.[6]

Lee's boyish enthusiasms get the better of him at times. He seems to have picked up such ideas from Western management books, which depict creativity as a messy informal process between like-minded individuals in unstructured environments. Lee apparently hopes to duplicate a similar milieu in tightly-controlled, intellectually arid and risk-averse Singapore.

Lee's Bohemian fantasies aside, the bureaucracy has also been told to lift its creative game. BG Lee told civil servants they must "show boldness, creativity and courage," adding that "change and innovation must become a way of life in the civil service".[7] Prodded by their political leaders, senior bureaucrats have felt compelled to echo similar sentiments. Civil service head Lee Ek Tieng stressed the civil service's need to build "a more proactive psyche".[8] Officers must be "willing to not just accept change, but to seek change with the aim of improving productivity and service," he declared.

The GIC is one government body that has claimed to walk the innovative style of talk. The GIC hires people with "fire in the belly", according to its managing director Ng Kok Song.[9] They are not there merely for the high pay and exciting prospects but because they have the national interest at heart, he insists. But few Singaporean employees, public or private, care about the national interest. Their opportunism and endless job-hopping shows self-interest comes first. Moreover, those with any fire in the belly are unlikely to stay with the GIC or any other state body for long. As has already been shown, elite AS officials are leaving the civil service to set up their own businesses.

The GIC chief's comments are typical of the verbal subterfuge that PAP leaders inflict on Singaporeans when urging them to be more "proactive" or "revolutionary". Were Singaporeans to ever take such sentiments seriously, the PAP state might well collapse.

Revolutionary mindsets can take many forms. They may not only motivate people to start their own businesses and develop new products, but may also generate desires for political reform and change. Creative people are not always satisfied with confining their creativity to the making of money.

Undeterred by such scenarios, Singapore's leaders continue to use incendiary rhetoric to try and transform Singaporeans into risk-taking entrepreneurs. In April 2001, the Government tried to kick-start the innovative "revolutionary" mind-set with a day-long brainstorming session on how to reinvent the country as an innovative nation.[10] The PAP cabinet, top civil servants and other public sector leaders attended, as did several US management gurus and CEOs. The talkfest made predictable calls for the development of an "innovative culture". PAP leaders regularly seek the advice of the world's top corporate executives on development strategies for Singapore.

In March 2003, yet another high-powered panel stacked with CEOs from major MNCs met in Singapore to ponder how it could deal with the harsher economic conditions after September 11, 2001.[11] During its deliberations the panel (the EDB's International Advisory Committee) devised the term "Global Entropolis" to describe what Singapore could become. The panel had given Singapore yet another buzzword to promote itself, this time as a global entrepreneurial economy.

Such gatherings do not just reflect the Singaporean fascination with Western buzzwords. They also reveal the obsessive concern that PAP leaders have for Singapore to stay competitive by becoming a global cutting-edge economy. Perhaps this obsessiveness blinds them to the near impossibility of Singapore achieving this goal under its present political, economic and social system.

It could be that the PAP leadership's free use of such terms as "revolutionary mindsets" and "creative destruction" is a cynical way of paying lip service to the ideals of entrepreneurial innovation for political purposes. Their near-desperate desire to develop Singapore's EICs suggests otherwise. When using such terms they seem to be genuinely oblivious of the political costs to the PAP state were Singapore to become a truly entrepreneurial economy. They also appear unaware of the implications of appeals for Singaporeans to adopt revolutionary mindsets and engage in such activities as "creative destruction". While they may use such terms in a certain sense, others could interpret them in ways that would alarm PAP leaders.

Whatever the case, Lee and his lieutenants are expounding views that deny reality in a way that can only be described as schizophrenic – a sharp contrast to the shrewd, hard-headed way they normally rule Singapore. They are very adroit at going through the motions of listening to the people and considering their proposals for re-engineering and reforming Singapore. But such measures are usually little more than diversions to deflect popular grievances.

2. Diversions

The constant formation of government-led committees and endless public debates on how to improve the country are a regular feature of public life in Singapore. In recent years such committees have exhaustively canvassed Singaporeans on ways to "remake Singapore" and galvanise its creativity. Chief of these has been the establishment of the Economic Review Committee (ERC) in October 2001 and the Remaking Singapore Committee (RSC) in February 2002. The ERC's brief was to examine how Singapore could be transformed to meet coming economic challenges, while the RSC's was to suggest ways to make the country's social, cultural and political life more creative.

The ERC's report appeared in February 2003. It called for greater economic liberalisation and tax changes that would benefit business.[12] Measures for promoting entrepreneurship were also proposed, including appointing a government minister for this purpose. Another was for SEs to follow the "Yellow Pages" rule and not start businesses already listed in the Yellow Pages.

RSC recommendations were of greatest interest. Its brief was to suggest ways to make Singapore a freer and more creative society through transforming its social, political and cultural landscape. Singaporeans' views were widely canvassed on hundreds of subjects including education, citizenship, the arts, political participation, freedom of expression and how to attract and keep foreign and local talent in Singapore. After

15 months of sustained effort the committee, headed by the Minister for National Development, Dr Vivian Balakrishnan, made over 100 suggestions on revitalising Singapore. They covered such areas as education, gender equality, freedom of expression, working hours, the CPF scheme and helping community groups.

On receiving the RSC report in July 2003, Prime Minister Goh piously promised that the Government would study the report "without blinkers" over the next few months.[13] But even before the Government had examined the report some government ministers had already dismissed several of its recommendations. They publicly rejected recommendations for a five-day week and for allowing the unemployed to access their CPF money.[14] The ministers also made it clear that restrictions on political debate would remain.

The ministers' comments disappointed many Singaporeans who, along with many RSC members, had had high hopes for the RSC. One committee member wondered if she had wasted her time. "If we cannot make changes after such a long process, then why were we there?" she asked. As *Straits Times* columnists Tan Tarn How and Helmi Yusof commented:

> *Cynicism is clear, with some even saying that the committee was just a new way of educating the new ministers of state* [who were sitting on the committee]. *In other words, the results don't matter as much as the process of "political bonding.*[15]

The real aim apparently was to give new PAP ministers the experience of dealing with important public issues, but RSC chief Balakrishnan denied this. Ministers who had shot down some of the RSC proposals were only musing aloud, he claimed; the proposals had not been "technically" rejected. But parallels were soon drawn between the RSC and its predecessor, the Singapore 21 (S21) program.

In August 1999, the S21 committee recommended ways to improve Singaporeans' "heartware". Boosting social and cultural cohesion and people's links with Singapore and also ensuring political stability were seen as the ways to achieve this.[16] The S21 ideals for Singapore were:

- Every Singaporean matters
- Strong families
- Opportunities for all
- Feeling passion about Singapore
- Active citizenship.

These aims were soon forgotten. "S21's success at that time might be considered as being mainly confined to discussion in the media while life went on as usual," remarked Singaporean educationalist Bastion:

> *The awful thing about S21 … is that after all the media blast and fury, nothing more was said or heard about it. It went the way of most of the national campaigns.*[17]

Values promoted during PAP campaigns last about as long as the campaign, she said. Their "shelf life is limited to that of the campaign's duration".

S21's apparent aim was to propose ways of transforming Singapore into a people-centred society whose citizens would feel at home. The real aim was to reduce the brain drain of talented Singaporeans migrating to other countries. Singaporeans who felt at home would be less inclined to do this, reasoned the Government. Once again the real purpose was primarily economic.

Some members of the S21 committee believed it was merely meant to endorse views already held by senior PAP ministers. Singapore drama director Alvin Tan believed that the S21 committee members "had become rubber stamps for the ideas that only some of the key people wanted" and so had resigned.[18] Some RSC members had told him that the RSC was no different.

Forming committees that ostensibly consult with many community groups to formulate proposals for dealing with current issues is a regular PAP government practice. Committees are set up, and after lengthy deliberations they produce numerous recommendations. The Government then goes through the motions of seriously considering them, but few are ever accepted unless they reflect current ministerial views. The Government merely wants to be seen consulting the people and "training up" new ministers to deal with current political issues. The basic structural reasons for Singapore's inefficiencies and lack of creativity and EICs remain unaddressed and unresolved. Only major political-economic restructuring can do this. The only real option left for the PAP state is to somehow work within the existing system to increase Singapore's EICs and overall prosperity.

3. Re-Engineering without Reform

Because structural reform is off the agenda for the PAP Government, other methods must be pursued to improve Singapore's productivity and competitiveness. Numerous state-sponsored schemes, strategies and projects have been launched in recent years to do this. Such measures are a substitute for the structural change the PAP state dares not make. The Government apparently hopes that they will be sufficient to "re-engineer Singapore" and transform it into a competitive 21st Century economy. These initiatives have been:

- Programs to help SMEs
- Frantic efforts to attract foreign talent
- Heavy R&D spending
- Education reform
- Developing a wired IT-smart society
- Reducing red tape
- Making the public service more innovative and proactive
- Continuing pursuit of "Second Wing" strategies for Singapore.

Promoting Enterprise

As the plight of Singapore's SMEs has become obvious the Government has felt compelled to appear to help them through various programs. The most prominent program was the SME 21 program launched in 2000.[19] Its aim was to create a vibrant and resilient SME sector to make Singapore more competitive. The program seeks to develop entrepreneurs with mentoring programs, promote business excellence through a National Best Practice Centre, provide SME support centres to give access to latest technologies and raise SMEs' profile through awards for outstanding local enterprises.

Funding to help SMEs with technology-based start-ups has been provided under the Technology Development Funds I and II since 1995. In addition, the Technology Incubator Programme has been launched to help hi-tech start ups with market feasibility studies and development, business planning, recruitment of venture capital and provision of administrative support.

More significant have been government schemes to improve SME access to finance. They are the Local Enterprise Finance Scheme (LEFS), the Local Enterprise Technical Assistance Scheme (LETAS) and the Micro Loan Scheme (MLS). LEFS is designed to help SMEs with fixed assets of up to S$50 million and 300 employees. In 2002, S$587 million of LEFS applications were approved along with S$80 million in SME grants. The MLS, which is for companies of 10 employees or less, approved S$56 million in loans in 2002.[20] The provision of such schemes to help SMEs and promote enterprise suggests a proactive Government at work energetically trying to boost entrepreneurship. While some SMEs may have been helped, how many and by how much is hard to say. Future chapters indicate that government schemes have provided only limited assistance to most SMEs. Whatever help these schemes may have given, the factors that retard their growth remain: SE/MNC competition, excessive red tape, heavy state imposts and depressed consumer spending caused by government policies.

Education for Innovation

Ruthless pragmatism always dominates PAP policies, and education is no exception. Education must serve the needs of national development. In recent years this has included entrepreneurship, which the Government has decreed, must start at school. The Technopreneurship-21 (T21) initiative for developing the technopreneurship sector reflects this thinking. T21 seeks to promote creativity in schools. The Government has been trying for years to cultivate this elusive quality.

While creativity begins in the classroom it can also die there as Singapore's education authorities have begun to realise. The rote-learning methods of Singapore's schools have killed creativity and stunted the development of problem-solving abilities. From the 1980s Singapore's schools and tertiary institutions began taking steps to counter this.

Edward De Bono and his lateral thinking theories have been particularly popular in Singapore since the 1980s. His methods were introduced into Singapore's schools in 1987 to teach lower secondary students critical and creative thinking. By November

1995, De Bono techniques were being taught in 103 secondary schools.[21] During the 1990s courses were also introduced into Singaporean universities and other tertiary institutions to promote creativity and thinking skills. New university students were to be taught how to think and analyse and to be weaned off rote-learning methods acquired in school. Meanwhile, polytechnics launched courses that required students to display innovation and initiative. In 2003, Singapore's newest polytechnic, Republic, launched problem-based learning courses. Groups of students had to solve problems teachers set them rather than being given lectures or sitting exams.[22]

At primary and secondary school levels, educational reform has aimed to stop Singaporean teachers' tendency to "over-teach", as an education panel put it in 1998.[23] Teachers were spending too much time drilling students to "produce the right responses" for tests and exams. Because students had too much to learn, teachers rushed to cover the courses. This discouraged students from asking questions and was turning them into passive absorbers of information. In 2000, new curricula were introduced for the A-level exams for 16-year-olds. Thinking skills, creativity, IT and independent learning were emphasised over rote-learning and regurgitation of information.[24] The curricula were to be phased in over three years.

However, some Singaporean educationalists are sceptical about the new "thinking skills" programs. "No amount of 'thinking skills' currently understood and taught is going to bring about a thinking culture," said National Institute of Education (NIE) Professor R. M. Nathan.[25] A homogeneous, externally produced "toolbox" of ready-made thinking skills could not do this alone, he said. The capacities of the teachers who were to implement such programs were more important and no major educational innovations could succeed without them. Two other NIE educationalists, Ho Boon Ting and Professor Toh Kok Aun, argued that if teachers could not practise the new methods they would revert to old teaching styles. Research showed that "teachers felt threatened when using new methods ... due to a sense of feeling incompetent and out of control", so "they often reverted to more familiar strategies such as the didactic style of the traditional teacher...they were already comfortable with".[26] This is a likely problem with Singaporean teachers who were not only trained to use didactic methods but were themselves taught by such methods at school.

In such a situation De Bono methods and Thinking School programs are unlikely to produce creative (and potentially entrepreneurial!) students without major changes in Singaporean teachers' mindsets, which itself will take time. Even then this may only be successfully done in a society where creativity, intellectual curiosity, risk-taking and innovation are respected; where the "one-mistake" mentality no longer prevails. Moreover, Singapore's average classes of 40 students make it difficult for teachers to implement new education methods for developing creativity and problem solving.

Singapore's hopes of producing growing numbers of creative students still seem remote. Reliance on foreign talent and ideas is likely to continue for some time.

Attracting Foreign Talent

First it was foreign capital, then foreign technology; now it is through foreign talent that Singapore seeks to maintain its international competitiveness. If Singapore cannot produce the indigenous innovative and technological expertise to do this then foreigners may. It is certainly a strategy that Singapore seems to be banking on heavily as it strives to become a knowledge economy. As Professor Arnoud De Meyer, dean of Insead's Asian campus, notes:

> *If Singapore wants to move up the economic ladder, it will have to become a place where ... skilled professionals can be attracted and a skilled workforce developed.*[27]

To lure foreign talent the PAP Government has been trying to make Singapore a more exciting place to work. Singapore is seeking to create a "Bridget Jones economy" to attract foreign talent, according to *The Economist*.

The Bridget character represents the well-educated, single professionals who increasingly dominate affluent city life from New York to Tokyo. "They are the main consumers and producers of the creative economy that revolves around advertising, publishing, entertainment and the media," claims *The Economist*. "More than any other social group, they have time, money and a passion for spending on whatever is fashionable, frivolous and fun." [28] Though Singapore has been energetically wooing talent since the early 1990s, the Bridget factor must now be considered. To attract these supposedly clever, free-spirited cosmophiles, Singapore has striven to transform itself into an exciting and "funky" place. Singapore's image must be changed from that of a repressive kill-joy society which bans the sale of chewing gum to one with an exotic and lively night-life. The Government, believing that creative spirits like to do "odd things" such as dance on bar counters, bungee jump and drink around the clock, lifted restrictions on these activities in mid-2003.

It also quietly lifted bans on employing gays in the civil service. This surprising reversal of long-held anti-gay policies was apparently due to the influence of such writers as US sociologist Richard Florida on Lee and the PAP leadership. Florida's book, *The Rise of the Creative Class*, was reviewed in *The Straits Times* about the time when the Government lifted its restrictions on gay employment. Florida argues that tolerance creates an open diverse society that welcomes everybody and attracts the innovative, creative talent critical to economic growth. He singles out gay friendliness as an indicator of tolerance. "To some extent, homosexuality represents the last frontier of diversity in our society and, thus, a place that welcomes the gay community welcomes all kinds of people."[29] Cities did not need shopping malls and convention centres to be successful, but eccentric and creative people, he said.

Singapore's leaders have come to believe that such people, gay or otherwise, are seen as essential to its survival. "Remember, this is not about gay rights. This is about economic competitiveness," noted a *Straits Times* columnist. There are clear parallels between the Government's sudden gay friendliness and the need to cultivate creativity for economic purposes. The Singaporean capacity to unquestioningly accept the latest Western ideas and fads never fails to amaze.

Government also began extolling the virtues of a freer, liberal and more swinging Singapore. During his National Day Address in August 2003, Prime Minister Goh proclaimed:

> *The Government will create the framework and the environment for you to thrive. But it should not and cannot micro-manage your life to guarantee your job and your wealth. You must create and seize opportunities yourself.*
>
> *To become a vibrant society with a strong and entrepreneurial streak, the Government will have to loose the apron strings.*[30]

On lifting bans on bar-top dancing and bungee jumping, he said:

> *What I had done was to signal a shift in our mindset to being more relaxed and open-minded, and less strait-laced and Victorian. I want Singaporeans to be self-reliant and robust. So I have to let you decide for yourselves the level of excitement and risk you want.*

It will take more than a few clumsy state-directed measures to transform Singapore into a tolerant cosmopolitan society. Its authoritarian and bureaucratic instincts are still intact, as was demonstrated by the ham-fisted way the police handled the introduction of bar-top dancing in August 2003. Police soon began warning bars that dancers could not mingle with patrons either "before, during or after their act", unless express permission was received from the Police Licensing Division.[31] Some of the dancers might be doubling as "hostesses" and soliciting for sex, feared the police. Dancers were not merely chatting to customers, but were hugging them and sitting on their laps![32] The police clamp-down confused and upset bar-owners. As one said:

> *They should tell us exactly what's going on because people still don't know how to interpret the rules. With so many kinds of licences, you end up applying for everything just to cover yourself.*[33]

While police said they would use discretion in monitoring bar top dancing, "the fact remains that the rule is still there," said another bar-owner.[34] The police's bureaucratic mindset had prevailed over the Prime Minister's call for greater personal freedom, displaying once again the ingrained bureaucratic and authoritarian mentality that dominates the Singaporean psyche. Singapore needs more than glib pseudo-liberal cant from its prime minister and a few stilted and trivial gestures to free up the place. More than bar-top dancing and bungee jumping are required to create a truly liberal society where creative energies are unleashed and which will attract talented foreigners.

Whether through wilful ignorance or a simple inability to understand, Government ministers just don't get it when trying to cultivate creativity. Perhaps it is expecting too much of them: after all, they have grown up in an authoritarian society where conformity, rote-learning education, "discipline" and hierarchical values prevail, where following the rules will get you ahead while being independent and taking a different view of things will not. That's how they got to be PAP ministers and senior bureaucrats. Clever conformists, not risk-takers, get ahead in PAP Singapore. But such attitudes are anathema to the creative process, which is highly individualised, often rule-breaking, usually eccentric and always questioning. As such the contrived attempts by PAP leaders to free up Singapore look more pathetic than proactive – and are very likely to fail.

Creative people seek culturally stimulating environments where information and ideas are freely shared and intellectual curiosity abounds. Staged opportunities to party are unlikely to appeal much to them. Singapore lacks the environment for creative endeavour. This can only be achieved by a sea change in values produced by substantially increased economic and political freedom. Until then the PAP's "soft authoritarian" rule will continue to deter foreign talent. As three NUS economists have noted:

> *The basic question is: why would world-class knowledge workers, who can take their skills anywhere, choose Singapore above other world-class cities? Singapore may need to change its image if it is to attract investors and innovators from the West's aggressively anti-authoritarian hi-tech community. The allegation that Singapore projects an "authoritarian" image to foreign innovators and talent deserves more serious investigation.[35]*

Singapore's lack of freedom and police-state image is not the only deterrent to foreign talent. Others are the problems faced by expatriate managers and others already employed in Singapore. Westerners in particular find they are often sabotaged by organisational and cultural values when working for Singaporean enterprises. A spate of high-level resignations (or sackings) of Western CEOs and managers of Singaporean GLCs from 2002 to 2004 demonstrated this. Their departures worried the government, including Prime Minister Goh. In January 2003, he expressed concern at the resignations of three high-level expatriate managers:

> *I am a little unhappy at the coincidence of events. One after another, you find that the GLCs have retired prematurely their CEOs. I am unhappy because it creates an impression that Singapore doesn't welcome foreign talent, but that impression must be removed.[36]*

In 2002, top foreign executives to resign included DBS Holdings' CEO Philippe Pailart and the Singapore Exchange's Thomas Kloet. In January 2003, the Danish group president and CEO of the GLC Neptune Orient Lines (NOL), Flemming Jacobs, resigned 18 months before his contract ended.[37]

When Jacobs took over NOL in 1999 it had suffered deep losses of S$297 million in that year and S$438 million in 1998. In 2002, when NOL was hammered by what some analysts called "the perfect storm", it lost S$435 million. They suggested that Jacobs was the victim of circumstance – that no CEO could have ridden such brutal economic weather better than he. "It will be very difficult for NOL to find a more capable CEO than Flemming Jacobs," said one Singapore shipping executive.

Previously NOL had been run mainly by Singaporeans. When Jacobs took over he had shaken up the organisation and brought in foreign executives to head various divisions. In Singaporean shipping circles, NOL was jokingly taken to mean "No Orientals Left". Clearly, Jacobs was having problems dealing with the GLC-style organisational culture and felt he needed foreign managers to help run NOL. It seems

Jacobs made enemies at NOL and when losses occurred that was the pretext needed to force his resignation.

Several other top-level foreign CEOs left Singapore in 2003. In March 2003, Chris Matten, a British manager described as a "capital management guru", resigned from Temasek Holdings nine months after joining it as managing director of corporate stewardship. In December 2003, a British senior manager, Peter Monksfield, prematurely left NTUC Income five months after being hired as the GLC's general manager for marketing and overseas business developments.[38] Company sources said Monksfield's departure was because of his difficulty fitting into the Income culture. He had also become frustrated because some of his suggestions had not been carried out.

Difficulties dealing with Singaporean organisational culture was a major reason for the resignations of Monksfield and other expatriate managers working for Singaporean firms. Unlike MNC expatriate managers, they are isolated and answerable to Singaporean superiors, not to Western bosses back home with similar cultural and organisational mindsets to their own. Being alone with few allies, they have little power to make improvements. The abilities they bring to their SE positions often remain under-utilised.

Temasek likes to point out that it hires top private sector and foreign talent for itself and its GLCs. The implication is that not only *amakudari*-style appointees and bureaucrats run its GLCs, but also the best executives that money can buy. But three of the above five CEOs, who worked for Temasek or its GLCs (DBS Holdings and NOL), felt compelled to resign.

Not only are many talented foreigners discouraged from coming to Singapore, but those who do have their effectiveness limited by local organisational and other cultural values. Even so, Singapore still attracts many expats, largely because of the attractive remuneration packages offered and because it's a safe and secure place to work. In fact, despite lacking creative fizz, Singapore lures more than its fair share of expats. The real question is whether they are permitted to use their abilities. Many clearly don't, and eventually leave Singapore in disgust for more interesting destinations.

The same observations may apply to the foreign, as well as local scientists working at Singapore's R&D establishments, including the vast state-sponsored Biopolis complex. There too the organisational culture has not been conducive to creative endeavours.

Biopolis and the R&D Push

Besides trying to create a Bohemian environment for free and creative spirits, Singapore has been buying foreign scientific talent with massive research funding. Billions have been spent creating world-class research institutes to which foreign scientists have been lured. Singapore's aim is to harness top scientific talent to produce major breakthroughs.

By March 2002, Singapore had 15 research institutes, many heavily staffed by scientists from Britain and the US. [39] The centrepiece of Singapore's R&D push is Biopolis, a purpose-built biomedical R&D hub. The S$15 billion complex covers 194-

ha, which was set up to hothouse biomedical talent. [40] Biopolis Phase 1 was opened in October 2003 and by September 2007 was home to 2000 scientists, researchers, technicians and administrators. Phase 1 accommodates seven institutes, of which five are controlled by the Agency for Science, Technology and Research (A*Star).[40a] Phase 2 of Biopolis was opened in October 2006 and houses two more biomedical research centres.

New Scientist described Biopolis as "every researcher's dream: a place with great career prospects, state-of-the-art labs and equipment, even a purpose-built city for scientists to live in and work together". [40b] Others have been less enthusiastic about Biopolis. Their view is that more than large R&D expenditures are required to transform Biopolis into a major centre for innovation. A culture that fosters risk-taking, initiative, creativity and sharing of information is also required. But this vital ingredient still seems largely missing in Biopolis.

Foreign commentators wondered how fast individual initiative can take root in an authoritarian culture of self-control where risk is avoided. "I do see a very conservative stance from scientists as a result of this top-down approach," said US Professor Paul Yager of the University of Washington, who heads his university's collaboration program with Singapore; "I don't see it as well-suited to a long-term healthy scientific environment".

Other sceptics included two Insead professors. Professor Yves Doz saw science parks such as Biopolis as "huge walled-in compounds".[41] Their physical space was not conducive to "messy interaction" between knowledge workers. His colleague, Professor Peter Williamson, noted that the Insead facility itself abuts the sprawling NUS campus but there was no interaction between the two. Both maintained that the smaller R&D clusters were, the more intense the interaction. "This is why the English pub is more important than the Internet," said Williamson.[42]

Scientists are not just bearers of knowledge; they possess links with like-minded colleagues. Knowledge is created as people interact, not only formally but around the water-cooler, coffee-maker or pub table. While you can relocate scientists, you cannot relocate their ties to other scientists. Their often untidy interaction with each other may produce serendipitous results and cutting edge discoveries. While scientists can be plugged into the Internet with access to vast amounts of data, tacit, uncodifiable knowledge can only be exchanged through face-to-face interaction.

Singapore's organisational culture isolates scientists and limits their interaction. Scientists have little opportunity to congregate informally within tertiary institutions. In Singapore's universities one sees row after row of academics' offices with the doors shut and lifeless corridors. They seem to stretch forever, especially at Singapore's National Technological University (NTU). There is also little contact between other scientific bodies in Singapore. The country's 15 research institutes operate "in splendid isolation", observed the head of Singapore's Biomedical Research Council, Louis Lim.[43] Professor Doz said that the links, both within and between organisations, were very weak in Singapore. Researchers needed to share ideas more readily. He and

Williamson thought that the local R&D culture was not yet conducive to building ties between scientists. This is not surprising: being open and sharing ideas is done reluctantly in Singapore because of low trust levels. Knowledge is seen as something to be hoarded, not shared.

Such cultural traits pose barriers to R&D at Biopolis and other research institutes in Singapore, especially for the many foreign scientists. By March 2002, half of the Republic's 18,000 scientists were foreign. Of the 3819 scientists who were post-graduates, 80 per cent were foreign.[44] Their scientific contributions could be reduced by cultural factors that discourage the interaction and information-sharing central to scientific research. Expat researchers who are cut off from their "native" communities of fellow scientists and companions and unable to form adequate bonds with colleagues in such places as Biopolis may begin to operate independently as if in "a bell jar", says Williamson. "One day the bell jar might be just as easily picked up and carried off to another place".[45] Already many Singaporeans feel little attachment to their country and migrate. This would be even more likely with expatriate scientists who have few links with colleagues at places like Biopolis.

A cowboy mentality has also reportedly been displayed by a couple of foreign scientists in Singapore – a UK researcher and his research assistant at the National Neuroscience Institute (NNI) which is a separate research body, independent from Biopolis. In April 2003, an NNI inquiry panel found that Dr Simon Shorvon and the assistant, an Indian national, had treated patients unethically. Dr Shorvon had administered the drug L-Dopa to 127 patients with Parkinson's disease, without their informed consent or their doctors' knowledge, risking their safety and well-being. Shorvon, the NNI's director, had failed to get an ethics committee approval for this research. He initially denied the reports' claims. But in July 2004, the Ministry of Health made public a letter from Shorvon in which he accepted the NNI panel's findings against him.[46]

However, Dr Shorvon said that he signed the letter under threat of being reported to the police. He would also have been prevented from leaving Singapore, which he was then anxious to do, he said. [47] The whole matter was subsequently referred to the Singapore Medical Council (SMC), but Dr Shorvon refused to attend its proceedings because he believed he would not receive a fair hearing in Singapore. The SMC concluded that Dr Shorvon had failed to safeguard the best interests and health of his patients and had exposed them to unnecessary risk. The SMC demanded that his name be removed from the register of medical practitioners in the UK and that he be censured. The Council also fined him S$10,000 which he paid under protest.

The General Medical Council (GMC), the UK equivalent of the SMC, got involved. The GMC examined the proceedings and comments and eventually ruled that it was not in a position to prove Shorvon guilty of misconduct. Singapore then appealed to the British High Court, where a Queens' Counsel, hired by Singapore, claimed they were there to "stop Professor Shorvon from getting away with it".[48]

During the High Court case, a UK neurological professor told the court he would not dispute "the clear-cut facts of the case" but said the alleged offences were so minor that they weren't worth bothering with. At "the level of professional misconduct I cannot find anything here that should cause serious concern about Professor Simon Shorvon," he said.[49]

In January 2007, the High Court quashed the SMC's bid to have the GMC's decision to discontinue proceedings against Shorvon over-ruled. Dr Shorvon claimed he had been vindicated and the slur on his reputation removed. However, the full story behind the four-year saga has never been told. Were experimental drugs administered to Parkinsons' patients at the NNI without their permission? And if so, was this done by Dr Shorvon and/or other researchers? Was he culpable and if so to what extent? The afore-mentioned neurological professor conceded the facts of the case but dismissed any possible offences by Dr Shorvon, or presumably anyone else, as too trivial to worry about. No media accounts of the trial, or of the whole saga, answer these questions.

Whatever the facts of the matter, various opinions about the case suggest some sort of power struggle was being waged at NNI between Dr Shorvon and Dr Lee Wei Ling, the Institute's deputy director and Lee Kuan Yew's daughter. This was the view expressed in July 2004 by a UK geneticist who had worked on Dr Shorvon's research team in Singapore.[50] The geneticist found the accusations against Shorvon as "nothing short of absurd", adding that, "It is hard to avoid the conclusion that Dr Shorvon fell victim to internal power struggles and personal vendettas".[51]

In January 2004, Dr Lee angrily rejected claims that she had acted against Dr Shorvon to take over his post. "I would have preferred someone else who is competent, dedicated and willing to do the job," she said.[52] She also accused Dr Shorvon of causing rifts in the NNI "using the very effective British colonial method of 'divide and rule'". She said he "tried his utmost to rapidly complete this unauthorised part of his research where he treated Singaporeans as subjects from a Third World country who can be easily manipulated".[53]

Whatever the truth, the Shorvon case prompted some soul-searching in Singapore about its R&D ambitions. Dr Shorvon's recruitment to the NNI in December 2000 was hailed as a coup for Singapore in its bid to become a biomedical hub. In an effort to attract top scientific talent, Singapore has been paying scientists such as Dr Shorvon from S$600,000 to S$1 million a year, along with generous housing, car and school allowances. However, the pressure to get results and the freedom to cut corners led to unethical behaviour, according to some Singaporean researchers.

Besides high salaries "there are a lot of implicit assurances that they will be given almost *carte blanche* to do a lot of things," noted one veteran researcher. Moreover, foreign scientists were not restricted by a string system of checks and balances in Singapore as they were in their home countries where robust peer-review procedures with established research cultures prevailed. In Singapore "they find they have almost demigod status because they have all the political and financial support and, in many ways, no peers. . . . It's quite easy for someone to be put in a position where he thinks he's only accountable to the paymaster – and that means intense pressure to deliver results, regardless of how you do it".[54]

The Shorvon case illustrates one danger that Singapore faces in catching up with more established research centres. It also reflects the short-term, fast results mentality that so often dominates Singaporean thinking, where principles are sacrificed for results. "Singapore's head-long rush into the [research] field risks turning it into something of a cowboy town, where scientists feel they can get away with a lot more, with less risk of being reined in," noted a *Straits Times* columnist.

How far such comments apply to Dr Shorvon is an open question, but the whole episode damaged Singapore's and NNI's reputation. It also discredited Biopolis's efforts to establish itself as a world centre for scientific research in some Western research circles. The UK-based Medical Protection Society, which provides advice to doctors facing legal problems arising from clinical practice in more than 40 countries, suggested that foreign doctors should not work in Singapore.[55] Such warnings would have discouraged some scientists from accepting appointments in Singapore, especially at the NNI, whose new director, following Dr Shorvon's departure, was Dr Lee.

After the Shorvon affair, Dr Lee said she would encourage more personal interaction between staff and maintain the open-door policy she had always practised.[56] But the challenge for her is whether she can change the NNI's R&D culture.

By February 2007, Ms Lee was having reservations about the Biopolis strategy.[57] She admitted that the spending of billions of dollars to create a biomedical industry had failed to achieve significant results. Research resources had been spread too thin, she said. "We need to choose the few research areas that we think we may have a chance with ... We have to be more focused." Singapore should invest in niche research areas such as Asian diseases, rather than compete with world-class scientific heavyweights in the West. "How many of the foreign stars have made any major discoveries after coming to Singapore?" she asked. Not many, it would seem. Clearly, Singapore's high hopes for Biopolis and the NNI have yet to be realised, despite the billions already spent on them.

The Biopolis initiative represents the latest stage in Singapore's quest for technology, which it now seeks to develop with imported foreign talent. Following failed efforts at technology transfer from the MNCs, R&D spending was stepped up from the early 1980s, as Chapter 3 showed. But this produced meagre results. Murray and Perera commented in 1996 that,

> despite the millions invested in R&D and other facilities, Singapore still does not have a broad ability to create its own technology base. One analyst has suggested that this is due to the fact that, while its people are skilled, they have had "the creativity and enterprise squeezed out by an over-protective, over-intrusive government". Singapore, therefore, will remain dependent on MNCs for some time to come and prey to adverse developments in the region and in the global business environment.[58]

Their comments may continue to be valid despite the establishment of Biopolis and related research projects. The economic, cultural and other factors that have sabotaged creativity in Singapore for decades are as strong as ever.

The Wired City

Though Singapore's R&D output remains modest its IT progress has been impressive.

Singapore has been a pioneer in developing IT expertise and becoming a "wired" economy. Its IT infrastructure is one of the world's best. The whole city-state has been wired up for the IT revolution. Under the Singapore IT2000 Masterplan, the Government plans to transform the country "into an intelligent island where IT is exploited to the fullest to enhance the quality of life of the population at home, work and play," according to a government website.[59] The aim is to deliver "a new level of interactive, multimedia applications and services to homes, businesses and schools throughout Singapore".

Computer access has soared in Singapore. By 2000, half of Singapore homes had Internet access and the number of registered websites had reached 17,200 by early 2001.[60] About 950,000 Singaporeans had broadband access from homes, offices and community organisations by early 2002, while 100,000 had been trained by a national IT literacy program by late 2002.

In 2004, Singapore was ranked the seventh most Web-savvy country in the world by US computer giant IBM and the intelligence unit of *The Economist* magazine.[61] Countries were assessed on such factors as the number and cheapness of Internet connections, software and technical support, legal and government frameworks and populations keen to use the Net.

With its wired economy, Singapore has the tools to develop into a more innovative society, but its IT capacity needs an innovative environment to be properly realised. Singapore has yet to achieve this. Like its education reforms and soaring R&D expenditure, Singapore's IT drive is only a first stage to this end. Being innovative remains an elusive goal for Singapore.

Reducing Red Tape

Since 2000 the Government has been trying to reduce the burden of red tape with the establishment of the Pro-Enterprise Panel which seeks to promote an easier regulatory climate for business. Although some progress seems to have been made, red tape continues to severely restrict Singaporean businesses. Moreover, statutory boards keep strongly defending their turf and fees. Despite government claims to being pro-business and lowering costs, Singapore is still more expensive and less competitive than its neighbours. Further major reductions in red tape will be required before Singaporean enterprises are as free of it as neighbouring Malaysia.

'Witless' Competitions

So often form overrides substance in Singapore, especially when new HRD and other strategies are launched. Often the means become an end in themselves. Getting qualifications without learning how to learn; creating hundreds of QCCs that do little to raise productivity and setting up impressive research institutes that fail to produce significant innovations are examples of this. The public service also demonstrates this very Singaporean paradox with its Work Improvement Teams (Wits) and Staff Suggestion Scheme (SSS), designed to cut waste and improve productivity. [62]

Too much time, effort and money are wasted on elaborate presentations for the annual Wits convention, according to Mr Bilahari Kausikan, the under-secretary chairing the committee that oversees Wits and the SSS. It was common knowledge "that Wits and SSS are widely perceived as a numbers game; an extra-curricula activity and an additional burden, not an integral part of work," he said. Departments would race to chalk up ideas and awards. Some consultants were paid up to S$200 an hour to vet and improve the presentation of Wits projects and reports. "No wonder some brilliant Wit has dubbed Wits as 'Waste Important Time'," Kausikan quipped. "Form has crowded out substance." [63]

Many civil servants lack enthusiasm for Wits. One survey found that almost half of the civil servants, if given the choice, would not take part in Wits. A survey five years previously had revealed the same disinterest. "I find this disturbing," Kausikan noted. The Wits competition has degenerated into an inter-departmental scramble to win medals rather than improve efficiency. The means have become the ends.

Singapore's Second Wing

Singapore has sought to re-engineer not only itself but its external economy. Central to this has been the "Second Wing" strategy, to develop an external wing to supplement the domestic economy. The strategy was initiated after the 1985 recession, prompted by the belief that Singapore needed a foreign source of income to reduce dependence on exports.

By 2000, Singapore's investments abroad totalled S$220 billion.[64] In 2001 these investments earned S$27.9 billion, but in 2002 earnings fell to S$25.7 billion.[65] In percentage terms, Singapore's Factor Income from Abroad (FIFA) was 15 per cent of GDP in 2001 and 14 per cent in 2002. This high FIFA has come at the price of indigenous entrepreneurial and SME development: income produced by Singaporean capital that could have financed the expansion of indigenous enterprise.

However, since the early 1990s Singapore's Second Wing strategies have become more ambitious. In April 1990, Deputy Prime Minister Goh Chok Tong said that the next phase of Singapore's expansion would focus on both developed and developing countries outside Singapore. The objective would be to transform "a mere city state" into "a great international city state", from "Singapore Inc" to "Singapore International".[66] Besides maximising FIFA, Second Wing strategies would include:

- Buying equity in foreign companies to gain access to their technology

- Facilitating foreign investment in Asia by such methods as setting up investment parks in other countries, including China
- Establishing the Johore-Singapore-Riau growth triangle with Malaysia and Indonesia.

Inevitably, the foreign investment aspect of the Second Wing strategy has diverted capital resources from developing local EICs. The same result comes from the strategy of buying of equity in foreign firms to acquire technology and overcome barriers to Singaporean exports. While Singapore may gain technology and boost exports by such means, once again the indigenous and SME sectors are deprived of capital. Developing home-grown, locally owned technology adapted to local conditions is far more beneficial to a country than acquiring off-the-shelf technology from abroad, but the PAP Government prefers the latter option. GLCs acquiring equity in foreign companies are much easier to manage than local SMEs whose independence may be hard for the Government to control, especially as they become bigger and stronger.

Industrial Parks

Facilitating foreign investment for other countries in Asia is another strand of Singapore's Second Wing strategy. Singapore believes that being part of Asia and investing there qualifies it to best help Western MNCs seeking to start operations in the area. Certainly Singapore can boost its regional and global role of serving foreign capital by such means. Industrial parks have been one way for Singapore to do this and the Singapore-Johore-Riau Growth Triangle was another way.

Since the early 1990s Singapore has been establishing parks in China at Suzhou, Wuxi, Chengdu and Chongqing. These parks are meant to generate investment opportunities for MNCs but will also showcase Singapore's "managerial software". The Suzhou project was the Republic's first major attempt to do this.

The Suzhou Project

Following a visit to Suzhou in September 1992, Lee Kuan Yew decided that Singapore should invest in an industrial and housing estate there to deepen bilateral ties with China and transfer Singapore industrial and managerial expertise: "With Singapore and Chinese managers working together ... we would transfer our methods, systems and knowhow."[67] The aim was to produce a "little Singapore" in China. The project would be a "software transfer," according to Singapore officials, in which a replica of Singapore's Jurong industrial park would be established in Suzhou, 110km west of Shanghai.[68] In February 1994, the Suzhou agreement was signed between the Singapore and Chinese Governments to launch the China-Singapore Suzhou Industrial Park Development. The 70 sq km industrial town was to cost US$20 billion to build, would create 360,000 jobs and house 600,000 people when completed in 20 years. The project was to be 65 per cent owned by a Singapore consortium; Chinese companies were to own the rest. Singapore's SEs were major investors in the project.

By the end of 1997 the first phase covering 8 sq kms had been completed. In November 1997, the marriage began to sour when the vice-mayor of Suzhou told

German investors to invest in the Suzhou New District (SND), a rival park set up in 1990 and owned by the Suzhou municipal government. On December 4, Lee told Suzhou officials to decide which industrial estate they wanted to support: the SIP or SND. Four days later on December 8, Lee got Chinese President Jiang Zemin to re-affirm his commitment to the SIP project. Lee elicited a promise from Jiang that the SIP would receive "special attention".[69]

Despite this support, Lee and the Singaporeans were soon to learn bitterly the old Chinese adage that "the mountains are high and the emperor is far away". While the central government issued decrees, provincial authorities continued to find ways around them. The Suzhou officials continued to promote the SND over the SIP, undercutting the SIP in land and infrastructure costs which they controlled. Lee fumed at the parochial attitudes of Suzhou officials. To his dismay he discovered that the Suzhou authorities were more interested in acquiring Singapore's "hardware" than its "software":

> We wanted to show them how to do things the Singapore way, with our emphasis on financial discipline, long-term master planning and continuing service to investors – our software. They wanted the "hardware" – the buildings, roads and infrastructure which we could build and the high-value investments we could attract using our worldwide connections and reputation....."Hardware" brought direct and immediate benefits to Suzhou and credit to its officials...[70]

The Suzhou authorities' uncooperative attitude towards the SIP could have been due to perceived Singaporean arrogance. As PERC noted, Suzhou officials were "somewhat miffed at tiny Singapore's attempts to teach China what to do".[71] As architects of the much-touted Singapore Miracle, Singaporeans felt they had the right to tell the Chinese (and others) how to run things.

The arrogance of Singaporeans doing business in China remains a problem. In November 2003, China's former ambassador to Singapore, Madam Chen Baoliu, told Singaporeans to drop their "air of superiority" if they wanted Sino-Singaporean relations to improve. Singaporeans had this attitude because of their better knowledge of English, affluent lifestyle, and greater familiarity with foreign cultures; but the Chinese were catching up and Singaporeans' superior airs would harm ties, she warned.[72]

Chinese business consultant and dealmaker Wang Wei echoes similar sentiments. Singaporeans still "act like professors" and think themselves superior to the Chinese, despite the relationship becoming more equal, he says. Singaporean businessmen had not realised that the Chinese had caught up.[73]

The biggest mistake that many Singaporeans made when doing business in China was to think they knew it all, says Canadian-Chinese John Chan, a Shanghai-based business consultant and author of *China Streetsmart*. They thought they understood China and so came with pre-conceived ideas: "I've seen a lot of Singaporeans who've not been that successful" because of such attitudes. Often non-Chinese foreign businessmen who did not speak Mandarin did better because they made a special effort to listen to staff and understand customers. Despite having a common language and cultural background, Singaporeans failed to listen and show respect to staff.[74]

Some Singaporeans working in China concur with such views. One is Ho Khee Tong, who had a design firm in Beijing and spent ten years in China. It is fatal to think the Chinese are "stupid and backward just because they are not as sophisticated as Singaporeans," he says. Today's Singaporeans, with their superior airs, remind him of himself when he was a China novice. "I thought too lowly of them and too highly of myself," he confesses.[75] After ten years and losing S$600,000 in China his attitudes to Chinese have become more realistic and respectful.

Singaporeans are, paradoxically, also perceived as naive by the Chinese. They are inclined to stick with each other rather than mix with the locals. Singaporeans are seen as having limited ability to build *guanxi* (links) with the Chinese. As Mr Ho says of his fellow Singaporeans, "Many of us are not good at building *guanxi*, even those whose jobs depend on it".[76]

Singaporean ignorance about doing business in China contributed to the Suzhou problems. As Lee Kuan Yew noted, "Both sides had believed that because of apparent language and cultural similarities there would be fewer problems in dealing with each other".[77] While Singaporeans took for granted the sanctity of contracts, the Suzhou authorities did not, believing they could be altered to suit changing circumstances. Singaporeans were understandably frustrated by the way Chinese officials changed rules to suit themselves. Besides promoting the SND over the SIP, Suzhou municipal officials withdrew tax concessions on capital equipment for investors in 1998, then reversed their decision a year later. They also undercut the SIP in land and infrastructure costs, making the SIP less attractive to foreign investors.[78] Eventually, after 19 months of negotiations, Singapore was able to wriggle out of the Suzhou agreement. In June 1999, it was agreed that the Singaporean and Chinese sides should swap their shareholdings, leaving China with 65 per cent and Singapore with 35 per cent of the project. The Singapore consortium would remain the majority partner in the project and complete the first eight square kilometres by the end of 2000. After that Singapore would remain as the minority partner until 2003, providing guidance for the Chinese management team which would then take over.

Apart from denting Singapore's reputation, the project began to take losses. By the end of 2001, while under Singaporean control, the project had lost US$77 million.[79] After the Chinese assumed 65 per cent control in 2001 the park reported a profit of US$7.5 million in 2002 and US$13.5 million in 2003. Having a larger share gave the Chinese greater incentive to sell the park to investors. Under Chinese control rentals fell to draw in Taiwanese technology firms. Suzhou park is now growing rapidly and there are plans to expand its size by another 250 sq km.

Singapore must be credited with the vision for launching the joint-venture park, but it only began to flourish under the Chinese. Although Suzhou revealed that Singapore's leaders can think and act in "big picture" terms, the country's managerial and other cultural values remain deficient. Its developmental "software", of which Lee Kuan Yew is so proud, is severely flawed.

The Singapore-Johore-Riau Growth Triangle

The growth triangle strategy encompasses Singapore, Johore (the southernmost state in Peninsula Malaysia) and Indonesia's Riau islands, especially Batam, off Singapore. It involves the creation of a tri-national industrial park that will counter the rising costs of doing business and hiring workers for both Singaporean firms and MNCs in Singapore. Both could shift their labour-intensive operations from Singapore to Johore and Batam where labour and business costs are much cheaper. Singapore would help MNCs make the shift because of its local knowledge and links with Malaysia and Indonesia.

The growth triangle initiative has yet to realise its potential. Although Batam has provided cheap labour for Singaporean and MNC firms, Johore's labour shortages and rising wages have limited its capacity to play a similar role.

Other problems have stemmed from Singaporean attitudes and managerial shortcomings. In promoting the scheme, Singapore depicted Johore and the Riau as providers of cheap labour, suggesting they were bereft of the technical and managerial expertise that Singapore could provide. Singapore seemed to be trading on its neighbours' weaknesses. The Malaysians especially were not impressed, particularly their government ministers and bureaucrats in Kuala Lumpur.[80] The marketing pitch of Batamindo, the Singaporean firm handling MNC start-ups in the Riau, was "the best of both worlds" – Singaporean "efficiency" and Indonesian cheap labour.

Singaporean managerial shortcomings have caused problems for MNCs in Batam. Batamindo promised foreign executives it would look after everything, but once in Batam they soon realised they had been misinformed. Indonesians would tell them, "well it's not quite like what they told you in Singapore".[81] Indonesians wanted their say and expected to be consulted and treated with respect. The situation was not as cut and dried as the MNCs had been made to believe. Arrogant and ignorant Singaporean managerial attitudes were again largely to blame.

In recent years there has been little publicity about the growth triangle, suggesting it has been put on the back burner by Singapore. Although the scheme has provided cheap labour for MNCs in Batam and allowed Singaporean firms to establish operations there, its achievements remain limited.

Trade Policies

Besides its Second Wing strategies, Singapore continues to pursue vigorous trade policies and has been an early participant in free trade agreements (FTAs). Singapore was the first Asian country to sign an FTA with New Zealand in 1999. By November 2003, it had signed FTAs with the European Free Trade Area (Switzerland, Liechtenstein, Norway and Iceland) and with the US, Japan and Australia.[82] At that time it was also negotiating FTAs with Mexico, Canada, India, South Korea, Jordan, Sri Lanka and Bahrain.

The preceding policy initiatives suggest an adroit government adapting Singapore to changing circumstances and ensuring it remains competitive. Closer examination reveals them as substitutes for the structural reform and transformation of cultural values that Singapore must undergo to become the efficient and competitive society its leaders so want it to be. So far these substitutes have only had partial success for re-engineering Singapore. They also display limited potential for doing the same in future.

4. Conclusions

The ten chapters in this and the previous section have revealed how exaggerated Singapore's claims are about its high efficiency. Its overall productivity is mediocre and a survey of major and minor sectors reveals many endemic inefficiencies largely the result of entrepreneurial, managerial and workforce shortcomings. These in turn are the result of PAP government policies and a range of cultural, organisational and other factors which also contribute to Singapore's second-rate productivity.

The next section examines long-standing claims about Singapore's economic freedom, transparency and favourable business climate. Further insights are also provided into the "miracle" economy's deficiencies.

References

1. *The Straits Times* (ST), August 30, 2000.
2. ST, August 21, 2000.
3. ST, March 31, 2004.
4. ST, April 10, 1999.
5. ST, March 19, 2000.
6. ST, March 2, 2002.
7. ST, April 1, 1995.
8. ST, November 23, 1995.
9. ST, May 23, 2001.
10. ST, April 22, 2001.
11. ST, March 1, 2003.
12. ST, February 7, 2003.
13. ST, July 15, 2003.
14. ST, July 5, 2003.
15. Ibid.
16. Lim, Levan and Tan, Jason: "Addressing Disability in Educational Reforms: A Force for Defining the Vision of Singapore 21", pp. 181-4 in *Challenges Facing the Singapore Education System Today*, edited by Jason Tan, S. Gopinathan and Ho Wah Kam (Singapore, Prentice Hall, 2001).
17. Bastion, Arlene: *Singapore in a Nutshell* (Singapore, Prentice Hall, 2003), p. 53.
18. ST, July 3, 2003.
19. Ho Kong Weng, Koh Ai Tee and Shandre M. Thangavelu: "Enhancing Technopreneurship, Issues and Challenges", p. 335-6 in *Singapore Economy in the 21st Century*, edited by Koh Ai Tee et al (Singapore, McGraw Hill, 2002).
20. *Economic Survey of Singapore 2002* (Singapore, Ministry of Trade and Industry, 2003), p. 75.
21. ST, November 23, 1995.
22. ST, July 7, 2003.
23. ST, March 22, 1998.
24. ST, October 5, 2000.
25. Nathan, J.M.: "Making 'Thinking Schools' Meaningful: Creating Thinking Cultures", p. 37 in *Challenges Facing the Singaporean Education System Today*, edited by Jason Tan, S. Gopinathan and Ho Wah Kam (Singapore, Prentice Hall, 2001).
26. Ibid, p. 76.
27. ST, July 19, 2003.
28. Ibid.
29. ST, July 9, 2003.
30. *Streats*, August 25, 2003.
31. Ibid, September 3, 2003 and ST, September 4, 2003.
32. Why the police would worry about this in Singapore seems strange. Singapore has dozens of karaoke lounges whose hostesses nightly engage in such intimate activities. Moreover, in Orchard Road there is Orchard Towers, a place filled with bars crowded with bargirls (and tranvestites) from Thailand, the Philippines, Indonesia, China and Vietnam. Sometimes called "four floors

of whores", Orchard Towers is the place to which droves of hormonally-driven males, expatriate and local (and even some western females), flock. One suspects that more places like that in Singapore would better attract expats than boring little bars where uptight Singaporean bimbos dance on the counter to induce customers to buy more over-priced drinks.

33. ST, September 4, 2003.
34. *Streats*, August 25, 2003.
35. Ho, Koh and Thangavelu in Koh et al, p. 339.
36. ST, January 13, 2003.
37. ST, January 21, 2003.
38. ST, December 24, 2003.
39. ST, March 23, 2002.
40. Ibid.
40a JTC Product Fact Sheet (Biopolis @ one north), September 2007.
40b. ST, December 11, 2004.
41. Ibid.
42. Ibid.
43. Ibid.
44. Ibid.
45. Ibid.
46. *Asia Sentinel*, January 22, 2007.
47. Ibid.
48. Ibid.
49. *The Financial Times* (FT), July 8, 2004.
50. Ibid.
51. Ibid.
52. "Lee Wei Ling's take on biomedical research in Singapore", (takcheck. blogspot.com) November 6, 2006.
53. ST, April 12, 2003.
54. FT, July 8, 2004.
55. ST, January 1, 2004.
56. *The New Paper*, February 1, 2007.
57. Murray, Geoffrey and Audrey Perera: Singapore the Global City State (England, China Library/Curzon, 1996), pp254-5.
58. *The New Paper*, February 1, 2007.
59. <www.s-one.gov.sg>.
60. Gomez, James: *Internet Politics: Surveillance and Intimidation in Singapore* (Bangkok and Singapore, Think Centre, 2002), p. 13.
61. ST, April 20, 2004.
62. ST, November 14, 2003.
63. Ibid.
64. *Business Times*, August 22, 2002.
65. Economic Survey of Singapore 2003, p. 23.
66. Tremewan, Christopher: *The Political Economy of Social Control in Singapore* (Britain, MacMillan, 1994), p. 39.
67. Lee Kuan Yew: *From Third World to First* (Singapore, Times Media, 2000), p. 720.
68. *The Financial Times* (London), January 9, 1996.
69. ST, June 11, 1999.
70. Lee, p. 721.
71. ST, June 23, 1997.
72. ST, November 20, 2003.
73. ST, November 21, 2003.
74. ST, November 17, 2003.
75. ST, March 30, 2003.
76. ST, February 22, 2003.
77. Lee, p. 723.
78. Ibid, p. 722.
79. *Streats*, April 5, 2004.
80. Murray and Perera, p. 55.
81. Ibid, pp. 66-7.
82. ST, November 1, 2003.

Section FOUR

. . . .

Myths for Multinationals

Singapore has an undeserved reputation for efficiency. What of the claims that it is a bastion of economic freedom and transparency and is a good place to do business? Singapore is rated highly on these attributes by always-supportive think-tanks and ratings agencies. This section examines the accuracy of their rankings.

CHAPTER 14

ECONOMICALLY FREE?

B eing one of the world's freest economies is a claim that has been made about PAP Singapore for many years. US think-tanks have been prominent in giving Singapore near-top rankings for economic freedom.

1. Ranking Freedom

When assessing efforts by ratings bodies to measure economic freedom, one needs to understand their reasons for doing so. Are they doing it for the benefit of foreign or local enterprises? And if for local enterprises then, in Singapore's case, whether for SEs or SMEs? It is widely believed in the West, especially among US neo-cons, that Singapore is a genuine free enterprise/capitalist society. Bello and Rosenfeld note that one of the myths about such Newly Industrialised Countries (NICs) as Singapore is that they are free market economies like the US.[1] US President Ronald Reagan, declared in his 1985 State of the Union address that:

> *America's economic success...can be repeated a hundred times in a hundred nations. Many countries in East Asia and the Pacific have few resources other than the enterprise of their own people. But through free markets they have soared ahead of centralized economies.* [2]

In 2002, Peebles and Wilson noted the pro-foreign capital bias of Singapore's economic freedoms:

> *To some observers Singapore is an economically free paradise of a corporately organized economy which provides an efficient pro-business environment, especially for chosen foreign investors.* [3]

Think-tank Ratings

Singapore is the darling of conservative think-tanks, especially in North America. They see the city-state as a shining example of economic freedom, second only to Hong Kong. The most prominent of these think-tanks are the US-based Heritage Foundation (HF) and Cato Institute (CI) and the Canadian-based Fraser Institute (FI). They compile periodic economic freedom reports for most countries, including Singapore.

The HF, with the Wall Street Journal (WSJ), produces the Index of Economic Freedom (IEF) report annually. The 2008 report surveyed 157 countries and was the

14th to appear since 1995.[4] The CI and FI publish the Economic Freedom of the World (EFW) report, which in 2007 covered 141 countries, and was the 11th since 1996.[5]

Almost invariably Hong Kong is ranked first and Singapore second for economic freedom in both reports. The IEF has placed Singapore second, behind Hong Kong for 14 straight years.[6] A similar pattern is evident with the 11 Cato/Fraser reports, where Singapore comes in just behind Hong Kong year after year.[7] Each report has a set of criteria for measuring economic freedom. The HF bases its criteria on the "ten economic freedoms". These are: business freedom, trade freedom, fiscal freedom, government size, monetary freedom, investment freedom, financial freedom, property rights, freedom from corruption and labour freedom.

In its 2008 report the HF said Singapore's economy was "87.38 percent free", just below Hong Kong's which was "90.25 percent free".[7a] For business freedom the HF scored Singapore 97.8 per cent; for trade freedom (90%), fiscal freedom (90.3%), government size (93.9%), monetary freedom (88.9%), investment freedom (80%), financial freedom (50%), property rights (90%), freedom from corruption (94%) and labour freedom (99%).

The Cato/Fraser criteria for economic freedom are similar: size of government, the structure of the economy and use of markets, monetary policy and price stability, freedom to use alternative currencies, freedom to trade with foreigners, freedom of exchange in capital and financial markets. The 2007 EFW report ranked Hong Kong No. 1 for economic freedom, with a score of 8.9 (out of a possible 10), while Singapore was ranked No. 2 with 8.8.[7b]

The criteria of both reports not only reflect corporate-sector concerns generally but, in many cases, those of the MNCs and foreign capital:

- Free trade (the degree of freedom that the host country gives MNCs to import and export from its borders)
- Freedom to use currencies and the development of financial markets (both dictate the capacity of foreign companies to remit profits, import capital and use financial derivatives)
- The quality of the legal system (this affects how much MNCs can ensure that contracts with local businesses and state authorities will be honoured)
- Property rights (how safe foreign-owned properties and plant are from confiscation and nationalisation)
- Wages and prices (how free foreign enterprises are to pay whatever wages they want to the locals without unions and/or government interference and to charge any prices they like for their products sold locally)
- Black market activity (to what extent foreign concerns must bribe local officials and sustain theft of stock by locals)
- Taxation levels (how low corporate taxes are).

Scoring highly on such criteria ensured Singapore's No. 2 spot in both economic freedom reports. However, each has acknowledged the heavy state involvement in Singapore's economy – a violation of a key benchmark for economic freedom.

The HF's 2008 report noted that the "state remains involved in the economy through Singapore's many government-linked companies".[8] In comparing Singapore with Hong Kong in its 2000 report, the HF said, "Hong Kong pursues a persistent laissez-faire policy. In Singapore there are government-directed investments, almost twice the rate invested in Hong Kong".[9] For such Singapore was ranked second behind Hong Kong for economic freedom, explained the HF.

The heavy role of the state has also been recognised in the Cato/Fraser reports. In the 1998 report, Singapore was ranked a lowly 30th for state presence in the economy (the lower the ranking, the greater state involvement was deemed to be).

In its 2001 report, the HF not only noted that GLCs "dominate Singapore's economy" but that they constituted "up to 70 per cent of Singapore-owned companies and generated up to 60 per cent of GDP", and that there was "increasing evidence of government intervention in Singapore's economy".[10]

Whether or not HF's 60 per cent estimate is accurate, this figure significantly discredits HF's claim that Singapore is the second most economically free country in the world out of the 156 countries surveyed in 2001. How can this be so when the state is supposedly controlling 60 per cent of the economy, far more than in most countries, especially the US and the Western democracies? How can an institute purportedly devoted to the cause of economic freedom rank a country where state control is extensive so highly? It would seem that state involvement in the economy is less important to HF and CI than the needs of foreign capital. What counts is how far foreign capital is accommodated.

By HF, CI and foreign capital yardsticks, Singapore is a truly free economy. MNCs there are not subject to high corporate taxes or threats of nationalisation, nor do they endure problems with theft, corruption, deficient judiciaries or militant unions. They face few restrictions on trade or the remission of funds. All these advantages give MNCs far greater overall economic freedom than they can find in almost any other country.

Despite the MNC-bias of the HF and CI economic freedom rankings, it must be recognised that they describe a business environment that also favours Singaporean firms: they too enjoy the benefits of low corporate taxes, minimal theft and corruption, an impartial judiciary (especially in commercial cases), nominal customs duties and few foreign currency restrictions. Even so, SMEs lack the resources to compete equally with MNCs and SEs. The MNC/SE dominance in Singapore restricts SME prospects, limiting their freedom to grow and prosper. When economic freedom is examined in such terms, along with the degree of state control of the economy, Singapore does not seem to be so economically free.

What Is Economic Freedom?

Debates about economic freedom usually focus on how far the state owns or controls the economy. This primarily depends on:

- The share of GDP produced by the state bureaucracies and enterprises

- The percentage of the economy's capital or land assets the state owns or controls
- The proportion of the workforce the state employs and/or controls by its power over the unions.

State involvement in the economy can also be measured by:

- How far the state regulates the economy through various monetary, fiscal and other policies and bureaucratic rules and red tape
- What percentage of the GDP produced by the private sector is taken by the state in the form of taxes, both direct and direct, to be spent as it sees appropriate.

Economic freedom is usually deemed as being greater the lower the state scores on the above criteria. For conservatives, a small state sector, low taxes and minimal regulation of the economy are fundamental to economic freedom. But they don't extend the same rights to labour. The conservatives' position is that a true "free enterprise" government firmly controls the unions, preventing them from striking and making "outrageous" wage demands.

More generally, economic freedom for the private sector means freedom from state control or interference. The fewer restrictions on business, the greater its capacity to respond to market demands quickly and efficiently. The PAP's statist development policies have restricted the private sector's freedom to do this, but seem to have counted for little with HF and CI. For them, truer measures of economic freedom are a lack of trade and currency restrictions, low corporate taxes and freedom from corruption: the kind of specific economic freedoms that benefit foreign and local corporate sectors.

2. A Not-So-Free Economy

The PAP state's pervasive presence in Singapore is described by Tremewan:

The Singapore state is the exclusive or major provider of infrastructure (utilities, communications, media, industrial estates, port and airport services) and of social services (housing, health and education). It is the country's largest employer, it sets wage levels, regulates labour supply and controls all unions. It holds approximately 75 per cent of the land and has the power to take the rest. It is a major actor in the domestic capital market, runs giant state enterprises, a trading company, and joint ventures with foreign capital.[10]

In December 1999, SEs owned 100 per cent of telecommunications, newspapers, taxis, mass transit, ports and airlines and nearly 100 per cent of TV and radio companies and marine services.[11] They also owned 80 per cent of healthcare companies and 50 per cent of supermarkets, 30 per cent of property development, 35 per cent of prime office space, 26 per cent of banks and 20 per cent of retail space.

The Singapore state not only controls a major share of the economy's capital resources but most of its land and workforce.

State Monopolisation of Land

The Government owns/controls the lion's share of Singapore's land. By 1998 the Government and GLCs owned 72 per cent of all land,[12] up from 40 per cent in 1960.[13] This has been achieved by extensive violation of Singaporeans' property rights, a principle which HF and CI hold dear for the MNCs but not for Singapore's local sector.

The free-marketeers not only support the unbridled operation of market forces, but demand strong property laws to protect gains from economic activity. While HF gave Singapore top ranking for property rights in 1995, this was mainly so for foreign-owned property. But all property rights, not merely those of MNCs, should be protected according to the principles of economic freedom. The strength of a country's property rights depends on how free *all* its citizens are to do what they want with their property, without it being confiscated or requisitioned by the state.

Singaporeans have few such protections. Their property rights have been severely compromised since Separation in 1965. In Singapore's constitution the "right to property" has been omitted. By contrast, Article 13 of the Malaysian constitution, which was also Singapore's until 1965, contains property rights.

Land requisition at nominal prices has been systematically practiced by the PAP state since the 1960s. In 1966, Parliament gave the Government power to acquire private land below market values for the public good, which then was deemed to include the new HDB and urban renewal schemes. An Act permitting such acquisitions "clearly violates the common laws that govern property rights," observes Singaporean sociologist Chua Beng Huat.[14] By abrogating Singaporeans' property rights, the Act eventually gave the state ownership of most of Singapore's land.

Occasionally Singaporeans are reminded of how completely the Acquisitions Act can overrule their property rights. In June 2003, the Singapore Land Authority paid a mere S$1 to acquire 200 sq m of freehold land from a church.[15] The land, which covered 17 parking lots, was for road widening purposes. The authority rejected the church's pleas for proper compensation. One property industry commentator described the Act as being "very powerful ... [it] favours whoever is acquiring the land. As an owner, unfortunately, you are on the receiving end".[16]

The Act also protects the Government from market disciplines, notes Bhaskaran:

> Section 5 of the Act is so broadly worded that it leaves non-state economic agents with little recourse, effectively diminishing their property rights, rights which are a critical core of the market economy.[17]

The Act contains such all-encompassing wording as "any public purpose" or "for any work". It has been so worded that "no property owner in Singapore can truly assume that his property is not safe from acquisition".[18] These draconian provisions were introduced in the 1960s when much of Singapore was still occupied by rubber estates and agricultural land, and where unused land was held by big companies or individuals. Rezoning or acquiring land at market prices would have given these owners big unearned profits at the expense of the average taxpayer.

Singaporeans accepted the Act because of Singapore's uncertain future after Separation and the need to remove any obstacles to rapid development. Now that such perilous times no longer prevail "there are few legitimate reasons to persist with such a draconian [act]". [19] It not only undermines property rights but is a further restriction on Singaporeans' economic freedom. The PAP Government's refusal to modify the Act means that most of Singapore's land is still owned by the state.

A State-controlled Workforce

The Government has extensive command of the country's workforce. In 1989, Clad reported that the state employed nearly 25 per cent of the workforce, [20] but major government publications such as its *Manpower Yearbooks* and annual *Economic Surveys* lack the information needed to calculate more accurately what percentage of the workforce is currently state-employed.

The PAP state also heavily restricts the freedom of Singapore's workers to fight for their interests compared to those in most free-market economies. This constitutes another clear denial of economic freedom. From the mid-1960s the PAP systematically broke the power of the unions. It brought them under government control via the NTUC, the state-controlled umbrella body that all unions must belong to and which is headed by government ministers. Strikes and other industrial action are virtually forbidden, and unions have been transformed into docile government mouthpieces, as the SIA retrenchments showed.

When think-tank conservatives talk of economic freedom, they usually mean the freedom of business, especially big business, to make profits, pay little tax, collude with each other, engage in monopolistic practices and be free of government interference. They rarely acknowledge labour's right to press its demands. This negates their version of economic freedom. The feeling is that companies should be permitted to pay whatever they want to workers, without fighting troublesome unions. HF and CI ratings reflect this mentality. True economic freedom would give labour the same freedom as the owners of capital to get the best return for their contribution to the process of production, but few MNC managements or the PAP leadership would concede this.

The 60 per cent Debate

The two fundamental components of an economy are its factors of production and what they produce. Hence, to measure the degree of state control one needs to ascertain not only what proportion of the economy's capital, land and labour are commanded by the state, but also what share of output the state is responsible for.

While state control of Singapore's economy is widespread, measuring how much output the state is responsible for is difficult. Estimates vary widely, ranging from one fifth to three fifths of the economy, depending on the source.

A 1998 study released by the US Embassy in Singapore put the public sector's share of GDP at 60 per cent.[21] Until 2001, the US Department of Commerce regularly cited this figure in its annual reports on Singapore. The figure itself was reportedly based on a 1993 Ministry of Finance estimate and HF's 60 per cent figure may also have been derived from that.

For years the Government would not comment on the 60 per cent figure, but since 2000 state control of Singapore's economy has become an issue and attracted growing disapproval, both foreign and domestic. A major reason for this growing foreign concern about state control stems from Singapore's FTA negotiations with the US.

In December 2000, the Americans raised concerns about fair competition, claiming that GLCs took up to 60 per cent of Singapore's GDP.[22] In 2003, the GLC sector was still an issue for Americans. GLC dominance had generated the perception that they enjoyed an unfair advantage over foreign and private sector competitors. Americans were pressuring Singapore to pass a competition law to allow US companies to compete on an even footing with the GLCs. Often the US requests were expressed in the guise of greater demands for transparency by Singaporean SEs. The US position was that the lack of transparency practised by the SEs gave them advantages over foreign enterprises, as the next chapter further explains.

Locally there was a growing tide of criticism about the prevalence of SEs in the economy. For years the local business sector and some PAP backbenchers had voiced increasingly strident complaints about the predatory business practices of SEs, as Chapter 16 describes. From February 2001, the PAP Government set out "to refute the view that GLCs have stifled local entrepreneurship".[23] Trade and Industry Minister George Yeo claimed that GLCs, in which the Government held 20 or more per cent of voting shares, contributed only 13 per cent to GDP. The US accepted this claim. The US Embassy in Singapore discarded its 60 per cent estimate as "redundant". A "presentation" by the Singapore Government had showed that GLCs and statutory boards only made up 23 per cent of GDP, the embassy conceded.[24] (As it was, the 60 per cent figure could easily have been disproved. Foreign-controlled companies generated over 40 per cent of Singapore's GDP in 1998 [see below]. If SEs accounted for 60 per cent of GDP, it would surely have been apparent that the entire local economy was state-owned!)

The Singapore Government's figure of 23 per cent for the state of the economy was slightly higher than 1998 figures showing that the state's share of GDP was 21.8 per cent. This figure was calculated by adding the public sector and GLC totals shown below. [25]

Table 14.1 – GDP percentages by sector

	% Share of GDP
Public sector	8.9
Corporate sector	87.5
Foreign-controlled companies	41.5
Local-controlled companies	46.0
GLCs	12.9
Others (private local firms)	33.1
Owner-occupied dwellings	3.6

These figures show that in 1998 foreign companies contributed 41.5 per cent of GDP; the local private sector 33.1 per cent and the state sector (public and GLC) 21.8 per cent. They reveal that the MNCs clearly dominated the economy, that the local private sector was quite small by the standards of a conventional market economy and that the GLCs and statutory bodies were a significant presence in the economy.

These figures, showing that the public sector was responsible for less than a quarter of GDP, require further examination. To begin with, the official claim that GLCs only accounted for about 13 per cent of the GDP is misleading. First, the government's definition of GLCs is suspect. A GLC "is a subsidiary or a associate, by virtue of share ownership, of Temasek Holdings (the government holding company) or a statutory board".[26] But as Peebles and Wilson noted in 2002, this "seems to ignore the fact that there are three other government holding companies [Singapore Technologies, MND and Health Corporation of Singapore] and that some companies are directly owned by government ministries".[27] The GLC-share of GDP is greatly increased when the GLCs of these other holding companies are included. Moreover, the GLC estimates of 12.9 per cent are limited to GLCs in which the Government has 20 per cent or more of voting shares.[28] If GLCs are included in which the Government holds less than 20 per cent, the GLC total would be even higher.

Moreover, there would be many GLCs where the government stake is greater than 20 per cent who would also not be classified as GLCs. The 20 per cent benchmark excludes many second and third-tier GLC subsidiaries. For example, if Temasek owns 50 per cent of a first-tier GLC, and that GLC owns 30 per cent of a subsidiary, the effective government ownership of the subsidiary is calculated to be only 15 per cent.[28a] As such the subsidiary is not considered to be a GLC, even though the government may still have an indirect stake in it that is well above 20 per cent.

There are also questions about the public sector, which consists of the central government and statutory boards, to consider. Government figures claim that the public sector was only responsible for 8.9 per cent of GDP in 1998, compared to 16 per cent of GDP in 1990, suggesting the public share of GDP had been almost halved. But this fall was more due to changes in definition than to any genuine reduction in the public sector. The decline "has mainly been accomplished by converting some statutory boards and companies, some of which, such as the Port of Singapore Authority, the government still completely owns," observed Peebles and Wilson.[29]

Thus while the Government insists that the public sector produces about 22 per cent of GDP, other data suggests that the public share of GDP is much higher. When non-Temasek GLCs and state-owned authorities that have been converted into "companies" are included (along with GLCs where the state has a less than 20 per cent share), the GLC and overall public share of GDP is significantly greater. The state sector could well be responsible for at least a third, while the local private sector's contribution would therefore be less than one third.

Besides minimising the public sector's contributions to GDP the Government also downplays the heavy state presence in the economy by claiming that GLCs operate as independent companies, despite government shares in them. But, as noted in Chapter Nine, the Government controls and monitors GLC boards' membership through the state-controlled DCAC, which approves GLC appointees, most of whom are retired politicians and military personnel and bureaucrats, past and present.

Often the Government has the controlling share in GLCs. As one Singaporean analyst told *The Straits Times*, "why would the Government want to own a controlling interest in these companies if it does not want to control them? Investors acquire controlling stakes in companies to influence or to control their direction".[30] Clearly the Government controls GLCs by dictating their board appointments and holding controlling interests in them. This suggests the Government controls GLCs almost as closely as it does statutory boards. Through control of so many SEs the state would probably account for over a third, not 23 per cent, of GDP.

Freedom for Foreign Capital

Extensive state control of Singapore's economy represents a major restriction to economic freedom. This discredits HF and CI claims that Singapore is one of the world's freest economies – until it becomes apparent that they are mainly measuring foreign capital's freedom to operate unfettered in the countries surveyed.

Besides their foreign-capital bias, the think-tanks seem subject to methodological errors. As Linda Low said, HF's weighting system is unclear, especially each factor's weighting.[31] Responding to such criticisms, HF's vice-director, Kim Holmes, claimed that its index was based on "'objective criteria" and political factors had been excluded from the survey.[32]

Another key problem with the HF and CI rankings is their misuse of words. "Economic freedom" really means "suitability for foreign capital"? Emotive terms such as "freedom" and "freedom indexes" obscure a foreign-capital agenda. Ranking countries in terms of their foreign investment climate instead of economic freedom would be more appropriate.

Though blinkered think-tanks may refuse to recognise the state-controlled nature of Singapore's economy, most Singaporeans, especially its SMEs, know otherwise. Strident criticisms from the local private sector since the 1980s and a realisation that Singapore must increase its entrepreneurial and innovative capacities (EICs), prompted the government to begin a privatisation program in the late 1980s.

3. Privatisation – Sort of

Singapore's extensive SE system has not only upset the local private sector since the 1980s but has come to be seen as severely stunting the growth of EICs. The Government felt that some sort of privatisation program was called for.

Half-hearted Steps

The push for privatisation gathered momentum after the 1985 recession, when the Government set up the Public Sector Divestment Committee (PSDC).[33] In February 1987, the committee submitted a privatisation program which identified 41 companies for partial or complete privatisation over a ten-year period. The PSDC recommended that 15 GLCs be listed on the stock exchange and that the government dispose of stakes in up to 17 GLCs. The committee's proposals were quite modest considering that there were several hundred GLCs in the 1980s.

By April 2000, fewer than two-thirds of the targeted GLCs had attained listed status, and privatisation had proceeded slowly for five of Singapore's biggest GLCs.[34] Singtel had gone from 100 per cent state control in November 1993 to 79.7 per cent by March 1998; SIA from 77 per cent in December 1985 to 53.8 per cent by June 1987; Neptune-Orient Lines from 62 per cent in May 1987 to 33.4 per cent in June 1993; Keppel Corporation from 58.5 per cent in January 1989 to 32.3 per cent in June 1993.[35] Few divestments have occurred since June 1993.

The Government also retains control of GLC board appointments through the DCAC which chooses and monitors directors. Once again the PAP state is going through the motions of reform. Regimes used to controlling everything find it hard to relinquish control of anything. The "privatisation" program has merely made its control of SEs and the economy less obvious. Linda Low's 1990 observation still applies:

> It would be too simplistic to assume that the government's "visible hand" would be less visible after privatisation. The government' known to be "high-handed", paternalistic, and interfering with a "government-knows-best" attitude, is not likely to just give up everything to the private sector.[36]

Thus "the privatisation move appears to have nothing to do with developing local entrepreneurship, at least not explicitly".[37] Apart from deflecting criticism about SEs, the Government has sought to use the privatisation program to raise more public money for them. By transferring ownership rather than control of GLCs, the Government could induce the public to buy shares in privatised GLCs. While state ownership of GLCs might be reduced through public offerings of shares, still "the major shareholder and hence control" was to "rest with the government".[38] The divestment of large firms like SIA or the International Trading Company (INTRACO) was unlikely to result in their being managed by single or small groups of local entrepreneurs. The real aim was to stimulate the stock market and give it depth, not to reduce state control and develop local entrepreneurship.

Complaints have been made about the slow pace of privatisation. A persistent critic has been PAP MP, Mr Leong Horn Kee. In March 2001, he said:

> Currently, the withdrawal of government stakes in government-linked companies is too long-drawn-out. There should be clear rules on the issue of whom to divest to, and how, because today we are not sure what the process is.[39]

Privatisation Sidelined

Renewed criticisms of GLCs prompted the Government to set up another committee in 2002 with a brief similar to the 1987 one. Called the Entrepreneurship and Internationalisation sub-committee, it sought to examine the role of the Government in business. The sub-committee also examined SEs. It recommended a "Yellow Pages rule" whereby SEs should not offer products or services already available in the local sector.[40] SEs should be confined to "strategic" areas of the economy such as public services and the development of new growth industries.

Though lip service was paid to the report, parliamentary debates revealed the Government planned little more privatisation of SEs, despite widespread SME calls for this. Defending the Government's tardy privatisation efforts, Deputy Prime Minister BG Lee said that it was in "no hurry to sell off the family silver".[41] GLCs were here to stay. There would be no Great Singapore Sale of them, merely strategic divestment. "We will restructure the GLCs, we will sell off pieces that do not fit," he said.[42] He rejected claims that GLCs would be made more efficient if privatised. Instead, the Government would strive to make them more competitive so they could compete abroad. Because the Government had created the GLCs it "had a responsibility to ensure they are well run, grow their businesses and contribute to the economy". He then told the private sector, "This may mean tougher competition for the non-GLCs. But so long as the competition is fair, that is good for the economy and for Singaporeans."

BG Lee airily dismissed long-expressed complaints that SEs competed unfairly, denying claims that they soaked up talent, tapped "old boy" networks and contacts in the public service, enjoyed cheap financing and crowded out the private sector. He also rejected calls for curbs on SE proliferation, saying the Government reserved the right to move into sectors that the private sector shunned.

To mollify both SE critics and the private sector, Lee spoke of a "Temasek Charter" where GLCs in the Temasek stable would be subject to clearer performance standards and focus on their "core competencies".[43] They would acquire new local companies in a less random way that better reflected their main strengths. Temasek would also be concentrating on two categories of companies.[44] The first would be those that were strategic enough to warrant state involvement, such as those providing water, power and gas grids, airport and seaport facilities and public goods like broadcasting subsidised healthcare, education and housing. Second, Temasek would focus on enterprises with the potential for regional or international growth. But as one Western journalist noted, "almost all of Temasek's existing companies fit into one or other, meaning there was not going to be much divestment in the near future". For him the Charter indicated that "far from stepping back from the marketplace, the government seems to be trying to improve its performance as an investor".[45]

Comments from the Temasek chairman and former government minister S. Dhanabalan have confirmed that the private sector will face even more vigorous GLC competition. Temasek's GLCs could still "crowd out" SMEs and were likely to become "even more dominant", he said.[46] His rationale was that the GLCs needed to be strong domestically to compete abroad.

These are indications that the Government's half-hearted privatisation program has been shelved. The private sector will continue to face tough competition. The state sector will remain large and Singapore will probably stay as economically unfree as ever. Vested interests explain much of the Government's resistance to privatisation.

Vested Interests

During the August 2002 debate on GLCs, PAP MP Dr Amy Khor told Parliament,

GLCs have proliferated and taken on a life of their own ...Hence any major attempt to divert or rationalise GLCs could trigger a chain reaction, upsetting an entire apple cart of entrenched interests, institutional arrangements, and corporate culture and agenda.[47]

Similar observations have been made by one of *The Australian*'s Singapore correspondents, Eric Ellis. In writing on the GLCs he noted the presence of "a merry-go-round of connected interests".[48] A Singaporean academic described statutory board and GLC posts as sinecures used to reward senior civil servants [and ex-government ministers] past their prime. This system could not be changed because it "would threaten the whole scholarship mandarinate class".[49]

The powerful vested interests of the SE sector have been documented in a report entitled "Why it might be difficult for the government to withdraw from business".[50] The report by a so-called "Tan Boon Seng", dated March 2002, was circulated over the Internet and to international journalists through email. The document represented a considerable research effort. It listed the extensive financial interests and the SE board and executive positions held by Lee Kuan Yew's family, current and retired PAP cabinet ministers and PAP MPs and active and retired senior civil servants and military personnel. The list included 50 senior government officials holding key SE appointments while still in government.

There were no allegations of corruption, but the document clearly showed the extensive web of vested financial and political interests between the PAP political and bureaucratic elite and Singapore's SE system. In commenting on the document, Rodan said, "Significantly, at no time did the government attack the factual accuracy of the document, something that it is generally quick to do when seeking to dismiss or deflect critical scrutiny". [51] Of particular interest was the document's identification of the leading roles played by Lee family members and relatives in major SEs, as Chapter Five has shown. At the time of the document's release in February 2002:

- Lee himself was heading the GIC, with the then deputy prime minister Lee Hsien Loong (BG) as its deputy chairman.
- Lee's second son, Lee Hsien Yang, was Singtel's CEO, director of Singapore Technologies Industrial Corporation and National Computer Systems (a Singtel unit).

- Hsien Loong's wife, Ho Ching, was director of such major SEs as Temasek Holdings and Sembcorp Industries (a unit of the now defunct Singapore Technologies), chairman of Chartered Semiconductor, ST Engineering, ST Capital and Starhub and deputy chairman of Singapore Technologies.

In addition to these positions, relatives of Lee Kuan Yew and of his wife and several in-laws held such positions as managing director, CEO, deputy chairman, senior vice-president and director of various key statutory boards and GLCs.

Lee Kuan Yew and Lee Hsien Loong are not paid for their GIC positions – an appropriate arrangement considering their huge parliamentary salaries – but other members of the Lee clan are handsomely compensated by the GLCs they head or help direct. Besides salaries and bonuses they receive shares and share options from the GLCs.

Many see nepotistic factors as accounting for the lucrative positions gained by the Lee clan and in-laws in the SE system, but the document also illustrates how the *amakudari* system is the main mechanism for ensuring that ex-ministers and senior public servants are rewarded with equally profitable SE sinecures. The document listed the SE positions of the following:

- Eight former senior ministers (including those for defence, foreign affairs, finance, trade and industry and education)
- Two parliamentary secretaries and 14 permanent secretaries
- Over 70 civil service CEOs who assumed executive positions with over 160 SEs.

The document listed 40 senior military officers, from lieutenant generals to lieutenant colonels, and the over 90 CEO and senior managerial SE positions that they were appointed to on their retirement. Finally, the document showed that 19 current and nine retired PAP MPs held key posts in SEs.

Much of Singapore's ruling elite benefits from the present SE system. Not surprisingly the document concludes that the "government's withdrawal from business could hurt the employment, income and ownership interests of people closely connected with it," especially senior cabinet ministers and civil servants. A "prestigious and lucrative destination" for them would be removed. Senior SE managers are compensated at globally competitive levels and many are shareholders of the SEs they manage. Non-executive directors are paid regular directors' fees and are often given substantial share options. "They may lose out if the government gives up ownership of GLCs," the document notes.

Apart from the vested financial interests of the PAP ruling elite, the Government's deep-rooted need for overall control of Singapore prevents any major GLC and SE divestment. For Rodan:

The problem is that a serious dismantling of the GLCs would represent a potential challenge to the established means by which the PAP has exerted social and political influence, no less economic. [52]

Powerful forces have undermined the privatisation program. It was never something the Government really wanted, which largely explains its tardy implementation and eventual shelving. As the Minister for Finance, Richard Hu, said in 1986, "We are not in a desperate hurry to accelerate this (privatisation) process." [53] The Government's subsequent slow and half-hearted privatisation program demonstrated this before it was eventually sidelined by the Temasek Charter.

It seems that Singapore's local economy and vast capital reserves will remain largely under state control, managed by retired politicians and rule-following bureaucrats, current and retired. As such, economic freedom in Singapore will remain as limited as ever, whatever US neo-con think-tanks may claim. For as long as their notions of economic freedom reflect foreign capital interests they will keep producing absurdly inaccurate rankings for Singapore that do not deserve serious attention.

References

1. Bello, Walden and Rosenfeld, Stephanie: *Dragons in Distress: Asian Miracle Economies in Crisis* (London, Penguin, 1990), p. 7.
2. Ibid.
3. Peebles, Gavin and Wilson, Peter: *Economic Growth and Development in Singapore* (Cheltenham, UK; Edward Elgar Publishing, 2002), p. 16.
4. *Index of Economic Freedom 2008* (The Heritage Foundation and the Wall Street Journal, Washington DC).
5. *Economic Freedom of the World 2007* (Cato Institute, Washington DC).
6. *Index of Economic Freedom reports 1996-2008.*
7. *Economic Freedom of the World reports 1995-2007.*
7a. 2000 report, (www.heritage.org/).
7b. 2007 report, (www.cato.org/pubs/efw/).
7c. *Index of Economic Freedom 2008,* country reports.
8. Peebles and Wilson, p. 67.
9. Ibid, p. 16.
10. Tremewan, Christopher: *The Political Economy of Social Control in Singapore* (Britain, MacMillan, 1994), p. 2.
11. Bhaskaran, Manu: *Re-inventing the Asia Model: the Case of Singapore* (Singapore, Eastern Universities Press, 2003), p. 33.
12. Ibid, p. 35.
13. Asher, Mukul G.: "Reforming Singapore's tax system for the twenty-first century", p. 402 in *Singapore in the 21st Century,* edited by Koh Ai Tee et al (Singapore, McGraw Hill, 2002).
14. Chua, Beng Huat: *Communitarian Ideology and Democracy in Singapore* (London, Routledge, 1995), p. 130.
15. ST, June 20, 2003.
16. ST, June 26, 2003.
17. Bhaskaran, p. 38.
18. Ibid, p. 39.
19. Ibid.
20. Clad, James: *Behind the Myth: Business, Money and Power in Southeast Asia* (Sydney, Allen & Unwin, 1989), p. 143.
21. *Country Commercial Guide* FY 1999: Singapore (Embassy of the United States, Singapore, July 1998), p. 6.
22. ST, March 3, 2001.
23. Peebles and Wilson, p. 13.
24. ST, March 3, 2001.
25. Peebles and Wilson, p. 14.

26. Ibid.
27. Ibid.
28. Rodan, Garry: *Transparency and Authoritarian Rule in Southeast Asia* (London, RoutledgeCurzon, 2004), p. 195.
28a. Ramirez, D. Carlos "Singapore Inc. Versus the Private Sector: Are government-Linked Companies Different" IMF Working Paper; (IMF Institute, International Monetary Fund, July 2003) p. 7.
29. Peebles and Wilson, p. 15.
30. ST, May 2, 2000.
31. Low, Linda: "The Elusive Developed Country Status", p. 387 in *Singapore: Towards a Developed Country Status*, edited by Linda Low (Singapore, Oxford University Press, 1999).
32. ST, November 28, 1995.
33. ST, May 31, 2002.
34. ST, April 29, 2000.
35. Ibid.
36. Low, Linda: "State Entrepreneurship", p. 159 in *Local Entrepreneurship in Singapore*, edited by Tsao Yuan Lee and Linda Low (Singapore, Times Academic Press; 1990).
37. Ibid, p. 155.
38. Ibid, p. 160.
39. ST, March 3, 2001.
40. ST, August 28, 2002.
41. ST, August 29, 2002.
42. *Business Times*, August 29, 2002.
43. *Today*, July 4, 2002.
44. Rodan, p. 69.
45. Ibid.
46. Ibid.
47. ST, August 28, 2002.
48. Quoted in Rodan, p. 66.
49. ST, May 1, 1999.
50. The report was summarised in a *South China Morning Post* article (March 4, 2002), "Web report reveals detailed state-private business links" by Jake Lloyd-Smith.
51. Rodan, p. 70.
52. Ibid, p. 68.
53. Low in Lee and Low, p. 154.

CHAPTER 15

A TRANSPARENT STATE?

After the 1997/8 Asian financial crisis, transparency became the newest buzzword of the world financial community. Lack of transparency (or too much opacity) was largely blamed for the crisis. Singapore's supposedly high levels of transparency did much to help it survive the crisis better than other Asian countries. Transparency is yet another attribute for which Singapore has received top rankings.

1. The Claims

After the Asian crisis Singapore's rulers quickly understood the importance of embracing notions of transparency. They could see that transparency was a key concern for foreign capital. In 1999, Senior Minister Lee Kuan Yew declared:

> *Because we are what we are, open and transparent, investors have confidence in us. The investors assess the situation and say, yes, this is a government and system that will continue to tick in an honest and efficient way.*[1]

However, Rodan notes, Lee was "conflating transparency with other governance factors important to international business".[2] The ratings agencies have followed Lee on this, with many claiming to measure transparency equating a lack of it with corruption. The agency most prone to doing this has been Transparency International (TI), a Berlin-based body which bills itself as an independent watchdog that seeks to fight corruption around the world. TI compiles an annual Corruption Perception Index based on countries' corruption as perceived by businessmen, financial journalists and bankers. Most of those polled are from developed countries who deal with foreign companies and governments worldwide. In 1995, Singapore was placed third out of 41 countries surveyed in one of TI's earliest corruption studies.[3] In subsequent years Singapore has continued to get top scores for transparency from TI. In 1998, Singapore was ranked 7th for transparency, while in 1999 it was 6th, 2000 (6), 2001 (4), 2002 (5), 2003 (5), 2004 (5), 2005 (5) and 2006 (5).[3] By 2007, when Singapore was placed 4th, TI was surveying 179 countries for its transparency rankings.[3a]

To justify TI's methodology TI vice-chairman Frank Vogl claimed that everyone understood that "people who are not transparent are corrupt".[5] But transparency (and opacity) are better assessed by such measures as ready access to information and open decision-making, whether at state or corporate level. Corruption, however, which can take many forms, most commonly involves the offer and acceptance of monetary or other inducements for special treatment. Those who pay bribes or provide other incentives usually seek favours or exemption from rules and procedures that aim to provide just and equitable treatment for all. The more such regulations are flouted the less likely they are to achieve such purposes. Corruption-prone countries display a range of political, judicial and other abuses, and of dysfunctional activities that inflict heavy social and economic costs on their societies.

Opacity does greatly facilitate corruption, so Vogl's equating transparency with reduced corruption may seem justified. But while transparency hinders corruption, and though opacity and corruption are often highly correlated, there are exceptions to the rule.

Opacity is not only used to hide financial corruption and favouritism. Rulers and other decision-makers may prevent the release of information that could discredit or undermine their policies or cover up abuses of power. Opacity is not only practised to conceal financial bribery and corruption but also to bury politically sensitive information and the misuse of power and privilege. As this book will show, such opacity is often displayed by the PAP state despite Singapore's low levels of obvious political corruption.

Unlike TI, other ratings bodies have been less inclined to use opacity as a synonym for corruption, though their foreign capital agendas are as obvious as ever. In November 2000, PERC ranked Singapore as having Asia's most transparent investment environment. PERC claimed that investors in Singapore-based companies had more access to information than those investing elsewhere in Asia.[6] The brokerage firm CLSA Emerging Markets has made similar claims.[7]

In 2001, Singapore was ranked No 1 for having the most transparent business practices in a global study by PriceWaterhouseCoopers (PWC).[8] The study used an "opacity index", with opacity defined as the lack of clear, accurate, formal and widely accepted practices. Countries were ranked on a scale from zero to 150, with zero being an ideal business environment of presumably perfect transparency. Singapore got the top score of 29 on this index. China, with a high degree of opacity, scored 87.

As usual, such surveys reflect the interests of foreign capital. The PWC study was seeking to quantify the cost of capital around the world caused by a lack of clear business practices. Legal protection for business, macro-economic policies, corruption, and government regulations were also considered, presumably because these were regarded as synonymous with transparency.

In 2004, Singapore was seen as providing a business and investment climate that was as open as that of the industrial nations, according to the Kurtzman Group, a US-based consultancy firm.[9] Singapore's opacity index was 24, the consultancy calculated, while the US scored 21 and Finland 13. Of the 48 countries surveyed those with the highest opacity were Lebanon and Indonesia with scores of 59 each, while China's was 50.

Kurtzman, like TI, seemed to directly equate opacity with corruption. The firm measured opacity in terms of business risks (the costs to business) that arise from fraud, bribery, legal and regulatory tangles and unenforceable contracts. Although fraud and bribery clearly constitute corruption, problems of a legal, regulatory and contractural nature are separate issues. Whatever the case, Kurtzman chose to measure Singapore's transparency levels by such largely irrelevant criteria. They are ones which Singapore can score well on: they are also those that reflect factors important to foreign capital.

Once again the ratings agencies have taken an attribute, this time transparency, and reinterpreted it to gauge a country's suitability for foreign investment. Surely it is more appropriate to measure a country for its transparency or corruption levels than for how well it serves foreign capital – which Singapore does very well. Because Singapore has been a top MNC venue for many years, it inevitably gets high scores when so assessed. But when a country's transparency is measured to reflect MNC concerns that have little to do with transparency, some very misleading transparency ratings are produced. The previous chapter's examination of Singapore's economic freedom rankings demonstrated this.

Countries like Singapore – and its PAP leaders – win undeserved praise from such bodies as TI for attributes they may not possess to the degree claimed. For example, in September 2000, TI awarded Lee Kuan Yew the Global Integrity Medal for honour, integrity and transparency because of his opposition to corruption and his promotion of transparency. [10] Do Singapore and its leaders deserve such accolades?

2. The Reality

Normally, transparency in business and politics is seen as the degree of access to information and the openness of decision-making. For example, to what extent can the public, NGOs or opposition politicians in a country examine and gain copies of official records and data without fear of persecution or prosecution? To what extent do government or corporate officials openly (and democratically) arrive at decisions and provide adequate reasons for them? How far do both public and private organisations regularly publish reports that fully describe their activities and financial positions? It is by such standards that Singapore's true transparency levels can best be assessed.

Coy GLCs, Evasive Ministers and Chastised Academics

Despite being ranked highly for transparency, "opaque behaviour" is widespread in Singapore's public, SE and corporate sectors. The GLCs and their holding companies especially have operated in great secrecy. "Very little is known about these GLCs," said Low.[11] While their funds come from budgetary surpluses, Parliament has direct control over only a few of the GLCs audited by the Auditor-General. Parliamentary control over most of them is minimal, particularly over their subsidiaries.

Singapore's two largest SEs, the GIC and Temasek Holdings, as well as most GLCs, can avoid parliamentary and public scrutiny. Nearly all GLCs are still privately held companies and do not have to submit publicly available annual reports to the Stock Exchange of Singapore (SES) or the Registrar of Companies and Businesses (RCB) though some GLCs are listed on the SES and must reveal routine information. Even so, with few exceptions, GLCs have been among the poorest performers in independent rankings for corporate transparency in Singapore, as a 1999 survey by Corporate Transparency Ratings Pte Ltd found.[12] The firm asked local business analysts to assess 100 listed companies for transparency. While one GLC (Natsteel Electronics) earned top billing, the vast majority of GLCs were well down the list. DBS Bank was at 54, Keppel Land at 55, NOL at 56, Natsteel at 60, Keppel Corp at 71, Keppel Finance at 74, Keppel Bank at 75, Times Publishing at 83 and Jurong Cement at 99. Not a single GLC gained an overall +A ranking.

SEs have been uncooperative with financial journalists and openly discriminate against foreign media, as has the SES. The foreign media have been excluded from press conferences of these bodies, resulting in letters of protest from the Foreign Correspondents' Association and individual media companies.[13] In recent years Temasek has regularly rejected requests from foreign publications for interviews with its chief, Ho Ching.

Various Acts protect the secretive nature of SEs. This has made it hard to get information on both the GIC and other SEs. GLCs' details are included in the Directory of Government Linked Corporations (DGLC), but the public are denied access to it because it is classified as a secret government document.[14] Even this directory excludes information about the GIC and its group of companies. These are listed in the GIC's own, equally secret, directory. Only in 2004 did the GIC begin divulging information about itself.

Getting a copy of the DGLC was impossible, Worthington found, when gathering information for his book *Governance in Singapore*. His attempt to buy a copy of the directory at a government office evoked near panic from desk staff:

> *The shocked receptionist could not deal with the enquiry and rushed out of the office for executive support. I was subsequently grilled by another officer as to how I had come to know about the publication. On being informed that it was mentioned in the academic literature, she was also shocked and informed me it was a top secret government publication and under no circumstances could I obtain a copy.*[15]

Any information that *is* provided on statutory boards and publicly-listed GLCs is given in a way that prevents their identification and individual examination by Parliament. Low observes:

> *Apart from the absence of consolidated corporate income and expenditure data, even broad indicators such as output, sales, value added and employment of the State enterprises are not easily available. Hence, it is not easy to measure the performance of GLCs in Singapore – particularly against that of private firms – using conventional efficiency rules as some studies have done.*[16]

Lack of information about SEs minimises scrutiny of their activities and allows them to side-step the aims for which they were originally formed. This has been particularly so when they have formed subsidiaries and associated companies, and embarked upon diversification sprees. "Many top civil servants and 'blue chip' SEs have increased and multiplied their stables as their corporate empires have gone from strength to strength."[17] Only the minister responsible for the specific SEs can control them. Not even the Minister for Finance need be informed when such SEs are set up with government funds. This situation has caused the Auditor-General "great concern" in the past, says Low.[18]

With subsidiaries, GLC operations are even less transparent because there are no regulatory mechanisms to check their corporate propagation. Private concerns, by contrast, have to submit audited returns every year and, if public companies, have to hold annual meetings to explain and justify their policies, plans, profits and losses to shareholders and to face hostile questions and criticisms – and even sanctions – from them. Such meetings are usually open to the media, ensuring widespread publicity for their successes or failures. Few SEs in Singapore get this degree of critical scrutiny.

The same applies to the GIC, whose secretive activities and investment operations have attracted much criticism in recent years. "What is troubling," Chee notes, "is that the public knows little about how these investments ...perform. The GIC does not account to anyone – not even parliament".[19] How and why directors were appointed was also not made public.

The GIC's proclaimed mission is to achieve healthy returns through "prudent investments worldwide", because these funds are "Singapore's assets". The problem is that few know much about these assets, as some investment experts have noticed.[20] "There is ...no transparency or public accountability concerning where these funds are invested," remarked NUS economist Mukul Asher. "These funds, however, are believed to be wholly invested abroad."[21]

Only after 2006, was any information released on these investments and then only in fragmentary form.

Generally though getting information on the performance of GIC investments has always been difficult. Every so often GIC chairman Lee Kuan Yew issues reassuring declarations about the GIC's returns on investment. "In the 15 years since 1985, the GIC has outperformed the relevant global investment benchmarks and more than preserved the value of our assets," he said in 2000,[22] while in that year Singapore's Minister for Finance claimed the GIC was "getting more than adequate returns".[23] However, the overall low returns that Singapore's reserves earned to 1995 cast doubt on such confident assertions. In 2006, Lee was making the same flattering claims about GIC returns, as Chapter Five shows.

Lee and son also trot out the usual national interest rationales to justify the GIC's secrecy – protecting the Singapore dollar from speculative attacks etc. When anyone questions this Lee replies that the GIC operates with "unflinching integrity".[24] He had set up the system for running the GIC and found the right people to operate it. Singaporeans should be satisfied with that. "There is total accountability," he said, stating that the GIC's accounts were monitored by a host of government agencies from the Accountant-General to the Council of Presidential Advisors.[25] But these assurances mean little when one considers that all such agencies and office-holders are tame PAP government appointees. They know their lucrative positions will be jeopardised if they dared to question or too closely scrutinise any anomalies in GIC accounts.

The GIC's opacity disturbs some Singaporeans.

Lee's claims of total accountability appear confusing, coming from a Government "that prides itself on transparency and accountability", wrote one Singaporean to *The Straits Times*. "Being exempted from even superficial annual reports, the GIC's position is neither transparent nor accountable to its shareholders – the electorate – which it claims to be accountable to." No matter how competent might be the bodies who examine the GIC accounts, they "are ultimately partial and fallible human beings who work within the Government's ambit". Should not a "totally accountable" system include independent auditors and observers? "Without even the most elementary disclosure of information, how could the people be assured that an elite group of individuals, behind a veil of secrecy, is handling their reserves properly?"[26] Lee and the Government have yet to satisfactorily answer such questions.

A former president of Singapore, Ong Teng Cheong, encountered a similar lack of transparency when trying to find the size of Singapore's reserves and assets. As president he had a constitutional duty to protect the reserves. Under the Constitution, the government of the day has to get his approval before it can spend any of the reserves. Ong took his responsibilities seriously and sought a complete list of the country's assets. He was told by the Accountant-General that it would take 52 man-years to do this.[27] The list was only given to him after a three-year delay, following complaints by him to the Government. At the end of his six-year term (1993-9), Ong complained about the "long list of problems" he had had with the Government. Ong had tried to do his job, but could not do so without complete data.

Inadequate information not only prevents tasks from being properly fulfilled: it can lead to erroneous conclusions, as two Singaporean NTU professors discovered in mid-2003. The academics had used what they thought were reliable government figures to point out that three quarters of new jobs created from 1997-2002 had gone to foreigners. The academics' finding caused a stir, because many Singaporeans were already upset at the number of local jobs being taken by non-citizens at a time when the Government was trying to lure foreign talent to work in Singapore during high unemployment. Realising the political sensitivity of the academics' report, the Government immediately countered by claiming that nine in 10 jobs went to Singaporeans and residents.[28]

The Manpower Minister attacked the two academics, one of whom had been a former National Wages Council chairman. He condemned them for failing to verify their figures with his ministry or the Department of Statistics before going public with "sensationalist" claims. Even if their figures had been correct they should not sensationalise them, he said. "But if your figures are wrong, it is irresponsible:

It is unprofessional to put out those figures and then when the damage is done, to expect others to check these findings," the Minister raged.[29] Suitably cowed, the two academics issued a statement the next day admitting they had made an "honest error of interpretation" in their findings.[30] In subsequent days it emerged that the two academics had used figures from the Ministry of Manpower's website, while to refute their findings the Government had drawn upon "classified" data to support its claim that 90 per cent of new jobs went to residents. It soon became apparent that this government figure could not be "validated independently – by academics and non-government economists – because the data is classified," noted *Straits Times* columnist Tan Tarn How.[31] It was impossible to get close to the Ministry's 90 per cent figure using publicly available data. The two castigated academics found that if the construction sector (which heavily employs foreign workers) was excluded when calculating changes in job creation, then it could be asserted that half the jobs from 1997-2002, not the Ministry's one tenth, had gone to foreigners.

The Ministry claimed that 90 per cent of the jobs went to Singapore *residents*, which covers citizens and permanent residents. It was "still a mystery how many of them were non-citizens," remarked Tan. "How many of the residents were already PRs when they landed the job, and how many were foreigners who were given PR status later?"[32] The Ministry refused to release the data that could answer these questions because it was in the "national interest" to keep the resident-vs-foreigner job statistics confidential. Revealing such data would supposedly give other countries leverage, as they would know how dependent Singapore was on their labour. But Singaporean economists have refuted this argument, contending that nationality-based job figures were unnecessary. All they wanted was a distinction between local and foreign. This would not have compromised national interest.

To deflect the debate from the issue, the Minister for Labour told Singaporeans to stop being fixated on the foreign/local job ratio and focus instead on solving the employment problem.[33] But without proper data it was difficult to tackle this problem, argued some Singaporean economists. As one said, if the Government wanted "a proper discussion, they ought to provide researchers with the proper figures". Another economist noted that other countries made comprehensive labour data publicly available. The inability of Singapore's labour economists to get accurate foreign job data caused problems for them at international conferences. While economists from other countries could present accurate findings on their countries' foreign worker numbers, the Singaporean delegation's conclusions were only estimates.

The Minister's rejoinder was to cite once more the usual national interest reasons for not giving out foreign job data, with the qualification that the Ministry might be prepared to release more sensitive data "to researchers who know how to handle" it, on a case-by-case basis.[34] Presumably only politically reliable academics would get access to such data. They could be trusted to not embarrass the Government as the NTU academics had done when they showed that the Government's efforts to recruit foreign talent was harming Singaporeans' job prospects. They both had to be vilified and their findings discredited. Confidential government data was trotted out which claimed to accurately describe the number of new jobs foreigners were taking, but the Government's lack of transparency prevented this data from being scrutinised. Opacity was practised to hide the evidence that foreigners were taking many jobs from Singaporeans and when any independent researchers proved otherwise, they were bullied into withdrawing their conclusions.

Secrecy Acts and Veiled Threats

Fear of being punished for divulging official information has done much to develop a culture of paranoia, secrecy and opacity among Singapore's civil servants.

The Official Secrets Act (OSA) of 1970 provides the main sanctions for the provision and receipt of unauthorised official information. The Act prohibits the communication of any information or document by any person holding a government office to another person not specifically authorised to receive it. The Act also makes it an offence to encourage another person to supply such a document or information.[35]

The Act harshly stipulates that the partners, directors or offices of a firm or corporation of a person found guilty under the Act are equally guilty unless they can prove that the offence of providing information illegally occurred without their knowledge or consent. Anyone suspected of contravening the Act can be arrested without a warrant. In addition, the Act allows for the president to confer the powers of a police officer on any person, including a civil servant, for the purposes of the Act. Those found guilty under the Act can be fined a maximum of S$20,000 and be jailed for 14 years.[36]

In commenting on this Act, Worthington observed:

> *The influence of this act on the maintenance of the culture of secrecy which defies accountability cannot be underestimated. In my interviews of public service officers, the inability or unwillingness of some officers to answer even the most simple of questions was based on reference to this act.*[37]

The Act appeared to induce acute paranoia in some bureaucrats. This prompted Worthington to try an unorthodox approach with one uncooperative senior official. To test the OSA's limits, Worthington asked,

> *whether the official could divulge the colour of the toilet paper used by that particular ministry – something that countless Singaporeans would have known. The official replied that this was impossible as it would infringe the act. When it was pointed out that this information could be gained by simply visiting the toilet in one of the ministry's buildings, the official replied that while that was so, nonetheless he could not divulge the information!*[38]

Further investigations of Singapore's bureaucracy by the intrepid Worthington revealed a Kafkaesque world of obsessive secrecy and surreal filing procedures. One civil servant complained that his ministry's filing system "had so many 'secret' categories, that it even had a category 'secret miscellaneous' in which everything that wasn't otherwise secret could be filed! In effect, in order to protect themselves, public servants classified almost everything as secret". The effects of the OSA had reduced the legitimate protection of the state's interests to "bureaucratic inanity".[39]

The OSA has been joined by other secrecy Acts including the Evidence Act of 1990 which forbids the production of any unpublished government records "relating to affairs of State" as court evidence without permission of the permanent secretary subject to the President's approval. It provides for civil servants to refuse to answer questions in court under several circumstances. These include disclosing written or spoken "communications made to him in official confidence...when he considers that the public interest would suffer by the disclosure".[40] The Act also prohibits a court from inspecting a document if it relates to "affairs of state". According to Worthington:

> This Act therefore provides for total control of the release of information by public officials which might be detrimental to the government and also provides substantial protection for both the government and its officials from investigation by the courts through an ambit claim of executive privilege.[41]

Another Act, the Statutory Boards and Government Companies (Protection of Secrecy) Act 1995, extends provisions similar to the OSA's to statutory boards and government companies, though the penalties are much less – a maximum fine of S$2000 and/or a year's jail. This Act applies to all 21 major statutory boards and the GIC.

In September 2003, the Evidence Act was amended to give employees of 23 statutory boards the right to withhold from the courts "sensitive information" deemed vital to national security or the national interest.[42] The "Flash Estimates" affair of 1992 demonstrates the punitive force of these Acts.

In June 1992, the SPH publication, *Business Times* (BT), carried a news report that "official flash estimates" – quick initial GDP calculations – suggested that the economic growth in April and May fell below the first quarter growth rate by 5.1 per cent".[43] Although it was no threat to national security, nor even embarrassing to the Government, the information had been leaked from the Ministry of Trade and Industry, for which Lee's son, Lee Hsien Loong, was the minister. A probe by the feared Internal Security Department (ISD), Singapore's secret police, was ordered to discover how BT had got the estimates. To justify the witch hunt, Lee Hsien Loong argued that "An open government does not mean that you condone and accept leaks of sensitive official secrets which are price-sensitive. They have to be investigated". Lee Senior chipped in by proclaiming, "You can't run a government which is leaking all over the place," smugly adding, "it would never have occurred on my watch".[44]

Eventually, in December 1992, four people, including BT editor Patrick Daniel, were charged on nine counts of breaching the OSA in connection with the news report. In March 1994, they and another BT journalist were fined the maximum of $2000 on each charge.

The BT case reveals not only the PAP state's obsession with controlling all official statistical data but its readiness to ruthlessly punish any leaks. As Cherian George notes, the prosecution of Daniel and the others was "a signal to civil servants that leaks would not be tolerated".[45] George's comments illustrate government concern about data getting into the "wrong hands" and possibly exposing the dubious nature of official statistics.

It can be seen how Singapore's secrecy Acts have produced a paranoid cover-up culture in the civil service. Suspicion can also fall on people seeking information from civil servants. Singaporean political activist James Gomez remarked:

> *Even when one seeks published information most officials may tend to be suspicious of the motives of the person or group seeking information.*[46]

Often the "researcher's problem is not so much getting the information, but fielding the questions about why he/she needs it in the first place".[47] The bureaucrats' paranoia becomes contagious. It can be so intimidating that the public may be too afraid to approach them for information. Requests for information might attract the unwelcome attention of Singapore's authorities, even the ISD. The ISD's influence is almost as pervasive in Singapore as was Stasi's in East Germany. Even such foreign stock brokerage firms as Merrill Lynch and Crosby Securities have been subjected to ISD attention. Both firms were questioned by the ISD over reports produced during 1992 that critically evaluated the Government's domestic savings policy.[48]

Such events, including the Flash Estimates case of 1992, have done much to intimidate private sector economists, foreign as well as domestic, from thoroughly analysing Singapore's investment climate. A foreign stockbroker in Singapore moved his valuables from his apartment before publishing a mildly critical article on the reasons for the Asian crisis for fear of being expelled for what he wrote.[49]

Journalists, both foreign and local, can feel inhibited from writing about Singapore because they know they must reveal their sources. This even applies in civil cases where their right to protect sources of information has been legally denied. In August 2002, Singapore's High Court ruled that journalists had to disclose their sources of information.[50] The court's judicial commissioner declared that the "newspaper rule" – a centuries-old English practice which exempts newspapers from disclosing sources of information – did not exist in Singapore. "The 'newspaper rule' has had no history in our jurisdiction for me to consider adopting purely as a matter of practice," he claimed. The commissioner made this ruling after hearing a case between a local door-manufacturing firm and SPH. The ruling meant that journalists and other commentators would be restricted in what they could report, even when covering private sector enterprises. With no guarantees of anonymity, sources would be unlikely to speak to the media in Singapore, impeding scrutiny of both private and public sector organisations. The net result is more opacity.

Past Cover-ups

Greater transparency in Singapore would expose questionable official data and also bad deals by SEs. So far governmental opacity has largely prevented this. Had such past deals been properly revealed, Singapore's rulers would have been grilled on them.

No official explanation was ever given for the Micropolis debacle, which cost S$630 million, except to say that the loss had resulted in a "diminution of the Government's assets".[51] Little information has been given about why Singtel paid such a high price for Optus in 2001 or about other corporate blunders. SIA's costly failure to acquire Air New Zealand has not been explained, nor the GIC's big loss in 2000 from its Macquarie Corporate Telecom deal in Australia, where 14 million shares bought for about S$3 each had to be subsequently sold for 18 cents.

For a long time the Government was coy about the problems in Suzhou. As late as August 1999, Deputy Prime Minister Lee Hsien Loong refused to give a full financial statement on the Suzhou project to Parliament, saying it was "not appropriate".[52] It was not for Parliament but the companies which had invested in Suzhou to examine the project's finances, he said.

Singapore's SEs have also been evasive about their more questionable mergers. First there was the tie-up between Keppel Bank, a GLC company, and Tat Lee Bank.[53] Tat Lee, a private bank, had loan exposures in Malaysia, Indonesia, Thailand and South Korea, amounting to $1.16 billion in 1997, and had incurred bad loans of up to $589 million.[54] At one point Tat Lee's share price dropped 35 per cent.[55] But Keppel, funded by public money, agreed to the merger. Few questions were asked or answers given.

In 1998, one of the Government's biggest GLCs, Singapore Technologies, merged with another GLC, Sembawang Corporation, which was "debt-laden".[56] In 1998 alone the company's debt hit S$1.2 billion, with only S$446 million cash on hand.[57] This "was not the first time the Government effectively stepped in to help such companies," said one analyst. The Government failed to properly explain this merger.

One of the biggest dubious mergers was between the Post Office Savings Bank (POSBank) and DBS. POSBank was a solid public bank which had served lower-income Singaporeans for decades without incurring debts or losses. But DBS was bleeding from bad investments throughout Asia. During a 12-month period amidst the Asian economic crisis in 1998 the bank's non-performing loans throughout Malaysia, Indonesia, Thailand, South Korea and the Philippines had exploded from S$1.1 billion to S$7 billion.[58] Thai Danu accounted for 41 per cent of the non-performing loans. DBS merely announced that the Thai Danu deal had been an "expensive mistake". Neither the government bank nor bank officials provided any answers, though the Government announced that DBS would take over POSBank. "By the time Singaporeans found out about this arrangement, the acquisition was all but a done deal," noted Chee. [59]

Opacity not only covers up bad deals but facilitates *fait accompli*. Policies can be implemented before they can be questioned or even reversed. Singaporeans have long complained about the Government's lack of transparency, but it is something that Singapore's neo-con cheer squads are usually unaware of. The Government's constant appeals for greater transparency obscure Singapore's opacity to foreign eyes. Even so, various domestic and international pressures are forcing Singapore to practice increased transparency.

Growing Demands for Transparency

After Asia's 1997/8 crisis, global business and financial circles called for greater transparency – along with increased accountability and corporate governance. Initially, to maintain Singapore's international image, PAP rulers paid the usual lip service to such calls. Finance Minister Richard Hu noted that the WEF had found that Singapore trailed developed countries in corporate governance (which includes transparency). If Singapore was to position itself as a world-class business centre, then high standards of disclosure and accountability were necessary, he said. [60]

In December 2000, a government committee called for greater corporate disclosures and transparency.[61] Soon after it became apparent that such openness would not apply to statutory boards or many GLCs. In July 2001, the Singapore Parliament passed a bill extending the provisions of the Official Secrets Act to 21 statutory boards, including the CPF Board, EDB, the MAS and the Defence Science and Technology Agency.[62] The legislation aimed to protect sensitive official information but perpetuated the opacity of state bodies and contradicted government calls for greater transparency.

Understandably, since 2000 foreign and local demands have been mounting for more transparency, especially by Singapore's SEs. First there were growing domestic pressures for information on how well the GIC was investing the country's reserves. Lee Kuan Yew's assurances in 2000 that the GIC was already outperforming global investment benchmarks were no longer deemed sufficient by GIC critics. A publication in 2001 commemorating the GIC's 20th anniversary revealed an unprecedented amount of information about its successes and failures,[63] but much about GIC operations and investment remained secret.

Meanwhile, such major Singapore SEs as Temasek faced foreign pressure for greater transparency. Initially this came from the bond ratings agencies and was mainly directed at Temasek, which was planning to expand into Asia and was seeking a credit rating for bonds it wished to market. This would have required greater transparency from this very secretive SE. Ratings agencies such as Standard & Poor and Moody's Investors Services would not issue credit ratings for Temasek until they had adequate information. A S&P report in late 2001 on Singapore's GLCs cited the lack of transparency in corporate credit as one of the obstacles to the development of the Singapore dollar bond market. The lack of information about Temasak made it difficult to identify its financial profile with certainty, S&P noted. [64]

Foreign corporate interests had also expressed concern at dealing with such a large and opaque Singaporean state entity as Temasek and its various GLCs. This was most apparent when two major Temasek GLCs – Singtel and SIA – sought to venture offshore to buy into industries of foreign countries with defence and security links. Failed bids by Singtel in Hong Kong and Malaysia after the 1997/8 Asian crisis were blamed in part on perceptions that the telco lacked independence from the Singapore Government.[65] The New Zealand Government refused to back an SIA bid to take a controlling share in Air New Zealand because of Prime Minister Helen Clark's reservations about the national carrier being "effectively controlled by the Singapore Government".[66]

In Australia, concerns about letting Singtel take over Optus were expressed by some Australian business leaders, including Australian media tycoon Kerry Stokes. They found Singapore's reputation as a police state worrying. Allowing one of Australia's biggest telcos to be owned by an "opaque" organisation controlled by a foreign police state was not to many Australians' liking. Singtel prevailed – but only after paying S$5 billion too much for Optus. Nonetheless, some governments are uneasy about enterprises controlled by a foreign government like Singapore's investing in their economies.

Pressure for greater transparency by Singapore has come from its FTAs with the US and Australia. During the two-year Singapore-US FTA negotiations Temasek and other GLCs came under increasing American scrutiny. US negotiators were being lobbied by the Coalition of Service Industries (CSI) to press for less opaque Singaporean SEs, especially Temasek. The CSI represented various US corporate interests who were seeking improved access to the Singapore economy under the guise of calling for a more transparent regulatory and licensing regime.[67] The CSI wanted the Singapore Government to remove the limit on the number of US banks allowed to operate with full banking licenses, and to permit American bank card issuers to have access to the automatic teller machine network of domestic banks. Engineering, legal and pharmaceutical firms and US financial institutions were also lobbying for access to the Singapore market on equal terms with local companies. The CSI said that licensing regimes should be open and include explanations by Singaporean regulators for unsuccessful applications. The US lobbyists also sought more details on how SEs were run and by whom, as well as other ownership information. Rodan noted, "The concept of transparency was at times a conspicuous means towards an end".[68] The real aim was to ensure a more level playing field for US concerns in Singapore.

In response to FTA and other pressures, such Singaporean SEs as Temasek became somewhat more transparent. In 2004, Temasek released its first report ever in 30 years. While it revealed some new information about itself, much remained hidden. Unlike normal company reports, there was nothing about how much Temasek directors and senior management were paid, complained analysts.[69] Also, S$13.5 billion had been spent on intangibles but there were no footnotes explaining what they were, as is customary in company reports. One analyst said the report still left "many questions unanswered". Not being a listed company, Temasek could disclose whatever it wished. Even so, on the basis of what Temasak had revealed, including its vast assets, S&P and Moody both gave Temasek a AAA rating.

Classified as an "exempt private company" by the Government, Temasek is not required to make its accounts public. Only Temasek's board of directors and its sole shareholder (the Ministry of Finance) receive its annual reports. When Temasek announced it would be making its annual report public for the first time the aim was to provide information "in a measured way ... to clear any misapprehension and misunderstanding concerning Temasek";[70] but it added that "Total transparency is not possible nor desirable".[71] The need for commercial confidentiality and "market sensitivities" were cited. Clearly, information was only going to be released in a "measured way" to satisfy credit ranking agencies and foreign capital.

A similar attitude is taken by the MAS regarding the divulging of information on Singapore's monetary reserves.[72] In response to requests for such information, the MAS replied that "our policies of not disclosing the annual rate of return on reserves is to avoid undue emphasis on year-to-year variations in returns that would detract from MAS' core objectives".

Such reluctance by Singapore's monetary authorities contrasts markedly with their support for an International Monetary Fund (IMF) scheme requiring countries to provide information about their reserves and foreign investments.[73] In 1996, Singapore was in the first group of 34 countries to subscribe to the scheme which obliged countries to reveal information about portfolio investment abroad, broken down into debt and equity assets and data on reserve assets. Even such disclosures to the IMF have not resulted in greater openness when the budget has been tabled in Singapore's parliament. The budget presented to parliament by the Finance Minister has excluded investment and interest income, capital receipts and net lending by the Government through budget and debt transactions.[74] None of these items has been debated by parliament. Singapore's readiness to sign on to IMF schemes may have impressed the IMF, but have not increased budgetary transparency back home.

A more recent demonstration of official opacity occurred when HDB Corp (a wholly-owned HDB subsidiary) was sold to Temasek in November 2004. No tender was called for the sale and both parties were tight-lipped about the price, merely announcing that it was a "mutually agreed" sum.[75] Only a week later, after much public criticism about the deal's opacity, did the HDB reveal that HDB Corp had been sold to Temasek for S$117 million.[76] This seemed well below normal market prices, according to local housing industry analysts.[77] They said a gauge of the transaction value would be the average price-earnings ratio of construction firms. Construction stocks were trading at an average price-earnings ratio of 23 in November 2004. Applying that to the HDB Corp's net profit of S$8.7 million, a price of about S$200 million emerged. The net asset value of HDB Corp was S$144.9 million and it had an issued paid-up capital of S$142.6 million. At S$117 million HDB Corp was a steal for Temasek.

In commenting on the deal, Singapore's *Business Times* asked why there had been no tender and no transparency on the price. The "lack of disclosure runs counter ... to the growing emphasis on corporate governance" in Singapore. In effect "it was a left hand to right hand deal – a shuffling of assets and holding companies by the government".[78] Would not a better price have been achieved had there been a tender, BT asked, implying it would have. That would seem to explain why no tender had been called. The deal was done secretly to ensure that Temasek acquired HDB Corp at nearly half the normal market price. Had tenders been called and the purchase been transparent, Temasek would most likely have had to pay a much higher price for HDB Corp. The opaque nature of the deal violated normal market principles of transparency and open bidding.

Despite conspicuous efforts to practise transparency, largely in response to FTAs, the Singapore Government's commitment to it remains limited. Opaque behaviour still prevailed in Singapore's SE sector in 2004. Nonetheless, Singapore continues to be pressured by the major economies, especially the US, for all its SEs, including the GIC and Temasek, to be more transparent. These pressures are likely to increase as Singapore seeks to increase its global economic integration through such means as FTAs. The USSFTA – and to a lesser extent the Singapore-Australia Free Trade Agreement (SAFTA) – have brought a significant degree of scrutiny to Singapore's SEs. This has forced them to display some increased transparency and to contemplate at least the prospects of competing on a more level playing field. But they are likely to fight a strong rearguard action. Rodan predicts that the "Singapore government may attempt to delay, deflect and finesse" any unscheduled FTA commitments on transparency and competition policy. "In any case, the strength of the GLCs within the domestic economy is such that even with the agreements they are unlikely to be dislodged in a hurry".[79] Any increased transparency would most likely be confined to the SE sector. For Rodan:

The government has been careful to distance its reforms from ideas about media freedom, political accountability and citizens' rights to information.[80]

Singapore's rulers continue to govern in opaque ways, and display a lack of personal accountability that would not be tolerated in a more democratic and transparent state. For example, government ministers have not been required to publicly record their financial interests and investments to identify potential conflicts of interest.[81] Such opaque practices are unlikely to change under current PAP rule.

But while the PAP state may be reluctant to practice greater transparency it has insisted that the local private sector do so.

Private Sector Secrecy

Not only the PAP state but also Singapore's private sector has traditionally displayed significant opacity. Singapore's banks have been particularly notorious for covering things up. This was revealed by a survey done in 1997 by ING Barings Securities of the banking systems of eight Asian countries. The study examined their disclosure policies – frequency of accounts released, balance sheet details, profit and loss details, cash flow statements and risk profiles. Singapore scored 21 for its disclosure policies while Hong Kong got 79, Malaysia 72, Indonesia 63, Philippines 57, Taiwan 47, Thailand 45 and Korea 42.[82]

Singapore banks' lack of transparency became apparent during the 1997/8 Asian financial crisis. As Lee Kuan Yew admitted, "we persuaded our banks to abandon their practice of maintaining hidden reserves and not disclosing their non-performing loans".[83] Even so, in October 1999 the MAS said that Singapore banks' disclosure standards were still some distance from top international practices.[84] In May 2001, the European Union named Singapore among 25 countries whose banking systems had poor transparency and supervision.[85] In 2000, a US State Department report noted that Singapore's banking system "provided opportunities for money launderers to conduct a wide range of illicit transactions".[86] But Singapore's banks could use the country's defamation laws against anyone who publicised such claims. This was the view of Phillipe Delhaise, a French financial analyst who wrote a book about the Asian financial crisis entitled *Asia in Crisis: The Implosion of the Banking and Financial Systems*. He refused to discuss Singapore banks because of fears that they, including the government-controlled ones, could sue him under Singapore law.[87] Delhaise recognised how readily Singapore's law punished commentators who wrote critically of private as well as state sector concerns.

Cultural Factors

Apart from Secrecy Acts and other forms of intimidation, legal and otherwise, cultural factors contribute to Singapore's high opacity levels. Singapore's low trust values discourage openness and the sharing of information. Such mindsets would largely explain the slow development of its credit bureaux. Since its establishment in mid-2002, a credit bureau for SMEs had only enrolled 100 members by May 2004.[88] The bureau was set up to provide a repository of SME credit information. SMEs were required to disclose information such as their account receivables and transactions with vendors and customers. Few Singaporean companies were willing to do this. A Citibank official put it down to the "Asian mentality" which was averse to transparency.

A credit bureau for banks established in November 2002 also made little progress. The refusal of Singapore's banks to share customer data delayed the bureau's development into a fully fledged credit agency. By March 2004, the agency was one of the region's least sophisticated, according to a senior Standard Chartered banker. "What's keeping it there is that the banks have decided they don't want to share information," he said.[89] Credit bureaux in Taiwan, Thailand, Malaysia and Hong Kong gather more customer information than Singapore's. Banks in Singapore were afraid that the bureau would be "turned into a fishing ground" for a bank's competitors to access its customer data, said one bank. The banks were displaying the Singaporean fear of sharing information.

* * * * * * * * *

Various ratings bodies have given the misleading impression that Singapore is very transparent. In TI's case such erroneous claims have been due to definitional deficiencies. TI has confused transparency with corruption. Because Singapore has little overt corruption, it supposedly has high transparency levels. Other agencies have also conflated low corruption with transparency, and with such factors as a favourable investment environment that has clear, accurate and widely used business practices.

Such notions of transparency once more reflect the interests of foreign capital and its need to locate profitable investment havens. Because Singapore serves foreign capital so well it inevitably scores highly on TI's and other "transparency" surveys. Despite this, Singapore was and still is a very opaquely run economy and society. For decades the operations (and failures) of its two biggest SEs, the GIC and Temasek, have been shrouded in secrecy, as have the activities of the state sector generally. The public are regularly denied access to official records and data, as Worthington and others have shown, and cultural factors accentuate Singapore's opacities, both official and otherwise.

Although the ratings bodies who presume to measure transparency have missed Singapore's many blatant opacities, foreign capital can quickly recognise Singapore's lack of transparency when necessary. US lobby group CSI demonstrated this when seeking a more even playing field for American firms wishing to compete with Singapore's SEs. CSI demands for more information on how SEs were run and by whom revealed its awareness of how opaque Singapore's state sector still was.

Despite Singapore's pervasive opacity, both local and external pressures are forcing such SEs as Temasek to become more transparent, though as Rodan pointed out, the PAP Government's policies for promoting transparency have "involved a limited and selective notion of transparency".[90] Greater media and public access to official information and more transparent political decision-making are excluded. Moreover, "the government has attempted to shield GLCs and other state economic interests from this process and to ensure authorities retain a significant degree of discretionary control over information".[91] Instead, the "bulk of the reforms have been directed at improving disclosures of private commercial interests and data facilitating them". In other words Singapore's local private sector is going to bear the brunt of the Government's transparency policies, not the state sector. Under the PAP, Singapore officialdom is likely to remain very opaque for some time despite government rhetoric to the contrary. Do as we say, not as we do, is again the real message.

Apart from being a secretive PAP state, much of Singapore's opacity is due to cultural factors that discourage openness. Were Singapore's rulers to vigorously implement transparency, it would take time for transparent mindsets to permeate non-government sectors. Cultural factors will slow down any move by Singapore towards a more transparent society.

References

1. *The Straits Times* (ST), February 15, 1999.
2. Rodan, Garry: *Transparency and Authoritarian Rule in Southeast Asia* (London, RoutledgeCurzon, 2004), p. 58.
3. Transparency International (TI) reports for 1998-2006; (www.transparency.org).
3a. TI 2007 report.
5. ST, January 3, 1999.
6. ST, November 28, 2000.
7. Ibid.
8. ST, January 27, 2001.
9. *Business Times* (BT), September 29, 2004.
10. Chee, Soon Juan: *Your Future, My Faith, Our Freedom* (Singapore, Open Singapore Centre, 2001), p. 72.
11. Low, Linda: "State Entrepreneurship", p. 147 in *Local Entrepreneurship in Singapore*, edited by Tsao Yuan Lee and Linda Low (Singapore, Times Academic Press; 1990).
12. Rodan, p. 196.
13. Ibid, p. 55.
14. Worthington, Ross: *Governance in Singapore* (London, RoutledgeCurzon, 2003), p. 200.
15. Ibid, p. 318.

16. Low in Lee and Low (1990), p. 148
17. Ibid, p. 153.
18. Low in Lee and Low (1990), p. 150.
19. Chee, p. 73.
20. Ibid.
21. Ibid, p. 75.
22. Lee, Kuan Yew: *From Third World To First* (Singapore, Times Media, 2000), p. 97.
23. ST, March 13, 2000.
24. ST, May 23, 2001.
25. ST, April 27, 2001.
26. ST, May 4, 2001.
27. ST, July 17, 1999.
28. ST, August 1, 2003.
29. Ibid.
30. ST, August 2, 2003.
31. ST, August 9, 2003.
32. Ibid.
33. ST, August 9, 2003.
34. ST, August 2, 2003.
35. Article 16 (3) of the Singapore Constitution.
36. Ibid.
37. Worthington, p. 137.
38. Ibid.
39. Ibid.
40. Worthington, p. 139.
41. Ibid.
42. ST, September 3, 2003.
43. Seow, Francis T.: *The Media Enthralled: Singapore Revisited* (Boulder, Colorado; Lynne Rienner, 1998), p. 218.
44. Seow, p. 218.
45. George, Cherian: *Singapore: The Air-conditioned Nation* (London, Landmark Books, 2000), p. 66.
46. Gomez, James: *Internet Politics: Surveillance and Intimidation in Singapore* (Singapore, Think Centre, 2002, p. 55.
47. Ibid.
48. Rodan, p. 53.
49. Ibid, p. 75.
50. *The West Australian*, August 17, 2002.
51. ST, January 15, 1998.
52. ST, August 20, 1999.
53. ST Interactive, January 13, 1998.
54. *South China Morning Post*, March 5, 1998.
55. ST Interactive, January 13, 1998.
56. Chee, p. 81.
57. *Far Eastern Economic Review*, June 11, 1998.
58. Chee, pp. 81-2.
59. Ibid.
60. ST, December 17, 1999.
61. ST, December 7, 2000.
62. ST, July 12, 2001.
63. Ellis, Eric: "Inching towards transparency", *Fortune*, August 13, 2002.
64. Rodan, p. 66.
65. Ibid, p. 65.
66. Ibid.
67. Ibid, p. 68.
68. Ibid.
69. *Today*, October 13, 2004.
70. ST, March 24, 2004.
71. ST, April 1, 2004.
72. ST, October 5, 2004.
73. Rodan, p. 61.
74. Ibid, p. 196.
75. *Business Times* (BT), December 1, 2004.
76. ST, December 7, 2004.
77. BT, December 1, 2004.
78. BT, December 2, 2004.
79. Ibid.
80. Rodan, p. 49.
81. Ibid, p. 72.
82. *Sunday Times* (Singapore), February 16, 1997.
83. Lee, p. 102.
84. ST, October 27, 1999.
85. ST, May 9, 2001.
86. Ibid.
87. Cited in Worthington, pp. 140 and 312.
88. ST, May 5, 2004.
89. ST, March 29, 2004.
90. Rodan, p. 49.
91. Ibid.

CHAPTER 16

GOOD FOR BUSINESS?

Singapore is not only one of the world's freest and most transparent countries but also a top business venue, according to the global ratings industry. Singapore is ranked highly, sometimes gets the top spot for a range of attributes that foreign capital considers important, and is depicted as a good place to do business. This chapter first describes these assessments and then considers whether Singapore provides a favourable climate for local enterprises, both government-controlled and private.

1. Good for MNCs

Singapore scores well on criteria used to measure its suitability as a venue for foreign capital, including profitability, risk levels, the ease and cost of doing business and quality of living.

High Profits

Singapore has been billed as a favourable and profitable venue for foreign capital since the 1960s. As Bello and Rosenfeld noted: "Whether American, Japanese or European, most investors have not been disappointed by the benefits accorded by the PAP's state foreign investment regime." [1] For example, from 1979 to 1984 the average rate of return for US investment in Singapore was 35.4 per cent, compared to 16.9 per cent for Hong Kong, 18.4 per cent for Taiwan and 15.2 per cent for South Korea. [2]

Since then, Singapore has remained a lucrative venue for foreign capital. In 1997 and 1998, BERI ranked Singapore as the second most profitable country after Switzerland for foreign businesses. [3] But from the early 1990s, the returns on capital for foreign enterprises in Singapore began to fluctuate significantly. The rate of return for US MNCs in Singapore fell below 20 per cent after 1992 and was only 8.7 per cent in 2002 and 11.6 per cent in 2003. [4] But by 2006 their return had risen to 21.3 per cent compared to a worldwide yield of 12.2 per cent. Elsewhere in the Asia-Pacific region, returns for US MNCs were 16 per cent in Hong Kong, 12.9 per cent in Japan and 6.2 per cent in Australia.

Singapore's profitability for MNCs is due to low wages and corporate taxes, which at 18 per cent are the second-lowest in Asia after Hong Kong's 16 per cent. Both factors are plusses for Singapore, according to its Department of Statistics (DOS), which admits that companies in Singapore have a "relatively low remuneration share and high profit share" compared to industrial economies and NIEs.[5] Deliberate efforts by the Government to keep down wages has ensured high investment returns. Singapore's wages' share of GDP is 42 per cent, the lowest of Asia's NIEs. But company profits are 48 per cent of GDP. Of the countries surveyed by the DOS only Thailand's profit percentage is higher.

The DOS also reported that Singapore had the highest profit-to-remuneration ratio among the industrial countries and NIEs. "This is consistent with the view that multinational corporations investing in Singapore have been able to obtain relatively high returns". But the MNCs have benefitted at the cost of the Singapore worker, whose wages are well below those of their peers in developed countries, as Chapter 23 shows.

Despite high profits, Singapore's business costs have been a periodic worry for MNCs operating there. By the mid-1990s, the island's booming property prices had pushed up rentals for offices and accommodation. But by 2002 property prices had fallen to make Singapore the 35th most expensive business district out of 92 surveyed.[6] By March 2004, Singapore had slipped to the world's 46th most expensive city, according to Mercer Human Resource Consulting.[7] However, with the surge in Singapore's property prices again from 2006, it had become, by 2007, the 14th most expensive city of 143 cities surveyed by Mercer.[8]

Low Risk

Apart from profitability, a country's business risk profile and ease of doing business are also important considerations for foreign enterprises.

Hong Kong-based Political and Risk Consultancy (PERC), compiles risk reports on Asian countries for foreign capital. PERC, which has been operating since 1976, sees business risk as being determined by:

- Existing markets
- Potential for economic change
- Systematic deficiencies and potential for socio-political change.

PERC rankings for the first two risk factors are derived from such variables as population, GDP growth, the inflation rate, historical data and forecasts. They are measured by PERC analysts and through surveys of 200 managers and bankers in the countries being studied. PERC ranked Singapore as the least risky country in 2006 of 12 Asian countries.[9] Singapore scored well in several areas, including domestic political risks, the quality of government policies and its institutions like the civil service, judiciary and police.

PERC also rated Singapore as the least corrupt of 13 Asian countries in 2007[10] and has been giving Singapore top scores for low corruption levels since the 1990s. Similarly, PERC regularly ranks Singapore, along with Hong Kong, as having the best judicial system in Asia. PERC also gave Singapore top ranking for personal safety in Asia in 1996.[11]

The World Bank has been another organisation to award Singapore top scores for attributes prized by foreign capital. In 2008, the bank ranked Singapore No. 1 for ease on doing business out of 172 countries surveyed.[12] The bank's prime focus was to measure how conducive a country's regulatory environment was for business. Criteria assessed included: starting a business, employing workers, protection for investors, paying of taxes and enforcement of contracts. Singapore's top ranking was largely because of its low corporate taxes, protection from nationalisation, a legal system capable of enforcing contracts and the freedom of employers to hire and fire at will.

Similar world corporate concerns were reflected in Mastercard's rankings of the Top 50 Cities for Business in 2007, when it gave Singapore 6th spot.[13] The legal and political framework, economic stability, ease of doing business and how well the city facilitates the flow of goods, services, people, finances and information were assessed.

Comfortable Lifestyles

Both a country's quality and cost of living (its "liveability") are other concerns for foreign enterprises and their staff. Here too Singapore scores well. Singapore was 34th for quality of living in 2007 out of 215 cities surveyed by Mercer Human Resource Consulting.[14] Singapore was also the highest ranked of all Asian cities, beating Tokyo and other Japanese cities. Criteria used included health and sanitation, schools and education, public services and transportation, recreation, consumer goods, housing, socio-cultural and natural environment.

However, since about 2006, Singapore's high cost of living, largely because of soaring rentals, has made it an expensive place to live for expats. Also, car prices in Singapore are several times more than those in most Western countries, further boosting living costs for expats, as Chapter 23 shows.

Even so, the prevalance of Westernised lifestyles and a population that speaks the best English in Asia makes Singapore a comfortable posting for expatriates. A PERC survey found Singapore to be Asia's least xenophobic country, noting that Singaporeans were "more patriotic than nationalistic".[15] Expatriates rated Singapore as one of the "very few places in Asia where nationalist sentiment rarely impinges negatively on the business environment".

Singapore's stable, if quasi-authoritarian state, with its strong support for foreign investment, provides a profitable, low-risk business environment for MNCs and an agreeable lifestyle for expatriates generally. Also, doing business in Singapore in much easier than in other Asian countries. Its legal system, sophisticated banking and finance systems and communications and transport infrastructures are user-friendly for foreign firms. Moreover, corruption is a minimal problem. The bureaucracy follows the rules and woe betide any public servant found taking bribes. The high scores for the legal system too are appropriate. In non-political cases, especially those of a commercial nature, the judiciary is equal to that of any in the West and Singapore's crime rate is generally lower. The streets of Singapore are much safer to walk at night than those of most Western cities.

Political representatives of foreign capital regularly pay homage to Singapore as a good investment venue. One has been Caspar Weinberger, former US Defense Secretary and Chairman of Forbes. He praised Singapore for maintaining a business environment conducive to "attracting multinational corporations".[16] He was particularly pleased with how the Singapore Government had reduced wages by "making cuts in bonuses and the required contributions to social security". Singapore's leaders bask in such US Republican accolades that confirm their country's attractiveness to foreign investment. Although wage cuts reduce the income of Singaporean workers, this matters little to MNC operatives such as Weinberger or Singapore's always eager-to-please-foreign-capital leadership. Being a tart for foreign capital requires such a mentality.

2. Good for SEs

Like the MNCs, Singapore's SEs have a privileged position in the economy. Both GLCs and statutory authorities have several advantages over the local private sector. They are:

- Political connections
- State support and favours, including cheap capital
- Artifically high credit worthiness and greater appeal to share market investors
- Protection from public scrutiny.

The biggest advantage for Singapore's SEs is the close liasion between them and the state political sector. "There is an almost incestuous relationship between the government and the bureaucracy as top civil servants have gone into politics to reach ministerial posts under the practice of meritocracy and elitism," observes Low.[17] Conversely, the *amakudari* mechanism provides cabinet ministers and ex-civil service heads with positions as CEOs or as directors on SE boards when they retire. Such cosy arrangements give SE managements ready access to government thinking and changing attitudes. All this constitutes access to inside information that the private sector rarely has. As Prime Minister Lee Kuan Yew said in 1987,

> *these government-owned companies at present are from a tight circle of administrators who share the thinking of the policy-makers. They share the Government's economic philosophy and have a firm grasp of the rationale for various policies since they are privy to background problems so that they can interpret signals accurately, and react swiftly and flexibly.*[18]

Lee's comments were prompted by his concern at plans to begin privatising GLCs in the late 1980s. He was afraid that once privatised, the senior managers of these former government enterprises "would be cut off from the inner sanctum of government *and would not react as insiders*"[19] (my italics). They could be more easily briefed about government policies if they remained in the state "family" of companies. Low noted, "This in turn implies that there is a real advantage in terms of information channels and connections enjoyed by these State managers, which may constitute a factor for their success."[20] As business people know, inside information confers enormous advantages over uninformed rivals. Acts were passed in 1973 and again in 1984 to restrict access to information about statutory authorities and GLCs, as Chapter 15 showed.

Besides inside information and contacts, GLCs enjoy state support and favours by firstly being granted licenses or concessions to operate. This is the case with such GLCs as Singapore Airlines and Primary Industries Enterprises (PIE). The Government has also arranged the purchase of products and services for Singapore Aircraft Industries (SAI) and Singapore National Printers (SNP).

The Government has also supported SE operations through cheap finance. Fernand and Nieman said that from the 1970s interest on government-directed commercial loans was 3 per cent less than the bank lending rate.[21] (But in the 1980s the Government stopped publishing such interest rate information.) Burton too reports that for GLCs, "the costs of capital are usually lower than for companies in the private sector".[22] And the US Embassy in Singapore notes that "GLCs were given preferential rates by DBS Bank, itself a GLC".[23]

Moreover, the Government bails out GLCs should insolvency loom, as already shown. "No large and few small GLCs have been declared bankrupt, despite some incurring serious losses," noted an Australian Foreign Affairs and Trade report.[24] The Government has also protected GLCs from the effects of open competition, as was shown with Singtel and Starhub in 2000, when the Government paid out S$2 billion to compensate them for the introduction of competition.

PAP state support for GLCs have done much to raise their credit worthiness and appeal to share market investors. "Being linked to Government is of course useful," noted one GLC manager. "It gives the company credibility and nobody will think you are a fly-by-night operation," he said.[25] Ramirez and Tan calculated, in a study of publicly-listed GLCs from 1994-8, that they enjoyed a stock market premium of more than 20 per cent.[26] They concluded that "performance measures aside, the capital markets seem to reward substantially the very fact that a company is linked to the government".

Another advantage for many SEs is not being listed on the stock exchange. Being unlisted, they do not normally pay dividends, which significantly boosts their bottom line. It also relieves them of the need to provide annual reports or practise other forms of accountability and transparency, privileges the GIC and Temasek have had for decades. In addition, Singapore's SEs have enjoyed the privileges of closed-door deals on occasion. Not only did Temasek acquire HDB Corp without tendering, but tenders have not been called on other SE deals. In 1998, Posbank was sold to DBS Bank, another Temasek company; the other local banks – United Overseas Bank, OCBC and Overseas Union Bank – were not invited to tender.[27] Two years later, DBS sold its stake in DBS Land to Pidemco Land, another GLC. No other suiters were reportedly allowed.

SEs have a charmed life and enjoy many advantages and privileges over the private sector. They face little competition, have access to inside information and often operate under a cloak of secrecy which shields them from scrutiny and censure. They also have ready access to state finance. The Government usually bails them out should insolvency loom. And not only are SEs cossetted but so are their staff. High salaries and other benefits make life as sweet for them as for the companies they run. Overall few market economies provide such a benign and lucrative environment for SEs – and MNCs – as Singapore's. But the same can not be said for Singapore's local private sector, especially the SMEs.

Not so Good for SMEs

SMEs have the hardest time in most market economies. Difficulties raising capital, limited resources for surviving market downturns, and often crippling competition from large corporations and MNC rivals are regular SME problems. Singapore's SMEs face these problems plus more: they are also hit hard by excessive red tape, high government charges and policies that curb consumer spending.

Crippling Competition

From the late 1960s the situation of Singapore's SMEs began to worsen with the rise of SEs and the Government's open-door policies to MNCs. Various policies were implemented which gave SEs and MNCs a central place in the economy at the expense of the local private sector. Often crushing SE/MNC competition has kept this sector, especially its SMEs, stunted and underdeveloped.

Initially, the greatest competition for SMEs came from the MNCs when they began arriving enmass from the mid-1960s. "Without the protection enjoyed by domestic producers in Taiwan and South Korea, the failure rate for local entrepreneurs was quite high," observed Bello and Rosenfeld.[28] By 1978, 38 per cent of wholly-owned Singaporean enterprises established since 1960 had gone under, revealed Lee Kuan Yew.[29] In 1986, a report by a small businessman's organisation blamed the paucity of local entrepreneurs on the Government's pro-MNC policies. As Clad remarked in 1989: "Singaporeans have been traditionally entrepreneurial. But an economic policy which stresses the role of foreign investment in manufacturing inevitably forces the local entrepreneur into a lesser role."[30] The Government's open-door policies for foreign capital not only unleashed MNC competition on local firms but denied them many new business opportunities. The Government's view was that MNCs, with their vast capital resources and global export capacities, could far more effectively industrialise Singapore than local enterprises.

The MNCs were allowed to pioneer new industries in Singapore which, at least to some extent, indigenous concerns could also have developed. MNCs which did this qualified for pioneer status and were given big tax breaks and other government help for developing new industries. While foreign enterprises received official support, indigenous concerns were neglected by the state. Not surprisingly, local "businesses resent not only the lack of protection in their home market but also the fact that government incentives have actively discriminated in favour of the multinationals."[30a]

Because of the Government's blatantly pro-MNC policies, foreign enterprises have taken a progressively more central role in the economy. In 1966/7, the foreign share of Singapore's GDP was 10 per cent but by 1998 it had risen to 42 per cent.[31] Had the Government protected local businesses from foreign competition and helped them as much as the MNCs, Singapore's local private sector would have been far more developed than it is.

However when the Government "opted for a strategy of making multinationals the engine of growth, the PAP technocratic elite envisioned a situation in which the foreign corporations would stimulate the growth of local industries that would service them," explained Bello and Rosenfeld.[32] But this strategy had very limited success, with foreign firms only sourcing 25 per cent of their input from local firms by the mid-1980s. "When [MNCs] did establish complementary relations with local entrepreneurs, it often ended with the former dominating and eventually buying out the latter."[33]

Also, as already shown, there has been little technological transfer between the MNCs and local concerns servicing them. Other benefits that MNCs have brought to the indigenous sector have been moderate at best as was revealed in a 1997 study of an Economic Development Board (EDB) scheme to "promote linkage development" between MNCs and local firms in Singapore.[34] The study, by NUS academics Perry and Tan, found that MNCs gave "a low priority to linkage localisation".[35] MNCs wanted to "retain flexibility in subcontractor selection" and had increased their ability to "manage spatially dispersed supply linkages".[36] The MNCs did not want to confine themselves to suppliers in one country but sought to be free to seek out the cheapest and best suppliers wherever they could. This has limited the development of long-term supply linkages between MNCs and Singaporean enterprises. "Locally owned supporting industries are typically confined to relatively low-value operations. For example, in the printed boards assembly sector, local firms account for 71% of total establishments and only 14% of value."[37] However, there have been "individual cases of local firms acquiring independent technological capacity in activities such as circuit board and other subassemblies".[38] Even so, Singapore continues to attract little of the MNCs' R&D capacity. "Without access to the core R&D process, Singapore SMEs are relegated to comparatively routine low-value production," observed Perry and Tan.[39] Moreover, the constant readiness by MNCs to relocate to cheaper locales keeps their Singaporean suppliers in a dependent and underdeveloped relationship to them.

Unlike those of Taiwan and South Korea, state policies in Singapore have largely failed to ensure MNC technology was transferred to local enterprises. "As a consequence the crowding out of SMEs by the more profitable and prestigious MNC sector has constrained the upgrading of the support sector."[40]

The MNCs not only failed to act as a locomotive for the growth of local enterprise but "competed with domestic entrepreneurs for the small Singapore market," observed Singaporean economist Lim Chong Yah.[41] The MNCs had brand-name advantages and access to the parent companies' resources in the areas of technology, finance, management and marketing expertise. This unequal battle, claimed a Singapore small businessmen's group, led to local enterprises being snuffed out by foreign competitors "through predatory pricing launched from protected home bases".[42] Local construction and retail companies, added Singaporean economist Lee Tsao Yuan, have had to contend with "the entry of large Japanese and Korean companies which have the ability to bid competitively and withstand short-run losses in order to gain market share."[43]

In the 2000s MNC competition continued to be a major problem for the local private sector. A 2002 survey found that Singapore enterprises believed they were much more highly affected by foreign competition than local enterprises in other countries, as data from the survey shows.[44]

Table 16.1 – Perceptions of foreign competition by Singapore companies.

	Company	Size	Sector			Totals	
	SME	Large	Mfg.	Distrib.	Finance	S/pore	Global
Degree affected							
Low	34.8	26.3	30.5	34.7	45.4	34.3	68.3
Moderate	31.1	24.9	17.0	38.7	15.8	30.8	15.7
High	34.2	48.9	52.5	26.6	38.8	34.9	15.2

This table shows that Singaporean companies see foreign competition impacting them far more than do indigenous enterprises in the nine other countries surveyed (US, Mexico, Brazil, Germany, France, Denmark, Taiwan, China and Japan). While 68.3 per cent of companies in the total sample thought that they were little affected by competition from foreign companies within their country, only 34.9 per cent of Singapore enterprises did. Also, while 34.9 per cent of Singapore companies said they were highly affected by foreign competition, only 15.2 per cent of all companies in the total sample said they were. In Singapore, local companies in the manufacturing and finance sectors, where foreign ownership is very high, experience foreign competition most intensely.

Domestic and foreign firms in Singapore also compete for indigenous talent, as well as market share. For decades, the local private sector has complained about how the MNCs, like the SEs, poach Singaporean talent.

SE competition has greatly accentuated the plight of Singapore's local private and SME sectors. While local firms were confronted with MNC competition from the 1960s, by the 1970s they also faced increased competition from the growing body of GLCs and other SEs that were assuming an ever-larger role in the domestic economy.

By the late 1980s growing SME complaints noted the predatory practices of SEs, especially GLCs. The "roast duck case" of 1991 exemplified private sector unease about GLC business practices. It arose when Singapore Food Industries (SFI), a GLC subsidiary of Singapore Technologies, teamed up with LM Food to go into the roast duck business. LM Food saw the deal with SFI as a means of becoming a regional player, but the plan was sharply criticised by local business people who asked why a giant GLC would want to enter the domain of the humble food-hall hawker. The roast duck case was debated in Parliament, and is still raised when GLCs' predatory practices are discussed.[45] In 1994, the roast duck company was divested by SFI following the furore its acquisition had produced,[46] but predatory GLC behaviour continues unabated. As one local executive complained to Chee in 2000:

> *How do you make headway when every time an idea comes up, the government sizes up whether the business is lucrative enough to barge in? I can understand if it's Singapore Airlines where you need the huge resources to get the business up and going. But the government even wants in on mom-and-pop grocery shops in the HDB estates.* [47]

PAP MP Penny Low echoed these sentiments:

> *Some SMEs avoid contact with the GLCs whenever a business opportunity arises – for fear that the GLCs may muscle them out ... Without the necessary financial muscle and network, the SME cannot set up companies with the same speed or size the GLCs can. It's not a level playing field.*[48]

Other MPs have also attacked GLCs. In March 2000, they condemned them for being uncreative and unethical and unnecessarily competitive against SMEs.[49] One MP said GLCs should seek new opportunities elsewhere and not "play in the backyard pond". Another accused them of being "deep in pockets but shallow in ideas" and said many smaller firms shunned partnering GLCs. "There is a perception that if you propose a good business idea to GLCs, they will take it and exploit it on their own with their strong financial resources," he said.[50]

The Finance Minister Richard Hu found it "startling" to hear these criticisms of GLCs. While admitting that some had been predatory in the past. He assured MPs that Temasek Holdings had reined in GLCs that deviated from their core business. He added, "In future, GLCs will be scrutinized carefully to ensure they don't venture into areas where their presence is not necessary nor where competition is unhelpful".[51]

Still, GLCs kept poaching in small business areas. In 2001, the huge GLC, Singapore Press Holdings won a tender for newspaper kiosks in Orchard Road and at bus stops. "The individual tender did not stand a chance in the tender exercise," said one bidder for the kiosks.[52] Appropriation of such small business prospects has meant that GLCs are prevalent at all levels of the economy. One Singapore MP complained:

> *The GLCs, the Government and union-affiliated organisations are involved in practically every sector of the economy. In fact one can't get through the day without having to have some business dealings with GLCs. For example, when we go to the bank, read the newspaper, buy food, use the telephone, or take a bus, taxi or Mass Rapid Transit, you can't throw a stone without hitting a GLC!*[53]

In 2002, renewed attacks were made on GLCs. Many focused on the NTUC Fair Price supermarket chain, a GLC owned by the NTUC, which besides being the government-controlled umbrella organisation for the unions also runs various cooperatives. By March 2002, there were no grocery or provision shops in Ang Mo Kio: they had all been closed down because of competition from NTUC Fair Price.[54]

Worse was expected by the 160 small shops in the area: the NTUC was planning to open a mega-supermarket in four years that would compete with many of them. Not surprisingly, NTUC detractors use such epithets as "Neighbourhood Tyrant Unlimited Corporation" to describe the NTUC and its squeezing out of small shops.[55] By October 2002, there were 68 NTUC supermarkets throughout Singapore.

In May 2004, Singapore Post (Singpost) began opening a string of 20 pawnshops throughout Singapore.[56] Here a statutory authority, not merely a GLC, was encroaching on a very traditional sector of the economy where "mom and pop" businesses had always operated. Singpost also proposed moving into investment and insurance products, home loans for HDB flats and cash flow management products. A state-owned post office was marketing financial products normally reserved for private sector enterprise. Such moves contradict government claims that SEs are being reined in: SEs not only grab SME business opportunities; they also cut SME profits and drive many out of business. The Government generally looks the other way when this happens.

Depressed Local Spending

Besides facing SE/MNC competition, SMEs have also been hit hard by a combination of government policies and, since the later 1990s, by external economic events that have depressed local consumer spending. SMEs have been particularly vulnerable to reduced spending because, unlike the MNCs, over 75 per cent of their markets are domestic.

Singapore's stagnating consumer demand started to become a problem for SMEs in the early 1990s. By the mid-1990s Singapore's retailers were being hit especially hard. But until the 1997-2003 economic crises Singapore's spectacular growth rates obscured this trend. In 1994, retail sales actually fell by 1.5 per cent and in 1995 rose by only 2.6 per cent.[57]

From 1994-6, one would hear such melancholy refrains from local shopkeepers as "business so bad", "how to make", "it's never been this bad". "All this talk about prosperity; it's a lot of crap," sneered one Orchard Road shop manager to me in 1995. Similar sentiments were widespread among local retailers in Singapore from early 1990.

In commenting on the lower retail figures the Government's Economic Survey for 1995 noted:

> Over the past few years, retail sales have been adversely affected by a number of factors. These are the diversion of consumer spending to asset purchases like car and private property [spending], slower visitor arrivals and lower spending per tourist and a growing tendency for Singaporeans to shop abroad.[58]

While soaring housing and property prices from the early 1990s drained away much consumer spending, new indirect taxes and rising health charges also contributed significantly. The introduction of the Certificate of Entitlement (COE) scheme for vehicles in 1990 pushed up vehicle prices, while the 3 per cent GST increased the cost of most purchases. Moreover, privatisation of health services from the late 1980s caused a surge in medical costs, which rose by 8.5 per cent in 1991, then by 2 to 2.5 per cent a year to 1995.[59] Tourist sector spending was severely cut during the 1980s until the mid-1990s because of the rising Singapore dollar. From 1988 to 1995, the US dollar fell from S$1.94 to S$1.41, Sterling from S$3.49 to S$2.19 and the Australian dollar from S$1.66 to S$1.05.[60] This not only discouraged tourists from coming to Singapore, but reduced the amount they spent while there. Lower tourist spending combined with reduced local spending to further hammer the retail sector.

By the 1997/8 Asian financial crisis Singapore's retail sector was already depressed. This and such external factors as growing terrorist threats in 2001, the Bali bombing of October 2002, the Iraq war and SARS in 2003 drove down consumer spending even more. These events were particularly devastating for the retail sector where one dollar in seven is spent by tourists.[61] Lower tourist as well as local spending pushed up unemployment, to further reduce consumer spending. In 2002, the jobless rate hit 5.5 per cent, the highest since the 1986/7 recession.

The amount the average Singaporean spent on shopping steadily fell from S$6362 in 1997 to S$5702 in 2001. Consumer spending also slumped severely in 2002 and 2003, but recovered by 2004.[62] Even so, the average retail profit margin in Singapore remained at a meagre ten per cent. Such a bleak retail scene saw growing numbers of shops and other businesses closing, often bankrupt.

A rising tide of bankruptcies has afflicted Singapore since the 1990s. Bankruptcies hit an 18-year high of 4484 in 2003.[63] From 1996 to 1999 they soared from 1200 to over 3000 cases a year and by 2002 the number hit nearly 3600.[64] The total number of undischarged bankrupts rose from 17,640 in 2003 to 20,553 by August 2004.[65] Part of this increase was due to the easing of bankruptcy laws. Because the changes made it easier for people to emerge from bankruptcy, people were more ready to declare themselves bankrupt. Another factor was readier access to credit cards in Singapore, which has increased the number of people running up credit card debts which they cannot meet. Recessionary conditions caused by externally generated crises also played a part. But these factors have only exacerbated the rise in bankruptcy levels, which is largely due to a long-term decline in consumer spending which has hit the retail/SME sector the hardest. This trend has been due to rising property prices, increased health-care costs and government charges.

More generally, depressed local spending has combined with SE/MNC competition to create an unfavourable and worsening business environment for SMEs. The problems of the SMEs became apparent in the early 1990s when they were already in the doldrums – well before the 1997/8 and later crises. The SMEs' share of manufacturing output had been steadily shrinking for many years. This share declined from 21 per cent of output in 1992 to 18 per cent in 1994,[66] and by 2001 had dropped to 14 per cent.[67]

The significance of this trend becomes more apparent when one sees that the number of SMEs and people they employed remained almost unchanged during this period. In 1992, SMEs made up 78 per cent of manufacturing establishments, and still did by 2001. In 1992, they employed 36 per cent of the manufacturing workforce; and 37 per cent in 2001 despite the SMEs' share of manufacturing output falling by nearly one quarter, from 18 to 14 per cent. Such trends indicate that the profitability of the manufacturing SMEs had been steadily declining since the early 1990s.

The low growth of Singapore's SMEs was revealed in a 2002 survey by business and credit bureau, DP Information Network. The bureau found that only four of the 50 fastest growing companies in Singapore from April 1 1998 to March 31 2001 were SMEs; only one SME made it into the top ten.[68]

Because of strong SE/MNC competition, falling consumer spending, and lack of venture capital, Singapore's SMEs have remained underdeveloped. As their situation worsened, calls were made to reduce SE involvement in the economy. The Government responded by launching a privatisation program in the late 1980s, supposedly to free up the economy and create more opportunities for SMEs. As already shown, this initiative benefited them little and has since been shelved.

Half-hearted Help

What of other government attempts to help the SMEs?

SME discontent has intensified as their situation has deteriorated. The Government responds by seeming to listen to their gripes and launching programs to help them, especially following economic downturns. In recent years schemes to aid SMEs have acquired an added impetus as the PAP state strives to boost Singapore's entrepreneurial capacities. Chapter 13 outlined these initiatives. But the Government has had schemes to help SMEs since the 1970s.

After the oil-induced recession of 1974 the Government established the Joint Venture Bureau within the EDB in 1975 to matchmake local and foreign partners.[69] To help with finance, the Small Industry Finance Scheme (SIFS) followed in 1976; then, following the 1985 recession, a privatisation program was launched ostensibly to create a more level playing field for SMEs. This initiative included the setting up of an SME division in the EDB. Finally, after a series of workshops in 1988 the SME Master Plan emerged in May 1989. It was the most comprehensive government statement until then on how the SMEs were to be helped. This plan was to be implemented by various state agencies headed by the EDB and its SME Division. By the mid-1990s more than 60 EDB-coordinated programs had been introduced over the previous two decades to promote the growth of local enterprises. They covered technology acquisition, business development, human resource management, marketing, design and R&D.[70]

How successful were these measures? The SMEs' reactions suggest they have so far received few benefits. In the early 1990s Lee and Low reported that there was "a dissatisfaction on the part of various groups in the private sector" with government efforts to help SMEs.[71] Many maintained that the Government had not done enough: that it should protect local firms from foreign competition, give local businesses more tax breaks and subsidies and remove unfair competition from the SEs. Others were sceptical of government commitment to develop local businesses, despite its claims.

They thought the efforts to help SMEs were mere "window dressing" and that the Government disdained local business people.

Small business people regularly complain about the problems of getting government support. In 1999, PAP MP Inderjit Singh described the obstacles he experienced launching his high tech company. He almost gave up when he received offers to start companies in Taiwan and the U.S., but he persevered even though he still had to raise 70 per cent of the funds from abroad.[72] He said the Government's pro-MNC, but SME-unfriendly policies discouraged the fostering of local entrepreneurship.

Four years later Singh was repeating the same criticisms. The reality was "that most local companies are left on their own to fight their own battles", he said.[73] Although government help was available, more still needed to be done to make it easier for start-ups to apply for the Government's incentive schemes. Local start-ups found it difficult to take full advantage of these schemes because the rules and incentives were designed for larger companies.

Raising capital from both state and bank sources is a major problem for Singaporean entrepreneurs and SMEs generally. One hi-tech entrepreneur said the National Science and Technology Board (NSTB) gave him a grant to research the production of hi-tech goods in Singapore. This was successfully completed.[74] When he asked the NSTB for funds to push the project to the commercial stage, he was told the board could not help him because its charter only permitted research support. "On scanning through the facilities that the Singapore Government has planned for home-grown companies and technical entrepreneurs I found almost 60 very attractive schemes which were available for me to tap," he said. But entrepreneurs could not approach the EDB or the Productivity and Standards Board (PSB). Instead the project had to be processed by an authorised bank before the funds were disbursed through either body.

The entrepreneur approached his bank and others but found "all of them were only interested in property business and trading – all heavily secured transactions. They had no desire to support a technical enterprise". When he spoke to the EDB and PSB again, "they again expressed their helplessness, saying that it is to be processed only through their bankers". The entrepreneur then asked a professional consultancy for help, who told him that "the local venture scene does not have an appetite for start-ups and it is not likely that we can generate interest from that front". Thus government programs to help SMEs often founder because of unhelpful rule-following bureaucrats and the conservative risk-averse mentality of Singapore banks. Both clearly lack the sympathy and the ability to deal with SMEs, especially those in hi-tech projects.

In March 2001, a small business bank was proposed for Singapore. The call came out of a government-chaired meeting between small business people and representatives from the PSB, four local banks and a finance company.[75] Two years later little had changed. In 2003, the Rotary Club president was complaining about how unhelpful banks were to SMEs, while the 2004 Spring Singapore survey revealed that banks had rejected over half of SME bank-loan applications.

Local business people see both banks and the Government as failing to help SMEs sufficiently. As Singaporean businessmen, Mr Lim Hian Hwa, complained to *The Straits Times*, before "a start-up can gain momentum, it is done in by government-linked companies".[76] He remembered fighting a price war with one of his company's main competitors – the PSB. Mr Lim was apparently referring to the PSB companies – PSB Corporation Pte Ltd and PSB Certification Pte Ltd. "And if anyone thinks that the PSB or the EDB will help start-ups with good ideas, think again," he said. Unless a company fell into the high-tech category or had over S$100 million in sales turnover, it could expect little government help. The emphasis was on large sales turnover, not product development. Contract manufacturers and components distributors were those most likely to get loans etc, Mr Lim noted.

Helping SMEs is a major problem for the EDB because it clashes with its role of attracting foreign investors. The EDB has been billed as a "one-stop" shop for foreign investors, a role it has performed well over the decades. "The EDB bureaucracy deals well with the multinational bureaucracy; they understand one another."[77] The question is whether the EDB's corporate culture is conducive to helping SMEs. This is a matter of priorities. MNCs sometimes represent billions of dollars of investment and thousands of jobs, compared to tens of millions of investment and a few dozen jobs by SMEs. Inevitably, the EDB gives precedence to MNCs.

Moreover, the skills for handling MNCs differ from those required for SMEs:

Patience, understanding, familiarity with Mandarin, Malay, Tamil or even specific dialects is required when dealing with some small local entrepreneurs. An attitude of sincerity is essential. These are not the communications skills required when dealing with multinational bureaucracy, where efficiency, speed and reliability are more appreciated.[78]

In the past, SMEs have distrusted government sincerity. This has impeded provision of any help it could have given them. Lee and Low report that many small business people complained to them about the EDB's SME schemes. Some were so heated "they would not approach the government for help even if they could benefit from it".[79] Reasons given included chagrin at the excessive paperwork, business plans and detailed statement of accounts required. Many small business people lacked the time or expertise to prepare them. The "high and mighty attitude" of some EDB officials also rankled many.

Another major SME grievance has been numerous and rising government charges. Here too government efforts to help SMEs are regarded as inadequate. Nominated (non-party) MP Lee Tsao Yuan told Parliament in 1998 that government fees and rates was the component of business costs that had increased the fastest since 1988. "While the unit business cost index as a whole had increased by 26 per cent, government rates and fees, which include property tax payments, increased by 93 per cent or nearly doubled," she said. "While businesses are all scrambling to cut costs this year, government charges should not contribute to costs".[80] Supporting her comments was Nominated MP Claire

Chiang. She said a freeze of present government imposts was not enough. Many SMEs believed the Government should cut levies, fees, charges and taxes.[81]

Even when the Government has appeared to do this, the benefits for the private sector have been minimal. In response to the 1997/8 economic crisis, the Government announced a S$2 billion package to reduce business costs and stimulate the economy.[82] This included cuts to government land rentals, electricity rates and petrol duties. Closer examination by the Singapore Chinese Chamber of Commerce and Industry proved the package was of little help to SMEs. The chamber's President, Mr Tay Beng Chuan, revealed:

> We did some calculations and found that our SME members can on average probably save only about $200 to $500 a month. The benefits to SMEs are very marginal. For example, the property tax rebate is not much gain to us because most SMEs do not own commercial property.[83]

Once again government policies to help SMEs were exposed as largely empty gestures. The Government clearly feels far more motivated to help MNCs and SEs. One suspects that previously the Government would have preferred the SMEs to fade away because they were too messy and demanding to deal with. It was better to work with big well-organised MNCs and bureaucratised GLCs than SMEs with their independent ways of thinking and doing things. However, the sudden realisation that Singapore must become more entrepreneurial and innovative to survive has forced the Government belatedly to recognise the need to cultivate SMEs. The result has been a plethora of schemes to help them. But there are still few signs that civil service attitudes to SMEs have changed appreciably. They will probably continue to feel more comfortable dealing with their customary clients, MNCs and SEs, than with SMEs. Such deep-seated bureaucratic mindsets are unlikely to change quickly in Singapore. Moreover, Singapore's need to retain and attract MNCs means they will keep receiving preferential treatment from its civil servants, especially as Asian, and particularly Chinese, competition for foreign capital heats up.

The PAP state sees not only MNCs but SEs as the mainstays of Singapore's economy. The 2002 debates on SEs have shown that further privatisation of them is unlikely. Instead the Government plans to use them to spearhead Singapore's efforts to compete abroad. In being prepared for international competition they keep getting preference over SMEs. Singapore will remain a good place for MNCs and SEs to do business in, but not for SMEs.

* * * * * * * * *

Strong claims about Singapore's economic freedom, transparency and business climate are certainly true as far as foreign capital is concerned. MNCs have enormous freedom to maximise profit with minimal government interference in a benign and transparent business environment – at least by their standards.

Singapore provides a similarly positive business environment for SEs, but this is largely because the Government flouts the principles of economic freedom and transparency to favour SEs at the expense of SMEs. Were SEs to compete in a genuinely free-enterprise transparent environment without state protection, life would be much harder for many of them. Some would probably go bankrupt or face "restructuring".

The SMEs and the local private sector generally do not operate in an economy which is genuinely free or transparent, nor where there is a level playing field for all. Such claims about Singapore are as hollow as those about its efficiency and the myth that it was merely a mosquito-ridden swamp after Separation in 1965. But understanding modern Singapore requires more than exposing these misconceptions about it, particularly when doing business there. An appreciation of the culture and values that determine Singaporeans' business behaviour is required, as the next section shows.

References

1. Bello, Walden and Stephanie Rosenfeld: *Dragons in Distress: Asian Miracle Economies in Crisis* (London, Penguin, 1990), p. 293.
2. Ibid.
3. *Straits Times* (ST), August 8, 1997 and August 8, 1998.
4. *Business Times* (BT), August 27, 2007.
5. ST, August 31, 2001.
6. ST January 2, 2003
7. *The Australian*, June 15, 2004.
8. *World Cost of Living rankings 2007/8* (Finfacts Ireland, www.finfacts.ie/costofliving
9. ST, February 27, 2007.
10. ST, March 14, 2007.
11. ST, May 5, 1996.
12. *Doing Business 2008 Report* (The World Bank Group, 2008), www.doingbusiness.org/economyrankings
13. Mastercard Worldwide Centers of Commerce Index 2007, www.mastercard.com.us/
14. *2007 Worldwide Quality of Living Survey* (Mercer Human Resource Consulting, New York, 2007), www.mercer.com/referencecontent
15. ST, February 21, 2000.
16. Chee, Soon Juan: *Your Future, My Faith, Our Freedom* (Open Singapore Centre, Singapore, 2001), p. 83.
17. Low, Linda: "State Entrepreneurship", p. 152 in Local Entrepreneurship in Singapore, edited by Tsao Yuan Lee and Linda Low (Times Academic Press, Singapore, 1990).
18. BT, June 12, 1987.
19. Ibid.
20. Low, in Lee and Low, p. 163.
21. Fernand, John and Brent Nieman: "Measuring the Miracle: Market Imperfections and Asia's Growth Experience" (Working Paper Series, Federal Reserve Bank of San Francisco, May 2006), p. 12.
22. Ibid.
23. Ibid.
24. "Changing Corporate Asia – What Business Needs to Know" (Economic Analytical Unit Report, Department of Foreign Affairs and Trade; Canberra, Australia, March 2002), p. 190.
25. Ramirez, Carlos D. and Ling Hui Tan: "Singapore Inc. Versus the Private Sector: Are Government-Linked Companies Different?" (IMF Staff Papers, International Monetary Fund, 2004), p. 513.
26. Ramirez and Tan, p. 526.
27. BT, December 2, 2004.
28. Bello and Rosenfeld, p. 294.
29. Ibid.
30. Clad, James: *Behind the Myth: Business,*

Money and Power in Southeast Asia (London, Unwin Hyman, 1989), p. 129.

30a. Bello and Rosenfeld, p. 296.

31. Ibid, p. 294.

32. Ibid.

33. Ibid.

34. Perry, M and Tan Boon Hui: "Global manufacturing and local linkage in Singapore" (Environment and Planning A 1998, Vol 30, pages 1603-24).

35. Ibid, p. 1603.

36. Ibid.

37. Ibid, p. 1608.

38. Ibid, p. 1609.

39. Ibid, p. 1619.

40. Ibid, p. 1608.

41. Bello and Rosenfeld, p. 296.

42. Ibid.

43. Ibid.

44. Wong Poh Kam and Ho Yuen Ping: "E-Commerce in Singapore: Impetus and Impact of Globalization" (Centre for Research on Information Technology and Organizations, University of California, Irvine; March 2004), p. 13.

45. ST, August 17, 1997.

46. BT, August 29, 2002.

47. Chee, p. 67.

48. ST, August 28, 2002.

49. ST, March 9, 2000.

50. Ibid.

51. Ibid.

52. ST, March 6, 2001.

53. ST, March 13, 2001.

54. ST, March 27, 2002.

55. ST, October 19, 2002.

56. ST, May 5, 2004.

57. *Economic Survey of Singapore 1995* (Singapore, Ministry of Trade and Industry), p. 68.

58. Ibid.

59. Ibid, p. 26.

60. Ibid, p. 137.

61. *Streats*, December 4, 2002.

62. Ibid.

63. ST, March 27, 2004.

64. ST, August 27, 2003.

65. *Today*, September 25, 2004.

66. *Economic Survey of Singapore 1995*, p. 54.

67. *Economic Survey of Singapore 2001*, p. 74.

68. *Today*, July 24, 2002.

69. Low in Lee and Low, p. 186.

70. Murray, Geoffrey and Audrey Perera: *Singapore the Global City State* (England; China Library/Curzon, 1996), p. 79.

71. Low in Lee and Low, p. 4.

72. ST, March 12, 1999.

73. ST, March 14, 2003.

74. ST, July 7, 1999.

75. ST, March 29, 2001.

76. ST, August 20, 2001.

77. Low in Lee and Low, p. 204.

78. Ibid.

79. Ibid, p. 207.

80. ST, March 10, 1998.

81. Ibid.

82. ST, October 29, 1998.

83. ST, July 24, 1998.

Section Five

Business Values and Realities

Singapore is not only perceived as a developed and efficient but also a very westernised society. This enhances Singapore's image as a good place for MNCs to do business. Singapore's visible efficiencies, its use of the latest technologies and HRD methods, Western-style planning and organisation, sophisticated financial, business, and legal infrastructures, transport and communications facilities and widespread use of English give the impression that it also has Western business values. In terms of business, financial, legal and social institutions, Singapore is well ahead of its neighbours whose business environments often range from mediocre to abysmal. Singapore looks good beside them.

Singapore's impressive business-financial infrastructures engender the belief that it also has high business principles. This would certainly be true compared to most Third World countries where business standards, like their business and physical infrastructures, are deficient and undeveloped. But do Singaporean business principles and practices match those of Western countries? To answer this question a general comparison of Western and Asian business values and attitudes would first be appropriate.

CHAPTER 17

A CLASH OF VALUES

Asia has always presented a challenge to Westerners, especially those doing business there. Whether operating as one-man shows or working for MNCs, Westerners soon learn that very different values, attitudes and trust levels dictate commercial activities in Asia.

The best way to learn about a country's culture is to do business with the people. Sojourning in a country can teach relatively little, no matter how long the stay. Those who work as journalists, academics or aid workers will usually learn more. They have greater access to the host country's political, business and intellectual decision-making elites. Aid workers gain further insight into a culture and its values through prolonged contact with its poor.

However, there is nothing like conducting business with the locals to understand them and how they think. Buying and selling, doing deals, delivering or taking delivery of stock, giving and getting credit and hiring staff give a far better appreciation of another culture than that provided by any other means. Each party is usually putting far more on the line than those employed in "non-business" occupations. Hands-on business encounters often provide the best opportunities to experience the real business values and trust levels of the locals.

1. Some Cherished Beliefs

Those doing business in Asia soon realise that the values of North America, Britain, Australasia, Scandinavia and Western Europe are largely specific to these regions. What are these values? Chief among them are:

- A belief in fair play and respect for others' feelings
- Truth and sincerity (saying what you mean and meaning what you say).

How prevalent are such values in Asia?

Fair Play and Empathy

In the English-speaking countries especially the belief in fair play is evident. In Britain this is called "playing the game", in Australia, "a fair go", in America a "fair (or square) deal". In the world of business it is manifested in the belief that the other party has rights and feelings, and is entitled to a profit or some benefit or to at least not having their time and money wasted by insincere offers and proposals. While screwing the other party to the eyeballs until he retaliates and takes your head off in a rage or bides his time until he can screw you back is not uncommon in the West, in Asia it is standard business behaviour.

The often total disregard for the other party opens a Pandora's box of negative possibilities for those on the receiving end. They generally involve money or stock being lost and/or time wasted.

Money lost can be due to being grossly underpaid or overcharged, unless one bargains hard. Such bargaining is *de rigueur* for Asia. The aim is to grind down the price of the other party or overcharge her/him as much as possible. Of course there are always exceptions, but such attitudes underlie most business negotiations in Asia, unless a long-term relationship has been formed between each party. Tough bargaining is based on the premise that the seller is over-charging or the buyer is trying to underpay. Either way it assumes that one or both parties is less than honourable or fair. While bargaining over prices of houses, cars, businesses and other major items is common in such Western countries as North America, Britain and Australasia, the same is much less so for smaller purchases.

Countries where hard bargaining is common are also those where over-charging is the norm. In 1992, Intramar polled 1450 travel agents world-wide to survey the incidence of over-charging.[1] Scores were based on the extent to which over-charging occurred in the countries surveyed. The higher the score, the greater the chances of being over-charged. Australia scored only 34 points, New Zealand 38, West German 39, and Denmark 41, while Asian countries such as Singapore scored 115, Hong Kong 182, Thailand 172, India 129 and the Philippines 97. But southern European and Latin countries scored even higher. Italy's score was a whopping 275, while Spain's was 171, Greece 171 and Brazil 163.

In all the countries with high scores hard bargaining was normal, while in such countries as Australia, New Zealand and West Germany, haggling for consumer and everyday items was uncommon. Many Westerners, especially those from Anglo-Saxon and some West European countries, find it distasteful, even demeaning, to bargain over small purchases though some find it exhilarating. They get a real thrill out of beating down the price of some impoverished stall-holder in Java or Bali with six kids to support in a shack overhanging a stinking canal. Many are the stories I have heard in Asia of eager Western tourists behaving in this manner. Fortunately, there are far more Westerners who find this behaviour contemptible.

Unfortunately, middle class and wealthy Asians do not share such sensibilities and will vigorously haggle for the lowest price, however obvious the poverty of the seller may be. One repeatedly finds that the affluent classes of Third World societies have few qualms about exploiting their own people. A social conscience for the poor and oppressed is a novelty for them, one the more westernised will sometimes assume as fashionable stance to show how Western they are. In Asia, haggling over the cost of small as well as major items is normal, except in such places as fixed-price supermarkets or department stores.

Hard-nosed bargaining is often the least of an expatriate's worries when doing business in Asia. More serious is the rather-too-frequent experience of not being paid, or being paid only after endless arguments and angry confrontations. This can be for goods or services provided or for wages or salaries due. Too often one's honesty and integrity may be questioned. Then there is the even more unpleasant experience of being cheated or ripped off. Money put into projects or businesses disappears or gets siphoned off or is simply stolen.

Apart from money, much time is frequently wasted. Projects initiated fail to eventuate because the Asian party too often has neither the money and time, nor the organisational and planning expertise, nor often the honesty and sincerity, to make it fly. Unfortunately, the hapless foreigner does not discover this for many months, by which time a lot of time as well as money has been wasted. But in the meantime his Asian partner has picked up numerous contacts, ideas, information and expertise that he may put to good use on his own. These he will use when the "joint venture" finally collapses.

Such situations in Asia were described by a *Straits Times* columnist and computer entrepreneur, writing from Silicon Valley in California. He quoted a fellow Singaporean entrepreneur who said, "some Asian bosses will tell you no to your face and then quietly steal your ideas. Or they have some hidden agenda somewhere". The columnist implied that while the same thing occurred everywhere, it had happened to himself so often in Asia that he had been prompted to "go somewhere else where things are different". The place he chose was America, where there was far more respect for ideas and intellectual property rights. He quoted another Singaporean who said, "Asians don't have an appreciation for intellectual property. Why is there rampant software piracy in Asia? We don't value ideas".[2] This denotes a ruthless, me-first attitude that has no regard or consideration for the other party. While similar callousness, especially at the corporate level, is now quite common in the West, it is an attitude that permeates most levels of business in Asia.

Often widespread poverty is the reason given for such cut-throat business tactics: so many people are so poor in Asia that they have to resort to sharp practices and even dishonesty to feed their families. But those who have spent much time in Asia will know that often it is the wealthier classes who are the most greedy, dishonest and unscrupulous. Such attributes are not the result of poverty but of obsessive greed and of mindsets where the individual feels compelled to put his own interests and those of his family and close kin, above any notions of higher or communitarian good. Anyone outside his kin circle is fair game.

Truth, Accuracy and Sincerity

Telling the truth, the whole truth and nothing but the truth is one of the mantras of the Anglo-Saxon legal system. It represents the Western search for certainty and veracity which began in earnest in the 17th Century with Leibnitz, Newton and Descartes. The quest for "objective truth" is central to the West's mindset. The more precisely and accurately physical reality, for example, can be understood, the better it can be controlled and manipulated to serve human ends. Being accurate and factually correct is deemed important in Western societies because it is seen as facilitating communication and efficiency.

In many non-western societies being truthful and accurate is not as important. Other aims such as maintaining social harmony, avoiding unpleasant truths and saving face take precedence, especially in Asian societies. Saying what you mean and meaning what you say may often disrupt social relations. Better to discourage such behaviour to minimise inter-personal tensions, however insincere this may be. Westerners place a much higher value on honest and sincere talk, despite the hurt feelings it can produce at times, but this can cause them problems in Asia where evasiveness is often preferred to sincerity.

The Japanese are masters at the art of indirect communication. Their practice of saying "yes" when they really mean "no" or "not likely" is well known, as is the way they can string someone along for weeks, if not months, without a definite reply. Such behaviour is based on the Japanese distinction between *tatemae* (the official stated position) and *honne* (real intent). Westerners tend to view such discrepancies as a negotiating ploy, notes Alex Kerr, a veteran American commentator on Japan. But they could be mistaken, he suggests:

> *It hasn't occurred to them that the fundamental Japanese attitude toward information might differ from what they take for granted in the West. But it does differ, and radically so.*
>
> *Traditionally, in Japan "truth" has never been sacrosanct, nor do "facts" need to be real, and here we run up against one of the great cultural divides between East and West.[3]*

Kerr contends that in Japan:

> *People will strive to uphold* tatemae *in the face of blatant facts to the contrary, believing it is important to keep the* honne *hidden in order to maintain public harmony....*Tatemae *helps to make Japanese society peaceful and cohesive, with a relative lack of aggressive violence, family breakups and law suits that plague the West.[4]*

Similar observations can be made about other Asian societies. They too have a strong desire to minimise interpersonal conflict by not voicing unpalatable truths. Because Asia is home to so many diverse cultures and peoples living so close together, maintaining social harmony takes preference over candour. Frank talk that might spark confrontation is to be avoided. It is far better to tell people what they want to hear and "give them face", especially if you want something from them.

However, respect for others' sensibilities, especially in Singapore, is usually confined to a person whom one wishes to impress. This is so whether he is an honoured guest, someone to do business with, or someone perceived as a socio-economic superior. Respect is rarely extended to those seen as socially inferior or subordinate. In

Singapore maids, waitresses, shop assistants and subordinates rarely receive much face-saving treatment. They are more likely to experience rude and thoughtless treatment characterised by a lack of empathy and callous insensitivity. Singaporeans will even treat Westerners like this if they are thought to be of lower socio-economic status. When not fawning to their superiors, Singaporeans may be bullying their subordinates. The same is regularly observed in Japanese society.

Normally Westerners are accorded deferential treatment because they are perceived as having higher prestige and more wealth than locals, but they still face the challenge of trying to understand what many Asians are really saying and to determine the sincerity of their sentiments. This can be very frustrating for Westerners, especially for Australians and Americans who value frank talk. So often they find – after wasting much time and effort – that seemingly sincere offers are merely hollow talk. Their Asian counterparts are only "shooting the breeze" with them. But there are hard-headed reasons why many Asian business people do this. They may be seeking to gain status and prestige in the other's eyes, to make themselves seem more substantial than they actually are.

Making empty proposals is an Asian way of getting you to show your hand. Your response will often reveal what resources, expertise, skills, or contacts you have. The offers may simply try and use you as an unpaid consultant. Having you doing the leg work, gathering information and feeling out markets for them, price and product-wise, will save them much time and effort. You may find that on presenting them with the information you have dug up, nothing more eventuates. Often you will not even be thanked.

Misinformation abounds in Asia. So often one is told things that are later found to be wrong or only half true. This may have been due to a desire to please or impress; or information may have been withheld because of the Asian fear of sharing information and telling others all they know. Knowledge is seen as a resource to be kept for oneself, not shared with others. Similarly, self-disclosure is avoided. What you reveal about yourself or plans can be used against you, giving others an advantage over you. People living in low-trust cultures are most likely to exhibit such behaviour.

2. Trust Levels

The extent to which fair play and honesty prevail in a society largely determine its trust levels.

When Westerners first arrived in Asia the lack of trust and chronically high levels of suspicion, bordering on paranoia, soon become apparent. Studies of Asian business attitudes confirm this. When commenting on Hong Kong Chinese business people, Redding noted:

> *The key feature would appear to be that you trust your family absolutely, your friends and acquaintances to the degree that mutual dependence has been established and face invested in them. With everybody else you make no assumptions about their goodwill. You have the right to expect their politeness and their following of social proprieties, but beyond that you must anticipate*

that, just as you are, they are primarily looking to their own i.e. their family's best interests. To know your own motives well is, for the Chinese, more than most, a warning about everybody else's. [5]

Redding's observations can easily be generalised to most other Asian societies but would exclude Japan, such writers as Fukuyama contend. He maintains that much higher trust levels prevail in Japan compared to China. He shares Redding's observations about the familistic mentality of the Chinese:

Familistic societies frequently have weak voluntary associations because unrelated people have no basis for trusting one another. Chinese societies like Taiwan, Hong Kong and the People's Republic of China itself are examples; the essence of Chinese Confucianism is the elevation of family bonds above all other social loyalties. [6]

Such views would also apply to most other Asian societies, whether Thai, Malay, Indonesian, Filipino, Korean, Indian, Sri-Lankan, Pakistani – or Singaporean. Doing business in Asia quickly teaches one this. Distrust is widespread while trust is hard won and quickly lost. Singapore is no exception. Its population comprises Chinese, Malays and Indians – all peoples from low-trust cultures. Usually only one's kin are trusted in such familistic societies. It means that one does not have to display the same honesty and fairness towards non-kin, who are fair game for sharp practices ranging from overcharging, avoidance of payment, or stealing their ideas to outright theft. Such behaviour between non-kin people in familistic societies inevitably breeds distrust between people who share no kin links, because each knows the other may treat him in unprincipled ways. Distrust in familistic societies is a result of familistic values which sanction unprincipled behaviour towards non-kin.

Clearly, trust and distrust do not exist in a vacuum. Both have to be earned. People's trust levels depend on how well they have been treated by others. A person will trust those who respect his trust by treating him in a fair and honest way. Conversely, if his trust is abused, then he will obviously distrust them. In societies where betrayal of trust is common, widespread distrust will prevail. They will be low-trust societies. This is so in Asia, as many a Westerner bitterly learns after doing business there as well as in other "low-trust" regions of the world. As one Australian aid worker who had worked in Sri Lanka and Cambodia once wearily told me, "To live in Asia is to be constantly disappointed". Western disenchantment with Asian business values is widespread.

Paradoxically, however, Westerners find that Asians are far more likely to trust them than fellow Asians. While the latter may have little trust in each other, they are often ready to trust Westerners, especially those from the Anglo-Saxon (North America, the UK and Australasia) and West European countries. Other Asians – or in fact people from any other Third World countries, where dishonesty and the corruption it breeds are rife – are much less likely to be trusted. Westerners, especially those from the aforementioned regions, are perceived as being far more honest and reliable than those from elsewhere – if sometimes too naive and trusting.

Asia's practical, hard-headed business people know their races and cultures: they are aware of which nationalities and ethnic groups are usually trouble, and which are easiest to deal with. Business people cannot afford the luxury of being politically correct and assuming all nationalities are the same. They stand or fall by how accurately they read people and to whom they can extend credit. If they are wrong, they lose money; if they are too wrong, they go bankrupt. Asia's low trust levels result from trust being constantly abused and betrayed due to cultural factors.

The preceding observations apply to Singapore as much as to most other Asian countries. Not only is it also a low-trust society; it is one where such virtues as fair play, truth and sincerity are lacking. The next chapter considers how these deficiencies affect Singaporeans' business psychology and practices.

References

1. *The Straits Times* (ST), June 29, 1992.
2. ST ('Life' section), October 12, 1998.
3. Kerr, Alex: *Dogs and Demons: The Fall of Modern Japan* (London, Penguin 2001), p. 104.
4. Ibid, p. 105.
5. Redding, Gordon S.: *The Spirit of Chinese Capitalism* (Berlin, De Gruyter, 1990), p. 66.
6. Fukuyama, Francis: *Trust: The Social Virtues and the Creation of Prosperity* (London, Penguin, 1995), pp. 28-9.

CHAPTER 18

SINGAPOREAN BUSINESS VALUES
AND PRACTICES

One Westerner who has proudly sung Singapore's praises is Jo-Ann Craig. Her book *Culture Shock! Singapore* provides a detailed guide to the island's culture and lifestyle for newly-arrived expatriates. "Singapore is modernized, industrialized, and, some might say, Westernized," she writes. After arriving at "the incredibly efficient Changi airport", being whisked by taxi through the island's skyscraper landscape "and dining later that evening on a truly gourmet meal with a sophisticated and high-tech Singaporean business associate" the "unwary business person, tourist or visitor" may be convinced "that there is little that is Asian about Singapore".[1] But she also notes:

> Airports, skyscrapers, taxicabs, hotels and other external trappings of industrialization, however, are only skin deep....While it may be true that some of the younger and more modern Singaporeans are forsaking their own Asian heritage, and losing touch with their own customs and culture, a careful study reveals that there is still a very strong Asian heart beating vigorously beneath the hot and humid atmosphere of the concrete jungle that is modern Singapore.
>
> Although Singaporeans may externally dress and behave in a Westernized way, the visitor would be wrong to assume that Singaporeans are like Westerners.[2]

How very true. Craig then devotes her book to providing a comprehensive account of the various social, religious, customs, beliefs and values of the Chinese, Indian and Malay communities of Singapore. Her thoroughness is commendable. Many newly arrived Westerners have valiantly sought to understand and follow such cultural guidelines when dealing with Singaporeans. Some are so conscientious in this regard that they tie themselves in knots. One former Western expatriate in Singapore got herself into quite a dither about doing the right cultural thing; but on expressing her consternation to Singaporean colleagues about this, she was told not to worry so much. They told her she really only had to be concerned about these things when she met their elderly parents and relatives. With the younger generation, she could just act normally.

While Craig's book gives a detailed coverage of traditional Singaporean customs and attitudes, it fails to prepare the average Westerner adequately for the often abrasive and stressful experiences he or she will have while living and doing business in Singapore. Much of this is the result of the low-trust *kiasu* values of Singaporeans, which Craig only mentions twice in her book, even though *kiasuism* is a central – and not terribly attractive – feature of the Singaporean personality. It is one which all Westerners coming to Singapore should quickly familiarise themselves with, along with a whole range of less-than-pleasant situations they may encounter while there. Culture shock-type books such as those by Craig fail to do this. Fear of offending their host culture may be the reason.

1. Kiasuism

Singaporean business and other values can best be understood in the light of *kiasuism*, a cluster of values, beliefs and attitudes which significantly determine Singaporeans' behaviour. *Kiasu* is a Chinese word which means "fear of missing out". Bjerke says that *kiasuism* sometimes gives Westerners the impression that "a Singaporean does not want to miss any opportunity which someone else is offered or taking (even if none of them gains anything)".[3] "Everything must also have" is one well-known Singlish (Singaporean English) phrase used to describe *kiasuism*. Key features of the *kiasu* personality are greed, materialism, selfishness, striving to constantly get something for nothing, insensitivity to others' feelings, paranoia, an obsessive desire to maximise every advantage from a business deal or friendship and a deep fear of failure. Not only many Westerners, but more sensitive and aware Singaporeans, deplore the *kiasu* personality.

Straits Times columnist Goh Buck Song noted that *kiasuism* grew out of "the nation's uneasy infancy and awkward adolescence".[4] While he once believed that *kiasuism* "makes people more alert and keener to work hard and do well" he no longer thought so:

> *It is time to recognise* kiasuism *for what it is: an awful social disease of self-centred disregard for community that will infect wherever allowed to and retard the Republic's progress towards a cultured society.*[4]

He was tired of Singaporeans who jumped taxi or canteen queues the moment you turned your head. "Such behaviour does not contribute to economic productivity, or help make people the best they can be. It just makes life here more unpleasant." To achieve a gracious society "Mr Singapore ... must see *kiasuism* for the monster it is".

Some Singaporeans are ashamed at the behaviour of their countrymen abroad, as one now living in Perth, Western Australia, has admitted. He could always tell a Singaporean "by the way he speaks and, sometimes sadly, from the way he conducts himself in a foreign land".[5] He said, "*Kiasuism* and a total disregard for the feelings of the locals come through loud and clear. It is embarrassing".

Displays of *kiasuism* are not pretty to watch, as several well-publicised examples have shown in recent years.

In January 1996, wealthy Singaporeans tried to get a S$60 *hongbao* (a cash gift given during Chinese new year) which was meant for the elderly poor aged over 60. One clan spokesman said that about a fifth of the 400 people who registered for the *hongbao* were well off. Some listed expensive private apartments as their addresses on the registration form. They often came dressed in costly clothes and jewellery. Some drove Mercedes Benzes, and a few even turned up with their maids. The spokesman said that when he tried to stop these people registering they told him off: "They tell me, 'Why do you care so much, the money is not yours'." [6]

In January 2000, an even more spectacular example of *kiasu* behaviour occurred when McDonalds began selling Hello Kitty soft-toy dolls at low prices to promote their burgers. Each meal and Kitty set cost $10. [7] Crowds mobbed the 24 McDonalds outlets in Singapore to get the kitschy little dolls which were dressed in wedding costumes.[8] Queues hundreds of metres long formed and became unruly when jostling began. In one day alone police authorities received nine calls about fights and people fainting. McDonalds assigned over 130 Cisco officers and other security to control the crowds from 4am onwards but they were sometimes unable to cope, and police were called in to help. Six people were arrested for fighting and a policeman was injured when three of the arrested threw stools at him.

Similar undignified scenes occurred in July 2001 when nearly 5000 customers with the Singapore telco M1 swore and jostled as they queued for hours waiting to swap their mobile phones for free ones.[9] M1 was closing down its CDMA network service and was permitting its 50,000 customers to swap their CDMA phones for GSM phones. They were to get free phones that would normally have cost S$498 each.

The *kiasu* fear of missing out was palpable. By 7am on the first day, four hours before the counters were due to open, 600 people were already queueing. By 11am several people had tried to jump the queue and a fight had nearly broken out. Security officers were called to control the crowd. Some female customers, fearing for their safety, fled the scene because of the violent crowd.

Company AGMs in Singapore have also been venues for *kiasu* mayhem by shareholders, especially when the buffet is served. As one eye-witness observed:

> *The moment the meeting's over and the door opens, you see 20 to 30 of them racing towards the buffet table, grabbing everything and yelling, "Don't push me!" at other people.*[10]

Seafood items – king prawns, lobsters and oysters – go first; then chocolate cakes, puddings and mango tarts. Last to go are the cheaper foods such as egg sandwiches and fried noodles. The greediest shareholders bring plastic bags and styrofoam containers to take away as much food as possible. Others merely choose big plates and grab far more than they can eat. Some even cart off the fruit displays and floral decorations. One company has decided to serve only tea and coffee at its AGMs to avoid such unedifying scenes.

While some Singaporeans are ashamed of their country's *kiasuism*, others have sought to cash in on it. Since 1989, Mr Kiasu comic books have been published in Singapore with such beguiling titles as "Everything Must Also Grab" and "Everything Also Want Extra".[11] Mr Kiasu "embodies traits that Singaporeans can relate to, such as always wanting to be first, being afraid to lose out and getting the most out of the least effort," *The Straits Times* blandly reported.[12] Following Mr Kiasu's success in Singapore, plans were announced in December 1995 for a venture called the Kiasu Company to export *kiasuism* throughout Asia by such media as satellite television. The company thought this would be a good way of introducing "the colourful character" of Mr Kiasu to Asia and help build brand recognition and demand for their merchandise.

Amazingly some Singaporean public figures and politicians seem captivated by the repulsive values of *kiasuism*. One who should have known better was prominent Singaporean writer Catherine Lim, who confessed to "having an enduring attachment to the 'kiasu' personage".[13] She was particularly chuffed that the term *kiasu* had even made it into an English language dictionary for international use. She felt "it is always nice to know that interest in local culture has actually moved on to a serious academic level".

Lim's vacuous sentiments were echoed by a Singaporean high school student, aged 18, who won a National Mandarin Elocution Competition in which he praised *kiasuism*.[14] He said that *kiasuism* was not a derogatory term but one embodying the spirit of meeting challenges and competition. "We cannot afford to lose. Therefore we must try to excel in the *kiasu* role," he declared to the applause of the 600-strong audience. Depressing stuff. Clearly many Singaporeans, young and old, see *kiasu* values as a worthwhile aid to nation-building, with their much-touted striving for excellence presumably boosting productivity.

While greed and a desperate desire to succeed are great motivators to work hard, *kiasuism* can cut productivity, as noted earlier. The paranoia that *kiasuism* generates undermines trust and discourages the sharing of information and resources in ways that reduce productivity within organisations. Such small-minded greed and selfishness within work groups damage team morale and breed further distrust, while the *kiasu* fear of failure cripples innovation and productivity because of the risk-averse behaviour it encourages.

While *kiasuism* may encourage risk-averseness, does it not push Singaporeans to aim for excellence? *Kiasuistic* values definitely motivate Singaporean students to strive for the best exam marks possible and to make as much money as they can; but their desire for top marks is motivated by materialistic status-seeking values. There is little desire to achieve greater knowledge and understanding of their subject, let alone to fulfil some higher aesthetic or intellectual goal, as noted earlier.

More generally, the apparent pursuit of excellence by Singaporeans is motivated mainly by an obsessive need to try and extract as much money or perks as possible from every deal, job or situation. When such incentives are lacking they often produce quite second-rate work when they can.

Kiasu values not only have a high social cost but harm Singaporeans relations with foreigners. Many Westerners find it especially hard to trust or respect Singaporeans practising *kiasu* values. *Kiasu* behaviour destroys trust, which is central to any joint projects and other ventures between Singaporeans and foreigners.

In many ways *kiasuism* is a local variation of the aforementioned Asian business values, insofar as it is based on distrust, disregard for other people and risk-averseness. After living and working in Singapore for some time, it becomes apparent that the nation's business ethics are similar to those of its less developed neighbours. In Singapore too there is a similar readiness to be dishonest, devious and insincere in business dealings.

On my first day in Singapore many years ago I met a Singaporean Chinese who cheerily observed that "If a Chinaman can't cheat someone every day he gets a tummy ache". Even then I didn't find his comment very amusing. Often such ruthless sentiments affect Singaporean business attitudes: "You look after yourself, I look after myself," seems to be the belief. Any advantage one party has over the other is to be fully exploited. Concepts of fair play mean little.

MNCs in Singapore are largely insulated from this behaviour by a government and bureaucracy that smoothes the way for them, as the EDB's treatment of MNCs shows. "The EDB bureaucracy deals well with the multinational bureaucracy; they understand one other, and multi-nationals appreciate the fact that the EDB keeps its word".[15] The EDB is always there to clear the path for MNCs in their dealings with the Government and civil service and with local partners.

Small foreign operations and individual expatriates doing business in Singapore find the going harder. They are less insulated from the *kiasu* mentality and deficient business ethics, as well as from poor planning, organisation and other "cultural" problems of doing business in Singapore. A Singaporean woman lawyer once told me how an Australian businessman bitterly complained to her how he always got ripped off when he did business in Singapore. She told him that he had to understand "the cultural differences" between Singaporeans and Australians. Such differences presumably made Singaporeans feel they could cheat Australians whenever possible.

Such cultural differences would perhaps explain this same Singaporean lawyer's treatment of an Australian expatriate who had been employed by an Australian firm for which she had been company secretary. When the company went bankrupt the expatriate Aussie was stuck in Singapore without money. She was holding money that was his which was still in the company's Singapore bank account, but refused to release this money to him so he could return home. Only when he got the Australian embassy in Singapore to speak to the woman did he get the money. The embassy official who dealt with this woman exclaimed to me, "I mean there are two sides to a story, but her behaviour was unbelievable," shaking his head.

Apparently the woman's need to fly to Perth every month on business was instrumental in her change of heart. Staying in the embassy's good books was more likely a key consideration for her, not any sense of fair play. When the proverbial hits the fan, Singaporeans are especially prone to run for cover. It's all part of the *kiasu* ethos of looking after Number One. But more on this later: First, a look at how *kiasuism* influences Singaporean business behaviour.

2. A Culture of Distrust and Disrespect

Singaporeans are often deeply distrustful in their business dealings, not only with other non-Western peoples such as Arabs and Africans, but also with each other. Even so, they are more likely to trust Westerners, especially the Anglo-Saxon variety, than other Singaporeans, Asians or Third World nationals. Being a trading people since Singapore's founding in 1819, Singaporeans are very aware of national differences.

"There are big differences between the nationalities," one ex-Orchard Road retailer emphatically told me. Tourists' treatment in his shop often depended on their nationality. Shop staff were far more polite to Anglo-Saxon Westerners than to other nationalities because the former tended to be more polite and appreciative and less likely to bargain ferociously. The Japanese got special treatment. "We used to fleece them like sheep," he smirked. They were overcharged more partly because they too did not bargain much, but also because bitter Singaporean memories from the Japanese occupation (1942-5) were operating. Of the three main ethnic groups and the Eurasians in Singapore, the Chinese (and Eurasians) received the worst treatment from the Japanese. Tens of thousands of young Singaporean Chinese men were killed by the Japanese in the Sook Ching massacres of March 1942 and in subsequent atrocities.

Singaporeans are quite specific about nationalities they trust the most – and the least. They generally think that Australasians, Americans, Britons and West Europeans are more honest and straight in their business dealings than other peoples, in ways already made clear; hence they are more likely to trust them. But they also think such Westerners, especially Australasians and Americans, are naive. Less scrupulous Singaporeans take advantage of this.

What is surprising in Singapore is the lack of trust within the main ethnic groups. Chinese, Indians and Malays often find it difficult to trust even people from their communities. For example, I have been repeatedly warned by the Chinese to not trust other Chinese in business. As Bo Yang, a caustic Taiwanese critic of the Chinese says, "Chinese people always think somebody is trying to take advantage of them. It is this constant suspicion of other people's motives that has made Chinese people as spineless as 'a bowl of sand', to borrow a phrase from Sun Yat-sen".[16]

Such comments suggest the Chinese often don't like each other much. Several times Singaporean Chinese have complained to me how selfish Chinese are. It is therefore not surprising to learn of the disdain Singaporeans generally (Chinese and non-Chinese) have for each other. This surfaced at a National Youth Council dialogue in May 2001. As a *Straits Times* report on the conference noted:

> Love Singapore? No problem. Especially because the country has achieved so much in so little time. But to love fellow Singaporeans? Well, think about the kiasu *people who cannot accept failure, colleagues who would not stop talking about money, or those who are just plain rude.*[17]

One young woman at the conference sparked off the debate when she exclaimed:

> *On the national level, we agree that Singapore is successful. But when you hear the word "Singaporean", do you get the same kind of admiration?*

Shocked silence greeted this utterance: she had apparently hit a nerve. But her comments did prompt the conference to discuss ways to make Singapore kinder and gentler.

Like the Chinese, Indians show a similar intra-racial distrust. One Indian Singaporean who had lived in Australia for some years said he understood the racist attitudes that Australians sometimes display towards Asians. When talking about the Indians and Chinese there he too complained how they "take over". Some Indians have even repeated to me the racist slurs and jokes against them.

Within each ethnic group, merely being Chinese, Indian or Malay is not enough to win trust. More specific socio-linguistic bonds are required. These usually relate to family and kinship links, dialect and ancestral origins. With more traditional Chinese business people, clan associations, based on some home village or town in China and dialect affiliation are still important. In Singapore the main Chinese dialect groups are Hokkien, Cantonese, Teochew, Hakka and Hainanese.

Similar links are important for Indians, who come from several main groups – the Tamils (who speak Tamil), and Punjabis and Sikhs (who both speak Urdu). Among the Malays, many of the main ethnic cleavage is between the Peninsula Malaysian Malays, many of whose ancestors originally came from Sumatra and Java; and Arab Malays, people of Arabic origin, who are also classified as Malays but still think of themselves as Arab.

Trust within the main ethnic groups in Singapore is consequently dictated by a network of sub-racial groupings based on kin and lineage, and linguistic and regional ethnic origins. Merely belonging to a common racial grouping is not enough to guarantee business trust. Predictably, trust is even less evident between Singapore's three main racial groups, especially between Chinese on one side and Indians or Malays on the other. Both sides regularly bad-mouth each other's business ethics. When one is an *ang moh*, each racial group feels safe to mouth off about other ethnic groups in one's presence – not to mention the PAP Government.

Singaporeans, like most Asians, see Westerners, especially Americans and Australians, as too trusting and gullible. As the editors of the New York-based Chinese language magazine *China Spring* told Bo Yang during an interview, "Many Chinese people in the US think that Americans are stupid, naive and easily taken advantage of". Bo Yang replied:

> *This is pettiness and ignorance. Chinese people think that being good to others is stupid. Actually, Chinese people who think this way make China the human jungle it is today. I feel ashamed whenever I think about these things.* [18]

Singaporean executives have similar attitudes to Australians, regarding them as "friendly but simple," according to an Australian Government report.[19]

3. Paranoia

In its extreme form distrust becomes paranoia, a key *kiasu* trait. Readiness to jump to negative conclusions – and clinging to them despite new evidence to the contrary – is one of its least attractive manifestations. Singaporeans are very prone to this. When problems arise in business dealings, they are depressingly ready to assume the other party is trying to cheat them. Bloodworth notes that the Chinese "will always look for an underlying motive (usually bad), a 'hidden agenda'..."[20] In similar vein, Bo Yang notes that "Chinese people are neurotic, belligerent and paranoid about people taking advantage of them. This makes Chinese people overly cautious, defensive and wary of others".[21] Singaporean educationalist Arlene Bastian says that her countrymen "only do things when there are rewards and goodies involved", adding that they are,

> *suspicious of free lunches, altruistic gestures and actions, and unconditional generosity. We only do things when there's something at the end of it for us, so we find it hard to believe anyone could be so silly as to do something with no ulterior motive.*[22]

Even when you have made it abundantly clear to Singaporeans that you are not trying to cheat or "bluff" them, apologies are rare. To apologise is to experience a loss of face, especially for the Chinese, who are normally most ready to make unfounded accusations. Sometimes, though, they will find some oblique face-saving way of making it up to you, such as taking you out to dinner or buying more stock than they need from you.

4. Hard Bargaining

Getting something for nothing, or the most for the least, is another key Singaporean trait. In business this makes them tough negotiators, using every tactic to screw the price down. Conversely, a fair price from them is the highest price they can extract from you.

Singaporeans like to bargain hard for everything and are obsessed with getting value for money, almost to the exclusion of all else. As one Singapore retailer sadly related, he was constantly criticised by Singaporeans for not lowering his prices, especially during economic downturns. These Singaporeans included the rich and employed.

> *I do have a few customers who never bargain. They tell me: "Make sure you earn enough." Sad to say almost all of them are foreigners. We need to follow their example.*[23]

Such pleas fall on deaf ears in *kiasu*-minded Singapore.

5. Opportunism

An Australian bar owner in Singapore once told me about friendships with Singaporeans: "At bottom it's all about money" – and, he could have added, how useful they think you will be to them. *Kiasu*-inclined Singaporeans are supreme opportunists and will readily use others to their advantage. One Singaporean Chinese woman told me her father discouraged her from playing with Malay children in the kampong where she grew up. He told her they would be of no use to her. The easy-going Malays, not being as money-obsessed as the Chinese and Indians, are unlikely to provide the business opportunities the latter deem so important. Friendship is heavily based on how well it may advance a business prospect.

Friendliness is something that many Singaporeans flick on and off like a switch. When they want something from you, niceness abounds. When they have what they want, a certain coolness, even downright rudeness, becomes evident. If, however, they believe you may again be useful to them, then the smiles magically reappear ("Where have you been? So long, not see you.") As a British public relations operative in Singapore said to me, "The trouble is with Singaporeans they think they are being so subtle, when really their intentions are so bloody obvious". One tolerates this base behaviour for a while, putting it down to "cultural differences", but in the end it becomes tiresome maintaining non-judgemental, "non-ethnocentric" poses or make excuses for such grossly opportunistic behaviour.

Networking is seen as a respectable way of using people in these days when the corporate ethos is so prevalent and Singaporeans are indefatigable networkers. At meetings, seminars and conferences their eyes may often glaze over during the speeches, but at intervals the name cards magically appear. The aim is to make as many contacts as possible through maximising business card exchange. Singaporeans, especially, see conferences as useful venues for making contacts and acquiring the latest HRD buzzwords.

6. Guangxi (Net-working)

The Chinese term *guangxi* can best be translated as "relationships" or "connections". As Bjerke remarks:

> Everywhere in the business world you need contacts. But you must magnify its importance many times to understand guangxi.... Hundreds of books have been written about guangxi, but it takes a lifetime to master. Every society in Asia is built around relationships and it is more than a matter of degree compared with the West. In the West, there is business first, then starts the networking: in Asia there is networking first, then starts the business... For the Chinese business boils down to contacts. [24]

A more caustic description of *guangxi* is provided by Dennis Bloodworth, a veteran British journalist who has lived in Singapore with his Chinese wife since the 1950s:

> At its best guangxi may be an "old boy" network of neighbours, of schoolmates, army comrades, members of the same club, including friends in official positions... But more often than not it is a coldblooded system of mutual exploitation, of exchanges of favours among useful "contacts", and sentiment does not come into it despite all the backslapping. Favours are strictly reciprocal, and if one Chinese does a service for another, it is on the clear understanding that the other must repay it when the debt is called in. Hand washes hand. It is simply a matter of moral bookkeeping. [25]

Various factors determine the strength of *guangxi* – whether of the nicer or more exploitive type – between the Chinese. Family and kin links are probably the most important. Members of extended families are mutually obliged to help one another: for example, wealthy family members help poor ones. In business organisations, family members will naturally use their connections to get jobs or other benefits. But *guangxi* goes beyond the extended family and can also be strengthened by ties such as clan membership, village and region or shared educational backgrounds.

The same applies to Indian and Malay communities where family and kin ties are also primary. With Indians too, such factors as shared origins from the same towns, villages or regions in India, common dialects and religious beliefs, such as whether Hindu, Moslem or Sikh, are significant factors determining Indian *guangxi*.

Until the 1997/8 Asian economic crisis, *guangxi* was seen as a largely beneficial practice. Since then it has come to be seen as a manifestation of cronyism, a key reason for the crisis. One writer to question the economic benefits of *guangxi* was Lingle. He saw it as having a similar zero-sum nature to corruption:

> *Ultimately, corruption is a best a zero-sum redistributive game. At worst, it may lead to a negative-sum outcome whereby the losses to one group exceed the gains to the rest of the community. Those who praise the virtues of the institution of* guangxi *seem to overlook its zero-sum nature, whereby if I have it, you cannot.*[26]

Guangxi is a form of favouritism which fosters corruption hinders transparency and the free working of market forces in Singapore and other Asian countries.

7. Avoiding Blame to Save Face

In Singapore's one-mistake society, avoiding blame to prevent loss of face is always a major concern, especially for *kiasu*-minded Chinese Singaporeans. There are two aspects to "face": one (*li-an*) concerns a person's moral character and honour. The other (*mian-zi*) denotes reputation and prestige. "The fear of losing face is nothing more than the fear of having one's ego and prestige deflated," remarks Bjerke. He adds that loss of face could be generated by a broad range of situations or events such as,

> *having an expected promotion fall through, one's child failing an examination, one's daughter marrying a poor man, one's brother working in a lowly position, receiving an inexpensive gift...In general, a person will lose his/her face if he/she is found to be unable, or unwilling, to satisfy the claims imposed upon him/her by his/her friends or subordinates...*
>
> *The logical counterpart to "losing" face is to "gain" face. The prestige of a Chinese may be inflated by working in a large company, surrounding him – or herself with influential "friends", showing off materially etc.*[27]

Losing face means deep shame for the Chinese: "The importance of shame for a Chinese makes it hard for him to admit a mistake ...or to ask for help".[28] Bo Yang also talks of the "utter reluctance" of the Chinese to admit mistakes:

How many of you have ever heard of a Chinese admit that he or she has made an error? If you have then break out the Maotai: it is time to celebrate the renaissance of China.[29]

Because the Chinese "are overly concerned about losing face ... they never surrender or admit to making mistakes".[30] This is especially so in Singapore's one-mistake society, and not only produces a fear of making mistakes but gives rise to a stubborn refusal to acknowledge those made. When screw-ups occur, it's everyone for himself. Pinning the blame on others is a standard tactic. Sometimes subordinates are required to accept the blame for superiors' mistakes. This behaviour most often occurs in Singaporean organisations where punitive managerial attitudes prevail.

Refusal to admit wrong-doing as well as simple mistakes is another less likeable Singaporean trait. When Singaporeans have failed in their obligations to you, or merely wasted your time, no apology or expression of remorse is likely. Cheques may bounce repeatedly; deadlines for payments may be missed; but no apology will be forthcoming. Occasionally, when reminded, defaulters will respond with bald denials, surly silence or even belligerent abuse. As Bloodworth drily notes: "the Chinese instinctively throw themselves into an orgy of righteous indignation whenever they know they are in the wrong, their object being to shift the blame for everything on to the other side".[31] This is apparently a long-standing Chinese tactic. Sunzi, a Chinese sage, "said that if your position is weak, use deception to pretend you are strong, and Chinese armies finding themselves outnumbered would create a systematic hullabaloo, beating drums, yelling defiance at the enemy, blowing discordant trumpets, waving a sea of intimidating flags, and doubling the number of camp fires at night (under cover of which they might safely sneak away)".[32]

8. Finding Fault

What happens if you are perceived to have fallen short? Singaporeans have little hesitation in complaining loud and rudely to you. You need to recognise, however, that this may be a tactic to put you on the defensive, to extract concessions. Singaporean retailers constantly moan about how fussy and picky Singaporeans can be. Not only do they always want things cheaper, but unless the product is absolutely perfect they will reject it – or want an even bigger discount. Retailers much prefer to deal with the more easy-going Westerners, especially from Australasia and North America and with the Japanese.

Singaporeans do love complaining. In December 2000, Prime Minister Goh remarked that Singaporeans were a nation of moaners. A *Straits Times* poll had just found that eight out of ten Singaporeans interviewed agreed with Goh's comment.[33] Those polled admitted that Singaporeans had a habit of complaining about everything from the humidity of the weather and traffic congestion to the high cost of living and poor service. "Singaporeans complain all the time. It's almost like a national pastime," one said. Another said: "Singaporeans whine about everything. In some sense we were brought up to be rather spoilt. We always want things our way."

9. Ingratitude

One particularly unpleasant aspect of the *kiasu* personality is to have a readiness to take advantage and take people for granted, but an inability to show gratitude for favours and help given. This again is particularly so with the Chinese, who will demand every assistance you can give in some business association or partnership. One can promptly and efficiently despatch stock and goods to them as per their specifications and get little appreciation. Sometimes they may not accept what you have supplied them because their requirements have changed, or they can't pay. Whatever the case, the inconvenience they have caused means little to them. This perceived ingratitude became the target of the 1987 Courtesy Campaign, where Singaporeans were urged not merely to be the passive recipients of other people's thoughtfulness.[34]

The Chinese especially don't like to acquire obligations. The old Chinese adage, "Before you drink from a stream, see where its source is," reflects Chinese thinking. Everything must be paid for, so be careful whom you take from. "What is given must be returned," observes Bjerke.[35] However, it is acknowledging, not merely accepting, favours that can pose problems, because such acknowledgement means recognition of an obligation. Failure to acknowledge a favour can free one from any sense of obligation. Singaporean Indians seem more appreciative of favours done and honesty demonstrated than others. While they display many of the *kiasu* traits mentioned, ingratitude is not one of them. They are also more ready to apologise if necessary.

10. Deceptive Behaviour

Smiles and deferential behaviour do not necessarily denote a friendly attitude, either in Singapore or elsewhere in Asia. In the West smiles tend to denote joy, friendliness or amusement; in Asia they more often mask a range of less-than-friendly emotions. "A Singaporean may hide nervousness, shyness, embarrassment, lose of face, sadness, hurt feelings, bitterness, cynicism or irony behind a smile," notes Craig.[36] Deferential behaviour can also mask disrespectful attitudes. As Tamney recalls; "the Chinese in Singapore tend to show respect for those in authority; I experienced this as a teacher at the local university, though I felt the formal expression of deference masked a variety of personal feelings, not all equally respectful".[37]

11. Short Attention Spans

An American expatriate journalist at *The Straits Times* once made this comment to me about the paper's management: "If you want to suggest something to them, you have got to get in quick before they move on to something else. They can only seem to focus on one thing at a time."

Lee Kuan Yew's Dutch adviser and friend Winsemius made similar and surprisingly critical observations about Singaporeans:

> *I don't know if you have ever noticed that Singaporeans and its government often behave like adolescents in a one-sided way, over-stressing a thing and forgetting the rest; then dropping the subject and focussing, once more one-sided, on the next thing.*[8]

Singaporeans have an exasperating tendency to express strong support for some scheme or project only to forget about it soon after. Subsequent inquiries merely elicit bland indifference. They often seem to completely forget about a proposal and their initial enthusiasm for it.

The preceding has described a range of less-than-attractive personality traits of Singaporeans. To this list could be added failure to listen (especially by bosses to subordinates), hierarchical attitudes and lack of initiative. Westerners especially need to know that Singaporean values, business and otherwise, are often very different from those practised in North America, Western Europe and Australasia. Such understandings better prepare them for doing business in Singapore which is the next chapter's focus.

References

1. Craig, JoAnn Meriwether (1993): *Culture Shock! Singapore* (Singapore, Times Editions), p. 92.
2. Ibid.
3. Bjerke, Bjorn: "Entrepreneurship and SMEs in the Singaporean Context", p. 276 in *Competitiveness of the Singapore Economy*, edited by Toh Meng Heng and Tan Kong Yam (Singapore, Singapore University Press, 1998).
4. *The Straits Times* (ST), August 14, 1995.
5. ST, June 1, 1999.
6. ST, January 25, 1996.
7. ST, February 1, 2000.
8. ST, January 28, 2000.
9. ST, July 25, 2001.
10. ST, April 18, 2004.
11. Murray, Geoffrey and Audrey Perera: *Singapore the Global City State* (England, China Library/Curzon, 1996), p. 243.
12. ST, December 20, 1995.
13. ST, March 11, 1995.
14. ST, October 3, 1997.
15. Low, Linda: "State Entrepreneurship", p. 204 in *Local Entrepreneurship in Singapore*, edited by Tsao Yuan Lee and Linda Low (Singapore, Times Academic Press, 1990).
16. Yang, Bo: *The Ugly Chinaman and the Crisis of Chinese Culture* (Sydney, Allen and Unwin, 1992), p. 41.
17. ST, May 13, 2001.
18. Yang, p. 32.
19. ST, May 21, 1995.
20. Bloodworth, Dennis and Liang Ching Ping: *I Married a Barbarian* (Singapore, Times Books International, 2000), p. 162.
21. Yang, p. 55.
22. Bastion, Arlene: *Singapore in a Nutshell* (Singapore, Prentice Hall, 2003), p. 104.
23. ST, September 10, 2001.
24. Bjerke in Toh and Tan, p. 274.
25. Bloodworth and Liang, p. 173.
26. Lingle, Christopher: *The Rise and Decline of the Asian Century* (Hong Kong, Asia 2000, second edition, 1997), p. 147.
27. Bjerke in Toh and Tan, p. 275.
28. Ibid, p. 275.
29. Bo Yang, p. 14.
30. Ibid, p. 29.
31. Bloodworth and Liang, p. 136.
32. Ibid.
33. ST, December 6, 2000.
34. "*Courtesy – More than a smile*" (Singapore, Ministry of Information and the Arts, 1999), p. 14.
35. Bjerke in Toh and Tan, p. 276.
36. Craig, p. 64.
37. Tamney, Joseph B.: *The Struggle Over Singapore's Soul* (Berlin, Walter De Gruyter, 1995), p. 82.
38. Barr, Michael: *Lee Kuan Yew: The Beliefs Behind the Man* (Surrey, UK; Curzon, 2000), p. 85.

CHAPTER 19

DOING BUSINESS IN SINGAPORE

Both Westerners and locals, especially individuals and small firms, often find it unpleasant and stressful doing business in Singapore. Even MNC operatives posted to Singapore cannot escape culture shock. They find they are dealing with business values often very different from those back home, where the other party is not always seen as an adversary to be fleeced or used but as a potential partner and someone to work and perhaps prosper with.

Besides dealing with a generally adversarial mentality, those doing business in Singapore must often endure evasiveness, insincerity and opportunism as well as unexpected inefficiencies, disorganisation and lengthy delays in making decisions. While there are many Singaporeans who conduct their dealings in an fair, honest and efficient manner they are far fewer than could be expected in a country which so vigorously espouses and apparently practises Western business values and procedures.

The difficulties of doing business in Singapore have intensified as the local private economy has found it increasingly hard to survive the number of recessions that have been afflicting Singapore since 1997. While Singapore as a whole has ridden out these downturns better than its neighbours, its SMEs have been hit hard, increasing such difficulties.

1. Survival Tactics

Though doing business is not easy in Singapore, the following may help.

Visit the Registrar of Companies

A visit to Singapore's efficient and well-run Registrar of Companies office in Anson Road can be an enlightening experience when checking out prospective partners or contemplating legal action against them. For S$5 you can get a print-out of a business, listing the full name, address and IC number of those who have registered that name.

Waving that print-out in front of Singaporeans who have been uncooperative or dishonourable can get results. They don't like you knowing that much about them. Knowledge is power; and the more you know about them the stronger you are vis-a-vis them. It will make them more amenable to settlement. Don't be put off by abuse: that's a standard reaction when they see you have out-foxed them. Interestingly, you will find that many a Singaporean businessman registers businesses in the name of his wife, who may have few assets of her own. Singaporean businessmen like to leave an escape hatch for themselves and keep creditors at bay should things go pear-shaped.

Being Nice

Niceness has its place in business, and Singaporeans can be very nice initially. When dealing with big companies and Singaporean corporations you will often find staff helpful, cooperative and professional, if somewhat bureaucratic at times.

Small business people in Singapore can also be hospitable. They may wine and dine you and give you the best of Asian hospitality. You can be nice back to them, be the appreciative guest, lavish in praise, restrained in criticism – but don't mistake any of this for genuine friendship or interest in you, except of course if they happen to be long-time friends going back many years. "Singaporeans – particularly the English educated – are hung up about staying in their comfort zone, and define relationships in clear terms a ('He's a business contact, not a friend') as one Singaporean executive told *The Straits Times*.[1]

Your new Singaporean acquaintances will often ask what you think of Singapore and its people. If you have just arrived you will probably be impressed by the place and find it easy to praise all things Singaporean. If, however, you have become a little jaded about Lion City, then a certain amount of dissembling may be required.

Being Nasty

What happens when problems arise: when, for example, you find your Singaporean partners have been less than co-operative or honest, or when your efforts to remain polite and patient have only elicited evasiveness or bloody-minded rudeness?

The standard cultural guides for Asia, including Singapore, stress self-control, keeping your cool, being patient and politely insistent. Craig belongs to the be-cool school. She primly observes that,

> *many an unwary expat still feels that the safest policy is to "be yourself: your open, friendly frank, outspoken, and up-front self". These qualities are supposed to be what Asians admire about Westerners.*
>
> *However, Asians are less likely to admire these "qualities", than they are to view the Westerners as lacking in grace, manners, and cleverness when these same qualities cause hurt feelings, lost face, business breakdowns and unwitting hostility.[2]*

The longer one stays in Singapore the more one sees that the locals often fail to practise such principles themselves. Chief among these is Lee Kuan Yew whose sneering comments about other Asian leaders and peoples, including Australians, is legendary. Singaporeans have no qualms about being very unpleasant when they want to be. Many are the abusive confrontations and phone conversations I have witnessed. Their phone manners also leave much to be desired; they are often terse to the point of rudeness when making or receiving calls.

Singaporeans are also prone to making rude comments about people still within earshot. It's embarrassing when they are talking to you about a person standing near you. On occasion Chinese will talk about you too in Chinese while you are in their presence. Sometimes the word *kweilo* can be heard. *Kweilo* is Cantonese for "white devil" and as a racist term is on the "wog-nigger-chink" level. Being referred to as an *ang moh*, however, is not so bad.

How therefore should the normally well-behaved *ang moh* respond to Singaporean rudeness, thoughtlessness and insensitivity? First, one should realise that niceness has its limits in Singapore, especially when one has been repeatedly asking nicely for something but has continued to be ignored or strung along. As one Chinese businessman told me, "The Chinese often look down on Westerners because they know they are too nice to make a fuss most of the time". He said Chinese are not so constrained to be nice to each other. Tough talk, even abusive behaviour, is acceptable. They will respect those with such traits more than they would most Westerners, especially the Anglo-Saxons and West Europeans. Italians, Greeks, Slavs and Russians, who are more capable of aggressive rudeness when necessary, are more respected by the Chinese.

Regarding the Slavic approach, one Bulgarian businesswoman comes to mind. She would buy bootleg cassettes and tapes at Sim Lim Towers in Singapore to send back to Bulgaria. The traders at Sim Lim spoke admiringly of how she was a "tough customer" and not someone they wanted to cross. She could be quite unpleasant if she thought she was being ripped off. As such, she always got good deals and made a lot of money. Unfortunately, she came to a sticky end during a business dispute in January 1998 with two Singaporean partners who ended up murdering her. Being too pushy and aggressive has its limits, even in *kiasu* Singapore.

Nonetheless, raising your voice a few octaves, banging the table and making legal threats, sad to say, seem to have more effect on many Singaporeans than being nice. When dealing with big companies in Singapore, the threat of going over their heads to superiors and complaining unless something is done also gets results. This ploy can work well because it is based on Singaporeans' fear of their superiors. Also, a Westerner has a certain credibility, and his complaints will usually be taken seriously. Singaporeans generally recognise that Westerners who are forced to go to such extremes must have a genuine grievance. Similarly, if a cheque has bounced in Singapore its a good idea to go to see the manager of the account-holder's bank. Ask the manager to speak to the account-holder and find out when funds will be put into the account to make the cheque good. Losing face with their bank manager is not an experience that Singaporeans relish.

None of these tactics are pleasant but they work depressingly often. On one occasion I had been politely requesting a big Singaporean company to do something for me for about four months. Eventually, my patience exhausted, I told a secretary at the company I would complain to the general manager unless something was done soon. Four days later my request was granted.

Countering Veiled Threats

"Are you PR here?" This seemingly innocent question from Singaporeans can merely be a polite inquiry. But it can also be a veiled threat from some of them, especially if they happen to be in business with you. They may want to cut you out and deal directly with the parent company back home. They want the whole cake for themselves, *kiasu*-style. If you are doing business on a Social Pass only, a word by them to Immigration can see you deported, leaving the field clear for them. If, however, you have an Employment Pass, or better still Permanent Residence, then you are safe and they know this. So always say "yes" when they ask if you are PR. If you have an Employment Pass, show this to them if necessary, just to ram home the point.

Singapore is a society where veiled threats are constantly used by the PAP regime against its citizens, so few Singaporeans have qualms about using them against foreigners. They usually don't act on them, but you can never be sure. Singaporeans, especially the Chinese, come from a culture where informing is a time-honoured pastime. According to their always unsparing critic, Bo Yang,

> the Chinese have been famous worldwide since ancient times [for] *informing on their friends. Indeed Chinese people are geniuses when it comes to snitching.*[3]

During the Qin dynasty (221-207BC), informing was so prevalent, that a law was passed to punish people guilty of false incrimination.

Employment passes usually are valid for from one to three years. In theory you are supposed to be earning at least S$2000 a month with a registered Singaporean company (not merely a business name). If you really are working for a Singaporean company then the company will get the pass for you. If you are basically self-employed, then a challenge presents itself. You must find a company, or at least a business name you can be employed under; but apart from Singaporean citizens, only PRs or those on an Employment Pass (EP) may register a business name or start a company. If you are already employed in Singapore and want to go it alone then make sure you register a business name while you still have an EP and you may be able to employ yourself under your own business name. Normally you are not supposed do this: Singapore Immigration rules stipulate that a company must employ you. But there are expatriates who have registered themselves under an already-registered business name. Your chances of doing this depend on several factors, such as having a university degree or some other prestigious tertiary qualification and/or a previous employment pass. Another is being a Westerner, especially if a British subject, which includes Australians, New Zealanders and Canadians. Almost as good is being an American or West European. Further down the pecking order are East Europeans. At the bottom are people from Third World countries, who find it hardest to get an EP on their own. (Most developed countries, including Australia, have similar immigration policies towards Third World peoples, but do not always wish to acknowledge this).

If you have omitted to register a business name while employed in Singapore, or are newly arrived and wish to work free-lance, then either a Singaporean citizen or a foreign resident holding PR or an EP must register a business name for you and be the

"First Precedent Partner" of that name. They are legally responsible for you or anyone else who is employed under that name, including making sure that you pay your taxes. But once having gained employment – and an EP – under that name you can eventually register your own business name and be employed under its name instead.

When you have an EP you will feel much safer conducting business in Singapore. No longer will you skulk around in fear of discovery. Neither will you have to go on visa runs every month or couple of weeks to Johore Baru in Malaysia (a 45-minute bus ride from the Queen Street bus terminus in Singapore) or Batam Island in Indonesia (a 40-minute ferry ride from the World Trade Centre). In recent years Singapore's immigration authorities have been giving Westerners, especially, longer social passes (up to three months for British subjects) to make it easier for them to stay in Singapore. It's part of the Government's drive to attract foreign talent.

Being Open?

Australasians and Americans suffer from this problem the most in Asia, including Singapore. Whereas frankness may inspire confidence, even affection in North America and Australia, such is not the case in Singapore, where being too open is seen as foolish. One expatriate Australian business woman in Singapore told me she cringes sometimes when Australian business people in Singapore make statements like, "Oh, I don't have a clue what to do about this" or "I don't know what to do, what do you think?" hoping naively that the Singaporeans they are negotiating with won't take advantage. They usually do. "Withholding information to gain or maintain power is acceptable among Chinese... Openness is, in fact, often considered to be a sign of weakness in the Chinese culture."[4] As Craig observes:

> To the Singaporean, the one who discusses emotions and feelings for all the world to hear, is seen as a person of little worth – a weak person of inferior status. Those who openly talk about sacred things reveal secrets, and they cannot be trusted.[5]

Much better to pretend to be open and naive while keeping one's high cards well hidden.

Being yourself can be a big mistake with superficial Singaporeans. As Bloodworth has found, the Chinese,

> tend to go by appearances, so that not only unsuitable clothes, but a high-pitched voice, an evasive manner, a mobile "monkey" face or an unfortunate nose... can quickly draw an invisible frown. As one sardonic commentator remarked, "They like everyone to be like everyone else."[6]

"Front" or image is important to Singaporeans. Dressing well and stylishly and giving the impression that one is wealthier and more successful than one actually is, is even more important than in the West. The question every expatriate must ask him or herself is the extent to which they wish to bend, twist and deform themselves to be acceptable to Singaporeans. Some Westerners do it with ease and back home in the West increasing numbers of ambitious people are forced to prostitute themselves in this manner to advance their careers and achieve corporate promotions. Others with personal integrity find this harder.

The Australian tendency to put themselves and Australia down does them little good in Asia, where assuming a tough, bold and successful front is seen as critical. Australian unpretentiousness and honesty are often viewed derisively in Asia, including Singapore.

Being on your guard is more important than being yourself in Asia. Big-hearted, open, honest and risk-taking attitudes cut little ice in a society of calculating, manipulative and small-minded opportunists.

Hands-on Approach

In Singapore, as in the rest of Asia, one needs to keep a constant watch on any investment, partnership or business arrangement. For example, if a Singaporean firm is distributing some product for you, make sure that it is being done properly by checking the outlets where it is supposed to be. Don't simply accept vague assurances that this is so.

Second, don't give distribution rights for a whole range of products you may have to market. While Singaporean firms like to get the franchise to distribute all your products, they may be able to distribute only a couple of them effectively. They want to have the rights to distribute the rest to deprive others from doing so. It's the *kiasu* mentality. Grab everything you can even if you don't need or can't use it.

Keeping tabs on any project is also important. Make sure you are getting a progress report on each stage. Singaporeans, like most Asians, have an aversion to staying in touch when you or they are abroad. Out of sight, out of mind is a common problem one encounters with them. The only way to find out the latest developments in any project or undertaking you may be involved in is by phoning them. Faxing or e-mailing is usually a waste of time. You have got to get them on the phone. Then fax or e-mail if necessary as a follow-up, and then phone again to make sure they got the fax/e-mail and know what's happening or what they are supposed to do.

The reluctance to stay in touch even occurs when one may owe them large sums of money, or hold large quantities of their stock. One can leave addresses and phone and fax numbers at all one's destinations, but often they will fail to contact you. They would rather sit and fume about you than get on the phone or fax and ask how things are going.

The desire to avoid contact, not surprisingly, applies doubly if they owe you money. The only time they will usually pay up is when you are standing in front of them, asking for your money. Expectations that they will TT money owed or pay it into your Singapore bank accounts are unlikely to be met unless you are dealing with large established Singaporean firms. To make sure you get paid it is sometimes best to ask someone you trust in Singapore to visit them to pick up the money and bank it for you. It's often preferable to have a Western friend do this. Singaporeans will often be more cooperative towards Westerners than each other on such occasions.

Hiring Staff

Singapore is regularly promoted as having the most efficient and best-trained labour force in Asia. Up to a point this is true. Singaporeans will certainly be more educated and speak much better English than most people in neighbouring countries; but wages will be several times higher than in Malaysia and much higher than in Indonesia, Thailand or the Philippines. As already shown, Singaporean employees have some severe deficiencies. Apart from their job-hopping propensities and limited initiative, there is the TPQ syndrome to contend with. Singaporean employers are usually more aware of this opportunistic mentality of their countrymen. This free rider problem makes many local companies reluctant to train staff because, once trained, they may let themselves be poached by competitors.

Western employers are often perceived as soft touches by Singaporeans because of their generally more considerate treatment of employees. Americans and Australians especially tend to have less hierarchical and more egalitarian attitudes to their employees than the average Singaporean boss. Many Singaporeans appreciate this, especially the women who, like women generally, tend to show more loyalty to their bosses and firms. But Singaporean male employees too often equate civilised treatment with softness and act accordingly. One Singaporean indignantly told me how an Australian friend of his had suffered this fate. He would sit down and have a few beers with his staff in the yard after work, in customary Aussie style. Soon they were taking all sorts of liberties at work. "I told him not to do that and said they will only shit all over him for that. They don't know how to respond to that sort of respect. You've got to have a firm hand with them, like Singapore bosses," insisted the Singaporean. Being treated in an egalitarian manner confused them, he contended. They would often abuse such treatment.

Living in a society where *kiasu* rudeness so often prevails does little for people's self-respect. Those with self-respect find it easier to treat others with consideration and equality. This is often not so in Asia, including China. Because "Chinese have never had much self-respect," remarks Bo Yang, "it is immensely difficult for them to treat others as equals. There are two alternatives: either you are my master, or my slave".[7] Such attitudes are inimical to egalitarianism.

Even so, Singaporean employees are good at performing complex technical and computer operations. They are also at their best when following a fixed set of rules and regulations where little initiative is required. But this can also be a problem as one expatriate banker noted when complaining about the poor quality of secretaries. He once gave his new secretary a list of ten people to call, but after an hour she hadn't put through a single call. He walked to her desk and found that she was still trying the first number. "What about the rest?" he asked. Flustered, she said: "Oh, I thought you wanted me to speak to them in this order".[8] As one British engineer said of Singaporean employees, "They are technically quite adept but ask them to use their judgement and so often they just don't have it". This is a recurring complaint made by expatriate bosses about them.

Singaporeans as Clients and Partners

Having Singaporeans for clients or partners as well as customers can also be taxing. Lack of ideas, readiness to criticise others' proposals and inability to make decisions are just some problems.

While Singaporeans may have few ideas of their own they will readily pick apart the ideas of others. As Singaporean columnist Jason Leow observed:

> *Anyone who has survived a Singapore client knows he waits for ideas to be handed to him, then spends all his time picking those ideas apart, instead of offering suggestions.*[9]

Leow was describing the frustration experienced by Singaporeans who have worked abroad before returning to work in Singapore. One Singaporean returnee recalled the problems he had running co-events with the locals. Many times "he had to wait – and wait – for decisions from the Singapore side. Getting orders from the top was like 'manna from heaven'," adding that, "No one wanted to stake his decision on a bad decision". By contrast Taiwanese and Hong Kongers were super-quick off the mark and business moved at breakneck speed, reported another Singaporean returnee.

Be Honest

Yes! Be as honest and straight as possible in your dealings with Singaporeans. Despite their less than perfect business ethics, the honesty policy is preferable for both practical and moral reasons. As mentioned earlier Singaporeans perceive Westerners, especially North Americans, Brits, Australasians and West Europeans, as far more honest than the locals. Anyone who belongs to this august set of nationalities should confirm the positive stereotype that Singaporeans tend to have of them. This involves such things as keeping your word, doing what you say you will do, delivering goods promptly, paying as quickly as possible and keeping in touch rather than avoiding contact if payments have to be delayed or if difficulties have arisen. It also includes drawing attention to any discrepancies in their accounts when you have been over-paid or given more stock than their records show. Such honesty can disconcert some Singaporeans who are used to operating in a business environment where dishonesty is common.

Get It in Writing

For expatriate businesses, Singapore's legal system alone makes the Republic one of the best places for business in Asia. Contracts can be signed, agreements enforced and business dishonesty minimised through the protection afforded by Singapore's laws. Accordingly, foreigners should remember this when doing business with the locals. Getting any agreement down on paper and signed, preferably with a company stamp, is an essential preliminary. Also important is ensuring that proper invoices and consignment notes are issued and signed by both parties for any goods received or delivered. Sometimes one will encounter a certain reluctance to do this by Singaporeans for obvious reasons.

The preceding may seem an unduly negative assessment about doing business in Singapore, perhaps suggesting that it is of Third World standard. But the people most cynical about Singaporeans are usually other Singaporeans. Much of the preceding is based on what they have written or told me about themselves. Even so, there are still some important differences between Singapore and most of its Asian neighbours. The first is its legal system, which is probably the best in Asia in terms of protecting local and foreign businesses. When it comes to commercial matters the courts in Singapore are as just and fair as anywhere in the world, and often more efficient than many in Western countries. Whatever disputes Westerners may have with the locals (or each other) they can be assured of fair hearings and objective corruption-free decisions. Singapore's commercial legal system is one of the great positive legacies that Lee Kuan Yew has left Singapore, as well as being a key factor attracting foreign capital to Singapore.

Of particular note is the Small Claims Tribunal, which has been set up to deal with disputes involving sums of S$10,000 or less. Many a Western tourist has received speedy justice there against less-than-honest local retailers who have overcharged them or sold them sub-standard goods.

Singapore's legal system has done much to ensure that the business ethics of Singaporeans are better than they would otherwise be. Their unscrupulous *kiasu* instincts are significantly curbed by the very visible and effective presence of Singapore law. Although criminals may have a strong propensity to rob a bank, the sight of well-armed guards, cameras and other security devices will deter them. Singapore's laws have a similarly deterrent effect on erring Singaporeans.

While many of Singapore's business people will readily engage in less than honourable business practices, a tough and reputable legal system does much to curb such tendencies. In addition, the Government's draconian anti-corruption measures have given Singapore one of the cleanest civil services in Asia.

2. A Word about Expats

No account on surviving Singapore's business jungle would be complete without a description of the many types of expatriate likely to be encountered there.

Dealing with so many *kiasu* Singaporeans can tempt many recently arrived Westerners to gratefully fall into the arms of the first *ang moh* they may meet. But they should not assume that such Westerners have similar outlook, values and viewpoints to themselves. Many of the "white men" (and women) you may meet in Asia, including Singapore, are usually not the same as those back home. Often their business values are more Asian than Western. They have been ripped off so many times by the locals (and other expats, quaintly referred to as "old Asia hands") that their principles have been bent and broken – they are often more deadly than the locals. Being Western they know how to press the right cultural buttons to make other Westerners, especially new arrivals, trust them.

Singapore's expatriates fall into six main groups.

1. The Organisation Men

Usually corporate and foreign government types who usually work for MNCs, big Singaporean enterprises or foreign embassies, trade organisations and banks. They are the standard issue organisation men, very concerned about perks and pecking order and rather cliquish. They certainly don't like mixing with anyone, expatriate or local, deemed to be of lower socio-economic status. Their lavish salaries and condo-country club lifestyle largely insulate them from the trials and tribulations endured by less exalted expats.

They are treated particularly well by Singaporeans, especially the PAP ruling elite and bureaucrats. Because such executives work for the MNCs, which are the lynch-pin of Singapore's economy, they are accorded special respect. Moreover, their high salaries and affluence automatically earn them high esteem from materialistic status-conscious Singaporeans. All this gives MNC executives favourable impressions of Singapore and its leaders.

2. The Respectably Employed

Academics, full-time teachers or instructors or computer consultants, book and newspaper sub-editors and commercial artists belong in this category. Although without the perks of the top group, they live comfortably enough in Singapore and have fewer pretensions.

3. The 20-something Hopefuls

Big numbers of these have been arriving in Singapore since the mid-1990s. They are often fresh from the universities and technical colleges in Australasia, the UK and North America and work for local wages under local conditions. They live in cheap rented rooms or share low-cost flats. The high cost of living and the need to "party" means they often save little. Even so, they are grateful to have a paying job in a foreign country where they can sometimes stretch their wings and be given more responsibility than in jobs back home. But dealing with *kiasu*-minded Singaporeans and the organisational and cultural peculiarities of Singaporean companies can often make life rather stressful for them.

4. The Off-shore Oilies

Mainly oil and construction workers, these hard-drinking, hard-playing men rejoice in the name "oil field trash" and sometimes wear T-shirts proclaiming this. They tend to live in cheap hotels and apartments, preferring to save their money for boozing and whoring when ashore. The North American variety, in particular, affect macho attitudes and strut around in cowboy boots and jeans. Often they are as pretentious in their own way as MNC operatives. They are great fans of Country and Western music and hang out at The Ginivy and hooker-type bars in Orchard Towers. They frequently have some Thai, Indonesian or Filipino bar girl in tow when in port. Rough and ready expatriates will get on with them, but those not of that type should look elsewhere.

5. The Entrepreneurs

This motley collection of individuals includes risk-takers, dreamers and con men. Some become successful entrepreneurs who have built up profitable businesses in Singapore. Others live on borrowed or absconded money. Singapore is a place where fortunes are regularly made and lost, where billion-dollar deals are common and multi-million ones occur daily. The sight of huge amounts of seemingly easy money sloshing around lures many expatriates to long periods of waiting in Singapore for the "big deal" to materialise. Most wait in vain and are always looking for unwary investors to finance their latest dream or project. This group you must be very wary of. They convincingly prove that a fool and his money are soon parted.

6. Down-Market Freelancers

Usually the poorest and most looked down on expatriate group, they can range from free-lance journalists and writers through fashion models and nude art models to part-time language teachers and instructors. They also include backpacker tourists working as airport touts to get guests for Bencoolen-Selegie Road crash pads. Among this group is a small but regular contingent of Western prostitutes from Australia, New Zealand, Russia and Eastern Europe. They normally work for Singapore's escort agencies and despite often being rather average-looking can get S$1000 or S$1500 a night from their clients. They are the "aristocrats" of Singapore's sex industry, compared to the thousands of bar girls from Thailand, Indonesia, the Philippines, China and Vietnam who freelance in nightclubs and karaoke lounges. Right at the bottom are Thai and Indian prostitutes servicing foreign workers in work camps.

Being on the make is endemic in Singapore. Most people, expatriates included, are affected by it. This is not a place where you can relax and enjoy yourself, nor make friends. You come to Singapore to work and make money – and to survive until you do. Real friends are few in such a competitive environment. Friendship is based on how useful you are to the other party and usually ends when they think they no longer need you. Help for expatriates with problems is usually limited, especially for expatriate wives who have to deal with philandering husbands. As one expatriate journalist, Paula McCoy, noted, "The support network for expatriate wives is minimal. The friends and family they could have turned to in a crisis are back home".[10]

This was dramatically demonstrated to me once when an ex-neighbour of mine, an American women living in Singapore with a baby and two teenage daughters, was abandoned by her husband. He disappeared into Indonesia for a few months, despite desperate efforts his wife could not locate him. Apparently the burdens of breadwinning had got too much for him and he had sought solace with some Indonesian lass. One day his wife phoned me and sought my help. She barely had money for food and was several months behind in the rent. I did what I could to help her and even managed to sell her one saleable item, an incomplete set of encyclopaedias, for a few hundred dollars. I was also able to locate alternative accommodation for her and the youngest child.

She and her husband had had a busy social life and often entertained a regular group of expatriates in their apartment, but none of these "good time" friends would help in her hour of need. Instead she turned to me, a mere acquaintance, for assistance. After helping her as best I could, I heard no more from her, but some months later I was told she had returned to the States. I later ran into her husband, who had subsequently returned to Singapore. He was once again strutting around its nightspots in his cowboy boots.

Singapore is a use-or-be-used society for both locals and foreigners. It is one where stress, anxiety and long hours await the newly arrived expatriate, especially the solitary entrepreneur or small businessman looking to develop new markets. However, a hard-nosed unsentimental attitude towards the locals and expats alike should improve one's survival chances and result in eventual prosperity.

For the MNC executive life is easier, though not without some culture shock. At least he can forget his worries at some over-priced country club's golf course or chill out in his company-supplied condo. But expatriates who have to work under local bosses and conditions find life far less salubrious.

* * * * * * * *

The first five sections of this book have critically examined the historical and economic aspects of the Singapore Miracle. This section has revealed the wide gap between Singaporean and Western business values and practices. The next section discusses how statistics produced by the PAP state in league with compliant think-tanks and ratings agencies have disguised this gap and obscured the Singapore Miracle's basic flaws.

References

1. *The Straits Times* (ST), February 8, 2004.

2. Craig, Jo-Ann Meriwether : *Culture Shock! Singapore* (Singapore, Times Editions, 1993), p. 48.

3. Yang, Bo: *The Ugly Chinaman and the Crisis of Chinese Culture* (Sydney, Allen and Unwin, 1992), p. 154.

4. Bjerke, Bjorn: "Entrepreneurship and SMEs in the Singaporean Context", p. 270 in *Competitiveness of the Singapore Economy*, edited by Toh Meng Heng and Tan Kong Yam (Singapore, Singapore University Press).

5. Craig, p. 78.

6. Bloodworth, Dennis and Liang Ching Ping: *I Married a Barbarian* (Singapore, Times Books International, 2000), p. 113.

7. Yang, p. 18.

8. *Singapore Swing*, Asia Inc, February 1996, p. 38.

9. ST, February 8, 2004.

10. ST, May 13, 2001.

Section Six

....

Mythical Statistics

Singapore's rulers live and breathe statistics and constantly use them to justify their policies and proclaim their success to the world. The aim is to sell the Singapore Miracle to both Singaporeans and the international business, financial and political circles. Singaporeans have to be convinced that PAP rule is best for them and Singapore has to be depicted as a choice haven for foreign capital.

Adroit use and tight control of statistics has been central to supporting the claims made about the Singapore Miracle, both domestically and internationally. Compliant ratings bodies have greatly helped in this task. The following chapters firstly consider how the PAP state manipulates statistics for domestic and foreign ends. Then the role that such bodies as the Swiss-based IMD and the Harvard-based WEF play in this process, along with that of other ratings agencies, is examined.

CHAPTER 20

LIES, DAMNED LIES AND SINGAPORE GOVERNMENT STATISTICS

In December 2000, a Singapore think-tank, the East Asian Institute (EAI), felt free to pour scorn on Chinese statistics. In its annual report the EAI said that the abundance of Chinese data and their prompt publication had ironically created "a common feeling outside China about their authenticity and reliability".[1] The report, titled "Lies, Damned Lies and Statistics", presumably inspired by Disraeli's famous quote about statistics, asked:

> *How can official statistics from a communist government which is often given to propaganda be trusted?*

How indeed? This question could just as easily be applied to Singapore, a country awash with dubious official statistics.

A recognition of the often malleable and misleading nature of statistics is appropriate when examining data that the PAP state relentlessly churns out for domestic and foreign consumption. One of the first researchers to cast doubt on Singapore Government statistics was UK academic Iain Buchanan, who spent several years in Singapore. He wrote:

> *Singapore's economic statistics are notoriously unreliable, and are characterized by a somewhat plasticine malleability – one statistic, relating to a specific item in a specific year, may undergo three or four permutations in following years, according to dictates of political expediency. Essential data go studiously unrecorded, statistical bases are often revised to alter recorded trends, different departments sometimes produce opposing sets of figures relating to the same item.[2]*

These observations were made in 1971. In 1984, former deputy prime minister Toh Chin Chye also questioned Singapore government statistics when asked about them by *Asiaweek*:

> *I don't believe the statistics put out by the Government. The man in the street doesn't know whether he is on thin ice or solid rock.[3]*

In December 1994, Singaporean political scientist Bilveer Singh, talked of the Government "massaging statistics" on living costs in an article in *The Jakarta Post* entitled "Singapore Faces Challenges of Success". While acknowledging that Singapore had made "very noteworthy" achievements in the areas of public housing, education, health and full employment, he added that what "the statistics hide through the law of averages and generalization, is that the majority of Singaporeans are basically living hand-to-mouth".[4]

Little has changed since. The PAP state's proclivity for manipulating statistics for political and promotional ends seems as strong as ever.

1. PAP Stats

In recent years the Government's readiness to distort official data has been most evident in data on the cost of living, income distribution, AIDS and trade, and on GDP figures.

Cost of Living Figures

Rising living costs have been a growing political problem for the PAP Government since the early 1990s. When housing and other prices took off, the Government sought to defuse public discontent over increased living costs. Consumer Price Index (CPI) figures until the mid-1990s showed inflation was under control and rising by only 2 to 3 per cent a year, but from daily experience the average Singaporean knew otherwise. Many were finding it increasingly hard to make ends meet. By the mid-1990s housing and car prices had soared, along with health and education costs.

By 1996, Singaporeans quite reasonably believed that living costs were outstripping their income. In July 1996, a *Straits Times* survey found that 57 per cent of young Singaporeans expected the cost of living to rise faster than their salary growth; 38 per cent thought both would rise at the same pace over the next few years, while an optimistic few believed their income would grow faster than living costs.[5] With elections in a few months, the Government took steps to mollify the voters. In August 1996, Parliament reconvened the Cost Review Committee (CRC) to investigate Opposition MPs' complaints about rising living costs. For over a month the committee ponderously reviewed Singapore's cost of living increases from 1988-95. A joint report by two opposition parties, the Singapore Democratic Party (SDP) and the Singapore Malay National Organisation (PKMS), claimed that cost of living increases had been "no less than phenomenal" in the 1990s, noting that household expenditure had risen by 76 per cent between 1988-93.[6] They maintained that government policies had driven up the prices of goods and services.

The Government countered, claiming that the cost of living had only gone up by 14 per cent while income had grown by 48 per cent between 1988-93.[7] The remaining 62 per cent of the increased expenditure (76 less 14 per cent) was largely due to greater spending by Singaporeans because of their higher incomes. People were buying more and better quality goods, the Government claimed. The Government used cost of living increases for all major expenditures from 1988-93 to prove price rises had been low. Government figures for household expenditure for these years were:

Table 20.1 – Household expenditure for 1988 – 93

	Percentage increase in spending	Percentage increase in prices
Food	32	6
Clothing	87	8
Housing	139	15
Transport	92	27
Education	101	26
Health	96	25
OVERALL	76	14

NOTE: The top and bottom five per cent of households were excluded. [8]

Opposition MPs argued that the low inflation rate claimed by these figures was due to "statistical massage" by the Department of Statistics (DOS). Much evidence supports this view, as an examination of housing costs will firstly show.

The Government claimed that while expenditure on housing had increased by 139 per cent, price rises had only accounted for 14 per cent. The rest was because Singaporeans had been buying bigger flats over the preceding seven years. To support this claim the Government cited figures showing that while the purchases of 3-room HDB flats had fallen by 29,100, those for four and five-room flats had risen by 71,300.[9] However, a housing price survey for 1985-95 and for 1990-95 revealed that HDB housing prices had increased by many times more than 15 per cent from 1988-93. From 1985-95, HDB prices increased by about 7 to 10 per cent a year, according to the HDB Yearbook of Statistics.[10] Four-room units rose by an average of 6.9 per cent, 5-room units by 9.5 per cent and executive class housing by 10.6 per cent a year. This meant that in any five-year period from 1985-95, HDB units would have risen by an average of 34.5 per cent, 47.5 per cent, and 53 per cent respectively – several times more than the 15 per cent claimed by the Government.

Moreover, a 1990-1995 study of the resale price of HDB flats showed that three-room HDB flats rose in price from S$43,000 to S$112,000 (160 per cent); four-room flats from S$89,000 to S$213,000 (139 per cent); five-room from S$127,000 to S$317,000 (249 per cent); and executive from S$183,000 to S$413,000 (225 per cent).[11]

Even more dramatic were the price rises for private property, especially in 1991 when they rose by 11 per cent, 1992 (15%), 1993 (36%), 1994 (42%) and 10 per cent in 1995.[12] Overall the cost of private residential properties increased by 25 per cent a year from the beginning of 1992 to mid-1996.[13]

One statistical tactic the Government used to prevent the soaring housing prices from being registered by the CPI index was to classify property purchase as an investment rather than an expenditure item. To pay lip service to the need to factor in housing costs (after all the CPI is supposed to track prices of consumption items) an "imputed rental" approach was used in tabulating housing costs.[14] A *Straits Times* columnist described how this worked:

This means that, rather than the purchase price of a property, its cost as reflected in the CPI is actually the amount of rental that it can fetch if it is rented out. The rental value is based on the annual value of the property as calculated by the Inland Revenue Authority.[15]

During the CRC hearings it was revealed that this "imputed" rental value was a mere S$348.72 a month,[16] but in the mid-1990s even cheap walk-up apartments cost at least S$1500 to S$2000 a month in Singapore. I know, because my 37-year-old walk-up apartment was costing me S$2000 a month at that time and it had risen to that figure from S$800 a month over five years. Renting one room only in an HDB unit would cost from S$300 to S$500 a month.

Not surprisingly, the IRA's S$348.72 figure "puzzled" one CRC member, Ms Lee Tsao Yuan, a Nominated MP (a non-party MP selected by the Government). She politely suggested to the Chief Statistician, Paul Cheung, that it "appeared to be on the low side". Cheung facetiously replied that he was "puzzled by her puzzle", adding that the number of people buying new houses was small. The only people affected would be those purchasing a new house. Those who stayed put in their houses would not be affected by rising house prices, he said. The tens of thousands buying houses, whether for the first time or to upgrade, apparently counted for little with Cheung – as did those renting accommodation.

Besides giving evasive and misleading responses to legitimate questions the Government turned the cost of living inquiry into an inquisition against opposition politicians whenever possible. This happened during the Select Committee (SC) hearings on health-care subsidies, which was held in conjunction with the CRC. (The SC was convened to examine SDP claims that health care was poorly subsidised by the Government in Singapore).

An inquisitional opportunity arose when a glaring error was found in an SDP submission regarding government health subsidies. The submission claimed that the Government's share of health care expenditure had dropped from 40 per cent in 1970 to 5 per cent in 1990, when it should have been 25 per cent.[17]

SDP chief Chee Soon Juan was portrayed by the Singapore media as being evasive in his responses. Press reports implied that he only admitted the mistake after sustained and ruthless bullying from the SC chairman and Minister Without Portfolio, Lim Boon Heng, and by the Minister for Health, Brigadier George Yeo. In commenting on Chee's treatment by the SC, Professor Garry Rodan, director of the Asia Research Centre at Murdoch University, said:

"The PAP had seized on Chee's error in misquoting NUS academic Mukul Asher's observation that there had been a declining contribution by the government to total health expenditure from 40.1 per cent in 1970 to 27.5 per cent in 1989, choosing to depict this as a calculated act of deceit rather than the more plausible explanation of a typographical error from an under-resourced opposition. It was the character assassination of Chee by the PAP, which the local media helped

execute, that took precedence over any serious engagement with the substantive issues raised by Asher and picked up by Chee." [17a]

Opposition MP Ling How Doong got similar treatment when he rejected Government definitions of what constituted a health funding subsidy. Ling maintained that it was wrong for the Government to say that it was subsidising health when private hospital patients were charged $100 but only had to pay $50. He said returning taxpayers' money to them should not be regarded as a subsidy. The Government not only totally rejected Ling's comments but had Parliament pass a motion expressing regret at attempts by him and the SDP to "mislead the public over health-care subsidies".[18]

Worse was in store for Chee and three other SDP members. They were dragged before the Parliament's Committee of Privileges and charged with contempt of Parliament by Health Minister Yeo because of the health costs mistake. The committee subjected Chee to a seven-hour cross-examination. Yeo accused Chee and his three SDP colleagues of "perjury, prevarication, misconduct and wilfully giving false evidence" to the SC. Simply proving that Chee and his SDP colleagues were wrong was not enough for this vindictive government; nor was publicly humiliating them. They had to be punished as well.

Vast tomes emerged from the CRC and SC hearings to give the proceedings an image of thoroughness and propriety. The CRC report was 167 pages and the SC report 600 pages. Predictably both reports gave no credence to the SDP/PKMS claims on cost of living and health subsidies. The CRC report also indignantly rejected allegations of statistical massage:

> *The allegation is a serious one, which stood to tarnish not only the reputation of the Department of Statistics ... but also Singapore's standing as a country where the business of government is taken seriously and is not subject to manipulation by corrupt officials for financial, personal or political gain.*[19]

From then on Lee Kuan Yew and the PAP Government lapsed into denial mode on rising living costs. In November 1996, Lee dismissed talk of rising living costs, claiming the strength of the Singapore dollar kept imports cheap and living costs down for Singaporeans.[20] "People say the cost of living has gone up. It's rubbish. We have the strongest currency in Asia," he declared. Many Singaporeans sullenly disagreed. They could do little else. The so-called CPI inquiry was a government whitewash and also a means of intimidating any Singaporeans who dared question official statistics. No real attempt was made to address Singaporeans' legitimate concerns about rising prices; the energy went into discrediting them with dubious government statistics.

The Income Gap

The PAP Government used questionable statistics to counter rising public concern at Singapore's widening income gap. Like soaring living costs, inequalities of wealth were becoming too obvious to ignore by the mid-1990s. The Government again resorted to obfuscation and denial. For years PAP ministers insisted that there was an increasingly equitable distribution of wealth in Singapore. The income gap was supposedly getting narrower.

In November 1994, government minister Lim Boon Heng said the gap between top and lower-income earners had narrowed since 1984.[21] He cited statistics that purported to show that in 1984, people in the top 10 per cent earned $7.40 for every dollar earned by the bottom 10 per cent. In 1994 it was only $6.10. In August 1995, the Department of Statistics released figures claiming that the share of total income received by the bottom 20 per cent rose from 3.6 to 4.7 per cent between 1980 and 1994. By contrast, the total share of income by the richest 20 per cent declined from 52 per cent to 49 per cent.[22]

In the same month Koo Tsai Kee, a PAP MP, cited figures and charts that made similar claims. Koo blustered that,

the charge that the wage gap in Singapore is one of the highest [widest?] *in the world, and is widening dangerously is ridiculous. Only an ignoramus devoid of any economics background would venture to tell such a lie. The truth is that, for the last 30 years, we are all growing richer together at more or less the same rate.[23]*

He proudly cited the World Bank's statement that Singapore's "low and declining level of inequality is a remarkable exception to historical experience and contemporary evidence in other regions". Senior PAP ministers such as Finance Minister Richard Hu also cited statistics to support this view. In May 1995, Hu claimed the wage gap between rich and poor had been stable over the last six years and that the top 20 per cent of wage-earners still only earned slightly more than three times that of average wage-earners in the bottom 20 per cent. [24]

Research by Singaporean academics refuted such confident mid-1990s claims by the Government about Singapore's supposedly low income gap. First, Gini coefficient (GC) figures from the mid-1980s to 1995 revealed growing income inequalities in Singapore (the GC is used to describe a country's distribution of income and ranges between two theoretical extremes – 0.0 representing total equality of income and 1.0 for total inequality). Gini figures compiled by NUS academics Linda Low and Ngiam Tee Liang [25] showed that the GC for Singapore was 0.450 in 1987. In 1990 it dropped slightly to 0.432 and then rose to 0.461 in 1997. The rises in Singapore's GC from 0.432 to 0.461 reflect a rising income inequality from 1990 to 1997. Low and Ngiam's figures also show that the share of household income for the bottom 20 per cent in Singapore was only 3.5 per cent in 1995 (not 4.7 per cent as Minister Lim claimed). Moreover, Low and Ngiam's figures for eight other countries (Japan, Taiwan, Holland, France, the Philippines, Australia, Britain and the US) show that the bottom 20 per cent in these countries received between 3.7 per cent of total income in the US to 11.5 per cent in Japan, according to income surveys from 1989 to 1995.[26] Singapore was at the bottom of this list with 3.5 per cent, showing it to be the least equitable of the nine countries surveyed.

Overall Low and Ngiam's data contradicted government claims that income inequalities were moderate and declining to 1995, but the economists' findings have attracted little attention or government criticism because they were buried in academic books that few Singaporeans would ever read. Bilveer Singh was the only Singaporean academic to publicly suggest that Singapore's income gap was widening; and he was pilloried by the Government.

In December 1994, an article by Singh on the Singapore Miracle appeared in a small English-language daily, *The Jakarta Post*. Dr Singh paid the usual homage to the Republic's dramatic progress but he also pointed out the growing disparity of wealth in Singapore and how badly off the majority of Singaporeans were:

> *What is now emerging in Singapore is a society that is faced with growing impoverishment even though a fortunate minority is still reaping profits and the queue for Mercedes 320s is still very long. What the statistics hide through the law of averages and generalisation, is that the majority of Singaporeans are basically living hand-to-mouth ...*[27]

The PAP Government was outraged. In a letter to *The Straits Times* from Singapore's ambassador to Jakarta, Simon De Cruz attacked Singh's claims, labelling them as "preposterous". He insisted that Singh substantiate his allegations or withdraw them.[8]

When Singapore academics face such governmental wrath they have little choice but to recant. This Dr Singh did with an abject apology. He "agreed unreservedly" with the points in the Government's reply and withdrew the offending allegations. "I admit that it was a gross error on my part and apologise for the negative impression created," he admitted. Since then the Government has conceded there is a wide and growing income gap in Singapore. Chapter 23 describes how big this gap has become.

AIDS Figures

In developed countries, AIDS has been mainly transmitted via homosexual sex or intravenous drug use. Relatively few people have been infected by HIV through heterosexual intercourse. In the US the main methods of AIDS transmission were homosexual sex (52%) and IV drug use (33%) in 1998.[29] Heterosexual sex accounted for only 13 per cent of infections. In other countries the figures were:

Table 20.2 – Methods of AIDS transmission

	Homosexual	IV Drug Use	Heterosexual
Russia	64%	1%	32%
Brazil	34%	25%	34%
China	5%	59%	17%
Southern Africa	7%	N/A	N/A

As these figures show, AIDS has still primarily been a gay-junkie disease, except in southern Africa. These percentages seem fairly constant. In China in 2003, 60 per cent of HIV/AIDS patients had contracted the disease through drug abuse.[30] In Malaysia, drug use accounted for 75.9 per cent of HIV infections and heterosexual intercourse for 10.6 per cent, in 2000;[31] in 2002 intravenously-caused AIDS made up 76.3 per cent of the total.[32]

Singapore's AIDS profile has been completely different. Most of Singapore's AIDS victims are heterosexual males, health authorities claim. They supposedly got it from unprotected heterosexual sex – mostly with prostitutes. Of the 199 new cases of AIDS reported in 1998, 163 had contracted it through heterosexual sex, 12 through homosexual sex, 19 from bisexual sex, four from mother to child and only one from drug use, official figures reveal.[33] Of the 185 new HIV cases reported to October 31, 2001, 97 per cent had been infected through sexual activity, a health official claimed. "The rest were drug-users or prenatal infections," she said.[34] Of those infected through sex, 80 per cent arose from encounters with prostitutes or from casual sex.

As the 2000s progressed the same pattern of AIDS infection was being reported by the Ministry of Health (MOH). Of 422 new infections in 2007, 93 per cent were males who had been infected through sex. [34a] As the following table shows, the mode of transmission had changed little over the years, except for a growing proportion of people infected by homosexual sex.

Table 20.3 – Methods of HIV transmission in Singapore 1985-2007

Mode of Transmission	1985-2000	2001	2002	2003	2004	2005	2006	2007
Heterosexual	979	181	181	177	188	185	222	255
Homosexual	169	22	30	40	72	87	94	130
Bisexual	130	16	12	14	22	14	14	15
Intravenous Drug Use	26	6	6	4	7	4	14	7

(Figures taken from Ministry of Health website)

Apart from an increase in homosexually-caused cases, the above figures show that the numbers infected through intravenous drug use have remained almost constant except for a one-year blip in 2006.

Official claims that heterosexual activity has caused most of Singapore's AIDS infections are questionable. First, HIV rates are very low among Singapore's prostitutes, especially when compared to those in other Asian countries. In 2000, the incidence of HIV infection among Singapore's sex workers was only 0.7 per cent.[35] Infection rates among prostitutes are much higher in other Asian countries such as Thailand, Burma, China and India, where heterosexual transmission of AIDS is recorded as significantly lower.

Intravenous drug use, not sexual activity, has launched many AIDS epidemics, especially in Asia. A UN AIDS official told an October 1999 conference in Kuala

Lumpur that the spread of AIDS in Asia was often closely linked to intravenous drug use. In many big cities an outbreak among injectors almost certainly preceded or would precede a wider epidemic. "It is arguable that only in the major cities of India and Cambodia did a sexually-transmitted epidemic occur first," he said. [36] Both countries were very poor, unlike Singapore which was small and rich and had far greater medical resources for treating AIDS outbreaks.

Questions have been asked about Singapore's AIDS statistics and official reluctance to release them. *Straits Times* columnist Alan John complained that "the secrecy over much that concerns AIDS here, and the paltry information that is released, combine to keep HIV infections and AIDS shrouded in mystery". [37] The newspaper's attempts to find out more about Singapore's AIDS victims, such as their education levels, socio-economic background and family details, had proved futile. The MOH said that such details "are not routinely captured" and so were unavailable.

Chris Beyrer, an epidemiologist at Johns Hopkins University in the US, found similar problems with getting AIDS data from Singapore's health authorities. In his 1998 book on AIDS in Asia[38] Beyrer said he omitted discussing AIDS in Singapore because "it has not consistently reported HIV statistics to international bodies". He also lacked first-hand experience of the place. [39]

Beyrer subsequently told *The Straits Times* that from 1994-6, while working through data by country, he found Singapore's policy was to target migrant workers by screening them every six months. Those infected were deported. This policy of keeping HIV-infected people out of a population "sharply skews statistics, since you are trying to test all of one population, and not testing (or testing and not reporting) others," he said. [40] The Government refused to release its foreign worker data or the numbers deported. Beyrer learned from a colleague who had worked for the health authorities how biased the data being released was.

The question remains: why is AIDS an overwhelmingly gay/drug-user disease in urbanised industrial countries – and over the border in neighbouring Malaysia – but a largely heterosexual phenomenon in equally urbanised and industrialised Singapore? Why has heterosexual activity accounted for about 80 per cent of Singapore's AIDS cases but only about 10 per cent of those in neighbouring Malaysia, where three-quarters of the rest have been due to intravenous drug use?

False reporting by HIV-infected people may well explain Singapore's peculiar AIDS figures. The intimidating effect of the country's draconian drug penalties and tough anti-sodomy laws discourage candour by HIV and AIDS victims. People can be hanged for possessing as little as 15 grams of heroin; lesser amounts can earn 10-15 years jail – plus an agonising caning with the rotan. Even heroin addicts who have relapsed more than twice are caned. Caning is excruciatingly painful. Even Singapore's most hardened criminals are said to prefer more jail time to the rotan. Drug-using AIDS victims have an enormous incentive to lie and say they got infected through sexual activity. This avoids police interrogation on how they get their drugs and risks of being punished for possession.

Singapore's health officials promise confidentiality to HIV/AIDS victims, but Singaporeans know such promises are highly conditional and would be readily suspended by the authorities, especially if drug-use was suspected. Better to lie than risk draconian punishment and being forced to "dry out" at a government drug rehabilitation centre where cold turkey is the preferred method.

Admitting to homosexual activity is also unwise for those with HIV or AIDS in Singapore where sodomy is severely punished. Section 377a of the penal code states that "Any male person who, in public or private, commits, or abets the commission by any male person, of any act of gross indecency with another male person, shall be punished with imprisonment for a term which may extend to two years".[41] Commenting on this in a July 2002 *Lancet* paper, Beyrer and Kass noted:

> *Singapore's sodomy statutes are enforced rigorously and widely feared. The government is known to use paid clandestine informants to obtain evidence of these acts.*[42]

Despite official promises of confidentiality, blood collection in Singapore is done by government agencies. Moreover, staff "interviewing subjects were civil servants of the same regime seeking to punish citizens for homosexual behaviour and drug use," they said.[43]

The HIV infection rate of Singaporeans tested before being permitted to donate blood was nine times higher in men than women, according to a Singaporean paper presented at the 1999 Kuala Lumpur conference,[44] yet nearly all HIV-infected males reported heterosexual sex as their only sexual activity. The Government has used this information to claim that most HIV infection was being caused by heterosexual activity. As Beyrer and Kass observed:

> *Since the nine-to-one prevalence pattern is typical of communities in which HIV infection is spread through male-to-male sexual or drug transmission, the interpretation of the study findings must be seen as highly suspect.*[45]

Two Singapore government health officials condemned Beyrer and Kass's comments as "frivolous allegations". They praised Singapore's low AIDS figures and the rigorous measures used to screen donated blood for AIDS and other viruses. They also claimed that "there are legal provisions to protect the confidentiality of HIV-infected persons".[46] But they failed to explain Singapore's peculiar AIDS profile. They refused to consider the effect that Singapore's climate of fear, caused by harsh drug and sodomy laws, has had on honest disclosures by HIV-AIDS victims. It is much simpler to claim they were infected by a prostitute abroad than tell the truth. Singapore's papers regularly run tragic tales of Singaporean men who got AIDS because they slept with one hooker too many in Bangkok or Batam.

The Government may well know that most AIDS in Singapore is due to drug use and homosexual activity, but finds it convenient to promote the idea that heterosexual sex is the main cause. The reasons may lie in governmental campaigns to promote "family values" and monogamous relationships, and encourage Singaporeans (especially the Chinese) to marry and breed to perk up the country's anaemic birth rate. Whenever new AIDS figures come out the Government lectures Singaporean men about consorting with prostitutes and the importance of monogamous (preferably married) relationships. A possible aim is to scare men from going to prostitutes. Better they slake their lust in a marital bed where babies (preferably Chinese) will be conceived. Frightening Singaporean men away from prostitutes and into matrimony is a likely motive. Using questionable statistics in such ways to promote official values is a common government tactic.

In fact, intravenous drug use, rather than heterosexual sex, would most likely account for far more of Singapore's AIDS cases. Since the mid-1990s Singapore has had four to six thousand registered addicts a year in an indigenous population of 3.2 million. While Singapore's drug addict numbers have been low by international standards they are still sufficient to contradict any perception of it having few intravenously-caused AIDS cases. Certainly there are sufficient drug-injectors in Singapore to explain the bulk of its AIDS cases. Out of an indigenous population of 3.2 million, Singapore had 3727 heroin addicts caught by police in 1998[47] and 3142 in 1999.[48] Morever, police would only catch a proportion of drug users of all types every year.

The longer erroneous notions about serious problems such as AIDS hold sway the more negative can the consequences be. AIDS prevention programs based on questionable findings result in "potentially unsound interventions and dangerous and inappropriate blood-donor criteria," warn Beyrer and Kass.[49]

Blood donors afraid of disclosing risky behaviours can increase the risk of contaminated blood supplies. This is especially so if they are HIV positive but still in the "window period" when HIV tests will show they are HIV-negative. This period can last several months before tests reveal they are HIV-positive. If they feel free to disclose risky behaviours such as drug use and homosexual activity, then their blood donations can be deferred until the window period has passed and a HIV test can conclusively confirm whether they are HIV-infected or not.

In Singapore, donor failure to disclose risky behaviours has resulted in two tragic HIV transmissions from HIV-positive donors who were still in the undetectable window period.[50] Had they admitted to such behaviours their donations would have been deferred until tests showed that they were positive.

Misleading information from HIV-positive people produces false AIDS statistics which lead to flawed anti-AIDS strategies. In Singapore, AIDS campaigns have been mainly directed at heterosexuals, especially males. The campaigns urge men to remain chaste before marriage, be monogamous when married and stay away from prostitutes. If they can't do this they should at least practice safe sex with condoms. But they are also told that condoms do not provide 100 per cent protection – only abstinence or monogamy can.

Such a strategy may be appropriate if AIDS victims were overwhelmingly heterosexual males. But if not, if most have contracted AIDS through drug-use or homosexual activity, then lecturing heterosexual males about abstinence and monogamous relationships only marginally addresses the problem, especially if it is primarily drug-driven. Malaysia has discovered this to its cost, according to the president of the Malaysian AIDS Council, Marina Mathathir. She said that Malaysia had missed its chance to prevent the spread of the disease because of a failure to target drug-users: "Ten years ago, if we had put in place programmes that prevented HIV transmission among drug-users, we could have contained the epidemic".[51] In the early days, AIDS campaigners had distributed very frank posters that talked about unsafe sex and the need to use condoms, but they failed to address the drug-users who were largely driving the epidemic.

By November 2004, there was growing concern that Singapore was facing an "alarming AIDS epidemic". A senior health minister said that in six years time new infections could reach 1000 a year unless something was done to stop the spread of AIDS. The number of new AIDS cases was rising and was set to exceed 300 in 2004, he said. He continued to claim that heterosexuals were responsible for 80 per cent of HIV cases though he did note that a growing number were homosexuals.[52] The promiscuous lifestyles of homosexuals as well as heterosexual men had to be targeted, he contended.

The minister's concern was well-founded because since 2004 the numbers of AIDS cases have continued to steadily rise. They were 311 in 2004, 317 (2005), 357 (2006) and 422 (2007).[53] Altogether, 3482 people contracted HIV/AIDS in Singapore from 1985 to 2007, of whom 1144 had died. Even so, apart from conceding that more homosexuals were being infected by AIDs, the minister maintained the official line that in Singapore the disease is primarily a male heterosexual one. No mention was made of strategies for drug-users, who are likely to comprise most of Singapore's AIDS cases, as they do in Asia and elsewhere. Instead, Singapore's health authorities have continued to target promiscuous behaviour since 2004 to curb the spread of AIDs. But as can be seen, the number of new AIDs cases rose by about 30 per cent, from 311 to 422, between 2004 to 2007. Clearly, government anti-AIDs strategies have continued to fail.

The only promising development has been some greater focus on homosexuals as well as heterosexuals. This approach coincides with a greater number of homosexual AIDS cases being recorded from 2004. This may not be because growing numbers of homosexuals are getting infected but because more are coming forward to be tested due to the Government's greater tolerance towards gays since 2003. Also, health officials have been working closely with AIDS NGOs on strategies to educate gays to reduce risky sexual behaviour and undergo regular testing.[54] However, the failure to recognise that intravenous drug use is probably responsible for most HIV infections means that the main cause of the problem remains unaddressed. Not only are AIDS victims still likely to lie about how they became infected but those who got it by intravenous means would continue avoiding going for any HIV tests because of the draconian consequences of admitting to drug use.

As such, there remain many undetected as well as undiagnosed HIV/AIDS cases in Singapore, as a February 2007 anonymous MOH survey of 3000 patients in public hospitals found. The survey showed that 0.28 per cent of adult patients in five hospitals had undiagnosed HIV.[55] This meant that 1 in 350 patients in public hospitals were HIV positive and did not know this, said a Government minister.[56]

When all of Singapore's possible cases are considered, its HIV/AIDS totals would probably double. According to UNAIDS estimates, there were 4700 people with HIV/AIDs in 2003 but by 2005 there were 5500.[57] At this rate of increase, which is about the same as that of the detected cases in 2006 and 2007, they would probably have hit about 8000 by 2008.

Singapore's AIDS numbers now exceed those of such countries as Hong Kong and Australia. Hong Kong had 414 new cases in 2007, compared to Singapore's 422, but Hong Kong's population is nearly double that of Singapore's.[58] Again, Australia had 960 new cases in 2006 but has five times Singapore's population.

The Government response to rising AIDS numbers has been directed at trying to control the sexual behaviour of high-risk groups such as gays and promiscuous heterosexuals. An uneasy combination of education and appeals for greater tolerance of AIDS victims, combined with the threat of heavy punishments, have been used. First, at-risk individuals are constantly urged to go for testing and advised on safe-sex methods, including condom use. Employers have also been asked to adopt a more understanding and supportive attitudes to HIV-infected workers.

However, the Government also amended the Infectious Diseases Bill in April 2008 making it an offence for any HIV/AIDs infected person or anyone who could have been exposed to infection through high-risk sexual behaviour to have sex without first informing his or her partner.[59] Fines of up to S$50,000 or 10 years imprisonment would be imposed on those who failed to do this. But instead of countering the problem of sexually-transmitted HIV, the Bill could encourage more anonymous sex by high-risk or infected people. One spokesman for AIDs victims said that those who were infected would not disclose the names of their partners to doctors for fear of being prosecuted.[60]

In summary, the Government keeps focusing its anti-AIDS strategy on controlling people's sexual behaviour, rather than targetting intravenous drug-users. Such strategies are likely to continue for as long as they are based on misleading statistics which claim that most of Singapore's AIDS victims are hetero or homosexual males who became infected through unsafe sexual activities other than from intravenous drug use.

GDP Figures

Singapore regularly releases impressive GDP figures to sell its success story. But some have queried Singapore's GDP figures. A financial analyst who wrote to the *New York Times* said that Singapore "habitually reports an 'errors and omissions' number that is disproportionately large in relation to its gross domestic product" in its annual financial accounts.[61] The analyst noted that this number is meant to account for discrepancies and should thus be comparatively small. But in 1996, Singapore's "errors and omissions" total amounted to 3.9 per cent of the GDP. This is a remarkable figure for an economy of Singapore's sophistication and supposed competence. Even China, with a much vaster and far less developed economy than Singapore, reports an "errors and omissions" number of only 3 per cent. Despite this a Singaporean think-tank believed it could ridicule China's statistics.

With improved statistical procedures and methods the Government's capacity to manipulate data for both foreign and domestic consumption has probably improved since Buchanan's 1971 observations. One can be sure that Singapore's rulers have developed state-of-the-art expertise in this regard. Prime Minister Lee Hsien Loong is, after all, a highly qualified mathematician and an expert in statistics.

The use of statistics for political ends involves not only doctoring them but restricting access to them. States are not content simply with issuing biased or misleading data: they also seek to prevent the release of information that could embarrass a government or challenge its policies. Singapore's rulers are adept at such opaque practices.

2. Controlling Information

All states manipulate official data for their own ends. How far they can do this depends on what access the public, NGOs and opposition politicians and parties have to information that can challenge official data. A citizenry who can acquire such information is far harder to mislead and "disinform" than one that can't. Controlling public access to government statistics becomes crucial when political leaders release false or misleading information. The aim is to prevent people getting hold of material that could reveal official mendacity or abuse of power. Should any unauthorised persons do so they are usually punished, especially in neo-authoritarian states such as Singapore.

As Chapter 15 showed, Singapore has a powerful combination of laws that ban or greatly limit public access to official records. These are the Official Secrets Act, the Evidence Act, and the Statutory Boards and Government Companies (Protection of Secrecy) Act 1995. They give civil servants the right to refuse to disclose official information to the courts or public. Often such laws induce acute paranoia in Singapore's civil service, as Worthington found. They seem terrified to release any information to non-government groups or individuals. The Evidence Act particularly prevents the release of any information that might be detrimental to the Government.

The 1992 Flash Estimates case involving *The Business Times* not only demonstrated the punitive power of these Acts but revealed the Government's readiness to prosecute any who published leaked information. Such leaks not only embarrass the Government but reveal the questionable nature of official statistics.

Besides punishing those who gain unauthorised access to official data, the PAP state vigorously persecutes those who dare challenge its statistics. As Chee, Singh and others have found, they are often publicly vilified and forced to apologise abjectly.

Singaporean university authorities also came down hard on two visiting academics who ruffled the Government's statistical sensibilities. An article by Christopher Lingle and Kurt Wickman called "Don't Trust the Reports of Supercharged Growth" appeared in the *International Herald Tribune* in January 1994.[62] The article questioned China's impressive economic growth figures and highlighted inconsistencies in these figures, cautioning that Chinese growth estimates should be treated with scepticism. Although there was no official complaint from the Chinese Government, Lee Kuan Yew had been championing China's case in world forums. Such articles might have prompted people to question Singapore's statistics.[63] Politically sensitive NUS authorities summoned the two academics and told them not to write such articles in future, nor identify themselves with the university when submitting future articles to the international press. As Lingle subsequently noted, "China's obsession for control over economic data is mirrored by a near-paranoid control of data in Singapore".[64] Neither state wanted maverick academics capable of discrediting official data. Even so, six years later Singapore's EAI felt free to belittle Chinese statistics.

Then there was the official castigation of two NTU academics in 2003. They were forced to make the obligatory apology after accidentally embarrassing the Government over the sensitive issue of foreigners taking local jobs. The Government subsequently made it clear that access to official data would be carefully controlled by only being available to "approved" academics. It appeared to be moving from the control to the fabrication of data when it began releasing "classified" data that could not be verified independently, to discredit the two academics' findings.

Politically inconvenient data, despite appearing on the Ministry of Manpower's website, was contradicted by other official but uncheckable data. Authoritarian states feel freer than democratic states to fabricate information because their citizenry have few means of challenging official data. In states such as Singapore, not only the distortion but even the falsification of data is common. This is done for domestic political purposes and also for international image-making.

Various international rating agencies play a central role in promoting Singapore internationally, especially the IMD and WEF. Both agencies often rely heavily on official data from the countries they survey when compiling their competitiveness rankings. This approach can be problematical when assessing such countries as Singapore, whose officials have few qualms about manipulating statistics for foreign or local consumption. Such PAP practices may significantly explain the very flattering competitiveness rankings that Singapore has received from the IMD and WEF for many years. These ratings will be examined in the next chapter.

References

1. *The Straits Times* (ST), December 11, 2000.
2. Buchanan, Ian: *Singapore in Southeast Asia* (London, Bell and Sons, 1972), p. 76.
3. Chee, Soon Juan: *Your Future, My Faith, Our Freedom* (Singapore, Open Singapore Centre, 2001), p. 80.
4. *The Jakarta Post*, December 6, 1994.
5. ST, July 7, 1996.
6. ST, July 8, 1996.
7. Ibid.
8. ST, August 7, 1996.
9. Ibid.
10. ST, September 21, 1996.
11. ST, August 21, 1995.
12. ST, May 11, 1996.
13. ST, August 22, 1996.
14. ST, May 11, 1996.
15. Ibid.

16. ST, September 23, 1996.
17. ST, July 16, 1996.
17a. Email comment from Garry Rodan to the author.
18. ST, October 11, 1996.
19. ST, November 2, 1996.
20. ST, November 4, 1996.
21. ST, November 1, 1994.
22. ST, August 24, 1995.
23. ST, June 6, 1995.
24. ST, May 1, 1995.
25. Low, Linda and Ngiam Tee Liang: "An Underclass among the Overclass" pp. 238-9 in *Singapore: Towards A Developed Status*, edited by Linda Low (Singapore, Oxford University Press, 1999).
26. Ibid, p. 239.
27. ST, December 21, 1994.
28. Ibid.
29. *Newsweek*, July 6, 1998.
30. ST, July 15, 2003.
31. ST, May 3, 2001.
32. ST, April 1, 2003.
33. ST, March 28, 1999.
34. ST, December 6, 2001.
34a. Ministry of Health (MOH), Singapore: www.moh.go.sg.mohcorp/statistics
35. UNAIDS, Epidemiological Fact Sheets, 2002 Update, Singapore, p. 2. <www.unAIDS.org/
36. ST, October 25, 1999.
37. ST, September 2, 1997.
38. Beyrer, Christopher: *War in the Blood: Sex, Politics and AIDS in South-East Asia* (London, Zed Books, 1998).
39. *Sunday Times* (Singapore), April 11, 1999.
40. Ibid.
41. Singapore Penal Code, Section 377a.
42. Beyrer, Christopher and Kass, Nancy E. "Human rights, politics, and reviews of research ethics", *The Lancet*, Vol 360, July 20, 2002, p. 248.
43. Ibid.
44. Chapman C., Leo Y.S.: "Risks for HIV infection from the ACURE@ database in Singapore" (MCD14 426]. (5TH International Conference on AIDS in Asia and the Pacific, Kuala Lumpur, 1999).
45. Beyrer and Kass, p. 248.
46. Chui, Paul and Suok Kai Chew: "Appropriateness of Singapore's HIV/AIDS control programme", *The Lancet*, Vol 360, December 14, 2002, p. 1982.
47. ST, March 24, 1999.
48. ST, September 24, 2000.
49. Beyrer and Kass, p. 248.
50. Beyrer, Christopher and Nancy B. Kass: "Appropriateness of Singapore's HIV/AIDS control programme" in reply to Chui and Suok's comment in the Correspondence section of *The Lancet*, December 14, 2002, Vol 360, p. 1983.
51. *Today*, December 2, 2004.
52. ST, November 11, 2004.
53. MOH website.
54. *UNGASS Country Progress Report*, January 2006-December 2007, (March 2008) p. 3.
55. Ibid. p. 4. and ST, July 17, 2007.
56. ST, July 17, 2007.
57. ST, April 23, 2007.
58. "HIV hits new high: Solution: punish" (yawningbread, May 1, 2008).
59. Inquirer.net (Philippines), January 14, 2007.
60. *Bloomberg*, February 12, 2008.
61. *The New York Times*, January 26, 1998 (quoted in Chee, p. 75).
62. *The International Herald Tribune*, January 19, 1994.
63. Seow, Francis T.: *The Media Enthralled: Singapore Revisited* (Boulder, Colorado; Lynne Rienner, 1998), p. 214.
64. Lingle. p. 228.

CHAPTER 21

RUBBERY RANKINGS

For many years the IMD and the WEF jointly published the World Competitiveness Report. The first report appeared in 1980 and over the years it gave Singapore very high rankings. In the 1994 and 1995 reports Singapore was ranked second and the US first for national competitiveness.[1] In 1996 the IMD and WEF parted company and began producing separate global competitiveness reports.

The IMD continued to rank the US (1) and Singapore (2) for competitiveness for every year from 1996 to 2001. The IMD was nothing if not consistent. Then in 2002, Singapore's IMD ranking plunged to (8), presumably to reflect the negative effect that international economic crises were having on its competitiveness.

However, in 2003 Singapore's IMD rankings recovered to 4th spot and did even better for the next five years. In 2004, the IMD ranked Singapore (2) and (3) in 2005, (3) in 2006, (2) in 2007 and (2) in 2008. The numbers of countries in these IMD surveys had risen to 51 by 2004 and to 55 by 2007.

WEF rankings initially showed a similar pattern to the IMD's, ranking Singapore (1) for global competitiveness in 1997, 1998 and 1999 and (2) in 2000. But in 2001, 2002 and 2003, Singapore's WEF ranking fell to (4) and from 2004-2007 they declined further to: (7) in 2004, (5) in 2005, (8) in 2006 and (7) in 2007. The WEF began by surveying 49 countries for its first competitiveness report in 1996, but by 1999 the number of countries had risen to 59 and to 75 by 2001, 102 by 2004 and 131 in 2007.

Despite occasionally lower scores for Singapore in recent years the WEF has, like the IMD, overall continued to award Singapore very high competitiveness rankings. Both bodies have done much to create the impression that the Republic has one of the world's most competitive and cutting-edge economies.

In ranking countries for competitiveness, what do the IMD and WEF think they are measuring? In 1995 the IMD/WEF report defined competitiveness as "the ability of a country or a company to, proportionally, generate more wealth than its competitors in world markets". This depends on a nation's capacity to create an environment which favours sustained value-added creation.[2] After the IMD/WEF split the IMD failed to define competitiveness in its reports, being content with saying that a country's competitiveness ultimately depends on how its environment sustains the competitiveness of its business sector. The IMD also assumed that "wealth creation takes place primarily at enterprise level (whether private or state-owned)".[3]

A country's political, cultural and educational conditions, as well as the economy, profoundly influence how effectively firms can do business. Countries compete with each other to provide an environment that supports firms through the provision of efficient political, economic and social institutions and policies. In reality, IMD competitiveness reports rank and analyses "the ability of nations to provide an environment in which enterprises can compete".[4]

The WEF does try to define competitiveness, seeing it as synonymous with productivity. A country's competitiveness is based on its productivity, "which is measured by the value of goods and services produced per unit of the nation's human, capital, and natural resources," the WEF says.[5]

The IMD/WEF competitiveness rankings are based on these rather loose conceptions/definitions of competitiveness, which are more thoroughly examined in the appendix on competitiveness. The credibility of IMD/WEF rankings largely rests on the hundreds of specific criteria which they claim measure competitiveness as they describe it.

In the IMD/WEF's 1995 World Competitiveness report, 378 specific criteria, covering a wide range of social, political and economic factors, were surveyed for 48 countries. Of these, 225 were used to compile rankings (the remaining criteria were used to provide background information on countries surveyed). In the IMD's 2000 and 2001 reports, 249 criteria were used to compile competitiveness ratings for 47 countries. The WEF was surveying 58 countries by 1999 and 75 by 2001, by which time it was using 174 criteria.

Both IMD and WEF criteria are either hard-data or soft-data based. Hard data is statistical material gathered from international and regional organisations, private institutions and partner institutes. In countries such as Singapore, the partner institutes are government or quasi-government authorities.

Soft-criteria data comes from in-country surveys. They are lengthy questionnaires sent to top and middle-ranking executives, both foreign and local, and to government officials in the countries studied. Respondents are asked to rank their country on a long list of criteria. Their responses are used to help compile that country's competitiveness ranking.

While hard-data criteria are based on statistics, soft-data criteria rankings are calculated from the perceptions of chosen respondents. How well do the IMD and WEF criteria, both hard and soft, measure the international competitiveness of countries surveyed? To answer this question selected criteria from IMD and WEF competitiveness reports are examined, starting with their last joint report in 1995. The separate reports of each body compiled in 1996, 1997 and 1998 and are also briefly assessed, while the 2001 report is examined in more detail. The aim is to see whether the later reports are an improvement on the 1995 report.

1. The 1995 Report

The 225 specific criteria used in the 1995 report were first grouped under eight "factors of competitiveness":

- Domestic economic strength (evaluation of the overall economy)
- Internationalisation (extent to which a country participated in international trade and investment flows)
- Government (how conducive were government policies to competitiveness)
- Finance (performance of capital markets and quality of financial services)
- Infrastructure (how adequate were resources to serve business needs)
- Management (extent to which enterprises were managed in an innovative, profitable and responsible manner)
- Science and Technology (scientific and technological capacity and success of basic and applied research)
- People (availability and qualifications of human resources).

The report gave composite rankings for these main factors, before rating countries on each of the 225 individual criteria. In 1995, Singapore's ratings for these general factors were: domestic economy (3), internationalisation (1), government (1), finance (4), infrastructure (29), management (4), science and technology (7) and people (5) (the more competitive a country, the lower its ranking for both general factors and specific criteria).

Assessing the value of IMD/WEF competitiveness ratings requires examining the specific criteria used to rank the factors they claim to be measuring. Selected criteria from the 1995 report, both soft and hard, will be discussed under "factors of competitiveness" headings.

GOVERNMENT

Singapore was ranked (1) for the extent to which its government policies were conducive to competitiveness, but of the 54 criteria used to produce the Government ranking, 11 seem unusually high. These were:

(3)   Government employment as a percentage of total employment. (A hard-data criterion [HDC] – No. 3.12)

Comment – This (3) ranking was based on a Singapore Government figure claiming that 3.8 per cent of the workforce was employed by the Government in 1992. This contrasts markedly with Clad's 1989 figure that state employment accounted for 25 per cent of the workforce (see Chapter 14). Clad was probably including all those employed by SEs. Were SE employees included, Singapore would have had a much poorer ranking than (3). Australia, where 22.8 per cent of the workforce was employed by the state in 1992, was ranked 35th on this criterion.

(3)   State interference does not hinder the development of business. (A soft-data criterion [SDC] No. 3.17)

Comment: Again Singapore scored (3); this time for being the country that was the third least likely to have a state that hindered business development. But by 1995, SEs and excessive red tape had significantly stunted the development of the local private sector for nearly three decades, as Chapters 9 and 16 show. Singapore's (3) rating for this is as debatable as its (3) for state employment.

(10)   State control of enterprises does not distort fair competition in your country. (SDC – 3.18)

Comment: SEs were clearly distorting fair competition in Singapore in 1995 far more than in such market economies as Australia's and Canada's, which were ranked (22) and (19) on this criterion. SEs had largely crippled the SME sector through unfair competition by then.

(1)   Government subsidies are directed towards future winners (SDC – 3.22)

Comment: Without detailed surveys and statistics the truth of such a claim cannot be confirmed; but complaints by local business people up to and after 1995 about the lack of government support for promising SMEs, as Chapter 16 shows, make a (1) ranking for this criterion unsupportable.

(1)   The government is transparent towards citizens (SDC – 3.27).

Comment: As Chapter 15 shows, Singapore was and still is anything but a transparent society with its secretive and paranoid bureaucrats. They, and the country's opaque SEs, dominate the local economy today as they did in 1995. Then as now a dictatorial and unaccountable cabinet ruled the country and few knew how it made decisions. The real reasons for government policies were often not revealed, let alone properly debated, in the government-controlled media. A (1) ranking for this criterion was nonsense.

(2)   The bureaucracy does not hinder business development. (SDC – 3.31)

Comment: Bureaucratic red tape, endless delays and problems for Singaporean businesses and entrepreneurs was even worse in 1995 than now. Only in 2002 did the Government start trying to reduce red tape. The report's (2) ranking for this criterion was indefensible.

(1)   Lobbying by special interest groups does not distort government decision-making. (SDC – 3.33)

Comment: Here the term "interest group" was not defined; if it included groups, whether social, political or economic, vying for government favour then Singapore had and still has several major players. Among these were SEs and MNCs, who have always been favoured by the Government over the local private sector. Then as now the opaque nature of the PAP state hid the extent of such lobbying – but it has always distorted government decision-making to the detriment of SMEs, discrediting the above (1) ranking.

(15)   Anti-trust laws do prevent unfair competition. (SDC – 3.35)

Comment: The more modest ranking for this criterion better reflected business reality in Singapore where the MNCs and SEs had numerous unfair advantages over the local private sector in 1995 as now. This enabled them to almost monopolise business opportunities, to the detriment of SMEs in particular.

(9)   Market dominance by a few enterprises is rare in key industries. (SDC – 3.36)

Comment: A much higher rating for this would be more appropriate for Singapore where SE/MNC dominance of major industries was and still is obvious. Most of the computer, hard-disk and petrochemical industries were and are MNC-dominated, while SEs control most defence-related industries. Moreover, the SEs especially, were expanding into "Mom and Pop" businesses in 1995.

(1)   Government policies are supported by public consensus. (SDC – 3.50)

Comment: Another bland assertion about Singapore that denied reality in 1995 and would still do so. In the 1991 elections the PAP Government struggled to get 60 per cent of the vote against a pitifully weak opposition crippled by second-rate candidates and a blatantly biased electoral system. Despite this the opposition managed to poll nearly 40 per cent of the vote in 1991, the last election before the 1995 report. This indicated a significant lack of public consensus on PAP policies, well below that required to justify a (1) ranking.

(9)   There is full confidence in the fair administration of justice in the society. (SDC – 3.52)

Comment: This score would be justified if applied to non-political court cases in Singapore in 1995 as now, but most Singaporeans know that anyone who upsets the PAP state has little chance of a fair trial, as has been regularly demonstrated since the early 1960s. The judiciary has supported the Government against opposition politicians and activists and publications, both domestic and foreign, which have offended it. By contrast Sweden was ranked (10), Hong Kong (12), Canada (13), the Netherlands (14), Germany (15) and the UK (21) – all strong democracies with established traditions of judicial independence far greater than Singapore's – yet the report ranked Singapore higher than these countries for fairer administration of justice.

MANAGEMENT

Singapore scored (1) for management in the 1995 report. As Chapter 10 showed, Singapore managers are mediocre at best. Giving them the world's top ranking in 1995 was ludicrous. Their lack of HRD skills and hierarchical and efficiency-sapping attitudes were probably even worse then.

(4)   Total quality management is comprehensively applied in your country. (SDC – 6.15)

266

Comment: Attempts to apply "total quality management" in 1995 were as widespread as now in Singapore. But as Chapter 10 shows, Singaporean management is severely deficient and was even more so in 1995. HRD has yet to significantly improve the quality of Singaporean management, largely for deeply rooted cultural reasons.

(9)   The customer orientation of domestic companies emphasises customer satisfaction adequately. (SDC – 6.17)

Comment: The "indifferent" quality of service in Singaporean shops and restaurants suggests that the (9) rating for customer orientation was excessive. The idiocy of this rating becomes fully apparent when one sees that the IMD ranked Australia (18), Hong Kong (13) and Thailand (29) for this criterion. These are all countries which Singaporeans have praised for having far superior service to Singaporean retail outlets, as Chapter Six shows.

(2)   Corporate credibility: companies do enjoy public trust. (SDC – 6.20)

Comment: While Singapore was ranked (2) on this criterion, the Australian and UK rankings were (30) and (38) respectively. Apparently Singaporeans regarded their companies as paragons of virtue while Australians and Brits viewed theirs with extreme distrust, even contempt, in 1995. In October 2002, an Asian survey by a US market research firm showed that 84 per cent of Singaporeans had become increasingly wary of which companies to trust, compared to 86 per cent of Asians overall.[6] Such figures show that Singaporeans, like most other Asians, deeply distrust local companies, making the above (2) ranking nonsense.

(9)   Social responsibility: Managers pay much attention to their responsibility to society. (SDC – 6.22)

Comment: In Singapore, any responsibility that managers display would only be due to government directive. In 1995 as now, when left to their own devices, Singaporean managers are likely to show little responsibility towards anyone but themselves. Their poor treatment of subordinates and readiness to job-hop show a narrow self-interest. Expecting them to care about the broader society would be unrealistic. In *kiasu* Singapore, it's every man for himself, unless made to behave less selfishly by the Government.

In 2004, two enterprises – Keppel Corp and the OCBC – were reportedly the first two Singaporean enterprises to set up formal whistle-blowing mechanisms to help detect in-house problems.[7] But Singapore lacked any laws to encourage and protect whistle-blowers, unlike the US, the UK and Malaysia, where such legislation existed. Prime Minister Lee Hsien Loong was lukewarm about legislation to encourage whistle-blowers in Singapore. He claimed that many corporate reforms had already been carried out in areas of internal control.

Even if a society has whistleblower laws it must also have the values to make them effective. This is something that Singapore lacks, according to local commentators. As one said, "How willing are Singaporeans to blow the whistle? The culture of Singapore is not to get involved and not to get into trouble. It is different in the West. You can have laws here but it doesn't help unless the culture changes."[8]

The absurdity of Singapore's (9) for managerial responsibility becomes apparent when one finds that the US was ranked (17) and the UK (29). Since the 1990s there have been vigorous debates about corporate responsibility and ethics in both countries as well as significant whistle-blowing activity, one of the most dramatic demonstrations of "social responsibility". There are probably far more corporate whistle-blowers per capita in Britain and the US than would ever be found in conformist, risk-averse Singapore, where taking unpopular public stands is akin to social and professional suicide. A survey by Singapore's Corrupt Practices Investigation Bureau in April 2003 revealed that three in five Singaporeans would be reluctant to report corruption to the Bureau. The reasons ranged from not wanting to get involved to fears of repercussions.[9]

(21)   Managers have a good sense of entrepreneurship and innovation. (SDC – 6.23)

Comment: A lowly (21) ranking for this criterion matched reality for Singapore in 1995 and probably still would. Singapore has an abundance of cautious risk-averse managers, especially in the SE sectors.

(11)   Risk-taking and individual initiative is [sic] fully supported and rewarded. (SDC – 6.24)

Comment: A ranking of (11) for this criterion seems high compared to the previous one where Singapore scored (21). As Chapter Nine shows there is little cultural support for risk-takers in Singapore. There was even less in 1995 before the Government began seriously urging Singaporeans to be more risk-taking. Then as now, those who fail and go bankrupt are shunned and find it almost impossible to borrow money or even get a credit card.

India, curiously, scores (6), ahead of the US (7). How did India, which still had so many bureaucratic obstacles to business and entrepreneurial activity in 1995, get a higher ranking than the US for risk-taking?

4)   The organisation of the workplace is designed more efficiently than those of foreign competitors. (SDC – 6.28)

Comment: Another nonsensical ranking, considering Singapore's relatively low levels of productivity compared with Western countries. Hierarchic managerial attitudes, bureaucratic rules and conformist mentality regularly sabotage efficiency in Singaporean companies far more than in the US, which scored (8) or Australia (21), Norway (7), Netherlands (9), Canada (14) or the UK (17).

(1)   Implementation of strategies: Management usually achieves the goals set. (SDC – 6.29)

Comment: Giving a (1) ranking for this criterion in 1995 was rubbish. As Chapters 9, 10 and 11 showed, the gap between theory and practice was and still is wide in

Singapore, especially for strategies which seek to improve organisational productivity and efficiency.

(12)   Willingness to delegate to subordinates is generally high. (SDC – 6.31)

Comment: This ranking of (12) may have been appropriate for Singapore's MNC sector, but the hierarchicalism of Singaporean organisations has always hindered delegation, especially in Singapore's more traditionally run concerns. The 1995 report's (13) for egalitarian Finland and (20) for Israel would have us believe less delegation occurs in these countries than in hierarchically minded Singapore.

(1)   Managerial rewards encourage long-term orientation. (SDC – 6.32)

Comment: Yet another vague criterion with a nonsensically high (1) ranking for Singapore. If long-term orientation applies to managers, does it mean they are less likely to job-hop? Such a ranking implies that inducements made Singaporean managers more loyal than those from any other countries. As Singaporean managers, like most Singaporeans, were and still are notorious job-hoppers always looking for greener pastures, they were and still are highly receptive to inducements to leave their present positions for better ones.

(2)   Intercultural understanding is well developed in the business community. (SDC – 6.33)

Comment: Many Singaporean business people have been educated in Western countries and so have a good understanding of Western values and business practices. They have a better command of English than almost all other non-western business people, which enhances their understanding of Westerners. Singaporean business people also have a clear and hard-eyed, if not always positive, understanding of non-western values, especially within Asia.

As Chapter 18 shows, there are high levels of inter-communal distrust in Singapore between the three main ethnic groups. While aware of each other's faults, they display little interest in learning about each other's cultures and virtues. Western lifestyles and values interest most Singaporeans far more than those of their fellow countrymen of different ethnic groups. Only during such state-sponsored events as Racial Harmony Day do Singaporeans show token interest in the other cultures of their own country.

Racial relations have been managed by the Government since the early 1960s. "Restrained and contained, the people lived safely under constant government protection and surveillance," noted Singapore playwright Kuo Pao Kun, but over time "the progress in inter-racial understanding was seriously impeded by the lack of full cultural dimension. Citizens grew ignorant of and indifferent to the extraordinary richness and complexity of their numerous races."[10] There were not even national institutions for translation and publication.

"It is understandable why the cynics say Singapore's multiculturalism is more an exercise to keep the different communities peacefully apart than draw them dynamically together."[11] Such attitudes are hardy conducive to racial harmony. If intercultural understanding includes appreciation of other cultures, then Singapore did not and still would not deserve a (2) for intercultural understanding.

(44)   Employee turnover is not a problem for business development. (SDC – 6.35)

Comment: A very poor ranking of (44) for this criterion is about right considering Singaporeans' notorious job-hopping. Sometimes the report's rankings reflected reality.

(8)   Industrial relations between employers and workers are generally productive. (SDC – 6.36)

Comment: The often poor worker-management relations in most Singaporean organisations was and still is a major factor depressing productivity. The full truth about the country's industrial relations is difficult to know because unions are tightly controlled by the government-run NTUC. Employees have to cooperate with management in Singapore because lack of union support gives them little choice to do otherwise. SIA's ongoing labour-management problems from the early 1980s would have provided a truer picture of Singapore's industrial relations than this (8) ranking in 1995.

SCIENCE AND TECHNOLOGY

Singapore was ranked (10) for its competitiveness in science and technology in the 1995 IMD/WEF report, while such technologically advanced and sophisticated countries as the UK scored (14), Australia (20), Belgium-Luxembourg (12), Canada (18), the Czech Republic (34), Denmark (11), Hong Kong (23), Italy (21), the Netherlands (15) and Russia (48). The report claimed that these rankings reflected countries' scientific and technological capacity and the success of their basic and applied research.

The report would have us believe that tiny, not-yet-fully-developed Singapore was, in 1995, well ahead of many developed, industrially advanced countries in science and technology. A look at some of the report's science and technology soft-data criteria and Singaporean scores on them might explain how the report awarded this remarkably flattering ranking for Singapore's scientific and technological capacity. Some of the criteria were:

- The education system meets the needs of a competitive economy. [SDC – 8.28]
- The extent to which science is adequately taught in compulsory schools. [SDC – 7.24]
- The level of compulsory education for the majority of people is superior to that of foreign competitors. [SDC – 8.34]

Singapore scored (1) on the first two and (4) on the third. By contrast, such developed countries as Australia scored (9), (12) and (12) respectively while Canada scored (24), (33) and (26); the US (30), (34) and (35); the UK (35), (39) and (33), and Russia (44), (42) and (34). How did Singapore manage to get top ranking for its education system (8.28) with such low rankings on the following education criteria in the same report:

- (18) in its public expenditure on education [SDC – 8.27] compared to (11) for the US, (15) for Australia, (16) for the UK and (12) for Italy.
- (37) in illiteracy for the over-15 population [SDC – 8.33] with an illiteracy rate of 13.7 per cent, compared to the US ranking of (5), Japan (2), Australia and the UK (6), and Italy (23).
- (33) in secondary school enrolment [SDC – 8.29], which is well behind rankings for all the OECD countries
- (37) in pupil-teacher ratio at the first level [SDC – 8.31] and 39 at the second level [8.32]. The same figures for Australia were (14) and (11); for the US (27 and 15), Canada (14 and 28), the UK (22 and 15), Japan (22 and 28) and Italy (4 and 4).

The 1995 report's education rankings for Malaysia and India show similar bizarre contradictions. Malaysia scored (22) for its education system's competitiveness, (26) for its science teaching and (25) for the superiority of its education system over foreign competitors. India scored (27), (7) and (42) respectively. Yet Canada's rankings for these three criteria were 24, 26 and 33; the US's (30, 35, 34); the UK's (35, 33, 39), and Russia's (44, 34, 42). How could Malaysia and India score so much better despite the four latter countries' more advanced technologies and education systems? How, for example, could India, which was ranked (45) for public education expenditure, (48) for illiteracy (51.2 per cent for the over-15 age groups), (44) for secondary school enrolment and (47) and (45) for first and second level teacher-student ratio, score (27) for its education system's competitiveness and (7) for the quality of its science teaching? The following chart reveals the absurdity of such rankings:

Table 21.1 – A comparison of some 1995 competitiveness rankings

CRITERIA	S/pore	M/ysia	India	Canada	USA	UK	Russia
(Education system's competitiveness)							
1) 8.28	1	22	27	24	30	35	44
(Quality of science teaching)							
2) 7.24	1	26	7	33	34	39	42
(Superiority of education system over foreign competitors)							
3) 8.34	4	25	42	26	35	33	34

How the report arrived at these scores is hard to fathom, especially when the rankings for its Nobel Prize criterion (SDC – 7.21) are also considered. The Nobel Prize rankings were based on awards for physics, chemistry, physiology or medicine and economics since 1950. While Singapore, Malaysia and India had never won any Nobel prizes by 1995, the US had acquired 164, the UK 44, Russia 9, Canada 6 and Australia and Italy 4 each; yet Singapore, Malaysia and India were still supposedly more competitive in general and science education.

A nation is only truly competitive in these areas when it encourages discovery and learning, the fundamentals of creativity and innovation. Failure to produce self-generated technological advances, as well as domestic entrepreneurial talent, condemns a nation to a perpetually dependent relationship with other nations. As Lingle noted:

Despite high scores in international competitions for Asian primary and secondary science and maths students, there is a dependency upon institutions of higher education in the West. Whatever the shifts in economic prowess, the West continues to have the greatest centers of higher learning, thanks to its tradition of intellectual freedom. As such, these centers attract and produce the bulk of the world's great scholars and innovators.[12]

While Singapore was scrambling in 1995 (as now) to attract as much international academic talent as possible, its universities had yet to be seen as centres for innovation and research. "Ironically, it is the West, and in particular Australia, which has the most established research institutions in the academic field of Asian studies," observes Chee.[13]

Singapore's (7) ranking for the report's criterion regarding the degree to which technical cooperation existed between companies in an economy (SDC – 7.37) requires examination. While this ranking was reasonable for Singapore, it should be realised that most of such cooperation would have been between state enterprises who would have little desire to share their expertise with the local private sector. Also, considering the distrustful *kiasu* mentality that prevails in Singapore, cooperation between rival private sector companies would have been as minimal in 1995, as now.

PEOPLE

Singapore was ranked (8) for this general variable in the 1995 report. Once again some of the criteria rankings used to measure this variable were questionable including those relating to attitudes to life, readiness to learn and work and to company loyalty.

(1) People have a positive attitude to life (SDC – 8.55).

Comment: According to this (1) ranking, Singaporeans were more positive and upbeat than any of the peoples from the other 47 countries in the 1995 survey. Anyone who lived and worked in Singapore then as now would find such a ranking ridiculous. Singaporeans are not only highly stressed, but are chronically anxious about the future. One of the main reasons Singaporeans migrated to countries such as Australia and New Zealand up to 1995 was because they wanted to have a more relaxed and secure lifestyle.

A May 1998 survey by *The Straits Times* found 51 per cent of Singaporeans interviewed found life "quite stressful" in Singapore, and 24 per cent thought it was "very stressful".[14] The same survey found that 81 per cent of professionals, including managers, found life stressful as did even more blue collar workers (84 per cent). Singapore's children seemed particularly unhappy. Besides also being highly stressed, one-third believed life was not worth living, according to a November 2000 survey by SPH.[15]

Singaporeans love to complain. As already noted in Chapter 18, Prime Minister Goh called Singaporeans a nation of moaners; and a *Straits Times* poll in that month found that 80 per cent of Singaporeans agreed with him. People who constantly whinge are not happy people.

(1)   The values of the society support competitiveness. These values are hard work, tenacity and company loyalty as opposed to pursuing individual interests at company expense. (SDC – 8.56)

Comment: Singaporeans work hard, especially when self-employed. While Singaporeans would score highly for tenacity in pursuit of individual wealth and material success, they rarely display the same dedication in serving the company, as their opportunistic job-hopping propensities reveal. While they may meekly accept existing corporate hierarchies and pay lip service to company aims, they are constantly seeking better prospects elsewhere. Unlike the Japanese, the Chinese and Indians particularly have individualistic values which put self and family before community and the wider society. Far more genuine company loyalty is demonstrated by Japanese than by Singaporeans, as Lee Kuan Yew has ruefully admitted. Despite this, Japan ranks (3) for this criterion to Singapore's (1)!

(9)   Employees truly identify with company objectives (SDC – 8.51).

Comment: The peculiar feature of this ranking was that four related criteria in the 1995 report contradict it. While criterion 8.56 ranked Singaporean employees (1) for company loyalty etc, they were ranked (9) for ability to identify with company aims. Is not this synonymous with company loyalty? The report correctly ranked Singapore (44) for employee turnover (SDC – 6.35). Such chronic job-hopping shows significant indifference to company aims, warranting a much worse ranking than (9) for this criterion.

(3)   Employees are generally receptive to learning new skills or a new profession (SDC – 8.50).

Comment: The Singapore Government has made strenuous efforts in recent years to encourage workers to upgrade their skills. But as Chapter Three notes, Singapore lags in skills upgrading, with four times more adults percentage-wise doing vocational courses in the US than in Singapore. Despite this, Singapore was ranked (3) and the US (22), Switzerland (7), Sweden (11) and Germany (16) on this criterion. Ranking such countries behind Singapore was nonsensical.

(1)   The major occupation of young people today is to learn and work. (SDC – 8.53)

Comment: The major aim of young Singaporeans in 1995, as now, was not to learn but get the necessary degrees to ensure them a highly-paid and prestigious job. Learning for its own sake interests them little unless it can be quickly translated into income and promotion. Young Singaporeans do have a desire to work, provided that does not mean postings to poor countries lacking Singapore's five-star comforts. But Singaporeans, young and old, always work very hard when working for themselves: in this regard they deserve a high ranking – along with Taiwanese, Hongkongians, Japanese and Koreans, whom many Singaporeans regard as being even more hard-working than themselves. Despite this, the report's rankings for Taiwan were (6), Hong Kong (4), Japan (37) and Korea (16).

Singapore's rulers always like to claim that the country's greatest resource is its people, but an analysis of the above criteria suggest this asset is over-rated, as shown by Singaporeans' *kiasu* mentality, mediocre work-skill levels and low employee loyalty.

The 1995 report also gave questionably high scores to Singapore's financial system

FINANCE

Singapore regards its financial system as another of its proudest assets. The IMD/WEF 1995 report agreed, giving Singapore a (1) ranking for this factor. Once again many dubious criteria scores, especially those relating to banking, contributed to Singapore's top ranking for finance.

(1)   The banking sector exercises a positive influence on industry. (SDC – 4.31)

Comment: The vague wording of this criterion gave ample scope for interpretation, as do many of the report's other "soft" criteria. Even so, Singapore's (1) score suggests its banks had a positively excellent effect on industry. This is surprising in the light of Lee Kuan Yew's gripes – several years after the 1995 report appeared – about how unprepared Singapore's banks were to compete against foreign banks. The complaints by SMEs on the difficulties involved in getting bank loans cast further doubt on this ranking for banks. SMEs found it even more difficult in 1995 than now to get bank loans.

More questions arise when the rankings of other countries are examined. Indonesia scored an amazing (8), Malaysia (10), Thailand (12) and the Philippines (20). By contrast, Australia scored (22), Germany (24) and Sweden (26)! The worthlessness of such rankings was revealed during the 1997/8 Asian financial crisis when the Indonesian and Thai banking sectors virtually collapsed, while Malaysia's was severely damaged. The main problem was numerous unsecured loans advanced by banks to vulnerable companies in these countries. Instead of controlling crony capitalism the banks encouraged it. They were definitely not exerting a positive influence on industry, yet the report's 1995 rankings suggest that Indonesian, Thai and Malaysian banks had a more positive influence on industry than banks in Australia, Germany and Sweden.

(1)   Public confidence in financial intermediaries is high (SDC – 4.32).

Comment: This soft data criterion presumably includes such financial intermediaries as brokers. Singaporeans display about as much faith in their brokers as Australians,

Americans or Germans. Singaporean investors have frequently expressed the cynical belief that brokers often collude with the "big boys" through insider trading to fix the Singapore stock market. Singapore got a (1) ranking while Australia scored (14), the US (17) and Germany (17).

In 1995 "bucket shops" had been rife in Singapore for many years, fleecing hundreds of investors weekly, yet the Government took years to close them down. Bucket shops were usually commodity trading firms who offered jobs to lure unsuspecting victims and pressurise them into get-rich-quick investment schemes. Even today some bucket shops still operate, though more furtively than before. "Financial intermediaries" of this sort would presumably evoke little confidence from Singaporeans.

Of special note is Colombia's score of (8) for this criterion. Could it be that Colombians living in a country where rampant corruption and violence prevailed in 1995 as now, where the "coke kings" were virtually a law unto themselves, would have more confidence in their financial intermediaries than those in the US? One of the report's strangest rankings.

(1)   Bankers enjoy public trust (SDC – 4.33).

Comment: For a country like Singapore to get a (1) ranking for this criterion suggests that its bankers positively bask in public approval. But *The Straits Times* frequently contains letters from Singaporeans complaining about poor service and heartless attitudes from their banks during recessions. In December 2003, banks, along with insurance companies, were at the top of the Singaporean consumers' hate list.[16] They attacked unfair bank contracts and banks for not being truthful about their products – this after years of ongoing efforts by banks to improve their customer service since 1995.

How did countries such as Malaysia score (6), Colombia (9) or Thailand (11) while Switzerland (yes, Switzerland!) scored (12) and Austria (15), Australia (36) and the UK (37)? The 1995 report is riddled with such inconsistencies.

Only 35 of the criteria from the 1995 report have been examined here, mostly those with dubiously favourable rankings for Singapore and other developing countries. Were sufficient data and information available to test all the report's criteria, it is likely that many more suspect rankings would have been found. But enough have been considered here to demonstrate that the report's rankings for Singapore and other countries were misleading and defective. It is especially disturbing that such egregious flaws were occurring in a report which was in its 15th year of publication by 1995.

Because the report was prepared over a decade ago, a significant body of data and information has accumulated in the intervening years to more thoroughly test its rankings. Despite its datedness, the 1995 report has been included in this chapter to provide a benchmark against which subsequent IMD and WEF reports can be compared to see how far they have repeated its weaknesses.

2. The IMD/WEF Split

After the 1995 report the WEF split from the IMD. A WEF board member said the WEF was unhappy with the report which "was found to be heavy and confusing",[17] and decided it could produce a better report on its own. Under the leadership of Harvard economist Jeffrey Sachs, the new WEF report was called the Global Competitiveness Report. Initially 155 criteria were devised by the WEF to measure the national competitiveness of 49 countries, but by 2001, 75 countries and 174 criteria were being surveyed. Both hard and soft data continued to be used. In recent WEF reports the ratio of hard to soft data criteria has been nearly five to one; in the 1999 WEF report, there were only 36 hard criteria compared to 138 soft data criteria; and in the 2001 report, 34 and 140 respectively.

In launching its 1996 report, the WEF claimed the criteria were selected according to data reliability and their correlation with growth rates based on evidence from dozens of academic studies. The WEF promised the reports would include the latest global thinking and research on international competition and a new method for measuring competitiveness and would be relevant to government and corporate decision-making.[18]

The IMD also made efforts to improve its report, still called the World Competitiveness Report. By 2001, the report was using 224 criteria (118 hard and 106 soft) to survey the competitiveness of 49 countries. Did these changes produce better reports? And did Singapore's rankings change much?

3. The 1996-8 Reports

Despite the changes they made to their competitiveness reports the IMD and WEF continued to give Singapore top competitiveness rankings, as the following summary of their 1996-8 rankings show.

IMD Reports – 1996 and 1997

In its 1996 and 1997 reports the IMD ranked Singapore (2) and (1) respectively for overall competitiveness. The rankings for the 46 countries surveyed for both years and also for 1995 were:

Table 21.2 – IMD competitiveness rankings 1995–7

	1997	1996	1995		1997	1996	1995
USA	1	1	1	Denmark	8	5	9
Singapore	2	2	2	Japan	9	4	4
Hong Kong	3	3	3	Canada	10	12	12
Finland	4	15	16	UK	11	19	18
Norway	5	6	10	Luxembourg	12	8	19
Netherlands	6	7	7	New Zealand	13	11	8
Switzerland	7	9	4	Germany	14	10	6

	1997	1996	1995		1997	1996	1995
Ireland	15	22	22	Philippines	31	31	35
Sweden	16	14	15	Portugal	32	36	31
Malaysia	17	23	21	Brazil	33	37	37
Australia	18	21	14	Italy	34	28	30
France	19	20	17	Czech Republic	35	34	38
Austria	20	16	13	Hungary	36	39	46
Iceland	21	25	25	Greece	37	40	43
Belgium	22	17	19	Turkey	38	35	40
Taiwan	23	18	11	Indonesia	39	41	33
Chile	24	13	20	Mexico	40	42	44
Spain	25	29	28	India	41	38	39
Israel	26	24	23	Colombia	42	33	36
China	27	26	34	Poland	43	43	45
Argentina	28	32	29	South Africa	44	44	42
Thailand	29	30	26	Venezeula	45	45	47
South Korea	30	27	24	Russia	46	46	48

The IMD's rankings for the eight main competitiveness factors for Singapore are listed in the following table.

Table 21.3 – IMD competitiveness factor rankings 1995–7

	1997	1996	1995
Domestic Economy	3	3	3
Internationalisation	1	2	1
Government	1	1	1
Finance	3	6	4
Infrastructure	27	30	29
Management	4	1	4
Science and Technology	12	8	7
People	8	5	5

Whatever changes the IMD made to its 1996 and 1997 reports, Singapore still retained the (1) or (2) overall competitiveness ranking. Many developing countries also continued to score oddly favourable rankings, and many developed countries curiously poor ones. Could Singapore in 1996/7 with its derivative and dependent economy, where risk-taking and innovation were minimal, really have been more competitive than large developed economies such as those of Western Europe, Canada, Japan and Australasia? Was Singapore really second only to the US in global competitiveness?

WEF Reports – 1997 and 1998

Like the IMD, the WEF produced flattering rankings for Singapore in 1997 and 1998, despite claims that it was using improved methods:[19]

Table 21.4 – WEF competitiveness rankings for 1997 and 1998

	1998	1997	Competitiveness Index (1998)
Singapore	1	1	2.16
Hong Kong	2	2	1.91
USA	3	3	1.41
Britain	4	7	1.29
Canada	5	4	1.27
Taiwan	6	8	1.19
Netherlands	7	12	1.13
Switzerland	8	6	1.10
Norway	9	10	1.09
Luxembourg	10	11	1.05

Like the IMD, the WEF first ranked countries on eight major factors. These factors, with Singapore's rankings for them, were: openness (3), government (2), finance (2), infrastructure (2), technology (2), management (7), labour (1) and institutions (1). All these rankings are questionable and some are ludicrous. A (3) for openness, considering Singapore's lack of transparency, is as absurd as the (1) for its mediocre workforce. Even the (7) Singapore got for management seems odd, given the many deficiencies of Singapore managers. Moreover, Singapore's (2) for technology ignores its inability to develop new technologies without MNCs. The (1) for government also failed to reflect the PAP Government's lack of transparency. Finally, the (1) for institutions could not have applied to Singapore banks. Their deficiencies were well-known when these reports were compiled in 1997 and 1998.

In 1999 and 2000, the IMD and the WEF continued to give Singapore top rankings. The IMD ranked Singapore (2) in the 1999 and 2000 reports. The WEF also ranked Singapore (2) in 1999. Then in 2000 the WEF introduced two basic indexes: the CCI and the GCI. Singapore got (2) on the first and (9) on the second. The WEF's Singapore rankings were beginning to reflect reality. Even so, WEF reports still shared many of the weaknesses of IMD reports, as an examination of the 2001 reports shows. They were both continuing to poorly measure the factors that they claimed determined competitiveness.

4. The 2001 Reports

In 2001, the IMD's sample group remained at 49 countries while the WEF's rose from 58 in 2000 to 75 in 2001 with the inclusion of more developing countries. The WEF's aim was to provide "a much richer platform for exploring the earlier stages of development".[20] Five of WEF's new countries came from central and eastern Europe, nine from the Western hemisphere, two from Asia and one from Africa.

The IMD 2001 Report

In the IMD's 2001 report, the 224 criteria used were grouped under four "competitiveness input factors". They and Singapore's rankings for them were:

- Economic performance (3)
- Government efficiency (1)
- Business efficiency (10)
- Infrastructure (5).

Despite this, some dubious soft-data criteria from previous reports – back to the 1995 report – appeared in the 2001 report.

(1)   The political system is well-adapted to today's economic challenges (Criterion 2.3.12 in the IMD's 2001 report and 3.29 in the 1995 report).

Comment: This criterion was also ranked (1) in the 1995 report and the same comments still apply. A repressive PAP state has transformed Singaporeans into risk-averse people lacking initiative and innovative capacities, the key ingredients for national competitiveness. The Government has striven to reverse this legacy of 40 years of PAP rule, demonstrating that Singapore's economy is not well adapted to meet current economic challenges. A (1) for this criterion is outrageous.

(1)   Values of society (hard work and innovation) support competitiveness. (4.5.05 – 8.56 in the 1995 report)

Comment: Singapore was ranked (1) on a similar 1995 criterion, but this one included innovation. While Singaporeans are generally hard (but often not smart) workers they certainly lack innovatory capacity, a key ingredient of competitiveness.

(1)   Labour relations are generally productive. (3.2.06 and 6.36)

Comment: A dramatic improvement from (8) in 1995, but was it justified? The chronic disputes between the SIA management and pilots in recent years suggest otherwise. Because all independent union activity remained suppressed in Singapore in 2001, labour was completely subservient to corporate and governmental aims. The low morale that this produced among workers at that time could only have undermined labour productivity, discrediting this (1) ranking.

(3)   Employees do identify with company objectives. (3.2.07 and 8.51)

Comment: Coming from (9) in 1995 to (3) in 2001, this 2001 rating seems even less credible. Chapters 10 and 11 show that Singaporeans were just as disloyal and job-hopping in 2001 as before, making this score ludicrous. Disloyal employees care little for company aims.

(7)   Business leaders do not neglect their responsibility towards society. (3.4.10 and 6.22)

Comment: In 1995, a score of (9) was given to a similarly worded criterion. The comments already made about this criterion apply in 2001.

(1)   Company managers are trusted by the public. (3.4.03 and 6.22)

Comment: In 1995, the IMD and WEF gave Singapore (2) for corporate credibility after respondents were asked to rank companies according to whether they enjoyed public trust. *Kiasu*-minded Singaporeans were no more likely to trust anyone, including company directors they don't know, in 2001 than they were in 1995. Moreover, Singaporean company managers, like their Western counterparts, have continued to show a capacity to put their own interests ahead of shareholders'. Singaporean company directors are as ready to award themselves excessive remuneration as their Western counterparts, as Chapter 23 shows.

Apart from these hardy perennials, there were some new and equally dubious soft-data rankings in the IMD's 2001 report.

(1)   Tax evasion is not a common practice in your country. (2.2.14)

Comment: Part of the reason for this top ranking for Singapore is because 70 per cent of Singaporeans are not required to pay tax because their incomes are deemed too low, as Chapter 26 explains. Even so, Singaporeans admit to being readier than most other Asians to evade tax, according to a 2004 *Readers Digest* survey of 1600 people in nine Asian countries, including Singapore.[21] Four in ten Singaporeans said they would not declare exactly how much they were earning to reduce their tax. This got them a ranking of seven for taxation honesty out of the nine Asian countries surveyed.

Some expatriates, especially self-employed ones, have paid no tax for years. One expatriate failed to pay income tax for nearly 10 years but managed to remain in Singapore and do business. He regularly had amicable meetings with Singapore tax officials who were very understanding about his plight, even when he failed to make the agreed re-scheduled payments on time. Another expat with a three-year employment pass managed to avoid paying tax for the last two years before leaving Singapore.

With so much government revenue being derived from indirect taxes and through HDB and CPF schemes, there is less pressure to crack down on tax evasion. A (15) or (20) ranking for tax avoidance would have been more appropriate.

One country however which does comes down hard on tax evasion is Sweden. Any politicians or other public figures found to be evading tax are expected to resign. The Swedes even have a uniquely Swedish word – "skattemoral" – for taxpayers' morality. The zeal of Sweden's tax authorities upsets special interest groups. Despite Sweden's tough and rigorous tax system it only ranks (28) on this criterion to Singapore's (1).

(1)   New legislative activity meets the competitive requirements of the economy. (2.3.09)

Comment: Bills for upgrading the economy, retraining the workforce and encouraging entrepreneurship are a regular feature of "legislative activity" in Singapore, but legislation that would break the stifling effect of SEs or reduce excessive indirect taxes on the local private and SME sectors is absent. Also missing is legislation for producing much greater genuine privatisation of the economy. Such measures are needed to unleash the Singaporeans' entrepreneurial energies and transform Singapore into an innovative and competitive society. Laws are also required to guarantee democratic rights and freedoms, to further engender the risk-taking mentality that Singapore so lacks. Singapore's legislative deficiencies in these areas makes its (1) ranking on this criterion unsustainable.

(11) The public service is immune from political interference. (2.3.14)

Comment: An (11) ranking for this is nonsense. Singapore's public service is tightly controlled by the PAP leadership and always has been. Selection of senior bureaucrats especially is closely monitored by Cabinet to ensure that only pro-PAP officials are appointed. Few Singaporean bureaucrats could ever stand up to the PAP leadership and hope to keep their jobs. A (30) to (40) ranking would be more appropriate.

(4) University education meets the needs of a competitive economy. (2.5.08)

Comment: With creativity and innovation synonymous with competitiveness, universities must cultivate such capacities in students. Although Singapore's universities have been trying to do this since the mid-1990s, the conformist mindset drummed into Singaporean students in primary and secondary schools has been difficult to overcome. Much more has to be done by the Republic's tertiary sector to try and meet the needs of a competitive economy. As earlier chapters have shown, the Singaporean workforce is deficient at the tertiary level. Only 14 per cent of Singaporeans have university degrees, less than half the percentage of such Western countries as Germany which was ranked (25), the US (5), Canada (11) and the UK (26).

(9) People in your country are flexible enough in adapting to new challenges. (4.5.02)

Comment: Although not as excessive as some IMD ratings for Singapore, Singaporeans' hierarchical, risk-averse values suggest that even (9) is too high for this criterion. Resistance to change by the young was demonstrated with the recent introduction of high school exams that required more thinking and problem-solving ability. Students expressed strident dismay at having to sit exams that would require them to think, not merely regurgitate rote-learnt information as before.

Again, government and corporate efforts have only had limited success in getting indifferent Singaporean managers and workers to retrain and upgrade their skills. As Chapter Three shows, only 10 per cent of Singaporean workers aged between 20 and 49 were undergoing education and training to gain formal qualifications in 1995. About 40 per cent of adults in the US and Europe were taking part-time courses. In addition, Singapore's SME managers are reluctant to provide training for their workers.

(4) Discrimination (race, gender, family background...) does not pose a handicap in society. (4.5.03)

Comment: A 1989 study of Singaporean Malays' work histories found that most contained detailed accounts of discrimination by Chinese employers regarding recruitment, pay, working conditions and opportunities for training and advancement. [22] Studies done in 1980, 1986, 1990 and 1995 highlighted Malay beliefs about the unequal opportunities they faced, often in the form of "glass ceilings" at work.

In the housing sector both Malays and Indians suffer discrimination. Each must often accept lower prices and wait longer to sell their HDB units because of PAP policies to maintain balanced race numbers in HDB blocks. As Chapter 24 explains, Malays must usually sell to other Malays and Indians to other Indians so that each block reflects Singapore's racial composition, which is about 70 per cent Chinese, 21 per cent Malay and 6 per cent Indian.

In the tertiary education sector, specific examples of racial and gender discrimination can be found. First, there was a 12 per cent quota that was still in force for Indian students enrolled in the Law faculty at the National University of Singapore (NUS) in 2001.[23] Second, until December 2002 there were restrictions on the number of women who could study medicine: for more than 20 years only one-third of the 230 places at the NUS's medical faculty went to women.[24] In 2001, the Government was still refusing citizenship by descent to children born overseas to female Singaporeans: only the children born overseas to wives of male Singaporeans had this right. Not until 2004 was this inequality removed.[25] Before 2004 the Government was not even considering equalising medical benefits in the civil service, which were granted to dependents of male but not female civil servants. Finally, Singaporean women's high illiteracy rates are further indications of gender discrimination. In 2000, the percentage of Singaporeans over 15 who could read and write was 96 per cent for males but only 88 per cent for females.[26]

(1)   Social cohesion is a priority for the government. (2.3.21)

Comment: While many countries could easily endorse this statement, Singapore is the one country which mysteriously scores best for it. The PAP Government promotes the need for social cohesion, but its policies often create division and racial tensions between the Chinese and the minority Malays and Indians. Lily Rahim's book, *The Singapore Dilemma*, provides detailed descriptions of the discrimination that the Chinese-dominated PAP regularly inflicts on Malays in such areas as education and housing.[27] The PAP's Speak Mandarin Campaign and promotion of Chinese values over those of Malays and Indians foment racial tension that undermines social cohesion. Singapore does not deserve a (1) for this criterion.

(8)   The health infrastructure meets the needs of society. (4.4.05)

Comment: The rankings of other countries for this criterion are Australia (10), Sweden (12), Netherlands (16), Canada (19) and New Zealand (22). With an (8) ranking, Singapore supposedly has a health system that better meets the needs of its people than those of developed Western countries where universal health-care is a non-negotiable reality. As Chapter 24 shows, whole categories of unwell lower-income Singaporeans fail to receive life-saving treatments, including AIDS victims and those requiring dialysis. All such people can get free treatment in most Western countries if necessary.

(2)   Employee training is a high priority in companies. (3.2.09)

Comment: The MNCs and SEs are the enterprises most likely to provide employee training, but no more than would be the case in most Western countries which the IMD ranks lower. Also, Singapore's SMEs lag in this regard, often being reluctant to train staff who may leave soon after. Despite this, most advanced countries with their highly skilled workforces, are ranked behind Singapore. Sweden is ranked (4), Japan (5), the Netherlands (7) and Germany (8). In Germany's case its training of apprentices and integrating them into the work force is second to none. Singapore has nothing comparable, yet is six rankings ahead of Germany.

(8)   Basic research and development does enhance long-term economic and technical development. (4.3.10)

Comment: Basic research, like pure research, is motivated by a desire to understand rather than gain immediate pay-offs. This negates the "pragmatic" results-oriented mentality of PAP Singapore where most R&D produces specific innovations for quick pay-offs. At the time of this 2001 report there was little basic research in Singapore despite the subsequent establishment of the Biopolis science park to remedy the deficiency.

Countries with far greater innovative capacity were ranked lower. The UK was ranked (9), Australia (13), Ireland (14) and France (15): the IMD would have us believe that in 2001 Singapore's shallow and derivative attempts at R&D, largely run by the MNCs, were somehow superior at enhancing long-term development than those of developed countries which have won a host of Nobel prizes.

(2)   Science and technology interests the youth of your country. (4.3.16)

Comment: The latest Western gadgets always fascinate Singapore's young, whether they be the newest mobile phones or IT products. Beyond that there is little interest in science and technology unless it leads to more money or a better job. Knowledge for its own sake has minimal appeal to Singaporeans, young or old, unless it produces some material benefit. Such a mentality does not produce inventions that boost competitiveness. This criterion is presumably another way of measuring innovative capacities. If so, a (2) for Singapore is excessive, as becomes apparent when such advanced and innovative countries as Britain score 49 (yes really!); the USA (22), Australia (27) and Japan (47). Such rankings suggest that the youth of these countries are largely if not completely indifferent to science and technology.

(3)   The educational system meets the needs of a competitive economy. (2.5.07)

Comment: Singapore is striving to transform its educational system at all levels to maximise its contribution to national competitiveness. But overcoming over three decades of rote-style education is difficult. While Singaporean students get top scores in science and mathematics in international competitions, they have minimal capacity for creative or problem-solving thinking. They have been made to do De Bono-type "lateral thinking" courses to improve their creativity, but so far with little apparent effect.

Besides low creativity, several hard-data IMD rankings reveal the deficiencies of Singapore's education system. As shown in Chapter Three, Singapore's literacy levels are similar to those of many Third World countries. The IMD ranked Singapore 37th for literacy, with 6.9 per cent of the population over 15 being illiterate. The Philippines, ranked (36), beat Singapore with an illiteracy rate of 5.4 per cent.[28]

Singapore also ranked an astonishing (37) for the pupil-teacher ratio in its primary schools, with one teacher for every 25 children. The ranking for its secondary schools is (34), with a 20:1 student-teacher ratio. (Colombia, which was ranked (33), had a ratio of 19.54:1).

Singaporean pupil-teacher ratios seem suspect, given that the teacher-student ratio for Singapore's primary schools was 1:40 in 2004.[29] Only in the wealthier independent schools has the teacher/student ratio even been 1:20.[30] Moreover, Singapore has no ranking on the IMD criterion for the percentage of population with tertiary education: why it could not provide hard data for this criterion is strange. But as already shown, the percentage of Singaporeans with degrees is well below that of Germans, Japanese and others.

Why Singapore was ranked (3) for the contribution that its education system makes to economic competitiveness despite its clear educational deficiencies is deeply puzzling. Few foreign educationalists are aware of the mediocre quality of Singapore's education system. In 2003, UNICEF chose Singapore to launch its State of the World's Children report to acknowledge the country's efforts in educating its children. "Singapore is a model to other countries," claimed UICEF's regional director.[31] Yet another undeserved accolade for Singapore.

(2)   Economic literacy is generally high among the population. (2.5.10)

Comment: What could "economic literacy" mean? Presumably this term covers the ability to use bank accounts and perform financial transactions, to have a knowledge of investment products and the ability to invest wisely. Being Southeast Asia's biggest centre for financial products might account for Singapore's (2) ranking on this criterion. But Switzerland scored (8) and Hong Kong (15) on this criterion and they are even bigger centres. Their citizens would surely be as educated as Singaporeans on all things financial. Yet Singapore is ranked way ahead of them.

Despite Singapore's (2) ranking, the Government felt compelled to survey the level of financial literacy in 2004.[32] Was this prompted by a realisation that Singaporeans' financial literacy was quite low? This could have been so. First, in 2001 Singaporeans still practised archaic investment strategies that suggested deep financial ignorance. Some older Singaporeans were still involved in tontines, primitive lottery-cum annuity systems prevalent in 19th-century Britain.

Second, Singaporeans were suckers for pyramid selling schemes. Banned in the Republic, promotions for pyramid selling schemes in Malaysia attract crowds of gullible Singaporeans. A Singaporean friend, a normally intelligent man, took me to one in Johor Bahru. Hundreds of Singaporeans were at the promotion. Its staging was as crude as it was stupid, and would have fooled only the most naive; yet many Singaporeans were signing up, including my friend. Only after vigorous protestations by myself did he re-think his decision.

Third, many Singaporeans have experienced big losses after being allowed to invest large portions of their CPF funds in securities. The widespread ignorance of investment basics among Singaporeans is significantly to blame. The co-author of a financial planning book started a course on the topic at the NUS in 1995 because he saw many floundering at managing their money. In 2004, he said that much more should be done to teach financial literacy in schools, universities and polytechnics: indeed, a 1999 NUS/Citibank survey of 1000 Singaporeans who earned more than S$2000 a month found that most Singaporeans do not plan for their future simply because they did not know how, he said.[33]

In 1996, I wrote and published a book entitled *Your Guide to Investment Trading* to give Singaporeans and Malaysians basic information on investment. The poor quality of existing investment books in Singapore prompted me to do this – a surprising situation in a country that scored (2) for the supposed "economic literacy" of its citizens. The US, which had produced a library of investment books by 2001, got (20) for economic literacy.

So much for the IMD's 2001 rankings for Singapore. Six of its most dubious criteria had apparently been recycled in every report since 1995. Further criteria with doubtful rankings had been added, 19 of which have been examined here. Were the WEF's 2001 rankings any better?

The WEF 2001 Report

The 174 criteria used in the WEF 2001 report were placed into 11 categories or indexes but rankings for some were omitted. Those that had rankings – and Singapore's scores for them – were:

- Macro-economic environment (1)
- Technological innovation and diffusion (12)
- Information and communications technology (4)
- Public institutions: contracts and law (7)
- Public institutions: corruption (5)
- Environmental policy (3).

The unranked indexes were:
- Aggregate country performance indicators
- General infrastructure
- Domestic competition
- Cluster development
- Company operations and strategy.

There were about as many questionable rankings in the WEF as in the IMD 2001 report.[34]

(10) How easy is it to obtain a loan in your country with only a good business plan. (2.08)

Comment: A ranking of (10) places Singapore in the top one-seventh of countries for this criterion. This puts it ahead of Australia (14), Hong Kong (15) and Canada (17), all of which are far more genuinely entrepreneurial than Singapore. Up to and after 2001, many SMEs expressed discontent at the lack of government and bank support they got for new ventures. Usually only property development or trading ventures, which could provide highly secured investments, got financing, as Chapters 9 and 16 show. Banks especially were not interested in start-ups or technical companies. A (10) for this criterion was too high.

(1) The composition of government spending provides necessary goods and services. (2.20)

Comment: Like the IMD criteria, those used by the WEF are often equally vague and ambiguous. One way of assessing this statement is to consider how well the state cared for the underprivileged in 2001. In Singapore's case, the minimal government spending on welfare and health continues to condemn its poor, aged and handicapped to far more miserable lives than are common in Western countries. Chapter 25 describes in some detail the wretched state that most of Singapore's disadvantaged, including the chronically ill, were and still are forced to exist in, because of mean-spirited PAP policies. Sweden is ranked (29), Denmark (14), Norway (32), Germany (20) and Australia (8). Could the WEF seriously suggest that in 2001 the governments of these countries which their extensive welfare systems lagged behind Singapore in meeting the needs of their peoples?

(13) Your country's position in technology is among world leaders. (3.01)

Comment: This ranking puts Singapore in the top sixth of WEF countries sampled regarding technological achievement in 2001; but if "position in technology" means the capacity for technological innovation, Singapore's (13) rating is far too high. Although Singapore has tried to improve its R&D performance, the MNCs still conducted the bulk of its R&D in 2001. The patents that emerge from Singapore were often for minor innovations and processes, nothing major. Countries with far greater claims to R&D capacities were Ireland which were ranked (14), Denmark (15), Australia (16), Norway (20) and Italy (31).

(5) In your business, continuous innovation plays a major role in generating revenue. (3.02)

Comment: A ranking of (5) puts Singapore in the top 15th of the countries surveyed for the 2001 report and way ahead of Canada, ranked (11), Australia (35), Sweden (13), Hong Kong (24) and the Netherlands (17). As repeatedly shown in this book, innovation, continuous or otherwise, has not been very evident in Singaporean organisations or companies, whether for generating revenue or raising productivity. Innovation requires initiative, creativity and company loyalty, qualities which few Singaporean companies found in their employees in 2001 and which are still lacking. Such measurements as productivity figures reflect levels of innovation, especially in highly industrialised countries. The WEF's rival, the IMD, had a set of productivity figures in 2000 for the workforce, industry, the services, and for productivity growth that reflected Singapore's innovation levels, as these figures show.

Table 21.5 – Productivity comparisons

	Labor Prod.	Industial Prod.	Services Prod.	Growth of Prod.
Singapore	26	29	26	43
Japan	18	22	12	35
USA	5	3	4	20
Australia	12	14	11	17

NOTE: These figures are based on GDP (PPP) for the year 2000 from the IMD's 2001 report.

(4) Women's participation in economy is equal to that of men's. (3.13)

Comment: Singapore was ranked 37th for the percentage of its women employed in the workforce, according to the IMD's 2001 report. This placed it far behind the workforce participation rates for all the OECD countries (except Italy) as well as for such countries as Indonesia, Thailand and Hong Kong.

On the managerial level also Singapore came in behind several Asian countries, according to a Grant Thornton International Business Owners Survey of medium-sized companies in 26 countries, conducted in 2003.[35] The survey ranked countries on the proportion of companies with women in senior management and women as a percentage of total senior managers. Singapore was ranked 13th for the first and 10th for the second, coming in behind Hong Kong, Taiwan and Indonesia.

Ranking Singapore (4) for female economic participation in the face of such evidence is difficult to justify. The absurdity of this ranking is further demonstrated when it is compared to the rankings of counties such as Sweden, which has vigorously practised sexual equality since the 1930s and which was ranked (8). The same applies to the comparative rankings of such countries as Canada (10), the US (11), Britain (15) and Australia (25), where patriarchal values are much weaker than in Singapore.

On the managerial level, the strong patriarchal values of Singapore ensure that the glass ceiling is very thick for Singaporean women, though Singapore seems to have more women in managerial positions than most other Asian countries, including Japan. Even so, ranking Singapore (4) for female economic participation when Sweden was ranked (8) is ridiculous.

The quotas on female medical students that operated at NUS until December 2002 further demonstrate the major occupational barriers women faced in 2001. Singapore's 88 per cent female literacy rate (compared to the male rate of 96 per cent) represents another restriction to female participation in the workforce.[36]

(8)   Minorities participation in the economy is equal to that of other groups. (3.14)

Comment: Trying to assess such a vaguely worded criterion is difficult. The presence of significant racial discrimination in Singapore in 2001 and now, especially in the jobs area, makes an (8) ranking questionable, especially when such liberal democracies as Sweden were ranked (55), Canada (12), the UK (16) and Australia (29). All were making, and still make, far more strenuous efforts to remove discrimination against minorities than Singapore has ever done for its Malays and Indians.

(7)   Public schools in your country are equal to best in world. (5.12)

Comment: Little credibility can be attached to this ranking of (7) for Singapore, considering the poor student-teacher ratios at its primary and secondary schools and its startling high illiteracy levels (see the comment on IMD criterion 2.5.07). It should be repeated that the student-teacher ratio was 40:1 or more in most of Singapore's primary schools in 2001. Only in 2005 was the Government planning to reduce class sizes to 30, for 70 primary schools – and only then for Primary 1 and 2.[37]

(13)   The difference in quality of public schools available to rich and poor children in your country is small. (5.13)

Comment: Singapore's (13) ranking means that it was in about the top 12 per cent of WEF countries surveyed for this factor. Singapore supposedly had greater equality of education in 2001 than Sweden which was ranked (17), Canada (19), New Zealand (28), Australia (29), Britain (40) and the US (42).

The teacher/pupil ratio in independent schools in 1998 was 1:20 compared to 1:40 for government schools in Singapore.[38] Rahim noted in 1998 that the independent schools often had an impressive range of facilities for drama, arts and crafts centres, gymnasiums, amphitheatres, computer and music laboratories and sports. Few Singaporean government schools could boast such facilities, she said. These inequalities were due to the PAP's elitist policies which seek to promote "excellence":

> *The movement towards "excellence" in education has resulted in a disproportionate sum of public resources being devoted to a few elite schools which serve an elite minority of the total student population.*[39]

In Australia, primary school class numbers were between about 20 and 26 in such states as South Australia, New South Wales and Victoria.[40] Low class numbers have also been evident for years in most Scandinavian and West European countries, where educational equality has been energetically pursued.

The plight of Singapore's educationally subnormal students, the physically handicapped, the autistic, and the academic "failures", was worse, noted Rahim. Such students were mainly catered for by privately run special education schools that "tend to be poorly funded, overcrowded, and offer poor educational facilities". The demand far outpaced supply at such schools. Even though the state paid half the cost of educating such pupils, parents had to pay three times the school fees of parents at mainstream schools. "The government's parsimonious funding of special education schools stands in stark contrast to its generous funding of programmes for 'gifted' children"[41] where classes are far smaller and resources far more lavish. By contrast, schools for the disadvantaged in Australia hold between five and 14 students per class.[42] Australia was ranked (29) to Singapore's (13) for educational equality.

(12)   The difference in quality of health-care available to rich and poor people in your country is small. (5.14)

Comment: Singapore's (12) ranking means that it beats Germany (14), Canada (15), Australia (17), New Zealand (23), and Britain (25) for equality of health-care.

Unlike Singapore, all these countries had and still have comprehensive health-care systems that guarantee medical treatment for all. Singapore still has no such system, as Chapter 24 shows. Many of its poorest and most disadvantaged receive no proper medical treatment, especially those suffering from AIDS or those who require dialysis, or the elderly sick who need treatment for chronic conditions.

(22)   The judiciary in your country is independent and not subject to interference by the government and/or parties to disputes. (6.01)

Comment: Although much lower than many WEF rankings for Singapore, a (22) still puts Singapore in the top third of the countries WEF surveyed for the 2001 report. While Singapore's courts may be politically independent in criminal, commercial and civil matters, this was certainly not so in 2001 for cases the Government considered political. Singapore's judiciary has been used repeatedly to persecute opposition politicians and any media outlets, domestic or foreign, that have displeased the Government since the 1960s. Since then Lee Kuan Yew and the PAP state have ensured that only pro-PAP judges and magistrates are appointed to the courts. This makes even the relatively modest (22) ranking of Singapore's judicial independence appear excessive.

(6)   Financial assets and wealth are clearly delineated and protected by law. (6.02)

Comment: While Singapore was ranked (6) for this criterion, Britain was ranked (12), Canada (14), Australia (16), New Zealand (19), and Norway (19). According to the WEF, assets and wealth were more clearly defined and better protected by law in Singapore than in these Western liberal democracies in 2001. But as already shown, private land can be requisitioned by the Singapore state whenever it wishes. There is nothing in the Constitution that guarantees property rights. This represents a far greater violation of freehold ownership than anything that would be tolerated in the above, more lowly rated, countries. Presumably this ranking is not based on the lack of freehold rights endured by Singapore's HDB owners, who comprise about 80 per cent of the country's homeowners. As Chapter 24 shows, the Government can re-possess peoples' HDB units for several offences. Singapore's laws protect land and property assets far less than in most Western countries, where freehold property rights are much stronger.

(4)   When deciding upon policies and contracts, government officials are neutral among firms and individuals. (6.04)

Comment: This (4) ranking would claim that Singapore's civil servants are more neutral in awarding contracts and the like than their bureaucratic counterparts in Britain which was ranked (11), Sweden (13), Australia (14) and Canada (17). The ranking suggested that Singapore's bureaucrats rarely favoured SEs over private-sector companies in framing policies and awarding contracts. This was despite the fact that statutory boards were run by bureaucrats, while many GLCs were often heavily staffed and usually headed by former civil servants and ex-PAP ministers. As already noted, this gave SEs marked advantages over the private sector in several ways in 2001. SEs could be granted licences or concessions and could have the Government arrange the purchase of products and services for them, as shown in Chapter 16.

(1)   The competence of personnel in the public service is higher than in the private sector. (6.06)

Comment: The PAP Government has always striven to recruit Singapore's best and brightest for the bureaucracy, but often it has merely recruited the safe and subservient, as demonstrated earlier. Entry to Singapore's civil service is heavily dependent on paper qualifications – proof of excellence at passing exams. People who have this gift may be adept at absorbing and regurgitating information and good at studying hard, but job competence requires much more than this, including people skills, street smarts and initiative. These are things that many Singaporean bureaucrats lack, as their often poor foreign investment decisions demonstrate.

While many of Singapore's smartest may initially join the civil service, they often leave for more challenging prospects in the private sector, as the many departures from Singapore's elite AS have revealed. This exodus of talent shows that Singapore's best are not always civil servants, the WEF's (1) ranking notwithstanding. Efforts to increase efficiency with ill-conceived "Wits-style" programs also demonstrate also some severe shortcomings in Singapore's civil service.

(1)   Tax evasion in your country is minimal. (6.11)

Comment: Like the IMD, the WEF survey ranked Singapore (1) for minimal tax evasion. The same comments apply to this WEF criterion as to the similar IMD criterion (2.2.14). Incidentally, Sweden, that tax-evader's hell, was ranked (24) in the WEF 2001 report.

(1)   Public trust in the honesty of politicians is very high. (7.07)

Comment: In its narrowest sense the honesty of politicians is usually measured by their capacity to resist corruption and bribery. In 2001, as now, Singaporeans probably have a high trust in their politicians, particularly cabinet ministers, whose astronomic salaries minimise any tendency towards corruption. High salaries also ensure that the best people lead the country, according to the PAP Government. Many Singaporeans reject such reasoning. They see the PAP Cabinet especially as self-serving and dishonest; some sneer that PAP stands for "personal action party". Because the PAP dominates Parliament and because the ministers dominate the PAP, they can easily rubber-stamp huge salaries for themselves. Singaporeans see this as simple greed and not something in the national interest, as the ministers would claim.

Singaporeans deeply distrust their political leaders, often believing them to be mean and tricky. Promises of greater openness in government, more consultation, or of no "punishment" from the PAP state for expressing dissenting opinions, evoke contempt. Singaporeans continue to see their political leaders as untrustworthy and dishonest.

They would certainly not rank them (1) for honesty.

(1)   Labour-management relations in your country are generally cooperative. (10.21)

Comment: It is interesting how the IMD and WEF Singapore rankings sometimes mirror each other. WEF ranked Singapore (1) for this criterion, as did the IMD for its criterion "Labour relations are generally productive" (3.2.06). The WEF's (1) ranking can be rejected for the same reasons as the IMD's.

(1)   Labour unions in your country contribute to productivity improvements. (10.22)

Comment: Because unions are government-controlled through the NTUC, they are required to go through the motions of implementing PAP exhortations to raise productivity. Workshop-style/Quality Circles discussions between unions and workers to improve efficiency are common, but walking the talk is not evident in Singapore's organisations. The workforce's lacklustre productivity suggests that union efforts to raise it have had limited success.

Despite this the WEF gave Singapore far higher marks for this criterion than they awarded countries such as Japan, whose ranking was (3), though Japan had pioneered the QC concept which Singapore had been trying to implement for over a decade. Other countries which have much greater claims to productive management-worker cooperation include Sweden which was ranked (2), Finland (4), Switzerland (5), Germany (29) and the Netherlands (6).

(1)   Environmental gains in your country are achieved through business-government cooperation and voluntary corporate action. (11.14)

Comment: The (1) ranking for this criterion suggests that environmental gains in Singapore have been achieved through government and business/corporate action, with environmental groups making no input. This is untrue.

Such groups as the Malayan Nature Society (MNS) have done much to raise Singapore's environmental consciousness since the early 1980s. They scored some success as a lobby group when they were able to persuade the Government to establish the Sungei Buloh nature conservation park. In 1991, an emboldened MNS released its own Conservation Masterplan which the Government endorsed, incorporating most of the proposals into its own Singapore Green Plan of 1993.[43] Although adopting a low-key, non-confrontational approach, the environmentalists' success throws doubt on the (1) ranking. A more recent success for Singaporean environmentalists was the preservation of the Chek Jawa mud-flats on Pulau Ubin from state redevelopment.

The preceding 18 WEF criteria show similar flaws to the IMD ones. The WEF criteria also share the IMD's propensity to give inflated rankings to Singapore. Despite revamps and revisions of its criteria, the WEF, like the IMD, continues to produce dubiously high rankings for Singapore and often for other countries.

It may be claimed that both agencies can only compile rankings from available information. The WEF admits to the difficulty of testing the soft criteria against hard data because "there are either no hard measures possible or else no international data available".[44] But as the preceding has shown, there is often sufficient factual material to cast doubt on many of the WEF and IMD rankings. Moreover, if Singapore were as transparent as claimed, there would be more official data available likely to refute even more IMD/WEF rankings than those assessed in this chapter. Nonetheless, the preceding has revealed that many of the IMD/WEF rankings for countries like Singapore are indefensibly high. Methodological deficiencies that would account for this are examined in the next chapter.

References

1. The international competitiveness reports used in this chapter were:
   - *The 1995 World Competitiveness Report* (Institute for Management Development and the World Economic Forum, Lausanne, Switzerland; 1995).
   - *The World Competitiveness Yearbooks 1996 to 2004* (Institute for Management Development, Lausanne, Switzerland).
   - The 1996 to 2004 WEF *Global Competitiveness Reports* (World Economic Forum and the Center for International Development at Harvard University, Oxford University Press, New York).
2. *World Competitiveness Report* 1995, p. 36.
3. *World Competitiveness Yearbook* 2001, p. 51.
4. Ibid.
5. *Global Competitiveness Report* 2001 -2 (WEF), p. 55. WEF definitions of competitiveness resemble those of MIT economist Paul Krugman, whose 1994 paper on national competitiveness sparked significant debate. Both Krugman and the WEF reject notions of competitiveness between nations as a zero-sum contest for export markets. A discussion of these conflicting conceptions of competitiveness is contained in this book's appendix.
6. *The Straits Times* (ST), October 9, 2002.
7. *Business Times*, October 9-10, 2004.

8. Ibid.
9. ST, April 4, 2003.
10. Kua, Pao Kun: "Contemplating an Open Culture", p. 52 in *Singapore: Re-engineering Success* edited by Arun Mahizhnan and Lee Tsao Yuan (Singapore, Oxford University Press, 1998).
11. Ibid.
12. Lingle, Christopher: *The Rise and Decline of the Asian Century* (Hong Kong, Asia 2000, second edition, 1997), p. 85.
13. Chee, Soon Juan: *To Be Free* (Melbourne, Monash Asia Institute, 1998), p. 340.
14. ST, May 25, 1998.
15. ST, November 21, 2000.
16. ST, December 21, 2003.
17. ST, May 25, 1996.
18. ST, May 25, 1996.
19. ST, June 5, 1998.
20. WEF 2001 report, p. 53.
21. ST, March 27, 2004.
22. Rahim, Lily: *The Singapore Dilemma* (Kuala Lumpur, Oxford University Press, 1998), p. 60.
23. Ibid, p. 177.
24. ST, December 6, 2002.
25. ST, March 11, 2004.
26. ST, December 12, 2003.
27. Rahim.
28. *World Competitiveness Yearbook 2001* (IMD), p. 437.
29. ST, June 12, 2004.
30. Rahim, p. 135.
31. ST, December 12, 2003.
32. ST, December 25, 2003.
33. ST, December 14, 2004.
34. Because the WEF surveyed 75 countries compared to 49 for the IMD, a WEF ranking of (10), for example, would be equivalent to an IMD ranking of (6) or (7).
35. *Today*, February 25, 2004.
36. ST, December 12, 2003.
37. ST, June 12, 2004.
38. Rahim, p. 135.
39. Ibid, p. 136.
40. *The Australian*, May 12, 2003.
41. Rahim, p. 148.
42. *The Australian*, May 12, 2003.
43. George, Cherian: *Singapore: the Airconditioned Nation* (Singapore, Landmark Books, 2000), pp. 142-3.
44. *Global Competitiveness Report 2001* (WEF), p. 176.

CHAPTER 22

SUSPECT SOURCES, MNC AGENDAS
AND SINGAPOREAN SCEPTICS

A constant problem for rating agencies and think tanks is getting accurate and reliable statistics from the countries they survey. Many developing countries are statistically underdeveloped. They often lack the organisational and bureaucratic infrastructures necessary to adequately gather statistics. Another problem is acquiring data untainted by political agendas. Authoritarian regimes are notorious for manipulating and even falsifying figures for propaganda purposes.

Official data from authoritarian states and neo-authoritarian ones such as Singapore should be treated sceptically.[1] Information is seen as a power resource that must be controlled, denied to NGOs and opposition politicians and only released in ways that would benefit the regime, as Chapter 20 shows. Consequently, official data from states such as Singapore should be treated with care. As Lingle warned when commenting on the high growth rates of East Asian economies,

> the supporting data are often supplied on a tightly controlled and selective basis by the governments themselves. Since this data is [sic] not amenable to extensive outside corroboration or detailed analysis by independent sources, such reports should be treated with healthy skepticism.[2]

Similar reservations should be held about the high competitiveness rankings that the IMD and WEF have given Singapore. Their deficient data-gathering practices and pro-foreign capital bias significantly explain the inflated scores they have given Singapore.

1. Data Deficiencies

Both the IMD and WEF competitiveness rankings, especially those for Singapore, are often unjustifiably high. The likely reasons for this range from questionable hard data sources to weaknesses in soft-data survey procedures that lead to biased results.

Suspect Hard Data Sources

Both agencies mostly compile their hard criteria rankings from statistics derived from national sources and international organisations. Much of their hard data comes from the "partner institutes", which in Singapore are state-controlled. The IMD's main partner institute in Singapore was initially the National Science and Technology Board (NSTB), but by 2001 included the Ministry of Trade and Industry (MTI). The WEF's partner institute is the Government's Economic Development Board. Government statistical yearbooks provide extra information for the IMD and WEF. Information is also obtained from international agencies, but it usually originates from national sources.

What is the relationship between partner institutes and the rating agencies? In its 2001 report, the IMD revealed that its network of partner institutes "guarantees the relevance of the data gathered". This arrangement gives partner institutes scope to adulterate, selectively release or even withhold data. Such opportunities would be fully exploited by Singapore's officials who have shown few qualms about withholding or doctoring statistics to promote Singapore internationally or to fulfil the PAP state's domestic political agendas.

Such rating agencies as the IMD and WEF can never be sure how far official data from Singapore have been "massaged" or even falsified. Moreover, hard data that partner institutes cannot supply come from other "national sources" – or from international bodies supplied with data from such sources.

In neo-authoritarian states such as Singapore, where data are tightly controlled, few independent means exist for checking official statistics. Most rating agencies simply accept information from such states because of the time and money verification would take.

Soft Data Surveys

The IMD and WEF's soft-data surveys do little to counter biased official data.

Survey data are meant to provide the "intangible" or "impressionistic" information that hard data cannot supply. According to the IMD, the results of the questionnaires "allow us to quantify questions that would otherwise not be measurable, but are nonetheless crucial to a country's competitiveness".[3] Surveys can only fulfil such aims if certain guidelines are met. First, questions should be clear and concise to prevent misinterpretation by respondents. Second, care should be taken to ensure the survey uses sufficiently representative sample groups of respondents. Third, procedures should exist to prevent respondents being, or feeling, pressured by government authorities to give slanted answers rather than honest opinions. Failure to adhere to such guidelines produces distorted results and rankings.

The IMD describes its respondents as representing,

a cross-section of the business community in their countries. They represent both domestic and international companies, as well as the local and expatriate perspectives. Respondents rank only the country in which they work, thereby ensuring that the evaluations reflect an in-depth knowledge of a particular environment. [4]

The usual WEF survey respondents are CEOs or senior managers. They come from local private sector enterprises, state-owned or government enterprises and MNCs. In its 2001 report the WEF provided a detailed table on the number of firms responding and distribution of respondents by firm size and type.[5] For the WEF the term "firm" covers not only domestic concerns and foreign companies but state-owned enterprises and government organisations.

WEF figures show that in Singapore, 67 firms responded to the questionnaire. Of these, 9 per cent were domestic firms (selling primarily in the local market), 27 per cent were domestically-based exporters (selling in foreign and local markets), 55 per cent were MNC subsidiaries, 3 per cent were state-owned concerns and 9 per cent government organisations.

Participation in the surveys is voluntary. This may explain why only a small proportion of the questionnaires sent out by each agency are completed and returned. The 1995 IMD/WEF report revealed that questionnaires were given to about 21,000 "international business executives" working in each country surveyed. Of these "more or less 20% returned the questionnaire completed".[6] In fact, it was 3292 executives.[7] With such a small percentage returning the questionnaire the sample is already biased. It consists only of self-selected respondents who either strongly wished or felt compelled to complete the questionnaire – for whatever reasons.

In subsequent years both the IMD and WEF have been coy about divulging the percentage of questionnaires that are returned. They only publish the numbers returned, not the total numbers sent out, making it impossible to calculate the per cent returned. Evidence suggests that the return rate for both agencies would still be around the 1995 figure of 20 per cent. In its 2001 report the IMD said that 3,678 "executives" returned the questionnaire,[8] while the WEF reported that 4601 executives had responded for its 2001 report.[9]

With only a small proportion of questionnaires being returned, data are coming from a limited and self-selecting sample. Respondents could either be those who genuinely support the survey and want to contribute or those who receive a questionnaire via a state authority and feel obliged to respond. It would be interesting to know what the response rate is for questionnaires distributed in Singapore: if government officials are involved in distributing and collecting the questionnaires then the response rate could well exceed 20 per cent.

Data Collection and Confidentiality

The partner institutes used by the IMD and WEF play an important role in gathering soft as well as hard data. The IMD merely says its institutes "helped distribute the survey questionnaires",[10] and says no more about their role in the surveys. However, one question begs to be asked: do the institutes ever collect the completed surveys? If so, institute staff could easily see how the respondents answered.

Once again the WEF is more forthcoming about the role its institutes play in the surveys. To ensure that surveys sufficiently represent each country surveyed, "we continue to work closely with partner institutes in most countries," the WEF says.[11] Partner institutes are first asked "to start with a comprehensive register of firms and then choose a sample whose distribution across economic sectors of the economy is proportional to the distribution of the country's labour force across sectors, excluding agriculture". The WEF then "asked our partners to choose firms randomly within these broad sectors …and to pursue telephone or on-site interviews, following up for clarifications where necessary".[12]

Obviously, the WEF's partner institutes are heavily involved in the whole data-gathering process. They not only largely choose the respondents but do interviews and follow up "for clarifications where necessary". This would give institute officials significant opportunity to ensure that respondents are giving the "appropriate" responses. It's hard to believe that Singapore's officials would not exploit such opportunities to boost WEF rankings for their country.

Intimidated Respondents?

Since the early 1960s the PAP state has created a climate of intimidation in Singapore. This has inhibited free expression of opinion, even among those filling in rating agency questionnaires. PERC is one rating agency that has expressed frustration at the fear of thinking critically in Singapore. In November 1995, the risk-assessment consultancy found that many respondents to one of its surveys were "at a loss to write anything" when queried about what most annoyed them about doing business in the Republic.[13] PERC asked:

> *Has the Singapore Government so cowed its private sector that businessmen are afraid to commit themselves to anything – even on an anonymous questionnaire – for fear of reprisals?* [14]

While PERC tactfully rejected this notion it added that "there certainly is a conscious effort on the part of the private sector in Singapore to avoid even a hint of public controversy". This would be especially so if respondents thought that Singapore officials were perusing the completed questionnaires for "inappropriate answers" before they were returned to the IMD and WEF. If so, it could well be that on occasion respondents would have found questionnaires being returned to them for "amendment" before being sent on to the IMD and WEF. Have foreign executive respondents in Singapore been subjected to similar pressures when completing the questionnaires? If they were, how far could they have resisted them? Like the locals, Singapore's expatriate sector has been intimidated into silence when commenting on both economic and business matters. Foreign journalists and publications have long since abandoned any efforts to report fully on Singapore. Having been so often and so successfully sued by the PAP Government since the 1980s for such large sums, most foreign publications play it safe. They only provide a partial picture of what is happening in Singapore, omitting much that would offend the Government. This is probably why no expatriate journalists have ever really exposed the major flaws in the Singapore Miracle.[15]

The same concerns are apparent in the foreign financial community. Rodan reports the story of a foreign stockbroker in Singapore who removed his valuables from his apartment before publishing an innocuous article about the reasons for the 1997/8 Asian financial crisis.[16] The prime concern of Singapore's MNC executives is to make money for their companies, not to upset the PAP Government. MNC interests are best served by maintaining good relations with their hosts, not making stands on principle. Moreover, were the NTSB involved in selecting respondents, it would most likely choose foreign executives who could be relied on to make the appropriate responses in the questionnaires. Both local and expatriate business people have legitimate reasons for not wishing to offend the Government. Ready praise rather than honest criticism is wiser, especially when answering questionnaires that might well be scrutinised by government officials. Such attitudes would explain the strangely high soft-data IMD/WEF data rankings for Singapore.

The WEF claims that the use of MNC executives checks the "perception" bias of indigenous respondents. Being the "voices of global business", the MNC executives provide "an important element of objectivity to the Survey" and counter "domestically biased distortions";[17] but the EDB's cosy relationship with many of Singapore's MNC executives, especially those responding to the questionnaires, could be expected to limit their capacity to counter "perception bias".

Even so, perhaps through partial success in countering perception bias, the WEF began giving Singapore lower rankings from 2000. This did not go down well with *The Straits Times*.

WEF Chastised

From 1996-9, the WEF, like the IMD, gave Singapore top or second-top rankings for competitiveness. Even when in 1999 the WEF switched to using two basic competitiveness indexes – the GCR and CCR – it still gave Singapore top billing. Singapore was ranked (1) for its GCR and (2) for its CCR in that year. In 2000, things began to change. While Singapore was still ranked (2) for its GCR, it was only ranked (9) on the WEF's CCR. In the WEF's 2001/2 report, Singapore's WEF rankings fell further to (4) on the WEF's GCR and (10) on its CCR.

Singapore's declining rankings irked *Straits Times* columnist Andy Ho, who sniped, "Singapore's competitiveness is slipping, if the World Economic Forum's 2001 Global Competitiveness Report is to be believed".[18] Ho criticised WEF reports for many of the methodological and other defects already mentioned in this chapter. While his barbs were justified, the irony was that he confined them to WEF reports. He avoided attacking the IMD, whose reports display the same weaknesses and more – but the IMD, unlike the WEF, was still giving Singapore top rankings for competitiveness.

Despite such journalistic admonishments, in 2002/3 the WEF again ranked Singapore (4) on its GCR and only (9) on its other major index, the Microeconomic

Competitiveness Index (MCI), which had replaced the CCR. *Straits Times* reports on the WEF's 2002/3 competitiveness rankings only mentioned that Singapore had scored (4) on the GCR. Singapore's (9) ranking on the WEF's MCI was omitted.[19]

The Government can rely on local media to not only to slant the news to favour Singapore but to chastise ratings agencies who step out of line. This accentuates the intimidatory atmosphere in which they must work in Singapore.

Soft Data Biases

Whether intentional or not, the IMD's and WEF's readiness to use criteria based on soft rather than hard data increases the potential for biased results. Soft-data are simply opinions, often vague ones, of compliant respondents. As the previous chapter shows, there were often hard data available that discredited some soft-data rankings. Survey-based data are often easier to manipulate than hard data, as their sources are readily intimidated respondents. Doctoring hard data, though regularly practiced by the PAP state, is more difficult. Hard data are often on public record and can sometimes be refuted by other data.

Lall has noticed that the WEF uses questionnaire data to measure variables when hard or quantitative data are often available. The WEF's failure to use widely published data on R&D to rank eight of its soft-data R&D criteria from the 2000 report surprised Lall.[20] Such information was readily available from UNESCO, OECD and national sources in most countries. Data on business-funded R&D as a proportion of GDP would be a good and widely used measure of relative research intensity. "It is difficult to understand why WEF ignores these data, particularly since their qualitative (soft) ranking differ significantly from that yielded by hard data," Lall said.[21]

Lall compared soft and hard data rankings for the R&D criterion – "private sector spending on R&D" – from the 2000 report. The hard data ranking was based on private enterprise-funded R&D as a percentage of GDP. Lall found that the two rankings for this factor differed markedly in the 39 countries he surveyed. Sweden led the hard-data rankings, but came sixth on the WEF survey ranking. Of the 39 countries Lall surveyed, 26 of them had higher hard than soft-data rankings for this factor, while for 13 the reverse was true. Among those with higher soft-data rankings was Singapore.

Table 22.1 – WEF R&D rankings from 2000 report

	R&D data Ranking	WEF Ranking	Ranking Difference
Singapore	21	12	– 9
Israel	16	7	– 9
USA	6	3	– 3
Sweden	1	6	+ 5
Switzerland	4	1	– 3
Finland	5	2	– 3

Notably, one of the largest ranking differences is for Singapore. When ranked on more verifiable hard data, Singapore scores much lower than when its rankings are based on the more manipulable soft-data. Although only five of the 39 countries have been listed here, Lall's table shows that the gap between Singapore and Israel's WEF and hard data rankings, in favour of the WEF ranking, were greatest.

In concluding his WEF survey, Lall noted that,

> *the subjective* [survey] *data that are at the core of the WEF index can be a very unreliable guide to the real world. The implications for the final rankings are, to say the least, disturbing. If the errors noted above are repeated over a large number of such* [survey] *questions, and the errors do not offset each other (there is no reason to believe that they do), the final effects may be highly distorting.*[22]

Such criticisms would apply even more to IMD competitiveness rankings.

New Methods, Same Results

Over the years the IMD and WEF have sought to improve their reports to better measure competitiveness. Both agencies have changed and updated their criteria, devised new indexes, and in the WEF's case, expanded the number of countries surveyed. These changes become apparent when the 1995 report is compared with the 2001 reports.

Both IMD and WEF competitiveness reports keep displaying the same defects. Data continue to be gathered from questionable sources, while flawed soft-data procedures remain and vaguely worded criteria are still apparent. It is therefore not surprising that Singapore still enjoys top rankings, especially in the IMD reports. Every year to 2001 (and sometimes after) the IMD ranked Singapore at least second-top for competitiveness. The WEF did the same until 2000. Although most of the criteria had been changed, the results were the same – because the same methodological flaws remained. The analysis of the now-dated 1995 report, along with later reports, in the previous chapter sought to show that six years later both IMD and WEF reports repeated the same defects.

Besides deficient criteria, suspect information sources and the biased data they produced kept being used by the IMD and WEF. In countries like Singapore partner institutes continued to play a major role in supplying data and choosing respondents for the soft-data questionnaires. There seemed to be few safeguards to ensure that respondents felt free to complete questionnaires as they wished without risk of being pressured by state officials to give the "right" answers. Certainly, the WEF has sought to reduce "perception bias" by respondents, and this may explain the lower competitiveness rankings it has occasionally given to Singapore since 2000; but the WEF reports' soft-data rankings still over-rate Singapore on numerous factors of competitiveness, giving it almost as unjustifiably favourable rankings as the IMD reports do.

A pertinent question to ask here is how well Singapore would score on IMD/WEF competitive rankings if they were "cleaned up". Singapore's rankings for many criteria would be much lower if unbiased data were used that accurately measured the factors being assessed, and if procedures were in place to ensure survey respondents felt free to answer the questionnaires honestly. This would likely result in Singapore scoring much poorer overall competitiveness rankings. How much worse would be hard to estimate; but some sort of guide could be provided by using the WEF's concept of competitiveness, which is based on productivity. According to the WEF, productivity basically determines a country's competitiveness.[23] However, it is the IMD, not the WEF, which provides the most comprehensive set of productivity rankings. In the IMD's 2001 report Singapore was ranked (24) for overall productivity based on (Purchasing Power Parity), (29) for productivity in industry and (26) for productivity in services. If Singapore's competitiveness rankings were based on these figures it would have been in the bottom half of the 49 countries surveyed by the IMD. Singapore would certainly not have got the (2) ranking from the IMD in 2001 for overall competitiveness, nor even the WEF's (4) and (10) rankings in that year.

Despite the WEF's emphasis on productivity, its reports lack the range of comprehensive criteria for measuring it, which ironically are provided by its rival, the IMD. Equivalent WEF measures of productivity would be its GDP per capita figures, which had Singapore ranked (20) out of 75 countries surveyed in 2000 for its 2001/2 report. Often GDP per capita figures are seen as proxy measurements for a country's productivity. Despite this, the WEF ranked Singapore (4) on its Growth Competitiveness ranking and (10) on its Current Competitiveness Ranking in its 2001/2 report.

Even by IMD/WEF measures, whether based on unbiased data or mere productivity/GDP criteria, Singapore's competitiveness rankings are excessive. This is probably the most telling criticism that can be made about IMD/WEF competitiveness rankings for countries such as Singapore. Their reliance on suspect state-supplied data undermines their credibility and casts doubt on the competence of the IMD and WEF to assess countries for competitiveness. Definitional and conceptual weaknesses also blight their surveys, as shown by this book's appendix on competitiveness.

Countries like Singapore have benefited from the methodological weaknesses of IMD/WEF competitiveness reports. Such flaws have made it easy for such an image-conscious state to boost its rankings. First, the heavy use of Singapore government statistics and reliance on state-run partner institutes as sources of data gives ample opportunities to control data received by the ratings agencies. Second, the institutes' involvement in the selection of respondents and the processing of their questionnaires provides further scope for influencing how the questionnaires are answered. Third, the intimidatory atmosphere that all respondents operate under in Singapore, as PERC noted, would also distort the responses of many respondents. Considering all the loopholes that the IMD and WEF provide – and the existence of a state highly motivated to exploit them – it is not surprising that Singapore attains such high competitiveness rankings.

Further proof of a pro-Singapore bias is demonstrated by the way the country's IMD/WEF rankings are always inaccurate in one direction – they unerringly favour Singapore. One can search in vain for any Singaporean rankings that should be higher than they are. If inaccurate rankings for a country were simply due to faulty or incomplete data, then one could reasonably expect there to be a mixture of too high and too low scores for that country: such data inadequacies could normally be expected to cleave both ways. In Singapore's case there seem to be no criteria rankings that are too low. All the defective rankings are flawed by being too high, on the basis of evidence available. By contrast, some criteria rankings for specific countries, especially many of the most developed countries, seem inexplicably low, especially compared to those for Singapore, as the previous chapter shows.

One is led to the conclusion that it is not so much a lack of data but a failure to use or gain access to all the data available that has lead to excessive IMD/WEF rankings for Singapore. Besides selective use of, or access to, available data, it could well have been the likely production of distorted data through the IMD/WEF soft-data questionnaires that has been the problem, so that both agencies have been using biased information to compile their rankings for countries such as Singapore.

The preceding discussion has identified flawed data-gathering methods that do much to explain Singapore's high rankings. However, the IMD and WEF's pro-foreign capital attitudes, which support countries like Singapore that strongly favour foreign investment, have also boosted Singapore's competitiveness scores.

2. MNC Agendas

The pro-MNC and free-market concerns of the IMD and WEF soon become apparent when perusing their competitiveness reports, as some commentators have noticed.

Reasonable Criticisms?

The WEF has been chastised for its foreign capital and corporate bias by Lall and MIT development economist Alice Amsden. In commenting on the 1996 WEF report, Amsden writes: "The first and second billings go to those city-states that are mainly locations for Western multinationals – Singapore and Hong Kong".[24] Similarly, Lall has noted a "free market bias" in the WEF 2000 report.[25] Criteria that measure government spending as a share of GDP, private as well as indirect taxes, union power and pension benefits are all assigned negative relations to competitiveness. Countries that score high on these criteria get poor WEF rankings.

Conversely, the greater freedom a country's firms have to hire and fire workers, the more positive its WEF competitiveness rankings. Russia gets one of the highest scores for such criteria because its employers have great freedom to hire and fire. By comparison, Sweden, Germany and Italy, whose employers have far less power over workers, score among the lowest. "Appealing as all this may be to the [2000] report's corporate audience, the economic validity of many of these propositions is debatable," noted Lall.[26]

Support for anti-trust legislation is another plus for competitiveness, says the WEF – along with commitment to free markets and competition. Moreover, the WEF endorses freer trade, stronger intellectual property protection and more liberal capital accounts across the board. But Lall remarked that this,

> *ignores valid arguments for interventions in all three, at least for developing countries with fledgling industrial sectors, weak capabilities and backward institutions. There is a good economic case for infant industry protection in developing countries, particularly in overcoming the initial costs of tacit learning and building new networks and skills.*[27]

Lall's call for infant industry protection coincides with the views of Cambridge University economist Ha-Joon Chang, who has rejected the claims of globalisation. Chang contends that affluent countries practised vigorous protectionism during the earlier stages of their growth but abandoned it once fully developed. Now, under the guise of globalisation, the developed world insists that developing countries abandon protection and open their economies to competition. The world economy's rules are not designed for underdeveloped countries but lock in advantages for the present industrial leaders.

Chang points out that data now show that Third World countries grew faster from 1960-80 (before they abandoned such development strategies as import substitution and tariffs) than during the period when they followed the advice of the IMF, the World Bank and free-trade evangelists. He says infant industry protection and trade barriers were used successfully to industrialise Britain, the US, Germany and Japan.[28]

Lall and Chang argue that underdeveloped countries require some protection to develop economically. Only then will they experience increased productivity and the capacity to provide the high and rising living standards that the WEF deems central to competitiveness. Conversely, a lack of protection means local industries will be crushed by foreign, often MNC, competition, which has occurred in Singapore since the 1960s and which partly explains its limited EIC levels. Despite this, there seem to be no WEF criteria that measure the negative effects of foreign competition on an economy, nor how that competition may reduce development and productivity. Such criteria are required to provide a fuller picture of an economy's competitiveness. If the WEF devised criteria to measure the downside of foreign investment and pro-corporate policies, then Singapore's competitiveness rankings would be lower.

The IMD shares the WEF's pro-MNC/free-market/globalisation position. The IMD believes that a country's competitiveness depends on how well it provides an environment in which enterprises can compete, nationally and internationally. The IMD also ranks countries as more competitive when they display a commitment to free-market policies, especially permitting foreign competition and minimising government interference. Like the WEF, the IMD lacks criteria that measure the negative effects that such policies have on a country's competitiveness.

In assessing the criticisms of the IMD and WEF's pro-foreign capital and corporate bias it must first be noted that the capacity to attract foreign capital is an important component of national competitiveness. Foreign investment can confer a range of benefits on the host economy, if properly used. The often mad scramble by developing countries to attract MNCs testifies to the value of foreign capital. Favourably ranking countries according to how well they accommodate foreign investment is a legitimate means for assessing their competitiveness. However, both the IMD and WEF deserve criticism when they lack criteria for measuring how the detrimental effects of MNC competition can cripple local concerns; nor do they consider the failure of governments to protect indigenous businesses from imports. Both situations can prevent the growth of the local and SME sectors, which are required for a country's long-term competitiveness.

When a country's SME sector is stunted, as Singapore's is, then its EICs will underdeveloped. This limits the capacity to produce local goods and services that can compete effectively on world markets. Countries in such a situation must then rely on MNCs to perform this role for them. For as long as foreign enterprises do this, the host economy will remain competitive. But should these enterprises depart for more profitable locations, then that country will suddenly become far less competitive. The question therefore is whether a country such as Singapore, which is so heavily dependent on MNCs and deficient in EICs, can be deemed competitive in the long term.

A Perplexing Exercise

Examining the IMD and WEF competitiveness rankings for Singapore is a perplexing experience. Firstly, much of the data they use to compile their Singapore rankings is likely to be suspect. Second, their foreign-capital bias prevents them from measuring negative as well as positive effects of foreign direct investment on the competitiveness of the host economy. Despite this foreign-capital bias, would it be fair to claim that a IMD/WEF competitiveness ranking for a country is merely a proxy for measuring its hospitality to foreign capital? Is a country with good competitiveness rankings also a prime venue for foreign investment?

It would be as easy to adopt this view about Singapore's IMD/WEF rankings as it would be to accept its rankings from The Heritage Foundation (HF) and the Cato Institute (CI). Although HF and CI claim to measure such attributes as economic freedom, they are really assessing a country's suitability for foreign capital. Because Singapore provides a very favourable environment for foreign capital it gets top scores for "economic freedom", the HF and CI's proxy for the quality of the foreign investment climate.

One suspects that many in the international financial community adopt the same attitude toward IMD and WEF competitiveness reports, seeing them as guides to locate the best countries for foreign investment, like the HF and CI reports. "Competitiveness", like "economic freedom", is seen as code for "suitability as an investment venue"; so when the IMD and WEF rank Singapore as one of the world's most competitive economies they are taken to mean that Singapore is a premium investment venue. When perceived this way, both agencies would seem to have got it about right. Singapore has been a very good place for foreign concerns, and this is reflected by its high IMD/WEF competitiveness rankings.

However, it would be simplistic to view IMD/WEF reports as merely being guides for locating profitable investment venues. First, only a minority of IMD/WEF criteria – around 10 to 20 per cent – reflect the concerns of foreign capital. The rest of their criteria genuinely seem to be trying to measure, however ineptly at times, countries' overall competitiveness, including Singapore's. Moreover, while the criteria may reflect an overall corporate bias, it is one that covers both local as well as foreign sectors of an economy. The criteria measure factors of equal concern to the business sector generally, though from a free-market corporate perspective.

The IMD sincerely seems to be seeking to rank countries' competitiveness by their capacity to provide a positive climate for business, while the WEF is trying to do the same by scoring the various factors that affect a country's productivity. Both assess a wide range of political, institutional and cultural factors to measure countries' competitiveness. It could truly be said that both bodies are measuring a country's competitiveness from much more than a foreign capital or even general corporate/business perspective and that their competitiveness rankings for a country reflect its overall national competitiveness, not merely its hospitality to foreign capital. Moreover, if the information being used by both agencies was accurate then the competitiveness rankings derived from it would have some credibility. However, the major problem with IMD/WEF methodologies remains: they still provide ample opportunities for a state such as Singapore to distort and manipulate the data it provides or processes for them.

Were Singapore to be ranked purely as an investment venue, it would score well, and no statistical manipulation by its officials would be necessary to boost its competitiveness rankings. However, Singapore is also being assessed on a much broader range of criteria by the IMD and WEF. These are often criteria upon which Singapore may not score well. As the previous chapter shows, Singapore would achieve mediocre scores on a whole range of criteria (by use of more accurate data) that have little to do with foreign investment, including those that determine EICs. Hence the need remains for data manipulation by Singaporean officialdom, including dubiously distributed and processed questionnaires. This ensures that Singapore continues to score top rankings on many of the IMD/WEF's non-foreign-investment criteria. Were such rankings compiled from all available and accurate information they would often be much lower, depressing Singapore's overall competitiveness rankings and reducing its appeal to foreign capital.

While the IMD/WEF competitiveness rankings measure more than a country's foreign capital (FC) climate, such rankings are still seen as a measure of such a climate by MNCs. They still use IMD/WEF rankings as a means of locating the best countries in which to set up operations, whatever other non-FC aspects of competitiveness such rankings may also be measuring. As such, Singapore must keep scoring well on all the IMD/WEF rankings that it can, not merely on those relating to FC, for as long as it remains dependent on FC. Moreover, scoring well on non-FC as well as FC criteria earns Singapore further accolades that boost its international status generally in many useful ways, including those relating to good government, R&D, and workforce and managerial quality.

Singapore's high competitiveness rankings are therefore most likely due to:

- High scores that accurately reflect Singapore's strengths as a top FC venue
- The IMD/WEF FC-bias which only measures the benefits of foreign investment to Singapore but not its often significant negative effects
- Suspect data and questionnaires that have greatly and undeservedly inflated Singapore's rankings for many "non-FC" IMD/WEF criteria.

Few so far have questioned Singapore's high IMD/WEF rankings. The prevailing view is that they show Singapore as highly competitive internationally in all ways, not merely in terms of attracting foreign investment. Even so, when these rankings are accepted at face value they sometimes elicit a sceptical "so what" response from Singaporeans.

3. Local Sceptics

While well-heeled expatriates and international "experts" are on hand to sing Singapore's praises, many of its citizens remain underwhelmed by their country's miracle economy and the high rankings. A few have directly questioned the real purpose of such rankings, asking who they are really for. One of these is *Straits Times* columnist Sonny Yap, who asked his fellow Singaporeans,

> *hand on your heart, what is your reaction whenever you come across yet another top rating for Singapore? Do you feel a turbo-charge of adrenaline or are you barely able to stifle a yawn.*
>
> *The more sceptical will ask if the average worker can really see the nexus between the Republic's pole positions and the need for continuing pay restraint. Or if evaluations by foreigners based on foreigners' inputs for a foreign audience necessarily coincide with the best interests of the country.[29]*

Yap's reference to pay restraint is understandable. This is one of the regular requirements that international capital imposes on countries such as Singapore – a demand to which the PAP Government readily agrees. Yap also asks whether Singaporeans should only be taking notice of ratings that flatter Singapore: "Should we not ....also pay heed to those which are less than flattering?" He referred to a February 1998 survey by Freedom House, a US-based agency that monitors political rights and civil liberties around the world:

> *Noting that almost all countries with a per capita GDP of above US$8000 were ranked at the top for political and civil freedom, it said that the only exceptions were Singapore and the oil-rich emirates of the Middle East. Ouch![30]*

What Yap did not (could not?) say was that the lack of political freedom is largely a function of the need to provide a politically stable low-wage climate for foreign capital. Keeping wages down for MNCs necessitates control of the workforce and the unions.

This in return requires political control, not only of parliament, but especially of the democratic right of association, which permits people (including workers) to freely organise and fight for better wages and conditions – and to be made fully effective, restrictions on such freedoms also need control of other sectors of society from which anti-government opposition may spring, including the media, the judiciary and the universities as well as a whole range of NGOs and civic bodies.

Yap queries the lack of attention focused on Singapore's failures concerning quality of life. He notes that Singapore comes only 28th in the 1998 UN human development index which ranked countries by overall health, educational level, life-expectancy and per capita income. While the local media trumpet Singapore's No. 1 scores for competitiveness, "not a single soul has breathed a word about why we are placed No. 28 on the latest UN index".[30]

As Walter Woon, one of Singapore's nominated MPs, carefully observed in 1996:

It's gratifying to know that foreigners feel Singapore is a good place. But I only see the positive, and I ask myself, is that all there is, or is there anything negative that doesn't get into the news?[31]

In similar vein, Graham Haywood, the executive director of the Singapore International Chamber of Commerce, noted that the rankings,

can be a tool to help sell Singapore. But they shouldn't lull people into a false sense of security. We should look at all of our faces in the mirror, and reflect on the warts as well.[32]

Singapore's competitiveness and other rankings obscure its warts to many in the West, especially neo-cons. They still see Singapore as an example for the developing world to follow with its open-door policies regarding foreign capital and its highly globalised economy. Their faith in Singapore is confirmed by its high rankings, prepared by ratings agencies and think tanks who have the same views. Those who work for such bodies are willing collaborators in the rankings game that Singapore plays with the world.

Think tank/ratings agency operatives must know they are really assessing countries for foreign investment potential, whatever else they are supposedly measuring them for. They prefer to claim they are measuring a country for such attributes as economic freedom, transparency or freedom from corruption or competitiveness, rather than for exploitability by foreign capital. It sounds better – and is less likely to arouse the nationalistic feelings of anti-globalisation activists in the countries surveyed.

Ratings bodies mostly seem to rely on information from published sources and partner institutes in countries being surveyed. Should any ratings agency staff visit Singapore, their task of giving the country top marks is made easier, one suspects, by the likelihood that they observe it through the spectacles of five-star accommodation and lavish expense accounts. Their likely lack of hands-on experience of Singapore makes it easy for government officials and ministers to mislead them. Such compliant "experts" are unlikely to display the capacity needed to check and sceptically evaluate official data

– should they ever want to determine how competitive or economically free Singapore really is.

Besides these shortcomings, the intellectual mediocrity of rating bodies is shown by their defective methodologies and lack of conceptual rigour – further explored in this book's appendix on competitiveness. This and their misuse of statistics border on incompetence. Not surprisingly many economists treat ratings agencies with a certain disdain. As Lall sniffs:

> *Academic economists have largely ignored the competitiveness "industry" and have been disdainful of its output: business school products based on weak or non-existent economic foundations.*[33]

Despite their evident failings, the rating bodies provide a useful service for international capital. While they may poorly measure what they claim to measure – such as economic freedom, transparency and national competitiveness – their reports do better at identifying countries that best meet the requirements of international capital.

MNCs, global finance bodies and international organisations provide a large and profitable market for rating agency reports. The WEF, for example, is funded by about 1000 corporations.[34] Moreover, astute countries such as Singapore have the opportunity to promote themselves to international capital. It's a cosy set-up that suits all three parties: foreign capital, rating bodies and countries like Singapore. It is also responsible for much of the statistical mirage that hides Singapore's severe flaws.

* * * * * * * * * *

Statistically the Singapore Miracle has been a brilliant success. Numbers have validated its achievements and all the myths that sustain it. Very early, Lee Kuan Yew and his team realised the importance of statistics for propaganda purposes, as Buchanan's 1971 observations suggest. Statistics were used not just to sell Singapore to the MNCs but also for domestic political purposes. The PAP state wanted Singaporeans to believe that it had delivered the good life to them and they were really experiencing high and rising living standards. The next section examines how far this is true. What has the Singapore Miracle given the average Singaporean?

References

1. Because of Singapore's regular quasi-democratic elections, a tiny though persecuted parliamentary opposition and limited freedom of speech and the press, the term "neo-authoritarian" rather than "authoritarian" more appropriately describes the Singaporean state.

2. Lingle, Christopher: *The Rise and Decline of the Asian Century* (Hong Kong, Asia 2000, second edition, 1997), p. 81.

3. *The World Competitiveness Yearbook 2001* (Institute for Management Development, Lausanne, Switzerland), p. 51.

4. Ibid.

5. *The Global Competitiveness Report 2001* (World Economic Forum and the Center for International Development at Harvard University, Oxford University Press, New York). p. 168.

6. *The World Competitiveness Report 1995* (Institute for Management Development and the World Economic Forum, Lausanne, Switzerland; 1995), p. 38.

7. Ibid, p. 358.

8. *The World Competitiveness Yearbook 2001* (IMD), p. 51.

9. *The Global Competitiveness Report 2001* (WEF), p. 169.

10. *The World Competitiveness Yearbook 2001* (IMD), p. 8.

11. *The Global Competitiveness Report 2001* (WEF), p. 167.

12. Ibid.

13. ST, November 18, 1995.

14. Ibid.

15. Even so, few foreign journalists have written about the failings of Singapore and its economic miracle even after having left it for other postings.

16. Rodan, Garry: "Asian crisis, transparency and the international media in Singapore, *The Pacific Review*, Vol. 13, No. 2, 2000, p. 34.

17. *The Global Competitiveness Report 2001* (WEF), p. 173.

18. ST, November 7, 2001.

19. ST, November 13, 2002.

20. Lall, Sanjaya: "Competitiveness Indices and Developing Countries: An Economic Evaluation of the Global Competitiveness Report", *World Development*, 29, 9, 2001, p. 1517.

21. Ibid.

22. Ibid, p. 1519.

23. This is despite the WEF's use of nearly 170 other criteria to measure competitiveness. The WEF justifies this by claiming that many of these factors correlate with productivity in some way or other, and it uses complex sets of statistical tables that purport to prove this.

24. Amsden, Alice: "Competitiveness and Industrial Policy: East and West", *JPRI*, Vol 3, No. 8, October 1996.

25. Lall, p. 1507.

26. Ibid.

27. Ibid, p. 1506.

28. Chang, H.J.: *Kicking Away the Ladder: Development Strategy in Historical Perspective* (London, Anthem Press, 2002).

29. ST, May 15, 1999.

30. Ibid.

31. ST, May 13, 1996.

32. Ibid.

33. Lall, p. 1502.

34. *The Australian*, October 14, 2004.

Section Seven

The Good Life?

The ultimate purpose of a country's economic growth, whether miraculous or otherwise, is to provide the best life possible for all its people. But what represents the good life? Materially it means high living standards, affordable housing, comprehensive social security and adequate health-care for all. The following chapters assess how far PAP Singapore has achieved this for all Singaporeans.

CHAPTER 23

AN AFFLUENT SOCIETY?

Singapore's claims to affluence are statistically supported by the island's developed world levels of per capita Gross National Income (GNI). In 2006, Singapore's GNI was US$29,320, the 18th highest out of 133 countries surveyed by the World Bank.[1] By comparison, countries such as France were ranked 13th (US$36,550), Canada 14th ($36,170), Australia 15th ($35,990), Italy 16th ($32,020) and New Zealand 21st ($27,250). The US was ranked 5th ($44,970) and the UK 9th ($40,180). However, a country's affluence rests not only on its per capita income but on how equitably that income is distributed and how much it buys. If income is very unequally distributed it can still condemn many to poverty. High living costs erode everyone's incomes and condemn poorer classes to even more poverty. A constant PAP government claim is that Singaporeans' living standards and material security have dramatically improved during its rule. Their affluence is clear for all to see. But affluence for whom? How many Singaporeans are enjoying the good life? This question can be answered by considering firstly the distribution of income and secondly the cost of living in Singapore.

1. Wealth and Income Distribution

Apart from lamentable road manners, a striking feature of Singapore's traffic is the many luxury cars on the road. Besides Mercedes (including the most costly), numerous Jaguars, mega-expensive Lamborghinis and even Rolls Royces are regularly seen. Their large numbers are surprising considering their astronomical prices in Singapore. On average all cars, cheap and expensive, cost three to four times more in Singapore than in Australia and the US. Further proof of the affluence of Singapore's wealthy is the endless stretch of high-rise condominiums, some costing over S$3 million.

But poverty is still visible in Singapore. Elderly people in their 70s and 80s can regularly be seen picking through rubbish bins and cast-offs on the roadside late at night. One also sees crippled and blind people sitting outside up-market department stores in Orchard Road selling tissues and pathetic trinkets to make a few dollars. Such socio-economic disparities indicate severe inequalities of wealth.

Inequalities of Income

Singapore's per capita GNI was S$45,353 (S$3779 a month) in 2006,[2] 59.4 per cent of the workforce was earning less than S$2500 a month, 47.7 per cent less than S$2000 a month and 33.8 per cent less than S$1500 a month.[3] A more detailed breakdown from the survey reveals the following:

Table 23.1 – Wage ranges of Singaporean employees in 2006

Monthly Wage Ranges	No. of Employees
Under S$500	94,800
S$500–$999	237,100
$1000–$1499	274,800
$1500–$1999	250,300
$2000–$2499	211,000
Total	1,068,000

(This total is 59.4 per cent of Singapore's 2006 workforce of 1,796,700.)

Besides individual wage rates, another measure of income distribution is provided by household income. A Department of Statistics (DOS) survey produced the following breakdown of monthly household income for Singapore's poorest groups for 2002/3.[4]

Table 23.2 – Household income ranges in Singapore for 2002/3

Income Ranges	% of Households	Individuals per Household
Below S$1000	11.5 per cent	2.2
S$1000 – $1499	8.2 per cent	2.8
$1500 – $1999	8.8 per cent	3.3
$2000 – $2499	8.5 per cent	3.5
$2500 – $2999	7.3 per cent	3.6

Nearly 20 per cent of Singapore's households lived on less than S$1500 a month in 2002/3. However, in 2000 the Government deemed that a Singaporean household of four people could exist on S$1000 a month.[5] But this would have been a pitifully small amount for a four-person household to live on in expensive modern Singapore as will be shown.

Even so, income averages only give an overview of income distribution in a country. Examining the pay-rates for specific occupations shows more clearly what the ordinary person earns. The following were median monthly gross wages for selected occupations in Singapore in 2006, according to Government manpower statistics.[6] These statistics define gross wages as including all overtime, commissions and other regular cash payments before deduction of taxes and employees' CPF payments, but exclude bonuses.

Tradesmen – Plumber (S$2000), Carpenter ($1757), Plasterer ($820), Electrician ($1856), Jeweller ($1620), Welder ($2197) and Sheet metal worker ($1420).

Other Blue-Collar – Crane operator (S$2680), Gardener ($860), Office cleaner ($657), Cook ($1854), Construction labourer ($800) and Manufacturing labourer ($913).

Service Workers – Restaurant waiter-supervisor (S$1650), Waiter ($1177), Hotel housekeeper ($1700), Motorcycle courier ($1395), Bus driver ($1506), Truck driver ($1659) and Shop assistant ($1500).

Clerical Workers – Bank tellers ($2107), Cashier ($1218), Ledger and accounts clerk ($1899), Typist ($1861), Filing clerk ($1763), Receptionist ($1550) and Storekeeper ($1893).

Semi-Professional – Social worker (S$2303), Pharmacist ($3492), Architectural draftsman ($2794), Personal/human resources officer ($2936) and Professional nurse ($2564).

These figures reveal how modest were the wages of most Singaporean workers, both white and blue collar. Singapore's average per capita income in 2006 was S$45,353 or $3779 a month.[7] But the median income was only S$2170 a month and the earnings of all the above-listed occupations, many for highly-skilled and trained personnel, fall below this figure; most are below S$2000.

Moreover, the earnings of Singaporean workers are normally based on 5 1/2 and six-day weeks, often with minimal annual holidays. In 2006, only 39.6 per cent of full-time employees worked a five-day week.[8] Of the rest, 41 per cent worked a 5 1/2 to six-day week. In addition, all Singaporean employees worked an average of 46.2 hours a week in 2006, with those in manufacturing working 50.5 hours and in construction working 51.9 hours a week.[9]

Also, annual holidays are limited for most Singaporean workers. In 2006, 60.1 per cent had 14 days or less of annual leave,[10] while the figures for manufacturing and construction workers being 65.5 and 91.6 per cent respectively.[11] By contrast, the higher-paid occupations – professionals, managers, executives and technicians – have shorter working weeks and longer holidays. For example, in 2006, 78.1 per cent of those in the information and communication sectors and 87.2 per cent of those in financial services had five-day weeks while 73.4 per cent had more than two weeks holiday a year.[12]

Besides differences in work-weeks and annual holidays, the major gap between Singapore's managerial and other elites and the ordinary worker is based on wealth and income. In 1999, the average income of the top 20 per cent was 18 times that of the bottom 20 per cent.[13] This trend has worsened in recent years, as the incomes of Singapore's poorest 20 per cent continue to decline – as shown later in this chapter.

Income inequalities have been accentuated by the enormously high salaries paid to Singapore's government ministers and senior civil servants, including those in such elite sections as the Administrative Service (AS). In July 2000, the Prime Minister's salary was raised to S$1.94 million, while salaries for cabinet ministers and top civil servants went to $968,000 and for senior civil servants (Superscale G) to $363,000.[14] In April 2007, ministerial salaries leapt by a further 60 per cent.[15] The average ministerial salary became S$1.6 million while the Prime Minister's salary rose to S$3.1 million.

Then in January 2008, ministerial and senior civil service salaries rose once more. The Prime Minister's salary went up to S$3.76 million, while salaries for ministers went to S$1.94 million and for senior civil servants to S$398,000.[16] Such stratospheric salaries for politicians and top bureaucrats are deemed necessary to ensure the PAP state recruits the best and brightest to run the country. Lower level civil servants are also offered attractive remuneration packages to discourage them from taking private sector appointments. Graduate newcomers usually start at S$60,000 a year or more and can quickly reach six-figure salaries.

With ministers, the Government seeks to retain them by benchmarking their salary to top earners in the private sector. The benchmark is set at two-thirds of the median pay of the top eight earners in each of six sectors: banking, law, engineering and accountancy, the MNCs and local manufacturers.[17] In April 2007, the benchmark was S$2.2 million. The 2007 pay rises brought it to 73 per cent of this sum and in January 2008 the benchmark was raised to 77 per cent. These latest increases were meant to keep public-sector salaries in line with the soaring salaries of top private sector earners, claimed the Government. There is also the implicit understanding that sky-high public sector salaries make ministers and public servants less susceptible to corruption – or as Linda Low delicately put it, "Sufficient pay would put private interests of ministers on hold while they serve."[18]

Salaries for Singapore's private sector executives and managers seem excessive even by international standards, as shown below. But before comparing Singapore's top-end salaries with those of other countries, its less respectable wealthy should be acknowledged. They are individuals who make their fortunes from the "underground economy", mainly gambling, prostitution and loan-sharking. This disreputable sector, which the Government would rather not recognise, caters for the bottomless appetite for such services in Singapore, despite its officially squeaky clean image.

Loan sharks do particularly well in Singapore, where a large and illicit gambling industry ensures constant business. One of Singapore's loanshark kings, "Big Brother", admitted to making S$250,000 to S$400,000 a month before he was caught and jailed for bribing police in July 2001. He owned several properties in Singapore and drove a S320 Mercedes.[19] Another loan shark reportedly earned about $600,000 in two years by making illegal loans to about 1000 people.[20] Those involved in illegal bookmaking for horse-racing and football matches also do well. One of note operated under the code name Har Tsai, ("prawn boy" in Mandarin). Although only 30, he made between S$500,000 and S$1 million a year for several years.[21]

Singapore's disreputable wealthy aside, its enormous inequalities of income are best highlighted by comparing the remuneration of its top and bottom earners with their equivalents in developed countries.

Comparing Inequalities

Singapore has far greater income inequality than almost all developed countries, as a comparison of their Gini coefficients (GC) reveals. Singapore's GC was 42.6, which was higher than that of 22 developed countries, according to the World Bank.[22]* The GCs of developed countries ranged from 24.7 for Denmark to 40.8 for the US (whose income and wealth inequalities are the highest in the West). Singapore's GC also exceeded the GCs of Russia (39.9) and all the East European and former Soviet republics.

Only Third World countries display Singapore's inequalities of wealth, with the GC's of most falling into the 40-60 range. For example, Thailand's GC is 42 while Malaysia's is 49.2, Turkey's (43.6), the Philippines's (44.5), Kenya's (42.5), Senegal's (41.3) and Nigeria's (43.7). Some of the highest GCs are Brazil's at 57, Argentina's (51.3), Chile's (54.9) and Colombia's (58).

While Singapore has per capita GNIs that match those of developed countries, its severe inequalities of income are more of Third World levels. Very high incomes for the top income-earners, combined with well-below Western wages for the workforce explain this. As shown above, remuneration for Singapore's political leaders and senior bureaucrats is astonishingly high by world standards, especially when comparisons are made with the top office-holders in major Western states. While Singapore's Prime Minister's salary was US$2.05 million in December 2007, the US president received $400,000, the UK prime minister ($375,000), the French president ($346,000), the Germany chancellor ($318,000), Japan's prime minister ($248,000),[23] and the Australian prime minister ($300,000).[24]

The salaries of Singapore's cabinet ministers are also several times those of their Western and Hongkongian counterparts. In 2006, Singapore's cabinet ministers received US$857,000 a year while cabinet salaries in the US were US$168,000; the UK ($231,000), Canada ($184,000), Australia ($200,000) and Hong Kong ($386,000).[25] At the other end of the income spectrum, Singapore's wage levels often approach those of the Third World, as already shown.

The pay rates for Singapore's manufacturing workers lag well behind those of other industrialised countries. The IMD's 2000 report ranked Singapore 22nd out of 45 countries for hourly rates paid to manufacturing workers.[26] All the developed countries paid their manufacturing workers more. The countries which Singapore surpassed included Russia, Thailand, the Czech Republic, Poland, Hungary, South Africa, Mexico and Zimbabwe (!) – certainly not affluent by Western standards in 2000. The countries which had higher manufacturing wages were Canada, Italy, Sweden, France, Britain, US, Australia, Japan, Spain, Greece and Germany.

Singapore's distribution of income is not only very unequal by developed country standards but is becoming even more so.

---

* The World Bank's Gini estimates in its 2007 report, were based on much earlier data from the countries surveyed, mostly from about 1998 and 2004. For example, Singapore's Gini data was from 1998. Also, the Bank did not specify whether its Gini statistics were for individual or household income. Even so, Singapore's GC is clearly much higher than those of virtually all developed countries.

A Widening Gap

Singapore had developed a sizeable income gap by the mid-1990s and this has grown even more since then. It has been a classic case of the rich getting richer and the poor becoming poorer.

The first two tables below – of individual monthly incomes – show how this trend had already become evident after the 1997/8 Asian financial crisis. While the incomes of the poor were falling from 1998 to 1999, those for managerial and professional positions were rising.

Table 23.3 – Falling incomes of Singapore's poorest workers, 1998 and 1999

Occupation	1998	1999
1) Helpers, cleaners in offices, hotels and other establishments	S$655	S$573
2) Housekeeping and catering service workers	$625	$503
3) Stall and market workers	$620	$461
4) Shop sales workers and sales demonstrators	$746	$492
5) Personal care and household service workers	$494	$418

Source: Straits Times, May 11, 2000.

Table 23.4 – Rising managerial and professional incomes in Singapore, 1998 and 1999

Occupation	1998	1999
1) Specialised managers	S$7643	S$8374
2) Statistical, administrative and related professionals	$5011	$5353
3) Company directors	$12,118	$12,527
4) Finance and sales associated professionals	$6581	$7566

The growing income gap became even more evident in the 2000s. By then wages were also falling for lower-middle and some middle-income employees in Singapore, not only the lowest paid, as the table below shows.

23.5 – Incomes of selected occupations in 2000 and 2005

	2000	2005		2000	2005
Plasterer	S$1226	S$820	Truck driver	S$1845	S$1659
Gardener	$1238	$860	Cashier	$1457	$1218
Office cleaner	$808	$657	Recep'st	$1932	$1550
Const. labourer	$893	$800	Storekeeper	$1905	$1893
Waiter	$1242	$1177	Nurse	$2682	$2564
Bus driver	$1890	$1506	Soc. worker	$2337	$2303

Not only the income of Singapore's poor but also that of many middle-income earners has been declining, though its millionaire numbers have continued to explode. They soared from 535 in 1996 to 1422 in 2001 and to 2121 in 2007.[27]

Singapore's household incomes have also been showing growing inequality since the 1990s, according to DOS surveys. They are the Household Expenditure Surveys (HES) and the General Household Surveys (GHS). The HES defines household income as that received from work or employment as well as income from rents, investment, pensions and cash contributions from relatives.[28] In the GHS, only household income is regarded as that "from work", from employment.[29] Each type of survey has not only revealed growing income inequalities, but actual declines in the income of the poorest third or so of Singapore's households. Both the 1997/8 and the 2002/3 Reports on Household Expenditure confirm this.[30]

23.6 – Average monthly household income by quintile, 1998 and 2003 (HES)

Household Income Group	1998	2003
Lowest 20%	S$933	S$795
Second Quintile	$2118	$2059
Third Quintile	$3374	$3379
Fourth Quintile	$5162	$5309
Highest 20%	$11,450	$12,792

(NOTE: From 1998 to 2003, the average household size for the lowest 20 per cent shrank from 2.7 to 2.4 persons, while that for the second quintile fell from 3.7 to 3.4.)

The 2000 and 2005 GHS surveys revealed similar growing inequalities in the incomes of Singapore's households.[31]

23.7 – Average monthly income by decile, 2000 and 2005 (GHS)

Household Income Group	2000	2005
1 – 10%	S$90	–
11 – 20%	$1470	$1180
21 – 30%	$2250	$2190
31 – 40%	$2950	$2990
41 – 50%	$3660	$3850
51 – 60%	$4470	$4850
61 – 70%	$5390	$5890
71 – 80%	$6520	$7260
81 – 90%	$8270	$9300
91 – 100%	$14,360	$16,480

(NOTE: Average household size for these studies was 3.7 persons in 2000 and 3.8 in 2005. Also, the $90 a month for households in the first decile in 2000 was because 87 per cent had no earned monthly income in that year. In 2005, the percentage of households without any such income was 10.1 per cent, meaning that the average income of those in the first decile was effectively zero – not withstanding money they may have received from pensions or family members etc.)

In both surveys, the incomes of the bottom 40 per cent of households had declined, especially for the poorest households. In the HES survey, the incomes of the bottom 20 per cent had fallen by 14.8 per cent from 1997/8 to 2003 while in the GHS, that of the second decile had plunged 19.8 per cent between 2000 and 2005.

It is worth noting that even the households in the middle income bands (the 40 to 80 percentiles) registered very modest income growth on both surveys. Only the top 20 per cent recorded even moderate rises, but this may well have been largely due to the surge in millionaire numbers that Singapore has experienced over the past decade. If this is so then income for Singapore's middle-class households has only been increasing slightly, if at all.

As Singapore's income inequalities become more glaring the Government claims they are the result of increased competition for sought-after skills and talent. Top salaries are required to get the best people to govern the country and run the economy etc. Yet despite the widespread evidence of a growing gap, the Government resents any journalists who comment negatively on this. One who did so was "Mr Brown", a columnist for *Today*. He was chastised by the Government for writing an article about the income gap it didn't like. He then felt compelled to resign from the newspaper. After the 2005 GHS figures (and cost of living increases) were released in June 2006, he wrote a sarcastic article titled "Singaporeans are fed, up with progress!".[32] Mr Brown (aka Lee Kin Mun) wrote:

> Household incomes are up, I read. Sure, the bottom third is actually seeing their incomes ... shrink, but the rest of us purportedly are making more money. Okay, if you say so. As sure as Superman Returns, our cost of living in also on the up.

He also noted that,

> We are very thankful for the timing of the good news, [about rising household incomes] of course. Just after the elections for instance. By that I mean that getting the important event out of the way means we can now concentrate on trying to pay our bills.

The news on housing incomes – and increased prices – "would have been too taxing on the brain if [they] were announced during the election period, thereby affecting our ability to choose wisely".

Three days later, a letter from a government official attacking Mr Brown's article was published in *Today*. She called him a "partisan player" whose views "distort the truth".[33] Three more days later *Today* suspended his column and Mr Brown resigned. The paper also refused to print any further letters that defended him.

On August 24, during his National Day address, Prime Minister Lee claimed Mr Brown's article "hit out wildly at the government and in a very mocking and dismissive sort of tone".[34] Lee was apparently upset at Mr Brown's claim that the Government had suppressed information before the elections. He said the Government had to respond "firstly to set the record straight, and secondly to signal that this is not really a way to carry on a public debate on national issues". Meanwhile, the income gap continues to widen and remains a national issue, and a rising source of discontent.

Further signs of growing income inequalities have been noted by Asher and Nandy.[35] First, the share of wages in GDP had declined from 47 per cent in 2001 to 41 per cent in 2006 while the share of capital has correspondingly increased.

Government policies which have cut tax on capital income and employers' CPF contributions have been partly responsible for the declining share of wages. Second, the ratio of the disposable income of the top 20 per cent of households to that of the bottom 20 per cent increased from 11.4 in 1990 to 20.9 in 2000.[36] Third, the Gini coefficient, the traditional measure for inequality, rose from 0.43 in 1990 to 0.52 in 2005.

However, the DOS's Gini figures for households have been somewhat lower. In 2006, the GC for household income was 0.472 and in 2007 it was 0.485.[37] Also, the GC in 1990 was 0.44 and had risen to 0.47 in 1999. But in 2000, the DOS computed Singapore's GC differently, and the GC fell back to 0.442. Despite this the GC had risen to 0.485 by 2007.

Even so, Singapore's DOS calculates household GCs from earned income. Income from dividends, rentals and interest is excluded.[38] If they were included, Singapore's GC would be significantly higher, because income from such sources is likely to accrue to high earners. Also, if the DOS included unearned income, such as that of pensioners and those on welfare (usually among the poorest), the distribution of household income would be even more extreme and household GC much higher.

Finessing the Facts

The PAP Government sought for years to deny Singapore's wide and growing income gap, but ultimately people's lived reality contradicts official reality. Singaporeans began rejecting the official line that the income gap was shrinking or at least stable. Their scepticism was revealed in February 1996 when a SPH poll asked them whether the income gap between rich and poor in the country (a) was widening, (b) had remained the same or (c) was narrowing, compared to five years previously. Of those interviewed, 46 per cent said it had increased, 34 per cent believed it was the same, while 19 per cent claimed it was narrowing. This revelation prompted *The Straits Times* to explain these findings by noting that:

> *Almost 60 per cent of those interviewed who were uneducated said the income gap had increased, while only four in 10 people with primary school education to anything above GCE O-level qualifications said this.*[39]

The article went on to say that how people viewed income distribution "boils down to personal perception". In other words the "uneducated" were too stupid to know the truth about income distribution, the article implied. But it was clear that they were more correct in their perceptions on this as NUS research subsequently showed. The poor especially know better than anyone whether their lot has improved, whatever elitist attempts are made to discredit their perceptions. The lives of the poor are a constant struggle for survival, in Singapore as elsewhere. Should they have marginally more money to spend, they would be the first to know. They are far more likely to detect a decline in income than someone with disposable income.

Soaring luxury car sales in the 1990s and the early 2000s were signs of the wealthy's ever-rising affluence. As early as 1994, NUS professor Dr Bilveer Singh noted that the waiting list for Mercedes was very long. Even the 1997/8 economic downturns failed to dampen demand for luxury cars. In December 1998, wealthy car-buying Singaporeans demonstrated how immune they were to the crisis – and also that their *kiasu* instincts were as sharp as ever. They snapped up 60 new Mercedes S-class cars for between S$300,000 and S$350,000 within the first hour of their unveiling in Singapore. "And in the subsequent hour ... it seemed as if a scuffle for the remaining 40 on offer was imminent," reported the *Business Times*:

> By the third hour, sales people were frantically asking their managers if more cars could be made available. Never mind that the display cars were all left-handed drive, and that no test drives were available. Never mind that the first cars will only be delivered in April. Never mind that the downpour and the overwhelming response slowed traffic to a crawl on the way to the showroom.[40]

The same pattern was even more apparent in 2003, several economic downturns later. Mercedes-Benz sold 55 per cent more cars in the first half of 2003 than for the same period in 2002.[41] The Mercedes E-class was selling for S$209,888. In 2003, vehicle sales' forecasts predicted that Singaporeans would buy 4300 Mercedes, 1700 BMWs costing S$211,500, 1400 Lexus (S$165,888), 1200 Volvos (S$204,000) and 400 Jaguars (S$278,000). Such volumes of luxury car sales are extraordinary for a country with only 3.2 million people, even though some of the cars would have been purchased by wealthy foreigners residing in Singapore.

While unedifying displays of *kiasu* greed in luxury car showrooms show that Singapore's wealthy are as recession-proof as ever, economic crises since the late 1990s have exposed a widening income gap and the plight of poorer workers. Public anger at the growing income gap intensified after ministerial and civil service pay rises. In July 2000, a *Straits Times* poll of 150 people found that 55 per cent of them said increasing ministerial pay from $861,000 to $968,000 was not fair.[42] They were angry at this being done when cuts to employers' CPF contributions to workers had not been restored. "At a time when people are talking about the widening income gap and the digital divide, the Government is talking about a pay rise," one Singaporean said. "It is bound to provoke strong emotions."

The Government realised that it had to manage mounting public discontent at the growing income inequalities. Recognising that denial was no longer plausible the Government, in April 2000, finally admitted that the income gap between top and bottom workers in Singapore was widening – about 15 years after this trend had become obvious to many. To dampen down public discontent, the blame was put on globalisation and the growing international competition for limited managerial talent.[43]

In June 2000, Trade and Industry Minister George Yeo explained that Singapore's Gini coefficient was,

> *likely to worsen because of globalisation. The top in our social ladder will command international wages. Those who are unskilled are competing with the unskilled in China, Vietnam, Indonesia and India and this has a depressing effect on the wages of unskilled labour in Singapore.* [44]

Government ministers also claimed that the income gap would get wider as Singapore's risk-taking culture took hold.[45] Successful entrepreneurs in the knowledge economy would earn big rewards while those who stayed in the old economy would have stagnant incomes. Both trends would widen the income gap. But as the Mr Brown case showed, the Government does not like journalists making sarcastic comments about this gap and the inadequate official responses to it.

Even so, PAP government claims that globalisation pushes up executive salaries as the hunt for managerial talent intensifies had some truth. This process has increased income inequality in many countries, including Singapore, since the 1990s. But from the late 1970s, growing inequalities of wealth were apparent in Singapore. This trend was initially due to the PAP policy of keeping workers' wages down to please the MNCs.

However, two other factors have accelerated the growth of income inequalities. The first is the government practice of paying extraordinarily high ministerial and civil service salaries. The second is the unbridled freedom of Singapore's GLC and private corporate executives to pay themselves enormous salaries. Unlike its workforce, Singapore's executives have few restrictions, governmental or otherwise, to prevent them from paying themselves very high salaries even when they fail to perform. There is no effective public opinion to limit this practice in Singapore, especially in the civil service and SE sectors.

A study by a Singapore consulting firm found that half the companies that had suffered a fall in profits still paid their executive directors an average of 59 per cent more over a seven-year period.[46] Some 410 Singapore-listed companies were examined for the period from December 31, 2001 to June 30, 2002 and the results compared with those for 1994/5. The study found that three out of four companies reporting higher profits paid their CEOs 81 per cent more. In addition, among the GLCs, median directors' remuneration rose 2.7 times from S$504,000 in 1994/5 to S$1.36 million in 2001/2. The Government may claim that the huge pay hikes for GLC chiefs were necessary to attract the best managerial talent. Even so, the degree of increase proves that there are less restrictions on salary increases for GLC directors when compared to those for CEOs in the private sector.

Thus while pressures to remain "internationally competitive" push up managerial salaries and force down workers' wages, there are also state policies in Singapore that allow ministers, senior public servants and SE executives to pay themselves exorbitant salaries. The Government has become increasingly adept at managing the discontent this causes among average Singaporeans.

Nonetheless, government claims that high managerial salaries are necessary to keep the best and brightest serving Singapore are starting to look threadbare, especially in relation to the civil service. Massive salary increases for elite bureaucrats have done little to stem their resignation levels. But huge rises in civil service salaries while the holding down of workers' wages have done much to increase income inequalities in Singapore.

Growing inequalities have produced two basic classes in Singapore – the condominium class and the HDB class. There are those who live in luxury apartments, and there is the mass of the population (about 80 per cent) who live in public housing estates on mediocre incomes, where life is often a hand-to-mouth struggle to survive, made tougher by high and constantly rising living costs. Living standards are determined not only by GNI per capita and how equally it is distributed, but by what it buys.

2. Living Costs

In Singapore, high and rising inequalities of income have condemned most of its people to live on rather low incomes, at least compared to citizens in most other modern industrialised societies. But poor incomes can be ameliorated by cheap living costs. Has this happened in Singapore?

Houses and cars are usually people's two biggest purchases. The prices of both significantly determine the cost of living, both directly and indirectly. An examination of Singapore's housing and motoring costs, along with those for groceries, consumer-durables and education can provide a comprehensive picture of its cost of living.

Housing

Housing is most people's largest expenditure, whether they are buying or renting. The family home is also most people's greatest investment. High housing prices have forced Singaporeans to over-invest in property. A 1985 NUS study by 12 local economists revealed that the average Singaporean spent 37 per cent of his income on paying off a home and paying for insurance, maintenance, property taxes and utilities.[47] This was compared to 15 per cent in the US, 14 per cent in Japan, 12 per cent in West Germany and 8 per cent in South Korea.

A house's true cost is also revealed by how many years of income are required to pay for it. The ratio between annual income and house price is called the median multiple (MM). The MM is calculated at the national level by dividing a country's median income into its median housing price. (The median is not the average, or mean, but the 50th percentile or mid-point in a distribution of prices, incomes or whatever is being measured.)

In Australia, New Zealand, Britain, the US, Canada and Ireland, the national MM for housing prices was 4.5 in 2007, according to the Demographia 2008 property survey.[48] Their median house prices were 4.5 times their median household income in

2007. The MM for the US was 3.6, Australia (6.3), Canada (3.1), Ireland (4.7), New Zealand (6.3) and UK (5.5).

Singapore's MM in 2007 was 6.5 because the median price of an HDB unit (the type of accommodation in which about 85 per cent of Singaporeans live), was S$380,000 in October 2007[49] while the median household income in 2007 was S$58,440. In 2007, Singapore HDB buyers had to spend an average of 6.5 years of median household income to buy an HDB unit, compared to 4.5 years for a home-buyer in the aforementioned Western countries. Only Australia and New Zealand's MM for 2007 almost matched Singapore's.

Even so, the 6.5 MM for Singapore could be an underestimate. First, in Western countries such as Australia median household income includes retirees and those receiving welfare. But Singapore's DOS median household income statistics for 2007, excluded retiree and pensioner households whose income is usually well below the median. As the 2002/3 HES revealed, retiree households constituted 3.9 per cent of all households and 18 per cent of the lowest 20 per cent of income recipients.[50] Moreover, as shown in the previous chapter, more than half of those aged 55 and over had no income of their own and had to rely on their families while a further 18.5 per cent received less than S$250 a month.

Second, Demographia's median housing prices are for all the houses within the housing markets it studies while in Singapore only HDB median prices have been used to calculate its MM. The private market was excluded because median house price data were not available. Even so, Singapore's private housing prices are always much higher than those for HDB units. Condominiums, which comprise about two thirds of private houses in Singapore, range in price from S$500,000 to several million, while landed houses go from about S$1.5 million to S$5 million or more. Though only comprising about 10 per cent of homes sold, they would push up the median house price by perhaps five per cent were they included in its calculation.

Overall, Singapore's housing MM would more probably be 7 rather than 6.5 if retirees's incomes and private home prices were included when calculating it.

Further proof that housing absorbs a higher percentage of Singaporeans' income than elsewhere comes from the US. A 2002 survey of US home-buyers showed that a typical Singaporean worker, aged 50 and above, had 73-77 per cent of his/her financial assets in housing and only about 20 per cent in CPF savings.[51] But in the US, where home-ownership is also high, only 20 per cent of household retirement wealth was held in housing.

The burden of costly housing for Singaporeans is eased in the short-term by their being able to meet home-loan payments from their CPF savings – to which their employers contribute. But paying for expensive HDB units drains their pension savings, leaving most with little to retire on. This situation will continue for as long as the Government seeks to maximise profits from HDB units by charging several times their cost price. For Singapore's poor, high HDB prices have become an unsupportable burden, especially as successive economic downturns have reduced their wages. In response, the HDB began building little three-room flats again in 2004, after having stopped doing so in 1984, to help the poor.

Vehicles

While housing prices are high in Singapore its vehicle prices are even more inflated, compared to those most Western countries.

Here are prices for some common car models in Singapore.[52]

Table 23.8 – Singapore car prices (2008)

Audi A6	S$172,300 – $189,800
BMW 1 Series	S$110,000
Honda Civic	S$73,500 – $83,000
Mercedes Benz Kompresser E200	S$204,000
Toyota Camry	S$89,000 – $96,000
Volvo V70	S$168,000 – $205,000

Numerous heavy imposts account for such high car prices. They are:

- Import Duty – 20 per cent of the vehicle's value
- Certificate of Entitlement (COE) – In May 1990 the Government introduced the COE scheme. Those wanting a vehicle must first obtain a COE through bidding. Aspiring car-owners must bid for a limited number of vehicle entitlements released every month. Prices for COEs have fluctuated widely over the years but for private cars have often ranged between S$40,000 to S$60,000 though since 2003 they have been between S$25,000 to S$30,000. COEs for commercial vehicles and buses are often about a third of those for private vehicles but in 2003 fluctuated within a S$6500 to S$13,000 range. COEs for most vehicles are valid for 10 years before they must be renewed. For taxis it's seven years.
- Additional Registration Fee (ARF) of 110 per cent of a vehicle's open market value, whether new or second-hand
- Registration Fee – S$140 for a car
- Road Taxes – These are calculated on cc engine capacity. They range from S$400 a year for cars with engine capacities up to 600cc, to S$3350 annually for cars with 1600cc to 3000cc engines.
- Licence Renewals for Vehicles 10 Years or Older – A surcharge of 10 to 50 per cent of the Road Tax is imposed on such vehicles, depending on their age.

Motorcycles have also attracted heavy imposts. By October 1995, COEs for motorcycles had hit S$4006.[53] Such amounts had to be paid whether the motorcycle cost S$5000 or $30,000. By 2003, motorcycle COEs had fallen to between S$300 and S$400.

The official justification for such imposts is to discourage private car ownership and use in order to reduce traffic congestion on Singapore's crowded roads. As shown in Chapter 26, this is a questionable rationale and means that cars and other vehicles are several times more expensive in Singapore than elsewhere, especially Australia, New Zealand and the US. Naturally, only a very small percentage of Singaporeans can afford to buy cars. But high imposts on commercial vehicles increase business expenses and push up consumer prices for all.

Motoring

Using vehicles, whether privately or for business, is also expensive in Singapore because of the road-tax fees imposed on motorists via the electronic road pricing scheme (ERP). The ERP was introduced in April 1998 and progressively extended to cover the island's expressways and CBD areas. Once again the official reason for this was to reduce traffic congestion – not to generate revenue. Under the scheme, every vehicle must have a smart card on its windscreen so that a toll or charge can be automatically deducted whenever a vehicle passes under gantries on main roads. The fee levied depends on the stretch of road used and the time of day, and ranges from 0.50c to $3 per entry into an ERP area.[54] When the ERP was officially launched in September 1998 numerous foreign transport experts were conveniently on hand to applaud the scheme, the world's first.[55] They came from Britain, the US, New Zealand and Holland; and they praised Singapore for being so advanced in traffic management and commented on how well the scheme worked.

Singaporeans viewed the scheme more cynically. They called the gantries "time bandits" and saw them as the PAP's slickest scheme yet for taxing motorists. City retailers complained at the ERP's negative effects on business. They said it discouraged people from entering the Orchard Road shopping belt because motorists had to pay S$2.50 each time they come into the area between 3pm and 5pm. Twelve of the retailers also said the ERP was also likely to drive up their business costs.[56] Making daily trips into the city for deliveries or meetings cost them an extra S$1000 to $8000 a month. Under the old area licensing scheme, which the ERP had replaced, they only had to pay S$60 a month to enter CBD areas.

Taxis are also subject to ERP rates despite being a form of public transport. This has raised taxi fares, discouraging people from using taxis.

Health

Medical care costs in Singapore are comparable to those in Western countries – and with bed subsidies for poorer Singaporeans may even be cheaper. The problem is that Singaporeans must pay the bulk of their medical costs themselves. In Singapore, 64 per cent of health-care expenditure comes from the private sector.[57] By comparison, 97 per cent of UK health expenditure is publicly funded, as is 84.3 per cent of Denmark's, 77.5 per cent of Germany's, 76.9 per cent of France's and 72 per cent of Australia's and Canada's. This means large out-of-pocket expenditures for Singaporeans compared to citizens of most Western countries. In 1997, the per capita out-of-pocket expenditure was US$481 for Singapore and US$37 for the UK. The next chapter explores Singapore's heavy health costs.

Groceries and other Consumer Items

In Singapore, prices for consumer items and whitegoods, and public transport costs are about the same or lower than those in most Western countries. Once, Singapore (along with Hong Kong) was renowned for cheap electronics and apparel: that was its big tourist drawcard. Those times are long gone. Now Singapore is only marginally cheaper than many Western countries for these items, and sometimes it is more expensive. For example, by 1995 mobile phones were found to be cheaper in Australia than in Singapore. Three main brands of mobile phone (Nokia, Ericson and Motorola) were slightly to significantly cheaper in Australia, Hong Kong, Britain and the US.[58] The same has sometimes been so for electronic goods.

Many basic consumer items, especially such grocery lines as eggs, meat, beverages, dairy products and most vegetables and fruit are also more expensive in Singapore than in Australia, Canada, New Zealand or the US. Alcohol is usually two to three times dearer in Singapore than in Australia and the US. But train, bus, and taxi fares are much cheaper in Singapore: taxi fares are only about 40 per cent of those charged in Australia.

Moreover, cheap meals are provided at Singapore's hawkers' centres. Most meals cost no more than S$5-$6 and help contain food costs for poorer Singaporeans. A 2008 survey by the Consumers' Association of Singapore (CASE) of 388 non-air-conditioned food stalls, found that 62 per cent had dishes for S$2.50 or less.[59] The other 38 per cent of food stalls had dishes between S$2.60 and S$5.

Groceries are much cheaper across the border in Malaysia at Johore Bahru (JB). Every weekend thousands of Singaporeans head to JB to shop. Groceries and consumer goods in JB usually are less than half what they cost in Singapore.

Education

Apart from the normal school expenses, many Singaporean parents must also pay sizeable coaching fees to educate their children. Coaching has become a heavy education expense for them. They feel coaching is necessary so their children can compete successfully in Singapore's relentlessly competitive, though often inefficient education system.

A *Straits Times* survey in 2000 revealed that 35 per cent of Singapore's primary and secondary students received private tuition.[60] Their parents were paying an average of S$135 a month in coaching fees, another sizeable financial cost on poorer families who have little choice if their children are to succeed in Singapore's pressure-cooker school system.

3. Conclusion

In surveying Singaporeans' costs of living it is clear that most food, and grocery items are higher in Singapore. Only public transport and perhaps some consumer durable items are cheaper. But lower outlays for these items cannot balance the high prices Singaporeans must pay for houses and cars, school tutoring costs, the burden of largely self-funded health-care and various vehicle and other imposts.

For many Singaporeans the good life has become increasingly elusive. Living costs are high, and rising. The average Singaporean must work much harder than most Westerners to live adequately. Compared to middle-income Westerners, Singaporeans' living costs are higher and their incomes generally lower. Despite having had a higher per capita income in 2007 than people in such countries as Japan and New Zealand and one approaching those of such countries as France, Germany and Italy, Singaporeans' living standards were often inferior.

This melancholy reality has not gone unnoticed by Westerners visiting Singapore. As Singapore opposition politician J. B. Jeyaretnam noted, "people coming from Australia, the United States, England and Europe [tell] me how expensive Singapore is..." They ask how Singaporeans manage. He replies,

> *they do that by holding down two or three jobs, moonlighting, working from 6am perhaps to 11pm, running from one job to another.*[61]

By such means they avoid the fate of the bottom 25 per cent of Singaporeans who have barely enough to live on. But what of the PAP Government's claims that 90 per cent of Singaporeans own their own homes, enjoy old-age security and comprehensive health care? The next chapter examines whether such benefits make up for their mediocre living standards.

References

1. *World Development Report 2008* (The World Bank and Oxford University Press), pp334-5.
2. *Yearbook of Statistics Singapore 2007* (Department of Statistics, Ministry of Trade and Industry, Republic of Singapore), Table 1.1.
3. *Report on the Labour Force in Singapore 2006* (Manpower Research and Statistics Department, Ministry of Manpower, Republic of Singapore), Table 23.
4. *Report on Household Expenditure Survey 2002/3* (Department of Statistics, Ministry of Trade and Industry, Republic of Singapore), p. 56.
5. *The Straits Times* (ST), May 31, 2000.
6. *Report on the Labour Force in Singapore 2006.*
7. *Yearbook of Statistics, 2007*, Table 1.1.
8. *Singapore Yearbook of Manpower Statistics 2007*, (Ministry of Manpower, Republic of Singapore), p. 69.
9. Ibid, p. 61.
10. Ibid, p. 71-2.
11. Ibid, p. 71.
12. Ibid.
13. ST, May 31, 2000.
14. ST, July 6, 2000.
15. *The International Herald Tribune*, April 9, 2007, www.iht.com
16. ST, December 14, 2007.
17. Ibid.
18. Low, Linda: *The Political Economy of a City State* (Singapore, Oxford University Press, 1998), p. 215.
19. ST, July 15, 2001.
20. ST, June 17, 1995.
21. ST, April 4, 1999.
22. *World Development Indicators 2007* (World Bank, Washington, DC).
23. Forbes.com, December 13, 2007.
24. Wikipedia.
25. Annual Salary of Major Office-holders in Selected Overseas Legislatures

and Governments (as of May 2006), Fact Sheet (Research and Library Services Division, Legislative Council Secretariat, Hong Kong).

26. *The World Competitiveness Yearbook 2001* (Institute for Management Development, Lausanne, Switzerland, 2001), p.464.

27. ST, September 2, 2003 and September 11, 2007.

28. *Report on Household Expenditure Survey 2002/3.*

29. *The World Competitiveness Yearbook 2001* (Institute for Management Development, Lausanne, Switzerland, 2001), p. 464.

22. ST, February 24, 1996.

23. Ibid.

24. ST, June 11, 1995.

25. ST, May 31, 2000.

26. May 31, 2000.

27. ST, September 2, 2003 and September 11, 2007.

28. ST, May 31, 2000.

29. *Report on Household Expenditure Survey 2002/3.*

30. *General Household Survey 2005* (Department of Statistics, Ministry of Trade and Industry, Republic of Singapore).

31. Findings of both reports are compared in the *Report on Household Expenditure Survey 2002/3*, p. 11.

32. *Today*, June 30, 2006.

33. Ibid, July 3, 2006.

34. ST, August 26, 2006.

35. Asher G. Mukul and Amarendu Nandy "Singapore's policy responses to ageing, inequality and poverty: An assessment" p. 46 in International Social Security Review, Vol. 61, 1/2008.

36. Ibid.

37. *Business Times* (BT), February 15, 2008.

38. BT, February 14, 2008.

39. ST, February 1, 1996.

40. BT, December 5-6, 1998.

41. ST, September 11, 2003.

42. ST, July 6, 2000.

43. ST, April 13, 2000.

44. ST, June 30, 2000.

45. ST, April 18, 2000.

46. ST, April 3, 2003.

47. ST, April 13, 2002.

48. Cox, Wendell and Hugh Pavletich: *4th Annual Demographia International Housing Affordability Survey: 2008* (3rd quarter 2007, Pavletich Properties Ltd), p. 10.

49. HDB InfoWEB: Median Resale Prices (4th quarter 2007).

50. *Household Expenditure Survey 2002/3*, p. 18.

51. Ramesh, M., "One and A Half Cheers for Provident Funds in Malaysia and Singapore," – Paper prepared for the UNRISD project on *Social Policy in a Development Context*, February 28, 2003, p16.

52. SGcarmart.com/new

53. ST, October 14, 1995.

54. *Expatriate Living Costs in Singapore 2004/5* (Singapore International Chamber of Commerce, 2004), p. 17.

55. ST, September 11, 1998.

56. ST, July 31, 1998.

57. Chia, Ngee Choon: "Health for all: Financing and delivery issues", p. 166 in Singapore Economy in the 21st Century edited by Koh Ai Tee et al (Singapore, McGraw Hill, 2002).

58. ST, May 25, 1995 and July 2, 1995.

59. ST, June 30, 2008.

60. ST, November 28, 2000.

61. Jeyaretnam, J. B.: *Make It Right for Singapore: Speeches in Parliament 1997-9* (Singapore, Jeya Publishers, 2000), p. 10.

CHAPTER 24

MATERIALLY SECURE? (HOUSING, PENSION AND HEALTH MYTHS)

The PAP state regularly contends that over 90 per cent of Singaporeans own their homes and also enjoy comprehensive health coverage and old age security. These are claims that have been readily endorsed by many Western commentators who also echo the view that in these areas too Singapore has much to teach the world, especially developing countries. The comments of the German business daily, *Handelsblatt*, reflect this thinking:

Singaporeans have a pension scheme, a functioning health-care system... and public housing, which are exemplary to its neighbours.[1]

The following examines how justified such claims are about Singapore's pension, health and housing schemes.

1. 90% Home Ownership?

After touring an upgraded HDB estate in October 1999, Prime Minister Goh felt moved to declare:

In my own humble opinion, I believe it [the HDB program] *is the best public housing program in the world.*[2]

He had seen public housing programs in many countries but never one better than Singapore's, he asserted.

Like so many other achievements of PAP Singapore its HDB scheme appears a brilliant success. The scheme was launched in the early 1960s to house the island's population, many of whom lived in kampongs in sub-standard conditions. Forty years later, impressive ranks of high-rise flats march to the horizon in many directions. But once again, all is not as it seems in Singapore. Not only are HDB flats very expensive by world public housing standards, but their conditions of ownership constitute a violation of freehold principles.

Not Quite Freehold

While the Government claims that about 90 per cent of Singaporeans own their own homes, only a tiny percentage actually do. Although 86 per cent of Singaporeans are housed in 800,000 HDB flats, none own them, despite government claims that most do – unless one accepts its peculiar conceptions of home ownership. To begin with, Singaporeans don't "own" HDB apartments in the normal sense of the word. Rather, they lease them for 99 years and so are denied a range of freehold rights that property ownership would normally confer on them. As Tremewan explains:

> HDB apartment owners are not owners in the sense of a private freehold sale. Rather they purchase equity in the flat in the form of a 99-year lease which reverts to the HDB on expiry. Owners are little more than tenants.[3]

The freehold rights denied HDB "owners" are several. First, they cannot rent out their entire HDB apartment as can normal freehold owners. They must live on the premises and keep at least one bedroom for themselves. Those who fail to do this have their units repossessed. In 1994, the HDB repossessed 16 flats and fined the owners of another 184 flats for having sublet their entire flats illegally in the past year.[4] The repossessed flats ranged from three-room units to executive apartments. Those who lost their flats did so because they either refused to pay fines imposed by the Board or continued to sublet their flats after being warned. The Board "bought back" the flats, paying the offenders an amount equal to the 1984 HDB price or the original selling price, whichever was higher.

For first-time offenders, the Board imposes a fine of 15 per cent of the 1984 HDB selling price of the flat. In 1994, the fines ranged from S$5000 to S$30,000. All 200 offenders were barred from applying for, or renting, any HDB flat for the next five years. These measures were inflicted on those who merely sought to exercise freehold rights on units for which they had paid high prices.

From 1992-4 the HDB took action against 670 flat-owners. The HDB,

> took a serious view against subletting of entire flats as HDB flats are meant only for owner occupation. Those who illegally sublet their flats show they do not need their flats. HDB should then take the flats back.[5]

In practice, people who rent out their HDB units leave one bedroom locked and let the tenants have free run of the rest of the apartment. Then the flat's leaseholders at least have some tenuous excuse for claiming that they were not renting out the whole flat, should HDB inspectors come knocking. But the Board is emphatic that flat-owners (leaseholders) who sublet rooms can only do so if they keep living in their flats. Those who rent flats out and give the excuse that they return occasionally to use the room would be caught out, warns the HDB: "Inspections by HDB officers would reveal the truth". The Board admits that some offenders have been nabbed by tip-offs from neighbours or from illegal tenants reporting flat-owners when they have had disputes with them.

Before October 2003, only those who had lived in their flats for at least 10 years and paid off the HDB loans on them were permitted to sub-let the whole flat. After that, however, the HDB eased the rules on subletting so that HDB owners who had lived in their units for 15 years could also sublet the whole flat.[6]

The HDB justifies its draconian violation of freehold property rights by claiming that the "government subsidises Singaporeans to own the HDB flats they live in". Despite these "subsidies" Singaporeans must still pay high prices for HDB units. Many HDB lessees are not only prevented from renting out their apartments but are also denied other freehold rights, including freedom from confiscation.

HDB units can also be repossessed if used for such illegal purposes as a gambling den or brothel, or for throwing "killer litter" from the balcony. In 1986, the Government passed a law which permitted HDBs to be repossessed if the occupants were found guilty of throwing objects from them.[7] Occasionally, during times of domestic or emotional turmoil, a TV set or other items may be chucked over HDB balconies. In October 2002, one disturbed HDB resident threw five cats, two chairs, a table and a pile of books out of her ninth floor HDB flat.[8] The Government is certainly justified in discouraging such reckless behaviour, but should punishment include repossession of a person's home? Normally in most developed countries freehold property is only repossessed if the owner has acquired it through the proceeds of crime.

Along with other laws allowing HDB flats to be repossessed, the killer litter law, "is a reminder that the laws of property are to be entirely subject to the government," notes T.S. Selvan, a Singaporean and former ISD officer who wrote *Singapore the Ultimate Island*. "The bill is ominously wide in its interpretation. This naturally strikes real fear into the home-owners," he observes.

The Government's race-mixing requirements for HDB blocks represent a further negation of freehold rights for HDB dwellers. The Government has always been keen to avoid the development of racial enclaves, especially of Malays and Indians, in HDB estates for political reasons. In 1989, the HDB instituted rules to ensure that a representative racial mix prevailed. Under these rules the HDB can, when a particular racial group is over-represented in a block, make flat-sellers in that block sell their flats to someone in the under-represented racial group.[10]

This requirement penalises the minority Malays who comprise 20 per cent of Singapore's population, and even more the Indians who make up only 6 per cent. The Chinese who comprise 70 per cent of the population can far more easily find other HDB buyers of their ethnic group than can Malays and Indians. Because the latter must sell their units to their own racial group, their potential pool of HDB-buyers is much smaller, especially for Indians. Sometimes Indians must accept 15 per cent below the normal market price for their HDB flats.[11] One Indian reported that he was offered a price 15 per cent below the market valuation of S$400,000. This represented a S$60,000 loss for him. He said, "the financial effect is especially pronounced on the minority races because we can sell our flats only to non-Chinese".[12] This meant that "our target market has shrunk by about 80 per cent".

Besides having to accept lower prices, Malay and Indian sellers need longer to sell their HDB units. While Chinese sellers require about two months, Malays and Indians must usually wait four to five months. "When Chinese families want to move or upgrade, it's very easy for them to find a new flat and sell the old one," said one

Indian housewife. "But when an Indian family wants to move, it takes a while to find a new flat and even longer to find a buyer for the old one."

The lower prices, delays and inconveniences that minority races face when selling their HDB units would not arise if they had proper freehold rights, including the right to sell to anyone and to get the best price for their property. For Singaporeans generally, HDB ownership is little more than a glorified long-term lease devoid of many property rights. Such "ownership" demonstrates the mythical nature of PAP claims about 90 per cent home-ownership by Singaporeans.

Value for Money?

By October 2007, Singaporeans were paying S$273,000 for a 4-room HDB flat. That is a lot of money to pay to lease a public housing flat for 99 years. This is especially so when nearly 60 per cent of Singaporeans earn less than S$2500 a month, even if they can buy and sell it. What do the leaseholders get for their money?

At first sight many HDB blocks look substantial and well-kept. Lawns and shrubbery usually separate them. But a certain desolation is apparent as one wanders around HDB blocks – even the newer and better ones. The ground floor of each block is left open and is called the "void deck" where residents can gather for weddings, funeral wakes and other social events. When vacant, they are little more than a large expanse of concrete floor interrupted by support pillars and occasional brick tables set into the floor.

HDB flats vary greatly in quality, depending on their age. Flats built in the 1960s are small, pokey and easily penetrated by noise from other residents, traffic and nearby hawkers' centres. The newer flats are much larger and far more spacious, but Lee Kuan Yew himself has admitted that the average HDB unit would be,

> well, "basic" for my class. If you ask me to live today in an HDB three-room flat, and I had to eat at a hawker centre every day, that would be a real problem.[13]

Not only Singaporeans of Lee's "class" find the HDB lifestyle irksome. "Ordinary" Singaporeans do as well, especially those forced to live in three-room HDB flats. One Singaporean described them as,

> box-like and built close together, so that one can see, and often hear, the comings and goings of one's neighbours to an embarrassingly intimate degree. Moreover, no matter how one copies ideas from Ideal Homes, a three-room flat remains as it is – a small apartment that takes only about 10 steps to walk from the front door to the kitchen or bedrooms, and often with a low ceiling that compounds the feeling of being boxed-in. If one lives with a large family in such a flat, then the lack of privacy can be felt more painfully. Only a few luckier ones get to have any sort of a view that can qualify as "scenery". More often than not one looks out to the next block, or to other buildings.[14]

Privacy is at a premium in most HDB blocks, as *Strait Times* columnist Chua Mui Hoong noted:

> *Far from being the proverbial castle, the Singaporean's home sometimes becomes a downright circus affording free entertainment to anyone who happens to walk down the common corridor. Or who happens to have a grandstand view of your living room from their windows across the block.*
>
> *Privacy is a scarce and precious commodity in this crowded nation-state and especially in the Housing Board heartlands.[15]*

This is the lifestyle the average HDB-dweller gets for S$200,000 to S$300,000 – on a 99-year lease.

Depreciating Assets?

During the 1990s, HDB units gave the impression of being sound long-term investments. Between 1990 and 1998, HDB prices soared 150 per cent. But such increases belong to the past. Prices for HDB values have risen only modestly, if at all, in recent years.

Stagnating prices for HDB units could be a prelude to a long-term decline in their value. There are several factors that make them vulnerable to major price falls. First, the purchase of an HDB unit merely gives the buyer a long-term lease whose value deteriorates every year. As Professor Koh Seng Kee, vice-dean of the NUS Business School, notes:

> *As most properties are sold with 99-year leases, Singaporeans are investing their lifetime savings in depreciating assets.[16]*

When Professor Koh made this comment in 1999 he predicted that the oldest leasehold properties, then only 25 years old, were likely to register a sharp drop in value in another 15 years.

Second, many retirees who lack sufficient money on which to retire may be forced to sell their existing HDBs and move into cheaper units or live with their families. This may become particularly apparent when the numerous baby boomers start retiring. With so many properties being dumped on the market, prices would plummet. This factor and deteriorating leases make HDB units poor long-term investments for Singaporeans – unless the Government decides to extend expiring leases on HDB units for, say, another 50 years or so.

A Means of State Control

For the PAP state, the HDB scheme is not only a major source of revenue but a potent means of social and political control. Buying an HDB unit represents the biggest investment most Singaporeans will ever make, and it is one they would not wish to jeopardise by upsetting the HDB. This gives the HDB great power over them. As Tremewan notes:

> *HDB ownership puts many in long-term debt to the state and ensures a disciplined labour force at home as well as in the factory. Even those who pay off their debt do not have exclusive rights over their equity and may be deprived of*

it at the government's discretion. The fear of losing one's home, which is usually also one's major asset, remains a fact of life for most Singaporeans. Under this constant threat, most Singaporeans are constrained to behave in their own homes as if everything is forbidden except what is expressly allowed. This fear and the mechanism which ties people into it have become one of the central pillars of the PAP-state's social control.[17]

Not surprisingly, there is always a big demand for private apartments in Singapore, where ownership really does confer freehold rights (for as long as the PAP state respects property rights). Over the last 30 years the state has normally done this, except when requisitioning land for its own needs.

2. The CPF: an Illusion of Security

The CPF has provided workers with a comprehensive self-financing social security fund equal to any old-age pension or entitlement programme, without shifting the burden to the next generation of workers. It is fairer and sounder to have each generation pay for itself and each person to save for his own pension fund.[18]

So claimed Lee Kuan Yew in 2000 when extolling the virtues of Singapore's CPF scheme, which he contended funds retirement better than the West's welfarist social security schemes – and once again an international body, this time the respected International Labour Organisation (ILO), was ready to support another self-promoting Singaporean assertion. The ILO's 1999 report praised Singapore and South Korea for having the "healthiest and most comprehensive" pension schemes.[19] During his 1996 visit to Singapore, British Labour Party leader Tony Blair expressed admiration for the CPF scheme and thought Britain could benefit from a similar one. Singapore's CPF scheme was even seen by one US business editor as a means for re-building post-war Iraq. Revenue from Iraq's vast oil reserves could be turned into a CPF-style fund for the purpose, according to UPI business editor, Martin Hutchison. The funds would be placed into individual accounts held by Iraqis rather than in a common pool, to prevent corruption and government inefficiency. Hutchison even suggested that Singapore's CPF Board should manage the Iraqi scheme. "It could best be managed by the staff of Singapore's CPF, who have 35 years' experience in running this type of scheme and are, as far as humanly possible, incorruptible,"[20] he opined. How risk-averse, rule-following Singaporean bureaucrats would cope in something like the chaos and carnage of post-Saddam Iraq doesn't bear thinking about.

Whatever the viability of Hutchison's proposal, it reflects the enormous prestige that Singapore's CPF scheme – and its civil servants – have in some foreign quarters. But like HDB-style home ownership, Singapore's CPF scheme promises far more than it delivers. Originally designed to ensure security for retirees, the CPF, in theory, is a sound method for ensuring security in old age; but its design reflects the Government's (and Lee's) obsession with the spectre of welfarism.

History

After the CPF's introduction by the British colonial administration in 1955, CPF contributions steadily climbed from 5 per cent for employers and employees to 25 per cent for each party in 1985. After the 1985/6 recession the employers' contribution was cut to 10 per cent to allow them to recover. During the next 15 years employee contributions were gradually reduced to 20 per cent, but employer contributions fluctuated markedly during this period. At first the Government progressively restored them up to 20 per cent in 1994; then reduced them to 10 per cent during the 1997/8 recession before restoring them to 16 per cent by 2001.[21] In October 2003, employers' contributions were again cut, this time to 13 per cent, while those for employees remained at 20 per cent.[22] However, in July 2007 employers' contributions were raised to 14.5 per cent. The CPF has generally paid 2.5 per cent interest on contributions, but savings in the Special, Medisave and Retirement Accounts have received an extra 1.5 per cent above the prevailing CPF interest rate.

The fund's functions, as well as its contribution levels, have increased over the years. The CPF's original intent was to help employees save sufficient to retire on so they would not be dependent on the state, but the fund has grown from a retirement scheme into an ad-hoc system for funding housing purchases, tertiary education, health-care and investment. The fund "now boasts an assortment of subschemes that allow members to use their savings to finance their homes, pay medical bills, service insurance policies and even punt on the stock market".[23]

The CPF's diversification began in 1968 when the Government allowed the fund's members to pay for HDB units with CPF savings. This measure aimed to boost sales for HDB units. The Government had been building HDB units at a furious pace since 1960 but few Singaporeans had any savings besides their CPF contributions to buy them. There were 52,408 applications for rental flats between 1960 and 1965 but only 2967 applications for purchases, leaving many of the for-sale flats vacant.[24] The Government had miscalculated. Building unaffordable flats meant the HDB would lack sufficient funds to build more.

Realising its mistake, the Government sought new ways of financing HDB flats and decided to use CPF savings to do this. The CPF Housing Scheme was launched in 1968: loans could be taken out with the HDB for down payments on units, with monthly instalments taken from buyers' CPF funds. Sales of HDB units soon soared, and have climbed steadily ever since. As a HDB CEO recalled, "We made a conscious decision in 1964 to sell the flats so we began our home ownership scheme, not to any great success. When we made CPF available in 1968 home ownership really took off".[25] In 1981, the HDB scheme was extended to allow purchase of private houses, boosting that property sector too.

Since 1978 the Government has increasingly permitted CPF savings to be invested in shares and other securities. In that year the Government let CPF members buy shares in the Singapore Bus Services (SBS). The aim was to give the people a stake in Singapore's future, said the Government. Then in 1986, 1993, 1997 and

1998 guidelines were progressively broadened to permit CPF funds to be used for a growing range of investments. Such measures did much to fuel Singapore's share market booms, especially from 1993 to 1997. Again the official reason was to give the people a stake in Singapore.

However, the CPF investments schemes have only had limited success. In July 2003, the CPF board revealed that 65 per cent of CPF investors were worse off since the schemes' introduction in 1993.[26] The losses were often due to contributors missing out on the 2.5 per cent interest they would have received had they kept their money in the CPF, not from any loss of savings. Only 35 per cent made profits that bettered the standard CPF interest rate.[27]

In August 2000, CPF rules were changed to curb risky investments and ensure that any profits made stayed in CPF accounts. Previously contributors had been permitted to invest up to 50 per cent of their savings in shares, but now it would only be 35 per cent. The remainder would have to be invested in government bonds, approved unit trusts and endowments. Investment profits could no longer be withdrawn but had to stay in the fund to maximise the savings of CPF contributors.

As the CPF's roles proliferated so have the number of accounts for contributions, which are now labelled Ordinary, Special and Medisave. Ordinary Account funds can be used for housing, education and investment purposes. The Special Account was set up to ensure that members would have at least some money for retirement. This account operates under the Minimum Sum Scheme, which requires that a specified minimum amount of a CPF member's contributions are retained from the total amount they are due to receive when turning 55 and returned to them in monthly amounts when they reach 60. In 2003, this amount was increased to S$80,000 and then in July 2007 to S$99,600 and was to be paid out to contributors at a maximum of S$345 a month from their 65th birthday. But in 2007, only 34 per cent had S$99,600 in their Special Account.[27a] The sums the remaining 66 per cent are pro-rated subject to a minimum of S$287 – which the Government deems to be sufficient for subsistence living in Singapore.[28]

The 20 per cent of earnings that employees contribute to the CPF is split three ways: 2 per cent is paid into the Special Account, 3.5 to 4.5 per cent into Medisave and the remainder into the Ordinary Account. But as will be shown, Medisave and associated medical funds fail to provide comprehensive health coverage; the degree of financial security the CPF gives retirees is limited despite increasing by 1 per cent the interest on the first $60,000 in members' accounts.

Significant Limitations

Because the CPF has mutated from being a retirement scheme to one for financing housing, education, health-care and investment, most Singaporeans' CPF savings have shrunk alarmingly. Paying for expensive and over-priced HDB units has been the biggest drain on their CPF contributions. In October 1998, a government minister told Parliament that 180,000 CPF members had used 90 per cent or more of their monthly contributions from their Ordinary accounts to service housing loans.[29] About half earned less than S$2000 a month. Low incomes and other calls on their CPF savings have left most Singaporeans with insufficient to retire on. This has been a worsening trend over the years. In 1983, CPF withdrawals amounted to 38 per cent of contributions; by 1998 withdrawals had risen to 85.1 per cent.[30] Even the sacrosanct Special Accounts are tapped when necessary. In early 1999, funds from these accounts were allowed to be used to plug mortgage shortfalls.[31] Thus whatever cash retirees may have in their Special Accounts is also depleted. The meagre payments of S$287 a month that they would receive from this account until it was exhausted would end even sooner.

With ever-greater withdrawals of CPF funds, far fewer Singaporeans have sufficient to retire on. By 1997, the average CPF balance was S$28,633, down from S$29,503 in 1996.[32] Balances for older CPF members were higher. In 2000, the average CPF balance was $50,000 for 50 to 55-year olds, noted Professor Leong Siew Meng, of the Faculty of Business Administration at NUS;[33] but one in four CPF members who had reached 55 in 1998 had balances of less than S$16,000.[34] By 2006, most CPF members still had little to retire on, with the average balance per member being S$40,598.[34a]

Even worse were the findings of a 1995 Ministry of Health survey which found that 57.3 per cent of those aged 55 and above had no income of their own.[35] They were totally dependent on their children or relatives. The survey also revealed the meagre income of most of Singapore's elderly. Their median monthly income was S$518, with 21 per cent receiving more than S$1000 a month, 59.6 per cent between S$250 and $999 and 18.5 per cent less than S$250.

Low interest rates on CPF investments partly explain the minimal retirement income of CPF contributors. A 2.5 per cent interest payment on Ordinary Account savings greatly limits savings growth. This rate compares poorly with those paid by private sector investments and foreign pension funds. In September 1999, a World Bank (WB) social security conference paper showed that in real terms, Singapore's CPF interest rate failed to meet the local bank deposit rate.[36] The CPF rate was 0.4 per cent below it, noted WB economists. Again, an unpublished study cited by Peebles found that the real return on CPF savings from 1987 to 1998 was only 0.07 per cent a year.[37]

Similar retirement funds in Malaysia, the US and India have produced far better yields. In Malaysia, the Employees Provident Fund (EPF) which began in 1952, produced dividends of 8 to 8.5 per cent from 1983-94 though they sank to 6 per cent in 2000 and 5 per cent in 2001.[38] When the EPF dividend fell to 4.25 per cent in 2002 there was an uproar. The country's Malaysian Trade Union Congress (MTUC) threatened to picket EPF offices. But no such scenes are likely in PAP-controlled Singapore, whose citizens have meekly accepted the CPF's 2.5 per cent interest rate for decades.

The CPF's low interest rate barely keeps pace with inflation. In real terms, from 1987 to 1998, the interest rate was zero because of inflation, according to calculations by

NUS professor Mukul Asher. In this situation savings only increase from contributions, not interest. The CPF rate was based on the one-year fixed-deposit, he said. There was "no economic rationale" to pay a one-year fixed deposit rate on what was essentially a saving plan of 35 years or more, the duration of most Singaporeans' working life. Much higher interest rates are normally paid on such long-term investments. The CPF was giving a short-term rate on what were in effect very long-term deposits. CPF contributors would have received at least 4 per cent returns if they had invested in the safest guaranteed financial products and funds. This would still be much better than the 2.5 per cent they have received on the Ordinary Account deposits,[39] despite the 2008 changes.

For years, numerous Singaporeans, including both PAP and Opposition MPs, have sought to discover what the Government does with CPF funds and where they are invested. Many believe that the GIC is the ultimate destination. Those that do constantly ask how the Government can pay Singaporeans 2.5 per cent on their CPF savings while the GIC claims to be earning 9.5 per cent a year on these funds.

The Government's standard reply is that the CPF board invests CPF funds in deposits and government bonds, through the Ministry of Finance (MOH), which earn modest risk-free investment. But the "gap between the return on what the Singapore Government gets for investments and what Singaporeans get from their retirement savings has fuelled speculation that the CPF provides a cheap source of funds for the Government's investment," pointed out Straits Times columnist Chua Mui Hoong.[39a]

However, when Opposition (Workers Party) MP, Low Thia Khiang, asked Government ministers whether the GIC invested CPF monies, he received evasive replies. "The answer is no," said one minister to Low's question in Parliament. The minister then explained that the Government bears the risk of investing CPF funds the same as a bank does. Rather than "lending" the money to the Government, the MOF assumes the liabilities and takes the risk of losing the money if the investments fail, the minister said, but would not elaborate further. However, PAP MP Sin Boon Ann, said that "CPF balances are indirectly invested by the Government through the GIC and other channels in external and real assets."[39b] Because the CPF funds go via the MOF, the Government maintains that the GIC etc are not using CPF funds, but those from the MOF. PAP sophistry aside, it is clear that Singaporeans are only receiving a fraction of what pension-fund contributors receive in other countries.

For as long as the Government's mean-minded CPF policies prevail, most Singaporeans will lack sufficient CPF savings to retire on. Asher has estimated that the CPF can at best only provide 20 to 40 per cent of a Singaporean wage-earner's pre-retirement income.[40] Because so many 50 to 55-year-olds have CPF balances of only S$50,000 or less, many elderly Singaporeans have minimal incomes. This may explain why 86.2 per cent live with their children.[41] And having to support elderly parents further explains why living costs are so high for many Singaporeans.

A 1997 NUS survey of 4000 Singaporeans aged 60 and above revealed that about seven in ten depended on their children for money.[42] The survey, by the NUS sociology department, compared data on the elderly in four Asian countries: Singapore, Thailand, Taiwan and the Philippines. It was part of a project sponsored by the US National Institute of Aging and tracked the spending patterns of the elderly over eight years.

Singapore compared badly with the other three countries studied (including the much poorer Philippines) despite having the world's highest savings rate. While about 70 per cent of Singapore's elderly relied on their children as their main source of income, in Thailand the percentage was 48.5 in Taiwan and 36 in the Philippines.[43] Moreover, only one in ten elderly CPF account holders in Singapore felt they had enough to meet daily expenses, compared to nearly a third of Taiwan's elderly.

Despite having the world's highest savings rate and a retirement scheme which embraces 86 per cent of its citizens, Singapore's CPF is clearly second-rate compared to pension schemes in other Asian countries – even such less affluent ones as Thailand and Taiwan. Singapore's CPF scheme fails to provide adequate security for most of its aged citizens.

The CPF may have severe deficiencies as a retirement plan, but it remains a potent tool of political control for the PAP Government. As Selvan notes, "one fears...the scheme has also become another institution for political control....Any government which can control the finances of the population can also regulate their lives the way it wants to".[44]

Old, Poor and Working

For many poor and elderly Singaporeans who can't or don't wish to be supported by their families, only two options remain – continue working or subsist on charity. Most choose the former until ill-health and disability force them to accept the latter.

Many Singaporeans keep working into their 70s and 80s, usually at menial and demeaning jobs. Between 1986 and 1996, the number of employed people aged 60 and above rose by over 60 per cent (from 39,136 to 62,664), according to Labour Ministry figures.[45] Even more startling was the soaring number of elderly working women – up by more than 80 per cent to 15,052 from 8,294 in 1986.[46] A significant number of these would be over 70. By June 2003, 35,727 Singaporeans aged 65 and over were still employed, a 57 per cent increase from 1993 when 22,699 were employed.[47] Of those in 2003, 35.7 per cent worked as cleaners or in other menial jobs while a further 21 per cent worked as sales assistants and serving staff.

The plight of the working elderly was once highlighted when 180 aged workers gathered outside a cleaning company's office to demand their overdue pay.[48] Most were over 60 years old and many had disabilities. One 72-year-old woman who earned S$830 a month, said: "If I don't work, I won't have money". Another elderly woman (75), a deaf mute, was afraid her brother might kick her out if she had no money to give him. No Singaporean family values there.

Other elderly people work as toilet attendants or rubbish collectors. Most public toilets in Singapore are staffed by old women, some in their 80s. Other aged people collect rubbish in the streets, usually late at night. You see them combing bins for saleable junk or newspapers, pulling their pitiful hauls behind them on little trolleys. As *Straits Times* columnist Chua Mui Hoong poignantly wrote:

> *I have seen old men and women in estates from Bedok, Ang Mo Kio, Holland, Toa Payoh and Chinatown, many of them bent over with age and perhaps pain, pushing solitary trolleys and collecting discarded cardboard boxes to sell. I often wonder how they cope.* [49]

Others cope by working as street cleaners. One Singaporean woman wrote movingly about the plight of an elderly woman street cleaner working in driving rain one morning during rush hour in a CBD area.

> *I witnessed recently a sight along Shenton Way that prompted me to write this letter* [to The Straits Times]. *It was the morning rush and raining quite heavily.*
>
> *Suddenly, I noticed an aberration in this somewhat cliched picture of commercial Singapore – a tanned-skinned woman in somewhat old and grimy looking clothes with her back so bent that she looked only half her height.*
>
> *She was the cleaner I see quite often along Shenton Way. I usually see her in the risky situation of sweeping leaves at the side of the roads in busy traffic, with cars whizzing past her. On this particular morning, she was badly ravaged [sic] by the pouring rain as she pushed her trolley of bins and brooms along the road, with only a thin plastic-like sheet to shield her.*
>
> *Singapore prides itself as a clean and efficient city. And rightly so. But perhaps it is time that we put some importance on the values of mercy and compassion.* [50]

At least some Singaporeans are disgusted at the wretched plight of elderly people left to fend for themselves.

Sometimes tragedy strikes old working people. One 77-year-old man was killed when hit by a car while walking home after working a midnight shift, to save a 25c bus fare.[51]

The plight of the *Samsui* women has been particularly poignant. For many years until the 1960s, single women were shipped in from China to perform labouring work in Singapore. When tower cranes were not in use they were the ones who had to carry heavy cement up as high as 12 storeys on construction sites. They performed this back-breaking labour day after day for years, even decades, on end. In 1996, one 79-year-old *Samsui* woman recalled the hardship of her life when she began working 60 years ago:

> *I earned only 60 cents each day. The heavy load blistered my shoulders and they bled. After work, I had to peel the clothes off the wound – very painful.*[52]

Most surviving *Samsui* women are now in the 75 to 90-plus age range. In February 2001, *The Straits Times* reported that the "60 or so *Samsui* women who remain in Singapore live alone, dependent on each other and the generosity of the public".[53] Lacking family – and CPF savings – they have been left to look after themselves and must pay for their medical needs when charity is not available. A few game old souls continue to try and earn a few dollars. One 88-year-old *Samsui* woman was still earning S$10 a month collecting cardboard.[54] But like other *Samsui* women she does at least receive donations of food and money from charitable individuals.

Other elderly people hawk such items as tissues around public areas, including food courts. "All had a hard luck story to tell, saying they resorted to selling tissues as they could not find proper jobs because of their age or physical disability," reported *The Straits Times*.[55] One weary 76-year-old man sold tissues to pay for his medical expenses. These sellers have to play hide-and-seek with the authorities. What they do is illegal, because such hawking is seen as begging by the authorities. Some basic old-age security would free many elderly from having to survive by such degrading means.

Many able-bodied elderly work in McDonalds and other fast-food outlets as food servers and table cleaners. The local press occasionally runs cheery stories about them, implying how wonderful it is that old people can still find a job. The belief that the elderly should be able to enjoy their final years in dignity and peace, doing things they have never had time to do before, is not widespread in Singapore. Flipping hamburgers or clearing tables for teenage junk-food addicts hardly qualifies as a lifestyle for old age.

Life is indeed forlorn for elderly Singaporeans who have no families to support them and lack CPF savings. They must work as hamburger dispensers, cleaners, toilet attendants, road sweepers or rubbish scavengers until forced to accept meagre charity.

Clearly, like the health-care system, the CPF has failed in its prime aims. It does not provide old-age security for most elderly Singaporeans, glowing assessments from such bodies as the ILO notwithstanding. This problem can only worsen as Singapore faces the problems of an ageing population now being experienced by most developed countries. As Singapore's population ages, a far more comprehensive scheme than the present CPF will be required to fund retirement for its elderly.

3. Comprehensive Health Care?

Yet another Singaporean achievement to win global acclaim is its health-care system. In 2000, WHO ranked Singapore 6th for "overall healthcare" in a survey of 191 countries.[56] Singapore and Japan were the only two Asian countries to be placed in the top 10. The US was ranked 27th, Britain 18th and Australia 27th.

In commenting on the survey a Ministry of Health (MOH) spokesman proudly noted that the WHO ranking was a recognition of the Government's successful health care reforms, which included "considerable autonomy over management decisions in public hospitals, the presence of a medical savings account and a subsidy scheme for low income groups". The spokesman added, "It was also commented that these reforms had succeeded in improving responsiveness to patients and efficiency in resource management".[57] The "salesmanship of Singapore's leaders," notes Hsiao, as well as high WHO rankings, explains much of the praise its health system receives.[58]

Acclaim for the apparent ability of Singapore's health system to deliver good health outcomes at seemingly low cost appears well deserved. In 1998, Singapore's health expenditure was 3.6 per cent of GDP, compared to 8.6 per cent for Australia, Sweden (7.9 %) and the US (12.9%), according to WHO.[59] WHO figures also showed the following:

Table 24.1 – Comparative longevity, infant mortality and health expenditure figures

	Australia	Sweden	US	Singapore
Life expectancy, males (2000)	76.6	77.3	73.9	75.4
Child mortality, males (2000)	7	5	9	5
Total spending on health per capita in 1998 (US$)	$1672	$2144	$4055	$792

Singapore seems to be providing top health care for a fraction of the cost of developed countries. PAP leaders would claim this is because the state has steered a middle way between a laissez-faire system and a government-owned national health service. They believe they have developed a health care system based on a judicious mix of private and public funding that adequately balances personal responsibility and government regulation.

The Government provides subsidised but not free medical care for a specified range of illnesses and treatments. In public hospitals the Government subsidises hospital bills by 80 per cent but patients must pay the balance, even those in the most basic wards. Private hospital patients must pay 100 per cent of all fees. Patients can either pay from their own pockets or, if employees, from government-run medical insurance funds to which they are required to contribute.

Whatever the case, the Government's aim is to reduce the "moral hazard" which arises when people overconsume medical services that they do not have to pay for. Singapore's rulers believe that free "cradle to grave" health schemes in Britain and elsewhere breed this problem and it is one they must avoid. Strenuous PAP government efforts to avoid moral hazards in the provision of health services are cited as the reason for Singapore's low health expenditures and the supposedly high levels of health care. An examination of Singapore's health system and its three MSAs (medical savings accounts) is first required to assess the validity of such claims.

The 3Ms

Apart from government medical subsidies three main schemes have been devised to fund health care in Singapore. They are the "3Ms": Medisave, MediShield and Medifund.

Medisave

Medisave was launched in 1984 and requires all employees to contribute to a personal but government-managed savings account which builds up over time to cover a contributor's share of hospital and medical bills. Contribution rates to Medisave "range from 6 per cent of monthly income for those aged 35 or less, to 8 per cent for 45 and older".[60] Contributions are equally provided by employers and employees, but the self-employed have to pay the entire designated rate themselves. A cap on monthly contributions protects high-income earners from having to pay excessive amounts to Medisave. Contributions are tax-free, earn interest and form part of one's estate after death. About 85 per cent of Singaporeans belong to Medisave.[61]

Medishield/Medishield Plus

In 1990, the Government introduced MediShield, "a basic low-cost, catastrophic illness insurance scheme to help Medisave members meet hospital expenses due to major or prolonged illness".[62] MediShield pays 80 per cent of the remainder of hospital bills after deduction of government subsidies. MediShield Plus is a more expensive version of MediShield and targets higher income earners. "It has very high deductibles [but] provides sufficient coverage for a patient to be treated at a private hospital or in one of the two top classes of ward in public hospitals".[63] While Medisave is compulsory for all employees, MediShield is a voluntary scheme, giving employees the option to opt out if they wish. MediShield premiums can be paid from the Medisave account. By November 1998, 61 per cent of Singaporeans were covered by MediShield or Medishield Plus.[64]

Medifund

In 1993, Medifund was launched by the Government to cover patients who have exhausted their Medisave and MediShield funds and have no immediate family to rely on. The Government set up an endowment fund to provide charity-style relief for such people. "The capital in the fund is left untouched and interest is distributed to public-sector hospitals which consider applications for assistance and allocate funds."[65] The extent to which the poor and deprived are helped by Medifund and other schemes is examined later.

In addition to the 3Ms, Eldershield was launched in September 2002. It is a Medisave-based insurance plan against long-term disability for those aged 40 and over. The scheme pays S$300 a month for five years to people who are physically unable to cope with such activities as walking, bathing or eating.

From its launching the scheme generated complaints, mainly because of its low monthly benefits, strict criteria for claims and the five-year limit on payouts.[66] Eldershield's defects prompted 40 per cent of the 40-69 age group eligible for the scheme to drop out. Many contributors only became aware they belonged to the scheme when Medisave started deducting premiums from their Medisave accounts. By January 2003, only 700,000 out of 1.2 million people eligible for the scheme were still in it.

These schemes would seem to provide overall comprehensive health coverage for Singaporeans, but further examination reveals otherwise.

Policies of Exclusion

A survey of Singapore's health schemes reveals that they exclude numerous illnesses and treatments and do not cover many people. The long list of exclusions demonstrates governmental indifference to the concept of universal health care for all. As Barr notes:

> *Although the government is committed to ensuring the provision of "basic health care" for the population, it is unembarrassed about excluding particular procedures from the definition.*[67]

First, Medisave does not cover most outpatient services. The exceptions are such outpatient services as radiotherapy, IVF, hepatitis B vaccination and surgery. Otherwise patients must pay for out-patient consultations themselves. In March 2001, private GP fees ranged from S$25 to S$35. The subsidised fee with a specialist was between S$19 and S$21, to S$80 if not subsidised. Medisave cannot be used to cover maternity ward and associated costs beyond the third child, nor long-term hospital care.[68]

MediShield does not cover a wide range of conditions, including congenital abnormalities, cosmetic surgery, maternity charges, abortion, infertility and contraceptive procedures, sex-change operations, mental illness and personality disorders, AIDS and drug addiction, or alcoholism. Also excluded are injuries arising from direct participation in civil commotion or strikes and self-inflicted injuries.[69]

To minimise liability, the Government runs MediShield according to private sector insurance underwriting principles. The scheme excludes a long list of illnesses if the patient has already been receiving treatment for them before joining Medishield. These illnesses are blood disorders, cancer, stroke, chronic liver cirrhosis, chronic obstructive lung disease, chronic renal disease (including kidney failure), coronary artery disease, degenerative disease, ischemic heart disease, rheumatic heart disease and systematic lupus erythematosus. As a result, thousands of poorer Singaporeans are burdened with crushing medical bills when forced to get treatment for these conditions. MediShield also refuses to enrol people aged 70 and over. Once again it follows the risk-minimisation policies of private insurance companies rather than the philosophy that the state must provide medical treatment for the aged and poor who cannot afford it themselves.

By 2004, MediShield's payout rate was found to be less than 40 per cent of the average hospital bill instead of the original target of 80 per cent.[70] The size of MediShield deductibles (the amount of a medical bill that an insured patient must pay) has ensured this. MediShield deductibles range from S$500 to S$1000 depending on the class of the ward the patient is in.[71] But what of Medifund, the last hope for many sick and impoverished Singaporeans? Barr found that:

> For the very poor, and for the lower and middle-income earners with insufficient Medisave funds, obtaining treatment for these conditions has been problematical in Singapore: Medifund helps some people, but there can be no assumptions that one will be treated.[72]

In 2002, 178,209 people were given S$26.62 million by Medifund.[73] This comes to a mere $149 per person. Some may have received little more than a Panadol script. What help the majority of recipients received from the scheme was probably minimal. The many illnesses and diseases excluded under Singapore's health care system account for a large share of health problems which could be alleviated with proper medical treatment.

A list of these problems was compiled by state and federal health authorities in Australia. The National Health Priority Areas (NHPA) list sought to identify illnesses deemed as adding to the nation's illness burden and for which assistance should be given. The NHPA list focused on "diseases and other conditions that contribute most significantly to Australia's burden of illness and for which there is potential for the burden to be significantly reduced".[74] Illnesses on the NHPA list accounted for 40 per cent of total hospital patient days in Australia in 1998-99. Two of the three most commonly treated conditions on the list – cardiovascular disease and control of cancer – are excluded by Singapore's MediShield. Kidney dialysis and treatment for HIV, mental problems and diabetes – also on the NHPA list – are among MediShield exclusions. The only illnesses on the NHPA list that are not excluded by MediShield are asthma and personal injury.

A similar pattern of exclusions is apparent with Medisave, which precludes patients from committing future Medisave funds to outpatient renal dialysis, radiotherapy, chemotherapy or AZT treatment[75] (presumably other more recent and effective AIDS treatments would also not be funded). All these procedures are on the NHPA list. The only item on that list which Medisave does cover is assisted conception procedures. This is probably prompted by government desires to boost the country's anaemic birth rate. Any procedure that can produce more babies gets full state support in Singapore.

Further Limitations

Besides excluding many illnesses from health-insurance coverage, the Government limits Singaporeans' access to health care in other ways. Those most affected are once again the elderly (this time old women) and children of Medishield members.

While Medishield excludes people aged 70 and over, most old women are further penalised through Medicare. Nearly all of them have been homemakers for most of their lives, whether as wives, widows or divorcees. Medisave only helps such women if their husbands have left money in their accounts or have voluntarily funded a Medisave account for them.[76] Otherwise, such elderly women must rely on their adult children.

Currently more than 65 per cent of private funding for acute care for those aged 65 and over comes from their children's Medisave accounts.[77] If the children are low-income earners themselves they will have little in their accounts. Medisave shifts the burden of poverty from an older to a younger generation, forcing one disadvantaged group to subsidise another.

While Medishield excludes those 70 and over, it also refuses to cover the children of Medishield contributors unless they are included in their parents' plans and the parents pay an extra premium.

Some Tragic Consequences

Besides the poor coverage offered by Singapore's 3M schemes they also display some startling and tragic anomalies, especially regarding kidney dialysis and AIDS treatment.

Over a four-year period, 130 Muslim Singaporeans died because they could not afford kidney dialysis.[78] This disturbing information was contained in a June 1997 report by the Muslim Kidney Action Group (MKAG). The report revealed that those who had died had not qualified for subsidised treatment in the centres run by the National Kidney Foundation (NKF) which charged between S$500 and S$1500 a month, depending on the patient's income. Those who failed to qualify were forced to seek private dialysis treatment, which can range from S$1495 to S$2990 a month at private hospitals.[79] A May 1997 report showed that NKF charges ranged from S$200 to S$1600 a month for subsidised patients and S$2200 a month for full-paying patients.[80] A rival kidney-treatment group in Singapore, the Kidney Dialysis Foundation (KDF), charged patients a flat rate of $260 to $715 a month.

The MKAG report contained more unsettling disclosures. It found that in 1993, the NKF had announced it would only treat Muslims who pledged their organs before they developed kidney disease. Muslims were not covered by the country's Human Organ Transplant Act, which allows doctors to remove their kidneys for transplantation if they are involved in fatal accidents. Muslims, presumably for religious reasons, had been excluded from the Act and they had to opt in if they wanted to pledge their kidneys, the report said. Between the Act's inception in 1967 and September 1997, only 7458 of 250,000 adult Muslims in Singapore had done so. Some 300 Muslim kidney patients had failed to qualify for NKF treatment because they had not made the pledge. Many of them could not afford dialysis treatment at private clinics, and because of this 130 had died.

A similar pattern of tragic and unnecessary deaths has occurred with AIDS patients over the years. By the end of 2003, official figures showed that Singapore had 1200 AIDS cases and 900 who were HIV-positive,[81] though WHO estimated that Singapore would have had about 4000 people with HIV by late 2004, according to the country's health minister.[82] As in most countries, large numbers of the HIV-positive remain unidentified in Singapore. Despite this, AIDS is one of the illnesses excluded from the country's Medisave list, and the Government refuses to subsidise the very costly drugs patients need to fight the disease.

By 2001, AIDS workers had, for 13 years, been calling on the Government to change its policies and help AIDS and HIV victims pay for their medication. By November 2001, three quarters of Singapore's 975 AIDS/HIV sufferers could not afford the anti-retroviral HIV medications, which cost up to S$1500 a month, said the charity group Action for AIDS (AFA).[83] Less than 10 per cent could afford the optimum treatment: an anti-retroviral triple-drug combination therapy which cost between S$1200 and S$1500 a month.

The MOH refused to budge on the matter. Its heartless response was this:

Anti-retroviral drugs are expensive and, more importantly, not a long-term solution for HIV and AIDS patients. It is hence not prudent for the Government to use public money on such subsidies, as drugs are not a cure for AIDS.[84]

The Ministry added that asking the Government to provide more health-care subsidies was not a solution to helping AIDS victims because it would mean higher taxes or less money for education and housing.

So far, the only success AIDS activists have had was in November 1998, when they managed to persuade the Government to allow HIV/AIDS victims to withdraw up to S$500 a month from their Medisave accounts to help pay for treatment: this amount was raised to S$550 in June 2001. Such victims still have to find nearly S$1200 a month to pay for treatment. If they can't they die.

By the end of 2007, 3482 people had contracted HIV/AIDS in Singapore of whom 1144 had died. How many more would still have been alive had they been given the necessary treatment? And of the survivors among the remaining 2338, how many would have been living productive, or at least bearable lives had they all had access to such treatment?

AFA provides subsidies to some HIV/AIDS patients through its own find-raising efforts. Also, by 2004 it was directing patients to Thailand for consultation and to buy generic versions of the AIDS drugs they required. An AFA spokesman said that government pharmacies in Bangkok sold the drug for S$60 a month, compared to S$1200 a month they had to pay in Singapore by November 2004.[84a]

A more comprehensive examination of the numerous "exclusions" in Singapore's health system would reveal many more tragic cases, especially regarding the elderly, especially those aged 70 and over who don't qualify for MediShield. Even so, it is clear from the above that Singapore's health services offer a far from blanket coverage for its citizens, tragically so in the case of kidney failure and AIDS victims. For such people only various charitable groups are left to help. For example, by 1998, AFA was able to subsidise the HIV treatment for 20 AIDS victims – with some justifiable reservations. As Dr Stuart Koh, an AFA committee member, indignantly noted:

As a non-government organisation, we feel strongly that we are not in a position to subsidise treatment. But nothing has been done for the patients so far, so we felt that we had to do something. [85]

Several Muslim community bodies have felt compelled to raise funds to help needy Muslims pay for dialysis treatment to keep them alive. Again, various voluntary welfare bodies focus on helping the poor and destitute. Without them, many people would be completely deprived of care. Although the Government does give some support to these charitable groups, clearly it falls far short of what is required.

Malaysia's treatment of its AIDS victims stands in dramatic contrast to that of Singapore's. In 2005, all Malaysians with HIV were to get free life-prolonging drugs once the medicines could be produced locally.[86] The drugs were already free for some HIV people, including mothers and babies. The drugs used are for the Highly Active Antiretroviral Therapy (HAART).

Through the efforts of charitable bodies some of the many gaping holes in Singapore's "comprehensive" health system are plugged. Were it not for such groups one wonders how many sick and destitute Singaporeans would be dying in the streets.

Soaring Costs

Singapore's health system is not only not comprehensive; it is also increasingly expensive. This is largely due to the privatisation of much of the Singapore hospital system, which began in the mid-1980s. Many former government hospitals have been corporatised and given greater freedom of operation. The Government thought that this would allow a much freer play of market forces, which would generate competition and keep down health charges, but the opposite occurred. Since the privatisation program began, medical costs have skyrocketed for Singaporeans. Between 1984 and 1989, medical costs rose by 3.5 per cent and total health expenditure by 11 per cent, while the CPI increased by only one per cent.[87]

More recent data confirms this trend. In September 2001, a *Straits Times* survey revealed that hospital bills had been increasing from 6 to 8 per cent a year, while the average amount spent on health care had been rising by 3.6 per cent a year in the five years to 2001.[88] In 2000, health care expenditure was S$1439 per person. Such increases have continued to eat into Singaporeans' incomes. As a percentage of household expenditure, health care costs rose from 2.6 per cent in 1993 to 3.3 per cent in 1998.

Much of the rise in health-care costs is due to increased doctors' salaries, nurses' wages and spiralling drug prices. In 2000, doctors' salaries rose by 22 per cent and nurses' wages by 10 to 21 per cent. Salaries and wages accounted for 60 per cent of operating costs and drugs for 15 per cent.[89] These costs were significantly boosted by purchases of new technology and competition for business and reputation between the newly privatised hospitals. "From Singapore we learn that providers [hospitals etc] compete by recruiting the best-known physicians with higher pay and by having the most sophisticated expensive technology," reported Hsiao.[90]

Rising health costs are a problem not only in Singapore but in most countries. Soaring prices for new drugs and more expensive treatments, have rapidly pushed up medical expenditures. In Singapore, there has been growing criticism of rising health costs. They have become one of Singaporeans' greatest concerns, especially for the elderly. A survey revealed that more than half of Singaporeans believed that health-care costs remained unaffordable.[91] Nearly 70 per cent indicated that it was too expensive to consult specialist doctors in government hospitals. This prompted one Singaporean observer to note that the survey "confirmed a long-known sentiment among ordinary Singaporeans that health-care costs here are simply too high for the average family to cope with".[92] High treatment and consultation fees led one medical practitioner to call on the Government to "put an end to the commercialisation of medical practice in Singapore".[93] Government policies which permitted the free play of "market forces" were driving up costs.

Singaporeans have complained to the Government through the government-instituted Feedback Units. Mr Wang Kai Yuen, a PAP MP and Feedback chairman, noted the people's unhappiness over how the Government "does not look after the old because they are 'no longer productive members of the community' and it 'cares only about profit'."[94] A 2003 poll supported Mr Wang's sentiments. Almost two thirds of over 2000 Singaporeans surveyed believed that health-care services for the elderly were not affordable.[95]

Lee Kuan Yew has little sympathy for such views. They embody a "sentimental approach" and were a "sure way to ruin Singapore".[96] Lee and the PAP are obsessed with preventing the development of a UK-style national health scheme whose free health-care, they believe, has been constantly abused by users. Lee recognises that "as we get older, [drugs get] more and more expensive" and there "comes a time when the bills become phenomenal".[97] But he had no ideas on how the Government might resolve the problem. He firmly ruled out using the nation's financial reserves to ease the burden for the elderly sick. The reserves were "out of reach, out of bounds," he proclaimed.

Health costs have become so high for many Singaporeans that they have been heading across the Causeway to Johore Bahru for medical treatment and to buy medicines. One JB pharmacist says that up to 95 per cent of his customers are Singaporeans.[98] Doctors and hospital chiefs on both sides of the Causeway say Malaysia's health costs are between 50 and 70 per cent cheaper than Singapore's.[99] Some Singaporeans even travelled to Malacca (about 120kms north of Johore Bahru). Besides undergoing simple surgeries such as appendectomies across the border, Singaporeans filled prescriptions for chronic illnesses such as diabetes and hypertension.[100]

Many Singaporean women go to JB for pre-natal check-ups and even to have their babies. JB pre-natal check-ups cost about half those in Singapore, while women have to pay two to three times more to give birth in a Singapore public hospital than in a JB maternity hospital.[101] One of these JB hospitals delivered about 30 babies a year for Singaporean couples.

Failed Policies and Band-aid Solutions

The *raison d'etre* for Singapore's health-care schemes is to provide a comprehensive medical coverage at affordable cost without burdening the state financially. The 3M schemes are supposed to do this, but have clearly failed. The same applies to affordable health-care. Singaporeans have been faced with ever-rising medical charges and PAP health policies have failed to contain government health-care spending.

Lee and other PAP leaders have been obsessed with preventing the growth of welfarist-type health-care systems. Making people contribute to their health costs would do this by keeping "moral hazard" at bay. When Medisave was introduced in 1984 the Government confidently believed it had found a way to curb health expenditure, but soon it was clear that Medisave was not achieving this. In fact, immediately following Medisave's introduction, health expenditure per capita jumped from 11 per cent to 13 per cent a year.[102] The share of GDP absorbed by health expenditure also increased, to pay higher physicians' fees and to purchase new technology due to greater competition between newly privatised hospitals.

Eventually in 1993 the Government sought to control costs. It reluctantly recognised that promoting personal responsibility and permitting the free play of market forces could not reduce or even contain health spending. A ministerial committee on health policies noted, "Market forces alone will not suffice to hold down medical costs to a minimum. The health care system is an example of market failure ... The government has to intervene directly to structure and regulate the health system".[103] To rein in costs the Government sought to control the introduction of technology and specialist services, and imposed price caps on medical procedures in public hospitals. It recognised that "to a significant extent health services are supply driven" and that "countries with more doctors tend to spend more on health care".[104] With medical services, the market is driven by supply rather than demand. Health providers such as doctors can induce demand by convincing patients that they need various treatments. Over the years there have been numerous reports from Australia and the US of "over-treatment" by doctors, dictated more by their personal financial considerations than by patient welfare. In such situations price competition is secondary. The main determinants of prices are the providers of medical services.

To counter this possibility the Government tightened the supply of doctors in the country, especially specialists, who were to number no more than 40 per cent of medical practitioners. It also controlled the supply of local medical graduates and cut the numbers of overseas medical schools whose degrees Singapore recognised from 176 to 28.[105]

Despite recognising the supply-driven nature of rising medical costs, the Government continued to "ration" health. This policy has been a virtual death sentence for some very ill Singaporeans, especially those needing kidney dialysis or

AIDS treatment. Not only has the Government kept denying help through subsidies to such patients: it has even blocked full access to their own Medisave funds to pay for life-saving drugs and treatments. Despite such callous and inhumane policies, health costs have continued to rise and the flow of Singaporeans across the Causeway to Malaysia keeps swelling.

The Government's hardline health policies are maintained even though under Medisave patients are often forced to pay sizeable sums for treatment from their own pockets, rather than getting MSA coverage. Compulsory savings comprise only a small fraction of total national health expenditure. In 1995, only 8.5 per cent of all health spending came from medical savings accounts, while 57.7 per cent came from patients in direct out-of-pocket payments.[106] Government subsidies and other expenditures would have accounted for the remainder.

Moreover, as already mentioned, by 1997, 64 per cent of Singapore's health-care expenditures was coming from the private sector.

This meant that Singaporeans were paying for nearly two thirds of their health costs themselves despite the Government subsidising hospital-bed costs by up to 80 per cent. Patients were still having to pay such expenses as outpatient fees, operations and drug costs. The PAP Government and its supporters proudly note that, at 3 to 4 per cent of GDP, its health spending is lower than that of most developed countries. One must ask what has been the "body count" price for this budgetary achievement. How many hundreds, if not thousands, of Singaporeans have died over the last decade or two, who would still be alive if not for the PAP's inhumane health policies?

Realising that the PAP regime thinks in cold-blooded financial terms, some concerned Singaporeans, in an effort to get greater help for such unfortunates as people with AIDS, have devised a pitch which tries to appeal to this mentality. Singaporean health economist Phua Kai Hong has suggested a cost-benefit analysis approach in supplying life-prolonging drugs to AIDS patients:

> We need to look at the cost effectiveness of these drugs to find out how many more productive life years HIV patients can lead. Have we done enough to measure their cost effectiveness?[107]

So far even these appeals appear to have fallen on deaf ears. Some Singaporeans are appalled at the PAP's merciless attitude, especially considering the country's affluence. As one Singaporean plaintively noted, "surely a tiny share of [Singapore's] prosperity should be allocated to a significant subsidisation of branded drugs for those with HIV or AIDS".[108]

Many Westerners – and Malaysians – cannot understand how such a wealthy country as Singapore (at least in terms of huge financial reserves) can deny life-saving drugs to patients simply because they can't afford them. Even more incomprehensible is how such a state even refuses to allow people to fully access their own Medisave funds to pay for life-saving drugs and kidney dialysis. Half of the money in Medisave has been deducted from their wages every month. The Government not only refuses to help such tragically ill people but only permits them to partially access their Medisave funds to pay for life-saving/prolonging treatments.

What explains such heartless policies, apart from an almost callous indifference to AIDS and kidney disease victims? Ensuring that such people will not be a burden to the state seems to be the basic reason, especially if they have drained their Medisave accounts to pay for treatment. This is likely, considering the Government decision to cap Medisave contributions at S$20,000 per person with contributions being channelled into people's CPF retirement accounts. In commenting on such PAP health-care policies, Hsiao observes:

> *Because our health declines as we age and health spending increases accordingly, any compulsory savings scheme based on the principle of self-reliance should ask people to save as much as they can during their working years for their health and long-term-care costs, particularly the high costs after retirement.*[109]

Hsiao argues that S$20,000 is insufficient to protect the elderly who have serious chronic diseases and need surgery. Medisave allows CPF contributors to withdraw some of their medical savings at 55, leaving only S$15,000 in the account to fund medical expenses. "These features defeat the whole purpose of compelling people to save so that they have the financial means to be responsible for their own health expenses," he notes, and are among the "several irrational and inconsistent features of the Medisave scheme that have caused financial hardship for Singapore's citizens and have adversely affected the cost-effectiveness of its health care system".[110]

Singapore's other MSA schemes possess little capacity for addressing these concerns.

Unhealthy Outcomes

Hsiao might also have mentioned how Singapore's deficient health system has adversely affected the population's health. In 2000, WHO ranked Singapore 30th out of 191 countries for the overall health of its population (as opposed to its health-care, for which it was ranked 6th).[111] Considering that Singapore is a highly urbanised society which had the eighth highest GDP per capita in the world in 2001 and the 16th highest GNI (PPP), being ranked a mere 30th for healthiness seems unimpressive.

The WHO report found that Singaporeans could expect to have a healthy life for 69.3 years before they succumbed to disability. A disability was defined as not being able to carry out daily living activities like taking a bath or feeding oneself without help. The survey found 24 countries where people could expect to remain healthy for 70 years or more. Japan topped the list with a healthy life expectancy of 74.5 years, followed by Australia with 73.2 years.[112] The far more comprehensive health-care systems of Australia and other Western countries would largely explain their higher healthy life expectancy than Singapore's.

In commenting on the WHO survey, the MOH said the incidence of such illnesses as cancer, heart disease, hypertension and diabetes largely determined how many years of healthy life Singaporeans could expect. Of these four illnesses, people suffering from three of them (cancer, several types of heart disease and diabetes) are excluded from MediShield coverage if they have already been receiving treatment for them before joining Medishield. Were these and other disabling illnesses covered by MediShield, Singapore's WHO ranking would undoubtedly be higher, especially for healthy life expectancy. But the Ministry is unlikely to endorse this view, preferring to make glib statements on the need for public education to combat such illnesses:

> *The ministry will continue to work towards reducing these diseases through promotion of a healthy lifestyle, including good dietary habits, regular exercise and not smoking, as well as early screening, diagnosis and treatment.*[113]

Such education programs will do little to save those already suffering from debilitating diseases, especially when they cannot pay for the treatment and may soon die as a result.

Though the MOH may praise the virtues of early screening, the health system seems to have failed with regard to tuberculosis, whose incidence and death rate appears surprisingly high in Singapore. The number of TB cases among Singaporeans and permanent residents rose steadily from 1434 in 1994 to 1821 in 1998, with 125 dying of TB in 1998.[114] The following year the number of new TB cases dropped to 1552 and 105 died of it.

The magnitude of Singapore's TB problem is only fully revealed when comparisons are made with the diseases developed countries. In 1999, Singapore had 58 TB cases for every 100,000 people, compared to six per 100,000 in Australia and eight in the US[115] – though in 2000 Singapore's TB numbers fell to 43 per 100,000.[116] Even so, the country's TB problem is still many times worse than that of developed countries with whom it shares similar levels of affluence.

When confronted with Singapore's high TB numbers a MOH spokesman baldly commented that some of the new cases were TB sufferers who had not completed their treatment and had had a relapse. "This has contributed to the higher TB rate, compared with the other developed countries."[117] The reasons why they had not completed their treatment were not considered. Perhaps they could not afford to continue the treatment for socio-economic reasons. Most of Singapore's TB cases are people in their 50s or older who are more likely to belong to lower-income groups. Many may have exhausted their Medisave accounts and be ineligible for MediShield assistance.

Chronically sick adults who require expensive on-going treatment, especially if elderly, are seen as unproductive by the PAP state. Their medical treatment must be strictly rationed, or even denied if they can't pay for it. This may explain why WHO's 2000 report ranked Singapore 101 out of 191 countries for fair health service financing.[118] The inequities of Singapore's health system are displayed by an absence of risk-pooling and an emphasis on personal responsibility supplemented by family support. Such a system condemns poorer classes to an inadequate and sometimes fatal lack of health-care. In the West, where more egalitarian health systems operate, health contributions are pooled and medical care is provided on the basis of need rather than merely the money contributed. A notable exception to this approach is the US, whose health system is recognised as one of the world's most wasteful and inequitable. Not surprisingly, US healthy life expectancy is rather average, being ranked 24th in the WHO 2000 report.

Healthy Despite the Health System

The lack of proper health coverage for many Singaporeans largely explains why Singapore was ranked 30 out of 191 countries for the health of its population by WHO. This is a mediocre score for a country with such a high GDP per capita. Even so, considering the major deficiencies in its "3Ms" system, the health of its population seems surprisingly good, at least in terms of low infant mortality rates (IMRs) and its still fairly high longevity.

Singapore's impressive IMRs may be linked to government concern with falling birth rates. Since the mid-1980s, the Government has been desperately trying to boost the birth rate and has ensured that pregnant women have full access to natal and post-natal health care. Such access has done much to keep down Singapore's IMRs, below those of the US and several other developed countries.

Singapore's longevity rates also compare favorably with those of most developed countries. In 2000, Singaporeans' life expectancy at birth was 78.1, putting it ahead of such countries as Britain (78), Belgium (77.9), Germany (77.8) and New Zealand (77.7).[119] This is despite Singapore's deficient health-care system, especially for its lower-income earners. Moreover, Singaporeans' overall health seems to be better than those of most Westerners, especially in terms of obesity. This is apparent when one sees Western tourists wandering around Singapore. So often the locals look much slimmer and fitter. This is more due to diet than to health-care. Singaporeans still have a largely traditional Asian diet based on vegetables, sea food and complex carbohydrates. They consume little red meat, and fewer dairy products, refined carbohydrates and sugars than most Westerners. How long such a diet will last is debatable. Singapore is being hit by the Western junk food invasion and sadly, the incidence of diabetes and obesity among Singaporeans is rapidly rising. Even so, Singaporeans still have a healthier diet than most Westerners and this may explain their better health.

Similar reasons may account for the good health of Japanese. As Chapter 31 shows, Japan's health system is also very deficient, yet its people have the world's highest life expectancy. In 2000, it was 80.3 years,[120] while in 1995 Japan had the world's lowest infant death of two deaths per thousand births.[121] Despite being a country "where medical malpractice is rampant" the "relatively low level of heart-disease-causing fat in the diet" explains Japanese's good health and longevity, Ben Hills argues:

> *Even with hamburger joints, pizza-on-wheels, fried chicken and the rest of the familiar Western junk food diet spreading across the country, the Japanese still eat more vegetables and get more protein from fish and less from red meat, than people in any other developed country. They have the lowest rate of death from heart disease in the developed world...[122]*

An OECD report found Japan had the lowest obesity levels of 17 countries from 1980 to 2001.[123] While only about 3 per cent of Japanese were obese in 2001, 22 per cent of Britains and over 30 of Americans were. Like the Singaporeans, the Japanese are at the low end of the obesity spectrum in industrialised countries. In Japan's case, too, this is mostly due to a diet which has been traditionally based on soy, fish, vegetables, fruit and tea, as well as rice and noodles. Japanese diets are also lower in animal fat and portions are smaller.

There are several other factors besides diet that would explain the good health of Singaporeans. Two of these have been noted by Barr:[124] the first is the comprehensive and free medical care received by Singapore's sizable numbers of "civil servants and retired civil servants who still enjoy free unlimited employer-sponsored health";[125] the second, is the operation of a National Service program in Singapore since the early 1970s, which has further contributed to national fitness:

> *The Singapore Armed Forces faced a regular problem with unfit reservists and even unfit raw recruits from school throughout the 1970s and 1980s, and in the process of trying to address this problem it incidentally inducted half the Singaporean population into consciousness of the need for exercise and healthy eating. ...This National Service driven fitness regime is probably only partially effective, but must nevertheless make some contribution to national health standards.[126]*

Finally, Singapore's rigorous public health and sanitation programs also contribute to its population's health. These range from comprehensive and ongoing measures to eradicate malaria-causing mosquitos to strict food-handling regulations that minimise food-poisoning. Such efforts would especially benefit the poorer classes who are normally most exposed to health threats posed by sub-standard housing and unhygienic food and water supplies.

The combined effect of these factors explain Singaporeans' longevity and good health despite their country's deficient health-care system.

Still the One

Many conservatives in the US health system share the PAP's rejection of welfarism and "socialist" medicine. For them Singapore is still the one to follow. Minimising health expenditure on the "undeserving" poor is preferable to developing a humane and fair health system for all. Singapore-style MSAs are seen as a means of rationing health resources, despite their many weaknesses. As Hsiao observes:

> *Unfortunately, Singapore's evidence was not adequate to alter the beliefs of those Americans who have unfaltering faith in the free market or those who believe the rich should get more favourable tax treatment than the poor.[127]*

Despite the deficiencies of Singapore's health schemes the US Congress passed its version of a tax-favoured MSA scheme in 1995:

Despite the clear evidence from Singapore, the proponents of the U.S. law argued that greater self-pay by patients would reduce insurance-generated moral hazard. Patients would demand fewer unnecessary medical services and thus curb health expenditure inflation.[128]

Hong Kong too has shown strong interest in Singapore's health system. A limited form of savings account was one of the proposed reforms to health-care funding released at the end of 2000.[129] This was contrary to the advice of a Harvard team hired to review health funding options for Hong Kong. Once again free-market ideology prevailed over reality. Singapore remains a magnet for health policy analysts seeking ways to reform health-care. They see Singapore as having struck a balance between a laissez-faire system and a government-owned national health service; but if they visit Singapore to study its health system they should first leave their ideological baggage at Changi airport, peruse several years' back issues of *The Straits Times*, talk to local welfare activists and visit some AIDS and dialysis patients and elderly poor. They might then better see through the glib sophistry of Singapore's health officials and PAP ministers and discover an inequitable and heartless health-care system that cares more about dollars spent than lives saved.

* * * * * * * *

The HDB and CPF schemes and the health-care system are supposed to be the three pillars that underwrite the average Singaporean's security. All are clearly deficient and have fallen well short of their original intentions. Singaporeans' HDB units are over-priced for the average Singaporean and could well be a depreciating asset into which many have been forced to sink their life savings. Singaporeans' CPF savings are totally inadequate for most of them to retire on. The health system provides patchy coverage at best for the average person.

Despite their failings, these schemes, especially the HDB and CPF, provide the PAP state with potent tools for ensuring social and political compliance. The PAP would only permit changes to them that would not jeopardise its political power. These schemes must be radically reformed if they are to serve Singaporeans rather than the PAP state's political and financial agendas.Until then they will fail to play the role they could perform in reducing the significant poverty that still exists in Singapore, the next chapter's focus.

References

1. As quoted in *The Straits Times* (ST), March 4, 1995.
2. ST, October 4, 1999.
3. Tremewan, Christopher: *The Political Economy of Social Control in Singapore* (New York, St Martin's Press, 1994), p. 57.
4. ST, September 20, 1995.
5. Ibid.
6. ST, August 30, 2003.
7. Selvan, T. S.: *Singapore: The Ultimate Island* (Melbourne, Freeway Books, 1990), p. 269.
8. ST, October 19, 2002.
9. Selvan, p. 269.
10. Initially, the PAP government broke up the Malay communities in the 1960s to neuter them politically. By preventing

them from concentrating in specific areas and electorates, the Malays would find it much harder to vote Malay MPs into Parliament. Despite this, Malays had begun congregating in some HDB estates by the early 1980s. (Tremewan, Christopher, *The Political Economy of Social Control in Singapore:* New York, St Martins Press, 1994; p. 65) After easing the rules governing flat allocation and resale it was found that the Malays were gradually moving back to their favourite districts. As Malays tend to vote against the anti-PAP, this would concentrate the anti-PAP vote in certain electorates, increasing the chances of opposition victories in them. The government was also afraid that increased racial concentrations of Malays, especially, and Indians in HDB estates, could re-ignite the inter-racial violence of the 1960s.

11. ST, November 11, 2003.
12. ST, November 15, 2003.
13. Han, Fook Kwang; Warren Fernandez and Sumiko Tan: *Lee Kuan Yew, The Man and His Ideas* (Singapore, Times Editions, 1998), p. 235.
14. ST, November 24, 1998.
15. ST, May 10, 1997.
16. ST, November 27, 1999.
17. Tremewan, p. 58.
18. Lee, Kuan Yew: *From Third World to First* (Singapore, Times Media, 2000), p. 127.
19. ST, April 16, 1998.
20. ST, March 18, 2003.
21. Ibid.
22. ST, August 29, 2003.
23. Chee, Soon Juan: *Your Future, My Faith, Our Freedom* (Singapore, Open Singapore Centre, 2001), p. 142.
24. Ibid, p. 146.
25. *South China Morning Post*, August 25, 2000.
26. ST, July 23, 2003.
27a. Asher G. Mukul and Amarendu Nandy "Singapore's policy responses to ageing, inequality and poverty: An assessment" p.52 in *International Social Security Review*, Vol. 61, 1/2008.
27. Ibid.
28. Chee, pp. 158-9.
29. ST, October 14, 1998.
30. ST, November 27, 1999.
31. ST, November 27, 1999.
32. Chee, p. 146.
33. ST, June 29, 2000.
34. *Far Eastern Economic Review*, May 25, 2000.
34a. Asher and Nandy, p. 52
35. Lim, Kim Lian "Enhancing the financial security of older Singaporeans", p. 68 in *Singapore Economy in the 21st Century* edited by Koh Ai Tee et al (Singapore, McGraw Hill, 2002).
36. ST, November 27, 1999.
37. Peebles, Gavin "Saving and Investment in Singapore", p. 384 in Koh et al.
38. ST, April 19, 2003.
39. Ibid.
39a. ST, September 20, 2007.
39b. Ibid.
40. *Asia Magazine*, August 16-18, 1996.
41. Low, Linda and Ngiam Tee Liang: "An Underclass Among the Overclass", p. 242 in *Singapore: Towards A Developed Status* edited by Linda Low (Singapore, Oxford University Press, 1999).
42. ST, August 18, 1997.
43. Ibid.
44. Selvan, p. 221.
45. ST, August 21, 1997.
46. Ibid.
47. ST, December 14, 2004.
48. Ibid.
49. ST, September 9, 1995.
50. ST, July 15, 1998.
51. ST, June 30, 1996.
52. ST, January 30, 1996.
53. ST, February 3, 2001.
54. ST, May 4, 1996.
55. ST, December 6, 2004.
56. Porter, Claire: "State of Health", *The Expat Magazine* (Singapore), September 2000, p. 18.
57. Ibid.
58. Hsiao, William C. "Behind the Ideology and Theory: What is the Empirical Evidence for Medical Savings Accounts", p. 733 in *Journal of Health*

Politics, Policy and Law: Vol 26, No 4, August 2001.

59. ST, September 17, 2002.
60. Barr, Michael D. "Medical Savings Accounts in Singapore: A Critical Inquiry", p. 712 in *Journal of Health Politics, Policy and Law*: Vol 26, No 4, August 2001.
61. ST, November 21, 1998.
62. Barr, p. 713.
63. Ibid.
64. ST, November 21, 1998.
65. Barr, p. 713-14.
66. ST, January 10, 2003.
67. Barr, p. 719.
68. Ibid.
69. Ibid.
70. ST, October 10, 2004.
71. *Business Times*, October 5, 2004.
72. Barr, p. 719.
73. ST, November 17, 2003.
74. Barr, p. 720.
75. Ibid.
76. Ibid, p. 722.
77. Ibid.
78. ST, September 3, 1997.
79. ST, May 11, 1997.
80. Ibid.
81. *The New Paper*, November 19, 2004.
82. Ibid.
83. ST, November 27, 2001.
84. Ibid.
84a. *The New Paper*, November 20, 2004.
85. ST, May 23, 1998.
86. *Today*, December 1, 2004.
87. Rahim, Lily: *The Singapore Dilemma* (Kuala Lumpur, Oxford University Press, 1998), p. 43.
88. ST, September 8, 2001.
89. Ibid.
90. Hsiao, p. 734.
91. ST, June 21, 2001.
92. ST, June 22, 2001.
93. ST, April 22, 1998.
94. ST, January 15, 2001.
95. ST, January 3, 2004.
96. ST, January 15, 2001.
97. Ibid.
98. ST, January 6, 2001.
99. ST, June 5, 2001.
100. *Far Eastern Economic Review*, February 15, 2001.
101. ST, June 6, 2004.
102. Barr, p. 716.
103. Ibid, p. 717.
104. Ibid.
105. Ibid.
106. Hsiao, p. 734.
107. ST, November 27, 2001.
108. ST, July 7, 2001.
109. Hsiao, p. 735.
110. Ibid, p. 733.
111. ST, June 21, 2000.
112. Ibid.
113. Ibid.
114. ST, March 24, 1999.
115. Ibid.
116. ST, February 18, 2002.
117. ST, March 24, 1999.
118. Ham, Chris: "Values and Health Policy: The Case of Singapore", p. 742 in *Journal of Health Politics, Policy and Law*: 26, 4, August 2001.
119. *The World Competitiveness Yearbook 2001* (Lausanne, Switzerland; Institute for Management Development), p. 505.
120. Ibid.
121. Hills, Ben: *Japan Behind the Lines* (Sydney, Hodder and Stoughton, 1996), p. 384.
122. Ibid, p. 385.
123. *The Australian Financial Review*, January 17-18, 2004.
124. Barr, Michael D.: "Singapore", in *Comparative Health Policy in the Asia-Pacific*, edited by Robin Gauld (England, Open University Press, 2005).
125. Ibid, p. 161.
126. Ibid, p. 165.
127. Hsiao, p. 734.
128. Ibid, p. 735.
129. Ham, p. 743.

CHAPTER 25

ALMOST POVERTY-FREE?

Officially poverty is a minor problem in Singapore. Sometimes its existence is even denied by such Singaporean spokesmen as Kishore Mahbubani, the Republic's permanent representative to the UN. Mahbubani asserted that Singapore "may be worth a study for those striving to bridge the growing divide in an increasingly troubled planet". After reciting the usual statistics about the country's soaring GDP growth and per capita income he declared, "Food is cheap and plentiful...Shelter is also plentiful... The population has become healthier every year... there are no homeless, destitute or starving people", finally proclaiming that, "Poverty has been eradicated".[1] While not perfect, the diplomat magnanimously conceded, Singapore was the best model on offer, especially for Third World countries. Once again Singapore was being billed as the example for developing countries to follow. This time its supposed lack of poverty was being cited as proof. Was this justified?

1. Poverty, Past and Present

For many years poverty was not a topic of polite conversation in the city-state. "To even use this word shocks many people in Singapore," noted Clammer in 1987. "Surely it doesn't exist there?" they would exclaim, believing it had been virtually eradicated. Certainly, poverty has not been a popular topic among Singapore's academics. Clammer wrote of "the deafening silence on the part of most local social scientists about problems such as poverty".[2] But poverty has been much studied in Singapore.

Early Poverty Surveys

The country's most comprehensive survey of poverty was done by none other than Goh Keng Swee, a leading PAP minister and Lee Kuan Yew's most senior lieutenant. Goh's 1953-4 Social Survey of Singapore was undertaken when he was Director of Social Welfare (Social Research) at the Department of Social Welfare. Goh conducted a major household survey in 1954 which found that between 22 and 25 per cent of households in Singapore were below the poverty line. They were those who lacked sufficient income to pay for minimum housing, utilities, food, clothing, transportation and education.[3]

In the early 1970s Buchanan re-examined Singapore's poverty when studying the socio-economic changes that had occurred between 1954 and 1968. While housing, health and education had improved, people were no better off socially or economically, he found. First, unemployment had doubled between 1957 and 1968 from 6 per cent to about 12 per cent. Second, resettlement in the new HDB estates often meant large and widespread increases in rent, fuel and power costs. Third, while wages and incomes of skilled workers and government workers had risen by 10 to 40 per cent, those for unskilled workers had remained stagnant or declined between 1959 and 1968. Average wages had fallen for those working in industries that manufactured food, textiles and paper and paper products; and in non-electrical machinery assembly, printing and publishing.[4] While people's housing may have improved, the poor's overall financial position had changed little in 15 years. While 25 to 30 per cent of Singapore's urban population lived in poverty in the mid-1950s, their numbers had declined little by the late 1960s, Buchanan contended.[5]

A 1977 study revealed that poverty had worsened in Singapore by the 1970s. The survey was conducted by Cheah Hock Beng, who followed Goh's methods and used his definitions of poverty. Cheah found that poverty levels had increased from about 25 per cent in 1954 to 34 to 39 per cent by 1973. Households in poverty had leapt from 19 to 21 per cent to 33 to 37 per cent during this period.[6] Moreover, rehousing people in HDB units from squatter dwellings and shophouses had worsened overcrowding for the poor: room-occupancy rates had risen from 3.6 people per room in some 1950s housing to 5 people after widespread rehousing in HDB flats.[7]

Clammer came to similar conclusions during research in 1987. He found over 30 per cent of the population were living below the poverty line and blamed the HDB for this:

> In the 1950s and 1960s most low income families (usually with an unskilled labourer as head, or a widow, or with a history of sickness and low education) could manage in the kampong environment on very little rent, employment in nearby cottage industries and communal facilities. Today the same family faces HDB rent, high utilities costs, rising transportation costs and the usual expenses for food, clothing, medicine and so on. A family that could survive on $400 a month in the kampong, would find it very hard to do so in their HDB estates, as the rising number of rent-arrears families indicates.[8]

Clammer's survey of poverty studies done to 1980 revealed that many poor families spent up to 60 per cent or more of their income on food, compared to 10 per cent for rich families. But poverty does not mean starvation for Singapore's poor. Rather it lies in "not being able to participate in the values that Singapore society has raised to the status of the sacred – consumption, employment, leisure, and luxuries".[9]

The HDB scheme and its urbanisation of Singapore seems to have worsened the poor's plight. While "low cost" housing can improve accommodation for the poor it can also increase their poverty. HDB policies appear to have "unwittingly promoted "shelter poverty" that is, poverty brought about when households had to deprive themselves of non-shelter basic necessities in order to meet the high costs of housing," noted Bello and Rosenfeld.[10] Pugh made similar observations in 1987:

> We have enough evidence ... to suggest that housing poverty is significant, mainly concealed in HDB one-room flats, in some older and dilapidated shophouses, and in some pre-modern dwellings. The HDB must have much current information on this, but it is not available for publication, and it is a subject largely ignored by Singapore's social science intellectuals.[11]

By the late 1980s Singapore's poverty had not so much been eradicated as relocated to HDB blocks. Although more hygienic than the kampongs, HDB accommodation may have actually worsened poverty for their dwellers in psychological as well as material terms. Soulless concrete boxes, they have sometimes been called "horizontal cemeteries for the soul" by Singaporeans. Those who dwelt in them have forever lost the freer more communitarian lifestyle of the kampong.

Lee Kuan Yew, with uncharacteristic empathy, wrote about the plight of displaced kampong dwellers in his autobiography:

> There were enormous problems, especially in the early stages when we resettled farmers and others from almost rent-free wooden squatter huts with no water, power or modern sanitation, and therefore no utility bills, into high-rise dwellings with all these amenities but also a monthly bill to pay. It was a wrenching experience for them in personal, social and economic terms.
>
> Difficult adjustments were inevitable and there were more comic, even absurd, results. Several pig farmers could not bear to part with their pigs and reared them in high-rise flats. Some were seen coaxing their pigs up the stairs![12]

Though the resettled people were paid compensation money, the older farmers did not know what to do with themselves and their money:

> Living in flats, they missed their pigs, ducks, chickens, fruit trees and vegetable plots which had provided them with free food. Fifteen to 20 years after being resettled in HDB new towns, many still voted against the PAP. They felt the government had destroyed their way of life.[13]

As Lee shows, poverty can be psychological as well as material.

Grudging Admissions

In 1985, the Government grudgingly admitted that poverty still existed in Singapore. Perhaps a former PAP minister's outburst about the growing inequalities of wealth in Singapore was the catalyst. In March 1985, Jek Yuen Thong, raised this issue in Parliament. He said the lives of low-income groups in Singapore had not improved in the previous 25 years. While the subsidies for MPs had risen six times and ministers' salaries ten times, the salaries of the average Singaporean had only risen two times, while the cost of living had gone up six times during this period.[14]

When Parliament opened in May 1985, the President, C.V. Devan Nair, read out a government position paper which said that 20 per cent of the population needed special help. He said: "At the tail end of Singapore's prosperity are a shocking number of Singaporeans who live on less than S$500 a month" (about US$250 at 1985 exchange rates). Of these, 400,000 "eke out a living".[15] The "government in response to the speech said it too was shocked, but it too was just a pose because the figures have always been there,"[16] mocked Selvan.

In recent years the PAP Government has insisted that Singapore's poverty rate is only 10 per cent – at least that's all the Government admits to.[17] Even the lot of this 10 per cent is tolerable, according to Prime Minister Goh, who in 2000 claimed they enjoyed a "modest but reasonable standard of living".[18] But how "reasonable" is Goh's claim? Do only 10 per cent of Singaporeans live in poverty. Answering such questions requires an examination of definitions of poverty and its prevalence in both developed countries and Singapore.

Measuring Poverty

Half a country's median per capita income is the usual international benchmark for measuring both individual and household poverty. As already explained, the median is the 50th percentile, which in a distribution of income marks the point at which half of income recipients fall below and half above that point.

By use of the half-median measure, individual poverty levels in most OECD countries from 2000-2004 ranged from about 5 to 17 cent of the population. Poverty rates for major OECD countries were: UK (12.4%), US (17%), Sweden (6.5%), Canada (11.4%), Switzerland (7.6%), Holland (7.3%), Germany (8.4%), France (7.3%), Italy (12.7%) and Spain (14.2%). Australia's rate was 12.2 per cent,[19] but by 2005/6 it had fallen to 11.1 per cent.[20]

In 2006, Australia's median individual weekly income was Aus$466 (S$560) and its half-median income was Aus$233 (S$280).[21] Apart from earned income, all income from pensions and various welfare payments is included. With the yearly individual median income being Aus$24,232, the half-median income would be Aus$12,116, which would be Aus$1009 (S$1211) per month.

Also in 2006, Australia's median weekly household income was Aus$1027 (S$1234).[22] It too included all retiree and other welfare income. With yearly household income being Aus$53,404, the half-median income was Aus$26,702, which was Aus$2225 (S$2670) a month.

How Singapore Compares

When the half-median method is used to measure Singapore's poverty a much higher percentage of the population seems to be living below the poverty line compared to that in the OECD countries. This becomes apparent when the method is applied to both individual and household incomes.

In 2006, Singapore's median income for all employed people was S$2170 a month, according to the country's Labour Force survey.[23] Half of this was S$1085 a month, which would mark Singapore's poverty line for individual income earners, according to the half-median income benchmark though Singapore's income statistics only consider earned income. As already noted, income from pensions, welfare or other transfer payments is omitted. Were Singapore to include such unearned income, its half-median income would be even lower. Before considering this point further, Singapore's poverty levels based on its own definition of median income will first be calculated.

From Table 23.1 it can be seen that 331,900, 18 per cent of Singapore's total workforce of 1,795,800 earned below S$1000 a month in 2006. But calculating the percentage of employees below the S$1085 median income mark would require an estimate of how many of the 274,800 who were earning between S$1000 and S$1499 a month were in the S$1000 to S$1085 income range. A fifth would be a reasonable estimate, adding another 50,000 or so to the 331,900 earning below $1000. This would bring the percentage of employees under S$1085, and therefore beneath the poverty line, to 21 per cent.

However, as already noted, the Labour Force survey only covers those who earn income, not retirees and others who receive unearned income. In Western countries such as Australia, income surveys, especially those for measuring poverty, include unearned pension and welfare income. In Singapore, only the Household Expenditure Survey (HES) includes any unearned income – and then only retiree income. The General Household Survey (GHS) and another DOS household income survey, the Key Household Income Trends (KHIT), 2007, do not.[24]

However, before seeing what per cent of Singapore's income recipients, both income earners and retirees, etc, fall below the poverty line, the proportion of households that do so will be calculated. But once again statistical problems present themselves. First, the 2002/3 HES report does not provide a median household income figure and while the 2005 GHS report does, it lacks the data necessary to ascertain what percent of households drop beneath the half-median mark. Only the KHIT survey provides sufficient data to do this. But then, like the Labour Force report for individual incomes, does so only approximately.

Table 25.1 – Distribution of earned household income in 2006/07

Income Level	Below S$1000	$1000 – $1999	$2000 – $2999	$3000 – $3999	$4000 – $4999	$5000 – $5999
% of H/hds						
2006	5.7	13.0	13.6	11.3	10.5	9.0
2007	5.4	11.9	12.2	11.6	10.0	8.6

The KHIT's median household income for 2006 was S$4500 and in 2007 was S$4870. This makes the half-median incomes for each year S$2250 and S$2435 respectively.[25]

The 2006 half-median S$2250 mark fell one quarter of the way between the S$2000 and $2999 range. This means that in 2006 all of the 5.7 per cent of households in the below S$1000 division, all 13 per cent in the S$1000-1999 division and a quarter (3.4 per cent) of the 13.6 per cent in the S$2000-$2999 division – a total of over 22 per cent of households – were under the half-median poverty line. In 2007, the respective percentages were 5.4, 11.9 and over a third of 12.2, making a total of nearly 21.5 per cent. The slightly lower poverty percentage in 2007 was due to higher employment in all households, including the poorest ones, according to the KHIT report.

At first glance it would seem that over 20 per cent of individual income earners, and up to 22 per cent of households, are beneath the half-median poverty line in Singapore. But if retirees and other unearned income recipients were included, the poverty percentages would be higher.

Retiree households, defined as comprised solely of non-working persons aged 60 and above, with no income from work, made up 5 per cent of Singapore resident households in 2007.[26] Moreover, in the 2003/3 HES report, retiree households constituted 18 per cent of the lowest 20 per cent of households – 4 per cent of total households.[27] Also, as shown in the previous chapter, more than half of retirees aged 55 and over whether individual or in households had no income of their own and had to rely on their families. A further 18.5 per cent received less than S$250 a month.

From all these data, it could be reasonably assumed that the incomes of most retirees, whether living in purely retiree households or with their families, would be well below the half-median income poverty measures mentioned earlier. As such, several more per cent could be added to the approximately 22 per cent of Singapore households beneath the poverty line. If this was done household poverty levels would have been about a quarter of all households in 2007. A similar percentage could be added to the 21 per cent of Singapore's individual income recipients in poverty, bringing this total to about 25 per cent.

Whatever the precise percentages for individual or household poverty in Singapore, they would often be double to nearly triple the 7 to 14 per cent of most OECD countries. Comparisons between Singapore and Western countries are valid because they have similar GNI per capita levels. Singapore's per capita GNI in 2006 was 18th (US$29,320) to France's 13th, Canada's 14th, Australia's 15th, Italy's 16th and Spain's 20th.[28] Despite sharing a similar GNI per capita level with these countries Singapore's poverty figures are much higher.

The same holds true when comparisons are based on PPP GNI data. As Chapter 23 showed, Singapore's PPP GNI per capita is slightly higher than its nominal per capita GNI. When the cost of living is factored in, Singapore's per capita affluence, both in nominal and PPP terms, matches that of many OECD countries. Hence developed country poverty standards can again be applied to Singapore. But largely because of Singapore's severe income inequality, its poverty numbers are about double those in the West. Nonetheless, while Singapore's poorest, as in the West, rarely starve they do lead lives of severe material deprivation.

As Chapter 23 also showed, the poorest 20 per cent of Singapore's households had an average income of less than S$795 a month in 2003. This was S$330 per person, based on the 2003 Household Expenditure Survey (HES) which found that households in this quintile averaged 2.4 members.[29] For people in the bottom 20 per cent of such households in 2003, this meant an income of S$300 a month.

Life is very difficult for anyone living on such minimal sums in high-priced Singapore, as a *Straits Times* examination of the incomes and expenditures of several poor people showed in 2000. One was a 73-year-old woman who earned S$300 a month as a cleaner working three hours a day, six days a week. Her total monthly spending was S$365. Of this S$250 went on food and S$58 for utilities; transport (S$25); household provisions such as soap, gas and cooking oil (S$20), and shopping expenses (S$12). Despite her frugality she still had a monthly deficit of S$65. Although she proudly spurned public assistance, she accepted help from relatives when necessary.[30]

A second case was a 42-year-old woman who was supporting an elderly mother in her 80s. She worked as a hawker's assistant for five hours a day, four to five days a week, for about S$340 a month. Her expenditure was: food (S$300); mother's expenses (S$157); utilities and phone bills (S$95); transport, including taxi fares to take her mother to hospital (S$80); rent and related charges (S$21.50); household necessities such as cooking oil, gas and soap (S$50). These items totalled S$720 a month, giving her a monthly deficit of S$380, which charitable groups, friends and family helped meet.[31]

Both examples indicate that the minimal amount needed by frugal individuals to survive (subsist?) in Singapore was about S$360-$370 a month. For two-person households it would be over S$700 a month, and several hundred dollars more for three-person households. With inflation accelerating in Singapore, especially since 2007, these monthly amounts would now be over S$400 for individuals and more than S$800 for a two-person household.

While poverty is a relative condition, it becomes clear that any household member forced to live on less than S$400 a month would be experiencing severe material deprivation in such a modern urban society as Singapore. Though Singapore may not be developed by conventional economic standards, it certainly has the GNI levels (and huge cash reserves) to provide the same level of material security for its poor as most developed countries. But a far greater percentage of Singaporeans are living in poverty than would be tolerated in the West.

However, most of the poor have housing with 75 per cent of the bottom 20 per cent being "home-owners," contends the Government.[32] The remainder are probably renting HDB apartments at nominal rents of about S$20 or so a month under the state's Rental and Utilities Assistance Scheme.

Moreover, among the bottom 20 per cent, 95 per cent owned a colour TV, 90 per cent had telephones and 77 per cent owned washing machines.[33] Even the poor are modest participants in Singapore's consumerist dream, though many household items may have been donated by family members or kind-hearted neighbours. Despite this, about 25 per cent of Singapore's households struggle to acquire sufficient income to pay for food and other basic necessities. Although shelter is critical for survival, you can't eat bricks as poor Singaporeans say. The same goes for whitegoods, even though they make life easier and TV may distract people from their plight.

The poor in Western countries also have access to low-rent housing and most also possess such basic consumer-durables as TVs and phones, and they are still classed as living in poverty when their income is less than half the per capita median for their countries. Cheap rent and the mere possession of some whitegoods does not mean they are not living in poverty, as defined by the standards of modern industrial societies – of which Singapore is one. By these standards, based on such measures as the half-median income method, around 25 per cent of Singaporean households are impoverished.

Singapore's poverty rate has only declined marginally since the 1950s to about 25 per cent – by modern benchmarks. These are the standards by which Singaporean poverty should be judged, because Singapore is a modern affluent society. The only real difference to Singapore's poverty is that it has been relocated into small cramped HDB units. Otherwise, poverty in Singapore today is nearly as extensive as it was in the early 1980s, in the 1970s, in the late 1960s and in the mid-1950s. Singapore's poverty is nearly three times what the PAP state will admit to: so how well are the bottom 25 per cent doing, in a society that offers itself as a model for dealing with poverty?

2. PAP-Style Welfare

In November 2001, Trade and Industry Minister BG George Yeo, lauded the Government's welfare policies:

> *Singapore as a society looks after its bottom 10 per cent better than most cities in the world.*[34]

Ignoring for the moment that perhaps it is Singapore's bottom 25 per cent that should be looked after, how is Singapore's bottom 10 per cent (about 320,000 people out of Singapore's 3.2 million citizens) being cared for? Better than most cities in the world? Answering these questions requires a look at PAP welfare philosophies.

Phobic Philistines

The PAP's welfare phobias find greatest expression when addressing the poverty problem. Like PAP policies on nearly everything, they stem from the private and often obsessive world-views of Lee Kuan Yew.

The first sign of Lee's opposition to the welfare state occurred on his taking power in 1959 when the new PAP Government banned free medicine. "We knew that free medicine was wasteful," recalled Lee in 1993.[35] Regular trips to Hong Kong from the 1960s apparently strengthened Lee's anti-welfare convictions. He visited the colony "to understand why Hong Kong people work with so much more drive and vigour than the people in Singapore". He concluded that "state welfare and subsidies blunted the individual's drive to succeed....I resolved to reverse course on the welfare policies which my party had inherited or copied from the British Labour Party policies".[36]

Lee's deputy Goh Keng Swee came to share Lee's anti-welfarist views. From 1966 he said that the welfare state was more appropriate "in an affluent society but largely irrelevant to a nation struggling to escape age-old poverty".[37] In 1976, Goh scathingly attacked the excesses of some West European welfare systems which, he said, were so generous that they left some workers better off unemployed.[38]

Then in 1984 came Senior Minister Rajaratnam's sentiments.

We want to teach people the government is not a rich uncle. You get what you pay for. We are moving in the direction of making people pay for everything...we want to disabuse people of the notion that in a good society the rich must pay for the poor.[39]

Helping the poor and unemployed contradicts the PAP state's anti-welfare views. It rejects the Western democratic view that every citizen is entitled to at least a minimum level of material security. The PAP state stresses self-reliance and individual responsibility. Families should look after their dependent or elderly members, not the state. Tamney, a US sociologist and former NUS lecturer, described the Singapore Government's welfare philosophy:

As the Government understands the situation, welfarism is bad because the money spent to provide social security could be more productively used. Moreover, welfare programs undermine the work ethic. In addition civil society is weakened when citizens no longer take responsibility for each other and instead assume the state will bear the burden of being compassionate.[40]

By contrast, the ILO sees social security as "the protection which society provides for its members ... against the economic and social distress that otherwise would be caused by the stoppage or substantial reduction of earnings resulting from sickness, maternity, employment injury, unemployment, invalidity, old age and death".[41] Singapore's rulers think otherwise. Charitable bodies should plug the gap between income and basic needs for Singapore's poor, according to the PAP Government. This builds self-reliance and creates a sense of community. Promoting such attitudes certainly cuts the state's welfare bill. While the Government funds 90 per cent of capital expenditure and 50 per cent of recurrent expenditure for projects by social service agencies, its social welfare spending is a small fraction of that of modern states.[42]

During Singapore's periodic economic downturns since the 1997/8 Asian economic crisis, Lee and his team have rejected calls for any of the country's huge cash reserves to be used to help the unemployed and poor. As already noted, such "a sentimental approach" was a "sure way to ruin Singapore," according to Lee.[43]

The low priority that Singapore and the PAP state gives to helping the poor is reflected in how social welfare workers are treated in Singapore. Despite having university qualifications they suffer from low pay and status. They usually get 25-30 per cent less than graduates in other fields such as marketing and public relations. *The Straits Times* interviewed 15 Singapore social workers past and present and 12 of these believed Singaporeans thought poorly of them.[44] One interviewee quit her job to become a PR operative because she felt that even her own family looked down on her. She remembers how, during a family gathering, a relative told her, "If you had wanted to become a social worker, you should not have wasted your parents' money by going to university".[45] Such Singaporean attitudes allow the Government to pursue minimalist welfare policies.

Dickensian Charity

Sanctimonious mean-mindedness characterises PAP attitudes to the poor. They are reminiscent of those displayed by the Beadle towards young Oliver in Charles Dickens' *Oliver Twist* in the "more gruel" scene. The PAP labels recipients of state aid as "underachievers", the implication being that they are responsible for their plight. In Singapore, Rahim described the poor as being,

> *stereotypically perceived as those who are physically or mentally handicapped, widowed, the aged who have no relatives to care for them, and culturally marred or social deviants who are able-bodied but refuse to extricate themselves from poverty...*
>
> *Little if any recognition is accorded to the possibility that ...there may be an institutional or structural basis which contributes to and helps perpetuate poverty.*[46]

The two main public schemes devised to help Singapore's poor are the Public Assistance (PA) scheme and the Citizens Consultative Committee Assistance Scheme (CCCAS). Only the absolutely destitute, because of chronic illness, disability or vagrancy, are entitled to PA – and how pitifully small the PA is!

Single adults get S$260 a month while a family of four receives S$825.[47] The single rate was 8 per cent of the average per capita GNI in 2005 and the family rate was 6 per cent of the per capita GNI for a family of four. By comparison, equivalent payments in OECD countries was 29 per cent of per capita GNI.[48]

The PA is consistently below the Minimum Household Expenditure (MHE), which is the poverty line as defined by the Ministry of Community Development (MCD). The MHE is set at about 25 per cent below the MCD's poverty line.[49] But at S$260 a month, the PA falls well short of the S$400 plus that an individual would need to just survive in present-day Singapore.

Whether or not the PA is sufficient to survive on is largely academic, because very few impoverished Singaporeans ever receive it. The scheme's stringent criteria ensure that. In September 1996, the MCD revealed that 1958 people were receiving PA, of whom 86.8 per cent were elderly, 5 per cent were handicapped and disabled, 5.5 per cent were medically unfit for work and 2.9 per cent were distressed wives or orphans.[50] The 1958 PA recipients were the 27 per cent successful applicants who had only received PA after being subjected to the most humiliating scrutiny by PA authorities to assess their eligibility. The loss of face that Singaporeans would experience at such times can only be imagined.

An examination of PA figures produces some bleak conclusions. First, only 6880, a tiny fraction of the 320,000 comprising Singapore's poorest 10 per cent in 1996 – the only poor the Government would acknowledge – actually applied for the miserable PA pittance. Only 1958, less than a third of these wretched few, got it.

Second, the situation would have been even worse if the 6880 applicants had all came from the poorest 100,000 Singaporeans (we're at destitution level now). If they had, then only 1.958 per cent of these (1958 of Singapore's poorest 100,000!) would have got PA in 1996. This was in a country with a GNI of over S$3000 a month in 1996, when cabinet ministers were being paid over S$600,000 and the Prime Minister was raking in S$1 million a year, and when total cash reserves were about S$140 billion. Almost a decade later the same obscene disparities still existed. In 2005, 2772 people were receiving public assistance, 86 per cent of whom were either old or destitute.[51] Mukul and Nandy commented that:

> *"Fewer than 5 per cent of households in the low-income groups are beneficiaries of state-funded systems. The amount of assistance is deliberately kept extremely low, at around 5-8 per cent of per capita income."*

When confronted with the PA's total inadequacy, the Government has tried to put a positive spin on it. While admitting, in 1996, that the lowness of the then S$185 PA was a common complaint, MCD permanent secretary Er Kwong Wah, brightly noted that the payment was only part of a "total package" received by recipients.[52] They also got food rations, supplementary financial assistance and help to pay medical fees, lifting the actual PA to about S$280 a month. These "extras" included government help with medical fees (S$15) and HDB flat rebates (S$12). In addition, food rations ($20), supplementary assistance (S$30), free meals and gifts etc ($20) were provided by various community groups. This pitiful rag bag of extras was the "total package" of S$280 received by 1958 successful PA recipients in 1996, and even then would probably have been below the 1996 equivalent of the S$350 plus needed in 2000 to subsist in Singapore.

But as noted, discussions of the PA's adequacy are mostly academic because so few impoverished Singaporeans receive it. Those denied PA are referred to other welfare agencies by the MCD, according to Mr Er. But they too often provide little help to the needy. While the PA has at least helped a couple of thousand poor, the same cannot be said for such bodies as the CCCAS. In January 2003, it was found that the scheme had helped only two people out of 14,161 needy people who had sought assistance.[53] One had received a payment of S$105 and the other $72!

Other public assistance agencies include the Community Development Councils (CDC) which provide needy families with short-term relief of about S$200 a month.[54] Equivalent amounts are provided by ethnic-based community organisations to destitute members of their own communities. By 1995, there were about 160 Voluntary Welfare Organisations (VWOs) and 50 charities in Singapore trying to help over 144,000 poor, sick, aged and handicapped.[55] Although this indicates there are many good-hearted Singaporeans striving to assist the underprivileged, the presence of so many VWOs is also used by the Government to justify its minimalist welfare policies. The Government invokes the "many helping hands" idea for tackling social problems. The purported aim is to help in ways that do not breed dependency or weaken the motivation to work. Self-reliance is encouraged; and when the underprivileged cannot help themselves, the family and community should fill the gap, claims the Government.

To avoid the financial burden of looking after the underprivileged the Government has largely delegated their care to the VWOs: hence the Government's minimalist welfare budget. In 1995, S$119.5 million was spent helping individuals and families in need.[56] A further S$70.2 million was given to needy families for education in the form of bursaries, tuition and grants, remission of fees, pocket allowance and scholarships. Another S$73.3 million went to providing social services for the disabled, children, youth and the elderly. Total government welfare expenditure for 1995 was S$263 million, or 0.015 per cent of the Government's total expenditure of S$15.555 billion in that year.[57] By contrast, Western countries spend five per cent or more of their budgets on welfare.

The PAP state cites such figures to prove its welfare policies are superior. After all, they "save" so much money that would otherwise be "wasted" on "unproductive" people. Clearly its "many hands" strategy which involves the community is better. But this strategy condemns three times more people to live in poverty than occurs in the "welfare democracies". While the latters' poverty rate is about 8-12 per cent, Singapore's is around 25 per cent. This has been especially so since the 1997/8 and 2002/3 recessions, despite Singapore's per capita GDP being equal to or higher than that of most Western countries.

But Fewer Homeless

While Singapore's poverty may be more widespread than in most Western countries, it is less extreme in one key way.

First, Singapore has far fewer homeless than in the West. Although the city-state, with an indigenous population of 3.2 million, seems to have several hundred homeless people at any one time, Western cities of the same size often have thousands. Moreover, most of Singapore's homeless appear to be older men, while in Western cities many of the homeless are children as well as the elderly. One sees few homeless children in Singapore. In many large Western cities, including those in Australia, thousands of children sleep in the streets every night. Such a situation is an appalling indictment of any society, especially an affluent one.

In this way most Western countries are well behind Singapore. There are several reasons for this. The first would be the pervasiveness of Singapore's HDB scheme. While HDB units are excessively expensive for the average Singaporean, there are enough of them to house anyone who needs accommodation. Even the poorest can have an HDB flat at a nominal monthly rental. Few developed countries, including Australia, can provide such comprehensive accommodation for the destitute. In the West, housing for them is patchy at best and often insufficient to shelter many such people. For them, the streets are the only option.

Second, a higher degree of family breakdown occurs in Western societies than Asian countries, including Singapore. In the West, children from broken homes, especially those in conflict with or being abused by step parents, are most likely to leave home. But in Singapore, despite the onslaught of Westernisation, the family unit is much stronger and more extensive. Fewer marriage break-ups mean far more families stay intact. Should parents separate, there are usually relatives who can care for any unwanted children. Strong family bonds in such countries as Singapore also mean that more elderly are looked after by their families, resulting in fewer living alone or sometimes homeless, if poor and dysfunctional.

Vigorous anti-vagrant measures by the Singaporean authorities also minimise homeless numbers. Every month MCD officers conduct raids looking for vagrants, especially elderly men, many of whom have held odd jobs most of their lives and often beg on the streets.[58] They are sent to one of Singapore's six welfare homes if the MCD cannot re-unite them with their families. About 300 people sleep nightly in the streets of Singapore and in 2002 authorities rounded up 287 such destitute people.[59]

Nonetheless, there is a particularly tragic component to Singapore's destitute – its homeless AIDS victims. They sleep in parks, at bus-stops, on the beach, or even in cemeteries. In December 1997, one AFA volunteer estimated that Singapore had about 100 homeless HIV and AIDS victims.[60] In December 2000, the Communicable Diseases Centre (CDC) reported seeing 10 homeless AIDS victims a year.[61]

Often homeless AIDS sufferers have been forced to leave home by their families, sometimes in the cruellest of circumstances. One such victim was a Mr Chan, aged 28. After he was diagnosed with HIV, his parents became suspicious when his girlfriend of five years dumped him. When they questioned him he told them the truth, and they told him to leave:

I asked them to let me stay, but they refused. There was frequent quarrelling and sometimes the police had to be called in.[62]

In the end, his family threw him out. His mother's parting shot was, "You cannot stay here because your sister and brother have young children and you may infect them. Go and solve your own problems". With these words ringing in his ears, Mr Chan left home. He slept wherever he could "find a place to rest my head and shut my eyes for a few moments". He earned a few hundred dollars a month doing odd jobs, but he could not afford medication and renting a room was impossible.

Anti-AIDS prejudice has been so great that AIDS groups such as AFA have struggled to find accommodation for people with AIDS (PWAs). In December 2000, there was no provision for such people at hospices, homes for drug addicts or the destitute or hospitals.[63] Only the CDC could accommodate them in its 25-bed centre.

Attempts to lodge PWAs elsewhere have had little success. Accommodation is difficult to find for AIDS victims because of anti-AIDS prejudice, even when money is available to rent rooms for them. One AIDS group had collected S$20,000 in donations to held AIDS victims but little of the money had been used by December 2003, despite having been collected in 2000. "The money should have been used by now, but no one wants to rent flats or rooms to HIV/AIDS patients," said a spokeswoman for the Patient Care Centre (Homeless) Fund. A Catholic nun remarked:

> AIDS is still taboo here. Many housing agents say home owners do not want to rent their flats to people with AIDS as they fear it will bring them bad luck.[64]

Government departments have often been less than helpful in accommodating PWAs. The MCD said that PWAs would only be accepted for communal living in ministry accommodation provided they were medically certified. But the MCD refused to clarify what "medically certified" meant. It said that PWAs could be admitted to MCD homes for the destitute "as long as they did not require nursing care".

Two half-way houses for drug addicts have accommodated PWAs, if not always knowingly. One half-way house initially admitted PWAs because they were thought to be drug addicts, only later discovering they were PWAs. Meanwhile, a hospice accepted 40 AIDS patients, but faced financial problems caring for them. The hospice had been trying to raise funds for the patients. "From a humanitarian point of view, it is correct for us to accept PWAs but the long-term nursing cost is prohibitive," a hospice spokesman said. Another problem for the hospice was the attitude of non-PWA residents there: "other patients still have a mindset against people with AIDS and might not be ready to have contact with them".[65]

Another AIDS group, The Cyrenes, have encountered similar bureaucratic and community indifference. Formed in January 1998, they tried for three years to find places for homeless PWAs to live out their last days.[66] By January 2001, they had written to government ministries, religious organisations, hospitals and half-way houses for drug addicts seeking accommodation for PWAs. They merely wanted an unused ward or school which they could convert into a home; but their requests were rejected. They even advertised in *The Straits Times*. About five people responded, but once they realised the accommodation would be for PWAs their interest evaporated. When visiting the PWAs, the Cyrenes would groom them, cut their nails and buy them meals. A Cyrenes spokeswoman said they would pay for food and shelter for homeless PWAs, themselves if necessary.

The Cyrenes saga epitomises the cruel paradoxes of Singapore's AIDS problem. Compassionate Singaporeans struggle with limited resources to help homeless PWAs in the face of callous government policies, bureaucratic indifference and cruel communitarian prejudice.

The tragic case of Mr T further illustrates this poignant dichotomy. Mr T (42) was a homeless PWA, living out his final days in the corner of a disused shopping centre, sleeping on a mat. He had no job, no home and no family to turn to. When *The Straits Times* publicised his plight, public sympathy was stirred so much that S$8000 was sent to the paper to help him.[67] One reader, a 58-year-old woman, offered him the spare room in her flat. Another reader offered him S$50 a week for his upkeep. Following the publicity he had to move from his disused building site to "avoid trouble". Also, his possessions were stolen. Soon after he found accommodation at the CDC where he died two weeks later. His death was not completely in vain: the publicity prompted the MOH to state that such public institutions as hospices, nursing homes and community hospitals could take in PWAs and receive the same subsidies for them as for other patients.

The Mr T case revealed the plight of PWAs in Singapore despite the readiness of some caring Singaporeans to fight for them and other underprivileged people. It also revealed a level of inhumane indifference to PWAs that would not be tolerated in most Western societies where those with AIDS are properly cared for. They are certainly not left to die in the streets if they seek accommodation.

Public Pressure

Many Singaporeans see their government as not only authoritarian and undemocratic but cruel and uncaring. Such perceptions can be inconvenient at election times when it can cost votes. The PAP is obsessed with winning crushing victories over Singapore's puny and miniscule opposition parties. Anything less than 60 per cent of the vote is seen as seriously questioning its policies and legitimacy to rule. Overwhelming endorsement for PAP policies is expected. Unfortunately for the PAP, the poor also vote. Indeed, because of compulsory voting, they must. Unfortunately too for the PAP, most Singaporeans think the state should care for the poor. A 1995 survey of 538 Singaporeans found that 87 per cent thought the Government should care for the poor while 56 per cent believed the Government had not done enough to help this group.[68]

The PAP "wants to be seen as compassionate at the very time it wants to minimize welfare costs," remarks Tamney.[69] It wants the kudos of compassion without paying the price. During election times especially, the PAP must appear to be caring and concerned to mollify the more humanitarian members of Singapore's middle classes as well as the voting poor. Both groups can cut the PAP vote. After the 1991 elections, the Government's miniscule welfare expenditure was increased to help the poor even though it clashed with "the PAP government's idea of welfare provisions as 'privileges' doled out at the discretion of a paternalistic government that expects gratitude from the citizenry," notes NUS sociologist Liew Kim Siong.[70]

However, the Government has made some meaningful efforts to help the underprivileged. While seeking to avoid "subsidising consumption" through charity to the poor, the Government has moved to provide assistance in education, healthcare and housing on the grounds that this would promote economic growth. Hoping to win over the lower classes was another likely motive.

Education bursaries for poorer students were introduced in January 1993 under the Education Endowment (Edusave) scheme. Students aged 6 to 16 were given an Edusave account to pay for education expenses, including school-based enrichment programs.[71] By 2004, primary school students were receiving S$170 and secondary students S$200 a year. Meanwhile, in 1995 the Edusave Merit Bursaries (EMB) were introduced to help the top 25 per cent of students who came from families with incomes of less than S$3000 a month. The aim was to assist bright but less well off students. A Constituency Top-up Bursary Scheme was established in 1995 for "poor but hardworking students" who were not among the top 20 per cent in school.[72]

In 1993, budget flats, which were smaller and cheaper than standard apartments, began to be made available and in 1994 the Government started buying old HDB flats and selling them at heavily discounted prices to families whose monthly income was below S$1000.[73] Units bought for S$80,000 to S$110,000 were resold for S$30,000 to S$40,000. The units were to be paid for out of the CPF savings of the buyers. During the first year of the program's operation 4000 families were assisted. It represented one of the most substantial government efforts to help the poor. The program's introduction was the result of public pressure for more help for the underprivileged.

However, it will take many more programs than these, and a far greater commitment to helping the poor, before Singapore's poverty levels drop below 25 per cent to those that prevail in most Western countries.Until then its poverty levels will be three times those in the West, while its aid to the poor and disadvantaged will remain pitiful by comparison.

References

1. Chee, Soon Juan: *Your Future, My Faith, Our Freedom* (Singapore, Open Singapore Centre, 2001), p. 194.

2. Clammer, John: "Peripheral Capitalism and Urban Order: 'Informal Sector' Theories in the Light of Singapore's Experience", pp. 192 and 196 in *Beyond the New Anthropology,* edited by John Clammer (London, MacMillan Press, 1987).

3. Ibid, p. 192.

4. Buchanan, Iain: *Singapore in Southeast Asia* (London, Bell and Sons, 1972), p. 229.

5. Ibid, p. 228.

6. Pugh, Cedric: "The Political Economy of Public Housing", p. 849 in *Management of Success: The Moulding of Modern Singapore,* edited by Kernial Singh Sandhu and Paul Wheatley (Singapore, Institute of

Southeast Asian Studies, 1989).

7. Ibid, pp. 850-1.

8. Clammer, p. 193.

9. Ibid, p. 195.

10. Bello, Walden and Stephanie Rosenfeld: *Dragons in Distress: Asian Miracle Economies in Crisis* (London, Penguin, 1990), p. 331.

11. Pugh, pp. 845-6.

12. Lee, Kuan Yew: *From Third World to First* (Singapore, Times Media, 2000), p. 120.

13. Ibid, p. 207.

14. Sai, Siew Min and Huang Jianli, "The 'Chinese-educated' political vanguards: Ong Pang Boon, Lee Khoon Choy and Jek Yeun Thong", pp. 165-6 in *Lee's Lieutenants,* edited by Lam Peng Er and Kevin Y. L. Tan (Sydney, Allen and Unwin, 1999).

15. Selvan, T. S.: *Singapore: The Ultimate Island* (Melbourne, Freeway Books, 1990), p. 222.

16. Ibid.

17. Chua, Beng Huat: *Communitarian Ideology and Democracy in Singapore* (London, Routledge, 1995), p. 206.

18. Tay, Simon, "The Coming Crisis: Domestic Politics in Singapore in and from 2001", p. 10 in *2002 Perspectives on Singapore,* edited by Chang Li Lin (Singapore, Times Academic Press, 2002). This quotation is from Prime Minister Goh Chok Tong's 2000 National Day Rally Speech.

19. *UN Human Development Report 2007/8,* p. 241.

20. *Australia Fair News,* October 23, 2007, www.australiafair.org.au

21. *Census QuickStats 2006* (Australian Bureau of Statistics, Canberra), p. 3.

22. Ibid.

23. *Report on Labour Force in Singapore 2006* (Manpower Research and Statistics Department, Ministry of Manpower, Republic of Singapore).

24. *Key Household Income Trends (KHIT) 2007* (Singapore Department of Statistics, February 2008).

25. Ibid.

26. Ibid, p. 1.

27. *Household Expenditure Survey 2002/3,* (Department of Statistics, Singapore) p. 18.

28. *World Development Report 2008,* (the World Bank and Oxford University Press), p. 334.

29. *Report on Household Expenditure Survey 2002/3,* p. 56.

30. ST, June 5, 2000.

31. ST, June 30, 2000.

32. Ibid.

33. Ibid.

34. ST, November 26, 2001.

35. Barr, Michael D.: "Lee Kuan Yew's Fabian Phase", *Australian Journal of Politics and History,* March 2000, 46, 1, p. 112.

36. Ibid.

37. Ibid, p. 113.

38. Ibid.

39. Tremewan, Christopher: *The Political Economy of Social Control in Singapore* (New York, St Martin's Press, 1994), p. 121.

40. Tamney, Joseph B.: *The Struggle for Singapore's Soul* (Berlin, Walter de Gruyter, 1995), p. 90.

41. Ibid.

42. ST, June 30, 2000.

43. ST, January 15, 2001.

44. ST, December 11, 1995.

45. Ibid.

46. Rahim, Lily: *The Singapore Dilemma* (Kuala Lumpur, Oxford University Press, 1998), pp. 40-41.

47. Ramesh, M. "Singapore's Multi-Pillar System of Social Security" KDI-World Bank Conference, Seoul, December 2006), p. 9.

48. Ibid.

49. ST, March 25, 1988.

50. ST, September 5, 1996.

51. Asher G. Mukul and Amarendu Nandy "Singapore's policy responses to ageing, inequality and poverty: An assessment" p.52 in *International Social Security Review,* Vol. 61, 1/2008.

52. ST, September 5, 1996.

53. ST, March 1, 2003.

54. ST, August 10, 2001.

55. ST, March 11, 1995.
56. ST, September 5, 1996.
57. *Economic Survey of Singapore 1995* (Ministry of Trade and Industry, Republic of Singapore), p. 30.
58. ST, February 5, 2001.
59. *Streats*, July 25, 2003.
60. ST, December 20, 1997.
61. ST, December 1, 2000.
62. ST, December 20, 1997.
63. ST, December 1, 2000.
64. ST, December 30, 2003.
65. Ibid.
66. ST, January 8, 2001.
67. ST, December 31, 2000.
68. ST, December 30, 1995.
69. Tamney, p. 90.
70. Liew Kim Siong, "Welfarism and an affluent Singapore", p. 54 in *Debating Singapore*, edited by Derek Da Cunha (Singapore, Institute of Southeast Asian Studies 1994).
71. Mukhopadhaya, Pundarik and Bhanoji Rao, "Income inequality", p. 104 in *Singapore Economy in the 21st Century* edited by Koh Ai Tee et al (Singapore, McGraw Hill, 2002).
72. Rahim, p. 143.
73. ST, March 1, 1995.

CHAPTER 26

MEAN AND TRICKY

M any Singaporeans realise they are much less affluent than PAP government statistics claim. Surveys conducted from 1990 to 1995 revealed that 50 per cent of Singaporeans believed their lives had not improved.[1] These surveys were done after decades of rapid growth and before Singapore was hit by the recessions of 1997/8 and 2002/3. Their chagrin is understandable considering the high cost of living, over-priced HDBs without freehold ownership, the CPF's failure to provide adequate retirement incomes and inadequate health insurance schemes.

It is also not surprising that Singapore was ranked 28th on the UN's human resource development index in 1998, placing it behind much poorer countries like Barbados and Malta. Despite the PAP hype, many Singaporeans appear to have missed the good life. Their gains from the Singapore Miracle have been relatively modest despite the country's high per capita income. The PAP Government's "nation-building" policies are the root cause.

1. Policies before People

The PAP state has pursued a range of economic and development strategies to ensure Singapore's survival and growth. A key one has been attracting and retaining foreign capital; a second has been balancing budgets and developing huge financial reserves to fund national development and provide a safety net during economic downturns.

The Government has always practised tight wage policies to please foreign capital: it has also minimised state expenditure and maximised revenue extraction to protect and increase the national reserves. But the cost of these policies has usually been paid by ordinary Singaporeans, as the following shows.

Pleasing the MNCs

For decades, the PAP Government has held down wages and more recently cut employers' CPF contributions to please the MNCs. The unions have also been brought under state control to prevent the workforce opposing such measures. Although these moves may have helped local businesses, they have been primarily designed to benefit MNCs, who must be kept in Singapore at all costs.

The 2003 recession strikingly revealed the Government's readiness to sacrifice workers' interests rather than government reserves to meet MNC demands. The Government decided that workers' wages must not only be held down but actually cut to prevent Singapore becoming "uncompetitive" for foreign capital. Employers' CPF contributions for their employees were reduced from 16 per cent to 13 per cent. The Government justified this by claiming that wages (which include employers' CPF payments) made up 40 per cent of business costs in Singapore. Wages were too high and had to be cut to retain the MNCs.

To support claims that Singapore workers were overpaid, misleading PERC statistics were cited by PAP minister Tony Tan. Normally one of the more reasonable PAP ministers, Tan quoted a PERC global study which claimed Singapore's workers were more expensive than those in the US and Australia as well as in eight other developing countries surveyed.[2] On a zero to ten labour cost scale, Singapore was ranked 5.5 compared to 5.07 for the US and 4.8 for Australia, claimed PERC. This was an "alarming" situation, blustered Tan:

> To me this is a profoundly important statistic. It's a simple one but it gets to the nub of the problem. We have priced our labour out of the market.[3]

Excessive wages rather than such "transitory factors" as the SARS crisis had caused the increased retrenchments in Singapore. PERC had crystallised the problem, he claimed. It was a structural one: high wages costs. Cutting wages would keep companies viable and save jobs. "We have no choice but to reduce our CPF rates substantially and quickly if we want to save jobs," Tan lectured. And this came from a cabinet minister on about S$800,000 a year. He was echoing similar calls made by Prime Minister Goh and Deputy Prime Minister Lee Hsien Loong. Hypocritical posturing aside, their claims were based on dubious PERC statistics and questionable assumptions that CPF cuts would save jobs.

A mountain of evidence refutes PERC's absurd assertions that Singaporean workers are better paid than those in the US and Australia. Even such pro-Singapore bodies as the IMD and WEF have demonstrated that pay rates for Singapore's manufacturing workers lag well behind those of other industrialised countries. For example, the basic adult wage in Australia is about S$2500 a month for unskilled workers. In Singapore, factory production workers are paid about S$800 to S$1000 a month, while wages can be as low as S$600 a month for cleaners and road sweepers.

Government claims that the CPF cuts would save jobs were as dubious as PERC's wage levels "findings". In September 2003, a survey of 200 Singapore employers revealed that most did not think the cuts would boost the job market.[4] Eight of 10 companies said it would not help them save jobs and nine out of ten said they would not hire in future. These findings did not surprise local human resource analysts, who said that the CPF cut was never intended to make companies recruit more employees. Rather, it was an important signal to foreign investors that Singapore was serious about boosting its competitive edge. This was the real reason for the CPF cuts. Government claims that Singapore wages were too high and that cutting them would create more jobs merely obscured the measure's pro-MNC purpose.[5]

Local representatives of foreign capital happily endorsed the CPF cuts, including Singapore's International Chamber of Commerce executive director, Phillip Overmyer. He thought the Government was "right on track" in identifying the problem of high local wages:

> *Over recent years, Singapore has become uncompetitive for a number of reasons. Wages and CPF are a very significant part of that.*[6]

To further please the corporate, especially MNC, sectors the Government reduced income tax. In 2002, Singapore's corporate tax was cut from 24.5 to 22 per cent while the top personal tax rate came down from 26 to 22 per cent. Moreover, by February 2005, MNCs that were given pioneer status by the Government could enjoy tax exemptions for 15 instead of ten years;[7] and when an MNC was viewed as a "development and expansion company" it could gain immediate tax relief for up to 20 years. In 2008, Singapore cut its corporate tax rate to 18 per cent.

Corporate tax cuts and tax exemptions aimed to attract and keep MNCs in Singapore, the Government claimed. Similarly, reducing the top personal tax rate sought to retain local talent and attract foreign talent.[8] The tax cuts were made despite shortfalls in the budget caused by the recession.

To help cover the shortfalls, the GST was raised in January 2003 from 3 to 4 per cent, and then to 5 per cent in January 2004. Again in July 2007 the GST was raised to 7 per cent to cover the latest corporate tax cut. NUS economist Mukul Asher noted that:

> *The official rationale for the GST is that its implementation permits reduction in income and property tax rates, thereby maintaining the international competitiveness of Singapore's tax system.*[9]

In other words, the GST was introduced to help pay for the tax cuts. Pressure to do this was strong during the 2002/3 economic downturn, when Singapore's economy was hit by falls in tourism numbers due to terrorism and SARS. Because of the slowing economy, revenue plunged by about 20 per cent in 2002 from 2001. This represented a revenue loss of about S$5 billion and contributed to 2002's S$2.3 billion budget deficit.[10]

The GST increases were badly timed for Singaporeans. The CPF had already been cut, and some workers had also experienced wage cuts, including SIA staff. Despite having about S$160 billion in financial reserves at the time, the Government pressed ahead with the GST increases to help cover the revenue shortfall. The GST would be raised to help make up for reserve shortfalls resulting from tax cuts that mainly benefited MNCs and highly paid foreigners. As always, the GST increases hit average and lower income earners the hardest.

Minimising Expenditure

The fiscal conservatism of Singapore's rulers is legendary. They are obsessed with budget surpluses and protecting the financial reserves whatever the cost to ordinary Singaporeans.

From 1985-99, Singapore experienced a budget deficit only three times: in 1986, 1987 and 1998 (all recession years). In many years, the overall budget surplus was sizeable, exceeding 10 per cent of GDP a year in seven consecutive years between 1989 and 1996.[11] In 2000, the budget was again in surplus with S$3.98 billion, though in 2001, 2002 and 2003 there were official budget deficits of S$2.7 billion, S$90 million and S$2.3 billion respectively.[12] These are official budget figures. Singapore's budget surpluses have actually been much larger, contends Asher. In fact its budget deficits may never have existed.

Official budgets exclude land revenues, investment income and profits from off-budget state bodies, Asher argues. For example, the Government received up to S$18 billion a year from land sales during the 1990s property boom.[13] Asher calculates that the average budget surplus for 1991-2001 was 9.7 per cent of GDP, not 3.6 per cent.[14] According to the IMF, Singapore actually had a surplus of S$7.9 billion, not the S$2.7 billion deficit claimed by the Government in 2001.[15] Clearly, publicly disclosed revenues understate real surpluses. It would seem the PAP Government was engaging in statistical disinformation.

A major aim of budget surpluses is to protect the sacrosanct financial reserves. Officially the reserves are there to provide a cushion in adverse times and generate a steady stream of overseas income for Singapore. The Republic's official foreign reserves in 2002 were S$160.9 billion. With an estimated 5 per cent return they would have been yielding about S$8 billion a year.[16] High reserves prevent the Singapore dollar from depreciating. As the MOF's budget director, Pek Beng Choon, declared in March 2000:

> We need large reserves to defend the Singapore dollar and be prepared for future downturns which may be even more severe than those of 1985/6 and 1998/9.[17]

A strong dollar also reduces the cost of imports. This not only keeps down living costs for Singaporeans but reduces the MNCs' import bill. MNCs must import large volumes of components for the goods they manufacture.

Moreover, cheaper imports from a strong dollar help reduce the cost of living. In this way at least, Singaporeans benefit from huge reserves. But such gains are heavily outweighed by the price the Government extracts from them to maintain the reserves.

Periodically some politicians plead with the Government to release some of the reserves to help less fortunate Singaporeans. But as shown, PAP leaders scornfully reject such appeals. The reserves must only be used for dire emergencies. Any reductions in government revenue that could reduce the reserves, such as those caused by tax cuts for the MNCs and wealthy (often foreign) income taxpayers, must also be met by ordinary Singaporeans. The tiniest portion of the reserves must be denied to impoverished

Singaporeans. They don't count in the PAP's grand scheme of things – not even AIDS victims, nor those requiring life-saving kidney dialysis. The Government's main aim is always to maximise revenue extraction and minimise expenditure. Over the decades the Government has devised a whole raft of measures to not only minimise expenditure but to maximise revenue.

Maximum Extraction

For jaded Singaporeans, PAP stands for the Pay And Pay party, a name that reflects the widespread resentment of the endless taxes, fees and charges the PAP state constantly levies on Singaporeans.[18]

Maximum extraction is the prime feature of PAP fiscal policies, whatever they might cost the people. Their ostensible aim has been to produce budget surpluses and build up the nation's reserves for adverse times. As well as endless imposts, the Government has zealously sought to maximise revenue from sales of land it has requisitioned and from HDB units, despite the inflationary effect this has on housing costs.

Land scarcity can be used to explain Singapore's high HDB and property prices generally. Land prices will invariably be high on a small, highly urbanised built-up island like Singapore, as they are in similar places like Hong Kong. The difference is that in Singapore the state has cornered the land market. Because the state owns 90 per cent of Singapore's land it has the power to control land prices almost totally. It has chosen to do this in ways that maximise the state's return no matter what burden this places on business and the people.

Though the Government acquired much of Singapore's land cheaply and through compulsory acquisition, it has since allowed market forces to dictate land values. This has ensured the state gets top dollar for whatever land it chooses to sell. In fact, the Government has been accused of "turning the property market into a property casino by acquiring land at low cost and auctioning it at very high prices," noted *Streats* columnist Conrad Raj.[19] Requisitioned land acquired at low, sometimes nominal, cost has been resold at high prices to Singaporeans for huge profits. As the former managing director of the MAS, Mr Wong Pakshong, remarks,

> *The government is the largest landowner. Apart from acquiring properties cheap, where they [sic] get a real windfall, the government owns the largest proportion of land in Singapore. All they [sic] have to do is put up a site and say, "99 years, please bid". Then people build on it.*[20]

The PAP Government "is a terrific moneymaking machine," especially when its profits from cheap land acquisitions are considered, he says. During the property boom until 1996, the Government's proceeds from land sales hit S$18 billion a year at the boom's peak.[21] The Government has got top dollar for state land not only from private property developers but from ordinary Singaporeans for HDB units. High prices for HDB units built on cheap land have meant big profits for the state. When criticised for this, the Government claims that the units' land-cost component is based on the land's market value. The "government factors in the 'cost' of the land which the buyers of the flats pay for. When 'costs' go up, flats become more expensive", a *Straits Times* columnist noted.[22] Were the land cost to be based on the prices the Government paid for the land, HDB units would be much cheaper.

The state's profit on HDB units is even greater when their low construction costs are considered. In Singapore, building costs account for 25 per cent of an apartment's cost and architects and engineers' fees 5 per cent, according to a Singapore construction firm boss, Jimmy Koh. The remaining 70 per cent pays for land and the builder's profit. [23]

Other figures have shown that a four to five-room apartment costs private developers about S$50,000 to build in Singapore[24] (to this could be added several thousand dollars for consulting and project management fees and pile-driving costs). With the price of four and five-room HDB units at S$200,000 to S$300,000, this means that the HDB is left with about S$150,000 to S$250,000 to pay for land. But land is auctioned to developers in Singapore at S$150 to S$250 psf. The land cost per unit would therefore be minimal in an average 500 to 1000-flat HDB development, even if the land was being purchased at market rates by HDB. But as shown, the Government has requisitioned land at well below market prices for decades, so that the land price component in each HDB unit is nominal, perhaps a couple of thousand dollars. Construction costs for HDB units are probably much less than S$50,000. Hundreds, sometimes thousands of HDB units are built at a time. This allows for enormous economies of scale, further reducing the units' cost.

Accurately estimating the cost of building an HDB unit is difficult. The Government has persistently refused to reveal its formula for computing the construction costs for HDB flats.[25] "How HDB flats are priced remains a murky area about which the HDB and National Development Ministry will say little," observed *Straits Times* columnist Lydia Lim.[26] Whenever questions are raised about HDB prices, the HDB claims that all new flats "enjoy a market subsidy", but it never reveals how large the subsidy is. During the November 2001 election campaign National Development Minister, Mr Mah Bow Tan, claimed that in 1999 and 2000 the HDB subsidies totalled more than S$800 million. There is no independent way of checking this because of the Government's lack of transparency.

The Government is clearly making huge profits out of HDB housing despite claims that it subsidises HDB flat prices. HDB units would be much cheaper if the Government adopted a less profit-driven policy towards public housing. Instead, the HDB scheme has been run like a business where market prices dictate unit cost. In most countries the state strives to make public housing as cheap as possible, often subsidising the price, but in Singapore public housing has become a cash cow for the state at the expense of the average citizen and has artificially inflated Singapore's property values. Housing will continue to consume a far greater share of Singaporeans' income than in comparable countries with similar per capita GDPs.

The low interest paid on CPF deposits – well below bank rates – has saved the Government billions more in interest payments. But by receiving such low interest payments on their CPF savings, while being overcharged for their HDB apartments, Singaporeans have less to retire on. Nonetheless, the Government always does OK. Such policies keep boosting its revenue and financial reserves.

Of the PAP's extractive policies, those pertaining to the HDB and CPF schemes have been most lucrative. Together they have provided the Government with scores of billions of cheap dollars over the decades to build up its reserves and finance the island's development in ways attractive to foreign capital as well as beneficial to the local economy.

The Government defends its revenue-extracting policies by claiming that over 70 per cent of Singaporeans don't pay income tax. But they must endure a heavy burden of government imposts including a wide range of indirect taxes and government charges. Over the decades the Government, through various departments and statutory bodies, has extracted revenue in numerous ways from Singaporeans. Having near total control of Parliament, the PAP can virtually do what it wants and impose whatever revenue-raising measures it likes.

Singaporeans must endure such heavy but disguised taxes as over-priced HDB units and very low interest payments on their CPF savings. Moreover, about 20 per cent of their wages and salaries are deducted for the CPF contributions that supposedly fund their retirement but are also used to pay for their flats and for very limited health coverage. By contrast, in the "welfare democracies" of the West, taxpayers are assured that they will all receive adequate social security and health-care when unemployed and in old age.

2. Mean and Tricky

Such terms readily come to mind when considering how the PAP rules. Its sustained and single-minded efforts to extract the last dollar from the people, especially through high HDB prices and vehicle and motoring imposts, demonstrate a degree of governmental greed that few Western democracies would dare practise. Moreover, its justifications for such avaricious policies are often as deceptive and tricky as its phony discounts on HDB units demonstrate. Its glib rationales deflect criticism of its crushing vehicle and motoring imposts. The Government's readiness to punish HDB estates that vote against the PAP also reveals this mentality, as shown below.

Reducing traffic congestion is the standard reason given for high vehicle imposts. This explanation is superficially plausible in land-scarce, densely populated Singapore. Not only does road space take up 12 per cent of land area, but also in 1998, 362,000 of the island's 683,000 vehicles were cars. Presumably by making cars more expensive, their owners will feel compelled to use public transport.

However, government rationales for high vehicle imposts and ERP fees are flimsy. The traffic congestion claim is most suspect when applied to taxis and commercial vehicles, especially those for small family-based enterprises. Should taxi fees not be cheaper to enable them to charge lower fares so that their use can be encouraged over private cars?. Despite such objections the Government continues to insist that taxis should be treated as private cars and pay the same COEs, not to mention other heavy imposts, including registration fees.

It is also difficult to justify heavy imposts on commercial and company vehicles. Although their COEs are only about one third of those for private vehicles, this still represents a heavy cost on business. Moreover, registration for company vehicles is five times that of private cars.

Often businesses need a certain number of vehicles to operate efficiently, and have little choice on this. How, for example, can businesses shift their goods without delivery vans? Must they use taxis or public transport to deliver furniture or refrigerators? While discouraging private car use is understandable, the same explanation cannot apply to businesses that need trucks, vans and cars and sometimes fleets of vehicles to operate effectively. MNCs can easily absorb high vehicle costs but not many SMEs are as fortunate.

Reducing traffic congestion is clearly second to maximising government revenue from vehicle ownership and use. Vehicle taxes, excluding COEs and licence fees, comprised 4.6 per cent of total tax revenue and 1.3 per cent of GDP in 1999.[27] With the introduction of the ERP and increased vehicle imposts generally, this percentage has probably risen significantly.

The desire for political control, as well as mere greed and meanness, explains the PAP Government's fiscal policies. Controlling people's money, or more precisely their access to it, ensures compliance. Their money can be returned to them if they behave and withheld if they don't. The PAP state is well practised in such Machiavellian methods of control. For example, electorates and more recently wards that vote against the PAP during elections are left out of upgrading projects that would have improved their HDB own estates. The monies they have paid via taxes and government charges is only used to upgrade their homes if they vote PAP.

Pork-barrelling is a time-honoured procedure in most Western democracies. Projects are often funded in marginal electorates to tip the balance in the ruling party's favour. Bribing voters to vote for the government is one thing; but punishing them if they don't is another. In Singapore the Government refuses to upgrade the HDB estates of any electoral wards that vote against PAP candidates in elections. That goes beyond bribery to intimidation, beyond pork-barrelling to denial of benefits that all citizens are entitled to. Citizens who pay their taxes like everyone else are being denied benefits because they voted against the government.

While most Singaporeans don't pay any income tax, they face hefty disguised taxes as well as numerous regressive taxes. Despite this they receive far less social and old age security and much more limited health coverage than in the West. Although Singaporeans can expect to be taxed and levied in many ways, they often cannot count on even minimal help from the state, even when destitute. Everything must be paid for – no free lunches. And if there ever are, recipients are given the smallest servings possible and made to feel like total losers for accepting them.

The PAP believes that Singapore should be run like a business where cash inflow is maximised and outflow minimised. As one PAP critic remarked:

In many ways, the PAP is materialism personified. It glorifies wealth accumulation as an end. It prides itself with .... increased budget surpluses year after year, most of which are derived from all manner of taxes, levies, fees and fines. It equates wealth with power, and in its relentless pursuit for more, the poor and underprivileged are often neglected and cast aside, after all the lower class has never fitted into their grand schemes.[28]

As one Singaporean taxi driver told me, "The Government loves Singapore, but doesn't love Singaporeans".

Western notions of social justice and welfare where the state is obliged to help the needy have little place in such thinking. Being "unprofitable", welfare should be left to "the private sector", i.e. overburdened charity groups and families of the disadvantaged. Health-care expenditures have been minimised by limiting Medisave and MediShield coverage, forcing their members to pay for many treatments themselves. The PAP has minimal sympathy for social-democratic notions that comprehensive health-care is everyone's right, and not merely for those who can pay for it.

PAP rulers could claim that their grand schemes have given Singapore the reserves needed to overcome various crises and attract the foreign investment which has transformed Singapore into a modern state envied by the world. Without such achievements Singapore would not have survived as an independent country but might have had to rejoin Malaysia. Singaporeans would also have been far less affluent – at least the top third or so of the population. Certainly such arguments are valid. Singapore may not have remained politically independent and without such large reserves would have been more vulnerable to currency crises and economic downturns. But the price of the PAP's grandiose nation-building has been a dependent economy of second-rate efficiency lacking entrepreneurial or innovative ability and a society of intimidated and risk-averse conformists.

Moreover, many Singaporeans have only had limited gains from the Government's schemes: their living standards remain mediocre and up to 30 per cent still live in poverty by the standards of modern developed countries. Those in need get little if any help. They often receive minimal social welfare and health-care, ensuring they remain well below the poverty line.

Singaporeans are now into their fifth decade of PAP rule. During that time some have prospered and many have experienced greater economic security than people in neighbouring countries. The PAP regularly cites such gains to convince Singaporeans how well off they are: how fortunate they are to have the PAP ruling them and how much the world admires Singapore for its achievements. But many Singaporeans find their country's affluence illusionary. The good life is largely out of reach for them. While their per capita income matches that of many Western countries, their living standards do not. Singapore's distribution of income is very unequal. While Singaporeans may have a per capita income of more than S$3000 a month, over half of them earn less than S$2000 a month, many much less.

The three pillars that supposedly underpin most Singaporeans' security – the HDB scheme, the health-care system and the CPF – are deficient. They provide little security for many Singaporeans and mask some serious shortcomings in health, housing and old-age security. Not 10 per cent, but up to 30 per cent of the population live in poverty, a damning indictment of a country whose per capita income, even on a PPP basis, is around the world's eighth highest.

The good life that Singaporeans supposedly enjoy is, like the Singapore Miracle, as much a statistical mirage as anything real. Their affluence is largely false. Many have never really experienced the good life, and those who have may find it has a limited shelf-life. The Singapore Miracle, which has underpinned whatever affluence they have, may soon run out of steam, as some uncomfortable parallels with Japan suggest.

References

1. *The Straits Times* (ST), February 11, 1995.
2. ST, August 27, 2003.
3. Ibid.
4. ST, September 7, 2003.
5. Cutting employers' CPF contributions benefits the MNCs as well as the Government, which employs perhaps 100,000 employees in its departments and statutory boards. The Government itself saved S$175 million from the CPF changes. (ST, August 30, 2003).
6. ST, August 19, 2003.
7. ST, November 18, 2004.
8. ST, April 20, 2002.
9. Asher, Mukul: "Reforming Singapore's tax system for the twenty-first century", p. 415 in *Singapore Economy in the 21st Century* edited by Koh et al (Singapore, McGraw Hill, 2002).
10. ST, January 6, 2003.
11. Asher in Koh et al, p. 404.
12. ST, February 21, 2004.
13. ST, November 22, 2003.
14. *Far Eastern Economic Review*, May 6, 2004.
15. ST, February 21, 2004.
16. *Economic Survey of Singapore 2002* (Singapore, Ministry of Trade and Industry, 2003), p. 23.
17. ST, March 13, 2000.
18. One Singaporean told me that for him, PAP stands for Personal Action Party. He was expressing his disgust at the astronomical salaries PAP ministers pay themselves.
19. *Streats*, June 30, 2003.
20. Low, Linda: *The Political Economy of a City State* (Singapore, Oxford University Press, 1998), p. 181.
21. Ibid.
22. ST, November 22, 2003.
23. ST, March 30, 2002.
24. ST, July 8, 2004 and July 12, 2004.
25. Gomez, James, editor: *Publish and Perish* (Singapore, National Solidarity Party, 2001), p. 178.
26. ST, January 19, 2002.
27. Asher in Koh et al, p. 409.
28. Gomez, p. 157.

Section Eight

A Second Japan?

Until the early 1990s Japan was billed to replace the US as the world's next economic super-power. The awe Japan inspired was understandable. Not only had it dramatically recovered from the devastation of World War Two but it had also transformed itself into an economic power-house. From the 1960s Japan had begun to become a global presence and by the 1980s seemed ready to surpass the US and the West.

As the seeming Japanese miracle continued to dazzle the world, such Asian leaders as Lee Kuan Yew came to see Japan as a role model for Singapore. He was not only captivated by its high growth rates but by the disciplined and hierarchical nature of Japanese society. It gratified his authoritarian instincts to see the subordination of individual interests to national ends.

However, the steady decline of Japan from the early 1990s to the mid-2000s has laid bare the defects of the Japanese miracle and Lee's infatuation with Japan has begun to wane. But while Japan may have ceased to be a role model for Lee, will Singapore share Japan's fate from 1990 to 2005? Certainly some Singaporeans have started to wonder this. The following chapters consider this possibility.

CHAPTER 27

INFATUATION AND REALITY

Until the early 1990s Japan seemed destined not only for super-power status, but to spearhead the imminent arrival of the Asian Century. The V-shaped "flying geese" concept was often used to describe Japan's leading role in Asia. As the head goose, it led the flock of Asian countries. Flying nearest to Japan were the four Asian "tiger economies" of Hong Kong, Singapore, Taiwan and South Korea. Then came other Asian countries, each at different levels of economic development.

By the late 1980s, Japan had become a leading example of successful economic development. Several US commentators encouraged this thinking, including Herman Kahn (*The Emerging Japanese Superstate*)[1] and Ezra Vogel (*Japan as Number One*).[2] They fostered the view that Japan's success was a demonstration of its superior values and economic organisation. Japan "appeared, to many observers, to be well on its way to global economic dominance," noted Krugman.[3]

Such breathless predictions about Japan's looming ascendancy were largely due to uncritical extrapolation of past growth trends. Dated data was being used from Japan's high-growth years, especially for the 1963-73 period when its real GDP was rocketing along at 8.9 per cent and per capita output at 7.7 per cent a year.[3] By contrast, during the 1973-92 period, its GDP grew at only 3.7 per cent annually and GDP per capita at only 3 per cent. As Krugman noted in 1994:

> The story of the great Japanese growth slowdown has been oddly absent from the vast polemical literature on Japan and its role in the world economy. Much of that literature seems stuck in a time warp with authors writing as if Japan were still the miracle economy of the 1960s and early 1970s.[4]

By the time the Japanese miracle was being hyped it had largely subsided. Through the 1980s writers kept promoting a miracle that had long run out of steam and was no longer a threat to US economic hegemony. A comparison of Japan-US labour productivity levels from the mid-1980s confirms this. First, Japan's productivity growth had slowed from between 4 and 6 per cent in the mid-1980s to about 3.5 per cent by the mid-1990s. "Despite a sustained investment effort that exceeded the pace of American capital accumulation over the past decade, Japan's productivity gains lagged behind those in America," Krugman said.[5] Second, surveys showed that Japanese workers were only about 55 per cent as productive as their American counterparts. Again, measures of capital productivity revealed that Japan's was only about two-thirds of US levels. Moreover, from 1985 to 1993 the productivity of US industry soared by 35 per cent while that of Japan's rose by only 4 per cent.[6] Despite the obvious flaws in the Japanese miracle, certain Asian leaders preferred, for political reasons, to ignore them.

1. Beguiled by Japan

So taken was Lee Kuan Yew by Japan that in 1990, when its miracle was about to implode, he confidently declared that Asia, especially Japan, was providing new development models to emulate:

> *Japan's successful economy is based on her political and social stability, her orderliness, low crime rates, negligible drug-taking, and strong communitarian values.*[7]

Despite himself and his family – and most of Singapore's population – having been traumatised and brutalised by the Japanese during their 1942-5 occupation of the island, Lee gushed:

> *I now respect and admire them. Their group solidarity, discipline, intelligence, industriousness and willingness to sacrifice for their nation make them a formidable and productive force.*[8]

Lee's eldest son, Brigadier Lee Hsien Loong has also shared his father's Japanese infatuations. In a 1987 interview with two US journalists he said the US must become more efficient to compete with Japan. "The quality of your output has to go up.... If the Japanese work like zombies, well, if you want to be in the same league, maybe you have to work like zombies too," laughed Lee Jnr – "without smiling", the two journalists noted.[9] So, for the Brigadier, a zombie-like consciousness was good for growth.[10]

As late as February 1995, the Brigadier was still endorsing Japan as a role model and yardstick for Singapore, even though the Japanese miracle was obviously unravelling.[11] Japan continued to inspire Lee and son until its decade-long decline became too apparent even for them to deny.

Perhaps the Brigadier has since had time to reflect on the virtues of zombie consciousness. Zomboid minds are bad for productivity and efficiency, as Singapore has shown. But whether he likes it or not a zomboid mentality is alive and well in Singapore, as was noticed by Professor Tommy Koh, Singapore's affable Ambassador-at-Large:

> *When I visited Myanmar last December [1997], I was struck by the fact that although the Mynamar people are poorer than Singaporeans, they seemed happier. One of my tour guides observed that Singaporeans struck her like a nation of robots, all rushing about their business with no smiles on their faces.*[12]

Even some Japanese think Singaporeans are robotic. As one Singaporean recalled: "One of my former bosses, who was Japanese, said that Singaporeans are like robots: We can work but cannot think".[13]

Will Singapore end up like Japan, a nation of robots whose miracle has run out of steam? Examining the Japanese miracle and the forces that drove it should provide some answers.

2. Explaining the Japanese Miracle

Lee and other commentators have ascribed the apparent successes of Singapore and Japan to such factors as "Confucian values". Others, including Lingle and Krugman, have explained Japan's miracle in less flattering terms. Their writings, which questioned the basis of the "Asian Tigers" success, have a special prescience, having appeared before the 1997/8 Asian financial crisis. Lingle gave these reasons for Japan's high post-war growth:

> [Japan's] *manufacturing powerhouses are technological "parasites". Although they are unquestioningly adept at applying mass-production techniques to processes developed elsewhere, they are unable to generate the true inventions that would allow them to mitigate or overcome business downturns.*[14]

(But it should be conceded that Japan may have borrowed heavily from foreign technologies it has used them to produce some of the world's leading brand names.)

Japanese companies were able to make big inroads into Western markets through its Ministry of International Trade and Industry (MITI) while promoting protectionist policies that insulated local enterprises from global competition. "As long as foreigners were kept out of the Japanese domestic market, Japanese companies were able to pass along to Japanese consumers the costs of 'lifetime employment'."[15]

The "heavily regulated nature of the Japanese economy discouraged true performance measurement in key sectors, especially banking".[16] Lingle added that the "deliberate lack of transparency allowed mediocrity and unsound business judgement to go undetected and undisciplined until reaching crisis proportions".

Lingle concluded that "all the above combined to prevent Japan from responding to the challenges posed by the stubborn recession of the 1990s".[17] Clearly Confucian values have had little to do with Japan's success – or subsequent stagnation since the early 1990s. In fact both outcomes were due to the centralisation of political and economic power under the Ministry of Finance (MOF), as subsequent chapters will show.

3. The Bubble Bursts

While Japan's GDP growth may have been slowed by the mid-1980s, its share market continued to boom. From the early 1980s to late 1989 the market more than trebled in value. By December 1989, the Nikkei had reached 39,000, generating the euphoric belief that the boom would never end. Some brokers were predicting that the Nikkei would hit 60,000 or even 80,000.[18]

In 1990, the new Bank of Japan (BOJ) head, Yasuhi Mieno, realised the situation was out of control and raised interest rates to slow the super-heated economy. This burst the Bubble and share prices crashed. By August 1992, the market had lost 60 per cent of its value and by April 2003 the Nikkei had sunk to 7607. As the market collapsed, so did property prices, which fell dramatically from 1991. By 2000, they were one-fifth or less of Bubble-era prices.[19] Banks found themselves saddled with an enormous number of non-performing loans.

The slump spread to all sectors of the economy. Rising unemployment and bankruptcies led to reduced domestic demand. Sales of manufactured goods fell and industrial production subsequently declined. Japan's debt levels rose to stratospheric heights and deflation engulfed the economy. The recession reinforced the Japanese propensity to save and consumer spending stalled. The economy entered a period of prolonged stagnation from which it would only begin to fitfully emerge after 2003.

4. The LKY View

In 1996, when pondering Japan's decline, Lee Kuan Yew claimed the lack of "strong government" was the problem. The rot had set in during 1993 with the ousting of the Liberal Democratic Party (LDP) that had ruled the country for 38 years, he concluded. Having to share power with other parties prevented the LDP from taking "decisive measures to get the people to accept hard decisions and to get the economy going again".[20] The possibility that Japan's miracle had crested because it had followed similar economic policies to Singapore's was not one that Lee wanted to contemplate. Better to blame Japan's demise on a lack of "strong government". Japan would have been OK if it had adhered to Singapore's authoritarian-style rule.

Perhaps Lee and his son could be excused for seeing Singapore as a potential Japan. Like Japan, Singapore has an industrious people who stress thrift and education, display obedience to authority, exercise self-discipline and practice hierarchical values. In addition Singaporeans, superficially at least, exhibit group conformity like the Japanese. Both countries staged apparent economic miracles in a short time. Japan developed after its war-time defeat in 1945, Singapore after Separation in 1965. Such similarities prompted Lee to think that Singapore not only should but could emulate Japan. His 1981 call for Singapore firms to adopt the paternalism of Japanese firms reflected such thinking, though it was an idea he later abandoned. "I wanted to emulate them but gave up after discussions with Singapore employers. We did not have their culture of strong worker loyalty to their companies."[21]

In recent years Lee has taken to lecturing his former mentors. While receiving an honorary degree from Waseda University in Japan in June 2003 he took the opportunity to give the Japanese a few pointers on how to remake their country. Creation of unique products was a major ingredient, he lectured. "You have to be like the Americans and invent products that others have not thought of that will be desired and bought by billions across the world," he declared, oblivious to the irony of the situation. [22] Here was the former leader of a small jerry-built country, largely devoid of innovative and entrepreneurial capacities, telling one of the world's oldest, biggest and richest nations that has produced many brand-name products, how it must become more creative. Lee could have more profitably spent his time devising strategies for avoiding Japan's fate. Singapore shares many of Japan's traits that bode ill for its future.

References

1. Kahn, Herman: *The Emerging Japanese Superstate* (London, Deutsch, 1971).

2. Vogel, Ezra: *Japan as Number One: Lessons for America,* (Cambridge, Mass.; Harvard University Press, 1979).

3. Krugman, Paul: "The myth of Asia's miracle", *Foreign Affairs,* November/ December 1994 (Vol 73, No. 6), p. 74.

4. Ibid.

5. Lingle, Christopher: *The Rise and Decline of the Asian Century* (Hong Kong, Asia 2000, second edition, 1997), p. 94.

6. Ibid, p. 224.

7. Seow, Francis T.: *The Media Enthralled: Singapore Revisited* (Boulder, Colorado; Lynne Rienner, 1998), p. 189.

8. Lee, Kuan Yew: *From Third World to First* (Singapore, Times Media, 2000), p. 587.

9. Kelly, Brian and London, Mark: *The Four Little Dragons* (New York, Simon and Schuster, 1985), p. 385.

10. BG Lee spoke of zombies while his father has referred to Singaporeans as being "digits" or "ciphers" – mere mindless cogs in the system. Clearly, BG is a chip off the old block.

11. Murray, Geoffrey and Audrey Perera: *Singapore: the Global City State* (UK; China Library/Curzon, 1996), p. 259.

12. *The Straits Times* (ST), August 9, 1998.

13. ST, October 22, 2001.

14. Lingle, p. 221.

15. Ibid.

16. Ibid, p. 222.

17. Ibid.

18. Kerr, Alex: *Dogs and Demons: the Fall of Modern Japan* (London, Penguin, 2001), p. 79.

19. Ibid.

20. *Fortune*, December 23, 1996.

21. Lee, p. 587.

22. ST, June 5, 2003.

CHAPTER 28

POLITICAL SIMILARITIES

While Lee Kuan Yew claimed that a lack of strong government explained Japan's problems, other factors may have accounted for them. Singapore displays many of these factors. They are political, economic and cultural. This chapter focuses on the political similarities that Japan and Singapore shared till the early 2000s and still largely do despite Japan's improved political and economic circumstances from 2003/4.

1. Iron Triangles

The separation of powers is a prime prerequisite for a healthy democracy. Each arm of government, whether the political, executive, legislative, or bureaucractic, balances the others to prevent a monopoly of power. Monopolised power is not only abused but leads to inflexible policies by rulers. There are few means to make such rulers reverse or change flawed or destructive policies. Many dictatorships have followed disastrous courses of action because there was no countervailing power to stop them.

Both Singapore and Japan are characterised by centralized political power. This is more obvious in Singapore where the PAP cabinet controls all major economic as well as political activities. A similar, though more subtle, centralisation of power has been evident in Japan where the bureaucracy rather than the political executive is supreme.

The term "iron triangle" has often been used to describe the political-economic system that runs Japan. This structure binds together Japan's political, economic, and business sectors through numerous invisible ties, including the *amakudari* mechanism. The triangle's apex is the bureaucracy, or more precisely the MOF, sometimes called the Ministry of Ministries. The MOF controls the rest of the bureaucracy, including the powerful MITI. The MITI has shaped Japan's external economy and devised many of the country's growth strategies, but despite its power, its plans cannot be implemented without MOF support.[1] The MITI may propose but the MOF disposes.

2. Methods of Control

Through control of the bureaucracy, the MOF dominates Japan's political system and the corporate and banking sectors. The MOF has been given various levers of power to do this and has developed others. Besides extensive regulatory powers, these include virtual law-making capacities. Decades ago Japan's parliament, the Diet, vested the MOF and other bureaucratic agencies with almost complete freedom to write and re-write laws without further approval from elected representatives. After the war, with the military and *zaibatsu* (large pre-war industrial conglomerates that dominated Japan's economy) discredited, politicians, the press and the public consigned their fate to the bureaucracy, allowing them near-dictatorial and unaccountable powers. All this solidified the MOF's power. "They can more or less make up the law as they go along," noted Fingleton.[2]

The MOF regulates the financial system and controls taxing, spending and defence. The Ministry administers the tax system through the National Tax Agency, an MOF division, and also determines the national budget. The Diet has no substantive powers and mostly rubber-stamps MOF legislation. The MOF also controls the Defence Agency, whose upper levels it staffs. The agency's top ranks are seeded with career MOF officials and is usually headed by an MOF man.

Up to the mid-1990s, the power of the MOF was largely hidden, especially to foreign commentators who usually thought big business ran Japan:

In the Confucian tradition, the MOF believes that power is exercised most effectively when it is least obstrusive.[3]

Previously Japan's civil servants sought to sustain the illusion of big business's supremacy. This helped the MOF-led bureaucracy disclaim responsibility for its sometimes controversial economic policies.

Japan is also supposed to be a democracy: so where do elected representatives fit in? In drafting the budget the MOF takes some soundings in the Diet, but the MPs' involvement only begins after the budget's main shape has already been determined. As Fingleton observes, the MOF is careful to create the impression that the MPs have the last word:

In drafting the Budget, for instance, the MOF is adept at including unnecessarily unpopular provisions as bargaining ploys. It later makes a show of bowing to pressure from politicians in removing the offending provisions, thus preserving the impression that the popular will prevails.[4]

The MOF controls politicians further by selective enforcement of Japan's electoral laws, especially those relating to election funding and vote-buying. The MOF can heavily restrict corporate funding for elected representatives and even impose limits on politicians' efforts to organise grassroots campaigns, but it and associated government agencies will only enforce rules on funding and other electoral regulations if they disapprove of certain politicians. Vote-buying is rife in Japanese elections, but if a politician is favoured by the MOF-led bureaucracy he can rest easy.

The MOF dominates not only parliament and its MPs but also its cabinet ministers. This is due to the MOF's vast law-making powers and also because of the revolving-door nature of Japan's governments and prime ministers. The MOF sees itself as the natural custodian of executive power in Japan, guided by the nation's long-term interests rather than the short-term expediency of politicians. It is made clear to each new batch of ministers and their prime minister that they must abide by MOF policies. Should any cabinet members upset the MOF, selective enforcement strategy is used. It is "the hidden dynamic behind most of Japan's political scandals," as was demonstrated by the Recruit and Nomura share scandals of the 1980s and 1990s, which forced cabinet and prime ministerial resignations. Such scandals have a century-long history in Japan and follow a standard pattern: "They begin with leaks to the press, usually concern securities violations or tax evasion, and are generally instigated by the MOF".[5] The usual victims are politicians or their business supporters.

The MOF has other equally effective methods for ensuring its dominance. These are usually exercised through the tax laws and banking and securities legislation. While very tough, the tax laws are normally only selectively enforced by the MOF's tax agency. Should corporations flout the MOF's guidance on various policies, its tax agency can reportedly "come in and ransack every single page of their books". Not without reason is the agency called "Japan's KGB".

However, the MOF-controlled tax agency can be surprisingly tolerant of dubious tax deductions by those corporations who have its favour. Japan's major companies are allowed to claim deductions for *shito fumeikan*, or literally "unaccounted-for-expenditure"; that is, expenditure without a receipt.[6] Payment of bribes would be one type of expenditure where receipts would not be used. Such deductions claimed by Japanese companies run into millions of dollars each year. MOF tolerance of such tax claims has encouraged corrupt practices in corporate Japan.

3. Elitist Mindsets

The MOF's power is enhanced by a strong *esprit de corps* due to its getting the cream of Japan's top graduates, usually from Tokyo University, the nation's best. Being the pinnacle of Japan's administrative system, only the finest graduates are recruited by the MOF. Fingleton contends that they are Nobel-prize calibre, describing them as "brilliant, creative, tenacious and public spirited". From Tokyo University come the rest of Japan's corporate and banking elite as well, so MOF officials can exploit a powerful network that permeates the top levels of Japanese society. It creates a strong community of interest among the university's old boys. Fingleton remarks that:

> *The university's graduates dominate not only the bureaucracy but also the major banks and many of the biggest corporations. The essential dynamic here is classic Japanese group logic: the Tokyo University people form a powerful clique, and through peer pressure they back each other almost automatically.*
>
> *By comparison, politicians generally come from a host of lesser universities. Thus they lack a deep sense of group loyalty and make easy prey for the Tokyo University crowd's divide and rule.*[7]

4. Amakudari

The MOF buttresses its authority via the *amakudari* mechanism, which has had harmful consequences for Japan. In Singapore senior public servants as well as former cabinet ministers are appointed to run GLCs and other SEs, but *amakudari* was pioneered in Japan and operates by having many ex-MOF and other former officials despatched to run banks and corporations. Japanese bureaucrats retire in their early to mid-50s and are encouraged by their former civil service employers to gain appointments in the private sector. This is especially so with many ex-MOF officials, 150 of whom headed Japan's top private banks in the mid-1990s. From July 1997 to early 1998 alone, 164 MOF staff were hired as executives by local banks, brokerages and insurers. In 1995, seven ex-officials of the Construction Ministry became directors on the board of Japan's second-biggest construction company, the Sumitomo Group's Kajima Corporation.[8]

There are rules against *amakudari* but they are rarely enforced. The public and media are critical of the practice but it continues. Some enterprises are so teeming with ex-bureaucrats that they are referred to as *amakudari* companies by the media.

The main aim of *amakudari* is to ensure that banks and corporations comply with MOF and bureaucratic policies, but *amakudari* is increasingly seen as a main cause of Japan's current plight by various Japan-watchers, including Chinese journalist and Japan specialist, Mr Wong Ping Fah. In a speech to Singapore's East Asian Institute he said *amakudari* would impede any reform of the Japanese bureaucracy. The *amakudari* tradition dictated that all the brilliant government officials who could not make it to the pinnacle of the bureaucracy should be channelled to private corporations to hold top positions. Bureaucrats thus farmed out were obliged to grant favours to their former colleagues, forming a mutual patronage relationship between the public and commercial sectors. This practice harmed Japan's bureaucracy by breeding corruption and cover-ups which, since the early 1990s, have been exposed in embarrassing profusion.[9]

Amakudari also fosters a more subtle two-way form of corruption. First, former bureaucrats working in the private sector are obliged to grant favours to ex-civil servant colleagues; but while still in the civil service they are often regulating corporations they expect to be working for when they leave the service. As such, they have every incentive to laxly monitor any corporation likely to employ them on an enormous salary when they retire from the civil service. Being over-keen in performing one's job would jeopardise their prospects for a lucrative post-retirement position. Moreover, existing bureaucrats are less likely to monitor the activities of their former colleagues closely; "To do so would be a considerable 'loss of face' for all concerned".[10]

The cosy collusive relationships that *amakudari* breeds mainly explains why regulatory agencies in Japan lack teeth. Such bonds sap the bureaucratic will to deal with corporate abuses, as shown by the impotence of the Free Trade Commission (FTC), Japan's sole fair competition body. The chairman of the FTC's five-member board usually comes from the MOF or MITI, both of which have displayed little enthusiasm for reforming Japan's collusive corporate culture. Sometimes the ministries have tipped off companies that are under FTC investigation or have exerted political pressure for investigations to be dropped.[11]

Such collusive bureaucratic-corporate relationships have flourished in Japan because it lacks sufficient independent sources of power to expose and challenge them. This has been due to the centralisation of power under the MOF-led bureaucracy, which has largely marginalised the Diet and Cabinet. Through various mechanisms, including *amakudari*, the MOF became the main locus of power in the iron triangle that ruled Japan. Only after Prime Minister Junichiro Koizami came to power in 2001 did the MOF's power over the political executive begin to decline.

5. Comparisons with Singapore

A similar political-business/GLC-bureaucratic nexus operates in Singapore, but one where the political executive (cabinet) rather than a MOF-led bureaucracy plays the leading role. All three elements are as closely linked in Singapore as they are in Japan. The PAP state, like the MOF, practises elite recruitment policies complete with its own version of the MOF – the Administrative Service (AS). While the MOF recruits the top graduates for its own ministry, the PAP wants them initially for the AS and eventually selects the best of these for the political executive.

Singapore's iron triangle has an *amakudari* "retirement scheme", but one where ex-cabinet ministers as well as senior, often AS, bureaucrats are appointed to the GLC corporate sector or the statutory boards.

Both countries have displayed a similar marked centralisation of political and economic power based on elitist civil service recruitment. While this can facilitate rapid growth and development in the short term, it has resulted in dysfunctional economic policies that have produced severe long-term structural problems for both countries, as the next chapter shows.

References

1. *Sunday Times* (Singapore), *The Sunday Review*, "The Invisible Hand" by Eamonn Fingleton, July 23, 1995.
2. Ibid.
3. Ibid.
4. Ibid.
5. Ibid.
6. Backman, Michael: *Asian Eclipse: Exposing the Dark Side of Business in Asia* (Singapore, John Wiley and Sons, revised edition, 2001), p. 130.
7. Fingleton, *The Sunday Times* July 23, 1995.
8. Backman, p. 134.
9. ST, November 15, 1998.
10. Backman, p. 135.
11. Ibid, p. 128

CHAPTER 29

ECONOMIC SIMILARITIES

W hen governments can intervene in the economy they usually do. Few rulers can resist the temptation to exercise all the power they have at their disposal, especially when they have pressing agendas to pursue. The barriers to their doing this include a vigorous political opposition, various constitutional checks and balances and a free press. Such things usually only exist in fully fledged democracies. Authoritarian regimes, and less than democratic ones like Singapore's and Japan's, lack such democratic safeguards. As a result, the governments of both countries have been free to pursue whatever economic policies they wish. These have been characterised by heavy state intervention in the economy. Their consequences are considered in this chapter.

1. Japan, the Tarnished Miracle

After Japan's real-estate bubble burst in 1989 the economy sank into prolonged stagnation. Occasionally the economy would briefly recover, only to stagnate again. From the early 1990s until the early 2000s the economy displayed little or no growth and often teetered on the brink of deflation. The Japanese miracle had become decidedly tarnished. Previously Japan's achievements had been uncritically lauded, but they were now receiving rigorous and unsparing scrutiny from several writers.[1]

Examinations of Japan's prolonged malaise have identified major flaws in its economic strategies, most of which were formulated by and conducted under MOF auspices. After Japan's property market crash in 1990, significant defects were exposed in the Japanese miracle, fuelled by astronomical debt levels. Largely because of MOF policies, huge amounts of credit were injected into an economy where corporate cronyism, questionable banking and accounting practices and widespread corruption prevailed. This began to emerge after 1990. Asset values crashed and the economy stagnated. Money was borrowed to prop up the economy but to little avail: it not only increased Japan's crushing debt burden, but starved the most entrepreneurial sectors of the economy of venture capital. It also bankrupted a number of pension funds, destroying the incomes of many retirees – incomes which had already been kept down by the MOF policy of low interest rates.

A fundamental MOF strategy was to provide cheap money for the corporate sector to promote rapid industrial expansion, especially since the 1970s slow-down.

The MOF encouraged listed companies to pay only minimal dividends to shareholders. It also ensured that bank and bond interest rates were equally minuscule. Interest rates were kept down and borrowing made easy. By the late 1980s the cost of capital in Japan was a mere 0.5 per cent, compared to rates of between 5 and 20 per cent in Europe and America.[2] Moreover, Japanese government bonds were yielding between 0.2 and 3 per cent, far below the US's 5 to 8 per cent at this time.[3] Such cheap money drove Japan's stock market and property boom in the 1980s. The MOF was also making loans independently to various companies through its own directly controlled budget called the Zaito or "second budget". The Zaito budget totalled as much as 60 per cent of the main budget and has been funded by the huge pool of deposits from Japan's postal-savings conglomerate – which the MOF's Trust Fund Bureau manages. This conglomerate, which Japanese Prime Minister Junichiro Koizumi planned to break up after his September 2005 election win, consists of the post office (*jucho*) and an insurance arm (*kampo*). Both have been required to buy government bonds, which the MOF can draw on to finance agencies and programs with no parliamentary overview. By such means, enormous amounts of cheap money were being fed into Japan's corporate sector. MOF economic policies not only ensured low-interest capital for industry but also allowed red tape to proliferate. As in Singapore, this impeded Japan's entrepreneurial growth, especially in the SME sector.

Keiretsu Cronyism

The heart of Japan's corporate sector is the *keiretsus*, huge publicly owned conglomerates. They replaced the pre-World War II *zaibatsu* that had dominated the economy until they were broken up after the war by the Allied occupation administration. The Allies outlawed the *zaibatsu*, seeing them as having collaborated with the Japanese militarists who had launched Japan into war. Former *zaibatsu* concerns Mitsubishi, Mitsui and Sumitomo survive as three of Japan's six biggest *keiretsu*.[4] The other three are Yasuda (sometimes called Fuyo), DKB-Itochu and Sanwa. These six *keiretsus* account for more than a fifth of Japan's economy. They consist of a series of core or inner companies and a raft of smaller and less important companies. Mitsubishi, one of the biggest *keiretsus*, has 28 core companies and about 1000 associates or companies of subsidiaries.

The companies within each *keiretsu* tie themselves together through such practices as cross-shareholdings, buying each other's output, exchanging staff, using common banks and real estate companies, setting up joint ventures and conducting joint research. They also use presidential councils where the heads of core companies meet regularly to discuss topics of mutual interest. Collectively, these practices have reduced efficiency and productivity and negatively affected shareholder value, a minor concern to many of Japan's listed companies. "Cozy cross-shareholding arrangements, where companies turn a blind eye to each other's inefficiencies, have seen to this," notes Backman.[5] Sticking together has reinforced their inefficiencies and mismanagement, he says, observing that:

In other economies, the market picks off those companies that are under-performing and have weak corporate governance, management and internal checks and balances.

They are taken over and knocked into shape or they go bankrupt. In Japan, weak companies have tended to huddle together to seek comfort and protection from other keiretsu *members, which ultimately leaves the whole group weakened.*[6]

Because inefficiencies and mismanagement were not admitted out of corporate pride, the whole group, not merely a couple of companies, might go under. Reluctance to write off the bad debts of affiliates has perpetuated this problem, which surfaced during the 1990s recession when bad debts not only increased but were allowed to accumulate. Had the debts been from non-affiliated companies it is unlikely they would have been carried for so long. While part of the reason was insufficient tax incentives to write down bad debts, it was also done to save "face" and honour, a matter of enormous importance in Japan. "Acknowledging a bad debt suggests defeat; to declare a low profit or even a loss is to confirm it."[7] Unsuccessful ventures then took, and still take, longer to kill off than they should in Japan, because to kill them is to admit failure.

Fear of losing face, plus the close links produced by cross-shareholdings, began to have dire effects on the *keiretsus* in the 1990s. "Cross-shareholdings in the 1980s meant concentrating wealth and success. In the 1990s, they have become the means for cross-infection."[8] Such companies as Sony, Toyota and Honda, which fared best from the financial crisis, were not usually directly attached to the *keiretsu*. Being more agile and focussed they could hide behind their affiliates to conceal poor management.

The *keiretsus* were largely instrumental in building Japan's economy after the war, and the big-government-big-business formula worked for many years. The anti-competitive practices of the *keiretsus* enabled many of them to grow into some of the world's biggest and best-known corporations. But as Backman observed in 2001,

through their system of mutual support and cross-subsidies, weak companies and poor management have accumulated and survived, clogging the arteries of corporate Japan and draining the reserves of stronger companies. What was once dynamic and instrumental to prosperity is now sluggish and a threat to it.[9]

However, it was not until the 1990s that these weaknesses in Japan's *keiretsu* system became apparent. Until then questionable accounting procedures had hidden them.

Questionable Accounting

For decades the cronyistic *keiretsu* system's operation was sustained by dubious accounting practices, often encouraged by MOF-led bureaucrats. Such practices did much to inflate *keiretsu* and bank assets and hide their insolvent operations, making them appear far stronger and more prosperous than they actually were; but this required the systematic violation of the basic auditing principles of corporate governance of modern market economies.

In Japan, auditing "can almost be as lame and ineffectual as other aspects of the country's corporate governance regime," remarks Backman.[10] *Keiretsu* accounting procedures illustrate Japan's indifferent auditing standards.

The diverse and complex nature of *keiretsu* subsidiaries makes it difficult to identify them and compile consolidated statements that accurately portray their performance. As a result, earnings and assets tend to be grossly understated. Listed companies are only required to report the assets and liabilities of enterprises in which they have a 20 per cent stake, though they may have smaller stakes in many enterprises.

While a company's books are supposed to reflect its financial health, in Japan "time and time again, they bear little relevance to reality".[11] In the cosy high-trust world of *keiretsu*-linked subsidiaries, they make verbal loan guarantees with each other which rarely show up on balance sheets. These guarantees are only revealed when the company gets into difficulties. Revised statements often show the company's situation to be much worse than has been indicated, sometimes even insolvent.

Japanese accounting creates distorted data through *tobashi* property transactions. Here a bank sells a troubled property to a subsidiary, to which it then lends the money to pay for the property. Such transactions are officially tolerated. The National Land Agency accepts *tobashi* sales as real ones, which falsely inflates land-value statistics. While agency figures may claim that land values have halved, for example, the fall may really be 80 per cent.

Tobashi deals are but one form of the cosmetic accounting widely practised in Japan. Such accounting is also used to hide such blights as unsightly liabilities and pension-fund deficits, generating more inaccurate statistics. Many banks and securities firms were adept at hiding growing debt problems for years, and when they went bankrupt in the mid-1990s they were found to have debts ten to twenty times greater than their liabilities.[12]

Auditors have little ability to pick up the deceptive accounting of Japanese firms and banks. Japan's accounting profession has low status compared to Western countries' and lacks the power to subject Japanese corporations to critical scrutiny. International accounting firms operating in Japan are forced to operate by lax local rules and with local partners. The Japan offices of the world's biggest accounting firms, including Ernst and Young, Arthur Anderson, Deloite Touche Tohmatsu, and Coopers & Lybrand, audited the companies that have been responsible for Japan's four biggest bank scandals in recent years.[13]

The government body that is supposed to regulate the accounting industry – the Business Accounting Deliberation Council – is a toothless tiger that lacks independence. This body is located in the offices of the MOF, whose policies tolerate *keiretsu* malpractice. MOF-sanctioned accounting methods often reflect disdain for conventional benchmarks for assessing corporate performance and asset valuation.

Besides *tobashi* transactions, other dubious Japanese accounting methods include "book value accounting", where companies count the increased market values of their assets as "latent profits". Such profits – the gap between the purchase price and current value of corporate assets – became more important to investors than the capacity to produce dividends. Mesmerised by apparently rising corporate asset values during the boom, investors ignored the miniscule dividends. They kept buying shares, propelling the Nikkei to ever-new heights.

With much money easily accessible to both private and corporate investors, a lot found its way into real estate, which was often used as collateral to buy shares. This further propelled the share market to giddy heights. From the early 1980s to late 1989 the market more than trebled in value. When the Nikkei reached 39,000 in December 1989, the euphoric belief that the boom was endless gripped the market.[14]

Fanciful P/E Ratios

As share prices soared, so did Price/Earnings ratios which express an equity's value. P/E ratios are based on company earnings and measure the ratio between the current yield of a share and its current price. The higher the ratio the lower the share's earning potential. In the US, when the Dow P/E ratios hit 30, market analysts claim the market is overheated. While investors can make capital gains from rising share prices, the yield they receive will shrink. Even in a soaring market most investors, as opposed to speculators, expect to be paid dividends either now or in future, but in Japan the common view has been that shares need not pay earnings.[15] Any reservations about such a view would have been dispelled by the Nikkei 1989 highs, fuelling brokers' expectations that it would eventually reach 80,000.

Before the Japanese Bubble burst in 1990, P/E ratios had also soared to incredible levels. The Dow Jones at its most inflated in early 2000 averaged P/E ratios of about 30 and this alarmed US analysts. In Japan they were hitting well over 100 in the 1980s, meaning that the average earnings per share of companies listed on the Japanese market were less than one per cent.[16] This is paradise for companies because it means they "can raise money from the public for practically nothing",[17] but such a situation only works for investors if share values somehow keep rising, despite producing no earnings. For many years, this did occur in Japan, until late 1989 when the Nikkei hit 39,000. When the BOJ intervened to cool the economy in 1990 the share and properties markets realised the hollowness of many Japanese company and reacted accordingly. Hell hath no fury like a securities market misled. It can wreak terrible financial carnage, as the Japanese discovered all through the 1990s. Japan was paying the price for "asset infatuation" to the exclusion of more concrete measures of value. Eventually when the crash came, the Nikkei plunged to about 8000 by 1993 and in 2002 was again at 8000 before slowly rising to over 11,000 in 2004.

Japan's real estate sector, where such distorted asset-valuing methods as *tobashi* transactions prevailed, was hit particularly hard. By 1996, official land prices for Japan were half what they had been in 1991, but real prices were 88 per cent less or lower at auctions.[18] The sustained share market surge had been driven by the Japanese financial community's belief in the "magic of assets" which MOF policies had done much to propagate. When this belief collapsed, not only *keiretsus* but the banks were savaged.

Ineffectual Banks

Japan's illusionary asset values had also propped up the banks. Previously, Japan's banks had enjoyed high status in world banking circles because of their assets. In 1995, when ranked by assets, the world's top ten banks were Japanese and 29 were in the top one hundred, compared to only nine US banks,[19] but when Moody's Investors Service quantified liabilities in 1999 it found that only five of Japan's 11 city banks had an excess of assets over bad loans. No banks rated A, only one rated B, three C and 26 banks D. By early 1999, the average rating of Japan's major banks had plunged to E+, meaning they were basically bankrupt. Clearly size was a poor measure of financial health with such banks, where liabilities often equalled or exceeded assets. The best measure of corporate health is profitability. By this yardstick not a single Japanese bank got into the top one hundred.

The banks, which were a major part of the *keiretsu* network, have contributed significantly to Japan's economic malaise. Initially this was due to their reluctance to enforce bankruptcy laws against insolvent companies. Japanese banks allowed hopelessly indebted companies to keep trading by rolling over loans and reducing the interest rates rather than having the loans declared "bad". The banks felt compelled to do this because by foreclosing on bad loans they too could go bankrupt, as they were often stakeholders in companies of their major, sometimes insolvent, clients.

Such concerns are called "zombie companies" because they cannot service their debt and so require life support. Normally it would be a doomed strategy for banks to fend off bankruptcy by keeping alive insolvent companies they have stakes in, as they would only be delaying their own bankruptcy. But the formidable MOF decided this must not happen.

Costly Rescues

The *keiretsu*/banking cronyistic network was not only being fostered by the MOF-led bureaucracy but was being increasingly rescued by it during the stagnant 1990s. When banks and finance companies faced insolvency from propping up *keiretsus*, the MOF and BOJ would save them.

The MOF even intervened to rescue insolvent banks and companies when they had violated lending limits. For example, the Tokyo Kyowa Credit Cooperative was one of two credit cooperatives which went bankrupt after exceeding their lending limits to a single client – the EIE International Group.[20] It was subsequently revealed that

Kyowa's head was also the head of EIE, which had also bankrupted itself buying over-priced foreign real estate in the early 1990s. Senior MOF officials insisted that Kyowa keep lending despite violating limits and being technically bankrupt. It transpired later that the officials had been wined and dined, provided with free weekends at EIE's golf courses and flown to casinos in Macau and Australia where they gambled with chips paid for by EIE. When Asian property prices crashed, so did EIE and Kyowa; but Kyowa was then merged with another credit cooperative to form a new bank which was given US$1.3 billion in the form of grants and low-interest loans by the Japanese government to keep it afloat.[21]

The MOF has even been involved in covering up illegal *keiretsu* behaviour. One senior MOF official was said to be involved in concealing a securities company's losses. Yamaichi Securities had been illegally compensating favoured corporate clients for share trading losses from early 1992. The ruses it used to hide the losses were suggested by the head of MOF's Securities Bureau, according to Yamaichi's president. "Given the ministry's track record, many were prepared to believe him [the president]," said Backman.

Like the MOF, the BOJ has been equally ready to prop up failing banks. In March 2003, the BOJ sought to boost share market confidence by buying huge quantities of bank shares. Financial commentator William Pesek Jr remarked:

> *Only in Japan could a central bank propping up stocks be seen as a confidence-boosting measure...It runs counter to virtually every principle of central banking and market economics. What in the world will the bank do with its huge portfolio of stocks? Is the BOJ a central bank or a hedge fund?[22]*

Clearly, BOF and MOF practices for bailing out insolvent banks and companies contravened free market principles. Japan's banks made many poor loans, failed to foreclose on them when they turned bad and hid the resultant losses, sometimes on MOF advice. When the banks' losses were too great to contain, the MOF and BOJ intervened to save them.

The BOJ's bailing out of troubled banks allowed them to delay disposal of bad loans. Instead of cleaning up their balance sheets during the 1990s, Japan's banks took the easy path and kept alive zombie companies. This significantly contributed to Japan's huge debt burden, widespread misuse of capital and a decade-long slump. Only from about 2002 did the banks start the painful process of shedding bad loans.

The regular practice of propping up insolvent companies and banks would largely explain why Japan's banks have had one of the lowest returns on equity in the developed world. In 1997, Japan's banks averaged a return of only 3.1 per cent, compared to 17.6 per cent in Britain, 16.9 per cent in the US and 15.9 per cent in Australia.[23] Japan's poor returns were due to the violation of market principles which resulted in the misallocation of capital to less efficient enterprises. When large amounts of an economy's capital is misused in this manner its overall capital productivity suffers.

Soaring Debt Levels

Japan built up high hidden debt levels until the 1990 crash because of the MOF's cheap money policies and *Zaito* loans to chosen *keiretsu*; but debt levels shot up further after the 1990 crash and subsequent stagnation during the 1990s – and once more the MOF was largely responsible.

Japan's total debt burden had hit stratospheric levels by 1999 and bad loans were a significant component. For years the MOF had claimed that bad loans totalled Y35 trillion (US$330 billion),[24] but by 1999 the MOF admitted they had hit Y77 trillion, which meant that the cost of rescuing Japan's banks would be 23 per cent of GNP. This was only a fraction of the country's cumulative debt, which had risen to Y395 trillion, 72 per cent of GDP. (The gross federal debt by contrast was 64 per cent of GDP). Moreover, when the Y160 trillion shortfalls of municipal and prefectural governments were added, the total came to Y555 trillion, or 97 per cent of GDP in 1999. If estimates on Japan's various sources of hidden debt had been included, this percentage would have been even higher.

When *Zaito* loans to various bankrupt authorities and agencies were included along with other MOF short-term loans, Japan's debt reached 118 per cent of GDP in 1999. By early 2002, Japan's public debt had risen to 140 per cent of GDP, largely because of government programs to stimulate the economy.[25] As a result, in May 2002 Moody's, the international credit ratings agency, reduced Japan's sovereign rating to that of Botswana and Latvia. The credit rating of the world's second-biggest economy was the same as two very small and underdeveloped countries.

In 2005, Japan's combined central and local government debt was expected to reach Y719 trillion (US$10.3 trillion) equalling 144 per cent of GDP, according to 2004 government projections.[26]

Japan's severe debt problems are a legacy of the MOF's long-term policies. Debt levels initially rose due to the MOF practice of providing cheap money to the *keiretsu*, and since the 1990s Japan's debt has been greatly boosted by MOF and BOJ loans to rescue insolvent *keiretsu* and banks. By 2000, the estimated cost of rescuing Japan's banks was still 23 per cent of GDP.[27]

Lack of Venture Capital

Because so much capital has been wasted propping up troubled *keiretsu* and banks, there has been little left for the entrepreneurial SMEs. Huge amounts of capital that small nimble companies could have used much more productively were tied up in large concerns.

Another barrier to acquiring venture capital has been the MOF-dictated listing requirements of the Tokyo Stock Exchange (TSE). The MOF believed that the building up of industrial capacity was a top priority for Japan and this could be best done through bigger and older companies;[28] hence only old established firms could ever get a TSE listing. Also, companies seeking a listing on the Japanese equivalent of the US's NASDAQ exchange are subjected to an average review period of 5.7 years; they are usually companies that have been around for decades, not merely a few years or months as with NASDAQ concerns. "It's a cold, hard fact that in Japan newly launched companies have had no way of raising direct capital. In America they can; in Japan they can't," observes Denawa Yoshito, the founder of an internet stock market for unlisted venture companies.[29]

Both directly and indirectly, MOF policies have starved the economy's most entrepreneurial sectors of capital. This has been done directly by restrictive TSE listing requirements and indirectly by having bankrupt *keiretsus* propped up.

Impoverished Pensioners

Besides massive debt levels, another consequence of MOF cheap money policies has been the impoverishment of many of Japan's retirees. The already low interest rates paid on bonds and bank deposits were reduced even further by the MOF in the 1990s to prop up the share market and banks. The new rates were close to zero – the lowest levels in world banking since the early 17th Century. From the mid-1990s, interest rates on ordinary bank deposits were less than 1 per cent, with some sinking to 0.25 per cent in early 2003.

While such low interest rates meant virtually free money for industry, savers were hit hard. The tiny returns on people's savings caused widespread hardship, especially for retirees. Many Japanese chose to put their savings in safety deposit boxes and piggy banks rather than banks. MOF policies reflected the view that impoverishing the people was acceptable: that payouts to the public wasted national resources. But this reduced the economy's access to the nation's savings, while low interest income cut consumer spending. Both factors further stagnated the economy.

Besides forcing down interest rates to stimulate the economy, the MOF made pension funds and insurance companies purchase very low-yielding bonds to boost the share market whenever it declined. After having to buy minimal-interest securities for years, insurance companies began showing zero or even negative returns. This, combined with billions of dollars of bad loans after the late 1980s bubble, forced the nation's eight biggest insurers to write off billions. Many Japanese suffered severely, as life insurance accounted for about 20 per cent of Japan's household savings.[30]

Very low interest rates also harmed Japan's pension funds. In 1991, US pension funds returned a massive 28 per cent on their investments, while Japanese funds only gained 1 per cent. By 1998, Japanese pension funds had the worst performance worldwide. They had declined to 3.2 per cent while US funds were yielding 14.6 per cent. By the mid-1990s the situation of Japan's pension funds was dire. A September 1996 survey revealed that only 4 per cent of corporate pension funds had enough reserves to make payments to pensioners. Since then dozens of pension funds have gone bankrupt and have been unable to pay their members. Even such huge Japanese concerns as Mitsubishi Electric, Honda Motors and Toyota Motors have had pension fund shortfalls of over half a trillion Yen – and most Japanese companies refuse to reveal their pension shortfalls. The extent of the problem was shown by a World Monetary Fund estimate that Japan's pension liabilities were about 100 per cent of GNI in 1997.[32]

Like the MOF policy of providing cheap capital for industry, its imposition of minimal interest rates to boost the share market and support banks has been disastrous for ordinary Japanese. Not only have they earned almost nothing on their bank deposits; they have often been denied some or even all of their pension savings on retirement. Like growing numbers of Singaporeans, they have to work until they die.

Excessive Red Tape

Extensive bureaucratic red tape has been another major obstacle to new entrepreneurial ventures in Japan, which "has become one of the most heavily regulated nations on earth," notes Kerr.[33] Former Japanese prime minister Hosokawa Morihiro once said that when he was governor of Kumamoto he could not move a telephone pole without calling Tokyo for approval. Just running a noodle shop requires filling out lots of forms in triplicate with stamps and seals. The same endless permits are required to open food kiosks in Singapore, as shown earlier. In Japan a store must wait three years to get a liquor licence before it can sell domestic beer – but vending machines can sell beer freely anywhere. The retail sector especially labours under layers of regulations and must also pay endless fees and charges in order to function.

The heavy bureaucratic imposts border on corruption. They are administered in ways that seem designed to line the pockets of *amakudari* appointees who operate "a vast web of semi-government agencies", often called "special government corporations" (*tokushu hojin*).[34] *Amakudari* appointees who run these agencies are separate from those who have been assigned to the *keiretsu* sector.

A major source of income for these agencies comes from the fees for permits and compulsory lectures and study seminars that businesses must pay for if they want to operate. "The fees do not go back to the public purse but straight into the pockets of the *amakudari* who run the permit agencies."[35] Many regulations have been created in Japan to maximise opportunities for *amakudari* to enrich themselves: the more red tape there is, the more fees they can levy.

All this has made it more expensive to do business in Japan. In both Japan and Singapore, excessive red tape and bureaucratic imposts have increased the difficulty and cost of starting and operating a business. This has discouraged entrepreneurial endeavours, especially by SMEs.

Conclusions

Power has been centralised in Japan around a bureaucracy which remains largely unchecked by a weak parliament and cabinet (or any other institution). Under MOF leadership, Japan's bureaucrats have heavily intervened in the economy in order to promote rapid growth in ways they deemed most appropriate. They not only mobilised large amounts of cheap money for the *keiretsus* but also sanctioned dubious accounting procedures which delivered further huge sums to *keiretsus* via inflated asset values. This greatly boosted the *keiretsus'* share prices giving them access to even more capital through the stock market.

However, the cheap money that *keiretsus* gained through minimal interest rates and a booming share market was often wastefully invested. Cronyistic practices led to inefficient capital use, particularly in the propping up of insolvent concerns.

For years a booming equity and property market and questionable accounting covered up the failings of the *keiretsu* sector. Japan's overheated markets, based on unreal values and low or non-existent dividends, were eventually exposed, as were the corporations they sustained. The boom was a massive bubble ready to burst and this happened in 1990 when the BOJ realised the situation was out of control and raised interest rates to slow the super-heated economy. This pricked the bubble and share prices crashed. By August 1992, the market had lost 60 per cent of its value and by March 2003 the Nikkei had hit 8000. As the market collapsed, so did property prices, which fell dramatically from 1991. By 2000, they were one-fifth or less of bubble-era prices.[36] Banks found themselves saddled with enormous numbers of non-performing loans, which they only began shedding from 2002.

While MOF policies achieved impressive results for many years, their serious flaws caused Japan's economy to unravel in the early 1990s. Despite this, insolvent *keiretsu* and banks continued to be rescued – with capital that should have been used for new ventures to reinvigorate a moribund economy.

Meanwhile, national debt levels kept soaring while vanishing pension funds reduced many retirees to poverty. Crippling red tape continued to hinder new ventures, especially in the SME sector. All these problems were due to policies sanctioned and often initiated by the MOF and related bureaucracies (with the *keiretsus'* eager connivance). The policies represented a consistent violation of free-market forces and modern business practices. The result was continued widespread unproductive use of capital, which condemned Japan's economy to over a decade of stagnation.

The centralisation of political and economic power has led to similar economic problems in Singapore.

2. PAP Policies and their Consequences

Like Japan, Singapore pursued economic strategies that produced high growth rates for several decades. In Singapore's case this was done through statist policies and an open-door policy towards foreign capital. As with Japan, the effective implementation of such policies was made possible through a centralisation of political power.

Three basic strategies guided Singapore's economic development: handing over much of the economy to foreign capital to develop and operate, heavily involving the state in establishing and running the economy's local sector, and building up large financial reserves. From these strategies flowed a range of statist and forced savings policies as well as policies for sweeping land requisition, keeping down wages, controlling unions, minimising state expenditure and imposing a regulatory regime to monitor and control the economy. These measures involved heavy state intervention in the economy, disrupted market mechanisms and bred long-term economic problems – low productivity (especially of capital), venture capital shortages, excessive regulation and reduced consumer spending, and also depressed living standards for the poorest half of the population. The following summarises how violation of basic market principles led to these problems.

Statist Strategies

Singapore may initially have had sound economic reasons for its statist and pro-MNC policies. After Separation in 1965 the fledgling state needed MNCs to industrialise and develop an export-oriented economy if Singapore was to survive and prosper. This created a pressing need to quickly provide an efficient infrastructure to serve the MNCs and support rapid national development. A range of statutory boards and GLCs was created to build the transport, communication, harbour and other components for such an infrastructure.

Over time a large and growing network of SEs developed which expanded into private sector areas. The SEs bred increasing numbers of subsidiaries which increasingly poached business opportunities from SMEs. The SEs could do this easily because of the many advantages given to them by the Government. Being part of the state sector, SEs had inside information and contacts. They also came to enjoy such benefits as being granted licences or concessions, having their products and services purchased by the state and getting easy access to finance. In addition, SEs could hide behind various secrecy Acts to protect themselves from scrutiny and criticism. Many GLCs had the advantage of not being listed on the stock exchange, which freed them from having to pay dividends and significantly boosted their profitability.

If, despite all these advantages, the SEs foundered, the Government often bailed them out instead of letting the market punish them for bad investment decisions. In Singapore, the Government permitted GLC banks and other GLCs to rescue each other when necessary. As already shown in Chapter 15, in 1997 Keppel Bank, a GLC funded by public money, merged with Tat Lee Bank, which was facing big losses after bad loan exposures in Asia. Again in 1998, Singapore Technologies, one of the biggest GLCs, merged with another GLC, Sembawang Corporation, which had S$1.2 billion of debt and only S$446 million in cash to meet its commitments. Another questionable merger was between the POSBank, a solid public bank, and DBS, another one of Singapore's largest GLCs. DBS was badly hit by poor investments throughout Asia. Over 12 months during the Asian financial crisis in 1998 the bank's non-performing loans in Asia exploded from S$1.1 billion to S$7 billion.[37] At government insistence, a healthy bank was sacrificed to prop up a vulnerable one in a way that defied market economy principles.

The many advantages that SEs had over the private sector – including a state readiness to bail them out when necessary – created a very uneven economic playing field. An all-powerful PAP government was able to easily ignore SME complaints. As a result of sustained and unfair competition with large, predatory and over-resourced SEs, Singapore's SME and private sectors shrank in relative terms, forming a smaller share of the economy. The local economy was increasingly run by inefficient SEs operated by civil servants, ex-civil servants and retired cabinet ministers who had limited entrepreneurial, managerial and innovative abilities. The private sector, which usually had and still has more of these abilities, was forced into smaller, less profitable areas of the economy.

The benefits conferred on SEs by the Government have given them unfair advantages over the private sector. This has not only contravened free market principles but also perpetuated economic inefficiencies that have reduced productivity – productivity that is also indirectly undermined by the Government's forced savings policies.

Forced Saving

The new PAP state required huge amounts of capital to finance its nation-building strategies to provide the infrastructure of a modern industrial economy. Forced savings were initiated through the CPF and later the HDB schemes to do this. Both employers and employees were compelled by the Government to make increased CPF contributions, which only began to level off in the 1980s; in the 1990s contributions by employers were reduced, with employees' payments kept at higher levels. Sales of HDB units have continued to yield huge profits for the Government.

The collective effect of the Government's forced savings policies was firstly to give it control of over two-thirds of total savings. Through the forced-savings policies of the CPF and the HDB programs, and by the payment of low interest on CPF savings, the Government was able to account for 70 per cent of national savings from 1970-90 while only contributing 30 per cent of domestic capital formation.[38] Moreover, the Government chose to invest a high proportion of public sector savings and CPF assets abroad in equities, bonds, foreign exchange, real estate and short-term financial assets, mostly through the GIC.[39] Capital that should have gone into developing Singapore's economy was used to develop someone else's. Income flows from overseas investments are no substitute for the wealth that comes from goods and services produced by locally owned and run firms. Only by such means do countries acquire the industrial and economic infrastructure, develop the R&D capacity and gain the skills, managerial competence and experience needed to achieve economic independence. This has not happened much in Singapore largely because the SME sector has remained underdeveloped.

Apart from crippling SE/MNC competition, a shortage of venture capital has also stunted the SME sector. This has been due to much of Singapore's capital being drained off to be invested abroad by the Government and its SEs.

Another reason for the venture capital shortage has been the way the Government has structured the CPF scheme. The CPF has reduced the availability of venture capital by discouraging private capital from being used for venture purposes. As Singaporean economist and merchant banker, Daniel Lian noted:

> *The present scheme is biased against the development of entrepreneurship. It favours the buildup of wealth via passive vehicles such as cash/deposits, residential properties, shares, unit trusts and investment-linked insurance and it disallows the employment of CPF as risk capital for the pursuit of enterprise development.*[40]

The CPF has not only delivered the bulk of the country's savings into state hands but has ensured that much of the remainder is absorbed by property-type investments. Thus, despite having the world's highest national savings rate – an extraordinary 58.3 per cent of GDP in 2000[41] – Singapore's SMEs especially have been kept chronically short of venture capital. The long-term effect of limiting SME development has restricted the growth of Singapore's EICs and of the greater productivity that this would eventually yield.

Imbalances in the distribution of capital resources does much to explain Singapore's poor capital productivity, but centralised control of so much of the economy's capital has further reduced its productivity through correlation of errors.

The yield produced by capital essentially depends on the abilities of those who allocate and manage it. Usually private sector entrepreneurs are better at playing this role than civil servants and *amakudari*-style appointees. Normally, the more an economy's capital resources are controlled by the former, the greater the return on capital. This is because the entrepreneurial abilities of private sector entrepreneurs usually exceed those in the public sector. Even if civil servants could match the private sector for entrepreneurial ability, as economic actors, they are far fewer and less diverse. Limited numbers of bureaucratic entrepreneurs cannot monitor the economy and its markets with the same sensitivity as their far more numerous and varied private sector counterparts.

Central to effective resource allocation and entrepreneurial decision-making are mechanisms for accurately monitoring the economy's requirements. Knowing what the market wants is necessary for the efficient allocation of land, labour and capital resources. Monitoring mechanisms that best play this role are economic players closest to the markets, specifically producers and consumers. They could be likened to "receptors", reflecting the ebb and flow of supply and demand and of economic cycles. The more diverse and numerous such receptors, the more accurately can the economy be monitored and the more efficiently can resources be allocated.

In top-down economies such as Singapore's, where the state dominates so much of local resource allocation, market sensitivity has been lost. This has impaired efficient resource allocation, argues Singaporean economist Manu Bhaskaran, and leads to what he terms "correlation of errors". Decision-making that is,

> *dominated in effect by a single brain may not be able to simultaneously understand and evolve responses to the myriad of bottom up micro-economic changes that hit us from all sides....*
>
> *In a normal economy, substantial numbers of economic agents operate, each making their own calculations and decisions independently and thereby in a diversified manner. However, substantial control over the factors of production and the corporate sector by a government that is highly unified and centralised in its thinking probably means inadequate diversity in economic decision-making.*[42]

Misallocations of resources by Singapore's mandarin-style bureaucrats have been accentuated by correlated errors. The top-down nature of so much of Singapore's economic decision-making has meant much less diversity in economic decision-making:

> *This raises risks — a mistake made by the government could be transmitted to a substantial part of the economy causing dislocation. In such an economy errors tend to be correlated, unlike in a more diversified economy where mistakes offset each other, not reinforce each other.*[43]

The operations of the GIC, which was responsible for investing Singapore's huge reserves, illustrate the all-eggs-in-one-basket risk.

> *This literally amounts to placing all our eggs in one basket and hoping that the board of directors is always astute and honest enough in future to prevent something going wrong. This does not sound like a good basis for the long-term management of Singapore's assets....Simple risk management requires that we have a diversified set of investment corporations.*[44]

However high the quality of staff and decision-making claimed for the GIC, it "represents the interests of a single investor with a single time horizon and a single set of risk preferences".[45] Bhaskaran questions the claim that a large institution such as the GIC would be more efficient and competitive than smaller investment institutions. Would management of over US$100 billion yield economies of scale? "Experience suggests that institutions as small as US$20-US$30 billion can command substantial scale economies," he says.[46] Moreover, it is debatable that such institutions would always command the respect of banks and the investment community and so gain preferential service.

The poor performance of several ultra-large funds suggests that there are diseconomies of scale in fund management, Bhaskaran contends. "Ultra-large institutions lack the nimbleness and flexibility needed to perform well in difficult equity and other markets." More generally the centralisation of economic power in Singapore through a network of large SEs has promoted the development of a herd instinct. The PAP government claims that such government holding companies as Temasek Holdings give its GLCs substantial autonomy, but as Bhaskaran notes, many GLC officials come from similar educational and career backgrounds and live, work and operate in a common milieu – one in which there is much exchange of information and views. Though this may build a useful consensus at times, it also leads to a uniformity of opinions and group behaviour. Market economies operate best where a diversity of attitudes prevail, reflecting the complexity of a modern economy.

A more powerful factor ensuring conformity of decision-making in GLCs is that the Government has shares in them all. "Even if boards of directors and executives do operate independently, it is only natural that they take the cue from the Government in many critical ways," says Bhaskaran.[48] For example, if PAP leaders called on Singapore companies to venture abroad to China the GLCs would respond because of their government links. Non-GLC companies that have been conditioned to follow PAP directives would also feel compelled to participate by forming joint ventures with GLCs. With many Singaporean companies moving into China en mass, especially if concentrated in one or two projects, any correlated errors would be substantial. Such an error was created with the simultaneous rush by GLCs and private companies into local property in the mid-1990s. The boom crested by 1997 and by early 2004 property prices were still well down on boom levels with many developers, both GLC and private concerns, losing billions. Bhaskaran notes that "the high prices paid by Singapore companies, especially GLCs, in making large overseas acquisitions could also reflect correlated errors".[49]

The cash positions of many Singapore companies, mostly SEs, which were out of sync with the 1990s economic cycle, constitute another example of correlated errors. When the economy was buoyant and returns high, SEs had large cash reserves, an inappropriate position at such times. These reserves should have been earning much higher returns as investments. Conversely, during subsequent deflationary periods when investment returns were low, so were the SEs' cash reserves. They were earning modest returns as investments instead of being held as cash reserves, as most companies would normally do during economic downturns. The herd instinct of SEs resulted in collective mistiming and correlated errors.

In an economy where there is a greater diversity of economic agents, a much wider range of decision-making occurs. Astute decisions by some agents will balance the bad decisions by others. Such a corrective mechanism has been largely absent in Singapore where the state controls the lion's share of capital resources and can compel the private sector to follow it on "investment excursions" into China and elsewhere.

This correlation of errors, which has further reduced Singapore's capital productivity, has been another negative consequence of Singapore's SEs having control of too much of the country's capital resources through the Government's forced savings policies.

So far we have considered how the PAP Government's statist policies and CPF scheme have produced a large inefficient state sector and a stunted SME sector, and how such heavy and often harmful state intervention in the economy largely explains Singapore's unimpressive productivity. A particular effect of such intervention has been to create an uneven playing field, making it difficult for the private and SME sectors to compete with the SE sector and to raise venture capital. The normal market mechanisms for mobilisation and use of capital have been distorted. Moreover, the way the Government has structured the CPF scheme has exacerbated these problems, as have widespread land requisitions.

Land Requisition Policies

With Singapore's decision to rapidly industrialise in the 1960s there was a pressing need to maximise efficient land use for both industry and housing. More land was required, not only to accommodate the proliferation of manufacturing concerns but to re-house the population in HDB estates. To achieve both aims the Government suspended property rights so that it could requisition land. Respect for property rights is the cornerstone of market economies. Without such rights the gains of economic activity are always under threat. All who engage in economic activity, whether entrepreneurs, producers or employees must know that property they acquire is safe from confiscation by the state or anyone else. Uncertainty about property rights reduces the motivation to engage in economic activities to acquire wealth.

Confiscation of property by the state also impedes private-sector efforts to accumulate capital. In Singapore, land requisition policies have diminished private assets. Compulsory land acquisition at below market value represents a partial state expropriation of such assets. By paying less than the current price for citizens' assets, the state has in effect requisitioned part of their wealth. This reduces their capacity to finance business ventures and inhibits the growth of local private enterprise. Bhaskaran comments that the Land Requisition Act,

> is so broadly worded that it leaves non-state economic agents with little recourse, effectively diminishing their property rights, rights which are a critical core of the market economy. The law is so worded that no property owner in Singapore can truly assume that his property is safe from acquisition, possibly at a price that is likely to be perceived as unfair to his interests.[50]

Such uncertainty has inhibited entrepreneurial activities in Singapore.

State land requisitions have acted to increase business sector costs generally by raising the capital needed to establish and expand a business. Extensive state requisition of land has forced up prices for remaining private land. This becomes apparent when requisitioned land has been sold back to the private sector at inflated prices during government land auctions. Costly land purchases leave businesses with less capital with which to grow.

Heavy government intervention in Singapore's property market through land requisitions and auctions has distorted the market's operation. Land has been made more expensive for the private sector than if such requisitions had been less extensive. Though many land requisitions may have been necessary to aid economic development in Singapore's early difficult years, they have increasingly harmed the private sector over time by forcing it to buy over-priced land. Moreover, expensive land has given the Government a convenient rationale for its high HDB prices. It can claim that high land costs have pushed up HDB prices though in fact its own land requisition policies have done this.

Wage Controls and Revenue-maximising Policies

Excessive Government intervention in the economy has not just distorted the allocation and mobilisation of capital. Government wage, CPF and other policies have also reduced consumer spending in ways that have especially harmed the local private SME sector and undermined living standards and retirees' security.

The Singapore state has always intervened heavily in the economy to keep down wages and control unions, largely to please foreign capital. Unlike unions in Japan and the Western democracies, those in Singapore have been largely deprived of any bargaining power with employers. Labour has lacked the same freedom as capital to fight for its interests within a mutually-agreed framework of arbitrational rules and procedures. In other words, labour has to compete on an uneven playing field against employers, as SMEs must do against SEs, because state intervention has favoured one side over the other. In the case of the workforce, the state's preferences have artificially forced down the cost of labour. Singaporean workers have been paid much less than their counterparts in Australia and other developed countries where union/management power is more equal and workers are able to bargain with employers. By depriving the workforce of bargaining power the state has once again distorted market mechanisms – this time by under-pricing labour.

The Government's wage and union policies have ensured that the incomes of the lower half of Singapore's workforce are much less than those of the bottom 50 per cent from equally affluent countries with similar per capita incomes. While this has benefited MNCs and local employers, it has denied many Singaporeans anything more than a basic living standard and given them less disposable income than their counterparts in the West. For example, in 2002, 20 per cent of disposable income was spent on retail items in Singapore, compared to 35 per cent in Britain and 30 per cent in Hong Kong.[51] Singapore's relatively low private consumption expenditure becomes even more apparent when compared with that of other industrialised countries since 1990.[52]

**Table 29.1 – Comparative private consumption
expenditure as percentage of GDP**

	1990	2001	Average 1990-2001
Singapore	46.4	39.8	42.3
Korea	54.9	51.2	53.3
Taiwan	57.3	62.0	59.3
Malaysia	52.2	46.4	47.9
Hong Kong	56.7	56.1	58.6

The local retail sector has suffered most from Singapore's low consumption rate. SMEs generally depend on local markets to survive. Domestic spending levels are important to them, especially for the consumer items which SMEs most often produce. Healthy local demand is necessary for the development of SMEs, but a range of government policies has stifled local demand and hindered the growth of retail concerns, especially those which service the non-tourist market. Policies that have aimed to maximise revenue extraction and minimise expenditure have further reduced consumer spending. The Government sees such deflationary effects as secondary to its need to maximise revenue from overpriced HDB units while minimising interest payments on CPF contributions. Both policies have also depressed consumer spending.

They represent additional breaches of market principles and have been economically dysfunctional. First, the Government's policy of charging too much for HDB units has meant that inflated values have been built into housing prices. The Government cannot reduce HDB prices because to do so would cause property and housing prices – HDB and private – to crash. Much of most Singaporeans' wealth, which is sunk into their HDB units, would be wiped out. As a result Singapore is locked into permanently high housing prices because of the government policy of overcharging Singaporeans for HDB units to maximise state revenue, as Chapter 32 further explains.

Second, paying below market rates on CPF savings represents another abrogation of market principles and has also had dysfunctional consequences. While cheap money from CPF contributors has saved the PAP state billions in interest payments and added tens of billions to its financial reserves, it has eroded Singaporeans retirement incomes to the extent that many Singaporean retirees must live in penury or rely on their families to survive. Moreover, the limited spending power of retirees has further depressed consumer spending.

Overall, both low interest rates on CPF contributions and over-priced HDB units, combined with low wages and numerous indirect taxes, have not only denied affluence to about half of the population but have also so reduced their retirement savings that even minimal aged security is often denied them. These factors have greatly reduced consumer spending, producing further negative economic consequences, especially for firms supplying the local market.

Red Tape Restrictions

The PAP state has devised a dense network of rules to regulate and monitor all economic as well as social and political activity. The original aim was to ensure the population's obedience to the PAP's nation-building goals and strategies, but excessive red tape has impeded the development of an entrepreneurial and innovative culture.

While all sectors of the economy have been adversely affected by the Government's layers of red tape, this burden has affected SMEs the worst. It has been most costly for SMEs because they have far fewer clerical and other resources than MNCs and SEs with which to handle red tape. Bureaucratic regulation has thus been one more factor to hold back Singapore's SME growth and EIC development.

Conclusions

The main feature of Singapore's government policies since the 1960s has been heavy and regular state intervention in the economy to facilitate rapid national development. While these policies may have done much to produce high growth rates they have also resulted in Singapore remaining a dependent economy with unimpressive productivity levels. Singapore is heavily reliant on MNCs, foreign technology, and expertise. It has limited indigenous innovational capacity to devise new products, services, or technologies and lacks entrepreneurial ability to successfully develop and market them.

These outcomes are largely because of excessive and inappropriate government intervention by the economy. Such intervention has distorted market mechanisms by favouring less efficient over more efficient enterprises by crippling the SME sector, and stifling the development of EICs through venture capital shortages due to forced savings policies and excessive red tape. PAP Government policies have also produced a property market made vulnerable by over-prices HDB units and land requisition policies and given rise to a generation of impoverished retirees who must rely on their children (if they have any) to support them.

3. Comparing Singapore and Japan

Heavy state intervention in the economy to produce rapid growth and development has characterised the economic policies of both Singapore and Japan. In Japan, interventionist policies by the state have been of the mercantilist variety. In the name of rapid development, the state has fostered a chosen sector (the *keiretsu*), rather than establish a new one as Singapore has done. In both countries the state has permitted a favoured economic sector to grow and operate at the expense of other sectors and in ways often harmful to the economy and people.

Dysfunctional Economies

While the interventionist policies of both Singapore and Japan have resulted in high growth rates and rapid development, they have also bred similar structural problems – and in Japan, long-term stagnation.

In Japan's case, the MOF's strategy of favouring the *keiretsus* and making them the main engine of the economy has fostered an increasingly inefficient and corrupt corporate sector that has greatly reduced Japan's productivity. This strategy has been detrimental to the development of the SME sector and has diminished Japan's EICs. Dubious MOF-sanctioned accounting methods that grossly inflated corporate assets created a bubble economy which burst in 1990. To deal with the astronomical debt levels that this produced, the MOF, until the early 2000s, allowed huge amounts of capital to be used to keep the *keiretsus* afloat. This starved the SME sector of venture capital, delaying Japan's development into a more innovative entrepreneurial economy and worsening Japan's chronic stagnation.

In Singapore, extensive state involvement in the economy has also produced major structural problems, often similar to Japan's. Government policies have produced a large, privileged, but inefficient network of SEs and a stunted under-resourced SME sector. Such an economic structure has inhibited entrepreneurial and innovative activity and kept Singapore at the level of a dependent economy of mediocre productivity. Although Singapore is not as dependent as many Third World economies, it still heavily relies on foreign capital, technology and talent. It is also very vulnerable to fluctuations in world demand for its products.

Singapore's SE and Japan's *keiretsu* sectors mirror each other. Both are state-protected and heavily staffed by *amakudari*-style appointees. The inefficiencies of these sectors drag down their economies' productivity and EIC levels. Even so, Singapore's privileged SEs have not yet produced Japan-style debt levels. Although they have occasionally lost hundreds of millions in bad deals and have even paid billions too much for new concerns, they have not yet swamped Singapore with a tsunami of bad debt, as Japan's *keiretsus* and banks have done. Still, unlike Singapore, Japan has the advantage of not having its economy dominated by MNCs. At least Japan still owns the farm.

The interventionist policies of both countries have also sacrificed ordinary people's savings and the welfare of retirees. National development strategies have been largely financed by cheap money extracted from the people. The imposition of low interest rates in Japan and Singapore largely explains why so many elderly in both countries lack sufficient to retire on.

Without doubt, pensioners are far worse off in Japan than in Singapore. In Japan there are insufficient funds to honour pension requirements. Many insolvent *keiretsu* cannot meet their pension obligations to employees because money which their employees have saved for retirement has vanished. The disappearance of their savings has been a result of Japan's structural indebtedness. At least Singapore's CPF can still fulfil its obligations to contributors despite the meagre interest rates they receive on their savings. While Singapore's SE sector continues to feed on cheap money from CPF contributors, the people have not been as impoverished by the process as their Japanese counterparts.

The plight of the elderly and disadvantaged in both countries is exacerbated by the lack of any proper welfare system. In Japan, the concept of public welfare is alien to Japanese cultural values. There is little tradition of public charity in Japan and this is reflected in an almost total absence of provisions for the poor and destitute. The situation is not so grim in Singapore where a variety of charitable groups struggle to help the less fortunate; but the PAP's bedrock opposition to welfarism has ensured that relief for the needy comes primarily from NGOs rather than the state. Moreover, minimal state welfare means the underprivileged have less to spend and so helps keep down consumer spending in Singapore as in Japan, deflating markets for domestic concerns, especially SMEs.

Excessive red tape has further stifled EIC and SME development in Singapore and Japan. The plethora of red tape has been generated by policies to maximise state revenue and to tightly regulate and monitor the economy.

Finally, Singapore and Japan have shared structural problems caused by state policies that have led to inflated asset prices. In Japan there have been asset-inflating policies aided by questionable accounting that have subsequently led to crushing debt levels. In Singapore, asset inflation has largely occurred through the HDB scheme and government land requisition policies. The immediate effect has been artificially high HDB housing prices, but this has also resulted in inflated private housing and property prices, which have permanently distorted the price structure of housing and property markets.

Japan has a debt-laden economy and Singapore a dependent one; and both are burdened with second-rate productivity, limited EICs, over-priced property assets and under-funded retirees. These problems are consequences of undemocratic political systems that are characterised by centralised political power.

Common Political Failings

In liberal democracies a wide range of interest groups, political, social, and economic, can influence and shape state policies. Political power is sufficiently diffused to prevent any one group, class, clique or arm of government from monopolising political power for its own ends – at least compared to such quasi-democracies as Singapore or Japan.

In modern democratic societies the main economic groups representing land, labour and capital and the entrepreneurial sectors have a far greater opportunity to express their views and influence government policies than in less-than-democratic ones. Western democratic governments must always strive to fashion policies that will be supported or at least tolerated by most major classes and other social and economic groupings. Governments who fail to do so adequately are voted out and replaced with those who can. Such a democratic political environment minimises or at least moderates any exploitation, discrimination, or the favouring of one group, class, or sector of the economy over others. In addition, the unemployed, the old, and the disadvantaged are properly cared for.

In fully-fledged democracies, legal and institutional mechanisms have been devised by the state to ensure that one group is not given preference over others – at least not to the extent that occurs in Singapore or Japan. Such mechanisms reflect the balance of power between competing groups in a democratic society whose parliaments can only pass legislation that is backed by a majority of such groups and has substantial public support.

Laws fashioned in a democratic political environment – where there is some rough parity between the contending groups – are most likely to provide equality of opportunity and a level playing field for all. Such laws guarantee the civil rights and individual freedoms of all participants against transgression by those who oppose them, including the state. This ensures that the main interests in society, particularly those representing labour, capital, the consumer and the individual citizen, can freely lobby to be heard and can organise to support or oppose government proposals, plans and policies without being prosecuted or suppressed.

Though the process of democratic government is often messy and time-consuming it is more likely to provide a level playing field than an authoritarian state where input by interest groups and the public in the decision-making process is far more limited and often discouraged. In democratic states, the confused melee of conflicting interests is better at preventing one group or class from getting too much of an upper hand than in undemocratic states. Various, often opposing groups, balance each other. This situation, along with the legal and institutional safeguards most often found in democratic states, prevents any one grouping from excessively influencing policy to the detriment of others.

A more level economic playing field emerges that reduces the chances of economic policies being implemented that unfairly favour state enterprises over SMEs, or MNCs over local concerns, or employers over employees and unions, or state needs for cheap capital over financial security for retirees.

A more equally competitive environment also maximises the chances of the most efficient and capable economic actors succeeding. On a level playing field "the best man" or business usually wins; but when the playing field excessively favours one side over others then pure ability is not always enough. Connections with the state matter more. The most efficient economic agents, whether they be entrepreneurs, producers or investors, are marginalised by less efficient but better connected operators. The less capable are permitted to play too great a role in resource allocation and use.

In theory, supremely wise rulers who intimately understand the mechanisms of the market and its constantly changing requirements can allocate resources far more efficiently than the rough and tumble of a free market. But do such rulers exist? History provides infrequent examples. Few contemporary economists would think economics has evolved to a stage where it could provide any ruler, gifted or otherwise, with a sufficiently precise understanding of the operations of a modern market economy to devise guidelines on the allocation and management of resources that are superior to those offered by the market. Nonetheless, there are rulers who think they can better perform these tasks than the market provided they are given free rein to intervene in the economy. They usually rule dictatorial regimes or undemocratic states such as Singapore or Japan, where insufficient democratic safeguards are in place to check such grandiose thinking. Few Western democratic governments are given such latitude. They face parliamentary oppositions and contend with powerful lobby groups and public opinion that usually stymie any grandiose economic schemes that the state might have for heavy and intrusive intervention in the economy, unless it would benefit a majority.

Only in authoritarian and less-than-democratic countries such as Singapore and Japan does the state have the power to implement far-reaching economic strategies that may lack popular support. While such states may achieve high growth rates, their policies usually produce major structural problems.

The elitist attitudes of Singapore's rulers and Japan's MOF have created feelings of infallibility. Both leaderships think they know what is best for the country and ride roughshod over those who would oppose them. Lack of effective political opposition removes the checks that would discourage such thinking and limit the economic problems it breeds. Currently, no one can effectively challenge their belief that a small group of like thinkers from a narrow social group can far more efficiently invest, allocate and manage resources than a market where such functions are performed by a multitude of entrepreneurs, investors and producers.

If the elite is gifted and the economy is still fairly underdeveloped then command-style statist and interventionist policies may work for a while, especially if the economy has been in a chaotic state or recovering from war, as was the case with Japan after 1945. But such strategies become increasingly untenable as an economy develops and becomes more complex. No ruling elite, no matter how intelligent they are – or think they are – can possess the omniscience required to run the economy better than the market and its many actors.

The more specialised and developed an economy becomes the greater the variety of economic actors there are. Because they are each operating in their particular sector, sub-sector or industry they are more likely to know what the market requires in their area of the economy than mandarin bureaucrats or *amakudari* entrepreneurs. This is so whether a market's actors are managers and employers, workers and employees, or entrepreneurs and investors: and, if investors, whether they run trust funds or are retirees or other individuals who give their savings to trust funds to invest for them. The number of potential players in a modern market economy is infinite, but those closest to the ground in their industry or sector know what is best required. Their collective interaction produces market dynamics that result in a more efficient allocation and use of resources than can be achieved by the top-down policies of undemocratic rulers far from the market and/or those running favoured enterprises that are shielded from vigorous market competition.

Nonetheless, some significant and carefully executed state intervention in the economy is required in modern market economies for several reasons:

- To regulate the economy and ensure its effective functioning

- To provide public goods and services that the private sector cannot supply (especially in developing countries where the state must take a leading role in national development)

- To protect the workforce from exploitation and poor working conditions, and care for the aged, vulnerable, unemployed and handicapped

- To prevent unfair trading practices and the provision of unsafe goods, substandard services and environmental pollution.

It is a constant challenge for governments to discover how far and in what ways they should intervene in the economy. Too much state intervention occurs with the centrally-planned communist states – eventually resulting in low productivity and stagnation. Too little state intervention can lead to an anarchic "Wild West" capitalist-type economy where virtually any economic activity can occur, no matter how unjust, disruptive or harmful to society. Britain during the Industrial Revolution and the US until the 1920s come to mind.

Ascertaining when, where and how far the state must intervene in the economy is an ongoing problem for most governments. Recent history has shown that liberal democratic governments are ultimately better at meeting this challenge than non-democratic governments, especially authoritarian ones. Democratic governments are far more likely to reflect and adjust to the changing needs of society and the economy than undemocratic states. This flexibility reduces social and economic imbalances that can develop in a changing and evolving society. The central democratic mechanism to achieve this is the feedback from the ruled to the rulers, via such mediums as free elections and independent media. The people communicate their needs, wants and desires to the government, which must then respond sufficiently to them to retain power. This ensures a far more sensitive response to the people's demands than anything authoritarian states are capable of. Such states usually have a monopoly of political power that enables them to easily ignore such demands. Over time the refusal to address legitimate grievances and requests from broad sections of society and the business community breeds dysfunctional socio-economic conditions. In Japan this has produced economic stagnation and mediocre productivity; in Singapore it has also caused mediocre productivity. In the former Soviet Union and its East European satellites it caused both these problems and political unrest.

The more that equality of competition prevails in a modern market economy, the greater its efficiency. A democratic state where political power is far more diffuse normally produces a more equal playing field than less-than-democratic states where power is much more concentrated and less accountable. Misallocation and inefficient use of resources is likely to be greater in undemocratic states. Eventually this leads to major structural problems, as Singapore and Japan have demonstrated.

Excessive centralisation of political power not only produces harmful policies but is also self-perpetrating. Rulers will always use their power to protect their position by destroying rivals and avoiding accountability. They resort to the politics of opacity to hide their mistakes or abuses of power. Both Singapore and Japan display such characteristics, as the next chapter shows.

References

1. Three of note include: Alex Kerr, *Dogs and Demons, the Fall of Modern Japan* (London, Penguin, 2001); Michael Backman, *Asian Eclipse* (Singapore, John Wiley & Sons, revised edition, 2001); and Ben Hills, *Japan Behind the Lines* (Sydney, Hodder and Stoughton, 1996).
2. Kerr, p. 81.
3. Ibid, pp. 257-8.
4. Backman, p. 137.
5. Ibid, p. 149.
6. Ibid.
7. Ibid.
8. Ibid.
9. Ibid, p. 136.
10. Ibid, p. 152.
11. Ibid.
12. Kerr, p. 110.
13. Backman, p. 154.
14. Kerr, p. 79.
15. Ibid, p. 82.
16. Ibid.
17. Ibid.
18. Ibid, p. 84.
19. Ibid, p. 85.
20. Backman, p. 150.
21. Ibid.
22. *The Straits Times* (ST), March 27, 2003.
23. Backman, p. 129.
24. Kerr, p. 80.
25. *Europa Yearbook 2004*, p. 2287. <www.europaworldonline.com>.
26. *The Australian*, July 22, 2004.
27. Kerr, p. 80.
28. Ibid, p. 83.
29. Ibid.
30. Kerr, p. 262.
31. Ibid, p. 263.
32. Ibid, p. 265.
33. Ibid, p. 137.
34. Ibid, p. 134.
35. Ibid, p. 137.
36. Ibid, p. 79.
37. ST, March 9, 1999.
38. Doshi, Tilak: "Chaining the Leviathan: A public choice interpretation of Singapore's elected presidency", p. 150 in Tan, Kevin Y. L. and Lam Peng Er, editors, *Managing Political Change in Singapore* (London, Routledge, 1997).
39. Ibid.
40. Lian, Daniel, "Global U, Pricing Power and Singapore Stones – Cyclical and Structural Challenge Confronting the Singapore Economy 2002 and Beyond", p. 96 in *2002 Perspectives on Singapore*, edited by Chang Li Lin (The Institute of Policy Studies, Times Academic Press, Singapore, 2002).
41. *The Global Competitiveness Report 2001-2002* (New York, Oxford

University Press, 2002), p. 359.

42. Bhaskaran, Manu: *Re-inventing the Asian Model: The Case of Singapore* (Singapore, Times Media, 2003), p. 31.

43. Ibid, p. 32.

44. Ibid, p. 56.

45. Ibid.

46. Ibid, p. 57.

47. Ibid.

48. Ibid, p. 32.

49. Ibid, p. 48.

50. Ibid, p. 38.

51. Ibid, p. 43

52. Ibid.

CHAPTER 30

OPAQUE SOCIETIES

I n the knowledge economy information is power. Factors that impede the free flow of information weaken a society, both economically and politically. Such concerns drive the constant calls for corporate and government transparency. In modern post-industrial economies, creativity is critical and access to information is essential. Markets rely on comprehensive, reliable and accurate information to make sound decisions – but such information is only readily available in democratic societies with strong independent media and cultural values that encourage openness and information-sharing. The opposite occurs in opaque and secretive societies such as those of Singapore and Japan's, where access to information is restricted and official data often limited, distorted and inaccurate. Both lack sufficiently independent media to expose questionable official data and critically scrutinise state decision-making. They also have cultural mindsets that discourage transparency and information-sharing and ultimately reduce productivity.

1. Unaccountable and Secretive

Most power-holders prefer making secret (opaque) decisions because this greatly reduces the need to be accountable. Secret decisions don't have to be explained or justified as transparent ones must. Opacity's benefits for decision-makers are most evident when problems or mistakes occur: cover-ups ensure power-holders escape blame or penalties for bad decisions. This cannot be done so easily in democratic states where leaders are usually required to explain and justify their decisions and failure to do so means criticism and a loss of popularity and even of power.

Similar principles apply to corporate governance by company boards and directors. They too must be transparent and accountable in their decision-making. If not, shareholders can have them penalised or even removed.

While most power-holders prefer opacity, only those in undemocratic states can easily practise it. Where power is heavily centralised and unchecked, weak oppositions and intimidated people cannot force their rulers to be transparent. In Singapore, an all-powerful PAP leadership and state can easily resist demands from the opposition or public for more accountability. As Chapter 15 shows, Singapore's bureaucrats have thickets of rules to prevent information being released. Not only cabinet decisions but also the operations of statutory boards and many GLCs are shrouded in secrecy. Only in Singapore's local private sector has transparency begun to be practised recently. This has been – ironically – due to government pressure, driven by international demands that Singapore become more transparent and practise better corporate governance.

In Japan as well opacity prevails on both the governmental/bureaucratic and corporate levels. As with many of Singapore's SEs, the "special government corporations" in Japan do not have to open their books to the public. Such bodies as the New Tokyo International Airport, Water Resources Public Corporation and "dozens of other huge special corporations" do not have to publish balance sheets but "function in near total secrecy," notes Kerr.[1] This secrecy has allowed many vast and hidden debts in these corporations to remain undetected, often with MOF connivance.

The MOF has regularly covered up for the scandal-prone corporate and banking sectors, especially during the corruption scandals of the 1990s. Not only do Japan's bureaucrats fail to practise transparency and accountability but so do its corporations, which regularly flout the rules of corporate governance. The MOF has also been repeatedly evasive about the severity of Japan's economic problems. Bankers have been instructed to avoid revealing information on the extent of bad loans.

The cover-up instincts of Japanese bureaucracy were revealed during the Daiwa Bank scandal in which the bank lost US$1.1 billion. Daiwa had breached US banking regulations by failing to notify US bank regulators of its plight. In September 1995, it emerged that the MOF had known of Daiwa's financial irregularities since April 1994. This omission by the MOF ignored an important inter-government protocol pertaining to such matters. The MOF and Daiwa's behaviour severely damaged Japan's credibility. In commenting on the Daiwa scandal, Lingle remarks:

> This lack of transparency is a common obstacle in economies that have deep traditions of bureaucratized regulations within a hierarchical political system. In this context, the system of accountability is designed to protect existing institutional arrangements, governments, or political figures rather than customers, shareholders, or citizens.[2]

During the 1990s Japan begun to pay a heavy price for bureaucratic-led cover-ups. While discussing the Japanese banking sector's response to the country slump, Lingle notes "a face-saving conspiracy of silence between the Ministry of Finance and Japanese bankers has prevented the kind of market scrutiny needed to force the resolution of the fundamental problems."[3] Such secrecy buries rather than resolves problems.

"Japan doesn't have a strong culture of corporate governance," says Backman.[4] In fact the concept is so new to the Japanese that they have only recently created a term for it: *koporeito gabanasu*. Few Japanese companies have independent non-executive directors to safeguard the interests of minority shareholders. Directors are not appointed for their ability or diligence, but as a reward for long service, not for any capacity to protect shareholders. Moreover, directors are not required to fully disclose their current or former relationships with the company or its affiliates. "Activist directors are unusual and are generally unwelcome."[5]

Minority shareholders are even more marginalised in Japan than in Western countries. Even annual general meetings (AGMs) in Japan cannot be used by them to air their views and question management. "Instead, what they are given is a farce," states Backman.[6] Most Japanese public corporations hold their AGMs during a single two-day period every year. In 1996, 94.2 per cent of listed companies which had closed their books in March 1996 held their meetings on June 27. Shareholders with a diversified portfolio had no hope of attending AGMs for all companies they had invested in. Not surprisingly, 90 per cent of AGMs concluded without a single question from shareholders. In 1996, the average AGM lasted 26 minutes.

Not only investors but financial journalists are disadvantaged by such practices, because they too cannot cover many AGMs. This suits corporate Japan admirably. As Backman notes:

> *Openness and scrutiny are really not part of Japan's corporate culture, whereas minimizing the opportunities for possible embarrassment is. That a shareholder should feel the need to ask a question might be construed as a loss of "face" to management.[7]*

Such unquestioning mindsets have perpetuated the opacity which permitted widespread corruption in Japan's bureaucratic and corporate circles to flourish unchecked for so long.

The 1990s' corruption scandals, which reached a peak in late 1997 and early 1998 when they engulfed the upper echelons of Japan's civil service, began when six of MITI's top officials were disciplined for allowing as many as 52 other MITI staff to be entertained in restaurants and on golf courses by an Osaka businessman notorious for his underworld connections, bribery and tax evasion. That was just the beginning:

> *It soon emerged that the nation's most prominent banks and insurance companies had systematically spent enormous amounts on entertaining government bureaucrats in exchange for confidential information, tipoffs when bank inspections were about to be made, advance notice of changes to banking laws, and helping to conceal damaging records.[8]*

Some 98 staff from Japan's central bank, the Bank of Japan, were disciplined for accepting lavish entertainment from private banks and other financial institutions. One official was arrested and both the bank's governor and his deputy resigned to "take" responsibility. Around the same time, an internal probe at the MOF, during which several ministry officials committed suicide, found that 112 of its officials had accepted "excessive" entertainment from private financial institutions. Some had even accepted cash bribes. Among the 112 was the vice-finance minister for international affairs. Two other officials were arrested and another resigned, as did the finance minister. One finance official of note had been entertained "excessively" on 170 occasions over a five-year period by insurance companies and other concerns. These were firms he was supposed to be regulating.

Such corruption best flourishes in societies where opaque decision-making prevails. Offering and accepting bribes is easiest when no one is looking. The same goes for the abuse of power and the pursuit of potentially unpopular policies. Unmonitored secret decisions can be implemented before they can be effectively opposed.

The same observations can be made about Singapore. As Chapter 15 shows, a pervasive lack of transparency, especially about the operations of SEs and especially such important ones as the GIC, is apparent. Even so, the PAP state seems to have kept corruption at much lower levels than Japan and other Asian countries. But both countries have similar levels of opacity and cultural and political/bureaucratic factors are to blame.

Like Singaporeans, the Japanese share the common Asian attitude that knowledge is power and should only be grudgingly divulged. As Kerr observes:

> *The facts about much of Japan's social, political and financial life are hidden so well that the truth is nearly impossible to know.*[9]

As in Singapore, bureaucrats in Japan do their best to limit public access to official records. Japanese citizens regularly discover this when seeking information from state bodies. In 1996, auditors at government agencies turned down 90 per cent of public requests for audits from 1985-94.[10] If citizens' groups press too hard, documents simply vanish, especially when officials wish to deny access to potentially embarrassing material. While civil servants everywhere try to cover up mistakes and dubious decisions, in countries like Japan and Singapore they can do so very easily. Japanese aversion to releasing information is reflected in the websites of their top universities and government departments, as Kerr found.

> *Log on to the Internet home pages of important Japanese entities and you will find a few meager pages, as poor in quality as in quantity, consisting mostly of slogans.*
>
> *From university home pages ... you will never get a clue to any serious data such as Tokyo University's budget, Keio University's assets, the makeup of the faculty, a cross section of the student body and so forth, only "What Our University Stands For". Most serious information about these schools is secret, not available in any medium, much less on the Internet.*[11]

Websites for such government departments as Japan's Construction Ministry and River Bureau are similarly deficient. The Ministry's website has a few pages of slogans and some dead links. By mid-2000, the Osaka and Tokyo stock exchange sites had "failed to offer any information of substance (for example, the value of new or secondary listings) and did not even have something so rudimentary as a ticker with current index levels".

The slowness with which the Internet has brought greater openness to Japan has been due to its secretive culture as illustrated by a vigorous practice of "industrial secrecy".[11] In the old manufacturing economy, companies would patent techniques and lock them in a safe, hidden from outsiders. Japanese have been good at that, believing in the adage, "Patents are only for a time; a secret is forever". Such mindsets are inappropriate in the post-industrial economy where the explosive development of software and new Internet technologies require collaboration and information-sharing. Computer engineers are often helped by colleagues and friends to find "the missing part" in some new software design. Someone finds the part and everyone benefits. In Japan, says Kerr, "such free and easy give-and-take is nearly inconceivable. Hobbled by secrecy, new ideas in Japan will continue to come slowly – and in the new economy there is no greater sin than to be slow".[13]

Cultural attitudes that condone opacity and the hiding of problems discourage not only information-sharing but whistle-blowing. A survey of Tokyo workers found that 99 per cent of them would not disclose any wrong-doing in their company.[14] Such silence can have serious consequences for public safety. In July 2000, Japanese police found that for 23 years Mitsubishi Motors had been hiding from investigators most of its documents on customer complaints.[15] At first Mitsubishi had kept its records in a company locker room, but after 1992 it created a computer system for storing dual records – those to be reported to regulators, and those to be kept secret. Only after police discovered the ruse did Mitsubishi start to deal with suspected problems in 2000, recalling over two million cars for defects including bad brakes, fuel leaks and failing clutches.[16] In June 2004, the firm recalled another 347,000 cars globally. This latest recall hit Mitsubishi share prices hard. Company plans to revive itself included shedding its opaque practices. The company's chairman hoped that by "coming clean" Mitsubishi would win back the trust of its customers. That the need for a second recall was required four years after the first demonstrates how difficult it is to change Japan's opaque corporate culture.

A similar scandal occurred in June 2000 at the giant milk producer Snow Brand. Tainted milk poisoned 14,000 people because of careless sanitation procedures that had remain unchecked for decades.[17]

Official and corporate opacity can cause harm in two ways. First, opacity permits cover-ups to bury problems that worsen over time. Second, opacity reduces both the quantity and quality of information circulating in a society. This impedes innovation and has other adverse economic effects.

2. Suspect Statistics

Economic efficiency depends on both access to information and its quality. How reliable and accurate is it? Here too Singapore and Japan share some unfortunate similarities. While Singapore's official statistics are suspect, in Japan both official and corporate data are. Kerr notes that "a lack of reliable data is the single most significant difference between Japan's democracy and the democracies of the West".[18] Initially cultural factors could account for this. As Kerr explains, "truth" in Japan has traditionally never been sacrosanct, nor do "facts" have to be real. In Japanese culture, ideal forms are regarded as being more true than reality which fails to fit the ideal. The ideal must be maintained. Brutal facts must not be allowed to prevent this. Such thinking may explain Japanese reluctance to admit blame for their war-time atrocities.

The Japanese desire to gloss over reality results in the production of misleading and erroneous data. Japan's dubious accounting methods have resulted in artificially inflated assets that bear little relation to reality. Kerr remarks that such accounting is "endemic" and a defining feature of Japanese industry,[19] as its asset-inflating and *tobashi* transactions reveal.

When the national debt has been calculated Japan's statistical discrepancies become colossal. Official estimates of its bad debts went from Y27 trillion in the early 1990s to Y35 trillion in 1996, Y60 trillion in 1997 and Y77 trillion in 1999."Even then the MOF was far from admitting the true figure, which might be double that amout," Kerr notes.[20]

Statistical distortion is the norm in Japan. "Skewed numbers are endemic in every field."[21] Karel van Wolferen, a well-known commentator on Japan, observes: "Systematic misinformation is a policy tool of Japan." Unsuspecting foreign economists, especially those of neo-classical (or neo-con) persuasion "are easy targets". "We simply do not know, even approximately, the level of employment, the amount of problem loans, assets and debts in most corporate sectors." [22]

Normally, misleading or false data would be probed and exposed by a free and vigorous press, as would attempts by authorities to hide behind walls of opacity. Such a press only exists to a limited degree in Japan and even less so in Singapore.

3. Muzzled Media

In Japan and Singapore, docile media have done little to make their societies more transparent or decision-makers more accountable.

In Western democracies, the media, "the fourth estate", fosters the separation of powers, but in Japan, and even more in Singapore, the media have become part of the collusive networks, the iron triangles, that rule both societies. A lack of media independence from existing power structures and widespread opacity have prevented the monitoring and exposure of abuses of power and so crippled efforts to reduce it.

In Japan, not only government officials but also the media are recipients of corporate largesse. Journalists too "are targets for being wined and dined, paid off, and compromised".[23] Other stratagems are also used to muffle the media. Media outlets receive such inducements as free telephone calls and temporary broadcasting facilities from organisations they cover. Journalists can join clubs to report on each company and even operate from offices that companies provide. Industry associations and government agencies even grant exclusive rights to chosen news organisations to cover their affairs. Such cosy arrangements deny other organisations access to interviews, information and news conferences. Should the news organisation become too investigative, its exclusive coverage rights are dropped and given to a competitor:

Investigative reporting in Japan all too often is confined to revealing the marriage plans of local rock stars, sumo wrestlers, and Japanese baseball players who make it big in America; rarely does it involve breaking stories about the misdeeds of Japan's corporations.[24]

While occasionally the Japanese media does expose and criticise such corporate malpractices as *amakudari*, corporate Japan usually escapes media scrutiny. Only when a scandal becomes too big to be ignored are teams of journalists assigned to cover it. Many smaller scandals receive little attention. Singapore's media cannot perform even this token journalistic role, being more docile than Japan's. The PAP state's tight control of Singapore's media is well known. Lee Kuan Yew and his ministers have repeatedly told Singapore journalists that they must consider "the national interest" first. Nation-building, promoting racial and community harmony, "educating the people", must be their priorities, not muck-raking and "embarrassing" Singapore's rulers and bureaucrats with unsavoury exposes. As a result, Singapore media coverage of bad investment decisions by SEs is minimal. Stories on the corporate shortcomings of Singapore's SEs get much better coverage in such publications as the *South China Morning Post*, the *Far Eastern Economic Review*, the *Asian Wall Street Journal* and *The Australian*.

Were it not for occasional critical commentaries by foreign writers and journalists, little would be published on the economic problems of Japan and Singapore. The journalists of neither country can do this well. Being kept in the dark and being misled certainly applies to Japanese and Singaporean journalists. Officials hide the truth and provide them with unsound and false information. Should journalists try to report critically, various governmental and corporate sanctions quickly discourage them. Intimidation prevents any meaningful checks on power-holders. Instead, Japanese and Singaporean media have disguised flawed economic policies and so helped to perpetuate them. Little publicity about failed government policies means minimal public pressure to reverse them.

Opacity is a practice all governments and rulers pursue to retain power: it permits the mistakes and abuses of power to be covered up, avoiding the popular hostility this can generate. A lack of tranparency can be most easily maintained in undemocratic and authoritarian states where power is most concentrated. In such states there are few democratic mechanisms to force rulers to be open and accountable or to provide public access to official information. Opacity not only results from the centralisation of power but preserves and even extends it. The greater the power that rulers have, the more secretive they can be in their decision-making, protecting themselves from political unpopularity for misrule or any misuse of power. Opacity therefore protects their power – and helps perpetuate any dysfunctional economic and other policies they are practising.

Opacity has operated independently as a cultural trait, one that has negative economic and other effects, in Singapore and Japan. These countries have discouraged openness and information-sharing, restricting the flow of information and the exchange of ideas necessary for creativity and innovation in the post-industrial knowledge economy.

Other cultural factors can also undermine economic efficiency as already shown in Singapore. Japan shares many of these factors with Singapore, as the next chapter explains.

References

1. Kerr, Alex: *Dogs and Demons: the Fall of Modern Japan* (London, Penguin, 2001), p. 110.
2. Lingle, Christopher: *The Rise and Decline of the Asian Century* (Hong Kong, Asia 2000, second edition, 1997), p. 93.
3. Ibid, p. 245.
4. Backman, Michael: *Asian Eclipse: Exposing the Dark Side of Business in Asia* (Singapore, John Wiley and Sons, revised edition, 2001), p. 147.
5. Ibid
6. Ibid, p. 148.
7. Ibid.
8. Ibid, p. 133.
9. Kerr, p. 104.
10. Ibid, p. 109.
11. Ibid, p. 128.
12. Ibid.
13. Ibid, p. 129.
14. Ibid, p. 122.
15. Ibid.
16. *The Australian*, June 4, 2004.
17. Kerr, p. 122.
18. Ibid, p. 104.
19. Ibid, p. 107.
20. Ibid, pp. 124-5.
21. Ibid, p. 124.
22. Ibid.
23. Backman, p. 155.
24. Ibid.

CHAPTER 31

COMMON CULTURAL AND ORGANISATIONAL FAILINGS

Efficiency and cutting-edge expertise have been central claims of Singapore's miracle as they were of Japan's until the early 1990s. Since then, productivity figures and other data have shown that the growth of both economies was less than miraculous. Japan's miracle had crested by the mid-1970s when increasingly wasteful allocation of resources because of extensive and inappropriate state intervention in the economy became the norm. That was at the macro-economic level. Japan, like Singapore, also has many endemic inefficiencies and shortcomings at the organisational and micro-socio-economic levels. Moreover, many seem to have similar cultural and organisational causes. Like Singapore, Japan has currently displayed limited capacities for innovation and new product development, despite past successes in this field. But also like Singapore, Japan has had some very visible efficiencies that have masked its severe shortcomings.

1. Endemic Inefficiencies

Singapore's endemic inefficiencies are described in Chapter Eight, where deficiencies are noted in such diverse areas as taxi and bus services, book publishing, government accounting, TB control, the quality of locally manufactured goods, laboratory management, swimming pool management and cinema projection. A range of cultural, organisational and other factors were cited to explain these deficiencies.

Japan displays similar specific failings in many areas. They have been most evident in Japan's inadequate handling of natural disasters and nuclear accidents, poor supervision of nuclear power plants, shoddy construction of bridges and expressways and other infrastructure, and sub-standard medical services and pharmaceutical products. Japan too has limited EICs, like Singapore. Similar cultural, organisational and educational factors are largely to blame – and in Japan's case, significant corporate-government corruption.

Sub-standard Construction

After visiting Los Angeles following its January 1994 earthquake, Japanese officials were shaking their heads at the destruction of high-rise buildings and highways, complacently remarking, "It could never happen in Japan": "our standards are far higher, our highways three or four times as strong". "It took just twenty-two seconds to destroy that hubris," remarked Hill when the Kobe earthquake hit on January 17, 1995, killing 6000 people.[1]

Not only did many old wooden structures and other buildings collapse, but so did half of Kobe's commercial buildings. Damage to government infrastructure was even worse. The supposedly indestructible bullet train – a symbol of Japanese technological pride for 30 years – had its tracks collapse in a dozen places. A one-kilometre section of the elevated Hanshin Expressway, built in 1970 and supposedly subsequently reinforced, snapped and fell over, crushing scores of vehicles and killing their occupants. Eighty per cent of Kobe's port fell apart, with cranes toppling into the sea and its concrete docks cracking up. Particularly disturbing was the collapse of the "quakeproof" underground tunnels of Kobe's subway system. Investigations found that many structures collapsed because of deficient government standards and dishonest and incompetent building contractors.

The Government had boasted that its earthquake standards were the world's toughest. They had been periodically upgraded since 1926, three years after the great Tokyo earthquake of 1923, which registered 7.9 on the Richter scale. Although standards were supposed to resist a quake of 7.9, they were clearly inadequate for dealing with the weaker 7.2 Kobe quake.

The devastation was widespread because political corruption; and the substandard work of unsupervised and inept building contractors had resulted in building standards being flouted. Contractors are one of the main sources of hundreds of millions of dollars of bribes that nourish the Japanese political system. "Contributions, not cost or competence, win the contracts," notes Hills.[2]

The elevated expressway collapsed because contractors had ignored the building code and used pre-cast concrete instead of welded steel beams to support the highway. This almost doubled the load on the supporting pillars, which snapped when the quake struck. Steel reinforcing was scrimped on, welding was substandard and wooden forming was left in the pillars. As a senior executive of one construction firm confessed after the Kobe quake, "We were told to build light, thin and cheap". The bridges especially were "too scary to cross, after what happened in Kobe".[3]

The Kobe quake and subsequent revelations demonstrated that in the earthquake-prone land of Japan "earthquake proofing" was a myth. Japanese had to face the chilling fact that almost every building, every bridge and highway in Japan, had been built to inadequate safety standards and would fall to bits if subjected – as, inevitably, one day they would be – to a quake as violent as the one that hit Kobe.[4]

After the Kobe quake building standards were tightened. A decade later in December 2005, Japan was rocked by another earthquake building standards scam.[5] A government probe found that a Japanese architect had falsified earthquake safety data on at least 40 hotels and blocks of flats to reduce costs. Some of his buildings would not even have withstood a moderate earthquake. Dozens were slated to be demolished.

Building experts believed the scandal was just the tip of the iceberg: Japan's construction companies had had to cut corners to survive more than a decade of recession. Japan was aghast that safety inspectors had failed to check the architect's work, allowing him to design deficient buildings for more than a decade.

The ongoing lack of proper regulation of the construction industry illustrates one of the many paradoxes about Japan. Despite being a rule-bound and safety-conscious society in often quite trivial ways, it frequently displays high levels of bureaucratic slackness in such critical matters as the enforcement of adequate building codes. The nuclear power industry has provided further examples of this.

Nuclear Plant Accidents

In September 1999, a nuclear reaction was triggered accidentally at the JCO fuel-processing plant at Tokaimura, 140km northwest of Tokyo. The Government had to admit that it had not planned for such a contingency. Worse still was the revelation that JCO had failed to warn staff of the cataclysmic consequences of having an excessive concentration of uranium in the manufacturing process to themselves and to the plant. The company had one manual to show government inspectors (who visited the plant irregularly, and always when the processing section was shut down) and a simplified one for the workers, designed to speed up uranium pellet production. JCO workers deviated from even this, resulting in Japan's worst-ever nuclear accident.[5]

Before the Tokaimura accident, another had occurred in 1995 at Monju, a fast-breeder reactor near Tsuruga which suffered a major leak from its cooling system.[6] Nuclear energy authorities claimed the leakage was "minimal" but it later turned out to be more than three tons, the largest accident of its kind in the world. The Monju plant was shut down for the rest of the decade.

Despite the 1999 incident at Tokaimura, a leak occurred at the plant in June 2004.[7] Ageing valves designed to prevent leaks had not been replaced for about 30 years. In August 2004, five workers were killed by a nuclear leak at the Mihama nuclear plant, 350kms west of Tokyo.[8] Non-radioactive steam leaked from a ruptured pipe which was 14 years overdue for replacement at the plant, which was operated by the Kansai Electrical Power Company (Kepco). "The accident not only showed scandalous neglect of safety at Mihama .... but that the problem extended to other Kepco plants which now have to be checked before they can go back online," reported *The Australian*'s Tokyo correspondent, Peter Alford. "Mihama is the worst of a series of egregious accidents, errors and cover-ups in the Japanese industry, not least because it showed that some operators had learned nothing from earlier mishaps." [9] Some 16 months previously Tokyo Power and Electric Company (Tepco) idled its 17 reactors for inspection and maintenance after admitting cover-ups of faults in some of its reactor walls.

Again in July 2007, further bungling by Japan's nuclear power industry was revealed after an earthquake battered a nuclear plant at Kashiwazaki, a northern coastal town.[9a] The plant was found to been built directly above an active earthquake fault line, causing atomic leaks when the quake hit. Leaks continued undetected for days and cast doubts on the plant's emergency measures. Damage to the plant was also under-reported by its officials.

Bullet Train Mishaps

Near-disastrous bullet train mishaps have revealed further organisational incompetence in Japan. In October 1999, a 225kg slab of concrete fell off a wall and on to the track of a bullet train tunnel.10 Three months previously falling concrete had damaged the roof of a bullet train, requiring all tunnels to be checked and reinforced where necessary. With Japan riddled with railway tunnels and subject to periodic earth tremors, there is a significant risk of concrete pieces being knocked loose. Investigations revealed that cracks had appeared in this particular tunnel soon after it was built. This had been conveniently forgotten during inspections, casting doubt on the Japanese reputation for thoroughness and attention to detail.

More tragically, 95 people were killed in a bullet train crash at Amagasaki in April 2005.[11] Investigations revealed that the train took a bend at 100kmh, where the speed limit was 70kmh. The driver had reportedly been speeding, after having been subject to a series of penalties for being late. In 2001, another bullet train driver hanged himself after being penalised for departing from a station 50 seconds late. His family said he had killed himself because of the humiliation of "re-education". Like Singapore, Japan has a punitive organisational culture that not only discourages initiative, but reduces morale in ways that at times can be tragically counter-productive.

Poor Disaster Management

A study of natural disasters in Japan found that communication problems, bureaucratic rivalry and multiple centres of administrative control hamper relief efforts. Professor of Japanese studies at the University of Queensland, Alan Rix, came to these conclusions after studying how Japan's multi-layered bureaucracy responded to disasters. In examining the Kyushu volcanic eruption of 1991, he found:

> *There were serious communications problems between the national and local governments and between the national governments and relief and emergency agencies.*

Professor Rix's experience from the devastating 1994 bush fires in New South Wales prompted his study of Japanese disasters.

> *The response to the NSW bushfires was quick and effective and all the more remarkable because one person was in charge, directing the entire operation free of undue interference from the various levels of government.*
>
> *This occurred in a country where people were thought by the Japanese at least to be happy-go-lucky and disorganised. In stark contrast, the Japanese have a reputation for being organised, efficient and able to cope, yet their disaster management is exactly the opposite.*[12]

The Kobe earthquake demonstrated the disorganization and inadequacy of Japanese relief efforts. Hills inspected the devastated city days after the earthquake and found chaos and disorder everywhere. He had witnessed earthquakes, cyclones, and bushfires before, but he had,

> *never seen an emergency where there was so little sense of urgency, such indifference by the authorities, such a lack of preparedness, such an unwillingness to take the initiative and such a deficit of every commodity from clean water to simple human kindness. The victims waited passively for the "authorities" to turn up – which, of course, they never did, at least not until too late.*[13]

Hills cited the case of firemen standing idly by while nearby residential areas were consumed by fire.

> *In Nagata ward, that densely packed district of wooden houses that was worst-hit by the quake, twenty-four firemen with four fire engines stood by helplessly without reinforcements for six hours as 3700 buildings went up in flames around them. The quake had ruptured the water mains, as might have been expected. However, there were no emergency reservoirs, no water tankers, no authorisation of pumps to take salt water from the ocean less than a kilometre away, no deployment of helicopters or planes to dump water on the flames, no despatch of extra fire units from nearby towns and cities until far too late. All the firemen did was watch and polish their engines, as twenty city blocks turned to ashes and nearly 1000 people were incinerated in the holocaust. The fires were still burning three days later.*[14]

Secondary fires erupted when ruptured gas mains ignited, apparently because the Osaka Gas Company, the private utility which supplied the region, refused for six hours to shut off the supply. The company's president said that if the gas had been shut off, it would have cost "an enormous amount of time and money" to reconnect them. Capacity to avoid or minimise disasters is a measure of a country's efficiency. Another is how quickly it can respond to them. Japan is deficient in both abilities. Lax supervision by its authorities has helped cause accidents and worsened the devastation of natural disasters. Response to such emergencies is also slow. And once again cultural and bureaucratic factors were to blame.

Sub-standard Drugs and Doctors

Besides poor disaster control and management, numerous other systemic inefficiencies afflict Japanese society. These include a malfunctioning health system and the poor quality of Japanese-produced drugs. Hills remarks that Japan is notorious for having "a first world economy with third world medicine".[15]

- Surveys show that in 1995, 76 per cent of Japanese doctors refused to tell their patients if they were suffering from a fatal disease. For example, scores of people were not told they were carrying the AIDs virus, resulting in many of them unwittingly infecting their partners.

437

- Japanese doctors have little training or interest in pain management. They prescribe only a fraction of such widely used painkillers as morphine, compared to the amount prescribed in other countries.
- Drugs dispensed by doctors and clinics are repackaged in plain plastic with no name or product information.
- Patients usually have to wait several hours to see a doctor.
- Patients are customarily required to hand doctors Y100,000 to Y200,000 in plain white envelopes before operations to make sure everything goes right.[16]
- Doctors use their patients as unwitting guinea pigs for experimental drugs. Drug companies pay up to Aus$2500 a head for "research" which would be deemed unethical, if not illegal, in most countries.
- Drugs continue to be used in Japan long after they have been banned elsewhere for harmful effects. These have included Enterovioform (an anti-diarrhoea drug which killed scores of people and may have blinded up to 11,000 in the 1960s and 1970s); Thalidomide (responsible for many birth deformities); steroids (causing sterility and violent outbursts), and Interferon (for treating hepatitis, despite being linked to chronic depression and dozens of suicide attempts, some fatal).[17]
- Most Japanese-developed drugs have been useless or even harmful to patients. By 1995, only two of hundreds of Japanese "anti-cancer" drugs had passed the rigorous standards needed to be approved for use in the US.
- Japanese vaccine has had a particularly deadly reputation. In 1988, a new vaccine to protect children against measles, mumps and rubella (MMR) was rushed onto the market after being tested on only 313 people. It killed and maimed thousands with meningitis before the Government withdrew it.[18]
- Japan's drug-approval bureaucracy is woefully understaffed, with only two inspectors to verify the integrity of clinical trials, compared with 100 in the US. This significantly explains why so many defective Japanese drugs are approved. In addition, "payoffs from drug companies to doctors are commonplace, with the result that Japanese medical results have become the laughing stock in world medical journals".[19]
- Japanese doctors "are generally abysmally ignorant about drugs," one Japanese doctor and health activist has told Hills. In 1995, only half a dozen of 80 medical universities in Japan even had pharmacology on the syllabus.

The above are the more striking deficiencies in Japan's health system, described by Hills and Kerr. Many of the system's problems stem from the failure of the Ministry of Health and Welfare (MHW) to regulate the health and drug industries. Instead, the MHW regularly collaborates with drug companies to hide deaths and illness caused by their drugs. Apart from the MMR vaccine of 1988, the MHW allowed drug firms in the 1980s to continue to distribute a polio vaccine even after it had killed dozens of children.[20] The aim was to protect the firms from the financial loss of recalling unused supplies.

So often one finds this attitude in Third World countries, where powerful vested interests collude with corrupt bureaucrats and politicians who sacrifice the community's welfare for their own gain.

Infrastructural Inadequacies

Often Japan's infrastructures (and building codes) resemble those of poor countries. For example, Japan is the only advanced country that still does not bury its telephone cables and electric lines, except in the CBD areas of such major cities as Tokyo.[21] One reason for this is that making concrete and steel pylons has become a profitable cartelised business. Sewerage lines were still lacking in about half of Japanese homes until 1995, and in a third by 2000.[22] The rest must use a hole in the ground or a septic tank. "Even in the back streets of glittering Ginza, rats as big as cats fossick in the garbage and you can smell the human faeces," says Hills.[23]

Japan's mediocre infrastructure is apparent even at its premier airport. Narita Airport at Tokyo features such poor design and management that air travellers have voted it the 42nd worst airport in the world out of 43.[24]

Japan has also fallen short in space technology. Japan's NASDA space agency has wasted billions of dollars developing a "Japan-only" rocket.[25] But the project has suffered a humiliating series of failures, especially in November 1999, when the launch of an H-2 rocket went so badly that ground control had to destroy it.

Low EIC Levels

Like most other 21st century economies, Japan must innovate to increase productivity and remain competitive. So far the going has been tough, notes a US thinktank. A study by the National Bureau of Economic Research (NBER), based in Massachusetts, observes that Japanese firms find it hard to move from refining existing technologies to forging more fundamental breakthroughs needed to create innovative products. This is partly due to the absence of a vibrant venture capital industry to nurture start-ups, the NBER study says,[26] but the excessive red tape that so hinders the launching of new businesses would be another factor.

Japan's poor record in incubating innovative firms was reflected in the 2002 Global Entrepreneurship Monitor, which ranked Japan bottom out of 37 countries it surveyed.[27] The survey, which identified the transformation of technological advances into marketable products as a key aspect of entrepreneurship, found that for every 1000 workers in Japan, only 18 were either involved in starting up a business or had done so in the previous 42 months. By comparison, the rest of Asia, including such countries as Thailand and India, had a ratio of entrepreneurs to workers that was ten times that of Japan's.

2. Cultural and Educational Weaknesses

Lack of government supervision increased the devastating effects of the Kobe earthquake and led to Japan's bullet train and nuclear reactor fiascos. Such slackness can be blamed on laziness and is common in less vigorous cultures, but the driven Japanese could hardly be so described. With them, other cultural and organisational factors seem to be operating. The desire to avoid responsibility, to not rock the boat or question authority, is combined with political corruption to produce the lax mal-administration that has caused or worsened disasters.

Organisational Ineptitude

The inadequacy of Japanese relief efforts is explained in cultural-organisational terms by Miriam Rohde, a Japan specialist from the Institute of Asian Affairs in Germany. She finds that relief efforts were delayed by:

- A lack of primary information for decision-makers
- Unclear definitions of legal responsibilities
- A fear of disputes about competence
- Difficulties coordinating relief activities
- Insecurity of decision-makers to proceed with actions beyond official guidelines.

Insecure decision-makers tend to be risk-averse, she adds:

> *In a cultural context, where spontaneous personal decisions without a framework of clear-cut rules and regulations might have unforeseen negative consequences for the people involved, the reluctance to act seems understandable. The basic problem appears to be one of responsibility and decision-making.*[28]

Japan's inadequate responses to disasters have further dispelled myths about its efficiency and organisational abilities. Despite this, Japan's perennial Singaporean fan tried to put a positive spin on the Kobe relief fiascos. While admitting that the "government's rescue efforts were slow", Lee Kuan Yew paid homage to Kobe people, describing their behaviour as "exemplary and impressive" and noting there was no rioting or looting as there was after the 1992 Los Angeles earthquake.[29] "I was amazed at how life was returning to normal when I visited Kobe in November 1996," he enthused. But Lee as usual was only seeing what he wanted to see, failing to recognise the prompt and efficient way in which Californian authorities responded to the 1992 quake and how this had minimised loss of life. He also seemed oblivious to how repeated violations of building codes had worsened the Kobe earthquake.

It would have been difficult for Lee or anyone to praise Japanese rescue efforts when a Japanese airliner crashed in August 1985, killing 520. While the crash site was quickly located by army jet planes, bureaucratic confusion and bungling meant the first rescue teams did not reach survivors for up to 14 hours.[30] Japanese handling of this crash and the Kobe and Kyushu disasters revealed a fear of taking responsibility, risk-averseness and failure to display initiative. But traditional Japanese hierarchic values and desire for consensus also help stifle initiative. Hierarchic values encouraged subordinates to wait for orders from superiors before acting, while the need for consensus further delayed decision-making.

Alan Lammin, a Western expatriate who has lived in Tokyo for 20 years, described the Japanese lack of contingency planning as "a total disaster", noting that "Japan's consensus building culture does not lend itself to the rapid response required in a crisis".[31] Singapore's initial tardy response to the SARS epidemic reflected a similar mindset.

Nanny-state Mindsets

Japan, like Singapore, has a nanny-state mentality. In Japan's case especially, this has weakened the capacity of its people to respond to disaster. Japanese writer Fukuda Kiichiro refers to Japan as a "Kindergarten State". Such emphasis is placed on personal safety that it strains credibility, says Kerr:

> Buses at Itami City urge riders to use soap. At Hayama, a beach south of Tokyo, a recorded voice tells bus passengers, "If you have come from a long way, please rest before entering the sea. If you are drowning please shout for help".[32]

An army of lifeguards at a swimming pool complex in Tokyo orders bathers to leave the water every four or five minutes while they check for any dead bodies. The complex has 20 guards on duty at all times.[33] Contrast this to the lackadaisical supervision of Singapore's swimming pools.

In Japan, security guards can be seen gathered around a hole in the road alerting pedestrians to the very obvious cordoned-off danger. About 400,000 security guards are employed to stand guard at public events or construction sites to protect people. There are police boxes at street corners in every neighbourhood. Despite this plethora of rules and controls there is often chaos in a real emergency, as Kobe and Kyushu demonstrated.

Singapore's nanny-state tendencies have a more authoritarian "do what you are told" rather than the "take care" tone of Japan. In Singapore the emphasis is on obeying the rules. The state tells people how to behave and how to save and spend their money. The operation of the CPF scheme and such rules as banning chewing gum, fining people for not flushing public toilets, spitting in the street or littering are examples. Singapore is not called "a fine city" for nothing.

Perhaps Singapore's authoritarian rule makes it better at responding to emergencies than Japan. During emergencies such as the SARS outbreak, an obedient rule-following population greatly facilitates rapid implementation of crisis measures by the government – once it has decided what to do. Nonetheless, this obedience has also produced a conformist risk-averse populace. Although the Japanese seem equally conformist, unlike Singaporeans they lack a response-ready political leadership ruling a small, easily-controllable island. Japan is not only less able to prevent emergencies but has trouble handling them when they do occur.

Authoritarian Schools

Both Singaporean and Japanese education systems have perpetuated cultural attitudes that sabotage initiative and creativity. Their schools have emphasised obedience to authority and extensive rote-learning. Both stifle the development of imagination, independent thinking and problem-solving skills. Obedience to authority is instilled in Japanese and Singaporean school children early on. In Japan, schooling is conducted along military lines throughout students' school years, as Kerr has described:

> At the beginning of each class, all students must stand up, hands at their sides, "at attention". Walking in unison, with announcements from loudspeakers, continues throughout the day, and as the children grow, new rules about dress and hair are added, and often uniforms are required.[34]

Group conformity is stressed through creation of a *kumi* or unit the child will stay with until graduation. *Kumi* members play, study and eat together at school. Most children make maximum efforts to be accepted by their *kumi* and stay securely within it. Those who fail to conform are subjected to vicious bullying at school. While officially discouraging it, teachers do little to prevent such bullying, believing it enhances group obedience.

Rote-learning is another central feature of Japanese education. "To pass examinations in Japan, students must learn facts, facts that are not necessarily relevant to each other or useful to life," notes Kerr. "The emphasis is on rote memorization."[35] While their "heads are filled to overflowing with facts ... Japanese students are surprisingly lacking in common knowledge". This was the finding of a US teacher's study of Japan's architect graduates. While they accumulate useless facts they are not taught how to think analytically or ask questions; nor are they encouraged to develop intellectual curiosity. Failure to develop these attributes ill prepares people to participate in the knowledge economy, as does mindless conformity to group norms. As in Singapore, obedience to authority, conformity and lack of interest in learning for its own sake is widespread in Japan.

The need for extensive after-hours tuition reveals further flaws in the educational systems of both countries. Singapore has a large coaching industry and Japan has its cram, or *juku*, schools. Further educational shortcomings are reflected by literacy deficiencies, both qualitative and quantitative. In 2001, Singapore's illiteracy rate for those over 15 was 6.9 per cent compared to Japan's 1.0 per cent,[36] but literacy can also be viewed in qualitative terms. What is being read can be as important as being literate. In commenting on Japanese reading habits, Kerr asks, "what is one to make of the fact that the favourite reading material of wage earners coming home on the evening trains is not books or newspapers but manga comics?"[37] Manga comics, which account for up to half the magazine market, are unlikely to contribute much to creating an informed workforce and a questioning independent citizenry, both requirements for a 21st century knowledge economy.

Like Singapore, Japan's rote-learning-based education systems have done much to impede the development of creative and innovative abilities. This partly explains why

Singaporeans have had to be great borrowers, and the Japanese expert copyists and improvers of foreign ideas and technologies.

3. Strengths that Mask

Like Singapore, Japan has conspicuous strengths that have hidden its failings for many years. From the time of the Meiji Restoration in 1871 when Japan began to rapidly modernise, it has periodically demonstrated formidable technological and industrial capacities. During its preparations for World War Two, Japan established a vast armaments industry. It built the world's two biggest battleships ever constructed – the *Yamato* and the *Mushashi* – and the Zero fighter-plane. After World War Two, Sony, Toyota and other big Japanese corporations developed a range of electronic products and motor vehicles that became world brand-names from the 1960s to the present, even though the technologies for these products was mainly imported – though the legendary Sony Walkman was a Japanese innovation. Japan also pioneered LCD screen technologies and such niche fields as precision engineering, in which it held commanding leads until the early 1990s. Its car manufacturers have remained a major presence in world markets, though not as strongly as in the 1980s.

Japan's productivity in the electronics, motor vehicle, steel and shipbuilding sectors, as well as its efficient urban transport system, have won international acclaim. Until the 1990s, Japanese managerial styles were studied and often copied around the world. Moreover, through such innovations as lean manufacturing, Japan perfected quality control on the assembly line and until the 1980s led the world in this practice.

Lean manufacturing was developed by the Toyota Motor Corporation's chief production engineer, Taiichi Ono, in the 1950s.[38] Essentially, lean production (also known as just-in-time manufacturing) gives workers the freedom to stop the production line if they see a problem. This greatly improves quality as problems can be fixed at their source rather than allowing defects to be incorporated into the final product, greatly improving quality. Devolving decision-making to assembly-line workers was a vast improvement on the mass production methods where workers were reduced to rigidly controlled cogs in the manufacturing process.

The industrial success of Japan's big corporations owes much to lean manufacturing and the efficient use and refinement of imported technologies. Such adapted technologies, maximising quality and output, drove the Japanese miracle. Apart from lean manufacturing and several other exceptions, innovation did not feature largely.

Even so, the manufacturing sector, especially the car, consumer electronics, steel and machine tools industries, have continued to display world-class productivity, according to James Kondo, co-author of the 2001 McKinsey Global Institute study of productivity in Japan.[39] Compared to the US, Japanese labour productivity in the auto sector is 45 per cent higher, 21 per cent higher in the steel industry and 15 per cent higher in consumer electronics. But these industries account for only 10 per cent of GDP and employment, Kondo points out. Most of the remaining economy is in the non-manufacturing sector, "which remains highly unproductive," notes a leading LDP member, Mr Yasuhisa Shiozaki.[40] The much larger domestic services sector, traditionally shielded from competition, is still struggling, especially in such areas as construction, retailing and health-care. These industries constitute a much bigger share of Japan's economy and account for 75 per cent of employment.

The domestically focused manufacturing sector, which has traditionally relied on protective trade barriers, also has low productivity. For example, productivity in the food processing sector is one third that of the US's. In the past, the brilliant success and high productivity of Japan's export-oriented manufacturing sectors and the extent to which they came to dominate world markets disguised the unimpressive performance of its domestic sectors.

Japan has other obvious strengths that have distracted attention from its weaknesses. These include efficient public transport, a people imbued with a rigorous work ethic, and a society awash with seemingly endless quantities of consumer-durable goods. As with Singapore, such highly visible achievements have demonstrated Japan to be an economy par excellence to many. Japan only began to be assessed more critically after its miracle started to unravel in the 1990s.

Singapore's miracle has not yet been subjected to such sceptical scrutiny from foreign journalists and academics. Their main focus has been on Lee Kuan Yew and his role in the creation of PAP Singapore; the authoritarian and undemocratic nature of the PAP state; its treatment of opposition politicians and activists, and how the judicial system has been twisted to persecute them and the media, especially foreign publications.

Other writers, especially Worthington, have exposed the oligarchic nature of Singapore's political economy and the hollowness of its claims to meritocracy and good governance. Much of Worthington's work rests on that of such theorists as Rodan and Deyo who have described the development of Singapore's economy since Separation, and the role foreign capital has played in this. Rodan too has exposed the emptiness of PAP claims on transparency, a central feature of good governance.

However, examinations of Singapore's miracle, especially its economic aspects, have been fragmentary at best. Singaporean economists such as Manu Bhaskaran and Linda Low have highlighted some major problems of the city-state's SE-dominated local economy while other economists such as Krugman and Peebles and Wilson have revealed Singapore's second-rate productivity at the macro-economic level. And sometimes articles by journalists in Asia, mostly Western, briefly summarise Singapore's economic shortcomings or focus on the latest problems being faced by Temasek and the GIC. But no systematic effort has been made, at both the macro as well as micro-economic level, to expose Singapore's constant claims to efficiency and cutting-edge excellence. Nor has there been any sustained attempt to critically assess Singapore's consistently high rankings for competitiveness; statistical rectitude, and for economic freedom and the other nation-building attributes deemed important by foreign capital.

Little effort has also been made to refute the PAP hype that poverty is almost non-existent in Singapore, apart from the writings of such political activists as Chee Soon

Juan and Jeyaretnam. Only they have made any overall attempt to reveal the extent of Singapore's poverty and how minimal have been the gains that most Singaporeans have made in exchange for the loss of their democratic freedoms and civil rights.

Perhaps because Singapore appears to have so far avoided Japan's fate, the central claims of the Singaporean miracle have not received rigorous critical assessment from foreign academics and journalists. Nonetheless, Singapore, like Japan, is already experiencing major structural problems – and for similar reasons. Singapore has displayed cultural and organisational factors that have undermined efficiency and fostered opacity, and which have combined with excessive centralisation of political power (usually unaccountable) to produce similar structural problems to those encountered in Japan. Like Japan, Singapore has been struggling for some time to resolve these problems. The next chapter examines how successfully each country has done this.

References

1. Hills, Ben: *Japan Behind the Lines* (Sydney, Hodder and Stoughton, 1996), p. 199.
2. Ibid, p. 201.
3. Ibid, p. 202.
4. Ibid, p. 200.
5. Kerr, Alex: *Dogs and Demons: the Fall of Modern Japan* (London, Penguin, 2001), pp. 117-8.
6. Ibid, p. 115.
7. *Sunday Times* (Perth, Western Australia), September 12, 2004.
8. Ibid.
9. *The Australian*, August 19, 2004.
9a. Ibid, July 20 and 21, 2007.
10. *The Straits Times* (ST), October 24, 1999.
11. *The Australian*, April 28, 2005.
12. *The West Australian*, February 23, 1995.
13. Hills, p. 203.
14. Ibid, pp. 203-4.
15. Ibid, p. 382.
16. Kerr, p. 125.
17. Hills, pp. 397-8.
18. Ibid, p. 399.
19. Kerr, p. 125.
20. Ibid, p. 373.
21. Ibid, p. 198.
22. Kerr, p. 150.
23. Hills, p. 142.
24. Kerr, p. 150.
25. Ibid, p. 374.
26. ST, January 28, 2003.
27. Ibid.
28. ST (Trends section), March 20, 1995.
29. Lee, Kuan Yew: *From Third World to First* (Singapore, Times Media, 2000), p. 588.
30. Van Wolferen, Karel: *The Enigma of Japanese Power* (New York, Alfred A. Knopf, 1989).
31. ST, August 27, 2003.
32. Kerr, pp. 311-12.
33. ST, August 27, 2003.
34. Kerr, p. 287.
35. Ibid, p. 295.
36. *World Competitiveness Yearbook 2001* (Institute for Management Development, Lausanne, Switzerland, 2001), p. 439.
37. Kerr, pp. 294-5.
38. Fukuyama, Francis: *Trust: The Social Virtues and the Creation of Prosperity* (London, Penguin, 1995), p. 258.
39. *The Australian Financial Review*, May 31-June 1, 2003.
40. ST, June 28, 2004.

CHAPTER 32

LIMITED CAPACITIES FOR REFORM

The capacity for reform varies widely between countries, but it primarily depends on the flexibility of their political-economic systems and whether or not they have social values that aid reform. Both factors largely determine a country's ability to renew and restructure itself economically and in other ways.

Usually, liberal democratic states are better at reforming themselves than those of the authoritarian and undemocratic kind. Change can only occur in any society when those pushing for reform have the political power to have long-held policies scrapped or amended, and to launch new ones that better meet society's requirements. This is more easily achieved in democratic societies where there is a more equal distribution of power. No one group can monopolise power sufficiently to thwart determined and widely-supported drives for reform.

Genuine democracies have institutional frameworks and bills of rights that protect all groups participating in the political process, including those seeking change. Vested interests can only oppose them through legal and constitutional means that guarantee the rights of all competing groups: reformist groups – provided they have sufficient public support – can have their proposals and programs approved and implemented by the state. In less than democratic countries like Singapore and Japan, reform is far more difficult. The powerful MOF-led bureaucracy and its corporate allies stymied reform efforts in Japan for over a decade while the PAP cabinet's near monopoly of power in Singapore still does.

1. Japan

Since the 1950s, Japan has been mostly ruled by the Liberal Democratic Party, often described as neither liberal nor democratic. As a largely subordinate part of the MOF-dominated iron triangle, successive LDP governments have helped sustain a corrupt hegemonic system that has been increasingly detrimental to Japan and has proven very hard to change. As Backman observes:

> The nexus between big business, the bureaucracy, and the LDP is one that is complex and mutually reinforcing, so much so that it is scarcely possible to treat each of the three as distinct entities. Moreover, the reform of any one pillar of the structure represents a direct attack on all the sections. It simply isn't possible to rope off one part of Japan Inc., remodel it, and then move on to the next

part. The interconnectedness of the client-patron relationship means that it is all or nothing. The buck doesn't stop there; it just keeps circulating, and any attempt at reform, even if relatively minor, is met with resistance from the entire establishment as each part moves to safeguard its self-interest.[1]

At present Japan's reform could only proceed very slowly. "The system simply won't allow anything dramatic to occur."[2] Half-hearted government efforts at reform have demonstrated this.

Deregulation Derailed

One of Japan's most sweeping attempts at reform was announced in 1996 when the need for drastic financial changes became apparent. The MOF came up with the idea of a Big Bang, similar to that of Britain's in the 1980s. Britain's Big Bang deregulated London's financial markets, sparking dramatic growth. In Japan it was soon clear that there would be major obstacles to implementing such a program.

Deregulation would have required the abandonment of various Japanese financial and auditing practices that had permitted the generation of grossly inflated asset values for decades. As Kerr pointed out:

The problem is that Japan's banks and securities firms rely for their very life on unreal values.....the banks are hooked on the narcotics of these unreal values, and kicking the habit will bring about severe withdrawal symptoms.[3]

Deregulation was scheduled to begin in 1999, but go-slow tactics soon became evident. The insurance industry was to be opened to newcomers in 1998, but won a reprieve until 2001. The MOF announced that banks must set aside capital against bad loans, but this plan was quickly watered down. It was phased in piecemeal and applied only to large banks; only later was it applied to small banks, the ones most affected by bad loans. Kerr found that when,

Japan entered the twenty-first century, the hype about the Big Bang had died out, and it was consigned to dusty shelves as just another government report. It was business as usual in Tokyo....Instituting a real Big Bang is simply out of the question, for the whole edifice of Japanese finance might crumble if the MOF allowed economic rationalism to infiltrate.[4]

More recent efforts at reform have been made by the Koizumi Government. In April 2001, Prime Minister Koizumi came to power pledging to deal with the root causes of Japan's problems. He was swept into office on a strong mandate by the Japanese people who believed they had elected a leader who would at last solve these problems. Koizumi planned to introduce major structural reforms that would reduce Japan's debt burden, compel the closure of bankrupt companies, and transfer the MOF-managed postal savings system to the private sector. But he soon faced immense opposition to such plans from elements within his own party, which had strong ties with powerful vested corporate interests and banks – and the all-powerful MOF-headed bureaucracy.

This web of vested interests has sabotaged economic reform. Their position has been strengthened by the perception that they – and the policies that fostered them – produced Japan's miracle and the high growth that gave Japan economic super-power status. "Nothing is more difficult to change than a policy which once worked and works no longer," Kerr noted,[5] adding that:

> *While the experts marvelled at how efficiently the well-oiled machines were turning, the ship was headed towards the rocks. Japan's cleverly crafted machine of governance lacks one critically important part: brakes.*
>
> *Once it has been set on a particular path, Japan tends to continue on that path and reaches excesses that would be unthinkable in other nations.[6]*

Even widespread bankruptcies, massive national debt, Botswana/Latvian-level credit ratings and a decade or more of mostly zero growth had done little to loosen the iron triangle's grip on the country by the early 2000s. Japan's political leaders have been unable to combat this nexus because they are largely controlled by it. Having very limited room to manoeuvre they have been too weak politically to implement reforms that would deal with Japan's on-going stagnation. This was demonstrated by Koizumi's frustrated attempts to cut back on the bureaucratic red tape strangling entrepreneurial activity. In late 2002, Koizumi tried to deal with the problem by proposing that specially deregulated zones be set up where businesses could operate with much less red tape. As the bureaucracy was mulling over the hundreds of proposals for these zones it was clear that Koizumi had little clout. Of 651 submissions made, ministries grudgingly approved only 27 per cent.[7]

Plans to improve the services provided by the Health Ministry and the Japan Medical Association (JMA) also had little success. The aim was to increase competition in the medical sector to improve the service in Japanese hospitals, but the JMA, a key LDP supporter, strongly opposed the scheme, restricting it to a few largely non-essential medical procedures.

Koizumi also faced determined opposition from powerful bureaucratic and political interests with his post office reforms. His plans to corporatize and privatise the hulking postal services/savings bank/insurance combine were strongly resisted by many in his party until his poll victory in September 2005.[8] The postal bank, Jucho, holds about Y230 trillion (Aus$2.8 trillion) of assets and is by far the world's biggest post office. Jucho's Kampo, the postal insurance arm (with assets of about Y125 trillion), is Japan's biggest insurer. Together, both entities control about one quarter of Japan's personal assets. Both entities were also compelled to buy huge amounts of government debt through the MOF-controlled *zaito* bonds which were used to fund public project spending. A PAP-type "applecart" of vested bureaucratic and LDP political interests would be threatened were the post office conglomerate to be dismantled and privatised. The *zaito* bonds and the budget they fund have been a potent source of political patronage for the LDP and of economic control for the MOF. The budget makes available funds for public works projects which are assigned to the corporate sector. Projects have been awarded to enterprises approved by the MOF, often according to their contributions to the LDP and its various candidates. Moreover, the postal service's 25,000 post offices are bulwarks of LDP influence. Privatising the various arms of the post office would disrupt such a situation: hence the strong opposition to Koizumi's post office reforms from many LDP MPs who were covertly supported by the MOF.

The reforms had been tentatively scheduled to be launched in 2007 and to be completed by 2017. Until mid-2005 the prospects of their being implemented looked bleak because of so much opposition, even from within Koizumi's own party. Frustrated with this opposition, Koizumi called a snap election in September 2005 to get a public mandate to press ahead with the post office reforms. His LDP party won decisively. This ensured that the post office's reforms were passed by Parliament in October 2005. Starting from October 2007, Japan Post would be broken into four parts, and over the next decade the postal savings bank and postal insurance company would be completely sold. On the post office issue at least the anti-reformists have been defeated.

Koizumi's post office victory gave new heart to the reformists, but future reform efforts are still likely to face stiff opposition from vested interests. In any case, the Japanese economy's sporadic revival since 2003/4 has weakened pressures for reform, as has Japan's legacy of past successes which continue to sustain complacent mindsets in some quarters.

Further Barriers to Reform

Japan's fitful recovery since 2003 has combined with Japan's still impressive post-war achievements to discourage reform. This recovery seems to be more sustained than before. However, this was initially not due to economic restructuring but to increased exports to China and Asia. By early 2004, exports to Asia had been increasing for nearly two years.[9] China was responsible for 80 per cent of export growth in 2003.

The rising foreign demand for Japanese goods forced manufacturers to invest heavily in capital equipment. Companies rushed to modernise factories and equipment that had become obsolete during Japan's decade-long economic slump. Capital expenditure was further boosted by demands for new technology: electronics companies were equipping factories to meet rising demand for digital consumer electronics and information technology products.

Consumer spending began to recover after more than a decade in the doldrums. Unemployment was down, and Japanese companies were ending an informal wages freeze. Following talks with unions, some companies agreed to modest wage and bonus increases. The spectre of deflation had begun to lift.

The 2003/4 recovery, for all its hopeful signs, was largely due to cyclical economic factors. It was the third recovery since the bubble burst. The upturn in Japan's exports and resultant increased capital spending by manufacturers had lifted the economy out of recession, but there had still not been much major change to the structural weaknesses that were holding Japan back. As the *Australian Financial Review* noted in March 2004:

> *One of the most worrying things about Japan today is that policymakers believe the heavy lifting is over. The government's reform drive, always fragile, is rapidly losing momentum. And there are more voices arguing that the current economic surge means the reform program wasn't really necessary after all.*[10]

Similar sentiments were expressed in the same month by the chairman and CEO of JETRO, Osamu Watanabe. He said the economy "has not yet come to the situation where full-scale structural reform is complete or when all companies can expect profitability for the future". The corporate sector "needs to go through one more stage of drastic reform by cutting off non-profitable businesses and further reinforcing profitable activities".[11]

Nonetheless, reform in the banking sector had shown significant progress by 2004. Japan's banks had been cutting non-performing loans from a March 2002 peak, though in April 2004 they still faced substantial credit risks from large, highly leveraged borrowers and small mid-sized enterprises, according to Fitch Ratings credit agency.[12] Bank profitability remained fragile and their lending balances continued to decline, the agency said, also noting that the "sustainability of current recovery remains uncertain".

By August 2004, the non-performing loans from Japan's major banks had fallen to Y13,600 billion (Aus$174 billion) from Y20,200 billion in 2003, according to the Government's Financial Services Agency (FSA).[13] The BOJ reported that Japan's percentage of non-performing loans to total loans had declined by 7.1 to 51 per cent. In 2004, banks were also beginning to make more loans to SMEs on which higher interest rates could be charged to boost banks' profits and provide much-needed venture capital for the SME sector. Nonetheless, Japan's economic recovery since 2004 has been fitful, with the economy lapsing into negative growth at times, largely because of fluctuations in export demand. Subsequent growth has been slow, usually ranging between 1 and 2 per cent a year. Other aspects of Japan's recovery remain mixed. While the banks have improved their situation by shedding many bad loans, the only big success of the reform process has been the Post Office privatisation.

However, reform stalled after Koizumi left office in September 2006 and little occurred under Prime Minister Shinzo Abe before he resigned in September 2007. And limited taste for reform has been displayed by his successor Prime Minister Yasuo Fukuda "a consensus style politician" who assumed office "at a time of apparent backlash against 'Koizumi reforms'".[14] However, the reform process must continue if Japan is to become an efficient high-growth economy that is not heavily dependent on fickle world export markets for its prosperity. While other Asian economies significantly reformed themselves after the 1997/8 financial crisis, Japan has yet to.

South Korea had a similar economy to Japan until the 1997/8 crisis. A network of cronyistic *chaebols*, like the *keiretsu* system, dominated the Korean economy, but the crisis forced South Korea to restructure. Not having the same high levels of industrial capacity and capital resources to rely on as Japan, South Korea had to make major changes. Within a couple of years its economy had revived and growth had surged. South Korea was not only far more entrepreneurial than before, but more entrepreneurial than Japan. By 2003, South Korea had eight times more entrepreneurs per capita than Japan, according to CSLA Emerging Markets.[15] The sweeping reforms that produced this outcome in Korea remain less likely in Japan despite Koizumi's reform successes. Reform will probably remain an arduous process till the power of the vested bureaucratic, corporate and LDP interests are checked and their ability to impede reform minimised.

Along with the iron triangle, entrenched cultural attitudes also pose barriers to the type of reform that Japan must have to acquire the innovational and creative capacities to compete effectively in the global economy. Japan's hierarchical/obedience-to-authority values do much to sustain the iron triangle nexus.

Moving Beyond A *Chuto Hanpa* Fate?

Chuto hanpa is the term coined in 2001 by Kerr to describe Japan's probable future. It means "neither this nor that" in Japanese; "in other words, mediocrity", he said.[16]

Countries that fail to deal effectively with major problems can face prolonged crises, even violent upheavals. This is particularly so with poor and underdeveloped countries which lack the economic resources and shared cultural values needed to survive prolonged political-economic crises. For them there is often a stark choice between reform and ongoing chaos.

More fortunate countries can endure chronic structural problems for decades without falling apart. Japan has been one. It has had the means to coast along as a stagnating economy for a long time before conditions became too uncomfortable. In 2001, Kerr likened Japan's fate to that of the proverbial boiled frog who, lulled into inactivity by luke-warm water, is cooked alive:

> *Radical change will only come when conditions have grown completely intolerable, and in Japan's case that day may never come. To put Japan's problems into context, we must remember that it remains one of the wealthiest countries in the world: the bankrupt banks and deflated stock market are not going to deprive most people of their television sets, refrigerators and cars. From this point of view, Japan remains a reasonably comfortable place to live.[17]*

...There is more than enough industrial power to support the population at roughly present standards. On the other hand, given its deep systemic weaknesses in finance and technology, Japan is not going to boom.[18]

The Government "croons the public to sleep with reassuring lullabies about Japan's unique form of government by bureaucracy, and its superiority over the degenerate West".[19] The 2003/4 trade-led recovery did much to fortify such smug attitudes and slow wholesale reform and continued to give validity to Kerr's observations.

Government policies that shored up insolvent *keiretsus* and protected vested interests were only beginning to change in 2005 after four years of strenuous reform efforts by Koizumi. By the time of his 2005 electoral victory only the banking sector had begun significant reform. As such reform efforts broaden to include more of the economy, Japan may achieve something better than a *chato hanpa* future. Even so, it has taken over a decade for the banking sector to begin a reform process which other economic sectors had yet to embark on by the mid 2000s. Powerful vested interests and other structural impediments continue to resist such reforms as the privatisation of bureaucratic monopolies, reduced red tape, and a fair and viable pension scheme. Should these and other reforms eventually prevail and Japan continues "comes good" it will be due to major restructuring in the face of bitter opposition. This would not vindicate the Japanese development model but demonstrate its limited capacity for rapid renewal. Not only has this model produced major structural problems over time: it has also required enormous effort, time and sacrifice to change. Similar observations can be made about the Singapore model.

2. Singapore

The PAP state's economic and development strategies since the 1960s suggest a proficient state quickly adapting to Singapore's changing circumstances. While there may be much truth to this, its freedom to manoeuvre is often severely limited by long-standing PAP policies which remain largely impervious to reform and also to difficult-to-change cultural attitudes.

The Need to Please the MNCs

Under the PAP, Singapore has been designed to serve foreign capital by being transformed into a profitable and stable climate for MNCs. The workforce has been kept docile and under-paid and corporate taxes have been repeatedly cut. Political stability has been achieved by violating democratic freedoms and sacrificing fair elections.

Though the MNCs have generated high GDP and export and job growth for Singapore, they have made the country heavily dependent on foreign corporations and world export markets. Should too many MNCs depart, the country would be in dire straits. Singapore must retain its pro-MNC policies to keep them. This means continued tight control of wages and the workforce and also giving MNCs the freedom to subject the local, especially the SME sector, to crushing competition that impedes its growth and development.

Corporate taxes also have to be kept low and even cut, to retain the MNCs and foreign talent. Unless the revenue shortfalls caused by low corporate taxes are financed out of the reserves, indirect taxes need to remain high to do this, but heavy indirect taxes, combined with depressed wages due to government wage-control policies, keep down consumer spending, reducing markets for Singapore's local private sector.

The Privatisation Problem

Another major barrier to economic reform is the SE system which dominates the local economy. Privatising many of the SEs would not only reduce state control of the economy but threaten the many lucrative *amakudari* positions SEs provide for current and ex-PAP ministers and senior civil servants. Such considerations would explain the shelving of the Government's half-hearted privatisation program originally launched to assuage SME discontent at SE predations.

For the Government, the SEs, not the local private sector, are the local economy's driving force and the spearhead for foreign entrepreneurial endeavours. The government focus is on how the SE sector can play this role and achieve greater economic independence for Singapore. The Temasek Charter reflects such thinking with its plans on how SEs will do this. Singapore's entrepreneurial bureaucrats have yet to show they can successfully perform such a role.

Land and Business Costs

The PAP Government has demonstrated limited capacity to reduce heavy business costs which are largely due to high land and property prices. While numerous government charges and imposts contribute significantly to both business and living costs, the fundamental factor driving them is land prices, according to a Singaporean think-tank. Land prices were the main culprit in rising business costs, concluded a December 2002 report by the Institute of Policy Studies on Economic Restructuring, which had been studying ways of reducing business costs.[20] Lee Kuan Yew himself admitted that land prices were the biggest factor driving business costs.[21] High land prices push up property prices. Properties not only cost more to buy but also require bigger loans that need greater interest payments to service them. Ultimately, higher property prices mean increased office, factory, retail and private rentals leading to higher business and living costs.

Constant pleas for the Government to cut land costs have been made by business people and MPs, including PAP MP Inderjit Singh, who argues that industrial land costs should be reduced and residential property prices cut by 30 per cent.[22] The Government has the power to do so, maintain some Singaporeans. As one Singaporean told *The Straits Times*:

> *While the Government's position has always been "let the market decide", the*
> *fact that it owns more than 90 per cent of all land in Singapore shows the*
> *direct role it can play (and it certainly has played) in setting property prices.*
> *Ultimately, it all leads back to how land is valued and sold by the Government.*
> *If the land were now to be valued and sold based on its true market and*
> *economic value, the possible result will be to bring down land cost by as much*
> *as 30 to 50 per cent.[23]*

Strong political reasons stop the Government doing this. Cutting land prices would substantially reduce the value of home-owners' properties. As Lee Kuan Yew admitted, bringing down land prices would be "very dangerous" because it would depress property values, both commercial and residential.[24] In fact, tampering with the property market generally was very risky, he said. For example, any move to bring down the cost of industrial land or commercial rent would eventually result in falling housing values. "It's all inter-linked and, finally you find your three-room flat may be worth less," he said. Most Singaporeans, especially the 85 per cent who have almost all their savings in their HDB units, would be hard hit. This would generate enormous anti-PAP hostility.

In similar vein, BG Lee said, "The last thing the Government should do is to destabilise the property market".[25] Calls for the Government to reduce land prices, especially for industrial land, were reckless and could cause alarm. He said that thousands of firms owned industrial land and used it as collateral for bank loans. Any reduction of industrial land prices would jeopardise such loan arrangements.

Apart from land prices, lowering HDB prices directly is also fraught with problems, as became apparent in early 2002. In January it was reported that Singapore had 17,545 unsold flats;[26] but the HDB could never lower prices to get rid of the excess units. The prices of new HDB flats form what one Singaporean property consultant described as the "psychological base tier of Singapore's housing price pyramid",[27] and cutting HDB prices would spill over into the private housing market. Such a move would also depress HDB prices.

The Government cannot reduce living or business costs by cutting land or HDB prices. If it did, property prices would plummet, pushing the economy into deep recession, even a depression. The PAP Government is trapped by a monster of its own creation. Its systematic attempt to acquire almost all of Singapore's land and then extract top dollar for it over the decades has led to very high land and property prices. Not only has this caused heavy living and business costs, but it has produced an almost insoluble problem for the Government.

In a spirit of commendable candour Lee Kuan Yew admitted, "We allowed, or we did not check, the rise in land prices and property prices. It went too high. That is a problem".[28] High land and property prices have become a structural problem which is very difficult for the Government to handle. Any ill-judged measures by the Government could lead to a property price crash, causing HDB home values to plunge, greatly devaluing the only asset most HDB-owning Singaporeans have.

The Transparency Problem

Both domestic and foreign pressures for greater openness have forced Singapore at least to try to be more transparent. The GIC and Temasek have released their first partial reports about themselves, but the operations of the PAP state and its SEs remain almost as opaque as ever. Singapore's media freedoms also stay curtailed. Instead, government efforts to implement transparency have been focused on the private sector, where greater transparency has become apparent.

Genuine transparency for the government and SE sectors would threaten PAP rule. "Glasnost"-type policies would compel greater accountability. The Government would have to explain more fully the reasons for its policies. Its failures, and abuses of power from the past, would be exposed. Many skeletons could come tumbling out of many closets. Those who monopolise power inevitably abuse it: Singapore's leaders are no exception. Their regular misuse of power over the decades would give them ample reason to fear greater transparency and accountability for political as well as economic reasons.

The longer the PAP state resists transparency, along with proper privatisation, the higher the price Singapore will pay in terms of productivity and competitiveness. To paraphrase Marx, the PAP state could be destroyed by its own contradictions. It needs and wants an innovative, entrepreneurial, risk-taking and transparent society, but such a society requires much greater decentralisation of political and economic power and far more governmental and state sector transparency, than the PAP could permit. Such measures would require a degree of political-economic restructuring that would undermine PAP rule and the vested interests it represents. The PAP state can only permit cosmetic changes. Anything more will jeopardise its political dominance. Major structural change would probably destroy PAP rule.

Substitutes for Real Reform

As a substitute for comprehensive reform the PAP Government has resorted to a range of specific and seemingly proactive policies to make Singapore more competitive and efficient. As Chapter 13 shows, the Government is expert at creating endless committees and launching numerous campaigns to renew and re-engineer Singapore, but their recommendations are usually ignored. Only those that do not threaten the status quo are implemented: they are also ones that fail to address Singapore's structural problems.

The Government's piecemeal reform efforts have sought to improve performance in particular areas of the economy and society but have done little to boost Singapore's EICs and its national competitiveness, as the following summary shows:

- Numerous government schemes which seek to promote SME entrepreneurial ventures have created the impression that the Government is fostering local enterprise. Such schemes will benefit most SMEs little until the Government protects them from unfair SE/MNC competition. The SMEs remain sceptical as to whether the Government's entrepreneurial schemes will help them.

- Policies have also been implemented to attract foreign talent by making Singapore a more "exciting" place where expatriate party animals will supposedly feel at home. While such measures may make Singapore fleetingly more attractive to the young cosmopolitans, its often deadening sterility and its lack of intellectual and cultural ferment and creativity will continue to turn them off. They will keep retreating into expat enclaves, eagerly adding up every month how much money they are making. They will still leave when they have accumulated enough money and when greener and more interesting pastures beckon. Contrived opportunities to party are unlikely to keep them in Singapore.

- Biopolis and other projects have aimed to hot-house foreign and local talent to boost Singapore's capacity for technological innovation. Importing over-paid scientists may produce some results, but often the greatest discoveries arise in small firms and in societies where intellectual curiosity and freedom of thought prevail.

- Educational reforms have sought to replace rote-learning methods with those that teach problem-solving and encourage critical thought and creativity, but this is only the first step to making Singaporeans more innovative. The social and political environment needs to be liberalised for such measures to be fully effective. Creative people need a liberal environment to function in, or they will leave.

- Turning Singapore into a wired city has been another major policy initiative. While this may increase IT capacity, its potential can only be fully realised in an innovative environment where people's rights and privacy are respected. Singapore lacks these preconditions.

- The Government's efforts to cut red tape may be reducing the regulatory overload for business, but thick layers of regulations still severely restrict Singaporean enterprises. Further major reductions will be required before they are as free of red tape as those in other countries like Malaysia.

- "Witless" competitions to boost efficiency in the civil service have yet to achieve significant results. These competitions have largely become ends in themselves.

- The Second Wing strategy's greatest success has been to generate a sizeable FIFA for Singapore, but at the cost of developing local private enterprise. Other Second Wing initiatives such as the Johore-Singapore-Batam triangle have yet to prove themselves. While Suzhou has eventually become a success, this was only achieved after the Chinese assumed a majority interest in the project.

Besides these measures there have been those aimed at freeing up the economy through deregulating the financial sector, liberalising the CPF scheme, and "reforming" the tax system to benefit the corporate and MNC sectors:

- The financial sector has been transformed, with banking and securities trading all deregulated. Foreign institutions can increasingly compete locally, and more flexible regulations have been introduced.

- The stock exchange has been demutualised and merged with the derivatives exchange to produce the SGX. The liberalisation of Singapore's capital markets is only partial, however, leaving the GIC's operations untouched. The GIC remains free to invest the bulk of the country's capital resources in what is still a mostly opaque and unaccountable manner. Capital which should be available for local ventures continues to be invested off-shore.

- The CPF scheme has been liberalised to permit CPF savings to be used to buy other financial assets. Though this has provided more capital for Singapore's investment markets, including perhaps a few local SMEs, it does little to improve financial security for Singapore's retirees. They still do not have enough to retire on. CPF changes fail to address this basic problem.

- The tax system has been reformed with a shift from direct to indirect taxation. While corporations and MNCs see this as an improvement, Singaporean wage and salary earners are unlikely to. Indirect taxation is regressive and falls hardest on the ordinary employee and reduces consumer spending and markets for local products.

The above measures create the impression of a vigorous leadership energetically re-engineering Singapore to improve competitiveness, but most have yet to boost Singapore's EICs substantially. Many of the measures have been hindered, if not sabotaged, by a strong network of entrenched PAP policies and vested interests. The Government has still to transform Singapore into an entrepreneurial world-class economy on its own terms, largely independent of foreign capital and expertise.

Genuine reform requires major restructuring of the economic and political system. Economic restructuring occurs when control of such fundamental resources as capital and land, and of entrepreneurial activity, passes from one major economic grouping, sector or class to another. In Singapore's case, this could generally be from the state-owned, GLC and MNC sectors, to the local private and SME sectors.

Political restructuring would require the PAP Government to dismantle the structure of repression and intimidation it has imposed on the people of Singapore since the early 1960s. This is a major precondition for the development of a free, democratic, innovative and fully entrepreneurial society where transparency and accountability prevail. It is unlikely to occur under Singapore's latest prime minister, Lee Hsien Loong, who is clearly committed to continuing the PAP's neo-authoritarian style of rule, despite suggestions to the contrary.

Because major restructuring is beyond the PAP state in its present form it has had to resort to substitutes for reform which are often little more than fine-tuning of existing structures and procedures. Any genuine reforms have been confined to specific areas or activities. Singapore's structural problems remain unaddressed. Government efforts have also failed to change Singaporean mindsets and organisational values that undermine productivity and EIC development. The risk-averse, hierarchical and *kiasuistic* attitudes of Singapore's managers and workers continue to sap organisational efficiency. Such attitudes are unlikely to change for as long as the PAP's style of rule perpetuates punitive, authoritarian and one-mistake values. The intimidatory atmosphere they create encourages excessive caution, obsessive rule-following and narrow *kiasu* selfishness. All of these traits undermine productivity and innovation.

Singapore's rulers may be superior to Japan's in handling specific and easily definable crises. However, like the Japanese leaders they have limited capacity to effect the reforms needed to transform Singapore into a genuinely innovative, entrepreneurial and competitive economy. Only major restructuring can do this – along with the development of appropriate cultural and organisational values to facilitate the process.

This chapter and the previous four have described the many political-economic and cultural-organisational features that Singapore and Japan share. Centralisation of political/bureaucratic power has produced dysfunctional economies and opaque and unaccountable governments. Structural problems bred by these factors are exacerbated by those of a cultural-organisational nature. With Singapore sharing these major similarities with Japan, the question is whether it will suffer a similar fate. The next chapter considers this.

References

1. Backman, Michael: *Asian Eclipse: Exposing the Dark Side of Business in Asia* (Singapore, John Wiley and Sons, revised edition, 2001), p. 127.
2. Ibid.
3. Kerr, Alex: *Dogs and Demons: the Fall of Modern Japan* (London, Penguin, 2001), p. 92.
4. Ibid, p. 93.
5. Ibid, p. 303.
6. Ibid, pp. 10-11.
7. *The Straits Times* (ST), March 7, 2003.
8. *The Australian*, February 16, 2005 and April 6, 2005.
9. *Far Eastern Economic Review*, January 29, 2004.
10. *The Australian Financial Review*, March 13-14, 2004.
11. *Business Times*, March 11, 2004.
12. *The Australian*, April 21, 2004.
13. Ibid, August 4, 2004.
14. Ibid, October 18 and December 9, 2007.
15. ST, January 28, 2003.
16. Kerr, p. 371.
17. Ibid.
18. Ibid, pp. 374-5.
19. Ibid, p. 370.
20. ST, December 21, 2002.
21. ST, July 24, 2003.
22. ST, March 13, 2003.
23. ST, April 18, 2002.
24. ST, July 24, 2003.
25. ST, March 13, 2003.
26. ST, January 19, 2002.
27. Ibid.
28. ST, July 24, 2003.

CHAPTER 33

WHITHER SINGAPORE?

In recent years some Singaporeans have begun to express concern about their country's future. During the 2002/3 downturn a *Straits Times* columnist asked whether the climate in Singapore had become "unbearably bleak". Sumiko Tan moaned that:

> *We have become a nation of tired people and frayed nerves. A cloud of fear hangs over us.*
>
> *We are fearful of losing our jobs, fearful our salaries will be cut further, fearful foreigners are chipping away at our rice bowls, fearful CPF rates will never be restored, fearful about whether there is a future for us here and, worse, whether there is a future for Singapore as a country.*
>
> *Where is the energy, the drive and the optimism that made us so self-assured, even cocky, in the past, despite being a tiny red dot in the South China Sea...*
>
> *How times have changed from the Singapore of the early to mid-1990s, when the economy was at its peak and nothing could go wrong.*[1]

The Silk air crash of 1997, the 1997/8 financial crisis, the SIA disaster of 2000, September 11, 2001, the Iraq war and SARS jolted Singapore out of its complacency. Sumiko mused about her own situation:

> *To be honest, it has occurred to me that perhaps I should invest in a second home, maybe in Perth where I have relatives, or in the United States where my sister is. Just in case. Who knows.*

Like so many Singaporeans, Sumiko is looking for a bolt-hole in some safe country if Singapore goes pear-shaped. Like so many Singaporeans her patriotism is highly conditional.

After her pessimistic ruminations in 2003, Singapore's economy began to recover and, superficially at least, a more optimistic mood started to take hold – though mostly confined to the country's ruling and managerial classes. Good times had returned for Singapore's privileged groups, so the official view was that things were looking up for everyone. Such optimism was not shared by average Singaporeans, whose living standards remained as modest as ever. In fact continued wage controls, reduced employer CPF contributions and an increased GST meant that they often had to struggle harder to maintain levels of affluence that were still below those of average income-earners developed countries. Little changed for them despite the return of growth. Increased GDP figures merely deflected attention from their mediocre circumstances and Singapore's ongoing economic malaise.

1. Disguised Mediocrity

Japan's stagnation became apparent during the 1990s. Its economy showed no growth at times, and there was limited entrepreneurial and innovative activity, high corporate and banking debt and depressed consumer spending. By the mid-1990s Japan's stagnation was obvious to the world. Singapore's malaise has been easier to hide because it has usually been disguised by steady and often high GDP growth rates and constant attempts to re-engineer the economy.

Singapore's basic economic problem has been one of ongoing dependence because of a failure to achieve a sustained and significant growth of indigenous EICs. This has been, firstly, because the local economy is dominated by a large state sector with limited EICs. Secondly, most of the manufacturing sector is run by MNCs which, being export-oriented, make little entrepreneurial or innovative contribution to the local economy. As MNC subsidiaries, their role is to manufacture standardised products for world markets, not to develop and market new ones for the host economy.

Singapore's still limited EICs has meant that it remains reliant on MNCs as well as foreign talent and technology to compete effectively in world export markets. While Japan's economic problems have taken the form of limited or non-existent GDP growth, Singapore's have essentially been those of ongoing economic dependence due to a continuing failure to develop significant EICs. The problems in both countries can only be solved through major structural reform. Both countries have lacked rulers who wanted to or could do this adequately, except perhaps Japan's Koizumi. Such reforms can only be undertaken by new political leaders who make a major break with past policies. In Singapore's case especially, the chances of this happening under the present PAP regime are remote. Singapore's problems, like Japan's, will persist for the foreseeable future. What consequences will this have for Singapore and how will its PAP leaders respond?

To try and boost Singapore's economic independence and international competitiveness the PAP Government is likely to launch more and bigger programs to boost R&D, entrepreneurial endeavours and import foreign talent. Such vigorous efforts to re-engineer Singapore will continue to create the impression of a rapidly developing, cutting-edge economy. The expansion of Singapore's EICs and its progress towards economic independence will nevertheless remain slow compared to its rapidly developing Asian neighbours and rivals. Certainly heavy and increased R&D spending and the importing of foreign talent and technologies could well lift local EICs to some extent in coming years. Moreover, the purchase of equity in foreign firms abroad by

Singapore's SEs to gain access to new technologies and business prospects might also boost national EICs.

However, Singapore's SME sector will probably remain stunted and unlikely to contribute much to the country's EICs. Unless major reforms are implemented to enable SMEs to compete equally with MNCs and SEs, its difficult to see how they might transform themselves into seedbeds of entrepreneurial and innovational endeavour. Singapore is unlikely to get much help from the MNC sector in developing indigenous EICs. While MNCs will keep devising products and services for the local market, most are likely to be minor adaptations of existing products, not anything representing new ground-breaking technology. MNCs, not local firms, will assuredly retain the patents for any innovations.

On balance though, Singapore's indigenous EICs should increase somewhat in the future despite minimal SME and MNC contributions. SEs do have some capacity for entrepreneurial activities, and through state-funded research via Biopolis and Singapore's tertiary institutions, SEs could gain access to marketable innovations. But Singapore will need more than modest increases in its EICs to survive without MNCs and compete in its own right in world markets as Taiwan, Hong Kong, South Korea and Malaysia have done. Singapore requires high and rapidly rising levels of EICs to do this. Having only an average degree of indigenous EICs will be insufficient to enable Singapore to compete effectively.

Competition to sell hi-tech/value products on world markets is intensifying, placing ever-greater premiums on rising EIC levels. Under the present political-economic system Singapore's EICs are likely to increase only slowly and the capacity to compete on world export markets will remain limited without MNCs.

Singapore will become increasingly uncompetitive globally if it relies on its own resources – entrepreneurial, innovative and production-wise. Without MNCs, Singapore would have to depend on its vast financial reserves and whatever income they earned to survive. But this would not be sufficient to save it from global irrelevance and eventual economic stagnation. PAP leaders realise this and know they still need MNCs to keep Singapore competitive and maintain GDP growth. The threat of the MNCs departing constantly haunts PAP leaders. They understand that Singapore still needs MNCs and with the global competition for foreign capital intensifying they feel pressured to make ever-greater concessions to them.

Singapore is facing increasingly vigorous competition for foreign capital from its near neighbours, especially Malaysia, Thailand and China. In 2002, Singapore lost Maersk Sealand and Evergreen Shipping to Malaysian ports; Egypt Air moved its base to Kuala Lumpur; BMW made Johor Bahru in Malaysia its regional headquarters and Shell moved its IT headquarters to Kuala Lumpur.[2] Other MNCs to move from Singapore to Malaysia have been Western Digital Technologies and Seagate Technology while Maxtor Corp has resettled in Malaysia, Thailand and China.[3] In 2004, Motorola and General Motors left Singapore. Motorola shut down its semiconductor and chip-design units in March 2004 and was planning to move them to China or India.[4] Motorola had been in Singapore for 30 years and employed 2000 staff. In 2003, it was awarded the "operational headquarters" status by the EDB to honour its commitment to Singapore; but sentiment plays little part in the decisions of foreign capital. Four years after receiving the EDB's operational headquarters status in 2004, General Motors, which had been in Singapore since 1993, was planning to move to Shanghai.[5]

Apart from Asian competition, globalisation has created a whole new range of competitors for foreign capital. The once closed economies of the former Soviet Union and the Communist bloc have opened up to world capital. Such countries as Poland, the Czech Republic and Hungary not only have more educated populations and better technological capacity than Singapore, but also they have much lower wages. Countries like India and Vietnam are also luring foreign capital – and their wages are even lower than Eastern Europe's.

Strong global competition for foreign capital has compelled the Singapore Government to provide ever-greater inducements to lure MNCs to Singapore and keep them there. The 2003 cuts to employers' CPF contributions and to corporate taxes and top-end income tax rates were prompted by such concerns. Attracting and retaining MNCs and foreign talent has never been seen as more important.

The Government may well feel compelled to repeat 2003-style measures for MNCs as global competition for foreign capital intensifies, but the 2003 GST increases were very unpopular with Singaporeans already hit hard by the 2002/3 recession. More increases in the GST or other regressive taxes would further anger them. The PAP knows that even politically docile Singaporeans can only be squeezed so much.

The Government is always looking for new ways to raise revenue, including ones it opposed in the past. The PAP has always rejected casinos for Singapore because of the social harm they cause; but as the Government exhausts all other ways of extracting revenue it will increasingly consider means previously spurned. In 2004, the Government announced plans to establish a casino on Sentosa Island, off Singapore. Various casino groups began bidding for the casino licence, including the Packer-owned Publishing & Broadcasting Ltd of Australia.

Whether the casinos pay off or not, the national reserves may still have to be used to finance further concessions to MNCs. Taxing long-suffering Singaporeans further would be politically unwise, especially if elections were looming. Dipping deeply into reserves would be a heart-wrenching decision for PAP leaders but political realities may require it, considering the PAP's obsessive fear of losing any seats in elections. The loss of even a few seats would be seen by PAP leaders as undermining their legitimacy.

Should a PAP Government use the reserves to meet budget deficits, rather than tax Singaporeans, the local private sector would benefit. Consumer spending would be boosted and local markets expanded, especially SMEs. But such a move would only be done in *extremis*. Protecting the reserves is a bedrock PAP policy and would only be changed under great pressure. The PAP may instead resort to devious ways of extracting further revenue from Singaporeans to try and avoid upsetting them.

In summary, then, Singapore is likely to remain a dependent economy with limited EICs. As such it will remain heavily reliant on MNCs to compete internationally and will need to offer ever-greater incentives to bring them and keep them. If bribed sufficiently the MNCs would be far more likely to stay; the necessary inducements can only be adequately financed out of national reserves. Retaining MNCs will ensure Singapore's survival and even its prosperity – at least in terms of continued steady GDP growth – but will keep it a dependent and underdeveloped economy unless it defies the odds and develops sufficient EICs to become an independent economy which can compete effectively on world markets without the MNCs.

While Japan's ongoing stagnation is obvious for the world to see, Singapore's major economic problems may well stay hidden. Its carefully cultivated image of a prosperous go-ahead economy could stay untarnished for some time. With MNCs driving the economy, especially the export sectors, for the foreseeable future, Singapore is likely to retain its export competitiveness. Being ever ready to make ever-greater concessions to the MNCs, Singapore should preserve its competitiveness in attracting foreign capital. This will do much to ensure that Singapore keeps scoring high IMD-WEF rankings. These will be inflated by Singapore's conspicuous efforts to practice transparency, accountability and corporate governance, and generally to re-engineer itself. Singapore's image as an efficient cutting-edge economy managed by apparently clever and astute leaders will probably remain intact. Its mediocrity and continued failure to transform itself into a genuinely developed and independent economy will stay obscured.

2. Some Bleak Scenarios

The preceding predictions envisage a *chuto hanpa* future for Singapore. Nothing much will change in a political-economic sense – provided Singapore uses its national reserves to keep the MNCs in Singapore and the PAP in power. Behind this façade, hollowing out processes will be operating. But one or two wrong decisions by the Government may be all that is required to plunge Singapore into potentially terminal economic and political crises.

A 'Hotel Singapore' Society?

PAP policies are transforming Singapore into a hollowed out and transitory hotel-type economy and society. Typically, hollowed out economies are heavily foreign-owned – as Singapore already is, and is likely to remain. Singapore may retain a sizeable industrial capacity with a high per capita GDP, but this will only be so if MNCs continue to be the economy's main generator.

Singapore will also continue to hollow out culturally, demographically and socially as more Singaporeans leave and transient foreigners come to work. Since the 1980s, growing numbers of educated and talented Singaporeans have migrated to other countries. This has rattled PAP leaders, who occasionally condemn them. During a 1989 National Day speech Lee Kuan Yew called such Singaporeans "washouts", depicting them as calculating opportunists (and this was when economic conditions were good). Prime Minister Goh Chok Tong expressed similar sentiments during a 2002 National Day speech:

> *Fair-weather Singaporeans will run away whenever the economy runs into stormy weather. I call them "quitters". Fortunately "quitters" are in the minority. The majority of Singaporeans are "stayers". "Stayers" are committed to Singapore. Rain or shine, they will be with Singapore.*[6]

PAP leaders' chagrin is understandable. Not only is much-needed talent being lost, but departing Singaporeans are demonstrating how there is little loyalty to Singapore. PAP leaders know that a country of stayers survives but one of quitters doesn't.

Because of Singapore's brain drain and limited innovative and creative capacities the demand for foreign talent will keep rising. As more of Singapore's talented leave, more expatriate professionals will be needed to replace them and provide the innovative, technological and managerial know-how that Singapore lacks. Under its present socio-political system Singapore is unlikely to display a sudden upsurge in innovation and creativity. Risk-averse mentalities and organisational attitudes will continue to retard the growth of such attributes. Educational reforms and other measures will take many years to produce a more creative and innovative society. This means that for some time yet Singapore will remain increasingly reliant on foreign talent to stay competitive. The Government will feel compelled to keep luring foreign talent to Singapore and many Singaporeans are likely to feel marginalised, especially as expatriate professionals take up more managerial and research positions.

"Hotel Singapore" is being used more to describe Singapore's future society. The term evokes a society increasingly run by transient and highly paid foreign managers or emigré Singaporeans who have returned briefly to work in Singapore before going back to their new homes in Australia, Canada or the US. PAP leaders often hail these transients as "cosmopolitans". Beneath these cosmopolitans are the ordinary Singaporeans who fill blue-collar and more mundane clerical positions. They are lauded as "heartlanders" by the Government and local media. Despite such accolades from both overpaid ministers and newspaper editors, most heartlanders have boring and mundane lives. They are stuck in low-paying jobs, often work long hours and frequently live in pokey HDB units on noisy estates with far less freedom than the average Westerner.

In reality the heartlanders are an increasingly sullen rump of indigenous Singaporeans who cannot migrate. Being less educated and/or older, they have little chance of being accepted as migrants to such developed countries as Australia, New Zealand or Canada. These heartlanders will feel increasingly excluded as more expatriates run Singapore. Heartlanders' marginalisation will intensify as they continue to be ruled by an all-powerful manipulative political elite that cannot be reformed or removed.

Transient cosmopolitans and resentful heartlanders are unlikely to have much sense of community, national loyalty or belonging. Hollowed out societies lack the resilience to meet adversity as Japan has done. Whatever Japan's structural problems, its people have great social and cultural strengths. Their deep sense of shared values and patriotism have always given Japan the capacity to bounce back from prolonged adversity. They still have a readiness to sacrifice themselves for the national good that few present-day Singaporeans display. Being adept opportunists, Singaporeans would be far more likely to jump ship (if they could) should things turn bad. They would be heading for whatever bolt-hole they could find. Sumiko Tan has been eyeing one in Perth, Australia. Singapore is still far from collapse, but its more qualified citizens continue to leave. High living costs, lack of democratic freedoms and a high-stress lifestyle prompt them to look elsewhere.

Besides the brain drain, Singapore is being hollowed out by demographic factors – primarily its disturbingly low birth rate. This has been a growing problem for both Singapore and Japan for many years. In 2002, only 40,800 babies were born in Singapore, the fewest in 16 years.[7] In 2003, the birth rate was heading for a 26-year low. Numerous government efforts to lift the birth rate have failed, including a baby bonus program in 2001 which gave cash for six years to parents who had second and third children. Singapore needs at least 50,000 births a year to sustain the economy and meet defence and manpower needs, but for many years Singapore has failed to achieve this birth rate and its population is beginning to age.

Several factors can explain Singapore's declining birth rate. Chief among these are high living costs, which often require both parents to work. The need to work six days a week, and often up to 12 hours a day, leaves little time for parenting. In addition, Singapore's stressful lifestyle further discourages couples from wanting to have many (or any) children. There is every reason to think that these factors will increase in future, causing further declines in Singapore's birth rate. A declining population means a shrinking workforce. Singapore's response has been to hire growing numbers of foreign workers, as well as expatriate professionals, to fill the gap. In 1990, non-citizens made up 13.9 per cent of the population, but by 2005 had risen to 28.4 per cent.[8] This figure was expected to rise to 50 per cent if Singapore's indigenous population continues to decline. Such a "foreignisation" of Singapore reveals how it is hollowing out demographically, as well as economically and socially.

Many Singaporeans already see their country as a way-station to some better place to live. They embody the mindset of a hollowed out hotel-like country with little real identity. This represents one final and very depressing outcome of Singapore's so-called economic miracle, but there could also be other bleaker outcomes for Singapore.

Rising Discontent and Political Change

The PAP Government may refuse to dip into reserves to keep the MNCs in Singapore. It may continue its revenue-extraction policies to cover budget deficits, if its obsession for protecting the reserves remains unchanged. The Government displayed a ruthless readiness to pursue such measures when it imposed further GST increases to pay for corporate tax cuts. This was despite having already reduced wages during a slump when the retail and tourism sectors were severely depressed. All this was done to gain an extra S$2 billion in revenue to finance the corporate tax cuts, rather than access the reserves. They had to be protected no matter what it cost the people, especially the poorer Singaporeans who would be hit hardest by the increased GST.

Future PAP governments may believe that they can still follow such policies at minimal political cost. Through over-confidence from half-a-century in power the PAP may continue to think that it can squeeze the people whenever it likes. The Government may assume that further rounds of GST increases, wage cuts, or excessive ministerial pay rises, etc, may be accepted as meekly as before - even during an economic downturn and/or when HDB prices are falling. A combination of all these variables would certainly produce an upsurge in anti-PAP feelings, as happened in 2003. But such feelings could be further intensified by a couple of "sleeper" factors that have been independently generating growing opposition to PAP rule for years.

The first is the growing income divide – and more specifically the stagnating and often declining income of the poorer classes. Like most Singaporeans they have traded their democratic freedoms for material security, if not always affluence. But this pact may be off if their living standards drop too far, making them feel much freer to oppose the PAP and support the opposition.

The second factor is the constantly growing resentment at the PAP's authoritarian style of rule. As Singaporeans' levels of education and political sophistication keep rising so do their demands for greater freedom and democracy and intolerance of authoritarian PAP policies. This thinking is especially prevalent among the middle classes. They could unite with a discontented working class and greatly strengthen any rising surge of anti-PAP discontent. This would produce soaring support for Singapore's opposition parties. Together they would achieve a numerically critical mass, transforming them from fragmented mini-parties into a broadly-based anti-PAP coalition. Such an alliance would also attract increased financial and organisational resources, greatly enhancing its capacity to effectively mobilise a major groundswell of opposition to PAP rule.

Already more educated and capable people are being drawn to Singapore's main opposition parties which are becoming increasingly professional in their operations. The anti-PAP vote was up from 27 to 33 per cent in the 2006 elections and record numbers, usually tens of thousands of people, attended their rallies reflecting growing demand for greater democracy and an end to the PAP's still authoritarian rule (despite limited liberalisation since the early 1990s) that are being made by a more informed and demanding populace.

However, a split in the PAP could be the decisive factor that removes it from power. Growing broad-based discontent could embolden some disaffected PAP MPs to leave the party and join an opposition coalition. Discarded and embittered PAP MPs who feel they were cast out before their time may also re-emerge as candidates for opposition parties. Buoyed by strong anti-PAP sentiment they may be prepared to endure the predictable wrath of the PAP establishment by joining the clash. Such a combination of factors may be sufficient to sweep the PAP from power.

Nonetheless, a new non-PAP government would face many severe challenges, especially if it takes over during a recession. The biggest task would be restructuring Singapore's economy to make it more efficient and competitive and less dependent on foreign capital. Managing such a transformation – and the dislocation it would cause – would test the skills of even the most competent and seasoned political leadership, let alone an inexperienced one. With luck such a post-PAP government may succeed and eventually, after much pain, transform Singapore into a viable independent economy. If not, other gloomy scenarios are likely.

A Consortium Scenario

Inept rulers and adverse economic conditions may be sufficient to reduce Singapore to such a parlous state that radical measures would be required. These could include turning the island into a complete outpost for Western capital or being forced to rejoin Malaysia.

A consortium of major MNCs and merchant banks could agree to take over Singapore and run it as a sort of "company town" for foreign capital. The consortium would have the right to organise the country's workforce as they saw fit and permit foreign banks and companies to operate unimpeded. They would not have to pay any tax but would have to maintain and improve the country's infrastructure.

Western military forces, especially from the US, could be provided to protect the new neo-colony. They could have naval and other bases on the island, perhaps with nuclear warheads. Singapore might become another Subic Bay and a lynchpin for a strong US and Western military presence in Asia.

Though Singapore might retain some nominal independence, its government would be reduced to an "advisory council". All major decisions about Singapore would reflect consortium interests, a 21st-century version of the East India Company. The island would have come full circle, once again being a colony, but this time privately owned.

Alternatively, a bankrupt unviable Singapore could simply rejoin Malaysia. Many would see this as a preferable option. Singapore was once part of Malaysia, and an organic component of it, economically, politically and culturally. It was largely Lee Kuan Yew's aggressive and insensitive attitudes to the Kuala Lumpur Government and its leader Tunku Abdul Rahman that had the city-state booted out of the Federation in 1965. Under a more moderate and reasonable leader, Singapore would have stayed in Malaysia and both would have benefited. Malaysia would have become a much stronger and more developed country much sooner, with Singapore as its financial and commercial heart. The island would have been a vital component of a prosperous and possibly progressive nation, instead of an underdeveloped economy dependent on foreign capital and expertise to survive.

3. Conclusion

Singapore and Japan have followed similar national development strategies. Each bears the marks of "steroid growth" and command-economy policies. Increased inputs and borrowed technologies rather than entrepreneurial innovation and productivity have determined their growth. Heavy and inappropriate state intervention in the economy has subverted market forces and created long-term structural problems that the leadership of Singapore has yet demonstrated the will or ability to solve and which Japan's has only begun to do so since 2001. In Japan's case such intervention produced prolonged stagnation; and in Singapore's, a dependent, hollowed out economy of second-rate efficiency. Neither outcome is desirable.

While Japan's failings have become increasingly obvious since the 1990s, Singapore still manages to hide its deficiencies. Its cutting-edge image remains intact; but Singapore, like MOF-dominated Japan, constitutes a development model that is best avoided rather than followed. In that negative sense Singapore is another Japan: but certainly not in the way Lee Kuan Yew had hoped.

References

1. *The Straits Times* (ST), August 17, 2003.
2. *Today,* April 8, 2003.
3. Bastion, Arlene: *Singapore in a Nutshell* (Singapore, Prentice Hall, 2003), p. 85.
4. *Today,* March 9, 2004.
5. ST, April 27, 2004. Singapore is facing greater competition for capital and also for opportunities to manage capital. In 2004, growing numbers of foreign fund managers were leaving Singapore because the market was too small. (*Today,* September 24, 2004). With the GIC and Temasek investing the bulk of the country's capital assets, there was not enough left for the private funds to manage. In August 2004, AIG Global Investment Corp (a unit of American International Group) closed 12 of its funds in Singapore and in September the Zurich-based Alianz Dresdner Asset Management was planning to wind up six funds.
6. "Remaking Singapore – Changing Mindsets", National Day Rally Address by Prime Minister Goh Chok Tong on August 18, 2002. <www.gov.sg/singov/announce/180802pm.htm>.
7. ST, August 20, 2003.
8. Asher G. Mukul and Amarendu Nandy "Singapore's policy responses to ageing, inequality and poverty: An assessment" p.42-3 in *International Social Security Review*, Vol. 61, 1/2008.

CONCLUSION
....

ECONOMIC MIRACLE OR
STATISTICAL MIRAGE?

T he Singapore Miracle still has much credibility in key global political and
economic circles. Singapore is seen as the one Asian tiger left standing.
Although the Asian financial crisis in 1997/8 punctured the Asian Century
hype, Singapore's reputation emerged largely unscathed. If anything, the city-state's
image was enhanced by the adroit way it handled this and subsequent crises.

Such timely responses suggested that Singapore was still ahead of the game
and a role model for the developing world – and for developed countries who still
questioned themselves. Singapore is as efficient and proactive as ever, its economic
miracle an undisputable fact to its many foreign fans. But as this book has shown,
Singapore's success and efficiencies are obvious and well-publicised; its economic
shortcomings and inefficiencies are less so.

This book has sought to reveal the less impressive aspects of the Singapore Miracle.
Despite Singapore's high growth and rapid infrastructure development it remains a
significantly dependent and underdeveloped economy of mediocre efficiency, lacking
in entrepreneurial values and any significant capacity for technological innovation and
where image usually triumphs over reality.

1. Myths for MNCs and Neo-cons

The PAP state has been developing its image-making abilities since coming to
power in 1959. From the beginning Singapore's rulers have promoted themselves as a
dedicated, efficient, hard-working, incorruptible team selflessly devoted to Singapore's
good. After separation from Malaysia in 1965 the need to promote Singapore to the
world gained new urgency. Lee and his ministers believed that the only way Singapore
could survive was through rapid export-led industrialisation – but this required large
infusions of foreign investment.

Several pre-conditions are necessary to attract foreign companies: political
stability, a docile labour force, generous tax breaks and other incentives. The PAP
delivered them all. Singapore's open-door policies were spectacularly successful.
Foreign capital poured in and development was rapid; industrial capacity exploded
and exports boomed. These achievements were then publicised to attract more foreign
capital.

Singapore became known as a clean, well-run, politically stable place that was good for foreign capital. Such claims were not without foundation, especially when compared to other Asian countries. Singapore is still a good place for foreign capital. Low levels of corruption, freedom for foreign companies to conduct operations as they wish, a legal system that guarantees property rights for foreign companies, a docile and reasonably literate workforce and a well-developed infrastructure still make Singapore a highly profitable, low-risk venue for foreign investors.

These achievements generated a chimera of myths about Singapore, including 99 per cent efficiency, high levels of economic freedom and transparency, an impartial judiciary and being a good place for business. Underpinning these claims was the strong implication that Singapore was developed and westernised.

Singapore's achievements, real and mythical, have been readily publicised by its Government – with the help of compliant ratings agencies, development experts and gullible foreign journalists. All this has confirmed Singapore's image as a choice haven for MNCs and a role-model for many countries.

However, Singapore leaves much to be desired as a blueprint for nation-building and economic development. Countries that see Singapore as an example to follow should look elsewhere, unless they want to become an MNC-dependent, state-controlled economy with limited EICs.

If Singapore is a model for anything, it is for its capacity for self-promotion and for producing statistical facades of success. Endless self-promotion is part of the Singapore model – along with the frequent denigration of its neighbours, including such countries as Australia, which along with Britain and New Zealand, have spent so much blood and treasure defending Singapore over the last 60-odd years, including the 1942 Japanese invasion, the 1948-60 Malayan Emergency and the 1963-6 Confrontation campaign with Indonesia.

Many who seek to promote themselves do so by belittling those around them in the belief this enhances their own status. This especially applies to individuals like Lee Kuan Yew with his arrogant, conceited and competitive mentality. Since the 1960s Lee has repeatedly done this, insulting the Malaysians, Thais, Filipinos and Indians, as well as Australians. He has mocked their intelligence and capacity for hard work and "discipline" (a major Lee obsession) and sneered at their inefficiencies.

Unfortunately, many Singaporeans have acquired Lee's attitudes towards their neighbours, ensuring that Singapore has few real friends in Asia. *Straits Times* columnist Koh Buck Song has lamented "the Republic's uninviting reputation for arrogance and self-righteousness" which some Singaporeans fear "is already entrenched in the minds of too many outsiders".[1]

Singapore and its leaders must expect rigorous criticism when they make such frequent and boastful claims about Singapore, and so often ruthlessly and dishonestly promote it at the expense of others. They can anticipate little mercy when they viciously attack those who dare chastise them. Opposition politicians Benjamin Jeyaretnam and Chee Soon Juan have not only been endlessly ridiculed and humiliated, but have been sued into bankruptcy: attacks as appalling as they are undemocratic. Others, such as Francis Seow and Tang Liang Hong, have been driven into exile by the PAP Government. Even those who have unintentionally offended the Government have been harshly dealt with. NUS academic Bilveer Singh and the two NUS dons who unwittingly published job figures that upset the Government were forced into abject apologies. Then there is an almost endless list of foreign and local newspapers and journals that have been forced to pay colossal damages and issue grovelling apologies on the most spurious of legal grounds for libelling the Singapore Government or its ministers.

Such readiness to inflict massive retribution on those who offend the PAP state is driven by an all-consuming desire to protect Singapore's reputation – its most precious asset – at any cost. Being a country that must constantly sell itself to the world and especially to foreign capital to survive and prosper, the PAP state will do whatever it takes to denigrate and discredit those whom it sees as harming Singapore's reputation.

Winning global approval is important for Singapore, to ensure that it maintains a high international profile where it can "punch above its weight" in world forums. When small countries are taken seriously by major powers, significant intangible economic and political benefits can be gained. High status ensures a strong bargaining position during the negotiation of trade, security and other agreements. Lee always understood this and has fully exploited it to win sizable gains for Singapore at world forums.

Besides Western nations, big states such as China keep drawing inspiration from Singapore. China's leaders (if not the Chinese, who must deal with arrogant Singaporeans on a daily basis in China) are apparently among those who admire Singapore's social engineering and managerial expertise. PAP leaders like to think that "Singapore software" is a source of nation-building ideas for such countries as China. Singapore-style development strategies are touted as likely to produce rapid development and prosperity for all.

By early 2007, the governments of China, Japan, South Korea, Malaysia and Vietnam were at different stages of "cloning" Temasek and the GIC.[2] China, Japan and South Korea in particular are sitting on huge foreign exchange reserves which are earning modest returns as US Treasury bonds. In February 2007, China was modelling a new state- owned company on Temasek and the GIC to invest the country's US$1.07 trillion in foreign reserves.[3] An asset management and foreign exchange investment company was being planned to jointly manage the foreign reserves similar to the Temasek/GIC structure.

Singapore's rulers have felt they need to prove that they have also achieved a New Jerusalem for the common man. The miracle economy must show that it has delivered the good life for all. This explains the constant PAP government propaganda about Singapore's affluence, and 90 per cent "home-ownership", and the superiority of its CPF and medical insurance schemes. PAP leaders like to suggest that Singapore provides the same level of health, aged care and security as the "welfare democracies" of the West for a fraction of the cost. Such claims win a ready audience among the West's neo-conservatives who are constantly seeking ways of reducing state welfare outlays by increasing self-reliance through "user pays" strategies. Were Singapore's foreign supporters to properly examine its HDB, CPF and assorted health schemes, they would feel compelled to revise their opinions of them – if they were intellectually honest.

2. Myths for Singaporeans

Selling Singapore's miracle to the locals is as important as promoting it to foreign capital and the international community. Singaporeans must be happy with their lot to make them more malleable. They will more readily accept restrictions the Government imposes on them to please foreign capital. The PAP never tires of telling Singaporeans how much they have benefited from its rule, how much happier they are in their HDB units than in the kampongs and how poverty has all but disappeared.

The rivers of dubious statistics the PAP state generates to back its questionable claims have often been uncritically accepted by journalists and Western neo-cons and the now discredited "Asia Rising" theorists. Both the myths and the statistics used to "prove" the Singapore Miracle are suspect. To what extent is the miracle a statistical mirage? If the statistics and myth-making used to promote this miracle are scraped away what is left? – A dependent and EIC-deficient economy, driven by MNC capital and expertise, with severe inequalities of wealth and income, high living costs and an often poorly paid workforce. Such truths about Singapore's miracle are not widely known abroad.

Negative foreign comments about Singapore focus on its authoritarian nature, the ruthless persecution of political opponents, its compromised and "compliant" judiciary, its lack of press freedom and its less-than-free elections. But Singapore is still seen as an economic success story that has delivered high living standards to its citizens despite democratic shortcomings.

Apart from Singaporean political activist Chee Soon Juan, few writers have exposed the many shortcomings of Singapore's economic miracle, and especially how little Singaporeans have gained from it. Were more commentators to do so, Singapore would no longer be regarded as a model for national development. It would lose its iconic "brand name" status around the world, particularly among neo-conservatives and the globalisation lobby. An MNC outpost serviced by underpaid locals and ruled by a manipulative and over-paid political elite is not an inspiring development model.

3. Myth versus Reality

Unlike Singapore's foreign friends, PAP leaders understand its real situation. Frantic government efforts to transform the country into an entrepreneurial, innovative, risk-taking society reflect this concern. However, such ends can only be achieved if the PAP state relinquishes much of its power over the economy and people.

While desperately trying to transform the economy, the PAP continues to deluge Singaporeans with assurances that everything is fine, using biased statistics to do this. Many Singaporeans see through such subterfuge, perceiving their society as one riven with privilege and inequality.

While the Government soothingly talks of cosmopolitans and heartlanders, Singaporeans name things differently. There is the "condo class" composed of highly-paid managers and professionals, at whose centre are the country's over-paid PAP rulers. And there is the "HDB class", comprising the vast bulk of the population, battling along on incomes of S$1500 to $2000 a month and often less, living limited and intimidated lives under a watchful and repressive state.

Another major socio-economic division in Singapore is between the privileged MNC-SE sector, protected at the expense of a stunted, marginalised SME sector. SME resentment at this intensifies with every economic downturn. They know well that there is no level playing field for them when competing against the MNCs and SEs.

Besides growing inequality, Singapore is hollowing out economically and socially. It will remain dependent on foreign capital and talent despite endless "re-engineering" efforts to make it more competitive. Singapore is becoming a transient hotel-type society. State-led efforts to inculcate patriotism and a sense of community merely disguise this process.

Eventually the truth may emerge that Singapore cannot be transformed into the economy the PAP wants unless the Government is prepared to relinquish significant economic and political control. The PAP cannot do this because it would undermine its rule and disrupt many powerful vested interests. However, without such reform Singapore is condemned to ongoing mediocrity. A vibrant MNC sector and huge national reserves will disguise this only for a while.

Nonetheless, a combination of internal and external factors could disrupt and tear apart Singapore's carefully cultivated image as a competitive cutting-edge economy. Some scenarios have been outlined on how this could occur. If conditions worsen, no amount of PAP spin, compliant ratings agencies or neo-con accolades will disguise Singapore's growing problems. Only then will the myths that have sustained PAP Singapore for so long be exposed; and only then will Singapore become a deservedly discarded development model for developing countries. Then, the Singapore Miracle will finally be seen for what it is.

References
1. *The Straits Times*, May 12, 1997.
2. *Australian Financial Review*, May 5-6, 2007.
3. *The Standard*, February 12, 2007.

. . . .

CONCEPTIONS OF COMPETITIVENESS

The competitiveness of nations only became a topic of serious concern in the early 1980s when US policy-makers began to see Japan and Europe as a threat to American economic dominance. By the early 1990s over a dozen books had appeared in the US expounding this alarmist view. One of the best-known was *Head to Head: The Coming Economic Battle Among Japan, Europe and America* by Lester Thurow.[1] The central theme was that a nation's fortunes were determined by its success on world markets. The notion that competitiveness was a contest-based activity is reflected in one of the most popular definitions of competitiveness. The US President's Commission on Industrial Competitiveness in 1984 described a nation's competitiveness as being,

> *the degree to which a country can, under free and fair market conditions, produce goods and services which meet the test of international markets, while simultaneously maintaining and expanding the real incomes of its people over the long term.*[2]

In 1994, MIT economics professor Paul Krugman challenged such conceptions of competitiveness.

1. The Krugman View

Krugman claimed that international competitiveness was an empty concept. To him, "competitiveness is a meaningless word when applied to national economies", declaring that "the obsession with competitiveness is both wrong and dangerous".[3] He dismissed the zero-sum view of competitiveness as a head-to-head contest between nations. But Krugman only discussed competitiveness between nations in terms of trade. He omitted any reference to the role of foreign investment and talent.

Questionable Zero-sum Claims

Krugman contended that when countries trade with each other they do not, as firms do, compete in a confrontational manner. They engage in non-zero sum activities that benefit all parties. Countries specialise according to the principles of comparative advantage, where they capitalise on their economic strengths and produce what they are best at. Nations must search for niches in world markets that will net them the greatest gains from their exports. Their productivity and prosperity improve the more they specialise in the products and services they can produce most efficiently and cheaply.

According to Krugman, the central dynamic of international trade is specialisation based on the principle of comparative advantage. Such concepts as competition become redundant, except as a synonym for productivity. Otherwise, notions of competitiveness, especially of the zero-sum variety, are conceptually empty. International trade can quite adequately be understood without reference to competitiveness. But Krugman, and those who support him, have conflated conceptions of trade with those of competitiveness. They have confused trade with competitiveness – two very different notions.

In its simplest form foreign trade involves societies exchanging their surplus production for goods and services they cannot produce themselves. For example, Country A produces product X best and Country B produces Y best. A exchanges its X for B's Y. Each country has specialised in producing what it can produce most efficiently, exporting the surplus in exchange for what it produces less efficiently or not at all. These are the essential principles of comparative advantage and foreign trade.

But what of competition between countries? When does trade become competition? Let's return to the above example. When Country A and B are trading X and Y with each other, trade, not competition, is taking place, but what happens if a Country C, which also produces Y and wants to exchange it for A's X, appears on the scene? Countries B and C are both trying to exchange Y for Country A's X.

Even here competition may not necessarily occur. For example, Country A may require five units of Y per year while B can only produce three units and C two units. Together, B and C can satisfy A's need for five Ys, so are not yet in competition. But if Country A only required 3 Ys, while B and C produced 5 Ys between them, then B and C would be forced to compete with each other for A's limited market of Ys. Every unit of Y that B can supply to A means one less Y that C can provide, and vice versa. A state of zero-sum competition would therefore exist between B and C for A's Y market.

Of course, it may be contended that any such competition between B and C could be dispelled if B or C were to develop some other product to export to A or to some other country. Either country could find some other niche in the international economy for some products other than Y, which it could produce more efficiently than any other country. In the real world of international trade, however, such a switch may not be so easy.

Often several countries or more may only be able to produce a certain range of goods or services, often of the same type. This would especially be so for the most underdeveloped countries that can only produce a limited variety of primary products, despite practising the principles of comparative advantage. In other words, several countries may end up producing the same exports. Despite having maximised the productive use of their resources, they may often be competing against each other to sell identical products on world markets. They lack the technological and other capacities to easily switch to developing alternative exports that would yield more for them. They may often have no choice but to compete with each other to sell the same products. Direct zero-sum competition would therefore be waged between them for market share.

This situation occurs with economies such as Singapore's and Malaysia's, which heavily depend on the world hard-disk drive market. By applying the principles of comparative advantage they have specialised in producing hard-disk drives for export, but they constantly compete against each other, and against computer chip producers generally, on world markets. Thus while countries may export according to comparative advantage principles, head-to-head competition still occurs. This has occurred in the zero-sum competition waged for the Japanese iron ore market between Brazil and the Australian state of Western Australia. If the Japanese had switched to Brazil for their iron ore, then WA would have experienced a massive decline in its iron ore exports – at least until it found other buyers. In other words, Brazil's gain would have been WA's loss – a classic zero-sum outcome. WA's continued capacity to win Japanese iron ore contracts has been at Brazil's expense.

Trade's Importance Minimised

Even if countries did lose out in zero-sum competition for exports, this would have little economic effect on them, according to the Krugman view. Krugman illustrated such claims by comparing corporations to nations. Corporations compete for market share. If they fail to sell sufficient of their products or services they cannot pay their workers, suppliers, or bondholders. They become uncompetitive and go out of business. This is their "bottom line", argued Krugman. Countries still exist whether or not they perform poorly economically. "They may be happy or unhappy with their economic performance, but they have no well-defined bottom line."[4]

Krugman condemned "the idea that a country's economic fortunes are largely determined by its success on world markets". Citing the US, Krugman noted that in the early 1990s exports constituted only about 10 per cent of GNP. The US was still an economy that produced 90 per cent of its own goods and services. "By contrast, even the largest corporation sells hardly any of its output to its own workers: the 'exports' of General Motors – its sales to people who do not work there – are virtually all of its sales."[5]

Such examples show that Krugman is only talking about what he terms "the world's leading nations", especially the US. His views are less applicable to many smaller trade-dependent nations such as Singapore, Hong Kong, Malaysia and Taiwan, as well as Third World exporters of raw materials, as the following table shows:[6]

Trade as a percentage of GDP

	Trade to GDP Ratio*	Exports of Goods (% of GDP)	Exports of Comm. Services (% of GDP)
	(1999)	(2000)	(1999)
Singapore	160:21	150.60	28.61
Hong Kong	130:64	123.64	23.85
Malaysia	111:60	114.76	15.22
USA	11:77	7.85	2.72
Japan	10:06	10.08	1.34
Australia	20:30	16.23	4.36

* (Imports + Exports) / (2 x GDP)

Clearly there is a vast gulf between trade-dependent countries such as Singapore and the "world's leading nations" but Krugman does not consider this. Should trade-dependent economies suffer significant declines in national competitiveness that reduce their exports, they face dire consequences, however much they may practice the principles of comparative advantage. They lose power and influence internationally, and their ability to negotiate favourable trade deals and attract foreign investment and talent declines. While such countries may not "go out of business" they suffer significant economic hardship from reduced competitiveness.

Foreign Investment and Talent Omitted

Krugman also fails to consider the extent to which some economies are heavily dependent on foreign capital and expertise. Diminished ability to attract foreign investment can reduce their productive capacity, making them less competitive. This is especially so for countries like Singapore, whose economy is largely driven by MNC investment. Were the MNCs to leave in large numbers and move elsewhere, the consequences, at least in the short-term, would be catastrophic.

Similarly, an exodus of foreign talent would be economically harmful to countries such as Singapore. For many decades the US benefited from foreign talent, especially during the 1930s and 1940s with the mass departure of top scientists from Germany and elsewhere. Einstein, von Braun and many other great minds conferred significant scientific benefits on the US when they came and worked and lived there (while in von Braun's case his Nazi past was judiciously ignored by US authorities). They gave the US a competitive pre-eminence in scientific research, especially in nuclear physics, that it still holds. The advent of the knowledge economy has made competition for scientific and creative talent a classic zero-sum situation for many countries, including Singapore. Every top foreign scientist Singapore lures to Biopolis is a loss for another country and a gain for Singapore. Conversely, every scientist that leaves Singapore to work in another country is to Singapore's loss.

Only a Benchmarking Exercise?

For Krugman there is no such thing as zero-sum competition between nations, and if there was it would not count for much because trade contributes little to the leading nations' GDP and overall economic welfare. The prosperity of such states as the US, Japan and the European Community rests on domestic productivity, not on trade – nor, presumably, the ability to attract foreign investment and talent. Krugman contended that "In each case, the growth rate of living standards essentially equals the growth rate of domestic productivity – not productivity relative to competitors, but simply domestic productivity."[7] And "Even though world trade is larger than ever before, national living standards are overwhelmingly determined by domestic factors rather than by some competition for world markets." Hence, "the major nations of the world are not to any significant degree in economic competition with each other".[8] Naturally there is always rivalry for status and power: countries that grow faster see their political rank and status rise: so while it is always interesting to compare countries, asserting that Country A's growth reduces Country B's status is very different from saying that it diminishes the latter's living standards. As such, assessing national competitiveness can be little more than a ranking or benchmarking exercise based on countries' productivity rates. For Krugman competitiveness was only "a poetic way of saying productivity, without actually implying that international competition has anything to do with it".[9]

It should be repeated that Krugman's views only apply to major world powers such as the US, which are not trade-dependent. His focus was on trade alone, and the refutation of claims that trade was an arena for zero-sum contests between nations. He paid little heed to the vigorous competition for investment capital between countries, especially those in the Third World. Demands for foreign capital and talent usually exceed the amount available, creating a zero-sum-type rivalry for such finite resources, where one country's gain is usually at the loss of others. This is illustrated by Singapore's determined struggle to retain and if possible increase the numbers of MNCs it has against competition from Malaysia, Hong Kong and Taiwan (not to mention China) and also its constant efforts to lure foreign talent.

Krugman's conception of competitiveness is flawed and limited to international trade. Better definitions are required.

2. Defining National Competitiveness

Conceptions of national competitiveness range between the benchmarking and the zero-sum variety. At the benchmarking end is the Krugman view that competitiveness is merely a "poetic" word for productivity where nations' productivity is compared. The only "prize" to be won is the honour of being ranked a highly competitive nation. At the other extreme is the belief that competitiveness is a zero-sum contest, where one party's gain is at the cost of its rivals.

If the aim is to merely compare countries in terms of their economic performance and productivity, then the Krugman approach might do; but as already shown, economic competition between countries is often zero-sum in nature and requires definitions that reflect this reality. This is so whether states compete for finite resources such as foreign capital and talent or for export markets. When many are competing for such limited resources as foreign investment or aid, demand almost always outstrips supply. The more that successful competitors get, the less is left for the rest.

A similar situation applies in competition for export markets. The least competitive get the smallest share, or even nothing. In time, the less successful may be able to develop new products and compete in different markets, according to the economic credo of specialisation and comparative advantage. However, this is often not a viable option for the least developed countries who depend on the export of one or two natural resources such as coffee, cocoa or bananas. Switching to producing other exports would be difficult for such underdeveloped countries with their limited technological capacities and low productivity levels, especially for manufacturing activities where a higher degree of workforce literacy and skill are required.

For major economies such as the US which have relatively little dependence on trade, the competition for foreign markets is less important than for smaller countries that need sizeable markets for their exports. For such countries as Singapore, Hong Kong and Malaysia, which depend heavily on trade as well as foreign investment and talent, being export-competitive in these areas is economically vital. This requirement greatly intensifies competition between them (and other Asian countries, including China), especially considering the zero-sum context in which it occurs.

While Singapore's leaders regularly deny they are competing with Hong Kong and Malaysia, it is clear they are. Efforts to deny the zero-sum realities that often dominate competition between nations are simply ploys to diminish international tensions that such competition generates and reduce threats of trade wars. In interpersonal relationships, as in international politics, unpleasant realities are often glossed over with euphemisms to minimise hurt feelings and potential conflict.

Krugman-type efforts to "euphemise" the term competitiveness have reduced it to a synonym for productivity. When used this way competitiveness is of little use in understanding the nature of economic competition between nations. When nations compete with each other for some finite resources vital for their survival they act very differently to each other then if they were merely competing for the status of being the most competitive nation in Krugmanesque productivity terms. If countries are to be ranked by economic performance alone then perhaps such terms as "achievement" or "performance" rankings rather than competitiveness rankings should be used. The term competitiveness is best used to describe what it originally meant – a contest-based encounter between two or more parties often with zero-sum elements. This would more accurately describe competitiveness, its outcomes and the mechanisms that drive it.

Little understanding of the processes of international competition can be gained by treating it as merely a benchmarking concept based on productivity. While productivity may significantly determine a country's competitiveness, especially in export markets, it cannot be used to describe how international competitiveness is a contest-based activity that occurs between countries. But while competitiveness can reasonably be regarded as the capacity to compete for such finite items as markets, investment capital, aid or foreign talent, the concept requires further qualification. First, zero-sum competition between nations is a matter of degree. While the winner takes all in a poker game, the situation is usually less extreme when nations are competing for trade or investment. Some nations are more and others less successful – though the former still are so at the expense of the latter.

Moreover, nations may cooperate with each other when belonging to trade blocks or through various trade and business agreements. This may reduce competition within such groupings, but those excluded would lose out. For example, when Britain joined the European Common Market in 1973, Australia and New Zealand's agricultural exports to Britain declined because Britain had to buy within the ECM.

These are merely a few dimensions to national competitiveness. Further examination would reveal many more, but that is beyond the scope of this appendix whose aim is merely to expose the inadequacies of existing conceptions of international competitiveness, especially those used by such bodies as the IMD and WEF, as well as Krugman. Nonetheless, from what has already been said, it can be seen that competition between countries is largely zero-sum and is waged not only for exports but for foreign investment and aid and talent. And compete they do and often vigorously, even ruthlessly on occasion. Krugman-like definitions at competitiveness that suggest otherwise are a denial of reality. The economic welfare of many countries, especially smaller ones with very open economies such as Singapore, heavily depends on how well they compete internationally for markets, capital and skills etc.

A country's competitiveness may be defined as its capacity to acquire such finite resources as foreign investment, aid and talent and to win the greatest possible shares of export markets in the international economy, often in direct zero-sum contests with other states.

By such a definition Singapore would seem to have been very competitive in the early 2000s. It continued to attract substantial foreign investment and talent and performed well in world export markets. However, luring and retaining MNCs in the face of vigorous competition from other countries has become much harder as Chapter 33 showed. Moreover, success in attracting foreign enterprises must be matched by a significant growth of indigenous EICs and of local firms which would be capable to compete globally. A country like Singapore which is lacking in these areas would quickly become uncompetitive were the MNCs responsible for its export success to depart.

In its most extreme form, competition between countries may involve head-to-head struggles by one country against others, but it can be moderated through trade blocks and other international bodies such as the World Trade Organisation. Whatever the case, conceptions of competitiveness that allow for a large zero-sum element are likely to provide a better understanding of competitiveness than those based on mere benchmarking, which is a far too general concept for analysing economic competition between nations. IMD/WEF views of competitiveness are muddled combinations of both conceptions.

3. Conceptual Confusion

Despite the limitations in Krugman's notions of competitiveness, they have been accepted by the IMD and WEF on occasion. In their 1995 report they denied claiming that world competitiveness was a zero-sum game. "We never said that," they insisted:

> On the contrary, an open world economy provides wealth creation for everybody, but at a different speed. In a 100m sprint, there is a first and second at the finishing line. But both have run 100m. Ranking competitiveness is the same dynamic process...[10]

In other words, assessing the competitiveness of nations was merely a ranking exercise. Later the report changed its definitional tack.

Conceptual Drift

After initally supporting the Krugman position, the 1995 report drifted towards backing the zero-sum position of competitiveness. Measuring competitiveness was apparently more than a ranking exercise. They rejected the Krugman notion that only corporations compete: nations compete too.

The report referred to "businessmen in many countries who are struggling with bureaucratic red tape, high operating costs, unskilled workers, deficient infrastructure, closed public markets, selective justice systems or political instability".[11] Countries that significantly suffer from these defects are less attractive to foreign capital and so less competitive internationally. They lose foreign investment to countries that are not so prone to such deficiencies.

The IMD and WEF also rejected the Krugman claim that trade was of marginal concern to national economies. Were this correct it would be "good news for those employees who are out of a job ... and who, naively, thought that the fact that some products or services now produced elsewhere had anything to do with it". Countries lose industries – and jobs – when they become less attractive for business and so more uncompetitive.

Claiming that only the domestic economy matters was "an extreme position", said the 1995 report. It "shows the bias of economists living in countries with large domestic markets"; but two-thirds of countries that the report surveyed had populations of less than 50 million. For them, being internationally competitive was central to their prosperity.

The report seemed to be adopting the position that countries that competed successfully on world markets for exports and investment, often in zero-sum contests, would benefit economically. Conversely, those that did not would suffer economic adversity. The report's definition of national competitiveness appeared to reflect these notions. It defined national competitiveness as "the ability of a country or a company to, proportionally, generate more wealth than its competitors in world markets".[12] In other words, a country's competitiveness depended on its capacity to generate higher per-capita earnings from trade than its competitors. Presumably too its competitiveness could be measured by how much foreign capital and talent had also boosted its per capita GDP. The less competitive a country was, the lower its per capita income would be. Thus the incentive to compete by whatever means would be very strong for a country.

The 1995 report's position should be qualified by recognising that the importance of international competitiveness to countries' economies depends on how reliant they are on the world economy. If heavily dependent, then an inability to compete would have severe economic consequences; but if only a small percentage of their GDP comes from trade and they have only a limited need for foreign capital and talent, then failure to compete would not be important. Nonetheless, the report did seem to more or less recognise the zero-sum element of competition between nations. Logically therefore international competitiveness would be a major economic determinant of most countries' prosperity, as measured by such yardsticks as the amount of per capita GDP earned from trade and the extent to which per capita GDP had also been boosted by foreign investment and talent. Such per capita GDP measures reflected a country's competitiveness. But then the report claimed that,

> competitiveness cannot be reduced to mere notions of GDP and productivity. Firms need also to cope with the political, economic, socio-cultural, human and educational dimension of a country.[13]

These aspects must be considered when measuring national competitiveness, the report said.

This observation confuses cause and effect. How well firms cope with political and other factors significantly determines productivity and their capacity to produce exports that can successfully compete on global markets. Moreover, such factors can also greatly affect a country's ability to attract foreign investment and talent and also can influence its GDP growth. This confusion of cause and effect, of dependent and independent variables, is characteristic of IMD and WEF reports, especially those produced since 1995.

Definitional Deficiencies

After the 1995 report, when the IMD and WEF split from each other, their views of competitiveness diverged. The IMD reports continued to endorse a quasi zero-sum view of competitiveness. The IMD's emphasis on the need for countries to attract foreign investment and talent reflected this attitude.

While admitting that nations really do compete with each other and rejecting the notion that national competitiveness can be reduced to GDP growth and productivity, the IMD refrains from clearly defining competitiveness. Instead it contends that a country's competitiveness ultimately depends on how its environment sustains the competitiveness of its business sector. The IMD "assumes that wealth creation takes place primarily at enterprise level (whether private or state-owned)".[14]

Political, cultural, and educational conditions, as well as the state of economy, profoundly affect how well firms can do business; hence countries compete with each other in terms of how well they can provide an environment that supports firms through the provision of efficient political, economic and social institutions and policies. This is recognised by the IMD competitiveness reports, which rank and analyse "the ability of nations to provide an environment in which enterprises can compete".[15]

The IMD contends that a country's competitive advantage is boosted by aggressive policies such as tax breaks, subsidies and the like devised by governments to create a more positive climate for foreign concerns. The greater such measures, the more likely a country is to attract foreign capital and enhance its competitiveness. The IMD also emphasises the growing need of countries to develop knowledge and expertise to remain competitive with the development of the global knowledge economy:

> *Knowledge is perhaps the most critical competitiveness factor. As they move up the economic scale, the more they thrive on knowledge to ensure their prosperity and to compete in world markets...Nation's do indeed compete.[16]*

Attracting foreign talent is central to remaining internationally competitive. Such thinking has driven Singapore to recruit the best brains for its R&D projects.

IMD references to the need to lure talent and create a favourable climate for foreign investment to remain competitive reflect its belief that nations actually compete, often in a zero-sum sense. Such vague notions are no substitute, however, for a coherent definition of competitiveness, which the IMD fails to provide. As Oxford University development economist Sanjaya Lall has noted, the IMD "chooses not to provide any measure of competitiveness".[17] Surely a clear definition of competitiveness is required to ensure appropriate selection of factors to measure it. Lall remarks that without any definition of the dependent variable (competitiveness),

> *it is difficult to see how to verify the analysis and the choice or relevant determinants. In effect, IMD appears to ask its audience to take its findings entirely on faith, to assume that "competitiveness" has a universally accepted meaning to which it adheres.[18]*

Valid measures of IMD conceptions of competitiveness are prevented when a definition is lacking.

WEF conceptions of national competitiveness are little better, and reflect the Krugman view. Like Krugman the WEF sees competitiveness as a synonym for productivity, and its measurement as mainly a benchmarking exercise. A country's competitiveness is based on its productivity, "which is measured by the value of goods and services produced per unit of the nation's human, capital, and natural resources," the WEF argues.[19]

Normally, productivity relates to economic performance while competitiveness relates to competition. Dictionary definitions of competitiveness use such words to describe a contest between rival parties for some finite resource, commodity, privilege, opportunity (such as access to export markets), item or status symbol of which the victor gets all or the greatest share. Productivity, however, comes from the word "to produce", which means to create and bring forth something. Productivity relates to the process of production, which in economics has been defined to mean the capacity to maximise output from a given amount of resources – i.e. land, labour and capital.

To compare countries' economic performances, productivity would probably be as good a benchmark as any. It is, after all, a very basic measure of an economy's productive capacity. But should productivity be used to define competitiveness? The WEF would have us think so. It seems to be suggesting that by being ranked for productivity, countries are somehow competing against each other for the accolade of being the world's most productive country – at least as assessed by the WEF. But even if countries being surveyed by the WEF were so competing, the prize would merely be the right to be deemed the most competitive according to the WEF. Nonetheless, it is true that a few of the countries that the WEF (and IMD) survey are probably vying for such a title for reasons of national prestige. Among these would be Singapore, which strives to do everything possible to promote itself, including being ranked top by various ratings agencies for every possible attribute and virtue. Most of the countries being surveyed, especially the larger ones, have little need for their countries to win IMD/WEF plaudits for competitiveness.

Whatever the case, the WEF's definition of competitiveness seems to be based on the tenuous assumption that the countries it surveys are competing for the highest possible WEF competitiveness rankings – which are based on their productivity levels as assessed by the WEF – and nothing more. Such feeble conceptual foundations underpin the WEF definition of competitiveness.

While productivity may profoundly affect a country's export performance and be regarded as a cause of competitiveness, it cannot be used as a means of identifying and defining competitiveness, especially of the zero-sum variety. Characteristics or traits that describe how a phenomenon manifests itself are different from factors which determine its causes.

A country's productivity significantly affects its capacity to compete on world export markets.[20] Higher productivity increases the ability to produce exports that meet market price and quality demands. But it is export success – along with the capacity to attract foreign investment and aid and foreign talent – that more precisely defines a country's competitiveness than its productivity.

If one wishes to stick to benchmarking notions of competitiveness which deny its zero-sum elements, then it would be appropriate to rank countries according to their per capita export levels and success in attracting foreign investment and talent. These criteria would more precisely describe a country's success in the international economy than productivity, even when used in a purely bench-marking sense. Productivity and the living standards it generates applies to the domestic economy, whereas export success, etc, relate to a country's external economic performance in the international economy. As such, it would be more appropriate to benchmark a country's economic performance in the world economy than in terms of its domestic productivity and living standards. Equating productivity with competitiveness is inappropriate. Even WEF-style benchmarking notions of competitiveness would be better served by a definition based on major indices of success in the international economy, even when zero-sum notions are rejected.

The WEF shares Krugman's rejection of the zero-sum view of competitiveness. Assessing a country's competitiveness by its share of world markets for its products is "deeply flawed", it claims.[21] Like Krugman, the WEF believes that specialisation and practicing the principles of comparative advantage minimise economic competition between countries. But again such an approach denies the reality of zero-sum competition between nations, the stakes involved and the methods some are prepared to use to compete.

IMD and WEF attempts to describe and define competitiveness are clearly deficient. The IMD fails to define it at all, while the WEF provides a tenuous definition that is second-rate even for benchmarking purposes. All that both bodies have really done is identify major factors that can cause or shape competitiveness. The IMD's favourable business environment and the WEF's productivity profoundly affect a country's international competitiveness, but neither could be used as benchmarks to define such competitiveness – certainly not contest-based conceptions of it. Only factors like export success, or the capacity to attract foreign investment and talent and so on, can play this definitional role. Krugman-style definitions of competitiveness fail to do this. Not only are the IMD and WEF notions of competitiveness conceptually flawed, so too are the criteria for measuring them.

3. Misconceived Criteria

Besides data deficiencies and defective conceptions of competitiveness, many of the IMD and WEF's criteria are poorly devised. The criteria often confuse cause and effect and are also vaguely worded.

Causal Confusion

Both agencies mix up criteria for measuring *causes* of competitiveness with those for *defining* competitiveness. After ranking countries for productivity the WEF ranks the factors that determine it. The rankings for both types of criteria are then conflated to produce overall competitiveness for each country. Such procedures ignore causal principles of measurement.

The WEF's violation of such principles has been noticed by Lall. In commenting on the 2000 WEF report, Lall observed that "the causation often runs the wrong way (from income to the independent variable)".[22] The reason why some of the variables have been used – and their causal role in relation to productivity – is hard to understand. For example, using GDP in its report to explain innovation, one of the WEF's three main groups of factors which are seen as determining productivity, is strange. "The causation is normally taken to be the other way round," noted Lall.

Again, the report used such criteria as "demanding regulatory standards" and "stringency of environmental regulations" to measure variables that supposedly explain higher per capita incomes. In fact, "common sense suggests that these are likely to be the result rather than causes of high income"[22] and high productivity. Lall suggested that the errors were because the WEF "never analyzes causal relationships for theoretical validity". The WEF 2000 report displayed "the problem of circular reasoning and causation".[23]

Problems of causality seem also to afflict IMD criteria. Like the WEF, the IMD has a group of productivity-related criteria that describe factors that are clearly caused by other factors ranked in its report. Overall productivity based on purchasing power parity (PPP), labour productivity (PPP), productivity in industry (PPP) and productivity in services (PPP) are the result of factors that IMD reports measure, such as the quality of management and labour in terms of competence, skill-levels and adaptability. These and other determinants of productivity are already measured by numerous alternative IMD criteria.

The WEF similarly confuses causality with correlation when measuring causes of competitiveness. The WEF often gauges factors that are only correlated with productivity but do not determine it. "There are problems with the causal relations posited by WEF and its handling of data," said Lall.[24] As WEF itself has admitted, some factors the criteria are measuring may be correlated with productivity (income) without being its cause. "High correlations cannot establish causation, if there is no theoretical justification for a relationship between variables."[25] Such correlations may simply show that variables move together with each other, and nothing more.

Superfluous and Vague Criteria

Another major deficiency of IMD/WEF criteria is that many are superfluous and vaguely worded, especially those that are used as survey criteria. First, survey questions are often repetitive. The same information is sought in several questions phrased slightly differently. This can cause respondents to interpret them in different ways and provide differentiated answers. "This can create 'noise' and redundant information, and [so] cloud rather than improve the rankings."[26] Lall cited six question-based criteria from the WEF's 2000 report that demonstrated this:

- Your country is a world leader in technology
- The business sector in your country spends heavily on R&D
- Companies in your country are aggressive in absorbing technology
- Competitive advantages of companies are due to unique products
- Companies develop their own products
- Product designs are developed locally.

The six questions "revolve around the intensity of business-financed R&D, asking essentially the same question in different forms".[27] This situation generates "statistical noise" that clouds rather than improves rankings.

Superfluous criteria also appear in IMD reports. Some IMD criteria in the 2001 report to display such tendencies were those relating to corporate rectitude. They were:

- "Ethical practices are adopted in companies" (3.4.02) [28]
- "Corporate boards prevent improper business practices in corporate affairs" (3.4.04) [29]
- "Companies' managers are trusted by the public" (3.4.03) [30]
- "Business leaders do not neglect their responsibility towards society" (3.4.10) [31]
- "Health, safety and environmental concerns are addressed by management" (3.4.11). [32]

Many soft data criteria in IMD and WEF reports are vaguely worded, making it easy for respondents to interpret (or misinterpret) them as they choose. For example, such bald statements as "bankers enjoy public confidence", etc. (4.33) [33] could mean:

- People believe their savings are safe with the banks
- Banks will stand by customers and not prematurely foreclose on their loans during difficult times
- Banks respect clients' confidentiality
- Banks efficiently serve customers.

These are the questions needed to measure public confidence in banks. Such thoroughness was clearly lacking in the questionnaires used to gather soft-data for the 1995 report. Of course, it could be argued that the criteria are deliberately worded in a vague manner to capture a variety of interpretations, but so often IMD/WEF criteria are so general as to be of little value in assessing whatever factors they are seeking to measure. That, along with the dubious data they get from countries such as Singapore, discredits their competitiveness rankings.

References

1. Thurow, Lester: *Head to Head: The Coming Economic Battle among Japan, Europe, and America* (New York, Morrow, 1992).
2. Quoted by Stephen Cohen in "Speaking Freely", *Foreign Affairs*, July-August 1994, 73, 4, p. 195.
3. Krugman, Paul: "Competitiveness: A Dangerous Obession". *Foreign Affairs*, March/April 1994, 73, 2, p. 44.
4. Ibid, p. 31.
5. Ibid, p. 34.
6. *The World Competitiveness Yearbook 2001* (Institute for Management Development, Lausanne, Switzerland), Tables 1.2.08, 1.2.11 and 1.2.18.
7. Krugman, p. 34.
8. Ibid, p. 35.
9. Ibid.
10. *The 1995 World Competitiveness Report* (Institute for Management Development and the World Economic Forum, Lausanne, Switzerland; 1995), p. 7.
11. Ibid.
12. Ibid, p. 36.
13. Ibid.
14. *The World Competitiveness Yearbook 2001*, p. 51.
15. Ibid.
16. Ibid, p. 43.
17. Lall, Sanjaya: "The Competitiveness Indices of Developing Countries: An Economic Evaluation of the Global Competitiveness Report"; 2001, *World Development*, 29, 9, p. 508.
18. Ibid.
19. *The 2001 WEF Global Competitiveness Reports* (World Economic Forum and the Center for International Development at Harvard University, Oxford University Press, New York), p. 55.
20. Another major factor that can give a country this capacity is simply a large store of sought-after natural resources such as oil. This too can assure export success, as OPEC members have demonstrated. Being resource-rich is a variable independent of a country's ability to efficiently or productively use its resources.
21. Lall, p. 1513.
22. Ibid, p. 1515.
23. Ibid, p. 1514.
24. Ibid, p. 1514.
25. Ibid, p. 1515.
26. Ibid, p. 1516.
27. Ibid. p. 1517.
28. *The World Competitiveness Yearbook 2001*, p. 468.
29. Ibid, p. 469.
30. Ibid, p. 468.
31. Ibid, p. 472.
32. Ibid.
33. *The 1995 World Competitiveness Report*, p. 560.

BIBLIOGRAPHY

··

Newspapers

Singapore
Business Times
City Weekly (a defunct *Straits Times* supplement)
The New Paper (afternoon daily)
Project Eyeball (a defunct afternoon daily)
The Straits Times (morning daily)
Straits Times Interactive
Streats (a defunct afternoon daily)
The Sunday Times (Sunday version of *The Straits Times*)
Today (afternoon daily)

Foreign
The Age (Melbourne, Australia)
The Australian
The Australian Financial Review
The Financial Times (London)
The Jakarta Post
South China Morning Post
The Sunday Times (Perth, Western Australia)
The West Australian
The Standard (Hong Kong)

Other Sources

Amsden, Alice: "Competitiveness and Industrial Policy: East and West" (*JPRI* 3, 8, October 1996).

Annual Salary of Major Office-holders in Selected Overseas Legislatures and Governments (as of May 2006), Fact Sheet (Research and Library Services Division, Legislative Council Secretariat, Hong Kong).

Asher G. Mukul and Amarendu Nandy "Singapore's policy responses to ageing, inequality and poverty: An assessment" *International Social Security Review*, Vol. 61, 1/2008.

Asia Sentinel, January 22 and August 4, 2007.

Asia Magazine, August 16-18, 1996.

Au, Alex: "Singapore joins banking top table", *AsiaTimes Online*. Jan 12, 2008, www.atimes.com.

Australia Fair News, October 23, 2007 www.australiafair.org.au/

Backman, Michael: *Asian Eclipse: Exposing the Dark Side of Business in Asia.* Singapore, John Wiley and Sons, revised edition, 2001.

Barr, Michael D.: *Lee Kuan Yew: The Beliefs Behind the Man.* Surrey, UK; Curzon, 2000.

Barr, Michael D.: "Lee Kuan Yew's Fabian Phase." *Australian Journal of Politics and History,* 46, 1, March 2000.

Barr, Michael D.: "Medical Savings Accounts in Singapore: A Critical Inquiry." *Journal of Health Politics, Policy and Law:* 26, 4, August 2001.

Bastion, Arlene: *Singapore in a Nutshell.* Singapore, Prentice Hall, 2003.

Beckerling, Louis: "Laggards." *Singapore Business,* October 1996.

Bello, Walden and Stephanie Rosenfeld: *Dragons in Distress: Asian Miracle Economies in Crisis.* London, Penguin, 1990.

Beyrer, Christopher: *War in the Blood: Sex, Politics and AIDS in South-East Asia.* London, Zed, 1998.

Beyrer, Christopher and Nancy Kass: "Human rights, politics, and reviews of research ethics." *The Lancet* 360, July 20, 2002.

Beyrer, Christopher and Nancy Kass: "Appropriateness of Singapore's HIV/AIDS control programme." *The Lancet* 360, December 14, 2002.

BERI Labour Force Evaluation Measure (LFEM) rankings for 2003-7, www.beri.com

Bhaskaran, Manu: *Re-inventing the Asian Model: The Case of Singapore.* Singapore, Times Media, 2003.

Bloch, Harry and Sam Tang: "Estimating technical change, economies of scale and degree of competition for manufacturing industries in Singapore." *The Singapore Economic Review* 45, 1, April 2000.

Bloodworth, Dennis and Liang Ching Ping: *I Married A Barbarian.* Singapore, Times Books International, 2000.

Yang, Bo: *The Ugly Chinaman and the Crisis of Chinese Culture.* Sydney, Allen and Unwin, 1992.

Brazil, David: *Insider's Singapore.* Singapore, Times Books International, 1999.

Buchanan, Iain: *Singapore in Southeast Asia.* London, Bell and Sons, 1972.

Byrnes, Michael: *Australia and the Asia Game.* Sydney, Allen and Unwin, 1994.

Carnoy, Martin: *The State and Political Theory.* Princeton University Press, 1984.

Census QuickStats 2006 (Australian Bureau of Statistics, Canberra).

Chang, H.J.: *Kicking Away the Ladder: Development Strategy in Historical Perspective.* London, Anthem Press, 2002.

Chang, Li Lin, ed: *2002 Perspectives on Singapore.* The Institute of Policy Studies, Times Academic Press, Singapore, 2002.

Changing Corporate Asia – What Business Needs to Know (Economic Analytical Unit Report, Department of Foreign Affairs and Trade, Canberra, Australia, March 2002).

Chapman C. and Y. S. Leo: "Risks for HIV infection from the ACURE@ database in Singapore" [MCD14 426]. 5TH International Conference on AIDS in Asia and the Pacific, Kuala Lumpur, 1999.

Chee Soon Juan: *Singapore: My Home Too*. Singapore, Melodies Press., 1995.

Chee Soon Juan: *To Be Free*. Melbourne, Monash Asia Institute, 1998.

Chee, Soon Juan: *Your Future, My Faith, Our Freedom*. Singapore, Open Singapore Centre, 2001.

Chew, Ernest C.T. and Edwin Lee, eds: *A History of Singapore*. Singapore, Oxford University Press, 1991.

Chua, Beng Huat: *Communitarian Ideology and Democracy in Singapore*. London, Routledge, 1995.

Chui, Paul and Suok Kai Chew: "Appropriateness of Singapore's HIV/AIDS control programme." *The Lancet* 360, December 14, 2002.

Clad, James: *Behind the Myth: Business, Money and Power in Southeast Asia*. Sydney, Allen & Unwin, 1989.

Clammer, John, ed: *Beyond the New Anthropology*. London, MacMillan, 1987.

Cohen, Stephen: "Speaking Freely." *Foreign Affairs* 73, 4, July-August 1994.

Communicable Disease Surveillance Reports. Singapore, Ministry of Health and Tan Tock Seng Hospital, 1998-2002.

"Country Commercial Guide FY 1999: Singapore." Embassy of the United States, Singapore, July 1998.

Courtesy – More than a smile. Singapore, Ministry of Information and the Arts, 1999.

Craig, JoAnn Meriwether: *Culture Shock! Singapore*. Singapore, Times Editions, 1993.

Crispin, Shawn W.: Fiscal finangling in Singapore *Asia Times On-Line*, April 13, 2007.

Da Cunha, Derek, ed: *Debating Singapore*. Singapore, Institute of Southeast Asian Studies, 1994.

Devlin, Will and Bill Brummitt: *A few sovereigns more: the rise of sovereign wealth funds:* (the Macroeconomic Group, the Australian Treasury, Canberra, Australia, 2007).

Doing Business in Singapore: A Country Commercial Guide for U.S. Companies: (US and Foreign Commercial Service and Department of State, 2005).

Doing Business 2008 Report The World Bank Group, 2008, www.doingbusiness. org/economyrankings.

Drysdale, John: *Singapore: Struggle for Success*. Singapore, Times Books International, 1984; 1996 reprint.

Economic Freedom of the World 2007 (Cato Institute, Washington DC).

Economic Survey of Singapore 2002. (Singapore, Ministry of Trade and Industry, 2003).

Economic Survey of Singapore 1995. (Singapore, Ministry of Trade and Industry, 1996).

Ellis, Eric: "Inching towards transparency." *Fortune*, August 13, 2002.

Ellis, Eric "Mdm Ho's Temasek in firing line after Thai coup" *Fortune*, September 25, 2006.

Er, Lam Peng and Kevin Y.L. Tan, eds: *Lee's Lieutenants: Singapore's Old Guard.* Sydney, Allen and Unwin, 1999.

Europa Yearbook 2004, www.europaworldonline.com

Expatriate Living Costs in Singapore, 2004/5 edition. Singapore International Chamber of Commerce, 2004.

Far Eastern Economic Review, December 18, 1997; June 11, 1998; May 25, 2000; May 6, 2004.

Fernand, John and Brent Nieman "Measuring the Miracle: Market Imperfections and Asia's Growth Experience" (Working Paper Series, Federal Reserve Bank of San Franscisco, May 2006).

Fingleton, Eamonn: "The Invisible Hand", *Sunday Times* (Singapore), *The Sunday Review*, July 23, 1995.

Forbes.com, August 2 and December 13, 2007.

Fukuyama, Francis: *Trust: The Social Virtues and the Creation of Prosperity.* London, Penguin, 1995.

Gauld, Robin, ed: *Comparative Health Policy in the Asia-Pacific.* England, Open University Press, 2005.

George, Cherian: *Singapore: the Air-conditioned Nation.* Singapore, Landmark Books, 2000.

George, T.J.S.: *Lee Kuan Yew's Singapore.* London, Andre Deutsch, 1973.

Global Entrepreneurship Monitor, GEM 2006 Summary Results (Babson College, USA; London Business School, UK, 2007).

Goh, Chok Tong: "Remaking Singapore – Changing Mindsets." Prime Minister's National Day Rally Address, August 18, 2002. www.gov.sg/singov

Goldstein, Andrea and Pavida Pananond: "Singapore and Thailand" (A contribution to the ICRIER Intra-Asian FDI Flows project; the OECD Development Centre and Thammasat University, Thailand, 2007).

Gomez, James: *Internet Politics: Surveillance and Intimidation in Singapore.* Bangkok and Singapore, Think Centre, 2002.

Gomez, James, ed: *Publish and Perish.* Singapore, National Solidarity Party, 2001.

Ham, Chris: "Values and Health Policy: The Case of Singapore." *Journal of Health Politics, Policy and Law*, Vol 26, No 4, August 2001.

Han, Fook Kwang, Warren Fernandez, and Sumiko Tan: *Lee Kuan Yew: the Man and His Ideas.* Singapore, Times Editions, 1998.

Hills, Ben: *Japan Behind the Lines.* Sydney, Hodder and Stoughton, 1996.

"HIV hits new high: Solution: punish", yawningbread, May 1, 2008.

Hofstede, Geert: *Culture's Consequences.* California, Sage Publications, second edition, 1984.

Household Expenditure Survey 2002/3 (Department of Statistics, Ministry of Trade and Industry, Republic of Singapore).

"How is Singapore Science Really Doing?", by "AcidFlask", March 28, 2005, www. newsintercom.org

Hsiao, William C. "Behind the Ideology and Theory: What is the Empirical Evidence for Medical Savings Accounts." *Journal of Health Politics, Policy and Law* 26, 4, August 2001.

Index of Economic Freedom 2008 (The Heritage Foundation and the Wall Street Journal, Washington DC).

Investment Climate Statement 2008 – Singapore (US Department of State) www.state.gov.

"International Housing Prices", www.treasury.gov.au/documents

Jeyaratnam, J. B.: *Make It Right for Singapore: Speeches in Parliament 1997-9.* Singapore, Jeya Publishers, 2000.

Jones, David Martin: *Political Development in Pacific Asia.* Cambridge, UK; Polity Press, 1997.

Kahn, Herman: *The Emerging Japanese Superstate.* London, Deutsch, 1971.

Kelly, Brian and Mark London: *The Four Little Dragons.* New York, Simon and Schuster, 1985.

Kerr, Alex: *Dogs and Demons: the Fall of Modern Japan.* London, Penguin, 2001.

Koh, Ai Tee, Lim Kim Lian, Hui Teng Tat, Bhanoji Rao and Chng Meng Kng, eds: *Singapore Economy in the 21st Century.* Singapore, McGraw Hill, 2002.

Krugman, Paul: "Competitiveness: A Dangerous Obsession." *Foreign Affairs* 73, 2, March/April 1994.

Krugman, Paul: "The Myth of Asia's Miracle." *Foreign Affairs* 73, 6, November/December 1994.

Lall, Sanjaya; "Competitiveness Indices and Developing Countries: An Economic Evaluation of the Global Competitiveness Report" *World Development* 29, 9, 2001.

Lall, Sanjaya: "Globalization and development, perspectives for emerging nations" (BNDES 50th Anniversary Seminar, Rio de Janeiro, Brazil, September 12, 2002).

Lee, Kuan Yew: *From Third World to First.* Singapore, Times Media, 2000.

Lee, Kuan Yew: *The Singapore Story.* Singapore, Times Editions, 1998.

Lee, Tsao Yuan and Linda Low, eds: *Local Entrepreneurship in Singapore: Private and State.* Singapore, Times Academic Press, 1998.

"Lee Wei Ling's take on biomedical research in Singapore", November 6, 2006 takcheck.blogspot.com

Lim Yoon Foo, "Singapore Workforce Tops BERI Rankings Yet Again", Productivity Digest June 2002.

Lingle, Christopher: *The Rise and Decline of the Asian Century.* Hong Kong, Asia 2000, second edition, 1997.

Lloyd-Smith, Jake: "Web report reveals detailed state-private business links." *South China Morning Post,* March 4, 2002.

Low, Linda: *The Political Economy of a City State.* Singapore, Oxford University Press, 1998.

Low, Linda, ed.: *Singapore: Towards A Developed Status*. Singapore, Oxford University Press, 1999.

Low, Linda and Douglas M. Johnston, eds: *Singapore Inc: Public Policy Options in the Third Millenium*. Singapore, TimesMedia, 2001.

Mahadevan, Renuka and Kali Kalirajn: "Singapore's manufacturing sector's TFP growth: A decomposition analysis." *Journal of Comparative Economics* 28, 4, December 2000.

Mahizhnan, Arun and Lee Tsao Yuan, eds: *Singapore: Re-engineering Success*. Singapore, Oxford University Press, 1998.

Mastercard Worldwide Centers of Commerce Index 2007 www.mastercard.com.us/

Minchin, James: *No Man Is an Island*. Sydney, Allen and Unwin, second edition, 1990.

Ministry of Health (MOH), Singapore: www.moh.go.sg.mohcorp/statistics

Murray, Geoffrey and Audrey Perera: *Singapore the Global City State*. England, China Library/Curzon, 1996.

Naisbitt, John: *Megatrends Asia*. London, Nicholas Brealey, 1995.

National Survey of R&D in Singapore 2006 (Agency for Science, Technology and Research, Singapore, November 2007).

NBER Macroeconomics Annual. Cambridge, Massachusetts, MIT Press, 1992.

Pearson, Cecil, and Samir Chatterjee: "Managerial goals and organizational reform in India, " *Asia Pacific Journal* 3, 1, June 1999.

Peebles, Gavin and Peter Wilson: *Economic Growth and Development in Singapore* Cheltenham, UK; Edward Elgar Publishing, 2002.

Perry, M. and Tan Boon Hui: "Global manufacturing and local linkage in Singapore", Economic and Planning A 1998, Vol 30, pages 1603-24.

Porter, Claire: "State of Health." *The Expat Magazine*, September 2000.

PSB Corporation press release, October 31, 2002 www.tuv-sud-psb.sg/news_release

Rahim, Lily Zubaidah: *The Singapore Dilemma*. Kuala Lumpur, Oxford University Press, 1998.

Ramesh, M., "One and A Half Cheers for Provident Funds in Malaysia and Singapore, " – Paper prepared for the UNRISD project on Social Policy in a Development Context, February 28, 2003.

Ramesh, M. "Singapore's Multi-Pillar System of Social Security" (KDI-World Bank Conference, Seoul, December 2006).

Ramirez, Carlos D. and Ling Hui Tan: "Singapore Inc. Versus the Private Sector: Are Government-Linked Companies Different?" (IMF Working Paper, IMF Institute, July 2003).

Rao, Bhanoji and Christopher Lee: "Sources of growth in the Singapore economy its manufacturing and service sectors." *The Singapore Economic Review* 40, 1, April 1995.

Redding, Gordon: *The Spirit of Chinese Capitalism*. Berlin, De Gruyter, 1990.

Report on the Household Expenditure Survey 1997/8. (Department of Statistics, Ministry of Trade and Industry, Republic of Singapore).

Report on the Labour Force in Singapore, 2003 and 2006. (Manpower Research and Statistics Department, Ministry of Manpower, Republic of Singapore).

Rodan, Garry: "Asian crisis, transparency and the international media in Singapore." *The Pacific Review.* 13, 2, 2000.

Rodan, Garry: *The Political Economy of Singapore's Industrialization: National State and International Capital.* London, Macmillan, 1989.

Rodan, Garry: *Transparency and Authoritarian Rule in Southeast Asia.* London, RoutledgeCurzon, 2004.

Sandhu, Kernial Singh and Paul Wheatley, eds: *Management of Success: The Moulding of Modern Singapore.* Singapore, Institute of Southeast Asian Studies, 1989.

Selvan, T. S.: *Singapore: The Ultimate Island.* Melbourne, Freeway Books, 1990.

Seow, Francis T.: *The Media Enthralled: Singapore Revisited.* Colorado, Lynne Rienner, 1998.

Seow, Francis T.: *To Catch a Tartar: A Dissident in Lee Kwan Yew's Prison.* New Haven, Connecticut, Yale Center for International and Areas Studies, 1994.

Shari, Michael: "Can Ho Ching Fix Singapore Inc?" *Business Week*, June 24, 2002.

Sessor, Stan: *Lands of Charm and Cruelty.* New York, Vintage Books, 1994.

"Singapore Swing." *Asia Inc*, February 1996.

Singapore's Corporate Sector 1999-2000 (Singapore Department of Statistics, December 2002), p. 6.

Singapore Country Brief (Department of Foreign Affairs and Trade, Australian Government, Canberra, April 2006).

Singapore: Selected Issues: IMF Country Report No. 04/103, (Asia-Pacific Department, International Monetary Fund, Washington DC), April 2004.

Singapore Yearbook of Manpower Statistics for 2001 and 2006. (Ministry of Manpower, Republic of Singapore).

Social Transformation in Singapore. Singapore, Ministry of Culture, 1964.

Tamney, Joseph B.: *The Struggle for Singapore's Soul.* Berlin, Walter de Gruyter, 1995.

Tan, Jason, S. Gopinathan and Ho Wah Kam, eds: *Challenges Facing the Singapore Education System Today.* Singapore, Prentice Hall, 2001.

Tan, Kevin Y. L. and Lam Peng Er, eds: *Managing Political Change in Singapore.* London, Routledge, 1997.

Temasek Review 2007 "Creating Value" www.temasekholdings.com.sg

"The Temasek Model": *The Wall Street Journal On-line*, March 21, 2007.

The 2007 Worldwide Quality of Living Survey (Mercer Human Resource Consulting, New York, 2007), www.mercer.com

Thurow, Lester: *Head to Head: The Coming Economic Battle among Japan, Europe, and America.* New York, Morrow, 1992.

Total Entrepreneurial Activity (TEA) Ranked by Country, Internationalentrepreneurship.com

Toh, Mun Heng and Tan Kong Yam, eds: *Competitiveness of the Singapore Economy.* Singapore, Singapore University Press, 1998.

Tremewan, Christopher: *The Political Economy of Social Control in Singapore*. New York, St Martin's Press, 1994.

UNAIDS, *Epidemiological Fact Sheets, Singapore*

www.unaids.org/EN/other/functionalities/search.asp

UNGASS Country Progress Report, January 2006-December 2007, (March 2008).

Vogel, Ezra: *Japan as Number One: Lessons for America*. Cambridge, Massachusetts, Harvard University Press, 1979.

WEF Global Competitiveness Reports, 1996 to 2004. (World Economic Forum and the Center for International Development at Harvard University, Oxford University Press, New York).

Wikipedia.org List of countries by GDP (nominal) per capita.

Wong Poh Kam and Ho Yuen Ping, "E-Commerce in Singapore: Impetus and Impact of Globalization" (Centre for Research on Information Technology and Organizations, University of California, Irvine; March 2004).

Wood, Justin: "Translucent Temasek", November 2004, *CEO Asia.com*

World Cost of Living rankings 2007/8 (Finfacts Ireland, www.finfacts.ie/cost of living

World Development Indicators 2007 (World Bank, Washington, DC).

World Development Report 2008 (The World Bank and Oxford University Press).

The 1995 World Competitiveness Report. (Institute for Management Development and the World Economic Forum, Lausanne, Switzerland; 1995).

The World Competitiveness Yearbooks 1996-2004 (Lausanne, Switzerland; Institute for Management Development).

World Development Report 1997 (New York, Oxford University Press, June 1997).

World Development Report 2007 (The World Bank and Oxford University Press, June 2007).

Worthington, Ross: *Governance in Singapore*. London, RoutledgeCurzon, 2003.

Yawning Bread, "DOS General Household Surveys", July 2006, www.yawningbread.org

*Yearbook of Statistics Singapore 2003 and 2007 (*Department of Statistics, Ministry of Trade and Industry, Republic of Singapore, February 2003).

INDEX

I

U

Made in the USA
Middletown, DE
11 February 2018